DICTIONARY OF JAPANESE CULTURE

by
Setsuko Kojima
Gene A. Crane

Heian

©1987 by Setsuko Kojima and Gene A. Crane

English reprint rights arranged with The Japan Times, Ltd. through the Japan Foreign Rights Center.

First American Edition 1991

91, 92, 93, 94, 95, 10, 9, 8, 7, 6, 5, 4, 3, 2, 1

HEIAN INTERNATIONAL, INC.
Publishers
P.O. Box 1013
Union City, CA 94587 USA

ISBN: 0-89346-336-1

Printed in the United States of America

FOREWORD

The age of "internationalization" has brought increasing attention to Japan and her people. Previously, Japan's "internationalization" consisted of the study of foreign cultures and ideas in Japan or the importation of foreign goods into the country. In recent years, however, many Japanese have traveled abroad, primarily as tourists. Despite this travel, few have engaged in person-to-person communication with non-Japanese to establish rapport or stimulate cultural exchange. Thus, to promote understanding between people of the world on a grass roots level, Japan must be introduced in terms of her culture and philosophy.

Japanese culture has been shaped in unique ways, both as a result of her geographical location and her self-imposed isolation that ended just over one hundred years ago. The people of Japan cannot assume that their ways are incomprehensible to others, however. The love of nature, the beauty to be found in the miniature or the imperfect, the transient perfection of the tea ceremony, the cultivation of self-discipline and self-control through the various traditional arts or religious practices—all these aspects of Japanese culture have found adherents and proponents throughout the world.

Perhaps one of the most puzzling aspects of Japanese society—as far as other peoples are concerned—is the emphasis on relativistic rather than universal values. The Japanese place great value upon human interpersonal relationships within such social frameworks as family, local community, factional group, and, say, work group. While previously they did not, in social context, aspire to such universal values as love of all mankind, fundamental human rights, liberty, equality, etc., most Japanese do realize that such values form the bond that will result in mutual trust between peoples of the world. And while cultures may indeed be different, people are people—even though each individual is a unique being.

The difficulty of interpreting concepts such as *wabi, sabi, ma, zen, haragei* and *kukan* (see each entry in the dictionary) lies in the fact that the essence of the concept lies outside mere words; it exists in what is unexpressed. And because of this, explanation is all the more necessary! To attempt this explanation in English requires tremendous effort, for as noted semanticist S. I. Hayakawa has said, "The symbol is not the thing symbolized; the word is not the thing; the map is not the territory it stands for." We hope that readers will look upon this dictionary as a "map" that induces further interest in the "territory" that is Japan.

*   *   *   *   *

This dictionary's antecedent, *A Cultural Dictionary of Japan,* was published in unfinished form—due to my illness—by The Japan Times, Ltd. in April, 1979. Much to my embarrassment, it ran through a number of printings. I planned a revision during my recuperation, and, shortly after my recovery, the project got underway. Over eight years have passed since that time. Working on this project has been an awesome task, and I often felt that I was creating a mountain, one pebble at a time. With the passage of time, the work has been transformed into an entirely new creation, thanks to the guidance and collaboration of many experts. It was my good fortune to meet Mr. Gene Crane who, by sharing responsibility and commitment, has played an integral role as advisor, contributor and proofreader through these many years.

Valuable comments have come from readers with regard to the earlier dictionary. For example, they cited the fact that the dictionary was appropriate for browsing through since entries were classified into different fields. However, when one was in a hurry, it was difficult to find a specific term. Thus, this dictionary has been arranged in alphabetical order. The earlier dictionary confined itself to traditional topics; this new edition has been expanded to embrace a wide range of up-to-date items, though by its very nature, it is probably already somewhat dated. No doubt it will require addenda in the future.

The more involved we became in this project, the more distant the final goal seemed. Realizing that we were like a ship on a voyage with no destination, we decided to drop anchor here at a temporary port. We would like to take this opportunity to ask that our readers continue to send comments and suggestions so that we may further enlarge and, indeed, improve our next edition.

I would like to express my deepest gratitude to Mr. Toshio Tojo and Mr. Akio Ishizawa, former and incumbent directors of the Publications Department of The Japan Times, Ltd., for their constant encouragement over the years. I also greatly appreciate the work of all the staff; in particular, Mr. Junichi Saito who patiently and thoughtfully guided me toward this achievement, demonstrating his excellent capabilities as an editor. Ms. Kazue Iizuka was extremely helpful with the galley proofs of the entire manuscript. Listed on the page following the "Guide to This Dictionary," are those who made substantial contributions in various roles. Further, I wish to thank the acquaintances and organizations that were kind enough to provide data and information or answer our occasional questions. This dictionary is the result of the support and cooperation of many people.

Setsuko Kojima

Tokyo, May 1990

FEATURES OF THIS DICTIONARY

1. Users

This dictionary is intended for two kinds of people—Japanese who wish to introduce their own country and culture to others and non-Japanese who are interested in Japan.

2. Entries

There are approximately 1350 entries arranged in alphabetical order, letter by letter rather than word by word. Entries were selected on the basis of specific terms and concepts, rather than all-inclusive topics. Each is translated into English, followed by a brief definition. This is a "dictionary for consultation" (a word finder or fact finder) rather than a comprehensive and exhaustive reference work.

3. Scope

A wide range of terms and concepts unique to Japanese culture and thought from the distant past up to the present day have been selected. Areas covered include art, history, religion, martial arts, annual events, manners and customs, food, clothing, housing, geography, literature, education, social affairs, psychological makeup, etc. Most of the items selected in each area are generally known by the average, educated Japanese citizen, with the exception of those special interest items that have been the contribution of experts in a given field.

4. Cross References

Users of the dictionary are encouraged to make use of cross references (indicated by the symbol ⇨) to amplify their understanding of many of the more subtle aspects of Japanese culture discussed herein.

5. Limitation of Definitions

This dictionary has only recorded meanings and interpretations as they existed at the moment of recording; there is no claim that these entries are to be considered final, authoritative definitions.

6. Style

Sentences have been written as concisely and plainly as possible, using modern American English.

7. Data and Information

Data and information came from hundreds of books and monographs, articles in newspapers and magazines, official documents and statistical reports. There has been an attempt to correlate definitions with pictures, exhibits, films and everyday observations. Of greater import has been the knowledge and expertise generously provided by advisors and contributors. In this manner, each entry has been researched and composed through a multiplicity of sources.

GUIDE TO THE DICTIONARY

1. Entries

a. All entries are arranged in alphabetical order.

b. Homophones or homographs are entered separately, each followed by a number in superscript (e.g., zen[1]; zen[2]).

c. Parentheses ( ) are used to indicate ellipsis or possible omission, and brackets [ ] to indicate common variants or possible alternatives.

2. Format

Generally, the definition for each entry is arranged as follows:

a. Lit.: Literal translation of the entry, when necessary.

b. Limited definition: Meaning translated in a phrase, beginning with a lower case letter. When two or more phrases appear, a semi-colon (;) is inserted.

c. Extended definition: Further detailed explanation in sentence form, as briefly as possible, to provide further information.

d. Cross reference: Suggested references to other entries for additional information. An arrow (⇨) is followed by suggested entries in caps.

e. Vocabulary notes: Selected explanatory notes for words and phrases that appear in the definition, rendered in Japanese.

3. Romanization

a. The romanization in this dictionary is based on the Hepburn system. (See entry *rōmaji*.) Long vowels are indicated by macrons, e.g. *fūrin*.

b. Generally, Japanese words appearing in the definition are set in italics; however, Anglicized Japanese words are in regular type, using the commonly accepted spellings, e.g.:

> Kabuki, Gagaku, Noh
> judo, kimono, saké
> Tokyo, Kyoto (cf. Ōsaka, Kyūshū)

4. Personal Names

Pre-Meiji names (prior to 1868) are given in the usual Japanese order (i.e., surname + given name), e.g., Tokugawa Ieyasu.

Names since the Meiji period (1868-present) are given in western order (i.e., given name + surname), e.g., Yukichi Fukuzawa.

5. Weights and Measures

The metric system is used for weights and measures. When the same measure appears more than once in the same definition, only the first one is spelled fully and the later ones are abbreviated, e.g.:

> centimeter(s) → cm
> square kilometer(s) → sq. km

6. Abbreviations

> lit. = literally
> r. = reigned
> i.e. = id est; that is
> e.g. = exempli gratia; for example
> C. = centigrade
> et al = et alii; and others
> ca. = circa; about
> etc. = et cetera; and so on

EDITORS AND COLLABORATORS

General Editors

Kojima, Setsuko	Instructor of English, Aoyama Gakuin University
Crane, Gene A.	Instructor of English, Aoyama Gakuin University

Advisory Editors, Proofreaders, Contributors

Comee, Stephen	Free-lance Editor
Crane (Kudaka), Hideko	Former U.S. Embassy Staff (Translator, Political Section)
Fukao, Tomoko	Lecturer of English, Aoyama Gakuin University
Gish, George W., Jr.	Missionary; Researcher of traditional Japanese performing arts
Hashimoto, Shinji	Former Senior High School Teacher of History
Hayashi, Hiroko	Former U.S. Embassy staff
Kikuchi, Takeshi	Attorney-at-law; Lecturer of Law, Aoyama Gakuin University (international transactions, industrial property)
Kojima, Satoshi	Graduate Student, University of Tokyo
Krantz, Ina	Staff, Editorial Department, The Japan Times, Ltd.
Moriizumi, Akira	Professor of Civil Law, Aoyama Gakuin University
Susuki, Ayako	Professor of English, Aoyama Gakuin University
Tani, Katsuji	Novelist
Ueda, Haru	Master of the Tea Ceremony
The 4th Generation Umeya, Fukutaro	Headmaster of the Umeya School (small hand drum)
Yamazaki, Zensei	Professor of Marketing, North Shore Junior College; Visiting Professor, Bern University, Switzerland
Yanase, Marion	Instructor of English, Aoyama Gakuin University

A

abekawa-mochi 安倍川餅 a rice cake coated with soybean flour. A rice cake is toasted until it becomes soft, and is then dipped in hot water. When it becomes very soft, it is coated with a yellowish powder made from roasted soybeans mixed with sugar and salt. This sweet originated somewhere along the Abekawa River in Shizuoka Prefecture. ⇨ MOCHI

〖注〗 soybean flour 黄粉. rice cake 餅. dip 浸す. sweet 甘い菓子.

abura(a)ge 油揚げ fried soybean curd; a thin oblong slice of deep-fried bean curd. It is used as an ingredient in soups, as a shell for vinegared rice, etc. ⇨ INARI-ZUSHI, TŌFU

〖注〗 soybean curd 豆腐. deep-fried 油をたっぷり入れて揚げた. ingredient 成分, (料理の)材料. shell 外皮, 包むもの. vinegared rice 酢をまぜた御飯.

aemono 和物 seasoned foods; a kind of Japanese-style salad of seafoods and/or vegetables. The seafoods and vegetables are either raw or boiled. They are dressed with sesame seeds, soybean paste, vinegar, soy sauce, or other seasonings and spices. ⇨ MISO, SHŌYU

〖注〗 seasoned ソース等をかけて味をつけた. sesame seeds 胡麻. soybean paste 味噌. vinegar 酢. soy sauce 醤油. seasoning 調味料.

agemaku 揚げ幕 an entrance curtain; a curtain hanging between the mirror-room and the passageway to the Noh stage. It is lifted up and pulled down by two bamboo poles when the actors enter and exit. ⇨ HASHIGAKARI, KAGAMI NO MA, NŌ, NŌBUTAI

〖注〗 mirror-room 鏡の間, 能役者の控室(＝green room). passageway 通路, (能舞台の)橋懸かり.

agemono 揚げ物 deep-fried foods; seafoods or vegetables deep-fried in vegetable oil. There are roughly two kinds of frying in Japanese-style cooking—the *tenpura* type and *karaage* type. ⇨ KARAAGE, TENPURA

〖注〗 deep-fried 油をたっぷり入れて揚げた.

aikidō 合気道 lit. the way of uniting forces. a Japanese art of self-defense derived from a type of *jūjutsu,* one of the traditional martial arts. In the 1920s Morihei Ueshiba (1883-1969), influenced by Zen Buddhism, established *aikidō* as an art of self-defense and self-cultivation based on "uniting with universal forces." He held that in true martial arts, strength should not be excessively relied on, and competition in mastery of skills should not be the main object. In keeping with this, the main technique employed is to grasp joints, resulting in throwing or pinning down assailants by using their momentum against them. Since two cannot be on the defensive at the same time, competition in the usual sense is not held, and one person must assume the role of assailant during practice. ⇨ BUGEI, JŪJUTSU, ZEN¹, ZENSHŪ

【注】 martial art 武芸, 格闘技. Morihei Ueshiba 植芝盛平. self-cultivation 自己修養. joint 関節. throwing 投げ(技). pinning 抑え(技). assailant 攻撃者. momentum 勢い.

aikyōgen 間狂言 a comic interlude; an interlude performed between the two acts of some Noh plays. It is performed in simple and comic language by a Kyogen actor who enters the stage after the first act to explain the development of the play in progress. It serves as a relief between the two acts of a Noh play while the main actor (*shite*) changes his costume. This term also refers to any other appearance or performance by Kyogen actors either before or during the acts of Noh plays as distinct from the normal Kyogen repertoire. ⇨ KYŌGEN, NŌ, SHITE

【注】 interlude 幕間, 幕間の演芸. the play in progress 上演中の劇. main actor 主役, (能の)仕手. repertoire 上演目録, レパートリー.

Ainu アイヌ an Ainu; an Aino; the Ainu race; aboriginal Caucasoid people on the Japanese archipelago, most of them living in Hokkaidō today. The Ainu people are thought to have formerly flourished over nearly the entire Japanese archipelago, but were driven far north to Hokkaidō and some northern islands. They are said to be of Caucasian roots with no racial affinity to the Japanese aborigines, the Yamato, although their way of living is greatly Japanized today. They make a living mainly by fishing and farming, and formerly hunting as well, but many have merged into mainstream Japanese society. The population of genuine Ainus has greatly declined, numbering 20,000 altogether today. The Ainu village in Shiraoi, Hokkaidō, is set up so as to show tourists their native way of life. ⇨ HOKKAIDŌ, HOPPŌ-RYŌDO,

NIHON-RETTŌ

〚注〛 aboriginal 土着の，その土地の．Caucasoid 白色人種．the Japanese archipelago 日本列島．Caucasian 白色人種の．affinity 類似点，類縁．aborigine 原住民，土着の人．

Aizu-nuri 会津塗 Aizu lacquer ware; lacquer ware produced since the 16th century around Aizuwakamatsu in the present Fukushima Prefecture. It is characterized by a method of undercoating with an astringent substance made from persimmons and sprinkling the lacquer with gold dust. ⇨ NURIMONO, SHIKKI, URUSHI

〚注〛 lacquer 漆．undercoat 下地を塗る．astringent substance 渋い物質，渋．persimmon 柿．gold dust 金粉，金泥．

Ajinomoto 味の素 a popular brand of monosodium glutamate; a powdered seasoning used in cooking, similar to "Accent" used in the U.S. A small amount brings out the natural flavor and taste of the ingredients.

〚注〛 monosodium glutamate グルタミン酸ソーダ(調味料)．seasoning 調味料．"Accent" 商標名．ingredient 成分，(料理の)材料．

akabō 赤帽 lit. a red cap. a porter at railway stations. They are on duty, wearing a dark-blue uniform and "red cap" at large railway stations. Some may still be seen, at Tokyo and Ueno stations, in Tokyo.

akachōchin 赤提燈 lit. a red paper lantern. an inexpensive drinking establishment. A huge, red paper lantern is hung at the entrance of such taverns. Though the lanterns vary in size, they may sometimes measure over one meter in diameter. Such taverns are usually located on side streets in busy sections of cities. Workers drop in at them on their way home to chat with colleagues over saké and food at reasonable prices, to release tensions from the day. ⇨ SAKE

〚注〛 establishment 店舗．tavern 居酒屋．

akadashi 赤出し reddish *miso* soup; soybean paste soup of a dark reddish color, containing *tōfu*, clams, vegetables, etc. The red *miso* is made mainly from fermented soybeans, and the white light-colored *miso* is made mainly from fermented rice; the former is favored in the Kansai area and the latter in the Kantō area. Originally, *akadashi* referred specifically to the reddish, soybean-paste soup cooked with steamed, ground fish, a specialty of the Ōsaka area. ⇨ MISO, MISOSHIRU, TŌFU

〚注〛 soybean paste soup 味噌汁．ingredient (料理の)材料．fermented 発酵

した. specialty 特産物.

akae 赤絵 lit. a red picture. the generic term for red enameled ceramic ware. In Japan, Sakaida Kakiemon (1596-1666) was the first potter to produce a persimmon-red color using enamel glaze for decorating ceramic ware. Gradually, other colors such as green, blue, purple, and yellow—along with the principal color of persimmon red—have also come to be applied on *akae* ceramic ware. Besides the representative Kakiemon type, *Kaga-akae*, *Kyō-akae*, and *iro-Satsuma* are famous. ⇨ KAKIEMON(-IMARI), KYŌ-YAKI, SATSUMA-YAKI

〖注〗 enameled エナメルをかけた, 上薬[釉]をつけた. ceramic ware 陶器. potter 陶工. persimmon 柿. glaze つや, 上薬[釉]. apply 薬・色などをつける.

Akahada-yaki 赤膚焼 Akahada ceramic ware; ceramic ware originally produced at kilns at the foot of Mount Akahada (the present Mount Gojō) near Nara, at the end of the 16th century. These kilns were among the seven most favored by Kobori Enshū (1579-1647), a great tea master and tea-garden designer, and thus produced mostly ware suitable for the tea ceremony. The body is white and is covered with a grayish-white glaze featuring small crackles and pinhole spots. ⇨ ENSHŪ-SHICHIYŌ

〖注〗 ceramic ware 陶器. kiln (焼き物を焼く)窯. Kobori Enshū 小堀遠州. tea ceremony 茶道. glaze つや, 上薬[釉]. crackle ひび目.

Akan Kokuritsu-kōen 阿寒国立公園 Akan National Park (905.4 square kilometers), designated in 1934; a natural park situated in eastern Hokkaidō, extending from Kushiro to Kitami. This park contains a number of caldera lakes. Among them are Lake Akan, noted for floating balls of mossweed; Lake Mashū, boasting of its transparency; and Lake Kutcharo with its alkaline thermal springs. The mountains are covered with subarctic primeval forests and alpine plants. Once inhabited by Ainu, this area features Ainu villages set up for tourists. ⇨ AINU, HOKKAIDŌ, KOKURITSU-KŌEN

〖注〗 caldera lake カルデラ湖, 噴火口からできた湖. balls of mossweed 毬藻. transparency 透明度. alkaline アルカリ性の. thermal spring 温泉. subarctic 亜寒帯の. primeval forest 原始林. alpine plant 高山植物.

Akazu-yaki 赤津焼 Akazu ceramic ware; ceramic ware produced at Akazu, near Nagoya. The ware is hard and thick, and glazed in dark brown or dark green, sometimes with shades or patterns of yellow, green or brown. Some pieces resemble Oribe ware in

texture and in color scheme. Its origin presumably dates back to
the Nara period (646-794). The Azuchi-Momoyama period (1568-
1603) in particular saw the production of many fine examples of
Akazu-yaki tea utensils.   ⇨ AZUCHI-MOMOYAMA-JIDAI, ORIBE-YAKI
〖注〗 ceramic ware 陶器. glaze 上薬[釉]をかける. shades 濃淡, 明暗, 色の
度合. texture 感触, 肌合い, 手ざわり, 生地. color scheme 色使い, 配色.
date back to（ある時期から）始まる, さかのぼる. tea utensils 茶道具.

aki no nanakusa 秋の七草 the seven grasses of autumn. They are
hagi (Japanese bush clover), *obana* (flowering eulalia), *kuzu*
(pueraria), *nadeshiko* (wild pink), *ominaeshi* (patrinia), *fujibakama* (eupatorium), and *kikyō* (*platycodon grandiflorum* or althea). While the seven herbs of spring have to do with food for
health, the seven grasses of autumn are selected for their flowers,
which bring out the atmosphere of the season.   ⇨ HARU NO NANA-
KUSA, NANAKUSA
〖注〗 秋の七草：萩, 尾花, 葛, 撫子, 女郎花, 藤袴, 桔梗.

Akō-gishi 赤穂義士 the Loyal Retainers of Akō (in the present
Hyōgo Prefecture); the 47 loyal retainers who avenged the death of
their lord in 1702. Asano Takuminokami Naganori (1667-1701),
lord of Akō, was compelled to commit harakiri and had his
domains confiscated, because he drew his sword in the shogun's
Edo Castle, in indignation over the unfair conduct of Kira Kōzu-
kenosuke Yoshitaka (1641-1703), a high-ranking shogunate official. Asano's loyal retainers, led by Ōishi Kuranosuke (1659-
1703), took vengeance on Kira in place of their lord. The loyal
retainers, except for one who had been sent to Asano's widow to
inform her of their action, were sentenced to commit harakiri.
They were buried close to their lord's grave at Sengakuji Temple
in Edo. This incident drew the people's sympathy, and shortly
after was adapted for a Bunraku puppet play (staged in 1706) and
Kabuki play (staged in 1748), which have been followed by many
other versions under the titles of *Chūshingura* or *Kanadehon
Chūshingura*.   ⇨ BUNRAKU, CHŪSHINGURA, HARAKIRI, KABUKI
〖注〗 retainer 家臣, 家来. avenge あだを討つ. domain 領地. confiscate
没収する. indignation 憤り. vengeance 復讐, あだ討ち. Sengakuji Temple 泉岳寺.

Akutagawa-shō 芥川賞 the Akutagawa Literary Prize; the most
prestigious Japanese prize in belles-lettres, established by the
writer Kan Kikuchi (1888-1948) in memory of the author Ryūnosu-

ke Akutagawa (1892-1927). The administration of this prize was first entrusted to the Bungeishunju Ltd.; from the seventh prize it was taken over by the Japan Literature Promotion Association (Nihon Bungaku Shinkōkai). Since 1935, the prize has been awarded twice a year, excluding several years during and after World War II. Recipients are selected by outstanding writers and critics, from among emerging writers whose works have appeared in newspapers or magazines. The selected works are published in *Bungeishunju* magazine. ⇨ NAOKI-SHŌ

〖注〗 belles-lettres 純文学. entrust 任せる. the Japan Literature Promotion Association 日本文学振興会. recipient 受賞者. emerging writer 新進作家.

ama 海女 a female sea diver; women who collect shellfish and seaweed by diving in the sea. This method of gathering abalone, turbo shellfish, agar-agar, etc., is of ancient origin, but diving for pearl oysters, such as at Ago Bay in Mie Prefecture, began in this century. *Ama* are often seen with a floating wooden tub, into which they put what they have collected from the sea.

〖注〗 seaweed 海藻. abalone あわび. turbo shellfish さざえ. agar-agar 寒天. pearl oyster あこや貝, 真珠貝.

amado 雨戸 rain doors or shutters; sliding doors made of thin sheets of wood or metal. They are closed at night and during storms or heavy rains to seal and protect the house.

〖注〗 shutter 雨戸, よろいど. sliding door 引き戸.

amae 甘え lit. sweet dependency. dependence wishes; to expect affection or acceptance from others. 1) to indulge in a feeling of security as a child feels with its loving mother. 2) dependency syndrome; a sense of dependency of expecting concern and acceptance from someone close in social life. In a close-knit Japanese group, it is regarded as natural that the dependent looks to the superior for acceptance and protection, both emotionally and practically, and the superior expects to be responded. This indulgent interdependency often works positively in Japanese society in maintaining harmony and unity, but is harsh for those going their way independently. This term was used to describe "a key concept for the understanding not only of the psychological makeup of the individual but of the structure of Japanese society as a whole"* by Dr. Takeo Doi (1920-), a scholar and psychiatrist, in his longstanding best-seller, *Amae no Kōzō* (1971; translated as *The*

Anatomy of Dependence, 1973), based on comparative observations of American society. He points out that, psychologically and sociologically, *amae* has been a dominant concept in Japanese society since ancient times, in connection with the language, culture, etc. He applies this phenomenon to the pathology of a Japanese neurosis caused by the rejection of *amae*. Edwin O. Reischauer (1910-) in *The Japanese* (1977) identifies *amae* as rooted in Japanese child-rearing techniques characterized by intimate contact with the mother, noting that "this attitude becomes expanded into acceptance of the authority of the surrounding social milieu and a need for and dependence on this broader social approval."**

* Doi, Takeo, *The Anatomy of Dependence* (1971), translated by John Bester (1973), Kōdansha International Ltd., p. 28

**Reischauer, Edwin O., *The Japanese* (1977), Harvard, p. 141 (Tuttle edition)

〔注〕 a feeling of security 安心感. syndrome 症候群. interdependency 相互依存関係. psychological makeup 精神構造. psychiatrist 精神科医. anatomy 解剖. pathology 病理. neurosis 神経症. child-rearing 子育て. milieu 環境.

amakudari 天下り lit. to descend from heaven. the descent of high-ranking government officials to private companies upon retirement. It has been revealed by a white paper that, particularly since the 1960s, quite a number of retired government officials have found second careers in large private companies, mainly in advisory positions. Large companies desire such personnel so as to benefit from their social influence and gain closer access to the government. This practice can be said to have developed from the close relationship between government and business, unique to Japanese society.

〔注〕 high-ranking government officials 政府高官. advisory position 顧問職. gain close access to 密接な関係に入る. practice 慣行.

Amaterasu Ōmikami 天照大神 lit. the Great Deity Shining Heaven and Earth. the Sun Goddess; the supreme deity of Shintoism and ancestral goddess of the Imperial Family. According to mythology, she was born to Izanagi and Izanami who created the Japanese islands, and ruled the High Plain of Heaven (Takamagahara). She ordered her grandson Ninigi no Mikoto to descend to the Japanese islands to establish an empire, investing him with the three sacred regalia (the mirror, the jewel and the sword). Thus, the Japanese imperial lineage is believed to trace back to Amaterasu Ōmikami, through Ninigi no Mikoto whose grandson Jinmu was enthroned as the first emperor. One legend has it that Amaterasu Ōmikami was born from the left eye of Izanagi while he was engaged in a purification rite in water. She is enshrined, with the sacred mirror which represents her, in the Inner Sanctuary of the Ise Grand Shrine in Mie Prefecture. There are numerous branch shrines dedicated to her throughout the country bearing the suffix "Shinmeisha." ⇨ KUSANAGI NO TSURUGI, MAGATAMA, SAN-SHU NO JINGI, SHINTŌ, YATA NO KAGAMI

〖注〗 deity 神のような人〔もの〕. regalia 王権の標章, 即位の宝器 (regaleの複数). imperial lineage 皇室の系図. purification rite 禊ぎ, 清め. enshrine 祀る. the Inner Sanctuary 内宮. suffix 語尾.

amazake 甘酒 lit. sweet wine. sweet beverage made from fermented rice. Boiled rice is mixed with malted rice and left to ferment overnight (or a day) at 60℃. The mixture takes on a sweet and slightly alcoholic flavor. Diluted with water, it is boiled and served hot. The alcohol content is so slight that even children may drink this beverage.

〖注〗 fermented 発酵させた. malted 発酵させた.

Amida (Nyorai) 阿弥陀 (如来) Amitabha (Sanskrit), the Lord of Infinite Light; the Buddha in Mahayana Buddhism, worshiped as the central being in the Jōdo and Jōdo-shinshū sects in Japan. He is believed to reside in the Paradise of the Pure Land in the West of Heaven, where anyone may be reborn by calling on his name in faith. He is usually depicted as sitting cross-legged on a lotus-flower pedestal with both hands resting on his lap or with his left hand on his lap and right hand raised (there are nine slightly different postures). During the late Fujiwara period (898-1185), a group of nine Amida statues was enshrined in a single hall—one example remains at the main hall of Jōruriji Temple, Kyoto. Other famous single statues can be seen at Byōdōin (Uji), Saidaiji (Nara), Hōkaiji (Kyoto), and Hōryūji (Nara) temples. ⇨ AMIDADŌ, JŌDO-SHŪ, JŌDO-SHINSHŪ

〖注〗 Amitabha 阿弥陀仏. Mahayana Buddhism 大乗仏教. the Pure Land 浄土. sit cross-legged 足を組んで座る, あぐらをかく. lotus-flower 蓮の花の. pedestal 台座. enshrine 祀る. Jōruriji Temple 浄瑠璃寺. Saidaiji 西大寺. Hōkaiji 法界寺.

Amidadō 阿弥陀堂 an Amida hall; the hall dedicated to Amitabha, built in the compounds of a temple. With the rise of the Jōdo sect of Buddhism in the Heian period (794-1185), such Amida halls came to be built as the most important structure in the compounds of many temples. The Hōōdō (Phoenix Hall) of Byōdōin Temple at Uji near Kyoto, and the Amida Hall of Fukidera Temple in Ōita Prefecture, Kyūshū, are fine examples built during the Heian period. ⇨ AMIDA (NYORAI), JŌDOSHŪ

〖注〗 dedicate to ささげる、奉納する、献納する. Amitabha 阿弥陀仏. compounds 敷地、境内、囲われた区域. Phoenix Hall 鳳凰堂. Fukidera Temple 富貴寺.

Amida-sanzon 阿弥陀三尊 the Amitabha Triad; a set of three statues consisting of the Buddha Amitabha and his two attendants. The Buddha Amitabha rests on a lotus-flower pedestal accompanied by two bodhisattvas, the left one being the Bodhisattva Kannon and the right one the Bodhisattva Seishi. The Amitabha Triad made of bronze at the Golden Hall of Hōryūji Temple is a representative example, and was dedicated in the late Nara period (710-94). ⇨ AMIDADŌ, AMIDA (NYORAI), BOSATSU, HONDŌ, KONDŌ

〖注〗 Amitabha 阿弥陀仏. triad 三つ組、三人組. lotus-flower 蓮の花. pedestal 台座. the Bodhisattva Seishi 勢至菩薩. the Golden Hall 金堂、本堂. dedicate 奉納する.

an 餡 sweet bean jam; strained or mashed bean paste boiled with sugar. Strained bean jam is called *koshi-an* and the mashed type *tsubushi-an*. Bean jam is most commonly made from red beans, but it is sometimes made from white or mottled kidney beans. It is the most widely used ingredient for Japanese sweets. Also called *anko* colloquially. ⇨ WAGASHI

〖注〗 strained 漉した. red bean 小豆. white kidney bean 隠元豆. mottled kidney bean 鶉豆. ingredient (調理の)材料.

andon 行燈 a paper lampstand; an ancient type of night lamp, consisting of a square or round frame of wood covered with strong rice paper, the top and bottom being open. It is lit with rapeseed oil and a rush-weed wick on an oil plate inside. It is not used today except as a decoration. ⇨ WASHI

〖注〗 frame of wood 木の枠. rice paper 和紙. rapeseed oil 菜種油. rushweed 蘭草. wick 燈心、ランプの芯.

anka 行火 a bed warmer; a foot warmer, which is kept inside the bed under a quilt. It used to be an earthenware pot containing a charcoal fire. Today it is an electric device.

〖注〗 quilt 布団. earthenware pot 土器製の壺.

anko 餡こ ⇨ AN

anma 按摩 a masseur; massage treatment; one of the traditional medical treatments for fatigue and minor pains. It eases muscle aches, stimulates blood circulation, soothes nervous tension, etc., thus giving relief from fatigue. It has been a popular profession among the blind. Formerly, blind masseurs with a stick in hand would walk the streets blowing a special kind of flute to notify people of their services.

〖注〗 masseur マッサージ師. blood circulation 血液の循環. soothe 和らげる.

Aoi Matsuri 葵祭 the Hollyhock Festival of Kyoto (May 15); the festival held in honor of Kamigamo Shrine and Shimogamo Shrine; one of the three grand Kyoto festivals, the other two being the Festival of Eras and the Gion Festival. Its origin dates back to the sixth century, when prayers asking the deities of these two shrines for the abatement of downpours and flooding were answered. On this festive day, a colorful procession marches from the Old Imperial Palace and back, by way of these two shrines, where worship ceremonies are conducted. The procession consists of an imperial messenger in an ox-drawn carriage, his suite and other followers, all elegantly dressed in Heian costumes. The carriage, the ox, and the headgear of the participants are decorated with "hollyhock leaves" (*aoi*), the sacred crest of the two shrines. ⇨ GION MATSU-RI, JIDAI MATSURI

〖注〗 hollyhock 葵, たち葵. date back to (ある時期から)始まる, ～にさかのぼる. deity 神, 神のような人[もの]. abatement 排除, なくすること. the Old Imperial Palace 京都御所. suite 従者の一行.

aotagari [aotagai] 青田刈り[青田買い] lit. harvesting unripened rice plants of the paddy field or purchasing fields of unripened rice plants. companies' picking-out of promising students for employment prior to the due time. Many major companies are keenly competitive in recruiting top-level students at leading universities ahead of schedule, despite a gentlemen's agreement among companies requiring employment interviews and formal contracts to start on officially designated days. This is evidently due to the education-oriented Japanese social structure and the lifetime employment system customary to major companies. ⇨ SHŪSHIN-

KOYŌSEI(DO)

〖注〗 due time 決められた期日. recruit 募る，新人を徴募する. lifetime employment system 終身雇用制度.

aragoto 荒事 lit. a rough thing. a masculine style of Kabuki acting, as opposed to *wagoto* (a feminine style). It is characterized by exaggerated movement, elocution and makeup in the portrayal of masculine roles possessing supernatural power. Ichikawa Danjūrō (1660-1704), who made his first stage appearance in 1673, created this style of acting in Edo (presently Tokyo), and gained popularity among Edo townspeople. His style has been handed down through his successors inheriting the same name. The Kabuki troupe headed by Danjūrō remains the most prestigious line of Edo tradition. ⇨ KABUKI, KUMADORI, SHŪMEI, WAGOTO

〖注〗 masculine 男性的な. elocution 舞台ぜりふ. inherit the name 襲名する. troupe（芸人などの)一座，一団.

aramaki-zake 新巻鮭 [荒巻鮭] lit. a fresh-wrapped salmon or a rough-bound salmon. a salted whole salmon. A freshly caught salmon is gutted and slightly salted. Wrapped in rush or straw, it is hung in the shade. Formerly, it was roughly bound with a straw rope, hence its name. Fresh *aramaki-zake* appear on the market with the approach of winter. As they could be preserved, they comprised an important part of the people's diet in winter and still do in the remote places. The Ishikari River in Hokkaidō is well-known for its *aramakizake*. ⇨ HOKKAIDŌ

〖注〗 gut はらわたを取り出す. rush いぐさ.

Arita-yaki 有田焼 Arita porcelain ware; porcelain ware produced in and around Arita in Saga Prefecture, Kyūshū. The origin of *Arita-yaki* dates back to the 16th century, when the manufacture of porcelain ware was begun in Arita by a Korean potter named Li Sanpei (?-1655), who was brought to Japan by Toyotomi Hideyoshi (1536-98) after the Korean expedition. His porcelain was characterized by blue designs on a white background (*sometsuke* design). Later, Sakaida Kakiemon's porcelain ware of enamel decorations in shades of a red-persimmon color made Arita ware famous worldwide. Together with other kinds of ware produced in northern Kyūshū, Arita ware is also called Imari ware because it was exported from the port of Imari. Today such ware fired at numerous small individual kilns in the Arita district is also known by the general term of *Arita-yaki*. ⇨ IMARI-YAKI, KAKIEMON

(-IMARI), SOMETSUKE

〖注〗 porcelain ware 磁器. potter 陶工, 焼き物師. Li Sanpei 李参平. Sakaida Kakiemon 酒井田柿右衛門. persimmon 柿. kiln 炉, (焼き物を焼 く)窯.

Ashikaga-bakufu 足利幕府 the Ashikaga shogunate (1336-1568); the government of the Ashikaga shoguns, established in 1336 by Ashikaga Takauji (1305-58). It lasted in name until 1573, when the 15th shogun, Yoshiaki (1537-97), was driven out of Kyoto by an influential feudal lord, Oda Nobunaga (1534-82), although most scholars give 1568 as the beginning of the Azuchi-Momoyama period (1568-1603). Despite being a period of disturbances, many of the Ashikaga shoguns pursued arts and letters. This shogunate is more commonly called the Muromachi-*bakufu* because in 1378 the third shogun, Yoshimitsu (1358-1408), built the so-called "flowering palace" as his administrative headquarters at Muromachi, Kyoto. ⇨ AZUCHI-MOMOYAMA-JIDAI, MUROMACHI-JIDAI, SHŌGUN

〖注〗 disturbance 動乱. letters 文芸, 文学. "flowering palace"「花の御殿」. administrative headquarters 政治の本拠.

Ashikaga-jidai 足利時代 the Ashikaga period (1336-1568); the period of the Ashikaga shogunate government established by Ashikaga Takauji (1305-58) at Muromachi, Kyoto. This period is formally called the Muromachi-*jidai* and the shogunate, the Muromachi-*bakufu*. ⇨ ASHIKAGA-BAKUFU, MUROMACHI-BAKUFU, MUROMACHI-JIDAI

〖注〗 shogunate (government) 幕府.

ashirai あしらい a supplementary stem or branch used in a flower arrangement. It may be added to each of the three principal stems. *Ashirai* is the term used in the Ikenobō school. Called *jūshi* in the Sōgetsu school and *chūkanshi* in the Ohara school. ⇨ CHŪKANSHI, IKEBANA, JŪSHI, SHUSHI

〖注〗 supplementary 補助的な, 追加の. flower arrangement 生け花. principal stem 主枝.

ashizukai 足遣い the leg manipulator; the third man of the Bunraku puppeteer trio. He manipulates the legs and feet of a single puppet, working together with the head manipulator (*omozukai*) and the left-arm manipulator (*hidarizukai*). ⇨ BUNRAKU, HIDARIZUKAI, OMOZUKAI

〖注〗 manipulator 操る人. the Bunraku puppeteer trio 人形遣いの三人組, 三人遣い. head manipulator 主遣い[面遣い].

Ashizuri-Uwakai Kokuritsu-kōen　足摺宇和海国立公園　Ashizuri-Uwakai National Park (109.7 square kilometers), designated in 1972; a natural park situated on the southwestern coast of Shikoku, embracing parts of Kōchi and Ehime prefectures and the surrounding waters. The area features rugged coastlines with eroded granite cliffs and capes, and provides spectacular scenery, combined with abundant subtropical vegetation including camellias and Japanese sago-palm trees. Its major feature is Cape Ashizuri where a lighthouse stands, behind which is the time-honored Kongōfukuji Temple, first built in 822 by Kūkai (774–835), founder of the Shingon sect of Buddhism. The waters in the park are noted for their coral reefs and a variety of fish and shellfish. A glass-bottomed boat permits visitors to view the underwater seascape.　⇨ KOKURITSU-KŌEN, SHIKOKU

〖注〗 rugged coastline リアス式海岸線. erode 侵食する. granite 花崗岩. subtropical vegetation 亜熱帯植物. camellia 椿. Japanese sago-palm tree 蘇鉄. Kongōfukuji Temple 金剛福寺. coral reef 珊瑚礁. underwater seascape 海底の景色.

Ashura　阿修羅　Asura (Sanskrit); a kind of celestial deity of early Indian mythology; a kind of demon in later Hinduism and in early Buddhism; a guardian deity in Japanese Buddhism. In Japan he is believed to protect the Buddhist realm. At Kōfukuji Temple, Nara, there stands a famous statue of the Ashura image, three-faced and six-armed, made in the late Nara period (710–94). ⇨ BUKKYŌ, NARA-JIDAI

〖注〗 celestial 天の, 天上界の. deity 神, 神のような人[もの]. guardian deity 守護神. Buddhist realm 仏界. image 像, 偶像.

Aso Kokuritsu-kōen　阿蘇国立公園　Aso National Park (724.9 square kilometers), designated in 1934; a natural park situated in Kumamoto and Ōita prefectures in central Kyūshū, centering around the volcano Mount Aso. Mount Aso boasts the world's largest crater basin, measuring 18 by 24 km. In the basin there are five cones, one of which is still active and smoking. On the slopes of the mountain, wild azaleas thrive, along with many kinds of alpine plants. This park is particularly well-known for its abundant hot-springs scattered from Mount Aso to Beppu along the eastern edge of Kyūshū. ⇨ KOKURITSU-KŌEN, KYŪSHŪ

〖注〗 crater basin 噴火口. cone 尖峰, 火山錐. azalea つつじ(ここでは「みやまきりしま」). alpine plant 高山植物. hot-spring 温泉.

atoza 後座　the rear stage portion; the back portion of the main stage in the Noh theater.　The *hayashikata*, or musicians, sit in a row across the front of the *atoza*, facing the audience.　⇨ HAYASHI-KATA, NŌ, NŌBUTAI

awamori 泡盛　a traditional distilled alcoholic beverage of Okinawa.　*Awamori* is a high-quality saké made from a type of rice grown in Thailand.　Chinese records report that *awamori* was first distilled in the Ryūkyū Islands around 500 years ago.　The rice is mixed with water and allowed to ferment.　It is then partly evaporated and begins to acquire a rather sweet smell.　*Awamori* must be aged for some time before it is ready to drink.　The beverage is drunk straight, with water, on ice, or used in various mixed drinks.　⇨ OKINAWA, RYŪKYŪ-SHOTŌ, SAKE

〖注〗 distilled alcoholic beverage 蒸留アルコール飲料.　ferment 発酵させる. age 熟成する.

Awa-odori 阿波踊り　the Awa folk dance; a folk dance performed during Bon week (August 12 to 15) in Tokushima, formerly called Awa, in Shikoku.　During this period, many large groups of people in uniform, summer kimono (*yukata*), merrily dance in lines down the streets of Tokushima City, to the accompaniment of *shamisen*, flutes and drums.　Its origin dates back to 1585 when people danced in celebration of the completion of Awa Castle.　⇨ BON, BON-ODORI

〖注〗 folk dance 民族舞踊.　to the accompaniment of 〜に合わせて、〜の伴奏で.　date back to (ある時期に)さかのぼる.

Awata-yaki 粟田焼　Awata ceramic ware; ceramic ware produced around Awataguchi in Kyoto since the 17th century.　Nonomura Ninsei (?1569–?1660) developed a purely Japanese style of pottery design.　His influence resulted in two new types of Kyoto ceramics: *Awata-yaki* and *Kiyomizu-yaki*.　*Awata-yaki* is glazed with a pale yellow color, the surface of which takes on a finely crackled texture after firing.　Multicolored decoration is elaborately painted on, often with gold outlines.　⇨ KIYOMIZU-YAKI, KYŌ-YAKI

〖注〗 ceramic ware 陶器.　Awataguchi 粟田口.　Nonomura Ninsei 野々村仁清.　pottery 陶磁器.　glaze 上薬[釉]をかける.　crackled texture ひびのはいった生地.

azekura(-zukuri) 校倉(造り)　a log storehouse; a storehouse built of triangular-shaped logs.　The floor of this type of storehouse is situated above the ground and the walls are made of logs piled up horizontally, without using nails.　In humid weather, the logs swell and shut up the openings between the logs, thus protecting what is stored from moisture; in dry weather, the openings between the logs provide ventilation.　The most famous example is the Shōsōin Imperial Repository (eighth century) in Nara, which has safely preserved time-honored treasures for more than 1,000 years.

〖注〗 storehouse 蔵, 倉庫.　ventilation 換気.　the Shōsōin Imperial Repository 正倉院.　repository 貯蔵所, 収納庫.　time-honored 昔からの, 由緒ある.

Azuchi-jidai 安土時代　the Azuchi period (about 10 years from 1568); a period of about 10 years during which Oda Nobunaga (1534-82), a warload, ruled over the country.　The name *Azuchi* came from his headquarters, Azuchi Castle built on the southwestern shore of Lake Biwa in 1579.　Together with the Momoyama period which followed, this period is more commonly called the Azuchi-Momoyama period (1568 to 98 or 1603).　⇨ AZUCHI-MOMOYAMA-JIDAI, MOMOYAMA-JIDAI

〖注〗 warlord 武将.　headquarters 本部, 本拠.

Azuchi-Momoyama-jidai 安土桃山時代　the Azuchi-Momoyama period (1568-98 or 1603); the period during which Oda Nobunaga (1534-82) and Toyotomi Hideyoshi (1536-98) reigned over the country respectively.　The name of the period is derived from Nobunaga's Azuchi Castle and Hideyoshi's Fushimi Castle at Momoyama.　The country secured political unification during this period following a chaotic condition of prolonged civil wars.　Encouraged by Hideyoshi, art flourished, having great impact on the development of Japanese culture.　It was characterized by grandeur in form and brightness in color as seen in the architecture, paintings and sculpture of those days; on the other hand, as a kind of reaction, simple and rustic tastes also came to be appreciated, as in the rustic tea ceremony and related fine arts.　⇨ AZUCHI-JIDAI, MOMOYAMA-JIDAI

〖注〗 be derived from ～に由来する, ～から生じている.　unification 統一.　civil wars 内乱.　sculpture 彫刻.　rustic taste 素朴な好み, わびれたものを好むこと.　rustic tea ceremony わび茶.

azumaya 東屋　a garden hut; a small rustic arbor usually open on all sides and sheltered by a low overhanging thatched roof.　Often placed in a large strolling garden, it is used for resting, viewing the moon or flowers, or conducting a tea ceremony.　It forms part of the landscape of the garden as well. ⇨ KAIYŪSHIKI-TEIEN

〖注〗 rustic 素朴な. arbor 東屋, 木蔭の休憩小屋. thatched roof 草葺きの屋根. strolling garden 散歩のできる庭, 回遊式庭園. conduct a tea ceremony 茶の湯を行う.

B

bachi[1] 桴   a stick or sticks used for beating drums.   They are used for drums, large and small, in Japanese folk music as well as in the traditional Noh and Kabuki theater.   ⇨ HAYASHI, TAIKO[1]

〖注〗 folk music 民謡.

bachi[2] 撥   a plectrum; a hand-held pick or plectrum, triangular in shape, used in playing string instruments such as the *shamisen* or *biwa*, producing a characteristic percussive sound.   It is made of very hard wood or ivory, and was originally used for the *biwa* until the 16th century when it was adapted for use with the newly introduced *shamisen*.   ⇨ BIWA, SHAMISEN

〖注〗 plectrum (楽器の)ばち，つめ.   pick つつく道具，(楽器の)ばち，つめ. string instrument 弦楽器.   percussive sound 打つ音，たたく音.

baiu 梅雨   lit. plum rain.   the same as *tsuyu* (the rainy season).   So called because the rainy season comes when Japanese plums ripen. ⇨ TSUYU

〖注〗 plum すもも，梅(=Japanese plum).

bakufu 幕府   lit. tent quarters.   the shogunate; the shogunate government as opposed to the imperial government.   Originally, *bakufu* referred to the headquarters of a battlefield camp.   This term was applied to the military shogunate government first established in Kamakura in 1185 by the shogun Minamoto Yoritomo (1147-99). The shogunate government continued from 1185 to 1867, covering the Kamakura, Ashikaga, and Tokugawa shogunate governments. ⇨ ASHIKAGA-BAKUFU, KAMAKURA-BAKUFU, SEII-TAISHŌGUN, SHŌGUN, TOKUGAWA-BAKUFU.

〖注〗 quarters 宿営，住居.   shogunate 将軍の，幕府(の).   headquarters 本拠.

bancha 番茶   coarse Japanese tea leaves; the lowest grade of Japanese tea made from large and tough leaves.   This tea turns out to be yellowish brown rather than green.   Unlike other kinds of green tea, it is brewed in boiling hot water.   *Bancha* leaves are often roasted to bring out a smoky flavor. Such tea is specifically known as *hōjicha* (roasted tea) and is brownish. Along with *sencha*, *bancha* is popularly used in everyday life. In Japanese restaurants it is served free of charge. ⇨ CHA, HŌJICHA, RYOKU-CHA, SENCHA

〖注〗 coarse 粗い，粗野な． brew（茶を）入れる． free of charge 無料で．

Bandai-Asahi Kokuritsu-kōen 磐梯朝日国立公園 Bandai-Asahi National Park (1,895. 6 square kilometers), designated in 1950; a natural park comprising mountainous regions of Yamagata, Fukushima and Niigata prefectures in northern Honshū. In addition to a large lake (Lake Inawashiro), it features a number of mountains including the dormant volcano Mount Bandai (1,820 meters). Many of the mountains are made up mainly of granite, with steep slopes and ravines. This park also abounds in dense forests and alpine plants, and is inhabited by wild animals, such as deer, bears, squirrels, etc. In winter, many of its slopes are used for skiing. ⇨ KOKURITSU-KŌEN

〖注〗 dormant volcano 休火山． granite 花崗岩． ravine 峡谷． abound in ～に富む． alpine plant 高山植物．

bangasa 番傘 lit. a number umbrella. an umbrella made of bamboo and oil paper. Before the spread of the Western umbrella of cloth, it was a common type of umbrella, generally used by men. It also served as an ad, with a shop's name and address painted on the oil paper. ⇨ JANOME(-GASA), KARAKASA

Banko-yaki 万古焼 Banko ceramic ware; ceramic ware produced around Yokkaichi, Mie Prefecture, since the late 18th century. This ceramic ware is characterized by the dark-brown grainy clay used and its decorations of Chinese origin: plants, animals, scenes from Chinese folklore, etc. These decorations are sometimes engraved without using color or glaze, and sometimes have a grayish cream color and are patterned in a reddish brown glaze.

〖注〗 ceramic ware 陶器． grainy clay つぶつぶのある粘土． folklore 伝説． engrave 彫る． glaze つや，釉．

banzai 万歳 lit. ten thousand years. 1) a shout or cheer addressed to the emperor meaning "May you live a long life!" During the war, it was a patriotic cry, especially uttered in triumph in battle. 2) an enthusiastic cry of celebration or triumph meaning "hurrah" or "three cheers." *Banzai* is often shouted upon the successful conclusion of a difficult achievement. In unison, it is customarily

repeated three times and the arms are usually raised in the air.
〖注〗 address to 〜に話しかける． in unison 一致して，声をそろえて．

banzuke 番付   a list ranking professional *sumō* wrestlers.   Three days after every tournament all wrestlers are reranked according to their win-loss records by a committee of *sumō* judges (*shōbukensayaku*).   The five column list, divided into east and west camps with the names of higher-ranking wrestlers listed in higher rows and in larger characters, is handwritten in calligraphy by one of the referees (*gyōji*) and later printed.   The names of *makuuchi* wrestlers appear in the first row, those of *jūryō* and *makushita* in the second, those of *sandanme* in the third, those of *jonidan* in the fourth, and those of *jonokuchi* last.   The official presentation of the new rankings takes place just before the next tournament.   ⇨ GYŌJI, JŪRYŌ, MAKUUCHI, ŌZUMŌ, SUMŌ
〖注〗 calligraphy 書道．

bashōfu 芭蕉布   abaca cloth; a hand-woven, dyed textile of Okinawa.   *Bashōfu* is woven from banana fiber.   Traditionally, it has been made only by women, and is prominent in the Kijoka district of Ōgimi village, near Okuma.   Banana leaves are stripped and dried.   The fibers are then spun and later dyed.   The colored fibers are then woven into a beautiful fabric.   ⇨ OKINAWA
〖注〗 abaca マニラ麻． banana fiber 芭蕉の繊維． fabric 織物．

Batō Kannon 馬頭観音   the Horse-Headed Kannon; the Kannon, or Deity of Mercy, worshiped as the guardian deity of horses or other animals.   His image is depicted as having the figure of a horse's head in his crown.   Unlike other kinds of Kannon, he has a fierce expression, with roots beyond Buddhism and having to do with Hinduism of India.   He is said to have the power to ward off evil spirits.   In the Golden Hall of Saidaiji Temple (originally built in 765), there is enshrined a famous statue of this kind, brought to Japan in the late Nara period (710-94).   ⇨ BOSATSU, KANNON
〖注〗 guardian deity 守護神． Hinduism ヒンズー教． ward off 追い払う，防ぐ． enshrine 祀る．

batsu 閥   a clique; a faction; a small exclusive group, informally made up of persons having the same background or the same purpose.   Such groups are formed based on school background (academic clique or *gakubatsu*), conglomerates (financial clique or *zaibatsu*), family ties (kinship clique or *keibatsu*), clans of feudal times (clan clique or *hanbatsu*), or factionalism in a political party (political faction or *habatsu*). There is a strong tendency to emphasize small-group affiliations. The intra-group structure is characterized by hierarchical relationships centering around a prominent person and close-knit interdependence among the members. Sometimes the terms *batsu* and *habatsu* are used synonymously. ⇨ GAKUBATSU, HABATSU, ZAIBATSU

〖注〗 clique 徒党, 閥. conglomerate 複合企業. kinship clique 閨閥. clan 氏, 藩. factionalism 派閥(主義). affiliation 加入, 所属. intra-group structure 集団内構造. hierarchical 序列の. close-knit interdependence 密接な相互依存.

beiju 米寿 lit. the rice congratulatory occasion. the celebration of one's 88th birthday; the 88th anniversary of one's life, one of the special ages at which one celebrates one's longevity. The Chinese character 米 (*bei*) meaning "rice" can be considered to be composed of 八十八, i.e., eighty-eight. Thus, the 88th birthday came to be called *beiju* together with *ju* meaning "longevity" or "congratulations". ⇨ HAKUJU, KANREKI, KIJU

〖注〗 congratulatory めでたい, 祝いの. longevity 長寿. Chinese character 漢字.

Ben(zai)ten 弁(財)天 the Goddess of Arts and Wisdom; the only female member of the Seven Deities of Good Luck. She is said to be a talented beauty and is depicted as playing a *biwa*, a string instrument. One legend says that she served Gautama Sakyamuni (fifth century B.C.) with her special wisdom and eloquence. There is a very popular shrine dedicated to Benten near Kamakura, called Zeniarai Benten (Money-Cleansing Benten). ⇨ BIWA, SHICHI-FUKUJIN

〖注〗 the Seven Deities of Good Luck 七福神. string instrument 弦楽器. Gautama Sakyamuni 釈迦牟尼. Money-Cleansing Benten 銭洗弁天.

bingata 紅型 lit. red patterns. a hand-woven, dyed textile of Okinawa. *Bingata* is the most well-known textile of Okinawa. It is handwoven from linen and, in a series of steps, dyed in a manner similar to the batik of Indonesia, but differs in that it uses a paste-resist (rice bran, rice flour and salt) instead of a wax-resist technique. After weaving, the resist is applied and dried in the sun. Then the dye is applied through a cut stencil and rubbed in with a brush, and fixed with a soy juice. The paste resist is then washed out and the textile is sun-dried. Favored motifs are from nature: flowers, grasses, rivers, birds, etc. Locales known for

particularly fine *bingata* include Naha and Shuri.   ⇨ OKINAWA,
RYŪKYŪ-SHOTŌ

〖注〗 batik ろうけつ染め.   paste resist 糊を用いた防染剤.   rice bran 米ぬ
か.   stencil 型紙、染め型.   soy juice 大豆の汁.

Bishamon(ten) 毘沙門(天)   the God of War and Defense; one of
the Seven Deities of Good Luck in Japanese folklore and one of the
Four Kings of Heaven in Buddhism.   He is clad in armor, holding
a spear in one hand, as if ready to fight against evil.   This spear is
said to have a magical power to protect people from evil.   ⇨
SHITENNŌ, SHICHI-FUKUJIN

〖注〗 the Seven Deities of Good Luck 七福神.   folklore 伝説.   the Four
Kings of Heaven 四天王.   be clad in ～を装っている，～を着ている.   armor
冑.   spear 槍.

biwa 琵琶   a Japanese lute; a pear-shaped lute with a bent neck,
usually having four or five strings with four or five frets depending
upon the type, and played with a triangular *bachi* (plectrum).
There are two basic *biwa* traditions in Japan, introduced from the
Asian continent.   One is the *mōsō-biwa* (blind-priest) type going
back to the seventh century, and the other is the *gaku-biwa* (court)
type introduced in the eighth century.   The former type is used to
accompany Buddhist sutras while the latter is used with Gagaku
court music ensembles.   A narrative style was developed in the
13th century and is known as *Heike-biwa*; *biwa* ballads also began
to be sung in the 16th century with *Satsuma-biwa* accompaniment.
Modern forms of *biwa* music were developed in the Meiji and
Taishō eras which gained wide popularity.   There was a rapid
decline after World War II, and the pre-modern forms have become
almost extinct.   However, recently there have been some efforts
at revival.   Today such composers as Tōru Takemitsu have
written contemporary works for the *biwa* and Western orchestra.
⇨ BACHI, GAGAKU

〖注〗 lute リュート(ギターに似た16，17世紀の弦楽器).   string 弦.   fret フ
レット(弦楽器のネック駒).   plectrum (楽器の)ばち，つめ.   *mōsō-biwa* 盲僧琵
琶.   accompany 伴う，伴奏する.   sutra 経文，お経.   ensemble 合奏.

Bizen-yaki 備前焼   old Bizen ceramic ware; ceramic ware produced
in Bizen, in the present Okayama Prefecture, since the 13th century.   The clay used is extremely hard and tenacious, its color
reddish brown, and its texture closely resembling bronze.   The
ware is never artificially glazed and even misshapen pieces are

esteemed. Originally, only seed jars and flower vases for everyday household use were made; however, accidental shapes created by the use of a bamboo spatula happened to appeal to the aesthetic sense of tea masters.

〖注〗 ceramic ware 陶器． tenacious 粘り強い． texture 肌合い，手ざわり． glaze 光沢をつける，上薬［釉］をかける． misshapen piece いびつの形のもの． bamboo spatula 竹べら． aesthetic 美的．

bokujū 墨汁 India ink or black liquid ink. It is made by rubbing an ink stick on an inkstone, and is used for writing calligraphy and black-and-white ink painting. Bottled ready-made *bokujū* is also available. ⇨ SHODŌ, SUMI, SUZURI

〖注〗 ink stick（棒形の）墨． inkstone 硯． calligraphy 書道． black-and-white painting 水墨画，墨絵．

bōkūzukin 防空頭布 an anti-air raid hood; a padded hood invented during World War II. It was worn to protect the head from dangerous objects. A similar type of hood, called *bōsaizukin* (anti-disaster hood), is thought to provide protection in the case of earthquakes.

〖注〗 anti-air raid 防空． anti-disaster 防災．

Bon 盆 the Bon Festival; the Buddhist All Souls' Days（July 13-15 or 16, or August 13-15 or 16）; the time when Buddhist rites are held for consoling the souls of ancestors, rites believed to have been observed since the seventh century. Today, the festival is mostly observed August 13-15 or 16, roughly corresponding to July 13-15 or 16 of the lunar calendar. The souls of ancestors are invited to their homes on the evening of the 13th and escorted back to the other world on the evening of the 15th or the morning of the 16th, though rituals vary according to the district. During this period, a priest is called to hold a Buddhist service, offerings of food and flowers are prepared for the altar, and graves are visited. It is also a time for family reunions for the living members of this world. On this occasion, people working away from home return to their hometowns. ⇨ BON-ODORI

〖注〗 Buddhist rite 仏事，法事． console 慰める． the lunar calendar 太陰暦． ritual 儀式． Buddhist service 仏教の儀式，法事． offering お供え． altar 祭壇，仏壇． reunion 再会．

bonkei 盆景 a miniature landscape on a tray; a miniature representation of a natural landscape arranged on a shallow dish or lacquer tray. It can be made of any material found in nature—pebbles, stones, sand, mud, moss and plants—combined with some manmade materials, such as miniature models of a house, a shrine gate, a bridge, etc.   Also called *hakoniwa* (lit. a box garden) when it is arranged in a box-like container.

〚注〛 representation 表現，描写． lacquer tray 漆塗りの盆． shrine gate 鳥居．

Bon-odori 盆踊り   lit. Bon Festival dances.   folk dances performed by all ages during the summer lantern festival (Bon) to welcome back, console and then send off the spirits of departed ancestors in mid-July or mid-August.   Traditionally performed in temple grounds or open areas in rural villages, the Bon dances are now also popular in urban areas.   The accompanying songs and *hayashi* music vary from region to region.   ⇨ BON, HAYASHI

〚注〛 console 慰める，供養する．

bonryaku-temae 盆略点前   a tray tea ceremony; an abbreviated tea ceremony prepared on a tray.   It is the most simplified way of preparing ceremonial tea and can be performed anywhere in a short time, with a minimum of tea utensils—a tea bowl, tea caddy, scoop, whisk and tea cloth placed on the tray, plus a waste-water bowl and a pot containing hot water.   ⇨ CHAIRE, CHAKIN, CHANOYU, CHASEN, CHASHAKU, CHAWAN, KENSUI, NATSUME

〚注〛 abbreviated 簡略化された． tea ceremony 茶の湯． tea utensils 茶道具． tea bowl 茶碗． tea caddy 茶入れ，なつめ． (tea) scoop 茶杓． (tea) whisk 茶筅． tea cloth 茶巾． waste-water bowl 建水．

bonsai 盆栽   a miniature potted tree or plant.   A potted tree or plant is dwarfed by artificial methods of culture such as pruning, wiring, or limiting root space.   A desired shape, size, or effect can be produced by the skillful expert with exceptional care over a long period of time, sometimes requiring many generations.

〚注〛 potted 鉢植えにした． dwarf 小さくする，発育をとめる． culture 耕作，栽培． pruning 刈り込み，枝打ち．

bonseki 盆石   a dry landscape on a tray; a miniature representation of a landscape arranged with rocks and white sand on a black lacquer tray, which is symbolic of mountains, rivers or the ocean. This art developed in the Muromachi period (1336-1568) along with the tea ceremony and flower arrangement.   Today, artificial stones are sometimes used.   ⇨ KARESANSUI(-TEIEN)

〚注〛 dry landscape 枯山水． miniature representation 縮小して表現したもの． lacquer tray 漆塗りの盆． tea ceremony 茶の湯． flower arrangement

生け花.

Bonten 梵天　Brahma; the creator, the primal source of all beings in the Brahminism of India; in Japanese Buddhism, a guardian deity who protects the land of Buddhism.　In Japan, he is usually depicted as wearing armor under a long Chinese-style garment, suggesting that he has a strong will under a gentle countenance.　Bonten was introduced from China to Japan along with Buddhism, and has been worshiped particularly in esoteric Buddhism.　⇨ MIKKYŌ

〖注〗 primal source 根源.　Brahminism バラモン教.　guardian deity 守護神.　armor よろいかぶと.　garment 衣服, 外衣.　countenance 表情.　esoteric 密教の.

bosatsu 菩薩　a bodhisattva (Sanskrit); a Buddhist saint; a buddha-to-be, a being who has attained enlightenment but who remains in this world for the salvation of all people.　This being is worshiped as an ideal for humans to follow in many sects of Mahayana Buddhism (*Daijō Bukkyō*).　There are several different *bosatsu*: Kannon (or Kanzeon) Bosatsu, Monju Bosatsu, Fugen Bosatsu, Jizō Bosatsu, etc., as portrayed in paintings and sculptures.　⇨ DAIJŌ BUKKYŌ, JIZO(BOSATSU), KANNON(BOSATSU), MONJU(BOSATSU)

〖注〗 buddha-to-be 仏になる人.　attain enlightenment 悟りを開く.　sect 宗派, 分派.　Mahayana Buddhism 大乗仏教.　Fugen Bosatsu 普賢菩薩.

botamochi 牡丹餅　lit. a rice cake in the season of the peony.　a sweet rice-dumpling made of glutinous rice coated with sweet red-bean paste or sweet soybean flour.　Steamed rice grains are coarsely crushed and kneaded into a round or oval shape, and then covered with a thick layer of red-bean paste (*an*) or soybean flour (*kinako*).　It is traditionally eaten or offered to family ancestors during the Buddhist festivals centering around the vernal and autumnal equinoxes.　The dumplings made in autumn are sometimes called *hagi-mochi* meaning "rice cake in the season of bush clovers."　⇨ AN, HIGAN, KINAKO

〖注〗 peony 牡丹, しゃくやく.　dumpling 団子.　glutinous rice 糯米.　red-bean paste 小豆餡.　soybean flour 黄粉.　knead 練る.　the vernal equinox 春の彼岸の中日.　the autumnal equinox 秋の彼岸の中日.　bush clover 萩.

bugaku 舞楽　the dance art of Gagaku; an ancient court dance with music, performed at court festivals and on other festive occasions. The Bugaku repertoire is divided into two categories, the first based on ancient dances native to Korea and performed to ancient Korean songs.　Most pieces, however, were introduced from other

parts of Asia such as Southeast Asia, China or India with masks
and costumes based on some foreign personage, event, or even
animal, and are accompanied by instruments from other countries
without the use of songs. It is preserved today by the Imperial
Household Agency, and some local shrines and temples as well as
amateur performance groups. Colorful costumes and the grace of
the slow and refined motions of the dance are the main features of
Bugaku.   ⇨ GAGAKU

〖注〗 court dance 宮廷舞踊． festive occasion 祭りの時． repertoire レパー
トリー，上演種目． piece（芸術上の）作品． personage 人物，役． accompany
伴う，伴奏する． the Imperial Household Agency 宮内庁． amateur performance group 素人の演奏グループ．

bugei 武芸 martial arts; the way of mastering samurai arts. These
arts include archery, judo, karate, swordsmanship, horseback-
riding, etc. Influenced by the ideas of Zen Buddhism, these traditional martial arts place stress on mental discipline, not merely on
techniques.   ⇨ JŪDŌ, KARATE, KENDŌ, KYŪDŌ, ZENSHŪ

〖注〗 martial 武勇の、戦の． archery 弓、弓道． swordsmanship 剣道，剣道
精神．

bugyō 奉行 a commissioner; an administrator; the official title
given to high-ranking administrators working for the Imperial
Court in the Heian period (794-1185) and for the shogunate government in feudal times. Particularly in the Edo period (1603-
1868), they played important roles, being under the direct control of
the shogunate government. Among others, important officials
were the *jisha-bugyō,* in charge of the supervision of temples and
shrines, the *kanjō-bugyō,* dealing with financial affairs of the government, and the *machi-bugyō,* overseeing the affairs, including
judicial problems, of towns and people of other than the samurai
class.   ⇨ BAKUFU, EDO-JIDAI

〖注〗 commissioner 長官，地方行政官． shogunate (government) 幕府． feudal times 封建時代． judicial 司法の，裁判の．

Buke Shohatto 武家諸法度 The Code of the Samurai; a number of
laws regulating feudal lords and their subordinate warriors,
imposed by the Tokugawa shogunate government (1603-1868).
They were first enforced in 1615 by the second Tokugawa shogun,
Tokugawa Hidetada (1578-1632). Each shogun issued a new code,
but the contents remained basically the same. The code dictated
ways to control feudal domains, feudal lords' alternate attendance

in Edo, attire appropriate for samurai, the prohibition of free marriage of samurai, etc. ⇨ DAIMYŌ, EDO-JIDAI, SHŌGUN, SANKIN-KŌTAI, TOKUGAWA-BAKUFU

〖注〗 code 法典. feudal lord 大名. subordinate 部下(の), 従者(の). shogunate (government) 幕府. enforce 施行する. domain 領地, 領土. alternate attendance 参勤交代. attire 服装.

Bukkyō 仏教 Buddhism; a religion founded in India by Sakyamuni Buddha (?565-?486 B.C.), which later spread to central and eastern Asia. It was roughly divided into two types: Mahayana (or Northern) Buddhism and Hinayana (or Southern) Buddhism, the former emphasizing universal salvation and the latter individual salvation. Each further developed into a great number of sects differing widely within individual countries. Buddhism teaches that life is full of suffering and that elimination of worldly desires through enlightenment will lead to salvation. Buddhism was introduced to Japan in the sixth century and took root through the support of Prince Shōtoku (574-622). It enjoyed national patronage in the Nara period (646-794). The Tendai and Shingon sects appeared in the Heian period (794-1185), and the Jōdo, Nichiren and Zen sects, etc., in the Kamakura period (1185-1336). Since the Edo period (1603-1868), when the parishioner system was enforced by the shogunate, Japanese Buddhism has emphasized ancestor worship. ⇨ DAIJŌ BUKKYŌ, SHŌJŌ BUKKYŌ

〖注〗 Mahayana Buddhism 大乗仏教. Hinayana Buddhism 小乗仏教. salvation 救い. worldly desire 煩悩. enlightenment 悟り. national patronage 国家の保護. the parishioner system 檀家制度.

bunka-kōrōsha 文化功労者 a person of cultural merit; persons recognized by the government for their contributions to the development of culture, in the sciences, arts, etc. They are honored annually around November 3 (Culture Day), and are granted through the Ministry of Education a life annuity of ¥3.5 million by the Law of the Annuity for Persons of Cultural Merit, enacted in 1951. Among the recipients, 10 to 20 particularly outstanding ones are awarded the Cultural Order Medal in the presence of the Emperor on November 3. As of 1986, there were 389 persons thus recognized, 231 of them recipients of the medal. ⇨ BUNKA-KUNSHŌ, BUNKA NO HI

〖注〗 merit 勲功, 功労. life annuity 終身年金. the Law of the Annuity for Persons of Cultural Merit 「文化功労年金法」. enact (法令を)発する, 制定す

る． cultural order 文化勲章． recipient 受賞者．

bunka-kunshō 文化勲章 a cultural medal; the order of cultural merit; a medal awarded to those who have made great contributions to the development of culture, in the sciences, arts, etc. The award was established in 1937. Since 1946 the selection of recipients has been conducted annually by the Cabinet, based on recommendations by the Education Minister. The medal is presented in the presence of the Emperor on November 3 (Culture Day). It is a gold medal in the shape of a five-petaled mandarin orange blossom and is attached to a purple ribbon. ⇨ BUNKA-KŌRŌSHA, BUNKA NO HI

〖注〗 order 勲章，勲位． merit 賞，功労． the order of merit 功労勲章〔位〕． recipient 受賞者． five-petaled 5つの花弁の． mandarin orange blossom 橘の花．

Bunka no Hi 文化の日 Culture Day (November 3); a national holiday designated to encourage the people to cherish peace and freedom, and to value culture as a whole. Various cultural ceremonies and activities are held both locally and nationwide on and around this day. As one of the notable national functions, the order of cultural merit is awarded to persons who have made either national or international contributions. Until the end of World War II, this day was called *Meijisetsu*, and was a holiday commemorating the birth of Emperor Meiji, the grandfather of the present Emperor. ⇨ BUNKA-KŌRŌSHA, BUNKA-KUNSHŌ, KOKUMIN NO SHUKUJITSU

〖注〗 function 儀式，行事． the order of cultural merit 文化勲章． order 勲位，勲章． merit 功労，賞． commemorate 〜の記念となる、〜を記念する．

bunkazai 文化財 cultural assets; cultural properties; cultural properties officially designated and protected under the Cultural Properties Protection Law enacted in 1950. Official protection is applied to five categories—tangible cultural properties (*yūkei-bunkazai*); intangible cultural properties (*mukei-bunkazai*); folk-culture properties (*minzoku-shiryō*); historic sites, scenic places and natural monuments (*shiseki, meisho, tennen-kinenbutsu*); historic buildings and structures (*rekishiteki-kenzōbutsu*). ⇨ MUKEI-BUNKAZAI, TENNEN-KINENBUTSU

〖注〗 assets 資産，財産． the Cultural Properties Protection Law 「文化財保護法」． enact 法律化する、（法律を）発する． tangible cultural property 有形文化財． intangible cultural property 無形文化財． folk-culture property 民族

資料. historic sites, scenic places and natural monuments 史跡, 名所, 天然記念物.

bunraku 文楽 the general term for the classical puppet theater. Bunraku consists of three elements—the *jōruri* narration originating in the late 15th century accompanied by the *biwa*, the *shamisen* instrumental accompaniment which replaced the *biwa* around 1560, and the addition of manipulated puppets (*ningyō*) introduced around 1600. It took its present form as *ningyō-jōruri* in the 17th century when Chikamatsu Monzaemon (1653-1724) wrote many plays for Bunraku. The main dolls (*ningyō*) are manipulated by three puppeteers while the narrator (*tayū*) recites the story to the accompaniment of *shamisen*. The unique charm of Bunraku lies in the harmony of the skillful actions of the puppets manipulated by the puppeteers and the deep voice of the *jōruri* singers telling a story to the sound of *shamisen*, which exquisitely conveys human feelings and moves the audience to tears and laughter. The stylized movements of the puppets can be seen in the acting techniques of the Kabuki theater, which has adapted many Bunraku plays. ⇨ BIWA, JŌRURI, SHAMISEN

〖注〗 accompany 伴う, 伴奏する. instrumental accompaniment 楽器による伴奏. manipulate 操る. puppeteer 人形を操る人, 人形遣い. exquisitely 巧妙に. stylized movement 様式化した動き. adapt 脚色する.

bushidō 武士道 lit. the way of the warrior. traditional Japanese chivalry, the unwritten code of ethics and behavior developing from the feudal warrior society. This concept took on importance with the establishment of the Kamakura shogunate (1185-1336), due to the need for the training of warriors in military skills and discipline to foster loyalty and bravery. In the Edo period (1603-1868), with the revival of Confucian studies and the spread of Zen Buddhism, the concept of *bushidō* was elevated to a basic ethical philosophy for warriors to follow and it influenced the commoners' way of thinking as well. There has been a variety of interpretations of *bushidō*. The *Hagakure* (lit. Hidden Behind Leaves, 1716), a collection of lectures given to warriors by Yamamoto Tsunetomo (1659-1719) and compiled by Tashiro Tsuramoto (1687-1748), states that "*Bushidō* means a way of dying." The Confucian scholar Yamaga Sokō (1622-85), who applied Confucianism to the principles of military science and samurai ethics, advocated the necessity of mental training to prepare for sacrifice in loyalty. Inazō

Nitobe (1862-1933), an educator and Christian, in his *Bushidō* (in English, 1905) attempts to explain the soul of Japan through *bushidō*, focusing on such virtues as justice, courage, benevolence, politeness, veracity and sincerity, honor, the duty of loyalty, self-control, etc.   ⇨ JUKYŌ, ZEN¹, ZENSHŪ

〖注〗 chivalry 騎士道. code おきて. ethics 倫理. Confucian studies 儒学. spread 普及. Yamamoto Tsunetomo 山本常朝. Tashiro Tsuramoto 田代(又左衛門)陳基. "*Bushidō* means a way of dying."「武士道といふは死ぬこと(と見つけたり)」. Yamaga Sokō 山鹿素行. Confucianism 儒教. justice, courage, benevolence, politeness, veracity and sincerity, honor, the duty of loyalty, self-control 義, 勇, 仁, 礼, 誠, 名誉, 忠義, 克己.

busshi 仏師 lit. a Buddhist master. a master craftsman of Buddhist images. In the Kamakura period (1185-1336), *busshi* was the occupational title given to skilled sculptors and painters of Buddhist images.   ⇨ BUTSUZŌ

〖注〗 craftsman 職人, 工芸家. Buddhist image 仏像. occupational title 職業上の肩書. sculptor 彫刻家.

butsudan 仏壇 a Buddhist household altar. Usually it holds a figure of the Buddha, and tablets with the posthumous names of ancestors and of the dead in the family. Flowers, offerings of food, and burning incense are regularly placed before the altar. A typical *butsudan* has a black lacquered body with gilted decorations.   ⇨ HONZON, IHAI

〖注〗 altar 祭壇. tablet 平板. posthumous name 死後の名前, 戒名. tablets with the posthumous names of ancestors 先祖の位牌. burning incense 線香. lacquered 漆を塗った. gilted 金箔にした.

butsumetsu 仏滅 lit. Buddha's death. a day of ill-fortune; the unluckiest day during a period comprising six days of the lunar calendar. Stemming from the Chinese philosophy of dual cosmic forces, the cycle of six divisions came to be applied to fortune-telling in Japan and is still observed for special occasions. A *butsumetsu* day is particularly avoided for weddings, moving, or starting long journeys.   ⇨ ROKUYŌ, TAIAN

〖注〗 six days of the lunar calendar 太陰暦の六曜, 六輝. dual cosmic forces 宇宙の二元力, 陰陽. fortune-telling 予言, 運命鑑定.

butsuzō 仏像 a Buddhist image; an image or likeness of the Buddha, sculpted or painted as an object of worship in Buddhism. Specifically, it refers to an image of the Buddha himself. More commonly, it includes images of various Bosatsu, Nyorai, Myōō and Ten, including Jizō, Kannon, etc. Sometimes, even figures of enlightened Buddhist priests may be included. ⇨ BOSATSU, JIZŌ (BOSATSU), KANNON (BOSATSU), MYŌŌ, NYORAI

【注】 sculpt 彫刻する. figure 人物像. enlightened 悟りを開いた.

byōbu 屏風 a folding screen; a screen consisting of a number of panels with a continuous picture or separate pictures on it. It is made of thick Japanese paper spread on a wooden frame and is used as a decorative blind or a room divider. There are two-, four-, six- and eight-panel screens.

【注】 folding 折りたたみ式の. panel 羽目板, パネル絵. wooden frame 木枠. blind ついたて.

C

cha 茶　tea; the generic, broad term for any kind of tea, also referring to the tea ceremony; specifically, green tea (also called
ryokucha), a beverage prepared by steeping green tea leaves in hot
water. Japanese green tea is classified into several varieties,
according to when the leaves are picked, the way it is prepared or
served, etc. Some kinds are *gyokuro*, *sencha*, *bancha*, etc., for
everyday use, and *matcha* for the tea ceremony. There are also
such popular kinds of tea as *hōjicha* (roasted tea), *mugicha* (barley
tea), etc., which are brownish rather than green. ⇨ BANCHA,
CHANOYU, GYOKURO, HŌJICHA, MATCHA, MUGICHA, RYOKUCHA, SEN-
CHA
〖注〗 tea ceremony 茶道．beverage 飲み物．steep（液体に）～を浸す，つ
ける．

chabako 茶箱　a tea chest; a wooden box used for keeping tea leaves
at tea shops. It is about a meter in length, 60 centimeters in width
and 60 cm in height, and is usually made of plain wood, lined with
tin to keep out moisture from the tea leaves. Formerly, some
special ones were covered with artistically designed fabrics or
paper. ⇨ CHA
〖注〗 plain wood 白木．line 裏張りする．fabric 布，織物．

chabana 茶花　lit. a tea flower. a simple flower arrangement for a
tearoom. It was developed by the 16th-century tea master, Sen no
Rikyū (1521-91). The beauty found in simplicity and purity is the
main theme of flower arrangements for the tea ceremony. Thus,
the arrangement used in a tearoom usually consists of a single
simple flower that is often only a bud. ⇨ CHANOYU, IKEBANA
〖注〗 flower arrangement 生け花．tea master 茶人，茶の師匠．tea ceremony 茶の湯．

chagama 茶釜　a teakettle; a kettle used for boiling water in the tea
ceremony. It is usually made of iron but can also be made of brass
or silver. The sound of the water boiling in the kettle calls to

mind the sound of wind through the pine leaves for devotees of tea.
⇨ CHANOYU

〖注〗 tea ceremony 茶の湯． brass しんちゅう． sound of wind through the pine leaves 松風の音． devotee of tea 茶人，茶の愛好者．

chaire 茶入れ a tea caddy; a small, usually ceramic, receptacle with an ivory lid for the thick, powdered tea used in the tea ceremony. It is kept in a bag made of old silk cloth called *shifuku*. In making tea, the bag is removed. ⇨ CHANOYU, NATSUME

〖注〗 caddy 小かん，小さい入れ物． ceramic 陶器(の)． receptacle 入れ物，容器． ivory lid 象牙の蓋． thick, powdered tea 濃い抹茶，濃茶． tea ceremony 茶の湯．

chajin 茶人 a tea master; a devotee of the tea ceremony. Devotees of tea regard the spirit of Zen as important, and appreciate both art and nature. Thus, practicing the way of tea makes a person of refined taste. ⇨ CHANOYU, ZEN[1]

〖注〗 devotee 熱中者，道に専念する人． tea ceremony 茶の湯． person of refined taste 洗練された趣味の人，風流人．

chakin 茶巾 a tea cloth; a small oblong piece of white linen or cotton used in the tea ceremony. It is roughly 30 by 15 centimeters in size. After being soaked in water, squeezed, and folded, it is used to wipe the edge and inside of a rinsed tea bowl, according to the prescribed rules of the tea ceremony. ⇨ CHANOYU, CHAWAN

〖注〗 prescribed rules 定まった規則．

chanoyu 茶の湯 the tea ceremony; the way of tea; an aesthetic pastime in which powdered tea is served in a ceremonial yet artistic way. Largely influenced by the ideas of Zen Buddhism, the tea ceremony cultivates a sense of inner tranquillity, and a proper frame of mind toward nature and man. The fundamental spirit of the tea ceremony is exemplified by the expression "harmony, reverence, purity and tranquillity." Thus, the traditional Japanese art of serving tea has its goal in attaining enlightenment through mental composure as well as acquiring elegant manners and etiquette. The drinking of powdered tea was introduced from China by the Zen priest Eisai (1141-1215) in the Kamakura period (1185-1336). But it was Sen no Rikyū (1521-91) who developed the rustic tea ceremony in the late Muromachi period (1336-1568). ⇨ SADŌ, WABICHA, WA-KEI-SEI-JAKU, ZEN[1], ZENSHŪ

〖注〗 aesthetic pastime 美的なたしなみ，風流の遊び． powdered tea 抹茶． cultivate みがく． tranquillity 平静，静寂． frame of mind 心構え． tea cere-

mony 茶の湯. harmony, reverence, purity and tranquillity 和敬清寂.
enlightenment 啓発, 悟り. mental composure 心の落ち着き. rustic tea
ceremony 侘茶.

chasen 茶筅 a bamboo tea whisk; a utensil used in the tea ceremony
for whipping up a mixture of green tea powder and hot water into
froth or paste. It is about 10 centimeters long, and is made of a
piece of cut bamboo, about two-thirds of which is finely split with
the tips slightly curled toward the center. The soft-headed type of
whisk is used for making foamy tea (*usucha*) while the coarse-
headed kind is for making pasty tea (*koicha*). ⇨ CHANOYU, KOI-
CHA, MATCHA, SADŌ, USUCHA
〚注〛 whisk 泡立て器. tea ceremony 茶道. froth 泡. the soft-headed type
of whisk 数穂. the coarse-headed type (of whisk) 荒穂.

chashaku 茶杓 a tea scoop; a spoon-like utensil for ladling out
powdered tea from a tea caddy to a tea bowl. It was originally
made of ivory, but from around the 16th century it came to be made
by whittling bamboo. A good tea scoop is whittled by a famous
tea master himself and bears his name. ⇨ CHANOYU
〚注〛 scoop ひしゃく, 掬うもの. ladle ひしゃくですくう, くみ出す. powdered tea 抹茶. tea caddy 茶入れ, なつめ. whittle 削る. tea master 茶人,
茶の師匠.

chashitsu 茶室 a tearoom; a structure or small room specially
designed for serving ceremonial tea, usually the size of a four-and-
a-half-mat room. It has a sunken square hearth fitted into the
floor where an iron teakettle is placed. There is also an alcove for
a hanging scroll and a flower arrangement suitable for the season.
With its small and humble appearance, it is intended to suggest
rustic simplicity and refined poverty. The first tearoom was built
at Ginkakuji Temple, Kyoto, by Ashikaga Yoshimitsu (1358-1408),
the third shogun of the Muromachi shogunate (1336-1568), who
devoted himself to the arts and literature. ⇨ CHANOYU, RO, TO-
KONOMA, WABICHA, WABI-SABI
〚注〛 four-and-a-half-mat room 四畳半. sunken square hearth 低くなった四
角い炉床, (茶室の)炉. iron teakettle 茶釜. alcove 床の間. hanging scroll
掛け物. flower arrangement 生け花. rustic simplicity わびれた簡素さ, さ
び, わび・さび. refined poverty 洗練された素朴さ, わび, わび・さび.

chatei 茶庭 a tea garden; a small Japanese landscape garden accompanying a tea-ceremony room. The tea garden is designed to
create an atmosphere conducive to the serenity necessary for full

appreciation of the tea ceremony.   Thus, it is composed of natural scenery with rusticity and simplicity.   Features include stepping stones, a stone washbasin, a stone lantern, and a middle gate to mark the inner garden and the outer garden, as well as evergreen trees.   Flowering trees are usually avoided.   Also called *roji* when referring especially to the tea garden containing a path leading to the teahouse for the tea ceremony.   ⇨ CHANOYU, CHŪMON[1], ISHI-DŌRŌ, NIHON-TEIEN, ROJI, TSUKUBAI

〖注〗 landscape garden 造景の庭園，日本庭園．tea-ceremony room 茶室．conducive ためになる，促す．serenity 静寂．rusticity さびれたさま，素朴さ．stepping stones 飛び石．stone washbasin つくばい．stone lantern 石燈籠．middle gate 中門．inner garden 内露地．outer garden 外露地．

chawan 茶碗 1) a rice cup; a porcelain cup for rice used for every-day meals.   It is around 10 centimeters in diameter and around 5 cm in height, and is cone-shaped, narrowing down to the base. With this, one can ask for extra helpings of rice.   2) a teacup, or a tea bowl; a ceramic tea bowl used in the tea ceremony, which is much larger than the teacup for everyday use called *yunomi*.   It is an artistic creation to be appreciated for its rustic simplicity and refined elegance.   A deep tea bowl is used with an ordinary sunken hearth (*ro*) in cold seasons, while a shallow one with a portable brazier (*furo*) is used in warmer seasons.   Hagi, Oribe, Shino, Raku and Seto ware, among others, are favored in the tea ceremony.   ⇨ CHANOYU, FURO, HAGI-YAKI, ORIBE-YAKI, RAKU-YAKI, RO, SETO-YAKI, SHINO-YAKI, YUNOMI

〖注〗 porcelain 磁器(の)．extra helping おかわり．ceramic 陶器(の)．tea bowl 茶碗．tea ceremony 茶の湯．artistic creation 芸術創作品．rustic simplicity ひなびた簡素さ，わび・さび．refined elegance 洗練された優雅さ，幽玄．sunken hearth 床にはめこんだ炉床，(茶室の)炉．portable brazier 持ち運びできる火鉢，(茶室の)風炉．

chawanmushi 茶碗蒸し a cup of steamed hodgepodge; steamed egg custard in a cup with various ingredients in it.   The ingredients may include chicken, seafoods, mushrooms, gingko nuts, etc., over which a mixture of beaten egg and seasoned fish broth is poured; the cup is then steamed.   When the custard is done, trefoil leaves are usually put on top as a garnish and for flavor.

〖注〗 hodgepodge [hotchpotch] ごった煮(肉と野菜の濃いシチュー)．ingredient (料理の)材料．gingko [ginkgo] nut 銀杏．seasoned 味のついた．fish broth 魚のだし汁．trefoil leaves 三つ葉．garnish 飾り，(料理に)添える

つま.

Chaya-zome 茶屋染 Chaya-style dyeing; a method of dyeing fabric, developed by Chaya Shirōjirō, a Kyoto draper and purveyor of textile goods to the shogunate in the Edo period (1603-1868). It is characterized by a simple color scheme, predominantly indigo on white. Its bold yet simple pictorial designs depict rustic landscapes. Well-bleached, high-quality hemp fabric is dyed, with the application of stencils pasted on both sides, leaving uncolored designs. This fabric was popularly used to make summer garments for women of the high-ranking samurai class of those days.
〖注〗 fabric 織物. Chaya Shirōjirō 茶屋四郎次郎. draper 反物業者, 呉服商. purveyor 御用商人. shogunate 幕府. color scheme 配色. indigo 藍. rustic landscape 田園風景, わびれた風景. hemp 麻. application of stencils 型紙をあてること. garment 着物, 衣服.

chazuke 茶漬け boiled rice with boiling hot water or green tea poured over it. It is served in a rice bowl, and garnished on top with broiled salted salmon, cod roe, pickles, pickled plum, small pieces of seaweed laver, bonito flakes or trefoil leaves. Often called *ochazuke*.
〖注〗 garnish (料理に)つまを添える, つけ合わせ. broiled 焼いた. cod roe たらこ. pickled plum 漬けた梅, 梅干し. seaweed laver 海苔. bonito flakes 削り節. trefoil leaves 三つ葉.

Chichibu-meisen 秩父銘仙 Chichibu silk fabric; coarse silk woven in the Chichibu area of Saitama Prefecture. *Meisen* silk was first produced in this area, famous for its sericulture, though production has recently declined. This kind of fabric is used to make casual kimono and bedding. ⇨ KIMONO
〖注〗 silk fabric 絹織物. sericulture 蚕産業.

Chichibu-Tama Kokuritsu-kōen 秩父多摩国立公園 Chichibu-Tama National Park (1,216 square kilometers), designated in 1950; a natural park extending over the Kantō mountains, straddling the borders of Saitama, Yamanashi and Nagano prefectures, and the Tokyo metropolitan area. Easily accessible from Tokyo, this park is visited by a great number of people on day trips. The mountains include Mount Kokushi (2,592 meters), Mount Kinbu (2,595 m), Mount Kobushi (2,483 m), etc. Through the mountains flow the Tama and Arakawa rivers, from which Lake Okutama and Lake Chichibu were constructed to supply water for Tokyo. The Daibosatsu Pass was made popular through the novel of the same name written by Kaizan Nakazato (1885-1944). ⇨ KOKURITSU-KŌEN

〖注〗 straddle またにかける. accessible 接近できる. Mount Kokushi 国師ヶ岳. Mount Kinbu 金峰山. Mount Kobushi 甲武信岳. Daibosatsu Pass 大菩薩峠. Kaizan Nakazato 中里介山.

chigaidana 違い棚 lit. shelves of different levels. staggered shelves built into the side-alcove of a Japanese-style drawing room. Some works of art are displayed on them.

〖注〗 staggered 交互にずらして配列した. side-alcove 床脇. Japanese-style drawing room 座敷. work of art 美術品.

chigi 千木 projecting rafter ends on a shrine roof; two pieces of wood forming the letter X on both ends of the roof of a Shinto shrine. Together with *katsuogi* (short logs placed in a row between the two *chigi*), *chigi* were originally fixed to secure the roof against the wind, but came to be used as ornaments as a feature of Shinto shrine architecture. ⇨ JINJA, KATSUOGI, SHINTŌ

〖注〗 project (建物の一部を)張り出させる. rafter たる木.

chikuwa 竹輪 lit. bomboo rings. a bomboo-shaped, broiled fish-paste cake. Fish paste of cod, shark or flying fish, mixed with starch, is molded around a steel rod (originally around a piece of bamboo), steamed and then scorched over a fire. It is usually served sliced into rings. *Kamaboko* (fish-paste cake on a wooden plank) is said to have derived from *chikuwa*. ⇨ KAMABOKO

〖注〗 cod 鱈. shark 鮫. plank 板片.

chimaki 粽 a rice dumpling wrapped in bamboo leaves; a traditional sweet, along with *kashiwa-mochi*, for Boys' Day (May 5). The dumpling is made of sweetened powdered rice, boiled and then pounded. Sometimes, shredded mugwort leaves are mixed into the dumpling, or it may be filled with red-bean jam (*an*). The bamboo-leaf wrapping adds flavor. ⇨ KODOMO NO HI, TANGO NO SEKKU

〖注〗 dumpling 団子. shred ずたずたに切る. mugwort leaves よもぎの葉. red-bean jam 小豆あん.

chindon'ya ちんどん屋 a traditional band of sandwich-board advertisers; a band for advertisement, walking in procession along busy streets. It consists of several men and women, some carrying advertising banners or placards and others playing noisy but merry tunes with drums, *shamisen*, etc. They are dressed in colorful showy costumes, either traditional or modern, with exaggerated makeup to draw the attention of people in the streets.　Nowadays they are rarely seen.

〖注〗　sandwich board サンドイッチマンが背と胸に下げる広告板．　banner 旗, のぼり．　showy 目立つ, けばけばしい．

chinju 鎮守　lit. to subside and guard.　a village guardian shrine; a shrine or deity of a community which protects the land and the people who are born and live there.　The shrine is a small, simple structure, often situated in a village grove.　This *chinju* grove serves to protect the farms surrounding it from wind and floods, and provides a rest area for people working in the fields.　⇨ JINJA

〖注〗　subside 鎮める．　guardian shrine 守護神社．　deity 神, 神のような人[もの]．

chirashi-zushi ちらし鮨　lit.　scattered *sushi*.　garnished *sushi*; vinegared rice with many kinds of ingredients arranged on top. The ingredients include sliced raw fish, mushroom, egg, sweetened mashed fish, seaweed laver, and vegetables.　It is usually served in a shallow, lacquer-ware box.　⇨ SUSHI

〖注〗　garnished つまを添えた, 具をあしらった．　vinegared rice 酢で味つけした御飯．　ingredient 成分, (料理の)材料．　sliced raw fish 薄く切った生の魚, 刺身．　sweetened mashed fish 甘味をつけてつぶした魚, でんぶ．　seaweed laver 海苔．　lacquer-ware 漆器．

chirichōzu 塵手水　a ritual of swearing to fight fairly performed by *sumō* wrestlers before a bout.　On entering the *dohyō* (ring), the wrestlers squat on their heels facing each other at the edges of the ring.　First they rub their hands together in an act of purification. Then they clap their hands twice, extend their arms to the sides with their palms facing upward, and proceed to revolve the palms downward, to show heaven and earth their bare hands in preparation for a clean fight.　⇨ DOHYŌ, SUMŌ

〖注〗　ritual 儀式．　bout 試合．

chirimen 縮緬　silk crepe; finely wrinkled fabric of silk.　This fabric is woven with a straight warp and highly twisted weft.　It is used to make kimono, *obi, furoshiki,* bedding, etc.　There are many kinds of *chirimen: hitokoshi-chirimen, futakoshi-chirimen, kodai-chirimen, omeshi-chirimen,* etc.　⇨ FUROSHIKI, KIMONO, OBI

〖注〗　wrinkled しわのよった, ちぢれた．　warp 縦糸．　weft 横糸, 縮緬の種類：一越縮緬, 二越縮緬, 古代縮緬, 御召縮緬．

chirinabe ちり鍋　a hot pot of fish and vegetables; fish—usually codfish or seabream—boiled with soybean curd, mushrooms, green onions, Chinese cabbages and other vegetables. It is cooked in an earthenware pot at the table and served with seasoned citron sauce and a few condiments—grated Japanese radish, minced green onions, red pepper, etc.

〖注〗 codfish 鱈．　seabream 鯛．　soybean curd 豆腐．　green onions 緑のねぎ，長ねぎ．　Chinese cabbage 白菜．　earthenware pot 土鍋．　condiment 調味料，薬味．　grated Japanese radish おろし大根．　minced こまかく刻んだ．minced green onions さらしねぎ．

Chishima-rettō 千島列島　the Kurile Islands; a chain of small islands off the northeastern tip of Hokkaidō, extending to the southern tip of Kamchatka. The chain consists of some 30 islands, including Etorofu, Kunashiri, Shikotan and Habomai. The islands contain rich mineral deposits and are surrounded by abundant fishing grounds. The islands officially belonged to Japan from 1875 until the end of World War II. They are now held by the Soviet Union.　⇨ HOPPŌ-RYŌDO

〖注〗 Etorofu 択捉．　Kunashiri 国後．　Shikotan 色丹．　Habomai 歯舞．mineral deposit 鉱物の埋蔵．　fishing ground 漁場．

chitoseame 千歳飴　lit. candy of a thousand years. a pack of candy given to children on the occasion of the Shichigosan Festival held November 15 to celebrate children's attainment of 7, 5 and 3 years of age. The candy comes in the shape of a stick, with red and white swirls like a candy cane. It is said that this candy, having the blessings of gods, will bring children happiness for many years.　⇨ SHICHIGOSAN

〖注〗 swirl 渦巻き．　candy cane ステッキ型の赤と白の渦巻きのキャンディ．

chiyogami 千代紙　lit. paper of a thousand generations. patterned paper; Japanese paper with brightly colored patterns originated in the Edo period (1603-1868). With the development of multicolored woodblock prints in the mid-18th century, *ukiyoe* artists also designed patterned paper in bright colors. These patterns were at first auspicious symbols, such as pine, bamboo, cranes, tortoises, etc., and then came in a wide variety, covering a range of subjects seen in those days. This paper was popular among women who then wore strictly regulated clothing, and was used for decorating boxes, covering books, wrapping gifts, and making dolls. *Chiyogami* crafts became part of their life. Thus, *chiyogami* reflects, in part, the essence of the Edo period.　⇨ EDO-JIDAI, UKIYOE

〖注〗 woodblock print 木版画． auspicious めでたい． regulate 規制する．

chō 町 1) a traditional unit for measuring area. One *chō* is 10 *tan*, 100 *se* or 3,000 *tsubo,* equivalent to 9,917.4 square meters. This unit is usually employed in measuring agricultural land, while the area of buildings and lots is measured by *tsubo,* regardless of size. 2) a traditional unit for measuring distance. One *chō* is 60 *ken* or 360 *shaku,* about 109.09 meters. This unit is often employed to denote the number of blocks along a street, one *chō* indicating a block regardless of the exact distance. ⇨ SHAKKAN-HŌ

〖注〗 lot 地所．

chobo ちょぼ the *gidayū* accompaniment in a Kabuki play; *Gidayū* narrators and *shamisen* players, or their music, in a Kabuki play of Bunraku puppet origin. They are seated on an elevated platform at the rear of the stage, with the scenario placed on a small stand. The parts they are supposed to chant or play are marked with dots (*chobo*), thus giving rise to the term. ⇨ BUNRAKU, GIDAYŪ, KABU-KI

〖注〗 accompaniment 伴奏． *gidayū* narrator 義太夫を語る者．

chōchin 提燈 a portable lantern; a lantern made of a bamboo frame covered with paper or silk. A candle is placed inside for illumination. *Chōchin* can be folded flat when not in use. Today, they are only used outdoors on festive occasions. Formerly, a portable *chōchin* was used like a flashlight when one walked at night.

〖注〗 lantern 提燈，燈籠． illumination 照明． flashlight 懐中電灯．

choku 〔choko〕 猪口 a saké cup; a tiny ceramic cup for drinking Japanese rice wine. It is about five centimeters in diameter and is wide at the top and narrow at the bottom. *Choku* is often synonymous with *sakazuki,* but the latter also comprises a larger, flat saké cup of lacquered wood. A small bowl used formally for raw fish (*sashimi*) or vinegared salad (*sunomono*) is sometimes called *choku.* ⇨ SAKE

〖注〗 ceramic 陶器(の)． synonymous with ～と同義の． lacquer 漆，漆を塗る． vinegared 酢で味をつけた．

chokudai 勅題 the theme for the New Year Imperial poetry party. The theme for the 31-syllable poetry (*tanka*) is announced the previous year. Anyone, even from abroad, may submit a 31-syllable poem for consideration. Several persons from the public whose poems are regarded as superior are honored with an invitation to this party held in the Imperial Court. The selected poems are recited aloud by specialists in a ceremonial way of chanting, along with the Imperial poems, in the presence of the Emperor and members of the Imperial Family. ⇨ UTAKAI-HAJIME

〖注〗 Imperial poetry party 宮中歌会. ceremonial way of chanting 吟詠. chant ～を歌う、(詩歌で)賛美する.

chōnin 町人 townsfolk; artisans and merchants who lived in towns, particularly in Edo, in the Edo period (1603-1868). Distinguished from the samurai, they were regarded as socially lower in class. Yet, they enjoyed great prosperity, benefiting from the economic growth of this period. It was the people of this class who gave rise to the blooming of the unique culture of Edo, as exemplified by Kabuki, Bunraku, *ukiyoe* painting, etc. ⇨ EDO-JIDAI, SHI-NŌ-KŌ-SHŌ

〖注〗 artisan 職人. give rise to ～を生じる、引き起こす.

chōninmono 町人物 a townsfolk novel; novels dealing with the daily life of townsfolk, emerging in the Edo period (1603-1868). Ihara Saikaku (1642-93) was the most representative writer of this genre; he depicted the merchant class in towns with realism as seen in his *Nippon Eitaigura,* 1688 (The Japanese Family Storehouse, translated in 1959), *Seken Munesanyo,* 1692 (Worldly Mental Calculations, 1976), etc. ⇨ CHŌNIN

〖注〗 townsfolk 町人、市民. emerge 現れる. genre 類型、ジャンル.

chonmage 丁髷 a topknot; the hairstyle for men in the Edo period (1603-1868). The head was shaved from the forehead to the top (though sometimes not), and the side locks and back were tied up into a knot at the top. The *chonmage* style was worn in slightly different ways according to social rank and occupation. In 1871 the *chonmage* was abolished by law, with exceptions for *sumō* wrestlers, actors, etc. ⇨ EDO-JIDAI, SUMŌ

〖注〗 lock 髷の房.

chōshi 銚子 a saké pot; a saké receptacle with a handle and a spout, made of lacquered wood, used on auspicious occasions today. The term *chōshi* is often confused with *tokkuri*, a saké bottle of ceramic. ⇨ SAKE

〖注〗 receptacle 入れ物、容器. spout (水さしなどの)口. on auspicious occasions おめでたい機会に. ceramic 陶器.

Chūbu chihō 中部地方 the Chūbu region; the central region of Honshū, one of the five geographical divisions of Honshū (the main island), the other four being the Tōhoku, Kantō, Kinki and Chūgo-ku regions. The Chūbu region consists of the nine prefectures of

Aichi, Gifu, Shizuoka, Yamanashi, Nagano, Fukui, Niigata, Ishikawa and Toyama. This region is further subdivided into three districts according to climate: the Tōkai district (on the sunny Pacific side), the Hokuriku district (on the snowy Japan Sea side) and the Chūbu-sangaku district (the central mountainous district). It contains seven national parks—Bandai-Asahi, Chichibu-Tama, Chūbu-sangaku, Fuji-Hakone-Izu, Hakusan, Jōshin'etsu-kōgen and Southern Alps.   ⇨ BANDAI-ASAHI KOKURITSU-KŌEN, CHICHIBU-TAMA KOKURITSU-KŌEN, CHŪBU-SANGAKU KOKURITSU-KŌEN, FUJI-HAKONE-IZU KOKURITSU-KŌEN, HAKUSAN KOKURITSU-KŌEN, JŌSHIN'ETSU-KŌGEN KOKURITSU-KŌEN, MINAMI-ARUPUSU KOKURITSU-KŌEN

Chūbu-sangaku Kokuritsu-kōen 中部山岳国立公園 Central Mountains National Park (1,697.7 square kilometers), designated in 1934, popularly known as Kita(Nihon)-Arupusu (Northern Japan Alps); a natural park situated in central Honshū, encompassing mountainous parts of Nagano, Gifu, Toyama and Niigata prefectures. Called the "roof of Japan", this is the loftiest mountain region in Japan, containing a number of towering mountains such as Mount Tateyama (highest peak 3,015 meters), Mount Shirouma (2,933 m), Mount Yari (2,890 m), Mount Yakushi (2,926 m), Mount Hotaka (3,190 m), Mount Norikura (3,026 m), etc. Between the steep slopes, deep ravines and rivers run through dense forests, among which Kurobe Gorge containing Kurobe Dam is most spectacular. Mount Tateyama is one of three sacred mountains, the other two being Mount Fuji and Mount Hakusan. This national park attracts many mountain climbers and hikers.   ⇨ KOKURITSU-KŌEN, MINAMI-ARUPUSU KOKURITSU-KŌEN
〖注〗 ravine 峡谷, 渓谷. gorge 峡谷(特に水の流れる).

chūgakkō 中学校 1) (in the postwar school system) a junior high school; a lower secondary school; the three-year second stage of compulsory education, following six years of elementary school. It is part of the 6-3-3-4 system adopted under the School Education Law (enacted in 1947). 2) (in the prewar school system) a middle school; the four- or five-year secondary school for boys, following six years of elementary school and followed by higher school (*kōtō-gakkō*), regular college, teachers' normal school (*shihan-gakkō*), etc. Middle schools were organized in 1886 with the issuance of the Middle School Order.   ⇨ KYŌIKU KIHONHŌ
〖注〗 the School Education Law 「学校教育法」. teachers' normal school 師範

学校. issuance 発布. the Middle School Order「中学校令」.

chūgen 中元 the midyear day (July 15). 1) Originally in China, it was the day to make offerings to a certain star to express thanks for protection during the first half of the year. In Japan, combined with the Bon Festival (July 13-15), it was the time to send something as an offering to the dead in appreciation for protection. 2) Nowadays, *chūgen* means simply gift-sending at midyear without regard to the Buddhist significance. It is customary to send gifts to those to whom one would like to express gratitude for special consideration, among individuals and business associates. This practice starts at the beginning of June, lasting until the middle of July. ⇨ SHOCHŪMIMAI, SEIBO

〖注〗 offering 供物, 奉納.

Chūgoku chihō 中国地方 the Chūgoku region; the region covering western Honshū, one of the five geographical divisions of Honshū (the main island), the other four being the Tōhoku, Kantō, Chūbu, and Kinki regions. The Chūgoku region consists of the five prefectures of Okayama, Hiroshima, Yamaguchi, Shimane and Tottori. The Chūgoku mountain range, stretching east and west, further divides the region into two districts—the San'yō district (on the sunny Pacific side, facing the Inland Sea of Seto) and the San-in district (on the Japan Sea side). It contains three national parks —San'in-kaigan, Daisen-Oki and Seto Naikai national parks. ⇨ DAISEN-OKI KOKURITSU-KŌEN, SAN'IN-KAIGAN KOKURITSU-KŌEN, SETO NAIKAI KOKURITSU-KŌEN

〖注〗 the Chūgoku mountain range 中国山脈. the Inland Sea of Seto 瀬戸内海.

chūkanshi 中間枝 a filler; a supplementary stem added to any of the three main stems of a flower arrangement. This term is used in the Ohara school. It is called *ashirai* in the Ikenobō school and *jūshi* in the Sōgetsu school. ⇨ ASHIRAI, IKEBANA, JŪSHI

〖注〗 main stem 主枝. flower arrangement 生け花.

chūmon¹ 中門 a middle gate; a simple gate between the inner garden and the outer garden of a tea garden. It is usually a small gate made of rush or bamboo with a rustic appearance. It marks the entrance to a yet more secluded place, the inner garden where the tearoom stands. ⇨ CHATEI

〖注〗 inner garden 内露地. outer garden 外露地. rush 蘭(い). rustic appearance ひなびた趣き. secluded place 閑静な場所.

chūmon[2] **中門** a middle gate; an inner gate of a temple; the gate located between the front gate and the central building in the compounds of an early large Buddhist temple. It is a roofed wooden structure, sometimes having two stories. From this gate extend corridors to the left and right, connecting the main hall with other buildings, and enclosing the inner compounds. Often statues of the two Deva kings (*niō*) stand guarding the temple on each side of the entryway. The *chūmon* of Hōryūji Temple, Nara, built in the eighth century, is the oldest existing example. ⇨ GARAN, NIŌ, SHICHIDŌ-GARAN

〖注〗 compounds 敷地、境内. enclose 囲む. statue 彫像. the two Deva kings 仁王.

Chūshingura 忠臣蔵 *The Treasury of the Forty-Seven Loyal Retainers* ; the common term for *Kanadehon Chūshingura* (lit. A Copybook of the Japanese Syllabary; the Treasury of the Models of Loyalty). *Chūshingura* or *Kanadehon Chūshingura* is the general title for Kabuki and Bunraku plays based on the historical incident of 1702 when 47 loyal retainers took revenge, in the form of assassination, on a shogunate official who had compelled their lord to commit harakiri. Three years later, the incident was adapted for a Bunraku puppet play (staged in 1706) by Chikamatsu Monzaemon (1653-1724) and shortly after for a Kabuki play (staged in 1748) titled *Kanadehon Chūshingura* by Takeda Izumo (1691-1756) et al. The term *kanadehon* is derived from the Japanese syllabary (*kana*) consisting of 47 letters, equivalent to the number of loyal retainers, and *dehon* (from *tehon*) meaning both "copybook" and "model". The original Kabuki version is composed of 11 acts. The background and names of those involved in the incident are disguised in the play, reflecting the strict censorship imposed by the shogunate government. Many other versions followed, attesting to the popularity of this tale. ⇨ AKŌ-GISHI, BUNRAKU, HARAKIRI, KABUKI, KANA

〖注〗 retainer 家臣、家来. syllabary 音標文字表、仮名文字表. revenge 復讐、あだ討ち. assassination 暗殺、やみ討ち. Takeda Izumo 竹田出雲. et al 他(=and others). disguise (本体を)隠す. censorship 検閲. the shogunate government 幕府. attest 証明する.

D

dadaiko 大太鼓 a huge drum used in Gagaku (ancient court ensemble). It is about two meters in diameter and colorfully decorated. The drum is hung in a frame carved with flaming patterns. On the Gagaku stage, a pair of *dadaiko* are used in formal performances of dance and music. One of the pair stands for the sun, the other for the moon. ⇨ GAGAKU

〖注〗 ancient court ensemble 雅楽. flaming pattern 炎の模様.

daibutsu 大仏 lit. great Buddha. a giant statue of Buddha. The standard for a *daibutsu* is a height of over 1 *jō* 6 *shaku* (4.85 meters) for a standing one and over 8 *shaku* (2.42 m) for a seated one. The two largest ones in Japan are the Rushana Butsu at Tōdaiji Temple in Nara with its seated height of 16.2 m (cast in 743), and the Amida Nyorai at Kōtokuin Temple in Kamakura with its seated height of 11.4 m (built in 1252). ⇨ AMIDA(NYORAI), RUSHANA BUTSU

〖注〗 Kōtokuin Temple 高徳院.

daibutsuden 大仏殿 a hall of the great Buddha statue; the hall which houses a colossal statue of Buddha. The hall of the Great Buddha at Tōdaiji Temple in Nara is the largest wooden structure in the world. Originally constructed in 752, it has been destroyed by fire and reconstructed a few times. Full-scale repairs were conducted recently (1974-80), called "the Great Shōwa Renovation." ⇨ DAIBUTSU, RUSHANA BUTSU

〖注〗 the Great Shōwa Renovation「昭和大修理」.

daifuku-mochi 大福餅 lit. a great-luck rice cake. a round rice cake stuffed with red-bean jam. Steamed glutinous rice is pounded and kneaded. A small amount is flattened, topped with red-bean jam, and rounded to form a dumpling. In the Edo period (1603-1868), it was called *harafuto-mochi* (fat-belly rice cake) from its round shape. But it gradually came to be called *daifuku-mochi* (great-luck rice cake), since it is a pleasant surprise to bite into the ample amount of tasty bean jam inside and it is considered that eating such cakes will bring great luck.　⇨ AN, MOCHI

〖注〗 glutinous rice 糯米.　knead 練る.

Daijō Bukkyō 大乗仏教 lit. Great Vehicle Buddhism.　Mahayana Buddhism; one of the two large categories of Buddhism, the other being Hinayana Buddhism (*Shōjō Bukkyō*).　Prevalent mainly in China, Tibet, and Japan, it has developed into many sects unique to each country.　Collectively, it teaches the importance of the universal salvation of all human beings, salvation which is considered to be attainable through faith in Bodhisattva (*bosatsu*) rather than self-discipline and moral efforts.　So it is for ordinary people to believe in.　⇨ BOSATSU, BUKKYŌ, SHŌJŌ BUKKYŌ

〖注〗 vehicle 乗物.　Hinayana Buddhism 小乗仏教.　Bodhisattva 菩薩.

Daikoku(ten) 大黒(天) the God of Wealth and Harvest, one of the Seven Deities of Good Luck.　He is represented as carrying a huge sack of treasures and holding a magical gavel that brings luck in his right hand.　Usually he is sitting or standing on two bales of rice as he also brings luck to farmers.　He has often been associated with Ōkuninushi no Mikoto, a hero who presided over the land in Japanese mythology, partly because both are depicted as carrying a huge sack.　⇨ SHICHI-FUKUJIN

〖注〗 the Seven Deities of Good Luck 七福神.　gavel 槌.　bale 俵.　preside 支配する.　mythology 神話.

daikon-oroshi 大根おろし grated Japanese radish.　It is served as a condiment for such dishes as *tenpura*, *nabemono*, etc.　It helps digestion as it contains a substance called "diastase."

〖注〗 grated おろした.　Japanese radish 大根.　condiment 薬味.　digestion 消化.　substance（化学）物質.　diastase ジアスターゼ.

daimoku 題目 the title of a Buddhist prayer, in particular the main prayer of the Nichiren sect.　It consists of seven Chinese characters, "*na-mu-myō-hō-ren-ge-kyō*," meaning "Glory to the Lotus Sutra of the Supreme Law" (namu = I pray; myōhō = the supreme law; renge-kyō = the Lotus Sutra).　In Mahayana Buddhism, repeated chanting of this prayer with all sincerity was considered to lead one to salvation and enlightenment.　In Japan, this concept was adopted as one of the Three Great Secret Laws by Priest Nichiren (1222-82) in the Kamakura period (1185-1336).　After World War II, some of the largest new Buddhist groups adopted Nichiren's teachings including the practice of chanting the

Lotus Sutra with *daimoku*. ⇨ BUKKYŌ, DAIJŌ BUKKYŌ, NENBUTSU, NICHIRENSHŪ

〖注〗 the Lotus Sutra 法華経, 蓮華経. Mahayana Buddhism 大乗仏教. enlightenment 悟り. the Three Great Secret Laws 「三大秘法」.

daimonji-yaki 大文字焼き lit. the burning of the letter "large." the grand bonfire festival held on Mount Nyoigatake near the city of Kyoto on the evening of August 16. As one of the Buddhist events of the All Souls' Festival (Bon), it is observed for the purpose of sending off the spirits of the dead as they return to the world beyond after the Bon days (August 13-16). On a slope of this mountain, the burning Chinese character 大 *dai* (large), formed by lines of giant torches, flares in the darkness. ⇨ BON

〖注〗 bonfire 大かがり火, (野天の)たき火. Mount Nyoigatake 如意ヶ岳. Chinese character 漢字. torch たいまつ.

daimyō 大名 lit. great name. a feudal lord; large land-holders or lords of provinces in feudal times. This term was first employed in the 11th century, generally for large land-holders. In the period of civil wars (1467-mid-16th century) it referred to military lords. Under the Tokugawa shogunate (1603-1868), *daimyō* status was clearly defined and granted to lords who ruled domains producing over 10,000 *koku* (1,800 cubic meters) of rice annually. Of about 250 *daimyō*, the richest was the Maeda family of Kaga Province with some 1 million *koku*. The *daimyō* were supervised by the shogunate and were subject to the Tokugawa Code of Warriors (*Buke Shohatto*) first enforced in 1615 by Tokugawa Hidetada (1578-1632). Depending on their relation to the Tokugawa family, the *daimyō* were classified into three categories: *shinpan-daimyō* (lineage feudal lords), *fudai-daimyō* (hereditary feudal lords) and *tozama-daimyō* (outsider feudal lords). ⇨ BUKE SHOHATTO, FUDAI-DAIMYŌ, KOKU, SHINPAN-DAIMYŌ, TOKUGAWA-BAKUFU, TOZAMA-DAIMYŌ

〖注〗 feudal times 封建時代. the period of civil wars 戦国時代. military lord 戦国大名. the Tokugawa shogunate 徳川幕府. domain 領地, 所有地. be subject to ～に服従する. enforce (法律を)施行する. Tokugawa Hidetada 徳川秀忠.

daimyō-gyōretsu 大名行列 a procession of a feudal lord and his retainers, especially when he traveled to Edo for alternate attendance to the Tokugawa shogunate (1603-1868). In the Edo period, feudal lords were required to reside periodically in Edo and serve the shogunate. It was customary on such an occasion to have a long procession for the march to Edo proceeding very slowly, as a demonstration of the lord's power and the wealth of his domain. Commoners were required to kneel at the road side whenever such a procession passed by. One of the shogunate checkpoints was at Hakone, where an annual festival featuring a colorful parade depicting such a feudal procession has been held since 1935. Another well-known one is held annually in Odawara, Kanagawa Prefecture. ⇨ DAIMYŌ, EDO-JIDAI, SANKINKŌTAI

〖注〗 feudal lord 大名. retainer 従者、郎党. alternate attendance 参勤交代. the Tokugawa shogunate 徳川幕府. domain 領土、領地. checkpoint 関所.

Dainichi Nyorai 大日如来 lit. great sun tathagata. Mahavairochana (Sanskrit); the Great Buddha illuminating the universe, the principal Buddha worshiped in esoteric Buddhism. Dainichi is regarded as the source of creation, personifying the absolute truth underlying all phenomena of the universe. He holds two unseparable aspects—truth as the fundamental law, and wisdom that manifests in the phenomenal world. The Tendai sect of esoterism interprets Sakyamuni as the manifesting aspect of Dainichi, while the Shingon sect worships Dainichi, considering them two different Buddhas. A typical image of Dainichi is characterized by the hair-knot tied on the top and the crown decorated with tiny images of Buddhas, as those at Tōshōdaiji and Enjōji temples (Nara). The colossal statue at Tōdaiji Temple (Nara), without a crown but with a halo, is a forerunner of Dainichi commonly called Rushana Butsu or Buddha Birushana. ⇨ MIKKYŌ, RUSHANA BUTSU, SHINGONSHŪ, TENDAISHŪ

〖注〗 tathagata 如来(世に来て真理を示す存在). the principal Buddha 本尊. esoteric Buddhism 密教. halo 光輪、後光.

Dainippon-teikoku Kenpō 大日本帝国憲法 the Constitution of the Great Japanese Empire; the official name of the former constitution of Japan. Today, it is officially called *Meiji Kenpō* (the Meiji Constitution). ⇨ MEIJI KENPŌ

dairibina 内裏雛 emperor and empress dolls; a pair of dolls portraying the emperor and empress, displayed on Girls' Day (March 3). They are attired in traditional imperial costumes for ceremonial occasions, tracing back to the Heian period (794-1185). Even today these costumes are worn by a bride and bridegroom at an

Imperial wedding ceremony.   On Girls' Day or Doll Festival Day (*Hina Matsuri*), they are placed on the top row of a tier of shelves with a golden screen behind them, along with their courtiers on the lower shelves.   ⇨ HINA MATSURI, HINA-NINGYŌ, MOMO NO SEKKU

〚注〛 be attired in ～を着飾っている、～で装っている. tier 段. courtier お付きの者, 従者.

Daisen-Oki Kokuritsu-kōen 大山隠岐国立公園   Daisen-Oki National Park (319.3 square kilometers), designated in 1936; a natural park situated in western Honshū, facing the Sea of Japan, in Shimane, Tottori and Okayama prefectures.   This park comprises a number of volcanic mountains, major ones being Mount Daisen (1,713 meters) and Mount Sanpe (1,126 m).   On the slope of Mount Daisen are the ruins of Daisenji Temple (built in 718), which was formerly the center of the Tendai sect of Buddhism. Japan's oldest Shinto shrine, the Izumo Grand Shrine, popularly known as a shrine of matchmaking as well as agriculture, is located in the center of the Izumo Plain.   The Oki Island chain, a rock formation off the coast of the Sea of Japan, was a place of exile for the retired emperor Gotoba (1180-1239).   The Shimane Peninsula is known for its beautiful coastlines represented by Mihonoseki and Hinomisaki.   ⇨ KOKURITSU-KŌEN

〚注〛 Mount Sanpe 三瓶山. ruins 遺跡, 廃墟. match-making 縁結び. rock formation 岩から成る地層. exile 流刑, 島流し. Mihonoseki 美保関. Hinomisaki 日御崎.

Daisetsuzan Kokuritsu-kōen 大雪山国立公園   Mount Daisetsu National Park (2,308.9 square kilometers), designated in 1934; Japan's largest natural park, situated in central Hokkaidō.   Called the "roof of Hokkaidō," Mount Daisetsu is composed of a large group of volcanic mountains.   Among them are Mount Asahi (2,290 meters), Hokkaidō's highest peak; Mount Tokachi (2,077 m), an active volcano which erupted in 1926 and 1962; and Mount Ishikari, noted for the Ishikari River running through Sōunkyō Gorge.   Numerous kinds of alpine plants thrive on the mountains. Hot springs abound and tour routes are well-developed.   ⇨ HOK-KAIDŌ, KOKURITSU-KŌEN

〚注〛 active volcano 活火山. the Sōunkyō Gorge 層雲峡. alpine plant 高山植物. hot spring 温泉.

daisu 台子   a tea stand; a shelf-like stand for tea utensils.   This formal decorative piece of furniture is used only when the tea ceremony takes place in a large room or a reception room, and is not used in a simple tearoom of four-and-a-half mats. ⇨ CHA-NOYU, CHASHITSU

〖注〗 tea utensils 茶道具. tea ceremony 茶の湯. reception room 客間. four-and-a-half mats 四畳半.

danka 檀家 a Buddhist parishioner; a family that supports a Buddhist temple. Derived from the Sanskrit word *dānapati* or "Buddhist follower," the term *danna* was first used to indicate a member of a specific Buddhist temple who supported it both spiritually and financially. *Danka* indicates such a family. The Tokugawa shogunate (1603-1868), in an attempt to prohibit Christianity, set up the *danka* system, under which each family was required to register at a specific temple. This system is still followed today as a family tradition. ⇨ KIRISHITAN, TERA, TOKUGAWA-BAKUFU

〖注〗 parishioner 小教区民. the Tokugawa shogunate 徳川幕府.

danmari 黙り mime; pantomime. In a Kabuki play this technique is used when the actors grope around or have a fight in the dark without saying a word. ⇨ KABUKI

〖注〗 mime 無言道化芝居, 無言の身振り. grope around 手探りで進む.

darari no obi だらりの帯 a dangling sash; an *obi*, tied with its long ends dangling at the back. The dangling parts are a meter or so in length, almost reaching the hem of the kimono. This type of *obi* is worn exclusively by young dancing girls called *maiko*, apprentice geisha, in Kyoto. ⇨ GEISHA, KIMONO, MAIKO, OBI

〖注〗 dangling ぶらぶらしている. apprentice 徒弟, 見習い.

daruma 達磨 from Dharma (Sanskrit); a red, rounded doll with no limbs, usually made of papier-mâchê or wood. This represents Bodhidharma (Daruma Daishi), a Buddhist priest from India who went to China in the sixth century. There he sat for nine years in meditation, losing the use of his legs, but attaining enlightenment, after which he founded Zen Buddhism. The round form represents him wrapped in his priest's robe. The *daruma* doll is considered a symbol of perseverance and thus a charm for achievement. It is often sold without the eyes painted in. The purchaser paints in one eye when starting something difficult and then paints in the other after successfully completing it. This custom is particularly seen during election campaigns. ⇨ OKIAGARI-KOBOSHI, ZAZEN, ZEN-SHŪ

〖注〗 papier-mâchê 紙でつくった，張り子(の)． sit in meditation 座禅する．
attain enlightenment 悟りを開く，悟りの境地に達する． charm お守り． election campaign 選挙運動．

daruma-ichi 達磨市   Dharma-doll fair. The *daruma*, a round red
doll without limbs, represents the Zen priest Dharma who lost the
use of his legs after years of sitting in meditation. *Daruma* dolls
are regarded as a symbol of good luck—particularly the tumbling
daruma doll which contains a weight at the base which returns it to
an upright position. It is the custom for many Japanese to buy
daruma dolls at the beginning of the year in hopes of a new year of
happiness and prosperity. In January a number of *daruma* doll
fairs are held across the country, especially in the Kantō district.
Well-known are the ones held at Darumaji Temple in Takasaki,
Gunma Prefecture, and Hajima Daishi Temple near Hachiōji,
Tokyo. There, hundreds of open-air stalls are set up selling
daruma dolls of various sizes. Among them, one-eyed *daruma*
dolls are especially popular, the other eye to be filled in when
wishes are fulfilled. ⇨ DARUMA, OKIAGARI-KOBOSHI

〖注〗 sit in meditation 座禅する． tumbling *daruma* doll 起き上がりこぼし．
open-air stall 露店．

dashi 出し   fish broth; the basic Japanese soup stock flavored with
bonito (*katsuo*) and kelp (*konbu*). First, water is heated and
steeped with a sheet of kelp. When it starts boiling, the kelp is
removed. Then, plenty of dried bonito shavings are added and the
water is brought to a boil again. By straining the shavings, clear
dashi is obtained, which is used to make clear soup or the like. A
second pot of *dashi* made with the same shavings is used for boiling
vegetables. Nowadays, powdered or instant *dashi* is also available on the market. ⇨ KATSUOBUSHI

〖注〗 stock 原料，(肉，魚などの)煮出し汁． kelp 昆布等大型の海藻． dried
bonito shavings 鰹の削り節． strain 濾過する，固体をこして除く．

date 伊達   dandyism; to behave or dress ostentatiously, referring in
particular to men, an aesthetic concept which developed in the
Genroku era (1688–1704). The term is said to derive from the
attire of Date Masamune (1567–1636), feudal lord of Sendai, and
his attendants, which was conspicuously showy. In the Genroku
era, a peaceful and stable time following a prolonged civil war,
people and in particular wealthy townsfolk dressed lavishly.
However, the shogunate's issuance of a sumptuary edict resulted in

a new trend, the pursuit of understated refinement known as *iki*. Since then, the term *date* has also taken on the connotation of untasteful showiness lacking in refinement. ⇨ GENROKU-JIDAI, IKI

〖注〗 ostentatiously はでに、これみよがしに. aesthetic concept 美的概念. attire 服装. attendant 家来. lavishly ぜいたくに. sumptuary edict ぜいたく取締り令. understated refinement 地味で洗練されていること. connotation 含蓄.

datejime 伊達締め an under-sash; a sash used to tie a kimono around the waist under an *obi* (sash). It serves as a foundation for holding the kimono in shape. It is a little narrower than the *obi*, and is usually made of stiff Hakata weave with cords at both ends or of soft silky cloth with a stiffener inside which wraps around the waist. ⇨ KIMONO, OBI

〖注〗 stiffener 固くするもの、芯.

datemaki 伊達巻き lit. a dandy egg roll. a roll often served on festive occasions, made of a thick, fluffy, sweetened egg that is prepared in a rectangular pan, browned on one side, and rolled. It is usually served in slices and is also called *tamagomaki*.

〖注〗 festive めでたい. fluffy ふわふわした. prepare 調理する. rectangular 矩形の.

debayashi 出囃子 the on-stage musicians in a Kabuki drama. Usually playing behind the black screen called *kuromisu*, they appear on stage when there is a dance in a Kabuki play or other classical dance performances. ⇨ KABUKI

〖注〗 on-stage 舞台上の. performance 上演、演技.

degatari 出語り the recitation or chanting of *jōruri* on the Kabuki stage. In some styles of Kabuki of Bunraku origin, *jōruri* chanters and *shamisen* players appear downstage to the right (as seen from the audience) on a revolving platform. In other cases, they are seated in a box behind a bamboo curtain. ⇨ BUNRAKU, JŌRURI, KABUKI, SHAMISEN

〖注〗 chanting 単調にくり返して謡うこと. revolving platform 回り台.

Dejima 出島 Dejima Island in Nagasaki harbor, western Kyūshū; an artificial island completed in 1636 by the Tokugawa shogunate (1603-1868) as a residence for Dutch traders. During the period of national seclusion (1639-1853), Nagasaki was the only port of entry for foreign traders. Trade was limited to the Dutch and Chinese; Dutch traders were restricted to this island under the strict supervision of the shogunate. The fan-shaped island lost its original form as a result of repeated land reclamation, along with the loss of the original Dutch residences and trade facilities. In 1958, a part of the trade facilities was restored. ⇨ EDO-JIDAI, SAKOKU(-SEISAKU)

〖注〗 the Tokugawa shogunate 徳川幕府. the national seclusion period 鎖国時代. the port of entry 入国港. strict supervision 厳戒. land reclamation 干拓, 埋立て. trade facility 貿易施設.

demae 出前 meal delivery service; simple dishes prepared by inexpensive local restaurants, ordered by telephone and delivered to workplaces and homes. This convenient service is popularly used at offices at lunchtime or for unexpected guests at homes. Types of foods thus offered may include noodles, bowl-rice dishes (*donburimono*), and a-la-carte Western-style dishes, as well as *sushi*. They are delivered quickly, arriving still warm or even hot, at a small extra charge (though formerly free of charge). Skilled delivery men can carry several layers of trays on one hand while riding bicycles or motorcycles. ⇨ DONBURIMONO, MEN(RUI), SUSHI

〖注〗 delivery 配達. a-la-carte dish 一品料理.

dengaku 田楽 lit. field music. one of the antecedent forms of Noh and Kyogen. It flourished especially in the 13th and 14th centuries, and was performed at shrines and temples, originally in relation to rice planting, harvesting and other agricultural events. ⇨ KYŌGEN, NŌ

〖注〗 antecedent 先行の, 前身の.

dezukai 出遣い the appearance of puppeteers, especially that of the main puppeteer (*omozukai*) in Bunraku. The main puppeteer appears in ceremonial costume with his face uncovered to greet the audience. Recently, the face of the main puppeteer in Bunraku is exposed even during the performance. ⇨ BUNRAKU, KUROGO, OMOZUKAI

〖注〗 puppeteer 人形遣い. main puppeteer 主遣い.

dō¹ 道 a region; a district; an administrative division. Under the Taihō Code of Laws (promulgated in 701 and in effect up to the time of the Meiji Restoration (1868) with numerous modifications), Japan was divided into several regions according to the roads extending from the area of the old capitals, Nara and Kyoto, with each region further divided into provinces (*kuni*). The regions consisted of the *kinai* (the capital district) and seven *dō*: Hokurikudō, Tōsandō, Tokaidō, San'yōdō, San'indō, Nankaidō and Saikaidō to which Hokkaidō was added later. Hokkaidō is the only region to retain the name *dō*, in the present system of administrative divisions. ⇨ HOKKAIDŌ, KUNI, MEIJI ISHIN, RITSURYŌ

〖注〗 administrative division 行政的区分. the Taihō Codes of Laws「大宝律令」. promulgate 発布する，施行する. in effect 効力を発する. the Meiji Restoration 明治維新. modification 修正. province（行政区画としての）国.

dō² 道 a district, as an administrative prefecture. Hokkaidō is the only prefecture still referred to as *dō*, the name for the former administrative divisions of the Japanese islands. Japan today is divided into 47 administrative units: one metropolis（*to*），two metropolitan prefectures（*fu*），43 regular prefectures（*ken*）and one district（*dō*）. ⇨ DŌ¹, HOKKAIDŌ, TO-DŌ-FU-KEN

〖注〗 administrative division 行政的区分. metropolis 主要都市，首都圏. metropolitan 主要都市の.

doburoku 濁酒 unrefined saké; raw saké made from rice with the lees unfiltered. It looks whitish and tastes sour compared with refined saké, due to the formation of lactic acid. The alcohol content is 10 to 13 percent. Formerly this kind of saké was often home-brewed, which is prohibited today. ⇨ SAKE

〖注〗 unrefined 精製していない. lees（酒類の）残りかす. lactic acid 乳酸. brew 醸造する.

dōfuku 胴服 a warrior's overgarment; an overgarment worn as everyday clothes in the past by such historical figures as Tokugawa Ieyasu (1542-1616) and Toyotomi Hideyoshi (1536-98) toward the end of the Muromachi period （1336-1568） and the beginning of the Edo period （1603-1868）. The colorful and lavish designs illustrate the move toward feminization in warriors' everyday clothing, in contrast to the manly armor of those days.

〖注〗 overgarment 外側に着る衣服. historical figure 歴史上の人物. feminization 女性化. armor 甲冑.

dogū 土偶 an earthen figurine of the Jōmon period （before 200 B.C.）. Most of the figurines depict fertile women. They are considered to be sacred objects connected with early fertility cults. ⇨ JŌMON-JIDAI

〖注〗 figurine 小立像. fertility cult 豊じょうを祈る儀式.

dohyō 土俵 the round ring on which a *sumō* bout is held. The area is surrounded by partially buried slender straw bags filled with earth forming a circle 4.55 meters in diameter on a 5.45-meter-square mound of hardened clay. There is also a line of bags forming a square along the edge of the mound. At the center of the ring are two white parallel lines that serve as markers where the wrestlers place their fists during the *shikiri*. Above the ring hangs a Shinto-shrine-style roof, a legacy of the days when *sumō* was held outdoors with the roof supported by pillars at the four corners of the mound. When the sport turned professional and was moved indoors, the roof was preserved as a symbol of sacredness while the pillars were removed to give the spectators a better view.   ⇨ DOHYŌIRI, ŌZUMŌ, SHIKIRI, SUMŌ

〖注〗 fist 握りこぶし. legacy 名ごり.

dohyōiri 土俵入り   the entering-the-ring ceremony; a ritual performed by all *sekitori sumō* wrestlers, wearing an elegantly designed *keshō-mawashi* of brocade, each day during a *sumō* tournament. Before their respective divisional matches, the *jūryō* and *makuuchi* wrestlers, other than the *yokozuna,* of the east and west camps step into the ring in reverse order of rank and form a circle facing the spectators. They proceed to face the center and simultaneously perform a simple ritual and step off in the same order. They are followed by the *yokozuna* (grand champion) wearing *yokozuna* (a grand champion's belt) over the *keshō-mawashi* led by the highest-ranking referee and accompanied by a "dew sweeper" and sword-bearer, two fellow *makuuchi* wrestlers. The *yokozuna* steps into the ring from either the east or west side and performs a ritual first facing the opposite direction then the north with his fellows looking on in a solemn sitting position.   ⇨ DOHYŌ, MAWASHI, ŌZUMŌ, SUMŌ

〖注〗 ritual 儀式. referee 行司. sword-bearer 太刀持ち.

dōjō 道場   lit. a place for the way. a place for the way to enlightenment or achievement. Originally, it was a seminary or hall for Buddhist services and training. Later it came more commonly to refer to halls where martial arts such as judo, karate, *kendō*, etc. are practiced. In Japanese martial arts, influenced by Zen concepts, spiritual training is regarded as most important for controlling the art, which requires training to a degree similar to that for attaining enlightenment.   ⇨ BUGEI, ZEN[1]

〖注〗 enlightenment 悟り. seminary 修養所, 僧院. Buddhist service 仏教の行事, 法事. martial arts 武術. attain enlightenment 悟りを開く, 悟りの境地に達する.

donburi 丼   a large bowl; a large, deep porcelain or ceramic bowl, 15 or 20 centimeters in diameter. A *donburi* with a lid is used for an a-la-carte dish containing rice, and is called *donburimono*; one without a lid is for noodles, or is used as a serving dish at the table. ⇨ DONBURIMONO

〖注〗 porcelain 磁器(の). ceramic 陶器(の). a-la-carte dish 一品料理.

donburimono 丼物 lit. a bowl thing. a bowl for rice; an a-la-carte rice dish, served in a large bowl, usually with a lid. The rice is topped with *tenpura,* egg, eel, or other ingredients. This kind of dish can be identified by the last suffix, *-donburi* or *-don* (abbreviation of *donburi*), such as *oyako-donburi* (lit. parent-child *donburi*; chicken-and-egg on rice), *unagi-donburi* (eel on rice), *ten-don* (abbreviation for *tenpura-donburi*), *katsu-don* (breaded cutlet on rice), etc. Along with noodles, *donburimono* is a very popular lunch dish and could be considered a fast food of Japanese cuisine. ⇨ DONBURI, KATSUDON, OYAKO-DONBURI, TENDON, UNADON

〖注〗 a-la-carte dish 一品料理. ingredient (料理の)材料. suffix 語尾. Japanese cuisine 日本料理.

dorayaki どら焼き a sweet-bean pancake; a pair of small pancakes with a filling of roughly mashed, sweet red-bean paste in between. The round shape is similar to that of a gong (*dora*), thus giving rise to its name. It is baked on a hot iron plate with shallow round molds.

〖注〗 filling 詰め物. sweet red-bean paste 餡. gong どら. give rise to 生じる，引き起こす.

dōtaku 銅鐸 a bell-shaped bronze article; a bronze bell which is considered to have been a symbol of community authority in the Yayoi period (c. 250 B.C.–A.D. 250). Its practical utilization is not definitely known; one theory holds that it was a musical instrument, another says that it served to give signals to the people. On the surface are primitive pictures depicting the life of the people in those days. The size ranges from 15 to 150 centimeters in height. Many were excavated in the Yamato district around the present Nara Prefecture, evidence that this area was one of the centers of early Japanese culture. ⇨ YAMATO, YAYOI-JIDAI

〖注〗 practical utilization 実際的利用方法. musical instrument 楽器. excavate 発掘する. evidence 実証，証拠.

doyō 土用 dog days; the period of 18 or 19 days before the beginning of spring, summer, autumn and winter on the lunar calendar. Today, *doyō* commonly refers to the period of 18 or 19 days before the first day of autumn on the lunar calendar (*doyō* of summer) which falls on August 7 or 8 on the present calendar. This happens to be the hottest period of summer. It is customary to eat nutritious eels on the day of the ox (one of the 12 signs of the zodiac cycle) during this period to stay healthy and to help tide oneself over the fierce heat. ⇨ UNADON, UNAGI NO KABAYAKI

〖注〗 the lunar calendar 太陰暦. eel 鰻. the day of the ox 牛[丑]の日. the 12 signs of the zodiac cycle 十二支. zodiac 12の星, 12の獣. tide over (困難などを)乗り切る, (人に)～を切り抜けさせる.

E

Ebisu 恵比寿　the God of Fishing and Commerce, one of the Seven Deities of Good Luck.　He is represented as holding a fishing rod in his right hand and a huge red seabream in his left hand.　He has a big smile on his face, thus giving rise to the metaphorical expression "*ebisu*-face" for a happy face with a big smile.　He is thought to bring prosperity and is especially worshiped by merchants.　⇨ EBISUKŌ, SHICHI-FUKUJIN

〖注〗 the Seven Deities of Good Luck 七福神．　fishing rod 釣り竿．　seabream 鯛．　give rise to 生じる，引き起こす．　metaphorical expression 隠喩表現，比喩表現．

Ebisukō 恵比寿講　the Ebisu Festival; a celebration observed by merchants in honor of Ebisu, the god of merchants and fishermen. It is said that Ebisu departs on business on January 10 or 20 and comes back with a large fortune on October 20 of the lunar calendar.　On the day of his return, or in some districts on the day of his departure, many merchants go to an Ebisu shrine and buy decorated bamboo rakes, symbolic of prosperity, as they may rake in fortune.　This custom started in medieval times and reached its peak in the Edo period (1603-1868).　⇨ EBISU

〖注〗 the lunar calendar 太陰暦．　rake in かき集める．

Echigo-jōfu 越後上布　Echigo fine linen fabric; fabric made from fine ramie, woven in the Echigo district, now Niigata Prefecture. It was first produced around Ojiya of this district in the Edo period (1603-1868).　Fine ramie threads, spun by hand, are woven into extremely thin and flat white, indigo, or indigo-and-white fabric. Today there are also kinds of *Echigo-jōfu* woven together with silk, cotton or hemp to make the fabric even thinner.　Summer kimono made of this *jōfu* are highly appreciated.　Along with the making of Ojiya ramie crepe (also produced in this district), the traditional skill of making *Echigo-jōfu* is designated as an intangible cultural property (*mukei-bunkazai*) by the government. ⇨ JŌFU

〖注〗 fabric 織物，布． ramie ラミー(皮から繊維をとる植物)． indigo 藍．
hemp 麻，大麻． crepe 縮緬． intangible cultural property 無形文化財．

Echizen-yaki 越前焼 Echizen ceramic ware; ceramic ware originally produced in the province of Echizen, in the eastern part of the
present-day Fukui Prefecture. Echizen was one of the "six
famous ancient kilns" (*rokkoyō*). The ware was made from the
Nara period(646-794)to the Heian period(794-1185). The Echizen
kilns produced thick, natural brown pottery for daily use, to be sold
mainly at local markets. The kilns of those days disappeared a
few hundreds years ago, but this district has maintained the traditional techniques, producing a variety of rustic ware today. ⇨
ROKKOYŌ

〖注〗 ceramic ware 陶器． the province of Echizen 越前の国． the six famous ancient kilns 六古窯． kiln (焼き物を焼く)窯． pottery 陶磁器． rustic
さびれた，素朴な．

edamame 枝豆 lit. branch beans. soybeans in the pod; green soybeans still attached to their stems. Pods separated from the stem
are rubbed with a bit of salt to bring out their green color and taste,
and then boiled in water. They go well with alcoholic beverages.
They are sold only during summer.

〖注〗 pod さや． alcoholic beverage アルコール飲料．

Edo-jidai 江戸時代 the Edo period (1603-1868); a period of 265
years during which the Tokugawa shogunate government ruled the
nation from Edo until the Meiji Restoration (1868); also called the
Tokugawa-jidai. In 1603, the shogun Tokugawa Ieyasu(1542-1616)
established this shogunate and began to consolidate a rigid feudal
regime based on Confucianism. The country was divided up and
placed under the total control of the shogunate, while society was
broken down into four classes—warriors, farmers, artisans and
merchants—aside from the nobility. The people's lives were
strictly regulated. To eliminate foreign influence, which was
considered a threat to the unity of the nation, Christianity was
banned and eventually a policy of national seclusion was enforced
in 1603 by the third shogun Iemitsu (1604-51). On the other hand,
peace and stability led to the blooming of the culture of the townspeople—haiku-poems, woodblock prints, Bunraku, Kabuki, Noh,
etc.—which had a profound influence on Japanese culture, continu-
ing to the present. ⇨ BAKUFU, JUKYŌ, SAKOKU(-SEISAKU), SHI-NŌ-

KŌ-SHŌ, SHŌGUN, TOKUGAWA-BAKUFU, TOKUGAWA-JIDAI

〖注〗 shogunate (government) 幕府. the Meiji Restoration 明治維新. consolidate 確立する. feudal regime 封建体制. Confucianism 儒教. warriors, farmers, artisans and merchants 士農工商. national seclusion 鎖国. enforce 施行する. townspeople 町人.

Edokko 江戸っ子 a Tokyoite; an Edoite; a native of Edo, the old name of Tokyo. Generally speaking, those born in Tokyo proper may be called *Edokko*. In particular, *Edokko* are those from the older section of Tokyo, which was called Edo in the Edo period (1603-1868), covering the Nihonbashi, Kanda, Kyōbashi, Fukagawa, Ueno and Shitaya areas. They are supposed to be at least third- or fourth-generation residents. *Edokko* were renowned for their enthusiasm for fires since Edo saw frequent fires. Their straightforwardness makes them contentious and prone to fight. At the same time, they are easily moved with compassion.

〖注〗 Tokyo proper 東京中心部, 古くからの東京. straightforwardness 率直さ, 竹を割ったような性格. contentious けんか好き, 議論好き. prone to fight けんか好き, 格闘好き.

Edo-komon 江戸小紋 lit. the Edo small pattern. a design of repeated small motifs on kimono fabric; also a kimono made of such fabric. The same as *komon*, but so called because it first became popular among women of the samurai class during the Edo period (1603-1868). ⇨ KIMONO, KOMON

〖注〗 motif 繰り返し用いられている意匠. fabric 織物.

eki(dan) 易(断) lit. changes. fortunetelling; divination based on the Oriental zodiac. Professional fortunetellers can be found on street corners. Dozens of slender sticks made of bamboo and diagrams of the zodiac signs are used for forecasting events and individual fortunes, including the proper direction for moving or building a house, the ideal partner for marriage, lucky days for travel, marriage or other undertakings, etc. An almanac written by the Takashima school based on the Chinese classic the *I Ching* (The Book of Changes) is popular among many Japanese.

〖注〗 fortunetelling 運命判断, 占い. divination 予言, 予知. Oriental zodiac 十二支. zodiac 十二星, 十二獣. diagram 図表, 図式. almanac 暦. *I Ching* (=The Book of Changes) 易経(五経の一つ；中国の易占いの書物).

ema 絵馬 lit. a pictorial horse. a votive picture of a horse painted on a wooden tablet. The tablet has the shape of a house, presumably a stable. It is offered to shrine deities as a token of gratitude when one's prayer has been heard, and today more often when one wishes a prayer to be answered.   Originally, it was said that feudal lords and warriors dedicated living horses to deities.   In the Edo period (1603-1868), *ema* painting developed to an artistic level.   ⇨ JINJA

〖注〗 votive（誓いによって）捧げられた，奉納の．tablet 銘板，平板．deity 神，神のような人［もの］．as a token of ～のしるしとして，～の証拠として．feudal lord 大名．warrior さむらい．dedicate 献上する．

emaki(mono) 絵巻(物)   an illustrated narrative scroll; a horizontal picture scroll, illustrating a story of a historical, legendary or religious subject.   It is roughly 30-40 centimeters wide and 9-12 meters long, with a cylindrical piece of wood attached at one end. A whole story comprises from one to a few dozen scrolls.   The earliest one found in Japan is *E-ingakyō* (The Illustrated Sutra of Cause and Effect) of the eighth century, but it is considered to be a copy of a Chinese original.   It was in the Heian (794-1185) and the Kamakura (1185-1336) periods that *emakimono* were very popular, influenced by the development of narrative literature. Some were for entertainment purposes and others were used for religious teachings.   Famous ones include *Genji Monogatari Emaki* (Scrolls of the Tale of Genji), *Chōjū Giga* (Scrolls of Frolicking Animals and Humans) and *Shigisan Engi Emaki* (The Scroll of the Legends of Mount Shigi).

〖注〗 scroll 巻物．The Illustrated Sutra of Cause and Effect「絵因果経」． sutra お経．narrative literature 物語文学．frolick 陽気にはしゃぐ，ふざける．The Scroll of the Legends of Mount Shigi「信貴山縁起絵巻」．

en 円   yen (¥); the monetary unit of Japan.   At present, bank notes come in denominations of ¥1,000, ¥5,000 and ¥10,000.   Coins are ¥1, ¥5, ¥10, ¥50, ¥100 and ¥500 pieces.   As a result of the floating exchange rate system adopted in 1973 due to the "Nixon shock," the yen rate has been tied to the American dollar, ranging from about ¥150 to about ¥300.   Prior to 1973, from 1971 the rate was ¥308 and from 1946 to 1971 it was ¥360, based on the official fixed exchange rate.

〖注〗 monetary unit 貨幣単位．bank note 紙幣, 銀行紙幣．denomination 単位名称，（貨幣・証券などの）額面金額．floating exchange rate system 変動相場制．official fixed exchange rate 固定為替相場．

engawa 縁側   a veranda-like porch; a veranda under the eaves of a roof projecting from a room.   Usually, there is a single groove along the outside edge on which rain shutters slide.　When there is no such groove for shutters, it is called *nureen* or a wet platform.　▷ AMADO, NUREEN

〖注〗 porch 建物の戸口に続く屋根付きの部分(＝(米)veranda).　eaves of the roof 屋根のひさし.　groove 敷居のみぞ.　rain shutter 雨戸.

enka 演歌　a Japanese popular song; the Japanese counterpart of "country western" in America or the "chanson" of France; a modern popular ballad with a distinctively indigenous Japanese melody and sentiment.　The origin of *enka* dates from the late Meiji era (at the beginning of the 20th century) when advocators of democracy sang on the street accompanied by a violin, in a melody modern at the time and yet blended with that of classical folk songs.　Gradually from the Taishō era (1912–26) onward, with its political aspect disappearing, the melody has taken on a sentimental mood, with ballads on love, nostalgia, etc.　The word *enka* is also written in other homophonic Chinese characters with the connotation of romantic sensuality or restraint broken-heartedness —艶歌 or 怨歌.　The sentimental tone of *enka* still induces pathos in most modern Japanese people.　▷ MEIJI, TAISHŌ

〖注〗 counterpart 対の一方，よく似たもの.　ballad 民謡，伝承的素朴な叙情的物語詩.　indigenous 土着の，土地固有の.　advocator 唱道者.　accompany ～の伴奏をする.　folk song 民謡.　nostalgia 望郷の想い.　homophonic Chinese character 同音の漢字.　connotation 含蓄，意味.　romantic sensuality 艶やかなこと，色気.　restraint broken-heartedness 耐え忍んだ怨恨の情.　induce ひき起こす，生じる.　pathos 哀感，もののあわれ.

Enma 閻魔　Yama (Sanskrit); the King of Hades.　Having his roots in Indian legend, he is a deity presiding over the underworld.　In Buddhism, he is regarded as the Lord of Hell who judges the dead and punishes them according to the deeds of their lifetime.　Japanese legend has it that he will pull out the tongues of those who tell a lie.　This expression is used by mothers in order to make their children not tell a lie.　▷ BUKKYŌ

〖注〗 Hades 死者の霊が住む地下界，黄泉，地獄.　deity 神，神としてあがめられる人[もの].　preside 統轄する，支配する.　the Lord of Hell 地獄の主.　Japanese legend has it that ... 日本の伝説によると.

ennichi 縁日　a fête day for a deity; a day set for worshiping the deity of a particular shrine or temple.　On this day when memorial services or other traditional events are held at a shrine or a temple, a number of open-air stalls are set up along the approach and in the precincts. People flock there not only to pay homage to the deity but also to buy the goods at the stalls. ⇨ JINJA, TERA

〖注〗 fête お祭り, 祝祭. deity 神, 神のような人[もの]. memorial service 記念法要. open-air stall 露店. approach 参道. precincts 境内. pay homage to に参拝する, に敬意を表する.

Enshū-shichiyō 遠州七窯 Enshū's Seven Kilns; the seven kilns most favored by Kobori Enshū (1579-1647), a great master of tea ceremony and flower arrangement. Enshū encouraged potters of many kilns throughout Japan to make utensils for use in the tea ceremony. Among the many kilns, seven are known as Enshū's specially favored ones: they are the kilns of Shidoro, Kosobe, Zeze, Agano, Takatori, Asahi and Akahada. ⇨ AKAHADA-YAKI, CHANOYU, IKEBANA, TAKATORI-YAKI

〖注〗 kiln (焼き物を焼く)窯. Kobori Enshū 小堀遠州. tea ceremony 茶道. flower arrangement 華道, 生け花. potter 陶工. 遠州七窯：志戸呂, 古曽部, 膳所, 上野, 高取, 朝日, 赤膚.

eto 干支 lit. stems and branches. the sexagenary cycle; the Oriental zodiac; the calendar cycle based on the Chinese *I Ching* (The Book of Changes). A full cycle of the zodiac combines a cycle of stem signs and a cycle of branch signs. The former has 10 signs consisting of five elements (*gokō*), i.e., wood, fire, earth, metal and water, that are represented as both positive and negative. The latter has the signs of 12 animals (*jūnishi*); i.e., rat, ox, tiger, rabbit, dragon, snake, horse, sheep, monkey, fowl, dog and boar. Thus, the zodiac embraces 60 years. Often the term *eto* is used as synonymous with the signs of the 12 animals. ⇨ JIKKAN-JŪNISHI, JŪNISHI

〖注〗 the sexagenary cycle 60年の周期, 干支. sexagenary 60の, 60を単位とする. zodiac 12宮, 12獣. *I Ching* (=The Book of Changes)「易経」(古代中国の易占いの書物). synonymous with ～と同義の. 十二支：子, 丑, 寅, 卯, 辰, 巳, 午, 未, 申, 酉, 戌, 亥.

F

fu[1] 府 a metropolitan prefecture; an urban prefecture, as one of the four administrative divisions of *to*, *dō*, *fu* and *ken*. Today, the two prefectures of Ōsaka and Kyoto are called *fu*. ⇨ TO·DŌ·FU·KEN
〖注〗 metropolitan 大都市の，首都圏の．administrative division 行政区画．

fu[2] 麩 wheat gluten bread; pieces of dried bread made of wheat gluten flour. Before cooking, the pieces are soaked in water, softening to a sponge-like state, and the excess water is squeezed out. They are used in soup, *nabemono* (pot dishes), etc. *Fu* is high in protein and easy to digest. ⇨ NABEMONO
〖注〗 gluten グルテン，麩質．squeeze out しぼり出す．

fudai-daimyō 譜代大名 a hereditary feudal lord; the feudal lords who were hereditary vassals of the shogunate, one of the three kinds of feudal lords (*shinpan-daimyō*, *fudai-daimyō* and *tozama-daimyō*) of the Tokugawa period (1603-1868). With Tokugawas' establishment of the shogunate government after victory in the Battle of Sekigahara (1600), feudal lords who had pledged loyalty prior to and during this battle were granted special privileges, including that of participating in government affairs. ⇨ DAIMYŌ, SEKIGAHARA NO TATAKAI, SHINPAN-DAIMYŌ, TOKUGAWA-BAKUFU, TOZAMA-DAIMYŌ
〖注〗 hereditary 世襲の，先祖代々の．feudal lord 大名．vassal（封建制度における）領臣，家臣．shogunate 幕府．

fude 筆 a writing brush; a brush used with India ink in calligraphy. It consists of a bamboo stem with a tuft of hair at one end. The hair is taken from a raccoon dog, rabbit or sheep. The oldest existing *fude*, made in the eighth century, is preserved in the Shōsōin Imperial Repository, Nara. ⇨ SHODŌ, SUMI
〖注〗 India ink 墨．calligraphy 書道．a tuft of hair 一房の毛．raccoon dog 狸．repository 保存所，蔵．

Fudoki 風土記 topographical records; accounts of natural and cultural features recorded by the provinces by the order of Empress

Genmei (661-721) in 713. They were the first topographical accounts in written form. Still existing are those of Izumo, Hitachi, Harima, Bingo and Hizen, among which that of Izumo is the only one in the form of a complete book.

〖注〗 topographical 地形の，地勢の． account 説明（書），記事． province （行政目的で分割した）国． 現存の風土記：出雲，常陸，播磨，備後，肥前（風土記）．

Fudō Myōō 不動明王 Acala (Sanskrit); the Deity of Fire in Hinduism; an incarnation of the Buddha Dainichi, the Great Illuminator, in Buddhism. He was originally one of the deities of Hinduism and was later introduced into Buddhism. In Japan, his image is usually represented with a fierce expression, sitting or standing on a rock, backed by a flaming halo. He holds a sword in one hand to cut away evil, and a rope to bind it in the other; in so doing, he is said to help people come to the place of salvation. ⇨ BUKKYŌ, MYŌŌ

〖注〗 Hinduism ヒンズー教． incarnation 化身． illuminator 照らす者． flaming halo 炎の光輪．

fue 笛 a flute; the generic term for the flute, most commonly referring to the horizontal flute. There are a variety of traditional flutes which vary somewhat in construction, ranging from the folk festival flute to the instruments used in Gagaku and the Noh theater. ⇨ GAGAKU, NŌ

〖注〗 horizontal flute 横笛． folk festival 民俗的祭り． instrument 楽器．

fuekiryūkō 不易流行 lit. constancy and change. changeability and changelessness, eternal truth in the depth of changing reality, a kind of poetical realization attained by the haiku poet Matsuo Bashō (1644-94). Bashō composed haiku (17-syllable poems) through communion with nature, mostly while traveling. By contemplating phenomena in nature changing with the seasons, he penetrated to the underlying eternity, perceiving it as unchangeable, and concluded that the eternal and the changing blend into one in depth. ⇨ HAIKAI, HAIKU

〖注〗 poetical realization 詩的把握． communion with nature 自然と融合すること． contemplate 観想する，深くみつめる． penetrate 透視する，内部に入る． underlying 奥にある．

Fugaku Sanjūrokkei 富嶽三十六景 *the 36 Views of Mount Fuji*; a series of woodblock prints of Mount Fuji, made by Katsushika Hokusai (1760-1849) and published in the 1830s. This series of prints, made in the artist's later years, drew public attention for its dynamic innovative compositions. Best-known among the series are *A View on a Fine Breezy Day* (also called *Red Fuji*) and *The Waves Near Kanagawa*, both of which are popular motifs for Christmas cards.   ⇨ MOKUHANGA, UKIYOE

〖注〗 woodblock print 版画. composition（絵の）構成. *A View on a Fine Breezy Day*「凱風快晴」（俗に「赤富士」）. *The Waves Near Kanagawa*「神奈川沖浪裏」.

fugu-ryōri ふぐ料理   globefish dishes. Globefish is usually served as *sashimi* (raw fish) very thinly sliced, or used as an ingredient in soup or stew. It has a superb delicate taste. Its preparation requires special skill, because globefish glands contain a deadly poison. Thus, *fugu* restaurants are required to be licensed by the government.   ⇨ SASHIMI

〖注〗 globefish ふぐ. ingredient 成分,（料理の）材料. gland 腺.

Fuji-Hakone-Izu Kokuritsu-kōen 富士箱根伊豆国立公園   Fuji-Hakone-Izu National Park (1,230.7 square kilometers), designated in 1936; a natural park on the Pacific side of central Honshū, comprising parts of Yamanashi, Shizuoka and Kanagawa prefectures, plus the Izu Islands under the jurisdiction of the Tokyo metropolitan government. This park embraces four regions: that centering around Mount Fuji (3,776 meters), Japan's highest peak, with the Fuji Five Lakes at its base along the northern slope; the wooded Hakone region comprising Lake Ashinoko and the volcano Mount Hakone (1,439 m), noted for a barrier station set up by the Tokugawa shogunate (1603–1868); Izu Peninsula with the city of Atami, a hot-spring and bathing resort, and the city of Shimoda where Commodore Perry and Townsend Harris arrived from America to open the closed doors of Japan; and the Izu Islands consisting of a group of active volcanic isles. Easy access from Tokyo and the variety of views it offers have made this park a popular vacation site.   ⇨ IZU-SHOTŌ, KOKURITU-KŌEN

〖注〗 the Tokyo metropolitan government 東京都. barrier station 関所. the Tokugawa shogunate 徳川幕府. hot-spring 温泉. bathing resort 海水浴場.

fukura-suzume ふくら雀   lit. a fat sparrow. one of the styles in knotting *obi*, with the bow tied at the back in the form of a sparrow. The bow is said to look like a plump sparrow flying with its wings spread. This style is appropriate for young women on festive occasions.   ⇨ OBI

【注】 bow りぼん． plump ふくよかな，丸々とした．

Fukurokuju 福禄寿 the God of Wealth and Longevity, one of the Seven Deities of Good Luck. He is represented as a very old man with a long, huge bald head, wearing a long, full beard. He holds a crooked cane with a rolled-up scroll attached to the top; the secret of how to gain wealth and longevity is said to be contained in this scroll. He is usually accompanied by a crane, symbolic of longevity. Fukurokuju is often confused with Jurōjin due to their similar appearance, but they have different origins; the former is said to have been an incarnation of a star in Chinese legend while the latter derives from a man of the Sung dynasty (960-1279) of China. ⇨ JURŌJIN, SHICHI-FUKUJIN

【注】 longevity 長寿． the Seven Deities of Good Luck 七福神． bald head 禿頭． crooked cane 曲がった杖． scroll 巻物，巻軸． incarnation 化身．

fukuro-obi 袋帯 lit. a sack sash. a double-weave *obi* (sash) for a kimono; a non-reversible woman's *obi* made of thick fabric, woven or sewn into a long sack. It is about four meters long and 30 centimeters wide, with a design on only the right half. This type of *obi* is worn with kimono ranging from formal ones such as *furisode* (with long, hanging sleeves) and *tomesode* (ceremonial kimono) to semiformal ones such as *hōmongi* (visiting kimono) and *iromuji* (solid-color kimono), depending upon the material and design. ⇨ FURISODE, HŌMONGI, IROMUJI, KIMONO, OBI, TOMESODE

【注】 fabric 織物．

fukusa 袱紗[帛紗] a silk napkin used in the tea ceremony; a square piece of silk cloth for wiping tea utensils—the tea caddy, tea scoop, etc.—and for holding hot utensils—the lid of the teakettle, etc. The host for a tea ceremony always carries it with him, hanging from his sash. There are prescribed rules for folding the silk napkin according to each school. The smaller kind of silk napkin is called *kofukusa*, which is used for different purposes. ⇨ CHANOYU, KOFUKUSA

【注】 tea ceremony 茶の湯． tea utensils 茶道具． tea caddy 茶入れ，なつめ． tea scoop 茶杓． lid 蓋． teakettle 茶釜． sash 帯． prescribed rule 前もって定められた規則． fold a silk napkin 帛紗さばきをする．

fukusa-zushi 袱紗鮨 lit. silk wrapping-cloth *sushi*. vinegared rice wrapped in an omelet crepe. The crepe is likened to *fukusa*, a square silk napkin used for wrapping precious things or for wiping tea utensils. *Sushi* rice mixed with fish and vegetables is wrapped in this crepe in an artistic way and tied with a ribbon of seaweed or dried gourd (*kanpyō*). It is also called *chakin-zushi*, or "*sushi* wrapped with a tea cloth." ➪ FUKUSA, SUSHI

〖注〗 silk wrapping cloth 袱紗. vinegared 酢で味をつけた. tea utensil 茶道具. dried gourd 干瓢. tea cloth 茶巾.

fukusuke 福助 lit. a good-fortune fellow. an ornament in the shape of a boy with an unusually big head. Dressed in a ceremonial costume for a samurai (*kamishimo*), he has a smile and is bowing while seated squarely on his legs. This ornament is often found in small shops, inns or restaurants, and looks as if it is politely inviting customers to enter. Its origin is unknown ➪ KAMISHIMO

〖注〗 seated squarely on one's legs 脚を折って座す，正座をしている.

fumie 踏絵 lit. stepping on a picture or a picture to step on. pictures of the Cross or Christian images, used to identify Chiristians in the Edo period (1603-1868). A major policy of the first Tokugawa shogun, Ieyasu, was to unify the country, which included the elimination of foreign influences and thus the suppression of Christianity. This prohibition was intensified during the days of the shoguns Hidetada and Iemitsu with the adoption of the *fumie* practice that was first employed by Mizuno Morinobu, a magistrate at Nagasaki, in 1626. Those who refused or hesitated to step on the *fumie* were presumed Christians and persecuted. The first *fumie* were a picture on paper or a wooden carving, and later elaborate cast bronze or brass images were used. This practice was abolished in 1857 upon an appeal by the Dutch. ➪ KAKURE-KIRISHITAN, KIRISHITAN

〖注〗 the Cross 十字架. Christian image キリスト教の肖像画. Mizuno Morinobu 水野守信. magistrate 奉行. cast 鋳造する.

fumi no hi 文の日 letter-writing days; the 23rd of each month, the date designated by the Ministry of Posts and Telecommunications to promote letter writing. This date is appropriate because 23 can be pronounced as *fumi*—by taking the *fu* of *futatsu* (two) and *mi* of *mittsu* (three)—which is the classical expression for the word "letter," today more commonly called *tegami*. The ministry issued two stamps on July 23, 1979, commemorating this designation. In older times, July was known as *fumizuki* meaning "the month of letters," according to the special names of the months given for their seasonal characteristics.

〖注〗 the Ministry of Posts and Telecommunications 郵政省. telecommunication(s) (電信，電話などによる)遠隔通信. commemorate 記念する.

fundoshi 褌 a loincloth; men's underwear made of a long piece of cloth. *Fundoshi* for everyday use is a white cotton cloth, though it is rarely used today. The one worn by *sumō* wrestlers in the ring is made of colored, tight-woven silk. ⇨ MAWASHI

〖注〗 loincloth 腰につける布，褌.

furikae-kyūjitsu 振り替え休日 a transferred holiday. When a national holiday falls on a Sunday, the holiday is transferred to the next day, Monday, when schools and public offices of the nation are closed. ⇨ KOKUMIN NO SHUKUJITSU

〖注〗 transfer 移す，移行する. fall on (ある日時に)当たる.

fūrin 風鈴 lit. a wind bell. a small hanging bell made to tinkle in the wind. It is made of metal or porcelain, and hung from the eaves of houses. A piece of paper underneath, on which a poem is sometimes written, catches the breeze. The sound of the bell and movement of the paper by the breeze brings a feeling of coolness in the hot and languid summer months.

〖注〗 porcelain 陶磁器. eaves ひさし，軒. languid ものうい.

furisode 振袖 lit. swinging sleeves. the hanging sleeves of a kimono with such sleeves; a silk kimono with very long sleeves, worn on formal or festive occasions exclusively by young unmarried women. It is lavishly decorated with traditional designs and colors, and usually worn with a *maru-obi* (reversible sash) or *fukuro-obi* (double-weave sash). *Furisode* sleeves with a length of around 115 centimeters or more are called *ō-furisode* (very long hanging sleeves), and those between 95 and 100 cm long are called *chū-furisode* (medium-size hanging sleeves). ⇨ KIMONO, OBI, ŌFURISODE.

furo 風呂 a bath. The Japanese wash themselves outside the bathtub, not inside. When they become thoroughly clean, they immerse themselves in water to warm up and relax. The *furo* for Japanese is a place not only to clean the body but also to refresh oneself and relax. A public bath is called *sentō*, and was formerly very popular. Most Japanese take a bath everyday. ⇨ SENTŌ

〖注〗 immerse 浸す，沈める.

fūro [**furo**] 風炉 a brazier; a portable brazier with a short tripod stand, used for the tea ceremony. It is made of pottery or iron, and filled with ashes. During the tea ceremony, an iron kettle is placed on a kettle holder over a charcoal fire in the brazier. In the warmer seasons, a portable brazier is used instead of the hearth set in the floor. ⇨ RO

〘注〙 portable brazier 持ち運びのできる火鉢[炉], (茶室の)風炉. tripod 三脚. tripod stand 五徳. tea ceremony 茶の湯. pottery 陶磁器. iron kettle 茶釜. kettle holder 釜をのせるもの, 五徳. hearth 炉床, (茶室の)炉.

furoshiki 風呂敷 a wrapping cloth; a scarf-like square cloth made of silk or cotton, or sometimes synthetic fiber today. It is used for wrapping and carrying things. When not in use, it folds into a small square. Most *furoshiki* are decorated with pictures—flowers, trees, scenery, or the family crest of the owner. *Furoshiki* literally means "bath cloth," because it was originally used to wrap clothes in a public bath or to sit on after bathing.

〘注〙 synthetic fiber 合成繊維. family crest 家紋.

fūryū 風流 lit. wind and stream or in the way of the wind. an aesthetic attitude toward life and nature; to live elegantly with refined tastes, contemplating nature and enjoying arts even in the midst of a busy life. It is the pursuit of a moment of tranquillity by detaching oneself from worldly strain. Though refinement had earlier been pursued by the aristocracy, it became a concept cultivated particularly by warriors in the period of prolonged civil wars (15th and 16th centuries). It was associated with the tea ceremony, flower arrangement, painting, poetry, etc., in the Muromachi period (1336-1568). In the Edo period (1603-1868) the concept spread widely even among commoners, and was linked with *haikai* (17-syllable poem) which requires seasonal inspiration. With various implications added over time, the *fūryū* concept has become deeply rooted in the aesthetic life of the Japanese. ⇨ CHANOYU, HAIKAI, IKEBANA, KADŌ, SADŌ

〘注〙 aesthetic 美的, 美意識の. contemplate 観想する. tranquillity 落ち着き, 静寂. aristocracy 貴族階級. the days of civil wars 戦国時代. tea ceremony 茶の湯. flower arrangement 生け花.

fusuma 襖 a set of sliding doors in a Japanese house; framed and papered movable partitions between rooms, running in grooves at the top and bottom. Both sides of a wooden frame are covered with thick paper on which decorative pictures—or sometimes a continuous panoramic scene—are painted. ⇨ SHŌJI

〘注〙 sliding door すべり戸. partition 仕切り. groove みぞ, 敷居のみぞ. panoramic scene 全景, 連続して表されている光景.

futaoki 蓋置 a lid rest; a rest used in the tea ceremony on which to place a ladle or the lid of a hot kettle. It is made of ceramic, bronze or bamboo. Sen no Rikyū (1521-91), who developed the rustic tea ceremony, preferred one made of bamboo. ⇨ CHAGAMA, HISHAKU

〖注〗 tea ceremony 茶道. ladle ひしゃく. ceramic 陶器. rustic tea ceremony わび茶.

futomaki(-zushi) 太巻き（鮨） a thick *sushi* roll; vinegared rice wrapped in a sheet of dried seaweed laver, with a variety of ingredients in the center. The ingredients include dry gourd (*kanpyō*), egg, mushrooms, mashed fish, green vegetables, etc. The long roll is sliced when served. ⇨ NORIMAKI, SUSHI

〖注〗 vinegared rice 酢で味をつけた御飯. a sheet of dried seaweed laver 乾燥した海苔. ingredient （料理の）材料. dry gourd 干ぴょう.

futon 布団 a thick quilt and mattress; a set of bedding stuffed with cotton. Today, synthetic fibers are usually mixed with the cotton. *Futon* are spread on the *tatami* floor at night, and stowed away in a large closet in the morning. A blanket may also be used together with *futon* in cold weather. ⇨ KAKEBUTON, SHIKIBUTON, TATAMI

〖注〗 stuff 詰める. synthetic fiber 合成繊維. stow away かたづける、しまう.

G

gabu がぶ a convertible Bunraku-puppet head. It is specially mechanized so as to depict a two-faced person. In one of the Bunraku plays, the face of a beautiful woman changes into that of a demon in an instant with the manipulation of a special lever. ⇨ BUNRAKU

〘注〙 convertible 転換できる. manipulation 操作.

gagaku 雅楽 lit. elegant music. ancient court music and dance. It comprises music and dances native to Japan along with repertoire introduced in the Heian period (794-1185) mainly from China, Korea and Southeast Asia. Gagaku generally refers to the ceremonial music and dance of the Imperial Court of Japan. It includes both the dances known as Bugaku and the orchestral music known as *kangen* performed with percussion, wind and string instruments. ⇨ BUGAKU, KANGEN

〘注〙 court music 宮廷音楽. repertoire レパートリー, 上演種目. percussion instrument 打楽器. wind instrument 管楽器. string instrument 弦楽器.

Gakkō Kyōikuhō 学校教育法 the School Education Law; the law concerning the school system of Japan, established in 1947, based on the Fundamental Law of Education (1947). Consisting of nine chapters, with 110 articles and a supplement, the law defines the schools of Japan as "elementary schools, lower secondary schools, upper secondary schools, colleges and universities, technical colleges, schools for the blind, schools for the deaf, schools for the handicapped, and kindergartens." Under this law, the 6-3-3-4 system was adopted, nine years of elementary and lower secondary education being compulsory. Later, after an amendment in 1975, special training schools were established in 1976. ⇨ KYŌIKU KIHONHŌ

〘注〙 the Fundamental Law of Education「教育基本法」. 110 articles 110条. supplement 補則. technical school 高等専門学校. school for the handicapped 養護学校. amendment 法改正. special training school 専修学校.

gakubatsu 学閥 an academic clique; academic sectarianism; a faction composed of graduates of the same college or university. Factionalism is very strong even in the academic world in group-oriented Japanese society. Graduates of the same school tend to share a group consciousness within corporations and support each other both emotionally and in practical terms. "School-clique" relationships may be effective in helping individuals find good positions and enjoy opportunities for promotion. ⇨ BATSU, HABATSU

〘注〙 clique 徒党, 派閥. sectarianism 派閥心. faction 党派, 派閥. group-oriented 集団志向の. group consciousness 集団意識. school clique 学閥. promotion 昇進.

Ganjitsu 元日 New Year's Day (January 1); a national holiday designated to celebrate the beginning of the new year. This day has traditionally been the most important day in Japan, when people make a fresh start with wishes for happiness and prosperity throughout the new year. Although only January 1 is an official holiday, the first three days of the year are traditionally recognized as the New Year holiday period. During this period, prayers are offered at shrines and temples; New Year greetings are exchanged; relatives and friends get together to celebrate; special dishes are served; homes are decorated with *shimekazari* (sacred straw tassels) and *kadomatsu* (gate pine), etc., symbolic of happiness and purity. ⇨ KADOMATSU, SANGANICHI, SHIME(NAWA)-KAZARI

〘注〙 tassel 飾りふさ. sacred straw tassel 注連縄飾り.

ganmodoki 雁もどき lit. look like wild geese. a variant of fried bean curd (*aburage*); soybean curd mixed with seaweed (*hijiki*) and bits of vegetables. The tiny pieces of black seaweed are likened to a flock of flying wild geese. Crumbled bean curd mixed with such ingredients is thickened with grated mountain yam. It is shaped into flat round patties and deep-fried to a golden brown. This is one of the main ingredients of *oden*. ⇨ ABURA(A)GE, ODEN, TŌFU

〘注〙 variant 変形物. fried bean curd 油揚げ. deep-fried たっぷりの油で揚げた. soybean curd 豆腐. seaweed 海藻. tiny pieces of black seaweed ひじき. crumbled ほぐした. ingredient (料理の)材料. thicken どろどろにする. grated mountain yam 山芋のおろしたもの.

garan 伽藍 a cathedral; a grand Buddhist temple with several fixed types of buildings in its compounds. The buildings include all or most of the following: a main hall, a pagoda (one or two), a lecture hall, a belfry, a library, a dormitory and a refectory (or a middle gate). Early great temples until the Nara period (710-94) followed an orderly layout consisting of seven buildings, called *shichidō-garan* (temple of seven buildings). From the Heian period (794-1185) on, the number and layout were not necessarily observed. Among others, Hōryūji Temple (607), Tōdaiji Temple (743) and Yakushiji Temple (680) in Nara were laid out in the *garan* style but have their own individual features.　⇨ CHŪMON[2], HONDŌ, SHICHIDŌ-GARAN, SHŌRO, TERA, TŌ

〖注〗 compounds 敷地, 境内, 囲われた地域. pagoda 塔. lecture hall 講堂. belfry 鐘楼. library 経蔵. dormitory 僧房. refectory (寺, 学校などの)食堂. middle gate 中門.

gasshō-zukuri 合掌造り lit. architecture in the form of praying hands. a house with a steep-sloping roof. The steep slope of the roof resembles hands clasped in prayer and thus arose its name. Shirakawa Village in Gifu Prefecture is well-known for this type of farmhouse, still well-preserved. They are huge wooden thatched houses. The roof is multistoried, providing enough space to hold many related families living together.

〖注〗 clasp in prayer 合掌する. Shirakawa Village 白川郷. thatched house 茅葺きの家屋.

geisha 芸者 lit. a person of arts. a traditional Japanese courtesan; a female entertainer, professionally trained in traditional dance and music. She wears an elaborate traditional coiffure and colorful kimono with a gorgeous *obi* (sash). A true geisha is highly accomplished in traditional manners and artistic performance of dance and music, and is not a woman of low morals. The training used to start early, often as young as 10 or under. There still exists a custom of inviting geisha to a Japanese-style banquet to wait on guests with saké (Japanese rice wine) and entertain with dances accompanied by *shamisen* (a string instrument). The most accomplished geisha are from Pontochō in Kyoto and Shinbashi in Tokyo.　⇨ RYŌTEI

〖注〗 courtesan (高級)娼婦. coiffure 髪の結い方, 髪型. accomplished ～に堪能な, たしなみのある. accompany 伴奏する. string instrument 弦楽器.

Genbaku Kinenbi 原爆記念日 the anniversaries of the atomic bombings; the annual memorial days for the victims of the atomic bombings, observed at Hiroshima (August 6) and at Nagasaki

(August 9). In 1945, an atomic bomb was dropped upon Hiroshima and one upon Nagasaki on these days, instantaneously killing over 80,000 and over 70,000 people respectively. It has been estimated that altogether close to 200,000 people eventually died, including victims of after-effects. Annually on each of these days, a huge city-sponsored memorial ceremony is observed for the dead, with silent prayers and peace declarations calling for the elimination of nuclear arms. ⇨ SHŪSEN KINENBI

〖注〗 after-effect 後遺症. city-sponsored memorial ceremony 市主催の記念式典. silent prayer 黙禱. peace declaration 平和宣言.

gengō 元号 the imperial era name; the era-naming system based on the reigning emperor. This system has been in use since the first emperor, Jinmu (r. 660-585 B.C., according to *The Chronicle of Japan*). When an imperial succession takes place, the era name is replaced by a new one; formerly, often more than one name was employed during the reign of an emperor, but in recent times there has been only a single era name for each emperor. The year in Japan can be numbered by either this imperial era system or by the Gregorian system. For example, since the present Emperor's era bears the name of Shōwa, the year 1985 corresponds to the 60th year of Shōwa. Official documents, registration, etc., usually require the use of the imperial era system. ⇨ TENNŌ

〖注〗 imperial era 天皇の御代. *The Chronicle of Japan*「日本書記」. imperial succession 皇位継承. reign 治世, 君臨. the Gregorian system 太陽暦, 現行の西洋暦.

Genji Monogatari 源氏物語 *The Tale of Genji* (1004-11). Japan's greatest novel, written by Lady Murasaki Shikibu (?978-?1016) in the Heian period (794-1185). Belonging to a minor branch of the aristocracy, Murasaki Shikibu served as a lady-in-waiting to Empress Akiko. Based on her experiences and observations, she depicted life and people in the Heian court through the characters Hikaru Genji, born to an emperor and a court lady, and his son Kaoru. Their amorous adventures and the responses of court ladies are described with a touch of courtly elegance, mingled with pathos and melancholy from a close association with nature as it changes from season to season. An underlying Buddhist theme, in terms of the transiency of life and the working of karma, is also found in the work. Consisting of 54 chapters, the story covers four generations spanning about 80 years, and deals with the lives of over 400 characters. ⇨ HEIAN-JIDAI

〖注〗 the aristocracy 貴族階級． lady-in-waiting 宮廷女房． amorous adventure 愛の遍歴． courtly elegance 雅び． transiency of life 人生のはかなさ． karma 因果，宿命．

Genkō 元寇 the Mongol Invasion (1274 and 1281); the Mongolian attacks on Japan during the regency of Hōjō Tokimune (1251-84). The Kamakura shogunate (1185-1336) rejected a Mongol demand that Japan become a tributary. Armed with catapults and cannons, Mongolian forces sent by Kublai approached northern Kyūshū in 1274 (Bun'ei War) and 1281 (Kōan War). The first group numbered some 30,000 and the second some 140,000. The outcome was total destruction of the Mongolian fleets due to timely typhoons on both occasions. The excess spending on defense that followed led to the gradual decline of the Kamakura shogunate. ⇨ KAMAKURA-BAKUFU, KAMIKAZE

〖注〗 Mongol 蒙古(人)． regency 摂政(職)． tributary 進貢国，属国． catapult 弩砲． Bun'ei War「文永の役」． Kōan War「弘安の役」． Mongolian fleet 蒙古艦隊． defense 防衛．

genpei 源平 the Genji [Minamoto] clan and the Heike [Taira] clan, the first two ruling samurai clans to emerge in Japanese history. The two great clans fought for military supremacy at the end of the Heian period (794-1185). At first the Heike were victorious, eventually gaining political influence over the Imperial Court. The defeated Genji reorganized their forces to fight back and ended 30 years of conflict with a great victory at Dannoura, at the western tip of Honshū, in 1185. The term *genpei* is sometimes used in reference to two opponents in games, especially in card games.

〖注〗 clan 氏． supremacy 至上権，主権． the Imperial Court 朝廷．

genpuku 元服 coming-of-age in olden times; a ceremony celebrating one's attainment of manhood. In the Nara (646-794) and Heian (794-1185) periods, boys of around 12 to 16 years of age changed the style of their dress and hair to mark their reaching adulthood. In feudal times, the coming-of-age rite was particularly important for boys among the samurai class; from then on they were allowed to carry swords, in addition to wearing the appropriate clothing and hair style. Today, both boys and girls who have reached the age of 20 are honored on January 15, Coming-of-Age Day (*Seijin no Hi*). ⇨ SEIJIN NO HI

〖注〗 feudal times 封建時代. rite 儀式.

genrō 元老 an elder statesman; the council of elders; chief advisers to the emperor who contributed from the Meiji (1868-1912) to the early Shōwa eras. They were selected unofficially from among top retired political leaders, and recommended new leaders to the emperor and advised him on the handling of politically important affairs. They formed a council of nine members, among whom were Hirobumi Itō (1841-1909), Aritomo Yamagata (1838-1922), Kinmochi Saionji (1849-1940), etc.

〖注〗 council 評議員会.

Genroku-jidai 元禄時代 the Genroku era during the Edo period (1603-1868); the name of the era lasting from 1688 to 1704, during which Emperor Higashiyama (r. 1687-1709) was on the throne. It is also commonly used to denote the culture that flourished during this period. With the disappearance of the warmongering spirit that prevailed during the previous 100 years, the Genroku era saw the prospering of urban life and the unprecedented blooming of arts enjoyed also by the common people: *haikai*, Noh, Kabuki, *ukiyoe*, pottery, etc. ⇨ CHŌNIN, EDO-JIDAI

〖注〗 on the throne 即位している. warmongering spirit 好戦的精神. urban life 都市生活, 町人生活. unprecedented 先例にない. blooming of arts 芸術の開花. pottery 陶芸.

geta 下駄 Japanese wooden footgear; a pair of wooden clogs with two wooden pieces under the sole, and V-shaped thongs between the big toe and the other toes. *Geta* for men are of plain wood and usually have black thongs while those for women are both lacquered and plain, and have beautifully colored thongs of silk or velvet. ⇨ HANAO, ZŌRI

〖注〗 footgear 履物. wooden clog 木靴, 下駄. sole 足底, 履物の底. thong 紐. lacquer 漆を塗る.

geza-ongaku 下座音楽 the offstage music for sound effects in a Kabuki drama. Instruments used include *shamisen* and *koto*, Japanese flutes, and a wide variety of percussive drums, bells, gongs, etc. ⇨ KABUKI, KOTO, SHAKUHACHI, SHAMISEN

〖注〗 offstage 舞台裏の, 観客から見えないところの. percussive 打楽器の, たたいて音を出す. gong どら.

gidayū(-bushi) 義太夫(節) the narrative style of vocalization in Bunraku and Kabuki of Bunraku origin. It is so called because it was developed by Takemoto Gidayū (1651-1714). Accompanied by *shamisen* music, a single singer can give life to each doll on the stage by providing the vocal expressions for each character and reciting the story.   ⇨ BUNRAKU, KABUKI, SHAMISEN

【注】 narrative 物語り風の． Takemoto Gidayū 竹本義太夫． accompany 伴う，伴奏する． character 人物，登場人物． recite 吟唱する．

gigaku 伎楽 the comical dance and ballad drama; an ancient style of performance employing masks, introduced from the Asian continent in the seventh century, now archaic.   Its influence can still be seen in the masks and style of performance of traditional folk dances and classical Bugaku.   ⇨ BUGAKU

【注】 ballad drama 伝承的物語劇，民謡劇． archaic 古風な．

Gion Matsuri 祇園祭 the Gion Festival of Kyoto (July 17-24); the festival held in honor of Yasaka Shrine, one of the three grand Kyoto festivals, the other two being the Aoi Festival and the Jidai Festival.   Its origin dates back to 869 when an epidemic raged in Kyoto and people dedicated scores of massive floats to Yasaka Shrine asking for protection. During the days of the festival, sacred portable shrines and elaborate floats with traditional themes, carried by a number of young men, are paraded in vigorous processions through the city to the accompaniment of flutes, drums, etc.   ⇨ AOI MATSURI, JIDAI MATSURI, MIKOSHI

【注】 date back to （ある時期から）始まる，にさかのぼる． epidemic 流行性の，流行病． dedicate 捧げる，献上する． float 浮く物，山車． sacred portable shrine 神輿．

go 碁 Japanese checkers; a board game for two players with the object of capturing more territory than one's opponent, also commonly called *igo*.   The players take turns placing round black and white stones on 361 lattice points formed by 19 vertical and 19 horizontal lines.   When one's stones completely surround the opponent's without leaving a vacant point within, the surrounded stones are regarded as captured and taken off the playing board.   This area is considered captured territory.   A stone cannot be placed inside an area surrounded by the opponent unless such a placement enables one to capture the opponent's stones.   The game ends when stones can no longer be placed on the board because the points are either occupied or inside captured territories.   The winner is determined by the amount of territory captured.

【注】 capture 獲る． territory 領分． lattice point 格子の交差点，碁盤の目．

gō 合 a traditional unit for measuring volume.   One *gō* is equivalent to 180 cc. There are three kinds of traditional square measuring cups (or boxes) made of cypress wood: a one-*gō* box (*ichigō-masu*), five-*gō* box (*gogō-masu*), and ten-*gō* box (called *isshō-masu* as 10 *gō* make one-*shō*, or *isshō*). This unit is still widely used for measuring grain, rice wine, soy sauce, etc. ⇨ MASU, SHAKKAN-HŌ, SHŌ

〖注〗 unit for measuring volume 容積計量単位. square measuring cup 升. cypress ひのき. soy sauce 醤油.

gofuku 呉服 lit. clothes of Go. traditional Japanese clothes and fabric. In the Edo period (1603-1868) it referred in particular to silk fabric. Originally, it indicated fabric woven using the skill developed in the country of Go 呉 (902-37) of ancient China, thus giving rise to its name, "clothes of Go." ⇨ GOFUKUYA

〖注〗 fabric 織物, 布. silk fabric 絹織物. give rise to 生じる, 由来する.

gofukuya 呉服屋 a shop selling traditional Japanese clothes. It sells not only many kinds of kimono and fabric but also kimono accessories such as *obi* (broad sash), *tabi* (socks for kimono), *juban* (kimono underwear), etc. In the Edo period (1603-1868), *gofukuya* referred in particular to a shop selling silk fabrics. ⇨ GOFUKU, JUBAN, KIMONO, OBI, TABI

〖注〗 silk fabric 絹織物.

gohei 御幣 a piece of white paper used in Shinto; a sacred staff with cut and plaited pieces of white paper hanging from it. It is used to purify and sanctify both persons and things by warding off evil spirits and inviting the sacred spirit of a deity, the color white being symbolic of purity and sanctity. Cut and plaited pieces of white paper may also be seen hanging at intervals from a straw rope to indicate sacredness when a Shinto rite is conducted. This is also called *nusa*. ⇨ JINJA, SHINTŌ

〖注〗 staff 杖, 棒. plait 編む. sanctify 聖別する. ward off さける, ぬぐいさる. deity 神, 神のような人[もの]. Shinto rite 神道による儀式.

gojūnotō 五重の塔 a five-storied pagoda; a five-storied tower-like structure erected in the precincts of a Buddhist temple. It is made of wood with five tiled roofs placed one over the other. The Buddha's or a Buddhist saint's ashes or relics are enshrined in the foundation stone or in an altar on the first floor. The Japanese pagoda is said to be a transformed grave marker, with its origin tracing back to the Indian stupa. The five-storied pagoda at Hōryūji Temple, Nara, is the oldest one existing today, constructed

in 607.   The largest one can be seen at Tōji Temple, Kyoto, first
constructed in 796.   ⇨ SANJŪNOTŌ, SHARI², TŌ

〖注〗 pagoda（東洋の寺院の）塔.   precincts 境内.   place one over the other
重ねる.   relic 遺品, 遺物.   enshrine 祀る.   grave marker 墓標.   trace back
to ~までたどる、~に由来する.   stupa 仏舎利塔.

gokaidō 五街道   five great roads; the five major roads opened in the
Edo period（1603-1868）to connect the provinces with Edo, the
shogunate capital.   They were mostly made use of by feudal lords
of the provinces for their processions to and from Edo under the
system of "alternate attendance"（*sankinkōtai*）.   They were: the
Tokaidō（extending from Edo to Kyoto along the Pacific coast）,
the Nakasendō（to Kyoto through the mountainous region）, the
Nikkō-kaidō（to Nikkō, in the present Tochigi Prefecture）, the
Kōshu-kaidō（to Fuchū, present Kōfu）and the Ōshū-kaidō（to
Aomori, northern Honshū）.   ⇨ SANKINKŌTAI

〖注〗 province 地方の諸国,（行政のため区分した）国.   shogunate 幕府（の）.
feudal lord 大名.   system of "alternate attendance" 参勤交代制.   五街道：東
海道, 中山道[中仙道], 日光街道, 甲州街道, 奥州街道.

Gokajō no Goseimon 五箇条の御誓文   the Five Imperial Oaths
（1868）; the five articles declared in 1868 in the name of Emperor
Meiji（1852-1912; r. 1867-1912）as the fundamental principles in
carrying out the reforms of the new Meiji regime, which aimed at
the establishment of a modern country.   This served as the first
step toward the parliamentary system and is sometimes regarded
as the Japanese counterpart of the Magna Carta of England.   The
five articles are as follows:
1.   All state affairs shall be decided by the people's opinions,
      obtained in widely convened deliberative assemblies.
2.   The administration of state affairs shall be carried out with
      perfect harmony between the government and the people.
3.   All people—officials, warriors and commoners—shall be en-
      couraged to pursue opportunities in accordance with their
      ambitions and abilities.
4.   Irrational old customs shall be discarded, and the righteous
      laws of heaven and earth shall be the basis of all things.
5.   Knowledge shall be pursued worldwide, by which the founda-
      tion of imperial glory shall be promoted.   ⇨ MEIJI ISHIN

〖注〗 oath 誓い.   article 条.   the parliamentary system 議会制度.   the
Magna Carta（英国憲法の基礎となった）勅許状.   convene 召集する.   deliber-

ative assembly 審議会． the administration of state affairs 国家行政．

gokenin 御家人 lit. men of the house. vassals serving the shogun. In the Kamakura (1185-1336) and Muromachi (1336-1568) periods, the term referred to hereditary vassals directly serving the shogun and having high ranks. Under the Tokugawa shogunate (1603-1868), they were poor low-level retainers, ranking below the *hatamoto*; they served the shogun as the standing military, together with the *hatamoto*. ⇨ HATAMOTO, SHŌGUN, TOKUGAWA-BAKUFU

〚注〛 vassal 臣下，家臣． hereditary 世襲的な． the Tokugawa shogunate 徳川幕府． retainer 従者，侍者． standing military 常備のさむらい，常備軍．

goki(nai)-shichidō 五畿(内)七道 the five central provinces and the seven districts; the system of administrative districts established in 646 by the Taika Reform. This system was retained until around the Meiji Restoration (1868) with modifications over the course of time. The five central provinces were centered around the former capitals of Nara and Kyoto. The seven districts were: Tōsandō (lit. Eastern Mountain Road), comprising northern Honshū and the mountain zone of central Honshū; Tōkaidō (Eastern Sea Road), along the Pacific coast of central Honshū; Hokurikudō (North Land Road), stretching along the Japan Sea coast from northern to central Honshū; San'indō (Mountain Shade Road), facing the Japan Sea along western Honshū; San'yōdō (Mountain Sunnyside Road), facing the Inland Sea of Seto on western Honshū; Nankaidō (Southern Sea Road), embracing Shikoku and the eastern part of the coast of the Inland Sea of Seto; and Saikaidō (Western Sea Road), covering all of Kyūshū. Each district was further divided into provinces (*kuni*). ⇨ DŌ[1], KINAI, KUNI

〚注〛 province (行政区画としての)国，県，管区． the Taika Reform 大化の改新． the Meiji Restoration 明治維新． modification 修正． 七道：東山道，東海道，北陸道，山陰道，山陽道，南海道，西海道．

goma 護摩 from the Sanskrit *homa*, meaning "fire ritual"; a ceremony in which wooden sticks are burned in esoteric Buddhism. The ceremony is performed in front of a statue of a Myōō deity, accompanied by prayers and bell-ringing. The idea is that the fire of wisdom burns up the wooden sticks which represent earthly desires and defilements. Prayers and wishes are written on the sticks. The one performed at Enryakuji Temple on Mount Hiei near Kyoto is well-known. The ceremony can be traced back to an ancient Indian fire ritual dedicated to the God of Fire. ⇨

MIKKYŌ, MYŌŌ

〖注〗 ritual 儀式. esoteric Buddhism 密教. deity 神のような人[もの]. earthly desire 煩悩. defilement 汚れ. Enryakuji Temple 延暦寺.

gomoku-meshi 五目飯 lit. rice of five things. rice boiled together with a variety of ingredients. The ingredients include small pieces of chicken, various kinds of seafoods, and bits of different vegetables. At least five kinds are used, particularly with a seasonal vegetable included, such as bamboo shoots, chestnuts, ginkgo nuts, etc. The dish is flavored with soy sauce and other seasonings. In the Ōsaka district, it is called *kayaku-gohan*.

〖注〗 ingredient（料理の)材料. bamboo shoots 竹の子. ginkgo nut 銀杏. soy sauce 醤油. seasoning 調味料.

gorin 五倫 the Five Norms of Ethics; the five basic human relationships in Confucianism. The Confucianism of ancient China teaches that the harmony of the universe is based on the reciprocal relationship of dual cosmic forces—plus and minus, light and dark, etc. In social terms, to ensure harmony the bond of five human relationships was considered all-important—between ruler and subordinate, parent and child, husband and wife, elder and younger, and that between friends. In turn, these relationships involve five virtues—justice, benevolence, propriety, order and sincerity. These concepts were adopted by the Tokugawa shogunate (1603-1868) and applied to feudal ethics, in an attempt to control the people's thought and conduct, and thus stabilize the country. There are a number of books bearing the title of *The Books of Gorin* (*Gorin no Sho*), among which the one by Kumazawa Banzan (1619-91) is noted. ⇨ JUKYŌ

〖注〗 Confucianism 儒教. reciprocal 相互の. dual cosmic forces 宇宙の二元の力, 陰陽. benevolence 恩. propriety 分, 立場の区別. feudal ethics 封建的倫理. Kumazawa Banzan 熊沢蕃山. 五倫：君臣の義, 父子の親, 夫婦の別, 長幼の序, 朋友の信.

gorinnotō 五輪の塔 lit. a five-ring tower. a pagoda or stupa consisting of five parts. It is constructed as a grave marker or as a monument to the departed. It is made of five stones set up vertically, each stone varying in shape:（from top to bottom) spherical with a pointed top, semi-spherical, triangular, spherical and square. They symbolize air, wind, fire, water and earth respectively. These were popular in the Heian (794-1185) and Kamakura (1185-1336) periods.

〖注〗 pagoda（東洋の寺院の）塔． stupa（円形，角錐の形の）仏舎利塔，卒塔婆． grave marker 墓標． the departed 死者，世を去った人々． spherical with a pointed top 頂上のとがった球形の． semi-spherical 半球形の．

Gōruden-wīku ゴールデン・ウィーク Golden Week; a seven-day period including three national holidays, coming in spring. The three national holidays are: *Tennō Tanjōbi* (the Emperor's Birthday), April 29; *Kenpō Kinenbi* (Constitution Day), May 3; and *Kodomo no Hi* (Children's Day), May 5.

gosanke 御三家 the three honorable families; the three branch families descended directly from Tokugawa Ieyasu (1542-1616), the first shogun of the Tokugawa government. With the establishment of the shogunate government, Ieyasu appointed three of his sons as feudal lords of Owari (around the present Nagoya), Kii (around the present Wakayama), and Hitachi (around the present Mito), and prescribed that the successors to the post of shogun be appointed from one of the three. Therefore, these three families and their descendants came to be called *gosanke*. ⇨ TOKUGAWA-BAKUFU

〖注〗 shogunate government 幕府． feudal lord 大名，藩主． successor 後継者． descendant 子孫． 御三家：尾張，紀伊，常陸の藩主．

goshinkō 御進講 lectures for the Emperor; an annual Imperial event of lectures given to the Emperor by distinguished scholars. It is held at the Imperial Palace at the beginning of the new year in the presence of the Emperor, accompanied by some other members of the Imperial Family. The subjects include important topical matters of the day and items in academic fields of special interest to the Emperor.

〖注〗 the Emperor 現天皇． annual Imperial event 恒例の皇室行事． the Imperial Palace 皇居． important topical matters of the day 時の重要課題事項．

gosho-ningyō 御所人形 a court doll; a doll portraying an infant with a chubby round face, made of clay. Originally, such dolls were used as toys for infants in the Imperial Court (*Gosho*). During the Edo period (1603-1868), the Imperial Court gave them to feudal lords in return for the tribute presented to the court in Kyoto.

〖注〗 chubby ぽちゃぽちゃした． feudal lord 大名． tribute 貢物．

goshuinsen 御朱印船 a ship with the official red seal; a ship for foreign trade, authorized with a red seal by the Tokugawa shogunate government (1603-1868). The official seal system was first established by Toyotomi Hideyoshi (1536-98) in 1592, and was continued by the Tokugawa shogunate, during which time the number of such ships greatly increased. From 1604 to 1635, some 350 ships granted such status carried some 80,000 to 100,000 Japanese abroad to the Philippines, Thailand, the Malay Peninsula, etc. They exported rice, lacquer ware, cloisonné, pottery, silver, iron, etc. and in turn imported silk, cotton, sugar, leather, etc. ⇨ TOKUGAWA-BAKUFU

〖注〗 the Tokugawa shogunate (government) 徳川幕府. official seal 公式な印. lacquer ware 漆器. cloisonné 七宝焼. pottery 陶磁器.

goyōhajime 御用始め the first work day of a new year (January 4); the resumption of business after the New Year holidays. Government offices and most large companies resume normal functions on this day. Most stores, though, open prior to this day. Schools generally resume around January 8. ⇨ GOYŌOSAME

〖注〗 resumption 再開始, 続行. function 機能, 職務.

goyōosame 御用納め the last business day of the year (December 28); the closing of business for the year. Government offices (except the post office) and large companies bring their operations to a close for the year on this day and officially enter the holidays the next day. People are kept extremely busy clearing up matters of the ending year. Banks and stores, though, are usually open until the next to the last or last day of the year. ⇨ GOYŌHAJIME

〖注〗 operation 運営, 操業. clear up ～を片づける, ～を解決する.

gozan 五山 lit. five mountains. the five principal temples of the Rinzai sect of Zen Buddhism. The idea of the *gozan* derived from five religious mountains in India and was introduced to Japan through the five official monasteries established during the Sung dynasty (960-1279) of China. In Japan, the Hōjō family regents and the Ashikaga shoguns, integrating the Rinzai Zen monasteries to organize a hierarchical system during the 14th and 15th centuries, designated three in Kamakura and two in Kyoto as official ones. They were Kenchōji, Enkakuji and Jufukuji temples in Kamakura, and Kenninji and Tōfukuji temples in Kyoto. Soon, Kamakura and Kyoto each came to have their own five official temples. ⇨ KAMAKURA-GOZAN, KYŌTO-GOZAN, RINZAISHŪ, ZENSHŪ

〖注〗 monastery 僧院. the Sung dynasty 宋王朝. regent 摂政. hierarchical system 位階制度. 五山：建長寺, 円覚寺, 寿福寺（鎌倉）, 建仁寺, 東福寺

（京都）.

guinomi ぐい飲み lit. one gulp. a large type of saké cup. It is the size of a small coffee cup (demitasse). With it, one is expected to drink saké in a single gulp. This kind of cup often comes in the form of Seto, Mino, Bizen or Karatsu ceramic ware. ⇨ CHOKU, SAKE

〖注〗 gulp ごくりと飲むこと，一飲み． demitasse デミタス（食後のコーヒーの小型コーヒー茶わん）. in a single gulp 一飲みに． ceramic ware 陶器．

gun 郡 a county; a geographical subdivision of a prefecture. A prefecture is divided into large cities and counties. A county is further subdivided into small cities, towns and villages. ⇨ KEN

〖注〗 subdivision 細分化．

gunki-monogatari 軍記物語 a war epic or tale; tales of medieval wars and warriors, a genre of literature appearing in the Kamakura (1185-1336) and Muromachi (1336-1568) periods. Generally, these works dealt with the vicissitudes of great men and great families based on historical facts, and at the same time presented views of life and fatalistic resignation based on Buddhist doctrine. Some of the tales were chanted to the accompaniment of the *biwa*, a lute-like string instrument. Famous works include *Taiheiki* (The Record of Great Peace, 40 volumes, 14th century) presumably by Priest Kojima; *Heike Monogatari* (The Tale of the Taira Clan, 13th to 14th centuries), author unknown; and *Genpei Seisuiki* (The Vicissitudes of the Minamoto and Taira Clans, 48 volumes, mid-13th to mid-14th centuries), author unknown. ⇨ BIWA

〖注〗 warrior さむらい． vicissitude 栄枯盛衰，変遷． fatalistic resignation 運命論的諦め． Buddhist doctrine 仏教の教義． chant 歌う，吟唱する． to the accompaniment of ～の伴奏で． lute リュート（ギターに似た15～17世紀の弦楽器）. string instrument 弦楽器．

gyōji 行司 a *sumō* referee. He stands in the ring facing the north, clad in a traditional costume of brocade with a ritual fan (*gunbai-uchiwa*) in his right hand. Before a bout he announces the names of the wrestlers and solemnly watches over the pre-bout *shikiri* ceremony. When the time for the *shikiri* is up, he informs the wrestlers and urges them into starting position. During the bout he shouts out words of encouragement. At the moment the match is decided, he points his fan toward the winner's side of the ring and proceeds to face the winner at the edge of the ring and annouces his name. As with the wrestlers, the *gyōji* also have ranks and they name. As with the wrestlers, the *gyōji* also have ranks and they referee bouts featuring wrestlers of corresponding rank, changing every two or three bouts. Their ranks are distinguished by the color of their breast cords and the tassels on their fans. ⇨ ŌZUMŌ, SHIKIRI, SUMŌ

〖注〗 referee 行司. ritual 儀式的な. bout 試合，勝負. tassel 房.

gyokuro 玉露 lit. jade dew. the finest green tea; green tea of the top quality made from the tenderest leaves of old tea shrubs. The flavor is mild and fragrant when the tea leaves are steeped in warm water at a temperature of about 60 degrees C., and never in boiling hot water. It is a tea to savor the fragrance. ⇨ CHA

〖注〗 fragrant 芳ばしい，芳香のある. steep 液体に浸す，煎じて出す. C.(= centigrade; Celsius) 摂氏. savor 賞味する.

gyōsho 行書 the semiformal style of writing letters and characters; the intermediate style among three styles of writing characters, the other two being *kaisho* (printing style) and *sōsho* (cursive style). This semi-cursive style is the most widely used, having both practical and artistic aspects. This term in particular refers to calligraphy, where there are certain prescribed rules in forming letters and characters. ⇨ KAISHO, SHODŌ, SŌSHO

〖注〗 calligraphy 書道. prescribed 規則にかなった.

gyūdon 牛丼 lit. a beef-bowl. a bowl of rice topped with thinly sliced beef and vegetables. Sliced beef is cooked in a soy-flavored sauce, together with *shirataki* (vermicelli), mushrooms, long green onions, etc; these ingredients are similar to those of *sukiyaki*. ⇨ DONBURIMONO, SUKIYAKI

〖注〗 soy-flavored 醤油味の. ingredient (料理の)材料.

H

habatsu 派閥 lit. branch clique. a faction; a factional clique; a political faction; a small exclusive group within a larger organization, referring in particular to a political faction. Factionalism is very strong within political parties. In a major party there are usually several factions, each centering around a leader who is vying for power with the leaders of other factions. The members share common interests and views, and make a commitment to increasing their leader's power; the leader, in turn, gives consideration to the promotion of the members. ⇨ BATSU

〚注〛 clique 徒党, 閥. exclusive 排他的な. factionalism 派閥主義. vie (優劣を)競う, はりあう.

hachi 鉢 a ceramic bowl, covered or uncovered. Larger types are used for the table for serving cakes, fruit, salads and other dishes. Smaller ones are used for serving individual portions. In a broader sense, *hachi* includes pots, basins and flowerpots, made of ceramic. ⇨ KOBACHI

〚注〛 ceramic 陶器(の). individual portion 個人の分け前. basin 洗面器, 水鉢.

hachijūhachi-ya 八十八夜 lit. the eighty-eighth night. the 88th day from the first day of spring (the New Year) in the lunar calendar. It falls on May 1 or 2 in the present calendar, counted from the first day of spring, which falls on February 3 or 4. Tea leaves picked around this day are considered to be tastiest. Scenes of people picking tea leaves give the Japanese a seasonal feeling that summer is really right around the corner. It is also said that this is the best time for sowing rice seeds. ⇨ CHA, SHINCHA

〚注〛 the lunar calendar 太陰暦. around the corner 間近である.

hachimaki 鉢巻き lit. to tie around a bowl. a headband; a cloth, often a towel-like cotton cloth, tied around the head. It is sometimes twisted like a rope. Many Japanese wear one when they apply themselves to an arduous task, to gather strength, both spiritually and physically. It also serves to absorb sweat. They wear one when carrying a portable shrine (*mikoshi*) at festivals, when selling items at street fairs, when doing construction work, or when studying for entrance examinations. Schoolchildren often wear red or white ones at athletic meets (*undōkai*) to distinguish teams. In the Kamakura (1185-1336) and Muromachi (1336-1568) periods, warriors used a white cloth to fix a hood on their heads under their helmets, and presumably also to brace themselves for battle. ⇨ MIKOSHI, TENUGUI

〖注〗 portable shrine 神輿. warrior 武士. hood（ここでは）烏帽子. brace 奮い立つ.

Hachimangū 八幡宮 a Hachiman shrine; a shrine dedicated to the deity of war or the deity of archery. Hachiman is the posthumous title of Emperor Ōjin (late fourth to early fifth centuries). It is told that he was born in 270 to Empress Jingū during her victorious expedition to Korea. Thus, Emperor Ōjin was later deified as the god of war. The headquarters of the Hachiman shrines is Usa Shrine in Ōita Prefecture, other famous ones being Iwashimizu Hachiman Shrine in Kyoto, and Tsurugaoka Hachiman Shrine in Kamakura.

〖注〗 deity 神, 神のような人［もの］. archery 弓道. posthumous 死後の. deify 神格化する.

hadajuban 肌襦袢 lit. a skin shirt. an undershirt for the kimono; a short shirt worn directly over the skin under a long undergarment (*nagajuban*) and a kimono. It is usually made of soft white cotton, with loose sleeves narrower than those of an ordinary kimono. ⇨ KIMONO, NAGAJUBAN

〖注〗 undergarment 下着.

Hagi-yaki 萩焼 Hagi ceramic ware; ceramic ware fired in the Hagi region of Yamaguchi Prefecture. It was first made at the end of the 16th century by a naturalized Korean potter called Kōra-izaemon. Thus, some quality Hagi ware still bears this inherited name. The basic type of Hagi ware has a rough crackle glaze in a yellowish or milky color, and the under-glaze takes on a pinkish or brownish tint turned out during the firing process. Hagi tea bowls have an especially high reputation among tea masters for their rusticity and soft texture. ⇨ CHAWAN

〖注〗 naturalized 帰化した. crackle ひび. glaze 釉. rusticity 素朴, わび, さび. texture 肌合い, 生地.

hagoita 羽子板　a battledore; a wooden racket used in playing the game of battledore and shuttlecock during the New Year holidays. It is rectangular in shape, widening toward the outer edge. The battledore is not only used for play, but is also appreciated as an ornament during the season. For the game, simple and light ones are used. The ones for display are large, sometimes measuring nearly a meter in length, and are elaborately decorated on one side with an embossed picture made of cloth. The most typical design portrays a Kabuki actor—particularly in female impersonation—in lavish costume. The game was first played with simple *hagoita* in the Imperial Court in the 15th century. In the Edo period (1603–1868), when Kabuki plays became popular, decorative ones gradually appeard. ⇨ HANETSUKI

〖注〗 battledore and shuttlecock 羽根つき． embossed 浮き上がった，盛り上がった． female impersonation 女形． lavish 豪勢な，ぜいたくな．

hagoita-ichi 羽子板市　a battledore fair. Battledores are used for games and also for display during the New Year holidays. Various types of decorative battledores are sold annually toward the end of the year, in the precincts of shrines and temples, or along streets. Among some famous traditional fairs are the ones held at Fukagawa Fudō Temple on December 15 and at Asakusa Kannon Temple on December 17–18 or 19. ⇨ HAGOITA, HANETSUKI

〖注〗 battledore 羽子板． precincts 境内．

hagoromo 羽衣　a robe of feathers; the feather robe in which a celestial nymph flew in the air, according to a Japanese legend. Legend has it that when a fisherman found such a robe hanging on a pine tree and was about to carry it away, a celestial maiden appeared and pleaded for it, and in return she performed a heavenly dance, then disappeared into the sky. This story has been adapted as one of the most famous Noh plays, *Hagoromo*. The design of the ceiling of the Hagoromo Hall in the State Guesthouse (Geihinkan) was inspired by the Noh play derived from this legend. ⇨ NŌ

〖注〗 celestial 天上界の． nymph 乙女，妖精． Legend has it that ... 伝説によると． adapt 脚色する，改訂する． be derived from ～に由来する．

haijin 俳人　a haiku poet; an expert in the art of the 17-syllable poem. It also refers to a person who is sensitive to the change of seasons and is moved by the exquisite phenomena of nature. ⇨ FŪRYŪ, HAIKAI, HAIKU

〖注〗 17-syllable poem 17音節の詩，俳句，俳諧． exquisite 微妙な．

haikai 俳諧 a witty 17-syllable verse; a traditional verse form of 5-7-5 syllables, derived from *renga* (a linked verse) but developed independently. At the end of the Muromachi period (1336-1568), Yamazaki Sōkan (1465-1554) and Arakida Moritake (1473-1549) established *haikai* as a genre of verse, independent from *renga*. As with *renga, haikai* emphasized wit and humor at the beginning stage. In the Edo period (1603-1868), this verse form was elevated as one of the most important serious literary genres by Matsuo Bashō (1664-94). Later it also came to be called haiku. ⇨ HAIKU, HOKKU, RENGA

〖注〗 linked verse 連歌. Yamazaki Sōkan 山崎宗鑑. Arakida Moritake 荒木田守武.

haiku 俳句 a 17-syllable poem; traditional short verse, consisting of three sections, of 5-7-5 syllables. Haiku may be one of the most compact verse forms in the world, but is also a most profound and evocative one. A word or phrase suggestive of a season is one of the required elements. It was Matsuo Bashō (1664-94) who brought this verse form to maturity. Through communion with nature during a solitary journey and under the influence of the concepts of Zen, he provided haiku with such aesthetic qualities as *sabi* (rustic simplicity), *karumi* (light beauty with subtlety), *shiori* (aesthetic feeling in solitude), etc., which became lasting elements. One of his well-known haiku goes:

Furuike ya	Ancient pond
Kawazu tobikomu	A frog leaps in
Mizu no oto	The sound of the water
	(translated by Donald Keene)

In the early Meiji era (1868-1912), Shiki Masaoka (1867-1902) developed the modern descriptive style of haiku, so that everyone could enjoy writing such poems. The term haiku was attributed to him and thereafter it came to also be applied to *haikai* (17-syllable poems prior to him and since Bashō). Along with *tanka*, haiku remains a major traditional poetic form today. ⇨ HAIJIN, HAIKAI, KIGO, SABI, TANKA

〖注〗 profound 意味の深い. evocative 感情を呼び起こす. communion with nature 自然に没入すること. aesthetic quality 美意識の要素. rustic simplicity さび. light beauty with subtlety かるみ. aesthetic feeling in solitude しおり. be attributed to ～の作とみなす, ～のゆえとされる.

hakama 袴 a long skirt-like ceremonial garment; loose-legged trousers or a long pleated skirt, worn over a kimono and tied around the waist. There have been many kinds of *hakama* for men's since around the Heian period (794-1185), the most common being a loosely divided one like culottes, sometimes still worn by the groom at a traditional wedding ceremony or at festivals. *Hakama* for women appeared in the Heian period, but soon went out of use. During the Meiji (1868-1912) and Taishō (1912-26) eras, a brownish-crimson *hakama* was in vogue, particularly for schoolgirls as part of their school uniform.   ⇨ KIMONO

〖注〗 garment 衣服, 衣料品.   brownish crimson えび茶.   in vogue 流行している.

Hakata-ningyō 博多人形   a Hakata doll; a painted clay doll, a special product of Hakata in northern Kyūshū.   As art objects, the dolls usually portray historical or legendary figures of Japan: heroes, warriors, aged men, beautiful women, children, etc.   They originated in the Edo period (1603-1868).

〖注〗 legendary figure 伝説上の人物.   warrior さむらい.

Hakata-obi 博多帯   a Hakata weave sash; an *obi* made of silk fabric originally woven in Hakata, northern Kyūshū.   The Hakata silk fabric is woven tight with thick warp yarn and thin weft yarn. It is coarse and solid enough to make an unlined *obi,* though recently, lined *Hakata-obi* have also appeared.   Unlined *Hakata-obi* are appropriate for summer kimono.   The typical design is of stripes or figured stripes woven into the background, which is called "the pattern of iron staffs," having a Buddhist connotation.   ⇨ KIMONO, OBI

〖注〗 sash 飾り帯, 帯.   fabric 織物, 生地.   warp yarn (織物の)縦糸.   weft yarn (織物の)横糸.   unlined 裏地のない.   figured stripe 模様つきの縞. iron staff 鉄の棒, 錫杖(しゃくじょう).   connotation 意味あい, 含蓄.

hakuji 白磁   white porcelain ware; white ware originally developed in Kōrai, one of the old names for Korea.   It is characterized by a flawless transparent glaze and gem-like translucent body.   Some take on minute glassy dust or have incised or relief designs under the glaze.   Such ware includes dishes, cups, vases, etc.

〖注〗 porcelain 磁器.   flawless 傷のない.   transparent 透明な.   glaze 釉. translucent 半透明の.   incised 刻みこんだ.   relief 浮き彫り細工.

hakuju 白寿   lit. white congratulatory occasion.   the celebration of one's 99th birthday; the 99th anniversary of one's life, one of the special ages to celebrate one's longevity.   It derives its name from the fact that by deleting "one" (一 in Chinese script) from the Chinese character 百 meaning "one hundred," the meaning *haku* 白 (white) is obtained.   ⇨ BEIJU, KANREKI, KIJU

〖注〗 longevity 長寿. derive...from ～に由来する，～からとられている. delete 差し引く. Chinese script 漢字の筆跡. Chinese character 漢字.

Hakusan Kokuritsu-kōen 白山国立公園 Hakusan National Park (476.8 square kilometers), designated in 1962; a natural park in central Honshū, encompassing mountainous parts of Gifu, Toyama, Ishikawa, and Fukui prefectures. This park centers around the extinct volcano, Mount Hakusan (lit. White Mountain), rising to 2,700 meters, with its highest peak covered with snow. From this mountain the Hakusan volcanic belt extends to northern Kyūshū. The area features a number of caldera lakes and deep ravines, along with primeval forests and alpine plants. Mount Hakusan is also renowned as one of the three sacred mountains of Japan, the other two being Mount Fuji in Shizuoka Prefecture and Mount Tateyama in Toyama Prefecture. ⇨ KOKURITSU-KŌEN

〖注〗 encompass 取り巻く，囲む. extinct volcano 死火山. The Hakusan volcanic belt 白山火山帯. caldera lake 火山の噴火口から出来た湖. ravine 渓谷. primeval forest 原始林. alpine plant 高山植物.

han¹ 判 a stamp or seal; often equivalent to *inkan* (a personal seal). *Han* refers to many types of stamps, of all sizes, as well as to personal seals. ⇨ INKAN

han² 藩 a feudal domain or a feudal clan; a fief or its people ruled by a feudal lord under the control of the Tokugawa shogunate (1603-1868). The first Tokugawa shogun Ieyasu (1542-1616), assessing the number of territories possessed by powerful feudal lords (*daimyō*), raised it from about 200 to about 250 (it later grew to about 300). He imposed the *han* system in an attempt to consolidate his power. He allowed autonomous rule within the domains by each feudal lord, but brought the lords under central supervision by means of *sankinkōtai* (the system of alternate residence of feudal lords in Edo and their domains), thus establishing strong vertical ties of loyalty and protection. The size of the *han* varied, ranging from the Kanazawa domain producing one million *koku* of rice annually to ones producing only 10,000 *koku*, with smaller ones or those with no heirs gradually disappearing. In 1867, as a result of the reforms of the Meiji Restoration, the *han* system was replaced by the *ken* (prefecture) system, and the rule of domains was taken over by the new Meiji government. As compensation, the feudal lords were given pensions. ⇨ DAIMYŌ, KOKU, SANKINKŌTAI, TOKUGAWA-BAKUFU

〖注〗 feudal domain 封建領地，藩．feudal clan 封建一族，藩．fief（封建時代の）封土，領地．feudal lord 大名．consolidate 一つにまとめる，固める．vertical tie 縦のつながり．loyalty 忠誠．heir 後継者．compensation 償い．pension 年金，恩給．

hanaire 花入れ a vase; the term for a vase used in the tea ceremony; a vessel for flowers more commonly called *kaki* or *kabin*. A modest flower arrangement is placed or sometimes hung in the alcove of a tea room. The container is usually small, holding only a single flower, or two or three at most, in the simple, natural, throw-in style, and is selected according to the kind of flower used and the hanging scroll displayed in the alcove. Besides ceramic vases, those made of old bronze, split bamboo, cut bamboo and bottle gourds are also used. Examples of ceramic vases used include celadon, Raku, Seto, Karatsu, Iga and Bizen wares. Unglazed ones are usually used after being dampened. The type of vase most favored by tea devotees of the rustic style is made of bamboo cut at a joint, which can be traced back to Jōō (1502–55) and Rikyū (1521–91), the developers of the rustic tea ceremony. ⇨ KAKI, NAGEIRE, TOKONOMA

〖注〗 alcove 床の間．natural throw-in style 投げ入れ．hanging scroll 掛け軸．bottle gourd 瓢簞．unglazed 釉のついていない．tea devotees of the rustic style 佗び茶人．joint（竹の）節．Jōō 武野紹鷗．

Hana Matsuri 花祭り lit. a flower festival. the birthday of Sakyamuni Gautama Buddha, celebrated during the cherry blossom season (April 8). On this day, Buddhist temples honoring Sakyamuni observe special services dedicated to him. The chief rite of the ceremony is pouring sweet tea (*amacha*) over a small statue of Buddha placed in a miniature shrine, which is decorated with flowers, generally cherry blossoms. The Buddhist term for this ceremony is *kanbutsue*. Other festive events are observed depending on the temple and the district. ⇨ KANBUTSUE

〖注〗 special service 特別法要．dedicate to ～に捧げる．rite 儀式．

hanami 花見 lit. flower-viewing. an outing for viewing cherry blossoms, at their best in spring. The cherry blossom is the national flower of Japan, and thus very often the word *hana* (flower) refers to the cherry blossom. From ancient times the

Japanese have had a special affection for this flower for its transient blooms—it comes out all at once in full bloom and is soon gone without hesitation. It has been a traditional custom to appreciate the coming of spring by enjoying cherry blossoms during the very short time of their bloom. Some contemplate the blossoms in a quiet mood while others make merry with a feast of drinking and singing under the trees.　⇨ SAKURA-ZENSEN, TSUKIMI
〖注〗 transient 束の間の． contemplate 観照する，じっと見つめる． make merry にぎやかにする，どんちゃん騒ぎをする． feast 饗宴，ごちそう．

hanamichi 花道 lit. a flower path. an aisle stage in the Kabuki theater; an elevated passageway extending from the stage through the audience, usually on the left side (facing the stage) but occasionally found on both sides. This passageway is used for special entrances and exits of actors to create a spectacular effect and for special performances in closer contact with the audience.　⇨ KABUKI
〖注〗 aisle 座席間の通路． elevated passageway 高くなった通路． entrances and exits 出入口． spectacular effect 劇的効果．

hanao 鼻緒 thongs for footgear; a V-shaped strap fitted onto footgear—*geta* or *zōri*—to secure the foot, separating the big toe from the others. Thongs are made of flax, hemp palm, or straw covered with cloth.　⇨ GETA, ZŌRI
〖注〗 thong 紐． footgear 履物． flax 亜麻． hemp palm しゅろ．

Hanasaka Jijii 花咲爺 The Flower-Blossoming Old Man; an old man who made dead trees bloom, a character in one of Japan's five most famous folk tales. A dog loved by an honest old man dug treasures from the ground. A greedy old neighbor tried to make the dog do the same for him, but instead the dog dug up garbage and odd creatures; thus the greedy man killed the dog in fury. A huge pine tree grew where the honest man buried the dog, from which he made a mortar. Grain pounded in the mortar turned into gold pieces. The greedy neighbor stole it and pounded grain, only to get odds and ends, and so he burned it. The ashes of the mortar, scattered by the honest man, made dead cherry trees bloom. A feudal lord passing by honored him for it. The greedy man tried the same thing, but the ashes which were scattered about ended up getting into the lord's eyes, and eventually he was punished. There are many slightly different versions of the tale.
〖注〗 character 人物． folk tale 民話． odd creature 奇妙な動物（虫けらやへ

び). in fury かっとなって. odds and ends がらくた. feudal lord 大名.

han'eri 半衿 a collar on a kimono; a replaceable neckband or cloth collar sewed on an undergarment. Its color and material should harmonize with those of the kimono, so that it gives layered effect at the collar of the kimono. ⇨ KIMONO

〖注〗 replaceable 代わることのできる, 取り替えられる. neckband 衿. undergarment 下着. layered effect 重ねた効果.

hanetsuki 羽根突き the game of battledore and shuttlecock; the traditional Japanese version of badminton, played during the New Year holidays. The shuttlecock is made up of a hard tiny ball of wood and several colored cock feathers stuck into it. The battledore is also made of wood; one side is usually decorated elaborately with an embossed picture made of cloth portraying Kabuki actors or the like, and the other side is used to hit the shuttlecock back and forth. The game of battledore and shuttlecock enjoyed by kimono-clad girls is a typical traditional scene during the New Year holidays. ⇨ HAGOITA, SANGANICHI

〖注〗 battledore 羽子板. shuttlecock 羽根. emboss 浮き彫り細工で飾る.

haniwa 埴輪 a clay figurine; earthenware figures and other objects made in the Tumulus period (250-552), excavated from and around the grave mounds of important figures. The earliest ones were of a simple, hollow, cylindrical shape. Later ones represented a variety of shapes—human or animal figures as well as buildings, boats, weapons, etc.—among which the most notable ones were soldiers and horses, having a hollow body and generally a cylindrical base. They range in height from 30 centimeters to over a meter high. There are roughly two theories as to their purpose. One involves legend, with no evidence to support it: such figurines were used in place of humans who were to be buried alive as sacrifices to console their deceased lord. The other is that they were lined up to mark the boundaries of a grave mound, while also serving to protect the dead from evil spirits. ⇨ KOFUN, KOFUN-JIDAI

〖注〗 figurine 小立像. earthenware 土器. the Tumulus period 古墳時代. excavate 発掘する. mound (墓などの)塚, 古墳. sacrifice 捧げ物, 生贄(いけにえ).

hanko 判子 a seal or a stamp; the colloquial term for *han* or *inkan*. ⇨ HAN, INKAN

hankō 藩校 a domain school; schools administered by feudal lords in the Edo period (1603–1868). Under the domain system of the Tokugawa shogunate, official schools were established, with at least one in each domain, totaling about 300 nationwide. They were first reserved for the education of the warrior class; gradually some came to admit commoners as well. The curriculum was generally based on Confucianism, and included other subjects such as calligraphy, history, swordsmanship, etc. They were abolished as part of the reforms of the Meiji Restoration (centering around 1868). ⇨ HAN, MEIJI ISHIN

〘注〙 domain 所有地、藩． feudal lord 大名． the domain system 幕藩体制．
Confucianism 儒教． calligraphy 書道． swordsmanship 剣道． the Meiji
Restoration 明治維新．

hanshi 半紙 paper for calligraphy; a sheet of traditional Japanese paper, approximately 25 by 33 centimeters in size, mainly used for calligraphy. Like other Japanese paper, popularly called "rice paper" in the West, it is made from fibers of the *kōzo* (paper mulberry) or *mitsumata* (paper bush). The size of the *hanshi* became the basis of several standard sizes of paper now used. ⇨ SHODŌ

〘注〙 calligraphy 書道． paper mulberry 楮． paper bush 三椏．

hanten 半天［半纏］ a short work-coat; a traditional workman's short livery coat in kimono style. It is made of coarse cotton, usually indigo with white patterns on the back (the crest or the name of the employer). Also called *shirushi-banten* or *happi*. ⇨ HAPPI, SHIRUSHI-BANTEN

〘注〙 livery（集合的）仕着せ、そろいの服． indigo 藍． crest 家紋．

haori 羽織 a short overgarment; a short coat worn over a kimono in cold weather. Commonly it extends to the knee or a little above it, and is tied loosely in front by short braided cords. The formal *haori* is black, usually with three or five family crests on the back and sleeves. Ordinary ones vary in color and design. ⇨ KIMONO

〘注〙 overgarment 上にはおる衣服． braided cord 編んだ紐． family crest 家紋．

happi 法被 a workman's livery coat; a short kimono-style jacket chiefly worn by workmen, which commonly bears the crest or the name of the employer on the back. This garment has become popular among foreigners, who call it a "happy coat" although *happi* has nothing to do with "happy" etymologically. A *happi* is also worn by youths during festivals, such as when they bear a portable shrine on their shoulders. The traditional workman's coat is also called *hanten*. ⇨ HANTEN, SHIRUSHI-BANTEN

〖注〗 livery coat そろいの上衣. crest 紋. garment 衣服. etymologically 語源的に. portable shrine 持ち運び出来る社, みこし.

haragei 腹芸 lit. the art of the belly. the art or technique of silent communication; communication by understanding what is in the mind—or inside the belly (*hara*)—by intuition without relying on verbal or logical expressions. Traditionally, the belly has been considered by the Japanese to be the core of the body from which both spiritual and physical energy come, thus making *hara*, symbolizing inner feelings, more trustworthy than outspoken words. Specifically, 1) in a play, *haragei* means the art of psychological acting. An actor's artful meditative pose, without action or lines, is expected to be appreciated as exquisite when his feelings are directly conveyed to his audience. 2) In human relationships, it refers to the technique of telepathic communication between individuals. It is often employed for problem-solving in negotiations, and is intended for averting open confrontation and maintaining surface harmony by protecting the other party from getting embarrassed or losing face. For example, instead of a frank flat "no," one may say "It may be difficult," "I'll handle it later in a better way," or cite allegorical expressions, or else may remain in meaningful silence. Essential things are expected to be sensed with only subtle hints in the same way the mysteries of an art are appreciated. Humanly concern and artfulness are likely to lead to toleration and concession. Effective *haragei* requires shared experiences and the thorough understanding of the other party's personality and background, as well as the whole situation of the negotiation. Such propensity is attributable largely to high Japanese homogeneity and interdependency in human relationships, and has been fostered through the Zen way of thinking where emphasis is placed on intuition rather than theory and truth lies between the lines. ⇨ ZEN[1]

〖注〗 belly 腹, 腹部. intuition 直感. artful meditative pose 黙想して芸術的表現をするポーズ. exquisite 絶妙な, 見事な. telepathic 以心伝心の. allegorical expression 寓意的表現, 比喩的表現. propensity 性質, 傾向. be attributable to 由来をたどることができる, 原因に帰すことができる. homogeneity 均質性, 同族性. interdependency 相互依存. between the lines 行間.

harakiri 腹切り lit. belly cutting. suicide by disembowelment.

Harakiri is commonly called *seppuku* by the Japanese, though the term "harakiri" seems to be better known to foreigners.　⇨ SEPPUKU

〖注〗 belly 腹．disembowelment 腹わたを取り除くこと，切腹．

haramaki 腹巻き　a stomach protector; a woolen waist-band worn for health.　It is not only worn to keep the abdomen warm, but is also used by men to carry money when traveling.

〖注〗 abdomen 腹部．

hari(-chiryō) 鍼(治療)　needle therapy; acupuncture; one of the traditional medical treatments of Japan, originally introduced from China.　It has been practiced from ancient times and is still very popular with evidence of success with a variety of pains and minor illnesses.　Licensed professional practitioners use extremely fine needles several centimeters long, inserting them into the skin and underlying tissues along specific meridians (*keiraku*) to reach certain points, called *tsubo* (acu-point), connected to the pain. The needles are seldom felt by the patient.　Masseurs and *shiatsu* therapists can practice acupuncture if licensed.　⇨ ANMA, KANPŌI, SHIATSU(-RYŌHŌ)

〖注〗 licensed professional practitioner 資格を持った専門治療士．underlying tissue 皮下組織．masseur マッサージ師．*shiatsu* therapist 指圧師．

harikuyō 針供養　a memorial service for needles; a rite for the repose of the spirits of broken needles observed on February 8 or December 8 at many Buddhist temples.　In this rite, broken needles are stuck into soft soybean curd (*tōfu*) to console the spirit of needles for having worked so hard.　On this day people used to avoid using needles in order to give them a rest.　This custom is said to date as far back as the fourth century.　Today it is observed chiefly by those who use needles in their occupations.

〖注〗 memorial service 追悼の儀式．rite 儀式，祭式．repose 休息，安らぎ，慰め．console 慰める．

haru no nanakusa 春の七草　the seven herbs of spring.　They are *seri* (Japanese parsley), *nazuna* (shepherd's purse), *gogyō* (cutweed), *hakobe(ra)* (chickweed), *hotokenoza* (henbit), *suzuna* (turnip leaves) and *suzushiro* (garden radish leaves).　Traditionally, since the Heian period (794-1185), these seven green herbs have been taken in soup or in rice gruel (*kayu*) on the seventh day of January, to ward off disease in the coming year.　In the Edo period (1603-1868) some districts observed a solemn rite in which a man in ceremonial costume sliced the seven kinds of herbs.　⇨

AKI NO NANAKUSA, NANAKUSA, NANAKUSA-GAYU

〖注〗 ward off 避ける, 追い払う. solemn rite 厳粛な儀式. 春の七草：芹, 薺, 御形, 繁縷, 仏の座, 菘, 清白.

hashi 箸 a pair of chopsticks; a pair of slender sticks, used as eating implements. They are made of ivory, bamboo or lacquered wood. In restaurants, disposable, splittable unpainted wooden chopsticks called *waribashi* are used. They are held in the hand much as a pencil is held between the thumb and index finger. However, in the case of *hashi*, one stick is supported between the index finger and middle finger while the other is supported between the middle finger and ring finger. ⇨ WARIBASHI

〖注〗 lacquered wood 漆塗りの木. disposable 使い捨ての. splittable 割りはなすことのできる.

hashibako 箸箱 a chopstick case; a long individual container for a pair of chopsticks. A pair of chopsticks is carried in it to accompany a lunch box (*bentōbako*). ⇨ HASHI

〖注〗 a pair of chopsticks 一対の箸.

hashigakari 橋懸かり a bridge-like extension in the Noh theater; a raised passageway leading from the actors' dressing room (green room) to the main stage. It is regarded as an extension of the stage, often used effectively as an additional stage area, not just as a passageway. ⇨ NŌ, NŌBUTAI

〖注〗 extension 延長部分. passageway 通路. dressing room 楽屋, 化粧室. green room （劇場の）役者控え室.

hashitate 箸立て a chopstick stand; a standing container for holding chopsticks. It is similar to a tall pencil holder in appearance —cylindrical or prismatical—made of porcelain, wood or bamboo. *Hashitate* holding disposable chopsticks (*waribashi*) are found on the tables of many noodle shops and other restaurants. ⇨ HASHI, WARIBASHI

〖注〗 chopsticks 箸. cylindrical 円柱形の. prismatical 角柱形の. porcelain 磁器. disposable 使い捨ての.

hatamoto 旗本 lit. the headquarters of the banner. direct retainers of the shogun under the Tokugawa shogunate government (1603-1868). Residing in Edo, they served as military guards, together with the *gokenin* (immediate vassals). ⇨ GOKENIN, TOKUGAWA-BAKUFU

〖注〗 headquarters 本部. retainer 家来, 郎党. vassal 臣下, 家臣.

hatsumōde 初詣 the year's first visit to a shrine or a temple.

Customarily, on one of the first three days of the new year many
people visit a nearby or noted Shinto shrine or Buddhist temple to
pray for happiness and prosperity in the new year.　From very
early in the morning or even at midnight right after the temple bells
have pealed out the old year, celebrated shrines and temples—Meiji
Shrine in Tokyo, for instance—become crowded with people, many
of whom are clad in traditional Japanese costume.　⇨ GANJITSU,
SANGANICHI

〖注〗 peal（鐘が）鳴り響く．celebrated 有名な．clad 着ている、装った．

hayashi 囃子　the instrumental music for traditional Japanese stage
and folk performances.　The kinds of instruments used are *shamisen*, Japanese flutes and percussion instruments（stick drums, hand
drums, shoulder drums, etc.）. *Hayashi* music is used primarily to
accompany dance performances in the classical Noh and Kabuki
theaters as well as such folk dances as *Bon-odori*.　⇨ NŌKAN,
SHAKUHACHI, SHAMISEN, TAIKO¹, TSUZUMI

〖注〗 folk performance 民俗芸能．Japanese flute 横笛，能管，尺八など．
percussion instrument 打楽器．stick drum 桴（ばち）で打つ太鼓．shoulder
drum 肩にかつぐ鼓，小鼓．accompany 伴う、伴奏する．

hayashikata 囃子方　the instrumental musicians for traditional
stage and folk performances.　In the Noh theater they sit in a row
at the front of the *atoza* rear stage portion and consist of the
tsuzumi and *taiko* drums and the Noh flute.　The *shamisen* is added
for Kabuki music while the *shakuhachi* or folk flutes may be used
with various-sized folk drums in folk performances.　⇨ ATOZA,
HAYASHI, KABUKI, NŌ

〖注〗 instrumental musicians 楽器を奏する人たち．folk performance 民俗芸
能．Noh flute 能管．folk flute 尺八．

hechima 糸瓜　a luffa［a loofah］; a sponge gourd or a sponge made
from a sponge gourd.　When a ripe gourd is thoroughly dried after
the outside skin is removed, it turns into a sponge of woven fibers.
It has been used for scouring pans and dishes in the kitchen, and for
scrubbing the body in the bath.

〖注〗 gourd 瓢簞．scour こすりみがく．

Heian-jidai 平安時代　the Heian period（794-1185）; the period from
the transfer of the capital from Nara to Kyoto in 794 until
Minamoto Yoritomo's establishment of his shogunate government
at Kamakura in 1185.　The Fujiwara family ruled for a large part
of this period.　This period saw the development of arts and

literature of courtly elegance and refinement, as exemplified by
The Tale of Genji. ⇨ MIYABI

〖注〗 the transfer of the capital 遷都. shogunate (government) 幕府.
courtly elegance and refinement 雅び.

Heiankyō 平安京 the ancient capital of Kyoto (794-1869); the capital of Japan for over a thousand years, in the present Kyoto, established by Emperor Kanmu (737-806). After being located briefly, for about 10 years, in Nagaoka, the seat of imperial residence was established in Kyoto until 1869 when it was moved to Tokyo. Like the capital of Nara (710-84), Heiankyō was laid out in checkerboard fashion along the lines of Ch'ang-an, the T'ang capital of China, but was larger, with the Imperial Palace at the center of the northern end. It covered an area of 5.3 by 4.6 kilometers. In the Ōnin War (1467-77), over half of the capital was swept away by fire, but was later restored by Toyotomi Hideyoshi (1536-98). ⇨ HEIAN-JIDAI, HEIJŌKYŌ

〖注〗 imperial residence 皇居. checkerboard 碁盤. Ch'ang-an 長安. the T'ang 唐.

Heijōkyō 平城京 the ancient capital of Nara (710-84); the first permanent capital of Japan, built in the western part of the present Nara, during the reign of Empress Genmei (661-721). Prior to this, the seat of the government had generally changed with each new emperor. Heijōkyō served as the capital for 75 years, during which seven emperors reigned, until the transfer of the capital to Nagaoka and then to Kyoto. Modeled after Ch'ang-an, the T'ang capital of China, it was laid out in checkerboard fashion, with the Imperial Palace at the center of the northern end. It covered an area of roughly 4 by 3.5 kilometers. At its peak, it had a population estimated at 200,000 and flourished as the center of Buddhist culture. ⇨ HEIANKYŌ, NARA-JIDAI

〖注〗 Empress Genmei 元明天皇. seat 本拠. transfer 移行, (ここでは)遷都. Ch'ang-an 長安. checkerboard 碁盤.

heika¹ 陛下 His (Her) Majesty or Your Majesty; the honorific title used when referring to or addressing the emperor and empress. "His Majesty, the Emperor" is expressed as "*Tennō-heika*" and "Her Majesty, the Empress" as "*Kōgō-heika*." When addressing them, it is common to use the title *Heika* alone for the emperor; *Kōgō-sama* is used for the empress. ⇨ TENNŌ

〖注〗 honorific title 敬称. address 呼びかける.

heika² 瓶華   a term used in the Ohara school; a flower arrangement in a tall vase; flowers arranged in a tall vase in such a manner that they seem to have been thrown in.   No metal holder is used.   Of the three principal stems for the *heika* arrangement, the longest stem measures about one-and-a-half times the height of the vase, the second stem measures two-thirds the length of the longest one while the shortest is one-half the length of the longest one.   Called *nageire* in the Sōgetsu and Ikenobō schools.   ⇨ IKEBANA, MORI-BANA, NAGEIRE, RIKKA

〖注〗 flower arrangement 生け花.   metal holder 金属の花留め，剣山，七宝. principal stem 主枝.   longest stem 第1主枝(流派により「真」「主」などと呼ばれる).   second stem 第2主枝(流派により「添え」「副」などと呼ばれる).   shortest stem 第3主枝(流派により「控」「体」「客」などと呼ばれる).

Heike Monogatari 平家物語   *The Tale of the Heike Clan* (the first version appearing around 1220); the historical tale of the rise and fall of the Heike clan (also called the Taira clan), written in the early Kamakura peirod (1185-1336), presumably by Shinanozenji Yukinaga (?).   It is a prose epic originally intended for blind minstrels to recite to the accompaniment of the *biwa* (Japanese lute).   Among many other versions, the present standard version, written in 1371, consists of 13 volumes.   Beginning with a description of the power and glory of the ruling Heike family, it deals with their gradual decline due to arrogance and extravagance, ending with sad scenes of their total destruction in 1185 at Dannoura (in the present Yamaguchi Prefecture) at the hands of the Genji clan (also called the Minamoto clan).   Through the tale runs the theme of the vicissitudes of fate and the working of karma, based on pessimistic Buddhist sentiments.   The descriptions are lyrical and develop in a way that induces pathos, particularly when recited with the *biwa*.   ⇨ BIWA, BUKKYŌ, GENPEI, KAMAKURA-JIDAI

〖注〗 Shinanozenji Yukinaga 信濃前司行長.   prose epic 叙事詩.   minstrel 吟遊詩人，(ここでは)琵琶法師.   to the accompaniment of ～の伴奏に合わせて. lute (ギターに似た)弦楽器.   arrogance 傲り.   extravagance ぜいたく. vicissitudes 栄枯盛衰.   karma 因果，宿命.   lyrical 叙情的な.

heimin 平民   the commoners; common people with no title.   Shortly after the Meiji Restoration (1868), the Japanese people were classified into three social classes under a government ordinance (1869): the nobility (*kazoku*), the gentry (*shizoku*) and the commoners (*heimin*).   The commoners constituted about 95 percent of the population. This system of social classes was abolished with the promulgation of the present constitution (1946). ⇨ MEIJI ISHIN, KAZOKU, SHIZOKU

〖注〗 the commoners 平民． the Meiji Restoration 明治維新． government ordinance 政府条令． the nobility 華族． the gentry 士族． promulgation 公布、発布、(法令の)施行．

hibachi 火鉢 a braizer; a box or pot half-filled with burning charcoal and ashes. It used to be the main source of heat in winter before modern heaters came into general use. Today, a charcoal-burning brazier with a grill used for cooking at the table at expensive restaurants is also called *hibachi*, but is quite different from the traditional one both in shape and purpose.

〖注〗 brazier 火鉢． grill 焼き網．

hichiriki 篳篥 a flageolet; a double-reed oboe-like wind instrument with nine holes in a bamboo tube—seven in the front and two in the back. It is played in Gagaku and also some Shinto services. ⇨ GAGAKU

〖注〗 flageolet フラジョレット(前に4音孔、後に2音孔のある縦笛)． reed (管楽器の)舌、舌楽器． wind instrument 管楽器． Shinto service 神社の祈禱．

hidarizukai 左遣い the left-arm manipulator; the second man of the Bunraku puppeteer trio. He manipulates the left arm of a single puppet, working together with the head manipulator (*omozukai*) and the leg manipulator (*ashizukai*). ⇨ ASHIZUKAI, BUNRAKU, OMO-ZUKAI

〖注〗 puppeteer trio 人形遣いの三人組、三人遣い． head manipulator 主遣い[面使い]． leg manipulator 足遣い．

hiden 秘伝 secret transmission; a traditional skill handed down from a master exclusively to his disciples through experience. The traditional Japanese way of mastering skills by artists and artisans is not by theory or words but rather through disciplined training—learning by doing—requiring a great deal of time and tremendous spiritual perseverance. A skill acquired in this way is difficult for outsiders to understand or to imitate quickly, and is thus kept a secret.

〖注〗 transmission 伝達． disciple 弟子． artisan 職人．

higan 彼岸 lit. the other shore. the equinoctal week, when Buddhist services are held in spring and autumn. These religious weeks begin on or around March 18 and September 18 respectively, with the equinox day falling on the middle day. According to

Buddhist belief, on the equinox day when the sun rises and sets in the most due directions, the dead can cross the river from the shore of this world to the other (*hi*) shore (*gan*), *higan* meaning "nirvana," or eternal paradise. Centering around this day, Buddhists pay a visit to their ancestors' graves and observe worship services at home or at temples. The coming of the equinoctal week signifies the advent of spring or autumn. It is said that no winter cold or no summer heat lingers past the equinox day. ⇨ BUKKYŌ, SHŪBUN (NO HI), SHUNBUN (NO HI)

〖注〗 equinoctal 昼夜平分(時)の、彼岸の. Buddhist service 法要. equinox 昼夜平分時、彼岸の中日. due direction 正しい方位. nirvana 涅槃. worship service 法要、礼拝. No winter cold or no summer heat lingers past the equinox day.「暑さ寒さも彼岸まで」.

higashi 干菓子 dry confectionery; dry sweets; a rice-powder biscuit or a rice jelly, pressed with sugar and dried. These sweets are artistically formed into the shape of flowers, leaves, etc., expressive of the season. With light foamy green tea (*usucha*) in the tea ceremony, dry sweets are served more often than wet ones. ⇨ CHANOYU, USUCHA

〖注〗 confectionery 糖菓類.

Higashiyama-bunka 東山文化 Higashiyama culture; the culture developed by the eighth Ashikaga shogun, Yoshimasa (1436–90), in the mid-Muromachi period, centering around the Higashiyama district of Kyoto. Yoshimasa, who pursued arts and letters rather than war, built a villa (Ginkakuji, or Silver Pavilion) in the Higashiyama district as a retreat in 1482 (with its pavilion added in 1490). To get respite during an age of civil disturbance, he devoted himself to aesthetic pursuits in a serene atmosphere —flower arrangement, tea ceremony, poetry, painting, etc., as well as Noh drama. Under his patronage, the arts flourished, characterized by elegant refinement, rustic simplicity, and the concepts of Zen Buddhism. These features continue to be lasting elements of Japanese culture. ⇨ ASHIKAGA-BAKUFU, MUROMACHI-BAKUFU, YŪGEN

〖注〗 retreat 隠れ家、別荘. respite (煩わしさからの)一時的休止、小康. disturbance 混乱、動乱. aesthetic pursuit 美的なものを追求すること. flower arrangement 華道. tea ceremony 茶道. elegant refinement 幽玄. rustic simplicity わび、さび.

hikicha 挽茶 ground green tea; powdered green tea; commonly called "*matcha*" in the tea ceremony. In the tea ceremony, this powdered tea is whipped to a froth in hot water. It is also often used to make a sweet iced drink or to flavor sherbet in summer. It is also used in some kinds of Japanese sweets. ⇨ CHA, MATCHA, RYOKUCHA

〖注〗 tea ceremony 茶道. whip 泡立てる，(茶を)たてる. froth 泡. sweets 甘い菓子.

hikite 引き手 a door pull; a metal fitting of a Japanese sliding door (*fusuma*), used as a pull. The sliding door of a Japanese-style room has a groove for the fingers, at eye level for one seated on the floor. This recessed groove is covered with a metal plate with an artistic design, engraved, embossed or lacquered. ⇨ FUSUMA

〖注〗 groove 凹んだところ. sliding door 襖，障子等. recessed 凹んだ. engrave 彫る. emboss 浮き上がった飾りをつける.

himono 干物 dried fish; salted dried sardines, mackerel pike, horse mackerel, etc. Bigger fish are usually cut open and then dried. *Himono* are broiled and eaten with grated Japanese radish as a condiment. ⇨ DAIKON-OROSHI

〖注〗 sardine 鰯. mackerel pike 秋刀魚. horse mackerel 鰺. cut open ひらきにする. grated Japanese radish 大根おろし. condiment 薬味.

Hina Matsuri 雛祭り the Doll Festival (March 3); the Girls' Festival, celebrated with the display of *hina* dolls. On and around this day, families with daughters display a set of dolls on a tier of five or seven shelves covered with a red cloth. The dolls portray the emperor and empress, three court ladies, five musicians, two ministers, three guards, etc., all attired in ancient court costumes of the Heian period (794-1185). Also displayed are miniature furniture, dinner sets, palanquins, etc., and real foods including *hishimochi* (diamond-shaped rice cakes). Girls, clad in pretty kimono, treat their friends and relatives to a sweet drink called *shirozake* and other foods in front of the display. The festival is also called *Momo no Sekku* (Peach-Blossom Festival), because peach blossoms, symbolic of women's virtues, are at their best in this season. ⇨ DAIRIBINA, HINA-NINGYŌ, MOMO NO SEKKU, SHIROZAKE

〖注〗 tier 列，段. attire 装わせる，着せる. palanquine 輿. clad 装っている，着ている. virtue 美徳.

hina-ningyō 雛人形 *hina* dolls; a pair or a set of dolls displayed on and around Girls' Day (March 3). A pair of dolls portray the emperor and empress. A set consists of about 15 dolls, usually representing the emperor and empress, three court ladies, five musicians, two ministers and three guards, all attired in ancient court costumes of the Heian period (794-1185). They are arranged on a tier of several shelves covered with red fabric. Gorgeously and elaborately made, they are usually treated as valuable heirlooms and carefully stored away after being displayed for a week or so. The form of an elaborate set of *hina* dolls as seen today dates from the middle of the Edo period (1603-1868). Prior to that, *hina* dolls—not like those of court figures—were made of paper or earthenware. Their origin can be traced back to primitive dolls made of straw; they were used for a religious ritual of purification and floated down a river with evil spirits transferred from people to the dolls. ⇨ DAIRIBINA, HINA MATSURI, MOMO NO SEKKU, NAGASHIBINA

〖注〗 two ministers 右大臣・左大臣． be attired in ～で装っている． tier 段． heirloom 家宝, 伝来の家財． earthenware 土器． ritual of purification 浄めの 儀式, みそぎ．

hiragana 平仮名 lit. a flat or easy script. the cursive or flowing form of *kana* script, one of the two sets of Japanese syllabary writing (*katakana* and *hiragana*). Each *hiragana* symbol is derived from a Chinese character of the same sound, without reference to meaning. This syllabary is said to have been invented by the Buddhist priest Kūkai (774-835) (controversy surrounds this, but a poem using all of the 47 *hiragana* syllables is attributed to him). The invention of *hiragana* contributed greately to the emergence of great literary works by women in the Heian period (794-1185), as represented by Murasaki Shikibu's *The Tale of Genji* (completed around 1004-11). Todays, *hiragana* is more commonly used than *katakana* and is usually used for writing inflectional endings and function words not represented by Chinese characters. *Hiragana* comprise the first stage for young children in learning to read and write. ⇨ KANA, KANJI, KATAKANA

〖注〗 script 書体, 筆跡． cursive 曲線的な． syllabary 表音文字表． be derived from ～から由来する． Chinese character 漢字． be attributed to ～の 作とみなす． emergence 出現． inflectional ending 活用語尾． function word 機能語．

hira-jawan 平茶碗 a flat tea bowl; a tea bowl, especially a shallow one, used in the tea ceremony in summer. It is thinner than an ordinary tea bowl. It is used with a portable brazier (*furo*), not with an inset hearth (*ro*), in a tea ceremony room. Also called *natsu-jawan* meaning "summer bowl." ⇨ CHAWAN, FŪRO, RO

〖注〗 tea ceremony 茶道． portable brazier 持ち運びの出来る火鉢[炉]，風炉．
inset hearth はめ込んだ炉床，炉．

hiraniwa 平庭 a flat landscape garden; a flat garden as opposed to a hilly garden (*tsukiyama*). It is characterized by an asymmetrical, yet balanced arrangement of trees, rocks, stone lanterns, and a water basin as decorative elements on a flat ground. One type of *hiraniwa* is laid out to be appreciated from the interior of a room, fine examples being the gardens of the *hōjō* (abbot's chamber) at Daitokuji Temple and Nanzenji Temple in Kyoto. The other type is meant for strolling through. The gardens of the Katsura Detached Palace, Kyoto, have characteristic features of the flat garden for strolling of the Edo period (1603-1868). ⇨ HŌJŌ-TEIEN, KAIYŪSHIKI-TEIEN, NIHON-TEIEN, TSUKIYAMA

〖注〗 hilly garden 築山． asymmetrical 非対称的の，不均整の． stone lantern 石燈籠． water basin 蹲踞(つくばい)． abbot's chamber 方丈，住職の部屋．
stroll ぶらつく，回遊する． detached palace 離宮．

hishaku 柄杓 a ladle; a dipper; a ladle made of bamboo or wood used in the tea ceremony. A bamboo ladle is used for the teakettle in the tearoom while a wooden one is used for the water basin (*tsukubai*) in the tea garden. ⇨ CHANOYU, CHATEI, TSUKUBAI

〖注〗 tea ceremony 茶道． teakettle 茶釜． water basin 蹲踞．

hitashimono 浸し物 parboiled greens; green leafy vegetables slightly boiled in water. After boiling, it is soaked in cold water or in slightly seasoned stock, and then the water is squeezed out. They are cut evenly into small sections and sprinkled with dried bonito flakes or sesame seeds. They are commonly eaten with soy sauce. Often called *ohitashi* by women.

〖注〗 parboiled お湯で軽くゆでる． season 味をつける． stock だし汁．
squeeze out しぼり出す． dried bonito flakes 鰹の削り節． sesame seeds ごま．

hiyamugi 冷麦 cold noodles; long, thin white noodles made from wheat flour and served in a bowl of iced water in the summer season. They are eaten by dipping into soy-flavored sauce mixed with some condiments—usually grated ginger and minced green onions. A cherry and a few slices of cucumber are usually placed on top as a garnish. ⇨ SŌMEN

〖注〗 soy-flavored sauce 醤油で味つけしたたれ． condiment 調味料，薬味．

grated ginger おろし生姜. minced 細かく刻んだ. minced green onions さら
しねぎ. garnish つま, 料理の飾り.

hiyayakko 冷奴 cold *tōfu*; cold soybean curd cut into cubes. It is
served with grated ginger, minced green onions, or other condiments, and eaten with soy sauce poured over the top or by dipping
it in soy sauce mixed with condiments. ⇨ TŌFU

〖注〗 soybean curd 豆腐. cube 立方形. grated ginger おろし生姜. minced 細かく刻んだ. minced green onions さらしねぎ. condiment 調味料, 薬
味. soy sauce 醤油.

hōgaku 邦楽 the generic term for traditional music, especially
music that developed during and after the Edo period (1603-1868)
in connection with the *shamisen* (three-stringed instrument) and
shakuhachi (Japanese flute). ⇨ SHAKUHACHI, SHAMISEN

hōji 法事 a Buddhist memorial service; a Buddhist service held
usually at home for the repose of the soul of a deceased member of
the family. Services are held every seventh day (not all are
necessarily observed) after a death until the 49th day, which is said
to be the day that the soul of the deceased departs for the other
world, when the family's period of mourning ends. Subsequently,
the first, third, seventh, 13th, 17th and 33th anniversaries are
observed. On memorial days, members of the immediate family,
relatives and close friends get together to offer prayers for the
deceased, while a priest chants sutras. Flowers and food are
placed at the altar and sticks of incense are burned. ⇨ BUKKYŌ

〖注〗 repose 慰め, 冥福. sutra お経. altar 祭壇. sticks of incense 線香.

hōjicha 焙茶 roasted tea leaves or tea made from roasted tea
leaves; roasted leaves of *bancha*, coarse tea, which have a brownish
color and pleasant smoky flavor. It is brewed in boiling-hot water.
While green tea tastes bitter when it cools, *hōjicha* does not. ⇨
BANCHA, CHA, RYOKUCHA

〖注〗 smoky flavor 芳ばしい香. brew 茶を入れる, 煎じる.

Hōjōki 方丈記 *An Account of an Abbot's Hut* (1212); a book of
essays written in the Kamakura period (1185-1336) by Kamo no
Chōmei (1153-1216). Becoming a Buddhist monk, he built a small
hut of about three meters square on Mount Hino near Kyoto to
spend a humble life in solitude released from worldly affairs, where
he wrote several books including the immortal *Hōjōki*. Largely
reflecting the eschatologic social conditions of those days, when
titanic struggles took place between two large ruling clans causing

upheaval, this book expresses his pessimistic view of life, based on the Buddhist way of thinking. He sees people and life in this world as "bubbles floating on stagnant water." ⇨ BUKKYŌ, GENPEI, KAMAKURA-JIDAI

〖注〗 abbot 住職. abbot's hut 方丈. monk 修行僧. eschatologic 終末的な. titanic struggle 大戦. upheaval 動乱. "bubbles floating on stagnant water"「淀みに浮かぶうたかた」.

hōjō-teien 方丈庭園 an abbot's garden; a garden to be viewed from the abbot's quarters (*hōjō*). It is usually laid out to symbolize the vastness of nature in a limited space. It is a garden for contemplating, not for strolling. The gardens at Daitokuji Temple (1324) and Nanzenji Temple (1293) in Kyoto are fine examples. ⇨ KARESANSUI(-TEIEN), NIHON-TEIEN

〖注〗 abbot's quarters 住職の住まい, 方丈. contemplate 観想する, 黙想する. stroll ぶらぶら歩く, 回遊する.

Hokkaidō 北海道 lit. north sea region. one of the four major islands of the Japanese archipelago, the other three being Honshū, Shikoku and Kyūshū. Situated to the north of the main island (Honshū), it is the second largest island, covering an area of about 78,500 square kilometers. With a sparse population, it is administratively dealt with as one prefecture. There are Ainu communities in remote areas; their population is now small. ⇨ AINU, DŌ², NIHON-RETTŌ

〖注〗 the Japanese archipelago 日本列島. sparse 希薄な. administratively 行政的に.

hokku 発句 the opening verse; the first 17 syllables of a linked verse (*renga*) or of a 31-syllable poem (*tanka*). This part, with sections of five-seven-five syllables, developed independently into the *haikai* form and later the haiku form. ⇨ HAIKAI, HAIKU, RENGA, TANKA

〖注〗 linked verse 連歌. 31-syllable poem 短歌.

Hokuriku chihō 北陸地方 the Hokuriku district; a district along the central part of the Japan Sea coast on the main island (Honshū). It is composed of the four prefectures of Fukui, Ishikawa, Toyama and Niigata. ⇨ HONSHŪ

hōmongi 訪問着 a visiting kimono; the semiformal silk kimono worn by women for social visits, tea gatherings, trips to the theater, weddings, etc. The material for a *hōmongi* is skillfully dyed and sewn, so that the kimono displays a whole picture or design flowing smoothly across the seams. Among a wide range of designs, the most typical is found in two parts, one on the lower half of the kimono in the front and the other extending from the left shoulder to the sleeve. An *obi* (sash) is chosen according to the occasion and the material used. A *haori* (an outer garment) is not worn over this kind of kimono. ⇨ HAORI, KIMONO, OBI

hondō 本堂   the main building of a Buddhist temple; the hall where the principal Buddhist image is enshrined.   The inside walls of the main hall of some grand temples used to be painted gold.   Thus, a *hondō* is often called *kondō* meaning "a golden hall," even if not painted gold. ⇨ GARAN, HONZON, KONDŌ

〖注〗 principal Buddhist image 本尊像.   enshrine 祀る.

Honshū 本州   the main island of Japan; the largest of the four major islands of the Japanese archipelago, the other three being Hokkaidō, Shikoku, and Kyūshū.   It is divided into five large districts —the Tōhoku, Kantō, Chūbu, Kinki and Chūgoku districts—and 34 administrative prefectures: the metropolis (*to*), two metropolitan prefectures (*fu*) and 31 prefectures (*ken*).   It covers an area of about 230,000 square kilometers. ⇨ NIHON-RETTŌ, TO-DŌ-FU-KEN

〖注〗 the Japanese archipelago 日本列島.   metropolis 大都市, 首都. metropolitan 大都市の, 首都圏.

honzen 本膳   the main table tray; the main tray of three served at a formal traditional Japanese dinner.   The three square trays have four short legs about 20 centimeters in height, the main one being a little higher than the other two and centered in front of an individual guest.   Generally, the main tray is arranged with a bowl of rice, a bowl of soup, a small plate of pickles, boiled fish or meat with vegetables, and some sliced raw fish or vinegared fish.   The saké cup may come on the main tray.   Often a full-course dinner of three trays is collectively called *honzen* as an abbreviation for *honzen-ryōri*. ⇨ HONZEN-RYŌRI, ZEN²

〖注〗 the main tray 一の膳, 本膳.   sliced raw fish 刺身.   vinegared 酢で味 をつけた.   abbreviation 省略.

honzen-ryōri 本膳料理   a traditional full-course dinner; the formal setting for a dinner served on very special occasions.   An individual setting consists of three low table-trays, and sometimes another tray of appetizers.   They are placed in front of a guest; the main tray in the middle, and the other two on the sides.   Foods on the three trays come in set combinations, such as a bowl of soup and three or five dishes, two bowls of soup and five or seven dishes, three bowls of soup and five or seven dishes, etc. (the dishes are served in odd numbers). The saké cup comes either on the tray of appetizers or on the main tray. This style originated among the nobles of the Muromachi period (1336-1568) and was later adopted by commoners in the Edo period (1603-1868). ⇨ HONZEN, ZEN²

〔注〕 formal setting of dinner 正式の配膳. appetizer 前菜, 口取り. odd number 奇数.

honzon 本尊 the principal Buddhist image; the central object of worship usually enshrined in the main hall of a Buddhist temple. It may be either a Tathagata statue (Sakyamuni, Amitabha or Vairocana) or a Bodhisattva statue (generally, Avolokiteshvara), depending on the particular sect. A miniature principal image is usually placed in a family Buddhist altar in the home. ⇨ AMIDA (NYORAI), BUTSUDAN, DAINICHI NYORAI, HONDŌ, KANNON (BOSATSU)

〔注〕 enshrine 祀る. Tathagata タターガタ, 如来, 仏陀の名の一つ(世に来て真理を示す人の意). statue 彫像. Sakyamuni 釈迦牟尼. Amitabha 阿弥陀如来. Vairocana 大日如来. Bodhisattva 菩薩(仏性に達していながらこの世の人々を救うために涅槃に入らないでいる人). Avolokiteshvara 観音菩薩. sect 教派, 分派. Buddhist altar 仏壇.

hoppō-ryōdo 北方領土 northern territories; four islands now under Soviet rule, located to the north of the Japanese archipelago. They comprise the islands of Habomai and Shikotan, off Hokkaidō, and the islands of Kunashiri and Etorofu in the Kurile Island Chain. With the end of World War II, the Soviet Union took possession of the Kurile Islands belonging to Japan, along with Habomai and Shikotan. In the late 1960s the Japanese government called on the Soviets to return these four islands, claiming that the ones off Hokkaidō are not included in the Kurile group and that Japan has a right to the Kurile Islands according to the Treaty of St. Petersburg of 1875. This has long been a tough issue between the two countries. ⇨ CHISHIMA-RETTŌ, HOKKAIDŌ

〔注〕 Habomai 歯舞. Shikotan 色丹. Kunashire 国後. Etorofu 択捉. the Kurile Island Chain 千島列島. the Treaty of St. Petersburg(=the Sakhalin-Kurile Islands Exchange Treaty) ロシアの St. Petersburg (今のソ連の Leningrad) で日本とロシアとの間で結ばれた「樺太千島交換条約」. tough issue 厄介な問題, 骨の折れる問題.

Hōraijima 蓬莱島 Elysian isle; the Isle of Eternal Life, which is said to be located far across the sea, according to Chinese legend. This idea is applied to the arrangement of a certain type of Japanese landscape garden as represented by the islet in the pond at Saihōji Garden, Kyoto.　　On the islet, aged pine trees and rocks are arranged so as to symbolize an everlasting land of bliss.　⇨ NIHON-TEIEN

〖注〗 Elysian 極楽浄土の，至福の． landscape garden 風景庭園． an everlasting land of bliss 永遠の至福の国，永劫の極楽浄土．

hotarugari 蛍狩り　firefly hunting.　It used to be a popular pastime on summer nights.　Holding paper fans and carrying cages, people young and old in simple summer kimono (*yukata*) enjoyed hunting and catching fireflies flickering near streams in the darkness.　It was something that gave poetic charm to summer.　Such a scene is beautifully described in a novel by Jun'ichirō Tanizaki (1886–1965), titled *Sasameyuki*, translated as "*The Makioka Sisters*."　⇨ YUKATA

〖注〗 firefly 蛍． pastime 気晴らし，娯楽． paper fan 団扇． flicker 明滅する，ゆらめく． poetic charm 詩的情緒．

Hotei 布袋　lit. cloth sack.　the God of Happiness and Prosperity, one of the Seven Deities of Good Luck.　He is represented with a fat potbelly and a smiling face with puffed-out cheeks, and as carrying a huge sack filled with treasures on his back.　It is said that this sack contains various treasures to ensure a happy and prosperous life, such as a treasure hammer, a money-producing purse, sacred keys used for treasure storage, and many more.　⇨ SHICHI-FUKUJIN

〖注〗 the Seven Deities of Good Luck 七福神． potbelly 太鼓腹，ほてい腹． puffed-out cheeks ぷっとふくらんだ頬っぺた．

hōzuki-ichi 酸漿市〔鬼燈市〕　Chinese-lantern plant〔ground cherry〕fair.　The *hōzuki*, a species of eggplant, grows to a height of 50 centimeters to one meter.　It bears lantern-shaped bags with a cherry-like fruit inside.　The plant is appreciated as a decoration in summer, when the bag and fruit turn a bright orange-red.　The fruit used to be enjoyed by girls as a kind of whistle; the seeds and meat are squeezed out in the mouth to make a hollow round ball. The bitter meat is said to have a medical effect.　A traditional *hōzuki* fair is held annually at Asakusa Kannon Temple, Tokyo, for a few days around July 10, where the plants are sold in clay pots at open-air stalls.　To some are attached a wind chime, the sound of which creats a cool atmosphere.

〖注〗 medical effect 薬効． open-air stall 露店． wind chime 風鈴．

hyakumantō 百万塔 the 1 million pagodas; a great number of pagodas dedicated to the many temples of Nara by Empress Kōken (718-70) in 764 in the hope of eternal peace. They were made of wood, each having a dharani, or a Buddhist charm, enshrined at its base. At present, about 30,000 of the pagodas are preserved at Hōryūji Temple (607), Nara. The shape of the Peace Tower at Japan Town in San Francisco was modeled after the *hyakumantō*. ⇨ TŌ

〖注〗 dedicate to ～に捧げる. charm お守り. enshrine 祀る.

hyakunin-isshu 百人一首 a hundred poems of a hundred poets; a collection of a hundred 31-syllable poems (*tanka*), adapted to the cards of a poem-matching game. A pack of game cards consists of two decks, 100 cards to be read and 100 cards to be picked up. On the reading card is a 31-syllable poem—originally the first 17 syllables of the poem—often with a portrait of the poet; on the card to be picked up only the last 14 syllables are written. The object of the game is to pick up as many scattered cards that match the ones read out as possible. This game is popularly enjoyed during the New Year holidays. This set of poems is also called *Ogura-hyakunin-isshu*. ⇨ KARUTA, OGURA-HYAKUNIN-ISSHU, TANKA, UTAGARUTA

〖注〗 31-syllable poem 31音節の詩, 短歌. poem-matching game 歌合わせ遊び. deck トランプ札などの一組(=pack).

hyō 俵 a traditional unit for measuring capacity. *Hyō* means "straw bag." The standard-size *hyō* bag was used for storing grain, charcoal, etc. One *hyō* of rice was further broken down into exactly 4 *to* (40 *shō*), equivalent to 72 liters. For grains other than rice, charcoal, etc., the *hyō* was not a standardized quantity. ⇨ SHAKKAN-HŌ, SHŌ

I

ichizoku-rōtō 一族郎党 lit. a family group and its members. a family-like group; a tightly linked social group based on the concept of a household, referring to either a kin group or a work group. Presumably rooted from ancient times in the agricultural life of the Japanese, this concept was firmly consolidated in feudal times. The head family, kinsmen and their retainers formed a cooperative group. The head and his subordinates were bonded together in a relationship of familial care and sacrifice. Such an intragroup structure can be seen even today in work groups in modern Japanese society. ⇨ OYABUN-KOBUN

〖注〗 household 家, 所帯. kin group 血縁関係の集団. consolidate 定着する, 固める. feudal times. 封建時代. kinsman 血縁者, 同族の者. retainer 家臣, 郎党. subordinate 部下. intragroup structure 集団内部構造.

Ido-chawan 井戸茶碗 an Ido tea bowl; a coarse ceramic tea bowl, originally produced in Korea and imported into Japan around the 15th and 16th centuries. It is characterized by a rough and solid surface, rustic enough to be favored by tea masters. There are a small number of pieces of this ware still in existence.

〖注〗 tea bowl 茶碗. ceramic ware 陶器製品. coarse（生地の）粗い. rustic 素朴な, さびれた.

iemoto 家元 lit. the origin of household. the headmaster or the main house associated with schools of the traditional arts. The *iemoto* descends lineally from the original founder of a school in the traditional arts, such as tea ceremony, flower arrangement, classical dance, theatrical arts, etc. The headmaster inherits the original principles and techniques attributed to the school. Not only does he enjoy the highest prestige in the art, but he also controls financial advantages by issuing certificates of proficiency to direct and indirect disciples. Succession to the position and the name are customarily hereditary (but not necessarily of the direct bloodline). ⇨ CHONOYU, IKEBANA

〖注〗 household 家族，所帯． lineally 伝来的に，世襲的に． be attributed to
～の作とみなす，～に由来する． certificate 証明書，免(許)状． proficiency 熟
達． disciple 弟子．

Iga-yaki 伊賀焼 Iga ceramic ware; ceramic ware produced in the
Iga region of Mie Prefecture. It is rich in rustic charm with
patches of thick glaze here and there. When dampened, the surface takes on an enchanting glow. Originally made for domestic
use, Iga ware caught the attention of great tea masters such as
Furuta Oribe (1544-1615) and Kobori Enshū (1579-1647). Since
then, *Iga-yaki* tea utensils and flower vases, particularly old Iga,
have been considered to rank among the best.   ⇨ HANAIRE, KAKI
〖注〗 ceramic ware 陶器． rustic charm さびれた魅力，素朴な魅力． patch
班点． glaze 釉． enchanting 魅惑的な． tea utensil 茶道具．

igo 囲碁   ⇨ GO

ihai 位牌 a Buddhist mortuary tablet; a tablet bearing the posthumous name of the deceased and the date of his death. Right after
one's death, such a tablet of unpainted wood is prepared and on the
49th day after the death, it is often replaced by a lacquered or gilt
one. It is placed at the Buddhist altar of the family or the family's
temple, and worshiped as the symbol of the spirit of the deceased.
⇨ BUTSUDAN

〖注〗 mortuary 埋葬の，死の． tablet 平板，銘板． posthumous 死後の，死後
生じた． the deceased 死者． unpainted wood 白木． Buddhist altar 仏壇．

ikebana 生け花 flower arrangement; floral art; the traditional
Japanese art of arranging cut flowers, branches, etc. Flower
arrangement has long been part of the Japanese way of life,
pursued not only for artistic purposes but also as a contemplation
of nature or the universe. Its roots go far back, deriving from the
offering of flowers to the Buddha or Buddhist altars. It was
around the 15th century that flower arrangement was formulated
as an aesthetic pursuit, simultaneously with the tea ceremony.
Together with the gifted Sōami (?1472-1525), the eighth Ashikaga
shogun Yoshimasa (1436-90) pursued the art at Ginkakuji Temple
in Kyoto. In the Edo period (1603-1868), it became popular even
among commoners and schools developed one after another.
Today, there are a few thousand different schools and styles, the
major three being the Ikenobō, Sōgetsu and Ohara schools. Common to all the schools, the styles of arranging can be divided into
formal and natural. The basic composition is made up of three

components, whether implicitly or explicitly, indicating heaven, earth and man, which are each named differently according to the school. The beauty of space created between branches is also emphasized. After World War II, an avant-garde abstract type emerged using driftwood, wire, painted materials, etc. ⇨ CHANOYU, KADŌ, SADŌ

〖注〗 contemplation 観照. Buddhist altar 仏壇. formulate 体系化する. aesthetic pursuit 美的追求. tea ceremony 茶道. school 流派. component 構成部分. avant-garde 前衛. drift-wood 流木.

ikezukuri 生作り[活作り] fish sliced and prepared while still alive and served in its natural form. Fish of a graceful shape such as *tai* (sea bream), *iseebi* (lobster), *ayu* (sweetfish), etc., are used for such cuisine. The flanks are separated from both sides of the spine, sliced into thin pieces, and arranged on the upper half of the body. The head and tail are skewered to make the fish appear alive. It is served together with decorative garnishes—flowers, vegetables, seaweed, etc.—in the background. Like other raw fish, it is eaten with *wasabi* (Japanese horseradish) and soy sauce. ⇨ SASHIMI, WASABI

〖注〗 sea bream 鯛. lobster 伊勢えび. sweetfish 鮎. flank 側面の肉. spine 背骨. skewer 串にさす. garnish つま, 料理の飾り. Japanese horse-radish わさび.

iki 粋[意気] lit. pure; essence. chic; sophisticated elegance; a polished, urbane form of understated elegance, an aesthetic ideal which developed among the townsfolk of Edo in the Edo period (1603-1868). Originally *iki* meant morale, manly pride, high spirits, etc. It gradually came to refer to the refined manners and appearance of a high-spirited and urbane person. A reaction to the extravagant and showy tastes which temporarily emerged after a long period of civil war, *iki* involves a preference for muted colors and the avoidance of a display of knowledge, culture, wealth, etc. For a man, *iki* means to behave with boldness, but at the same time with attentiveness to human feelings. In the case of a woman, *iki* involves a sensual type of beauty or elegant coquetry with inner restraint, such as a polished geisha might possess. Literary works by Tamenaga Shunsui (1790-1843) describe the complicated atmosphere of *iki* in the love affairs of the townsfolk of Edo. ⇨ CHŌNIN, EDO-JIDAI, GEISHA

〖注〗 sophisticated 洗練された, 凝った. urbane 都会的な, あかぬけした.

understated おさえた，地味な． aesthetic 美的な． townsfolk 町人． morale 士気，意気． extravagant ぜいたくな． muted color 地味な色． attentiveness to human feelings 人情深い． a sensual type of beauty 色気． elegant coquetry いやみのない色気． inner restraint 慎み，控え目．

ikō 衣桁 a clothes rack; a rack to hang kimono on. It is about 1.5 meters high, and is made of two vertical poles and two crossbars —one around the middle to hold the rack together and the other across the top. The material used is usually lacquered wood. Several pieces of clothing can be hung on the crossbars for daily use. But this rack is primarily used to spread a single kimono by inserting the outstretching top crossbar through the sleeves, so that an entire kimono can be displayed and appreciated.

〖注〗 vertical pole 縦の棒． crossbar 横木． outstretching 外の方に延びている．

Imari-yaki 伊万里焼 Imari ceramic ware; the generic term for the ceramic ware of northern Kyūshū, including ware from the kilns of Arita, Nabeshima, Hirado, etc., collectively so called because they were once exported from the port of Imari in Saga Prefecture, Kyūshū. Among the many types of ware of northern Kyūshū, best known are the products of the kilns around Arita; therefore, the terms Arita ware and Imari ware are very often synonymous. Generally, Imari ware is white porcelain of a fine texture. The color scheme varies from white and blue to brocade-like patterns of many colors; the decorative patterns vary from pure Chinese to pure Japanese, plus some of European origin. ⇨ ARITA-YAKI, KAKIEMON(-IMARI), NABESHIMA-YAKI, SOMETSUKE

〖注〗 ceramic ware 陶器． kiln（焼き物を焼く）窯． porcelain 磁器． fine texture こまかい肌ざわり，滑らかな手ざわり． color scheme 配色，色彩構成．

Inari 稲荷 lit. a load of rice plants. the fox deity; originally, the deity of harvests. Inari is said to be the posthumous name given to the person who first cultivated rice plants. In some districts, foxes living in the fields and mountains were believed to bring rich harvests and came to be widely worshiped as deities of agriculture called Inari. Later, the Inari came to be considered the deity of commerce and industry as well, as the Hata clan (naturalized Japanese from Korean nationality) prospered under the protection of the Inari Shrine of Fushimi near Kyoto. Inari shrines are guarded by a pair of white stone foxes, and have numerous red *torii* gates leading to the sanctuary. ⇨ TORII

〖注〗 deity 神，神のような人［もの〕．　posthumous 死後の．　naturalized 帰化
した．　the Hata clan 秦氏．　sanctuary 聖所，神殿．

inari-zushi 稲荷鮨　lit. fox *sushi*.　a vinegared rice ball wrapped up
in a bag of fried bean curd (*aburage*).　The fried bean curd is
seasoned with sugar, soy sauce and sweet rice wine.　Sometimes
cooked mushroom and other vegetables are mixed in the rice.
Inari means "a fox deity"; the fox is said to like fried bean curd,
according to Japanese legend.　⇨ ABURA(A)GE, INARI, SUSHI
〖注〗 fried bean curd 油揚げ．　season 調味する，味をつける．　soy sauce 醤
油．　sweet rice wine 味淋．　deity 神，神としてあがめられる人［もの〕．

inekari 稲刈り　rice harvesting; the work of cutting rice plants in
the field when the heads ripen.　Rice is harvested in autumn from
late September to early November depending on the district.
Traditionally, rice plants were cut by hand with a sickle and
husked at each farmer's house or at a community rice mill.　Today
combine harvesters are commonly used.　⇨ TAUE
〖注〗 sickle かま．　husk 皮（穀）をとる．　rice mill 稲脱穀機．　combine har-
vester 刈り取り脱穀機．

inkan 印鑑　a personal seal; a seal used in Japan for personal
endorsement, instead of one's signature.　The seal is usually affixed at the end of one's written name, when required, as a mark of
approval.　A family name or a full name is engraved on the end of
a stick made of wood, ivory, crystal, or sometimes precious gem
stones.　The impression of a seal is generally oval in shape with a
diameter of 1 or 1.5 centimeters.　Usually, each family holds one
registered seal (*jitsuin*) and a few unregistered seals (*mitomein*).
Also called *han*, and colloquially *hanko*.　⇨ HAN, JITSUIN,
MITOMEIN
〖注〗 endorsement 是認，確認．　affix（印などを）押す．　engrave 彫る．
impression 捺印，押印．　registered seal 登録された印鑑，実印．

inniku 印肉　lit. stamp meat.　stamp paste; ink paste in a small
container used for stamping a seal, a kind of ink pad.　Authentic
ink paste is vermilion in color and is also known as *shuniku*
(vermilion paste).　It is generally made of mugwort leaf fibers
mixed with a certain kind of resin.　⇨ HAN, INKAN
〖注〗 seal 印鑑，判．　vermilion 朱．　mugwort leaf fiber よもぎの葉の繊維．
resin 樹脂，松やに．

inrō 印籠　a case for a seal; a small case hung from the waistband
of a samurai in feudal times.　It was originally used to carry a seal

and ink pad, later also to contain medicine.   It is usually made of lacquered wood, elaborately designed.   ⇨ INKAN, INNIKU

〖注〗 feudal times 封建時代.   seal 印形.   ink pad 印肉.

ippansanga 一般参賀 congratulatory greetings to the Imperial Family by the general public.   The Imperial Palace grounds are open to the public only two days a year: on one of the New Year days (January 2 or 3) and on the Emperor's Birthday (April 29).   On these occasions the Emperor, the Empress and other members of the Imperial Family appear on the balcony of the palace to receive greetings from well-wishers.   ⇨ KŌKYO, TENNŌ, TENNŌ-TANJŌBI

〖注〗 the Imperial Palace 皇居.   well-wisher 幸福を祈る人，好意をよせる人.

iriaiken 入会権 common rights; a traditional practice of co-ownership of mountains, forests, etc., by members of a community.   Those belonging to the community have entitlement to such places and the natural resources therefrom, such as edible plants, firewood, natural fertilizers, etc., under strict regulation according to local custom rather than by contract.   This practice was established in the Edo period (1603–1868), and has supported have-not farmers, while at the same time imposing restrictions and obligations on them.   The system has declined as a result of land reforms.   There has been a similar practice, concerning the right to fishing grounds, called *nyūryōken*.

〖注〗 co-ownership 共有.   entitlement 資格, 権利.   natural resources 自然資源.   obligation 義理，恩義.

Iriomote Kokuritsu-kōen 西表国立公園 Iriomote National Park, situated in the Yaeyama Islands of Okinawa Prefecture, established in 1972.   The park covers an area of 445 square kilometers (land area 125.1 sq. km), about three quarters of which is water, consisting of Iriomote, Kobama and Taketori islands and their surrounding waters.   The park includes the largest coral reef in Japan, dense subtropical forests and mangrove swamps.   It is noted for rare butterflies, poisonous snakes, terns and a species of wildcat, the *Iriomote yamaneko* (*Mayailurus iriomotensis*), discovered in 1965.   ⇨ KOKURITSU-KŌEN, OKINAWA, RYŪKYŪ-SHOTŌ

〖注〗 the Yaeyama Islands 八重山諸島.   coral reef 珊瑚礁.   mangrove マングローブ(熱帯の湿地に密生する森林性植物).   tern 鯵刺.

iroha いろは the Japanese syllabary; the Japanese alphabet or the Japanese version of the ABCs; one of the two fixed orders of the

Japanese syllabary system, the other being the one beginning with *a, i, u, e, o* used officially today. The *iroha* is the older system, adopted from a poem composed by the Buddhist priest Kōbō Daishi (774-835), which covers all 47 syllables of the Japanese phonetical system. The phrase *i-ro-ha* is used to refer to a first step or the basics of something, just as the English "ABC" is. ⇨ IROHAUTA, KANA

〖注〗 syllabary 音節文字表，字音表． phonetic system 音標組織．

iroha-garuta いろは歌留多 a card game of the Japanese phonetic alphabet; a pack of cards consisting of 47 pairs of cards to be played as a card-matching game. One pack of cards consists of two decks, 47 cards to be read and 47 cards to be picked up. (47 is the number of Japanese *kana* script, but one is excluded.) On the reading card is written a maxim or a short phrase, and on the card to be matched is a picture and the first *kana* of the phrase in the upper corner. The game is played by picking up the scattered picture cards that match the ones read out. The one who collects the most pairs wins. Children enjoy this game during the New Year holidays. ⇨ IROHA, IROHAUTA, KANA, KARUTA

〖注〗 phonetic 表音式の． deck カードの一組． script 書体，筆記体活字． maxim 格言．

irohauta いろは歌 the Japanese syllabary poem; a poem composed of all 47 syllables covering all the *kana* of the Japanese phonetic alphabet. This had long been the fixed order by which to memorize all the *kana* letters, although another order beginnig with *a, i, u, e, o* is officially used today. The poem is said to have been written by the Buddhist priest Kūkai (774-835), also called Kōbō Daishi, based on the conception of Buddhism. The poem begins: "*Iro ha nihoheto ∕ Chirinuru wo ∕ Waka yo tareso ∕ Tsune naramu*" and is translated (by Donald Keene) as: "Though the color be fragrant ∕ The flower will fall ∕ Who in this world of ours ∕ Will last forever?" ⇨ IROHA, KANA

〖注〗 syllabary 音節文字表． phonetic 表音式の． conception 考え方，認識．

iromuji 色無地 solid color fabric; a kimono or kimono fabric of a solid color without a colored pattern. Often it has a woven design of patterns of the same color. A silk kimono of this type of fabric can be worn on various occasions: one with three family crests (*kamon*) on it, ranking next to *tomesode*, is worn on formal occasions; one with a single crest is regarded as similar to a *hōmongi* (visiting kimono), and is worn on semiformal occasions; one with no crest is for tea ceremonies, courtesy visits, ordinary outings, etc. depending on the material used and the *obi* (sash) used with it. ⇨ KAMON, KIMONO

〖注〗 fabric 織物. solid color 無地色. pattern 模様. crest 紋, 家紋. tea ceremony 茶道. courtesy visit 表敬訪問.

iro-tomesode 色留袖 a colored formal kimono for women; a very formal silk kimono, ranking next to the most formal one called *kuro-tomesode* (black *tomesode*). It has one, three or five family crests (*kamon*) on it, depending on the degree of formality, and is lightly colored with the lower part decorated with a picturesque pattern in gold, silver, and some other colors. It is worn by both married and unmarried women of middle age and older and is appropriate to attend a wedding or other formal occasions. ⇨ KAMON, KIMONO, KURO-TOMESODE, TOMESODE

〖注〗 family crest 家紋. the degree of formality 正式の度合.

Ise-Shima Kokuritsu-kōen 伊勢志摩国立公園 Ise-Shima National Park (555.5 square kilometers), designated in 1946; a natural park covering the southern part of the Shima Peninsula and its surrounding waters. This area includes the city of Ise, famous for Ise Shrine where the Sun Goddess, mythological ancestor of the Imperial Family, is enshrined, along with the city of Toba, known for Mikimoto cultured pearls, and Ago Bay dotted with rafts of pearl oysters. The coastline is rugged and the seascape is varied. Off Futamigaura beach are two "wedded rocks" linked with a sacred rope, representing a pair of gods, Izanagi and Izanami, who are said to have created the Japanese islands, according to mythology. ⇨ KOKURITSU-KŌEN, YŌSHOKU-SHINJU

〖注〗 the Sun Goddess 天照大神. enshrine 祀る. cultured pearl 養殖真珠. pearl oyster 真珠貝, あこや貝. rugged ぎざぎざしている, リアス式の. seascape 海の風景. wedded rocks 夫婦岩.

ishidōrō 石燈籠 a stone lantern; lanterns made of granite or the like, placed in the compounds of temples and shrines, or in landscape gardens. The structure consists of a flat hexagonal roof, a hollowed part to hold a light, and legs or a foundation. Originally, they were used to provide illumination on special occasions at temples and shrines. Tea masters began to use them in tea gardens in the 16th century, and thus the *ishidōrō* has also become an essential art object in the landscape of a Japanese garden. ⇨

CHATEI, NIHON-TEIEN, TŌRŌ

〖注〗 lantern 燈籠. granite 花崗岩. compounds 境内. landscape garden 風景庭園. hexagonal 六角形の. illumination 照明.

ishiyaki-imo 石焼き芋 stone-baked yam; a sweet potato baked in hot stones fired from underneath. Pulling a cart equipped with such an oven, a vendor calls out *"yaki-i-mo"* during the cold season.
〖注〗 cart 荷車, 手押し車. vendor 行商人.

Issun Bōshi 一寸法師 One-Inch Boy, a Japanese folk tale character; a tiny figure who defeated giant fiends (*oni*). Through prayers, a couple was blessed with a son, who somehow never grew beyond a few centimeters (one inch). When the boy became of age, he set out for the capital of Kyoto, using a soup bowl as a boat and a chopstick as an oar, to seek his fortune. There he became the retainer of a court minister. While escorting the minister's daughter on a journey, two giant fiends attempted to kidnap her. Drawing his needle-sword, he defeated them. By waving the mallet the fiends had left behind, he grew into a normal-sized, handsome young warrior. He married the minister's daughter and they lived happily ever after. This tale became very popular in the early 18th century when it was retold in *Otogi Zōshi* (A Book of Fairy Tales).
〖注〗 folk tale 民話. character 人物. fiend 悪鬼, 鬼. chopstick 箸. retainer 家臣. court minister 宮中の大臣. mallet 小槌.

Iyo-gasuri 伊予絣 Iyo splashed-pattern weave; coarse cotton weave with splashed patterns on an indigo background, originating in Iyo Province in the present Ehime Prefecture. White cotton threads tied at intervals are dyed repeatedly in the sap of natural indigo plants, the tied parts being left white. (Chemical indigo is also used today.) When the threads are woven into fabric, the undyed parts form white splashed patterns. Strong and simple in color, *Iyo-gasuri* fabric has been widely used to make traditional work clothes. Its use may be compared to blue denim in the US. ⇨ KASURI
〖注〗 splash とび散る, 散らばった模様にする. indigo background 藍色の地. province 地方の諸国, (行政目的で分割した)国. sap 樹液, 植物の液. indigo plant インド藍(まめ科の熱帯産の低木). fabric 織物.

Izu-shotō 伊豆諸島 the Izu Islands (290 square kilometers); a group of volcanic islands located in the Pacific Ocean southwest of Tokyo. They consist of seven main islands, Ōshima, Toshima,

Niijima, Kōzujima, Miyakejima, Mikurajima, Hachijōjima, and some smaller ones. They are administered by the Tokyo metropolitan government. The area is included as part of Fuji-Hakone-Izu National Park (designated in 1936). ⇨ FUJI-HAKONE-IZU KOKURITSU-KŌEN

〖注〗 the Tokyo metropolitan government 東京都庁. 伊豆諸島(伊豆七島)：大島, 利島, 新島, 神津島, 三宅島, 御蔵島, 八丈島.

J

jabisen 蛇皮線 a string instrument of Okinawa. The stringed instruments of Japan comprise various types of zithers, lutes, and an eighth-century harp. The *jabisen* of Okinawa is a long-necked lute (the *biwa* being an example of a short lute). The *jabisen* has three strings which are plucked. The soundboard is covered with snakeskin, unlike the similar *shamisen* of the main Japanese islands which is covered with catskin. It is a modified form of the Chinese sanxian which was introduced to Okinawa late in the 13th century. Traditional folk and court music of the Ryūkyūs is often accompanied by the *jabisen* (also known as *jamisen* or *sanshin*). Even today's pop-folk music of Okinawa often employs the unique sounds of this instrument. ⇨ SHAMISEN

〖注〗 stringed instrument 弦楽器. zither ツィター(琴・三味線のような弦楽器). lute リュート(ギターに似た15-17世紀の弦楽器). pluck ひっぱる，はじく. sanxian 三味線. accompany 伴奏する.

janken(-pon) じゃんけん(ぽん) the "stone-scissors-paper" game often used to decide the winner or loser; the Japanese counterpart to "heads or tails" played by throwing a coin. While shouting "*jan-ken-pon*," all the participants simultaneously, hold out a hand: making a fist, outstretching the index and middle finger, or extending a palm—each representing a stone, scissors, or paper respectively. The stone cannot be cut with scissors, the scissors can cut the paper, and the paper can wrap up the stone; thus each sign wins over one and loses to another.

〖注〗 counterpart 相当するもの，相対物. heads or tails 表と裏(表が出たら勝ち，裏が出たら負け). hold out さし出す. outstretch さし伸ばす.

janome(-gasa) 蛇の目(傘) lit. a snake's eye. an umbrella made of a bamboo frame and oiled paper. It has a white circle on a dark background, suggesting a snake's eye. It is used by women when wearing a kimono. ⇨ BANGASA, KARAKASA

〖注〗 bamboo frame 竹の骨組み. oiled paper 油紙.

Jidai Matsuri 時代祭   the Festival of Eras in Kyoto (October 22);
the festival of Heian Shrine to commemorate the founding of the
ancient capital of Kyoto in 794; one of the three grand Kyoto
festivals, the other two being the Aoi Festival and the Gion Festival.   This festival started in 1895 with the founding of Heian
Shrine.   It features a procession over a kilometer long through the
streets from Heian Shrine to the Old Imperial Palace (Kyoto
Gosho).   More than 2,000 people attired in historical costumes
participate in the parade, representing notable historical events
over the period of 1,100 years from the beginning of the Heian
period (794–1185) to the Meiji Restoration (1868).   The events in
procession come in reverse chronological order.   ⇨ AOI MATSU-
RI, GION MATSURI.

〔注〕 commemorate 記念となる，祝う． procession 行列． the Old Imperial
Palace 京都御所． be attired in ～で装っている． the Meiji Restoration 明治
維新． in reverse chronological order 時代順と逆の順序で．

jidaimono 時代物   a historical play; Kabuki and Bunraku plays with
historical backgrounds.   They deal with the samurai and nobility
as seen in *Kanadehon Chūshingura* (The 47 Faithful Retainers),
Sugawara Denju Tenarai Kagami (The Sugawara School of
Penmanship), etc.   ⇨ BUNRAKU, KABUKI

〔注〕 the nobility 貴族(階級)． retainer 家臣． The 47 Faithful Retainers
「仮名手本忠臣蔵」． The Sugawara School of Penmanship 「菅原伝授手習鑑」．

jikatabi 地下足袋   lit. socks worn on the ground.   a pair of split-
toed shoes, separating the big toe from the other four in the shape
of *tabi* (socks for the kimono).   Tough cloth is used for the uppers
and rubber for the sole.   Many Japanese laborers, particularly
carpenters, used to wear them; covering the entire foot, they secure
one's footing and have the comfort of *tabi*.   ⇨ TABI

〔注〕 split-toed つま先の分れた． tough cloth 厚地の布． sole 底．

jikkan-jūnishi 十干十二支   lit. 10 stems and 12 branches.   the sexagenary cycle; the Chinese zodiac made up of a combination of 10
stems and 12 branches, the calendar cycle based on the Chinese *I
Ching* or *The Book of Changes*. This calendar has been used to
denote time, month, year and direction.   In China, with archaeological evidence going far back to before 1000 B.C., it is said to have
been first employed in the first or second century, and in Japan
since the early seventh century.   The stems consist of five elements (*gokō*)—wood, fire, earth, metal, water—each having a

positive and negative side; the branches consist of 12 animal signs (*jūnishi*)—*ne*(rat), *ushi* (ox), *tora* (tiger), *u* (rabbit), *tatsu* (dragon), *mi* (snake), *uma* (horse), *hitsuji* (sheep), *saru* (monkey), *tori* (cock), *inu* (dog) and *i* (boar). Thus, for example, the full cycle embraces 60 years. It is more commonly called *eto* in Japan. ⇨ ETO, JŪNISHI

〖注〗 sexagenary 60の. zodiac 十二宮, 十二支. *I Ching*(=The Book of Changes) 易経(五経の一つ, 古代中国の易占の書物). archaeological evidence 考古学的に実証されていること. five elements 五行. 12 signs of animals 十二支 (子, 丑, 寅, 卯, 辰, 巳, 午, 未, 申, 酉, 戌, 亥).

jingi 仁義 1) humanity and justice; benevolence and righteousness; a virtue in human relations, originally as interpreted by a Chinese Confucian, Mencius (Mōshi in Japanese). In the Confucian concept, this term denotes the balance between humanity and justice to make human relations smooth, the balance to be maintained by emphasizing humility, fidelity to superiors, and mutual concerns in a group or in society. With the influence of Confucianism, this concept deeply permeated Japanese society, especially in feudal times. 2) obligation and duty in an outlawed society. In the Edo period (1603-1868), this term was reinterpreted by gangsters. In return for protection, the boss compelled his subordinates to fulfill a series of obligatory codes in their closed society. ⇨ JUKYŌ

〖注〗 benevolence 慈悲心, 善意. Confucian 儒者, 儒教的. humility 謙遜. fidelity 忠誠. mutual concern お互いの気くばり. Confucianism 儒教. feudal times 封建時代. obligation 義理, 恩義. outlawed society やくざの社会, 無法者達の社会. obligatory 義務的な. code 掟.

jinja 神社 a Shinto shrine; a sacred compound containing a Shinto shrine, dedicated to mythological gods, ancestors of the Imperial Family, or historically celebrated figures. The *jinja* usually includes several structures—a sanctuary, an oratory, etc.—within its precincts. The construction of the shrine is extremely simple, using unpainted natural wood and thatched roofs, and retains the style of indigenous Japanese architecture. A *torii* gate marks the entrance to a Shinto shrine. Often situated among trees, the shrine has an atmosphere of solemnity and serenity. ⇨ SHINTŌ, TORII

〖注〗 compound 敷地. dedicate to 捧げる. celebrated figure 有名人物. sanctuary 神殿. oratory 拝殿. precincts 境内. unpainted natural wood 白木. thatched roof 茅葺きの屋根. indigenous Japanese architecture 日本古

来の建築. solemnity 厳粛. serenity 静寂.

jinrikisha 人力車 lit. a man-powered vehicle. rikisha; rickshaw; a small vehicle for one or two passengers, pulled by one man. It consists of a seat, a convertible top, two wheels and two long poles for pulling. There are two theories as to its invention: one, that it was an invention of Yōsuke Izumi, and the other that it was invented by Jonathan Goble (died 1898), an American Baptist missionary. They first appeared in Tokyo in 1870 as a public conveyance replacing the *kago* (palanquin). Later they were introduced to the Philippines and other parts of East Asia. In Japan, they disappeared as public transport with the spread of motor vehicles. Today, they are used only by some geisha or as a tourist attraction.

〖注〗 passenger 乗客. convertible 屋根のたたみこめる. Yōsuke Izumi 和泉要助. conveyance 交通機関. palanquin 駕籠.

jitō 地頭 the head of an estate. 1) a local land administrator appointed by the lord of a manor in the Heian period (794-1185). 2) an official in charge of an area appointed by the shogunate in the Kamakura period (1185-1336). When Minamoto Yoritomo (1147-99) established the Kamakura shogunate government, he brought local land administrators, along with the heads of provinces, under shogunate control. The *jitō* were also entrusted to collect taxes in the form of rice for the shogunate. During the long period of civil wars that followed, this function gradually disappeared. ⇨ KAMAKURA-BAKUFU, SHUGO

〖注〗 manor 領主の館, 荘園. the lord of a manor 荘園領主. shogunate 幕府. province (行政目的で分けた)国. entrust まかす. taxes in the form of rice 年貢米. the period of civil wars 戦国時代. function 役目, 慣習.

jitsuin 実印 lit. a real seal. a registered seal; a master seal; a personal seal whose impression is officially registered at a local public office. This seal is used exclusively for official documents and important transactions. When used, it must be accompanied by an official certificate of the seal impression for legal identification. The design of the ideograph of a family name or a full name on this seal is extremely elaborate so as to prevent duplication. ⇨ INKAN, MITOMEIN

〖注〗 seal 印, 判. impression 捺印. transaction 取引. official certificate 公式証明書. legal identification 法的に同一物とみなされること. ideograph 表意文字, 象形文字. duplication 複製.

jiutai 地謡   the chorus in the Noh drama.   The chorus is composed of four to eight singers seated to the right of the Noh stage (as the audience faces it), who chant Noh texts to the accompaniment of the Noh *hayashi* (orchestra).   This solemn style of singing is thought by some to have developed from Buddhist chanting.   ⇨ HAYASHI, NŌ

〖注〗 chant 歌う、詠唱する.   accompaniment 伴奏.   solemn 荘重な.   Buddhist chanting お経、声明.

jiutaiza 地謡座   the chorus seating area on the Noh stage.   It is the porch-like area located to the far right of the main stage of a Noh theater (as the audience faces it).   Four to eight singers are seated there.   ⇨ JIUTAI, NŌ, NŌBUTAI

jiyūminken-undō 自由民権運動   the liberal movement for people's rights; a political movement which emerged in the 1870s, inspired by Western liberal ideas.   This movement was started by former samurai who were not recognized by the new Meiji government, including Taisuke Itagaki (1837-1919), Shōjirō Gotō (1838-97), Shinpei Etō (1834-74), etc., in protest against absolutist tendencies of the government.   Supported by a large number of sympathizers nationwide, it eventually led to the establishment of a national assembly (1881) and later the promulgation of the Meiji Constitution (1889).   Ideas embraced by the movement were from Western works translated into Japanese: John Stuart Mill's *On Liberty* (translated in 1872), Jeremy Bentham's *Theory of Legislation* (1873), Jean-Jacques Rousseau's *Social Contract* (1882), etc. Japanese intellectuals including Yukichi Fukuzawa (1835-1901), enlightened by democratic ideas, also indirectly influenced this movement.

〖注〗 sympathizer 共鳴者.   national assembly 国会.   promulgation 公布、発布.   *Theory of Legislation*「立法論」.   *Social Contract*「社会契約論」.   intellectual 知識人.   enlighten 啓発する.

Jizō (Bosatsu) 地蔵 (菩薩)   Ksitigarbha (-bodhisattva) (Sanskrit); a being in Buddhahood who leads people to salvation and particularly protects children.   He is believed to save people from suffering in the six transient worlds that are thought to exist on the way to the realm of enlightenment.   As the guardian of children, he is said to protect them at the River Styx leading to the other world. His image is represented as one with a shaved head, holding a staff in one hand and a gem stone in the other.   Small stone statues of him can often be found on the roadside, with bibs placed around his neck by worshipers. ⇨ BOSATSU

〖注〗 bodhisattva 菩薩(悟りを開いて仏性をもっているが人を救うために現世にいる者). Buddhahood 仏性. salvation 救い. transient 束の間の，一時の. the realm of enlightenment 悟りの境地. the River Styx 三途の川，(ギリシャ神話)ステックス川. staff 棒，杖. bib よだれ掛け.

Jōdo-shinshū 浄土真宗 True Pure Land Buddhism; a sect of Buddhism founded in the 13th century by the priest Shinran (1173-1262), a disciple of Hōnen, the founder of the Jōdo sect. According to Shinran's teachings, humans can achieve salvation not by pursuing religious practices or studies, but by relying simply on the "other great power"—the gracious mercy of Amitabha—admitting that human beings are so weak and sinful that belief in "great mercy" is needed. This sect is often viewed as a Japanese Buddhist form of Protestantism. It has come to be one of the most influential sects in Japan, comprising millions of adherents and thousands of temples with its headquarters the Honganji Temple in Kyoto. ⇨ AMIDA(NYORAI), BUKKYŌ, JŌDOSHŪ

〖注〗 sect 宗派. disciple 弟子. salvation 救い. gracious mercy 崇高な慈悲. Amitabha 阿弥陀仏. Protestantism (キリスト教)新教. adherent 信者.

Jōdoshū 浄土宗 Pure Land Buddhism; the Jōdo sect of Buddhism, founded in the 12th century by the priest Hōnen (1133-1212). He taught that humans could achieve salvation not through their own efforts but by Amida's gracious mercy, and that they may be reborn in the Pure Land by praying to Amida, repeating a phrase from a sutra, "*Namu Amida Butsu*" (I sincerely believe in Amitabha). Later, this sect was divided into several new branches, the most influential one being Jōdo-shinshū. ⇨ AMIDA(NYORAI), BUK-KYŌ, JŌDO-SHINSHŪ

〖注〗 salvation 救い. gracious mercy 崇高な慈悲. sutra お経.

jōfu 上布 fine linen fabric. Hand-spun, fine ramie threads are woven into a very thin, flat fabric. It is usually white or indigo in color, or has simple patterns of these colors. This fabric is appropriate for making midsummer kimono. Famous kinds of *jōfu* are *Echigo-jōfu* of Niigata Prefecture, *Satsuma-jōfu* of Kagoshima Prefecture, *Noto-jōfu* of Ishikawa Prefecture and *Miyako-jōfu* of the Ryūkyū Islands. ⇨ ECHIGO-JŌFU, OKINAWA-JŌFU, SATSUMA-JŌFU

〖注〗 fabric 布，織物. ramie ラミー(皮から繊維をとるアジア産の植物).

hand-spun 手で紡いだ.　indigo 藍.

jōkamachi 城下町　a castle town; a town centering around the castle of a feudal lord.　A castle not only served as a fortification but also had great influence on the growth of a town.　Many of today's cities and towns derive from castle towns that emerged in feudal times, though very few of the castles survive.　Some examples of such castle towns are: Sunpu, which developed under the Imagawa clan; Yamaguchi under the Ōuchi clan; Kōfu under the Takeda clan; etc.　⇨ SHIRO

〚注〛 feudal lord 大名.　fortification 防御，要塞.　feudal times 封建時代.

Jōmon-jidai 縄文時代　lit. the straw-rope pattern age. the Jōmon period (?10000–?200 B.C.); the Japanese neolithic period, the first recognized culture of the Japanese islands.　This period was characterized by the use of distinctive earthenware bearing straw-rope patterns (*jōmon*).　People of those days are thought to have lived in caves, relying mainly on hunting and fishing, and not yet on farming.　⇨ JŌMONSHIKI-DOKI

〚注〛 neolithic 新石器時代の.　earthenware 土器.　straw-rope pattern 縄文.

jōmonshiki-doki 縄文式土器　Jōmon-style earthenware; straw-rope pattern earthenware estimated to have been made in the Japanese neolithic period (?10000–?200 B.C.).　This type of earthenware is the oldest ever excavated in the Japanese islands.　Fired at a low temperature, it took on a brownish-gray color.　The decoration is generally elaborate, with curved lines or straw-rope patterns (*jōmon*) on the surface.　The shape varies depending on the district.　Some of the earliest vessels are conical in shape, narrowing at the bottom.　⇨ JŌMON-JIDAI

〚注〛 earthenware 土器.　the neolithic period 新石器時代.　excavate 発掘する.　conical 円錐の.

jōruri 浄瑠璃　a traditional epic-like ballad; a narrative ballad originally accompanied by the *biwa* (a Japanese lute) and later by the *shamisen* (a three-stringed instrument).　This latter style was combined with puppets to develop a musical drama of highly artistic quality called Bunraku.　Many excellent dramas were written for this new dramatic form by the celebrated playwright Chikamatsu Monzaemon (1653–1724), the Shakespeare of Japan.　Today, the term *jōruri* refers mainly to the music of Bunraku.　⇨ BIWA, BUNRAKU, SHAMISEN

〚注〛 epic 叙事詩.　ballad 伝承的物語詩，叙事的歌謡.　narrative ballad 物語

的な詩または歌謡. accompany 伴う,伴奏する. lute リュート(ナシ型,ネック付き弦楽器). playwright 劇作家.

jōshikimaku 定式幕 lit. the formal curtain. the stage draw curtain, used in the Kabuki and Bunraku theaters. It is made up of vertical stripes in black, green and persimmon colors. This color combination was designated to represent formal Kabuki stages at the beginning of the Meiji era (1868–1912). The curtain is drawn to the sound of wooden clappers. ⇨ BUNRAKU, KABUKI

〖注〗 vertical stripe 縦縞. persimmon 柿. wooden clappers 拍子木.

Jōshin'etsu-kōgen Kokuritsu-kōen 上信越高原国立公園 Jōshinetsu Highland National Park (1,890.3 square kilometers), designated in 1949; a natural park situated in central Honshū, encompassing parts of Nagano, Gunma and Niigata prefectures. This park can be divided into two sections: the Jōshin'etsu and Myōkō-Togakushi regions. The former includes the Sugadaira Plateau (1,300 meters), Shiga Heights (1,400–1,700 m), Mount Tanigawa (1,963 m), and two famous active volcanoes, Mount Asama (2,542 m) and Mount Shirane (highest peak 3,192 m). The latter comprises Mount Myōkō (2,446 m), Mount Kurohime (2,053 m), Mount Togakushi (1,911 m), etc. Hot springs can be found scattered around these areas. Crowds throng to the park, since its entrance is situated at the foot of Mount Asama which is close to the international resort town of Karuizawa, accessible in only a few hours from Tokyo. ⇨ KOKURITSU-KOEN

〖注〗 encompass 取り巻く, 囲む. the Sugadaira Plateau 菅平. the Shiga Heights 志賀高原. active volcano 活火山. hot spring 温泉.

joyanokane 除夜の鐘 night-watch bell; temple bells ringing out the old year at midnight on New Year's Eve. The temple bells peal 108 times to announce the passing of the old year and to welcome the new year. (This is televised today.) According to teachings of Buddhism there are 108 earthly desires, and it is said that the peals of the temple bells release people from each and every one of them for the new year. ⇨ ŌMISOKA, TSURIGANE

〖注〗 night watch 除夜. peal (鐘などを)鳴り響かせる, とどろかせる. earthly desire 煩悩. release 解き放す, 解放する.

jōyō-kanji 常用漢字 Chinese characters in common use; Chinese characters used in the Japanese language which must be learned in the nine years of compulsory education. In 1946, as one of the postwar reforms of the writing system, the Cabinet officially listed

1,850 Chinese characters (called *tōyō-kanji*) for daily use, as selected by the the Council on National Language (Kokugo Shingi-kai). In 1981 the number was raised to 1,945 and they came to be called *jōyō-kanji*. The use of these characters is encouraged in public notices, newspapers and magazines, with only minor modifications. In fact, though, more Chinese characters are used in specialized fields. Among the 1,945 *jōyō-kanji*, 996 are designated as *kyōiku-kanji* (Chinese characters in education), which must be learned in the six years of elementary school. ⇨ KANJI, KYŌIKU-KANJI

〖注〗 Chinese character 漢字. compulsory education 義務教育. public notice 公示. modification 修正.

juban 襦袢 underwear for a kimono. There are two kinds: a short cotton undershirt and a long colorful undergarment worn between the undershirt and the kimono. The latter *juban* has an interchangeable silk collar, or neckband, called *han'eri* which should be harmonized with the kimono. ⇨ HADAJUBAN, HAN'ERI, KIMONO, NAGAJUBAN

〖注〗 long undergarment 長い下着, 長襦袢. interchangeable 取り替えできる. neckband 衿.

jūdō 柔道 lit. the way of gentleness. weaponless self-defense as a sport derived from *jūjutsu*, a traditional martial art. Shortly after the Meiji Restoration (1868), Jigorō Kanō (1860-1938) modified *jūjutsu* into a modern sport form by standardizing techniques, especially those that could easily be applied to competition without sacrificing the spiritual aspect. He set three main goals: strengthening of the body, cultivation of the mind, and mastery of skills. The sport was first introduced abroad toward the end of the 19th century and since has gained worldwide popularity. Its status as an international sport was established when it was adopted as an official Olympic event at the time of the 1964 Tokyo Olympics. The basic techniques are: the throw, pinning the opponent down, the strangle hold, the joint lock, and the knockdown blow which includes the kick, thrust and hit. Since this blow at vital points can be fatal, it is not allowed in competition. ⇨ BUGEI, JŪJUTSU

〖注〗 martial art 武芸, 格闘技. cultivation of the mind 精神修養. throw 投げ(技). hold 固め(技). pin-down 抑え(技). strangle hold 締め(技). joint lock 関節(技). knockdown 当て身(技). kick 蹴り(技). thrust 突き(技). hit 打ち(技).

jūdō-obi 柔道帯 a judo belt; a sash tied at the front of a coarse *happi*-style jacket of cotton to keep it together. In judo there are five classes (*kyū*) and 10 grades (*dan*) that indicate degree of proficiency, and the color of the belt differs according to the degree. White is for the fifth (beginner) and fourth classes, brown for the third to the first class, black for the first up to the fifth grade, red and white stripes for the sixth up to the eighth grade, and red for the ninth and tenth grades. Those holding a grade are considered experts. Promotion at the grade level is difficult, depending not only on improvement in skills but also length of experience. ⇨ JŪDŌ, JŪJUTSU

〖注〗 proficiency 熟練.

jūgoya 十五夜 lit. the fifteenth night. the full moon of the 15th night, particularly on August 15 in midautumn in the lunar calendar, falling around September 29 in the present calendar. In ancient times, nobles and men of letters enjoyed moon-viewing parties, composing poems and drinking rice wine (saké) under the moonlight on this night in midautumn. People pray to the moon for a good harvest of rice, offering rice dumplings together with the seven grasses of autumn, particularly pampus grass (*susuki*) and bush clover (*hagi*). ⇨ TSUKIMI

〖注〗 the lunar calendar 太陰暦. men of letters 文人. dumpling 団子.

Jūichimen Kannon 十一面観音 the Eleven-Faced Kannon Bodhisattva; the Deity of Mercy, crowned with 11 small faces. Of the 11 faces, the one at the top represents the face of Buddha, and the other 10 around the head represent benevolence, compassion, laughter, wrath, etc., symbolic of the range of human feeling. The Eleven-Faced Kannon has been popularly worshiped since the Nara period (646–794). ⇨ KANNON (BOSATSU)

〖注〗 Bodhisattva 菩薩. the Deity of Mercy 観音. deity 神, 神のような人 [もの]. benevolence 慈悲. compassion 情. wrath 怒り.

jūjutsu 柔術 lit. the art of gentleness. the weaponless art of self-defense, one of the traditional martial arts. It is said to have developed in medieval times as a combination of *sumō* wrestling and Chinese unarmed combat. Originally it was employed in battle by warriors as a means of felling an enemy even without a weapon. After the establishment of a feudal system in the Edo period (1603–1868) following a long period of war, it developed into a martial art of self-defense and mental training with the emergence of schools teaching systematized techniques under the influence of Zen Buddhism. Unlike other martial arts, it prevailed not only in the samurai class but also among commoners. After the Meiji Restoration (1868) it was modified into the popular sport of judo. The basic idea in self-defense is to make use of the enemy's strength and weight with a throw (*nage-*), strangle hold (shime-), kick (*keri-*), pin-down (*osae-*), joint lock (*kansetsu-*), thrust (*tsuki-*) or hit (*uchi-*) technique (*waza*). ⇨ JŪDŌ, ZEN[1], ZENSHŪ

〖注〗 martial art 武芸, 格闘技. unarmed combat 素手の戦い. fell 打ち倒す. feudal system 封建制度. throw 投げ(技). strangle hold 締め(技). kick 蹴り(技). pin-down 抑え(技). joint lock 関節(技). thrust 突き(技). hit 打ち(技).

juku 塾 a school for private tutoring after regular school hours. There are two types of such schools: one for learning arts such as the piano, calligraphy, etc., and the other, cram schools, (also called *gakushū-juku*) for extra studies with the aim of passing entrance examinations for higher schools of learning. It is estimated that over half of elementary and secondary school students are enrolled in *juku*, the latter particularly in cram schools. Cram schools for college examination preparation are more commonly known as *yobikō* (lit. preparatory school); they also offer full-time courses for young people making a second or third try for the college of their choice. Most of the cram schools concentrate on rote memorization and techniques in taking exams rather than academic education per se. ⇨ RŌNIN, YOBIKŌ

〖注〗 cram 詰めこみ. calligraphy 書道. enroll 登録する, (学校, 団体などに)入れる. rote memorization 機械的記憶, 暗記. per se ＝itself

Jukyō 儒教 Confucianism; ethical teachings developed by Confucius (551–479 B.C.) in China and followed by his disciples to maintain social order and consolidate political power. With no god or worship services, Confucianism is often considered a philosophy rather than a religion. The teachings are related in *Gokyō* (the Five Books) compiled by Confucius, and in *Shisho* (the Four Books) written by his disciples. The virtues emphasized are benevolence, righteousness, propriety, wisdom and faithfulness. The five basic human relationships are prescribed as loyalty between ruler and subject, affection between father and son, distinction between husband and wife, order between elder and younger, and sincerity between friends. Confucian concepts entered Japan around the sixth century and contributed to the consolidation of central imperial power but, with the spread of Buddhism, they did not come into prominence until the 17th century. The Tokugawa shogunate (1603-1868) utilized Confucianism to form an orderly feudal society by blending it with the indigenous samurai code of ethics. Thus, Confucian concepts dominated social behavior, and still strongly influences Japanese society and human relations. ⇨ GORIN

〔注〕 ethical 倫理上の. Confucius 孔子. disciple 弟子. the Five Books 五経. the Four Books 四書. benevolence, righteousness, propriety, wisdom and faithfulness 仁, 義, 礼, 智, 信. the five basic human relationships 五倫の道(君臣の義, 父子の親, 夫婦の別, 長幼の序, 朋友の信). indigenous 土着の, 固有の.

jūnihitoe 十二単衣 lit. a twelve-layered costume. a ceremonial costume for a court lady in the Heian period (794-1185). Today, imperial princesses wear it at their weddings. It consists of 12 unlined robes worn one over the other. The beauty of the complex effect at the collar and sleeve openings is emphasized.

〔注〕 unlined 裏地のついていない. sleeve opening 袖口.

jūnishi 十二支 the 12 signs of the Oriental zodiac; one of the two calendar cycles based on the Chinese *I Ching* (The Book of Changes). This cycle of 12 signs consists of nine beasts, two reptiles and one fowl. They fall in the order of *ne* (rat), *ushi* (ox), *tora* (tiger), *u* (hare), *tatsu* (dragon), *mi* (snake), *uma* (horse), *hitsuji* (sheep), *saru* (monkey), *tori* (cock), *inu* (dog) and *i* (boar). It takes 12 years to complete a cycle. These animals are used in referring to a particular year, very popular even today; formerly they were also used for indicating directions and hours of the day. As in the West, personalities of people are said to have much to do with the zodiac sign under which they were born. ⇨ ETO, JIKKAN-JŪNISHI

〔注〕 zodiac 十二宮, 十二獣. *I Ching* (The Book of Changes) 易経(古代中国五経の一つ). boar いのしし.

Jurōjin 寿老人 the God of Longevity, one of the Seven Deities of Good Luck. He is represented as a very old man with a long huge bald head, wearing a long, full beard. He holds a flat fan in one hand and a holy cane with a rolled scroll attached to the top. A prescription for longevity is said to be written on this scroll. He is usually accompanied by a stag. Jurōjin is often confused with

Fukurokuju due to their similar appearance, though they have different origins; the former was derived from a man of the Sung dynasty (960-1279) of China while the latter is said to have been the incarnation of a star in Chinese legend. ⇨ FUKUROKUJU, SHICHI-FUKUJIN

〖注〗 longevity 長寿. the Seven Deities of Good Luck 七福神. rolled scroll 巻き軸. prescription 処方箋. stag 雄鹿. the Sung dynasty 宋朝. incarnation 化身.

jūryō 十両 the second highest division in professional *sumō*, formally called *jūmaime*. This division, ranking below *makuuchi* and above *makushita,* is limited to not more than 26 wrestlers. The wrestlers are divided into east and west camps, and are ranked from one down to about 13 with the east wrestler positioned higher than the west's counterpart of the same rank. Wrestlers of the *makuuchi* and *jūryō* divisions are collectively called *sekitori*. ⇨ MAKUUCHI, ŌZUMŌ, SEKITORI, SUMŌ

jūshi 従枝 a subordinate branch [stem] in a flower arrangement; supplementary flowers or branches added to the main branches. These are cut shorter than the main branches and any number can be added to complete the arrangement. Yet, the effect of open space between the branches should be taken into consideration. This term is used in the Sōgetsu school. Called *ashirai* in the Ikenobō school and *chūkanshi* in the Ohara school. ⇨ IKEBANA, SHUSHI

〖注〗 subordinate 付随的な. flower arrangement 生け花. supplementary 追加の. main stem 主枝.

Jūshichijō no Kenpō 十七条の憲法 the 17-article constitution; the Constitution of the 17 Ariticles; Japan's first written code of laws, promulgated by Prince Shōtoku (574-622) in 604, when he was regent. The 17 articles are actually moral teachings based on Buddhism and Confucianism. The teachings emphasize: the value of harmony, respect for the three treasures (Buddha, the law and the priesthood), loyalty to imperial authority, good human relations, the responsibilities of ministers and officials, etc. ⇨ BUK-KYŌ, JUKYŌ

〖注〗 article 条項. code 法典. promulgate 発布する、施行する. regent 摂政. Confucianism 儒教. priesthood 僧職、仏の道. loyalty 忠義.

jūyō-bunkazai 重要文化財 important cultural properties; tangible cultural properties, designated as important by the government.

They are officially protected under the Cultural Properties Protection Law promulgated in 1950.   The categories include buildings, sculptures, paintings, archaeological articles, objects of academic value, etc.   Among the Important Cultural Properties, rare ones of especially important cultural significance are designated as national treasures (*kokuhō*).   ⇨ BUNKAZAI, JŪYŌMUKEI-BUNKAZAI, KOKUHŌ, MUKEI-BUNKAZAI

〖注〗 property 財産, 資産.   tangible 感知できる, 有形の.   the Cultural Properties Protection Law「文化財保護法」.   promulgate 公布する, 発布する, 施行する.   sculpture 彫刻.   archaeological article 考古学的発掘物.

jūyōmukei-bunkazai 重要無形文化財   important intangible cultural properties; intangible properties of traditional and artistic value designated as especially important by the government.   The 65 general categories of time-honored arts and crafts include pottery, dyeing, lacquer ware, textile-weaving, sword-forging, doll-making, etc., as well as musical and theatrical arts.   Individuals who preserve the spirit and skills of these arts and crafts are officially designated as bearers of important intangible cultural properties, commonly called living national treasures (*ningen-kokuhō*).   The idea of broadening the scope of preservation of cultural properties was proposed by General Douglas MacArthur shortly after World War II, resulting in the Cultural Properties Protection Law promulgated in 1950.   ⇨ BUNKAZAI, JŪYŌ-BUNKAZAI, KOKUHŌ, MUKEI-BUNKAZAI, NINGEN-KOKUHŌ

〖注〗 intangible 無形の, 触れられない.   property 財産, 資産.   time-honored 伝統的な, 由緒ある.   arts and crafts 美術工芸.   pottery 陶磁器.   dyeing 染色.   textile-weaving 織物.   sword-forging 刀の鋳造.   theatrical arts 舞台芸術.   bearer 保持者.   Cultural Properties Protection Law「文化財保護法」.   promulgate 発布する, 施行する.

jūzume 重詰め   foods packed in a lacquered box; a collection of foods artistically arranged in a square lacquered box.   For New Year celebrations, many kinds of foods are arranged in four lacquered boxes placed in tiers and served with Japanese rice wine.   ⇨ OSECHI-RYŌRI

〖注〗 lacquered box 漆器の箱.   tier 段.   Japanese rice wine 日本酒.

K

kabayaki 蒲焼 barbecued fish; fish broiled over a charcoal fire (or a gas fire) after being dipped in sweetened barbecue soy sauce. Eel *kabayaki* is most popular. ⇨ UNAGI NO KABAYAKI

〖注〗 soy sauce 醬油. eel 鰻.

kabuki 歌舞伎 Kabuki drama; a highly stylized traditional play with singing and dancing. Kabuki was developed by a women dancer, Izumo no Okuni, in the 17th century. Since the Tokugawa shogunate (1603-1868) prohibited women from acting in public, the Kabuki drama has been performed exclusively by males, including female roles. The music for Kabuki employs a variety of singing and *shamisen* styles as well as combining percussive and flute music adapted from the Noh and folk theater. Kabuki dancing is also influenced by Noh and a variety of folk performance styles. ⇨ JIDAIMONO, KIZEWAMONO, SEWAMONO, SHAMISEN

〖注〗 stylized 様式化された. percussive 打楽器の. folk performance 民俗芸能.

kabuki-jūhachiban 歌舞伎十八番 the 18 best plays of Kabuki. Eighteen plays which proved most successful on the Edo stage have been selected from the repertoire of the great actor Ichikawa Danjūrō I (1660-1704) and his successors. Of these 18 pieces, only about 10 are still performed, seven of which are very popular even today—*Sukeroku* (The Love of Sukeroku), *Kanjinchō* (The Faithful Retainers), *Shibaraku* (Wait a Minute), *Yanone* (The Arrowhead), *Kenuki* (Hair Tweezers), *Narukami* (Thunder God) and *Kamahige* (Shaving with a Large Sickle). ⇨ KABUKI

〖注〗 repertoire レパートリー, 上演種目. Ichikawa Danjūrō I 初代市川団十郎. piece (芸術上の)作品. retainer 家臣. sickle かま. 歌舞伎十八番：「助六」,「勧進帳」,「暫」,「矢の根」,「毛抜」,「鳴神」,「鎌髭」等.

Kachi-kachi Yama かちかち山 *Raccoon Dog on Mount Kachi-kachi*; a tale of a raccoon dog and a rabbit, one of Japan's five most famous folk tales. There was a raccoon dog (*tanuki*) troubling an old man and woman, and it finally killed the old man. A rabbit, to avenge the old man's death, tricked the raccoon dog into carrying firewood on its back in the mountains. It then struck a flintstone, making the sound *kachi-kachi* (click-clack), thus setting the wood afire and burning the raccoon dog's back. And then on another occasion, the rabbit lured the raccoon dog into a boat made of mud, which began to sink at sea, after which the raccoon dog pledged never to harass people again. The original story appeared in the Muromachi period (1336–1568).

〖注〗 raccoon dog 狸. flintstone 火打ち石. lure さそう. harass 悩ます.

kachō 家長 a household head; a patriarch; the person of authority in the traditional Japanese household. In the system of the extended family, the male successor usually took over this position. The authority of the head was once regarded as absolute, extending over the conduct and ideas of the entire household.

〖注〗 household 家族, 所帯. patriarch 家父長, 長老. extended family 大家族.

kadō 華道 floral art; the way of flower arrangement. The same as *ikebana*, but *kadō* has more philosophical and spiritual connotations. It focuses on the way to pursue and develop mental composure rather than technique. ⇨ IKEBANA

〖注〗 flower arrangement 生け花. connotation 含蓄. mental composure 精神の平静.

kadomatsu 門松 lit. a gate pine. a New Year decoration set up on both sides of the entrance to a house or building. Originally it was made only of pine branches. Later on, a combination of pine branches, bamboo stalks and plum-tree twigs, which symbolize longevity, constancy and purity respectively, came into use. Nowadays, one of these or a combination of two or of all three is used. ⇨ GANJITSU, SANGANICHI, SHŌ-CHIKU-BAI

〖注〗 bamboo stalk 竹の茎. plum-tree twig 梅の小枝. longevity 長寿. constancy 忠実, 貞節.

kagami-biraki 鏡開き lit. the opening of a mirror. the cutting or breaking of the New Year's rice cake, an annual event held on January 11. It has been customary on this day to cut or break mirror (*kagami*)-shaped rice cakes which have been used as offerings to Shinto gods at homes or at shrines, and then to eat them. The word *biraki* (open) is used instead of *wari* (break) to avoid the phrase *kagami-wari* (mirror-breaking), a taboo. A grandiose ceremony of *kagami-biraki* is held at the Nippon Budōkan Hall, Tokyo, along with demonstrations of traditional Japanese martial arts such as judo, karate, *kendō* (swordsmanship), etc. ⇨ KAGAMI-MOCHI

〖注〗 offering お供え. martial art 武芸.

kagamiita 鏡板 lit. a mirror board. the panels of the backdrop of the Noh stage upon which an old dignified pine tree is painted. All Noh plays are performed in front of this single backdrop, the main purpose of which is to create the resounding effect of chanting and music. ⇨ NŌ, NŌBUTAI

〖注〗 backdrop 舞台正面の背景, (一般に)背景. dignified 荘重な.

kagami-mochi 鏡餅 mirror-shaped rice cakes; a pair of round rice cakes offered to the gods on New Year's Day. The two cakes are slightly different in size, and stacked one upon the other, and often decorated with auspicious symbols such as a sheet of kelp, a citron (*daidai*), sacred straw (*shimenawa*), etc. Symbolic of seats for gods of the year to sit on, they are placed in the alcove of the main room of the house, or on the household altar or shelves set up especially for this purpose. The cakes come in various sizes. ⇨ MOCHI, SHIME(NAWA)-KAZARI

〖注〗 auspicious symbol めでたい印. kelp 昆布. citron 柑橘類(ここでは橙). sacred straw しめ縄. household altar 家庭内の祭壇.

kagaminoma 鏡の間 lit. a mirror room. called the "green room" in English. It is a room where Noh actors wait, contemplating their appearance and making a final check on their costume in front of a large mirror, until they are ready to go on stage. ⇨ NŌ, NŌBUTAI

〖注〗 contemplate 黙想する.

Kaga-yūzen 加賀友禅 Kaga painted silk fabric; a silk fabric dyed in the Yūzen fashion, developed at Kanazawa in Kaga Province, presently Ishikawa Prefecture. Originating with Miyazaki Yūzen-sai (?1680-?1710) in Kyoto in the Edo period (1603-1868), Yūzen dyeing also developed in Kaga a short while later, basically with the same techniques but slightly different in terms of design and coloring. Compared with *Kyoto-yūzen*, *Kaga-yūzen* uses more abstract designs and brighter colors with shadings, including vermilion, green, purple, etc. ⇨ YŪZEN

〖注〗 fabric 織物. shadings ぼかし. vermilion 朱.

kagura 神楽 dance and music for the Shinto gods; sacred dances and songs of ancient origin, still performed at Shinto shrines by shrine maidens and/or priests for a variety of festivals and Shinto rituals, from rural villages to the Imperial Court. It is accompanied by the music of drums, flutes, zithers, etc. According to legend, *kagura* originated when the Goddess Ame no Uzume no Mikoto danced merrily in order to lure the Sun Goddess, Amaterasu Ōmikami, from a cave where she was hiding. ⇨ JINJA, KAGURADEN, MIKO

〚注〛 shrine maiden 巫女. Shinto ritual 神社の儀式. accompany 伴う，伴奏する. flute 尺八. zither ツィター（琴に似た弦楽器）. lure 引き寄せる，誘惑する. cave 洞窟（天の岩戸）.

kaguraden〔kaguradō〕神楽殿〔神楽堂〕 a sacred stage in the precincts of a shrine for Shinto music and dance. On special occasions, several young shrine maidens perform a sacred dance of ancient origin on this stage. ⇨ JINJA, KAGURA, MIKO

〚注〛 precincts 境内. shrine maiden 巫女.

Kaguya Hime かぐや姫 Shining Princess; a character in a Japanese folk tale, who was born from a bamboo stem. An old bamboo cutter found a radiant little girl, about 10 centimeters tall, in the joint of a bamboo stem. She grew up to be a most beautiful maiden of ordinary size, to whom many young men proposed marriage. Five selected from among them were assigned by her to different tasks, but none succeeded. She explained to her foster parents that she was from heaven, and on a night of the full moon, a flying carriage came and took her back to heaven. This *Taketori Monogatari* (The Tale of the Bamboo Cutter) was written in the Heian period (794-1185, author unknown). Many elements from different sources of folklore are incorporated into it.

〚注〛 folk tale 民話. the joint of a bamboo stem 竹の節. assign 課す. carriage 馬車. folklore 民話（集合的）. incorporate 合併する，混ぜる.

kaimyō 戒名 lit. a name for taking Buddhist commandments. a posthumous Buddhist name; a name given to a deceased person by a family's Buddhist priest. It consists of several Chinese characters, suggestive of the deceased's personality and virtues, and is written on his memorial tablet to be placed in the family Buddhist altar and engraved on his tombstone (though tombstones are often engraved with secular names today). Originally, the *kaimyō* was for those who entered the priesthood, the custom starting around the 14th century in Zen Buddhism. In the Edo period (1603-1868) receiving a *kaimyō* had already become very common even among laymen in almost all sects of Buddhism. ⇨ BUKKYŌ, BUTSUDAN, IHAI

〖注〗 commandment 戒律. posthumous 死後の. Chinese character 漢字. memorial tablet 位牌. secular name 俗名. layman 俗人.

kaiseki 懐石 lit. with a stone in the pocket. a simple but sophisticated meal served before a very formal tea ceremony in which a thick pasty tea (*koicha*) is served as well as thin foamy tea (*usucha*). The term *kaiseki* derives from the small heated stone that Zen monks held against their empty stomachs during long hours of fasting when meditating. It then became a modest treat served to a guest in preparation for a prolonged tea ceremony. It consists of a bowl of soup and three dishes—clear soup to rinse the chopsticks and small bits of seafood and vegetables served on a wooden plate, accompanied by rice wine. The food and dishes are selected so as to be expressive of the season. The food is served and eaten piece by piece according to meticulously prescribed rules. It is proper manners not to leave any food uneaten. Nowadays, called *kaiseki-ryōri*, this type of cuisine minus the tea ceremony is available at certain restaurants. ⇨ CHANOYU, KOICHA, USUCHA

〖注〗 sophisticated 洗練された、凝った. fast 断食する. meditate 瞑想する、座禅する. meticulously 細かいところに気をつかって. prescribe 規定する. cuisine 料理.

kaiseki-ryōri 会席料理 banquet cuisine; Japanese-style party dishes served with saké (rice wine) when entertaining guests. Starting off with appetizers, several different kinds of courses, each arranged in an artistic way, are served, usually on an individual lacquered tray along with saké. Rice, soup and pickles are served at the end of the courses. This banquet cuisine is different from a simple meal served at a formal tea ceremony, also pronounced *kaiseki-ryōri*. ⇨ KAISEKI

〖注〗 cuisine 料理. start off 着手する、始める. appetizer 食欲をそそるもの、前菜. course 料理のコース(dinnerのひと皿ひと皿をいう). lacquered tray 漆塗りの盆.

kaishi 懐紙 lit. pocket paper. a set of sheets of white, napkin-like paper. It is made of traditional Japanese paper, and is used to place sweets on and to wipe the tea bowl in the tea ceremony. Guests are expected to bring their own *kaishi* to the tea ceremony.

It is thicker than pocket tissue, and is carried in a special cloth bag.
〖注〗 tea ceremony 茶道、茶の湯． cloth bag 布の袋(懐紙入れ)．

kaisho 楷書 the print style of writing letters and characters; the most formal among the three styles of writing Japanese, the other two being *gyōsho* (semi-cursive style) and *sōsho* (cursive style). *Kaisho* requires accurateness of every line, angle and dot. This term refers in particular to calligraphy. ⇨ GYŌSHO, SHODŌ, SŌSHO
〖注〗 character 文字． calligraphy 書道．

kaiyūshiki-teien 回遊式庭園 a landscape garden designed for strolling through; a landscape garden laid out to be viewed from various vantage points while strolling along the garden paths. Gardens of this type reached their highest degree of development in the Edo period (1603-1868) and were mostly laid out for the residences of feudal lords. ⇨ NIHON-SANKŌEN, NIHON-TEIEN
〖注〗 landscape garden 造景の庭、日本庭園． vantage point 見晴らしのよい所． feudal lord 大名、藩主．

kakashi 案山子 a scarecrow; a traditional Japanese scarecrow standing on one leg in the rice field. A scarecrow is made of bamboo sticks and rice straw, wearing a straw hat or a towel tied around its head, and is clad in shabby clothes. The style is that of farmers working in the fields of bygone days. A modern type of *kakashi* might be clad in a T-shirt and jeans. When the ears of rice are beginning to ripen to a golden color, it serves to keep birds, usually sparrows, away.
〖注〗 be clad in ~を着ている． shabby みすぼらしい． bygone days 昔、過ぎ去った日々．

kakebuton 掛け布団 a covering *futon*; a thick coverlet stuffed with cotton. It is placed over the body, sometimes together with a blanket. A traditional *kakebuton* is not quilted but simply stitched here and there to keep the cotton in place. It is covered with a fitted cover sheet (*futon-kabā*) which is generally white, although they are sometimes found in other colors. ⇨ FUTON, SHIKIBUTON
〖注〗 coverlet 掛けるもの． stuff 詰める．

kakei [kakehi] 筧 [懸け樋] a water spout; a pipe made of half-cut bamboo, placed in a Japanese garden. Through the bamboo pipe, water is carried between rocks and foliage, and then falls into a stone water-basin (*tsukubai*) sometimes to sounds created by a bamboo fixture. It is a characteristic feature of one type of tea garden. ⇨ CHATEI, NIHON-TEIEN, TSUKUBAI

〖注〗 spout 樋口, 雨どい口. foliage 樹木の茂り. fixture とりつけたもの.

kakejiku 掛け軸　a hanging scroll; a long vertical hanging scroll with a painting or calligraphy (or both) on silk or paper. It is usually displayed on the wall of the alcove in a Japanese-style guest room. The painting or calligraphy is selected to suit the season or occasion. It is so called because it has *jiku* (an axis or roller) on the lower end and on the upper end, enabling it to be rolled up when not in use. Also called *kakemono* (a hanging thing). ⇨ KAKE-MONO, TOKONOMA

〖注〗 calligraphy 書道. alcove 床の間. axis 軸.

kakekotoba 掛け詞　a paronomasia; a kind of pun; the use of a word in such a way as to suggest two or more different meanings, found particularly in Japanese short verses. The Japanese language contains countless homophones. Taking advantage of this, Japanese short verses depend largely on the effect of *katekotoba*, which compress many images and subtle shadings with a minimum of expression. For example, the use of the word *matsu*, meaning "pine tree," can also suggest the feeling of *matsu*, "to wait," blending the two ideas with a single word. When such use of a word achieves a humorous effect in everyday language, it is also called *share*. ⇨ HAIKU, MANZAI, SHARE, TANKA

〖注〗 paronomasia (同音異義語, 類似語による)掛け詞, 地口, しゃれ. pun 地口, 語呂合わせ, 同音異義語の語句によるしゃれ. verse 詩形, 詩の一行. homophone 同音異義語. subtle shadings 微妙な陰影. a minimum of expression 最小限の表現.

kakemono 掛け物　a hanging scroll; a scroll made of silk or paper with a roller at the top and at the bottom, which is hung on the wall in an alcove. The painting or calligraphy on the scroll is generally chosen to suit the season or occasion. ⇨ KAKEJIKU, TOKONOMA

〖注〗 scroll 巻物, 巻軸. alcove 壁の一部をへこませた小室, 床の間. calligraphy 書道.

kake-soba 掛け蕎麦　buckwheat noodles in soup; a bowl of buckwheat noodles in a fish broth seasoned with soy sauce, served hot. Minced green onions and red pepper are used as condiments. ⇨ SOBA

〖注〗 buckwheat noodle 蕎麦. fish broth 魚の煮出し汁, だし. season 味をつける. soy sauce 醬油. minced 細かく刻んだ. minced green onions さらしねぎ. condiment 薬味.

kaki 花器　a flower container; the general term for a flower container—a vase, basin, basket, etc. A Japanese flower arrangement involves a harmonic combination of flowers with the container that holds them. The container represents the earth, and flowers should be arranged as if they sprang from the earth and were still growing. ⇨ HANAIRE, IKEBANA

〖注〗 basin 水盤. flower arrangement 生け花.

Kakiemon(-Imari) 柿右衛門（伊万里） Kakiemon porcelain ware; porcelain ware with enameled pictures, originally developed by Sakaida Kakiemon (1596-1666). He succeeded in applying enamel coloring to porcelain ware for the first time in Japan, in the 17th century at Arita, Kyūshū. As the name *Kakiemon*, given him by the local feudal lord, suggests, his basic color was persimmon (*kaki*); in addition, yellow, green, purple and blue were also used. Typically, flowers and birds are arranged on a milky white body with the greater part the space left white. This arrangement, along with the use of sharp brush lines, reflects the scheme of a traditional Japanese painting drawn on white paper. ⇨ AKAE, ARITA-YAKI, IMARI-YAKI

〖注〗 pocelain ware 磁器. feudal lord 大名. persimmon 柿. scheme 配置, 構成.

kakure-Kirishitan 隠れキリシタン hidden Christians; those who adhered to the Christian faith in secret during the period of official prohibition of Christianity (mid-17th century-1873). In an attempt to eliminate Christians after the Shimabara Uprising (1637-38) of Christians and farmers, the Tokugawa shogunate (1603-1868) set up the Inquiry Office in 1640 where every man was required to register his religion. Christians were forced to undergo apostasy to avoid being persecuted. This practice followed the imposition of national seclusion (1639), and appeared to have put an end to the Christian religion in Japan. However, many Christians survived in secret, remaining true to their faith in remote places in western Japan. Some disguised themselves as Buddhists by keeping an image of the Virgin Mary which looked like the Bodhisattva Kannon (Maria Kannon), or by concealing a crucifix in a Buddhist altar. After the prohibition was lifted in 1873, some "hidden Christians" joined new Catholic churches while others continued with their own peculiar worship practices. ⇨ KIRISHITAN, SAKOKU(-SEISAKU), SHIMABARA NO RAN, TOKUGAWA-BAKUFU

〖注〗 the Shimabara Uprising 島原の乱. the Inquiry Office 宗門改役. apostasy 背信, 改宗. the national seclusion 鎖国. the image of the Virgin Mary 聖マリア像. the Bodhisattva Kannon 観音菩薩. crucifix 十字架. Buddhist altar 仏壇. lift とり除く, 解く.

kama 釜 a teakettle; an iron teakettle used to boil water for the tea ceremony. According to Sen no Rikyū (1521-91), the great tea master of the 16th century, it is the most important utensil in making tea. A larger kettle is heated on an inset hearth in winter, while a smaller-sized one is used with a portable brazier in summer. ⇨ CHANOYU, FURO, RO

〖注〗 tea ceremony 茶の湯. inset hearth はめこんだ炉. portable brazier 持ち運びのできる火鉢, 風炉.

kamaboko 蒲鉾 a fish-paste cake; a steamed fish-paste cake in the shape of a half-cylinder. Fish paste placed on a piece of wood is steamed, and sometimes also slightly roasted to get a burned brownish effect on top. The cake is cut into thin slices when served. Often the top of *kamaboko* is dyed red, and the combination of red and white is regarded as a felicitous one.

〖注〗 fish-paste 魚のすりみ. half-cylinder 半円筒型. felicitous 適切な, めでたい.

kamakura かまくら the snow-hut festival; an annual event in which snow huts are built in Yokote, Akita Prefecture, February 15-17 (the New Year period in the lunar calendar). In this district of heavy snowfall, children build igloo-type huts of snow containing a Shinto altar dedicated to the god of water. By the light of candles on the altar, they spend evenings chatting and eating around a warm brazier. Visitors, both children and adults, are treated with rice cakes and a hot saké-flavored sweet drink called *amazake*. The festival is said to have originally begun as an occasion to pray to the god of water for a good harvest in the coming year. ⇨ AMAZAKE, HIBACHI, KAMIDANA

〖注〗 the lunar calendar 陰暦. igloo イグルー(雪で作った半円形のエスキモーの家). Shrine altar 神棚. brazier 火鉢.

Kamakura-bakufu 鎌倉幕府 the Kamakura shogunate (1185 or 1192-1336); the government of the Kamakura shogun, with its headquarters in Kamakura, south of Tokyo. It was the first military government, established by Minamoto Yoritomo (1147-99) in 1192 when the title of highest ranking general (*seii-taishōgun*) was conferred upon him after the fall of the Taira clan.

He distributed land confiscated from the Taira clan to his vassals, and secured loyalty in return with the enforcement of the samurai code of ethics and behavior. After Yoritomo's death, his wife's family, the Hōjōs, took over the administration, acting as regents under puppet shogun until they were overthrown in 1333. Yoritomo was followed by eight puppet shoguns—two more from the Minamotos, two from the Fujiwaras and four from imperial relatives. ⇨ BAKUFU, SEII-TAISHŌGUN, SHIKKEN, SHŌGUN

〖注〗 headquarters 本拠. confer 授ける. confiscate 没収する. vassal 家臣, 領臣. loyalty 忠誠. the samurai code of ethics and behavior「武家諸法度」. regent 摂政. puppet shogun 傀儡将軍.

Kamakura-gozan 鎌倉五山 the five principle temples of the Rinzai sect of Zen Buddhism, located in Kamakura. They are the temples of Kenchōji, Enkakuji, Jufukuji, Jōchiji and Jōmyōji. They were designated by the shogun Ashikaga Yoshimitsu (1358-1408), together with the Hōjō regents, in the Muromachi period (1336-1568). ⇨ GOZAN, KYŌTO-GOZAN

〖注〗 the Rinzai sect 臨済宗. regent 摂政. 鎌倉五山：建長寺, 円覚寺, 寿福寺, 浄智寺, 浄妙寺.

Kamakura-jidai 鎌倉時代 the Kamakura period (1185-1336); the period in which the Kamakura shogunate government controlled the country. With the fall of the Taira clan, Minamoto Yoritomo (1147-99) established his shogunate government in Kamakura in 1192. This marked the start of the age of domination of the country by the samurai class. After his death, power was seized by the Hōjōs, his wife's relatives, who acted as regents. The reign of the Hōjōs saw the attempted Mongolian invasions of 1274 and 1281 and the total destruction of the enemy's fleet both times, thanks to timely tempests which have been called "winds sent by gods" (*kamikaze*). This age was followed by a period of struggle between imperial loyalists and the Ashikaga clan, resulting in victory by the latter. ⇨ GENKŌ, KAMAKURA-BAKUFU, KAMIKAZE

〖注〗 the Kamakura shogunate government 鎌倉幕府. domination 支配, 統治. regent 摂政. the Mongolian invasion 蒙古襲来. total destruction 全滅. fleet 艦隊. imperial loyalists 皇室に忠誠をつくす人達, 官軍.

kamameshi 釜飯 rice in a small clay pot; boiled rice in an individual pot with a wooden lid. The rice is cooked in fish broth seasoned with soy sauce, and mixed with small pieces of chicken or seafoods (shrimp, crab, scallop, etc.), mushroom, bamboo shoots and some other vegetables.　Some of the ingredients may be placed on the top.

〖注〗 fish broth 魚の煮出し汁，だし．　season 味をつける．　soy sauce 醬油．
scallop 帆立貝．　bamboo shoot 筍．　ingredient 成分，(料理の)材料．

kamidana 神棚　a household shrine; the shelf the household Shinto shrine is placed on.　On this shelf, a miniature model of a Shinto shrine, made of plain cypress wood, is placed in which talismans from shrines are enshrined.　Offerings of food, saké, twigs of *sakaki* tree, etc. are placed in front of this miniature shrine.

〖注〗 household 家族(の)．　plain cypress wood 白木の檜．　talisman お守り，
護符．　enshrine 祀る．　offering お供え．　twig 小枝．

kamikaze 神風　a divine wind; winds sent by the gods to save the country from the Mongolian threat in the 13th century.　During the regency of Hōjō Tokimune (1251-84), a large Mongolian force, armed with catapults and cannons, attempted to invade northern Kyūshū in 1274 and 1281.　The invasions were thwarted by typhoons which totally destroyed the Mongolian fleets both times.　The Japanese thus believed the typhoons were sent by the gods.　This *kamikaze* idea exerted a great influence on Japanese myth, spreading the belief that Japan was a country especially protected by the gods.　World War II saw the emergence of *kamikaze* suicide corps (*kamikaze-tokkōtai*).　⇨ GENKŌ, KAMAKURA-JIDAI

〖注〗 the Mongolian threat 蒙古襲来．　regency 摂政(職)．　catapult 弩砲．
cannon 大砲．　thwart 裏をかく，妨げる．　fleet 艦隊．

kamishibai 紙芝居　lit. a paper stage. a picture-card story show.　It used to be a very popular form of entertainment for children before the advent of television.　At the sound of wooden clappers made by an entertainer, children would gather at a street corner and pay a small fee for a lollipop or the like as a treat.　The showman would narrate a story dramatically, while changing scenes one by one, using a set of picture cards in a wooden-frame miniature stage, the size of a standard television screen.

〖注〗 wooden clapper 拍子木．　lollipop 棒つきキャンディ．　wooden-frame
miniature stage 木の枠の超小型ステージ．

kamishimo 裃　feudal ceremonial costume; a suit consisting of a sleeveless jacket and loose-legged trousers (or a pleated skirt) made of the same material.　Appearing in the Muromachi period (1336-1568), it was adopted as the formal costume for samurai in the Edo period (1603-1868).　Gradually, it came to be worn by commoners as well, but only for ceremonial occasions. The sleeveless jacket has wide, square shoulders, with a family crest on the back and two on the front. Long trailing trousers were reserved for high-ranking samurai. ⇨ HAKAMA, KAMON

〖注〗 feudal 封建時代の. family crest 家紋. trailing 長く尾を引いた.

kamiza 上座 a head seat; the seat of honor; the highest-ranking position in a room. In a traditional Japanese guest room, it is situated in front of the *tokonoma* (alcove) where a hanging scroll and an ornamant or flowers are displayed. The lowest-ranking seat is nearest the entrance, and farthest from the *tokonoma*. This order is observed on formal occasions. Customarily, visitors tend to avoid taking this seat of honor unless it is strongly offered. ⇨ SHIMOZA, TOKONOMA, ZASHIKI

〖注〗 alcove 床の間. hanging scroll 掛け軸.

kamon 家紋 family crest; hereditary insignia for a family or business firm. The motif of Japanese crests is generally a plant, a bird, a fan, a Chinese character, etc., most commonly contained in a circle. The imperial family's is composed of a chrysanthemum with 16 petals, and the Tokugawa family's the hollyhock. In feudal times, nobles and warriors were permitted to have crests, and upon the Meiji Restoration (around 1868) all Japanese families were encouraged to have one. The crest is put on formal kimono, lanterns, *noren* (business curtain), etc. ⇨ NOREN

〖注〗 crest 紋章. insignia 記章, しるし. motif 意匠. Chinese character 漢字. chrysanthemum with 16 petals 16花弁の菊. hollyhock 葵. feudal times 封建時代. the Meiji Restoration 明治維新.

kan 貫 a traditional unit for measuring weight. One *kan* is 1,000 *monme*, about 3.75 kilograms. In medieval times the *kan* was also a monetary unit equivalent to 1,000 *mon* (1,000 silver coins), 960 *mon* in the Edo period (1603-1868). The monetary *kan* is considered to have become a standard weight. ⇨ MONME, SHAK-KAN-HŌ

〖注〗 medieval times 中世期. monetary unit 貨幣単位.

kana 仮名 the Japanese syllabary; a Japanese system of syllabic writing in the form of characters that stand for clusters of sound. The system consists of 48 letters. Phonetically, each letter represents one or two consonants followed by a vowel with the exception of six letters pronounced *a, i, u, e, o* and *n*. There are two kinds of *kana* syllabary—*katakana* and *hiragana*, the latter being for general use in the present writing system. *Kana* are commonly used in combination with Chinese characters; they are used mainly for functional words and functional parts of the language while Chinese characters are used mainly for content words and the stem part of a word. The *kana* system is of native origin (although derived from Chinese characters) and dates from the eighth or ninth century. ⇨ HIRAGANA, KANJI, KATAKANA

〖注〗 syllabary 音節文字(表)、字音表． character 文字、記号． cluster 群． Chinese character 漢字． functional word 機能語． content word 内容語． the stem part of a word 語幹．

kanbun 漢文 Chinese readings; reading classical Chinese literature; Chinese prose and verse to be read in the particular Japanese way. *Kanbun* is not the Chinese language as it is spoken in China, but written Chinese to be read with the Japanese reading, the word order following Japanese syntax with specific Japanese particles (a part of speech, functioning similar to prepositions) supplemented, and with the Japanese sound system. High schools and colleges may offer a course of *kanbun*, whose materials are selected from well-known classical Chinese works of literature.

〖注〗 prose 散文． verse 韻文． syntax 構文． specific Japanese particles てにをは． part of speech 品詞．

kanbutsue 灌仏会 the Buddhist service held for Gautama Sakyamuni Buddha's birthday (April 8); the ceremony in which sweet tea is poured over a small statue of Sakyamuni, observed at Buddhist temples in commemoration of his birth. This ceremony is said to have begun with perfume used instead of sweet tea in the Nara period (646–794). The small standing statue placed in a miniature temple represents Sakyamuni at his birth, with his right hand pointing to heaven and his left hand to earth. This celebration is commonly known as the "Flower Festival" (*Hana Matsuri*), because cherry blossoms are in bloom around this day and the miniature temple is generally decorated with their blossoms. ⇨ BUKKYŌ, HANA MATSURI

〖注〗 Buddhist service 仏教の儀式、法要． statue 彫像． in commemoration of ～ ～を記念して．

kanga 漢画 lit. paintings of the Western Han dynasty (206 B.C.–A.D. 8); Chinese-style paintings; the generic term for any Chinese-style paintings as opposed to Japanese-style paintings; specifically, Japanese paintings in Chinese style or of Chinese subjects which emerged from around the Muromachi period (1336-1568). The term is often synonymous with *karae*, but this word specifically refers to Chinese-style paintings popular from the Heian (794-1185) to the early Muromachi period. The Kanō school of painting, which flourished from the mid-Muromachi period, has its roots in *kanga*. ⇨ KARAE, YAMATOE

〘注〙 the Western Han dynasty (中国の)前漢王朝.

kangen 管絃[管弦] the orchestral music of Gagaku consisting of wind instruments (*kan*) and string instruments (*gen*). The term Gagaku covers both *kangen* (instrumental music) and Bugaku (dance music). ⇨ BUGAKU, GAGAKU

〘注〙 wind instrument 管楽器. string instrument 弦楽器.

kanji 漢字 Chinese characters; a Japanese system of writing based on characters borrowed or adapted from the Chinese language. Chinese characters are ideographs which stand for objects and ideas. In Japanese they are usually used for writing content words or root elements with other parts supplemented by *kana*. ⇨ KANA

〘注〙 adapt 適合させる. ideograph 表意文字. content word 内容語. root 語幹. supplement 補う.

Kannon (Bosatsu) 観音 (菩薩) Avalokiteshvara (Sanskrit); the Deity of Mercy; the deity of infinite compassion who is believed to deliver people from suffering. Kannon is primarily male or neuter. Very feminine and merciful in form and expression, he is very commonly referred to as a goddess. He is said to manifest himself in 33 different incarnations to save people in 33 different ways to meet their particular needs. There are six representative types of Kannon—Shō, Nyoirin, Fukūkenjaku (or Juntei), Jūichimen, Senju and Batō Kannon (categorization slightly differs according to sect). Famous Kannon statues are Guze Kannon (seventh century) at Hōryūji Temple, Nara, and Senju Kannon (12th century) at Sanjūsangendō Temple, Kyoto. ⇨ BATŌ KANNON, JŪICHIMEN KANNON, SENJU KANNON

〘注〙 deity 神, 神のような人[もの]. infinite compassion 無限な情け. neuter 中性. incarnation 化身. sect 分派, 宗派. Guze Kannon 救世観音. 六観音：聖観音, 如意輪観音, 不空羂索観音(または准胝観音), 十一面観音, 千手観音, 馬頭観音.

Kanō-ha 狩野派 the Kanō school of painting; a school of traditional Japanese painting of Chinese origin, founded by Kanō Masanobu in the middle of the Muromachi period (1336-1568) and which flourished as the mainstream of the art form until the end of the Edo period (1603-1868). Masanobu (1434-1530) was talented in black-and-white painting (*suibokuga*) in the Chinese style; his son Motonobu (1476-1559) incorporated indigenous Japanese styles (*yamatoe*) into the form. Later, Kanō painters added decorative qualities, using gold and other bright colors. Patronized by the shogunate government and the Imperial Court, this school produced a number of distinguished painters including Eitoku (1543-90), Sanraku (1559-1635), Tan'yū (1602-74), etc. Among a variety of works are particularly well-known large-scale screen paingings, such as *Chinese Lions* by Eitoku preserved at the Imperial Household Agency; *Tree Peonies* by Sanraku at Daikakuji Temple, Kyoto; *Tiger* by Tan'yū at Nanzenji Temple, Kyoto, etc. ⇨ SUIBOKUGA, SUMIE, TOSA-HA, YAMATOE

〚注〛 Kanō Masanobu 狩野正信. black-and-white painting 水墨画, 墨絵. Motonobu 元信. incorporate 融合する. indigenous 土着の, 土地特有の. the shogunate government 幕府. Eitoku 永徳. Sanraku 山楽. Tan'yū 探幽. screen painting 屏風絵, 襖絵. *Chinese Lion*「唐獅子図」. the Imperial Household Agency 宮内庁. *Tree Peonies*「牡丹図」. *Tiger*「虎図」.

kanpaku 関白 a regent or a counselor for an emperor; the title for the direct adviser to the emperor and the supervisor of all court officials, first granted in the Heian period (794-1185). Fujiwara Mototsuna (836-91) was the first to receive this title in 880 after serving as *sesshō* (a regent for an underage emperor) for Emperor Yōzei (866-949). Thereafter the Fujiwara family held a monopoly on this position until the Meiji Restoration (1868), though their political power largely declined after the Heian period. Fujiwara Michinaga (966-1027) was the most renowned *kanpaku*, enjoying the utmost in splendor of court life in connection with art and literature, as well as political affairs. Besides the Fujiwaras, Toyotomi Hideyoshi (1536-98) and his son Hidetsugu (1568-95) were the only two to be granted this title. ⇨ SESSHŌ

〚注〛 regent 代理で政務を司どる人. Fujiwara Mototsune 藤原基経. the Meiji Restoration 明治維新. the utmost in splendor of court life 宮廷生活の栄華の極み. Hidetsugu 秀次.

kanpōi 漢方医 a doctor of Chinese-style medicine. He prescribes herb medicines and practices some kinds of traditional Chinese-style treatment such as acupuncture (*hari*), moxibustion (*kyū*), finger-pressure therapy (*shiatsu*), massage (*anma*), etc. ⇨ ANMA,

HARI(-CHIRYŌ), KYŪ, SHIATSU

〖注〗 medicine 医療. prescribe 処方する. acupuncture 鍼. moxibustion 灸. finger-pressure therapy 指圧(療法).

kanpyō 干瓢 dried gourd shavings; long, ribbon-like shavings made from the bottle gourd or calabash (*yūgao*). Bottle gourd pulp is shaved into long strips and dried a day in the sun, or nowadays, in a dryer. Tochigi Prefecture produces about 90 percent of the total output of *kanpyō* and the countryside there used to offer distinctive local scenes of *kanpyō* hanging from bamboo poles. *Kanpyō* is mainly used as an ingredient in *sushi* after being softened in water and boiled in seasoned soy sauce. It also serves as a handy edible string for tying a variety of foods including cabbage rolls. ⇨ SUSHI

〖注〗 gourd 夕顔, 瓢箪など. shaving 削ったもの. bottle gourd 夕顔(=calabash). pulp 果肉. ingredient (調理の)材料. seasoned 味をつけた. edible 食べられる.

kanreki 還暦 lit. the complete cycle of the calendar. the celebration of one's 60th birthday; the 60th anniversary of one's birth, marking one of the special ages of one's life. According to *The Book of Changes* of China, a complete life cycle based on the zodiac calendar spans 60 years. Formerly, the average span of active life was considered to be 60 years, and at this age one was said to enter upon a new phase of life or to return to the beginning, or childhood. There used to be a custom of presenting a person of 60 with a red jacket and red hood, symbolic of childhood, in celebration of this second life. Today, even with the lengthening life span, 60 years marks a turning point in life; many start a second career upon retirement. ⇨ BEIJU, HAKUJU, JIKKAN-JŪNISHI, KIJU

〖注〗 *The Book of Changes* 「易経」. zodiac 十二支. life span 寿命. turning point 曲がり角, 転機.

Kansai chihō 関西地方 the Kansai district; a district in the western part of central Honshū. It roughly encompasses Osaka-Kyoto and surrounding prefectures, as opposed to the Kantō district which comprises several prefectures centering around Tokyo. The Kansai district is not an official division whereas the Kantō district is. From the Kamakura period (1185–1336) until the Meiji Restoration (around 1868), Kansai consisted of Kinai (the five central provinces surrounding Nara and Kyoto), the two provinces of Ōmi and Iga, and 31 provinces covering the San'in, Sanyō, Nankai and

Saikai districts, totaling 38 provinces in all.   ⇨ GOKI(NAI)-SHI-
CHIDŌ, KANTŌ CHIHŌ, KINAI, KUNI
〖注〗 the Meiji Restoration 明治維新.

kanten 寒天   agar-agar; Japanese gelatin made from a kind of
seaweed called *tengusa*.   It is used to mold dishes and sweets in the
same way as gelatin, but unlike gelatin, it does not melt at room
temperature even in summer.
〖注〗 agar-agar 寒天, 天草. seaweed 海藻. mold 型に入れてつくる, 固
める.

Kantō chihō 関東地方   the Kantō region; a region in the eastern
part of central Honshū, one of the five geographical divisions of
Honshū (the main island), the other four being the Tōhoku, Chūbu,
Kinki and Chūgoku regions.   The Kantō region consists of Tokyo-
to and the six prefectures of Kanagawa, Saitama, Chiba, Tochigi,
Gunma and Ibaraki.   It contains five national parks—Jōshin'etsu-
kōgen, Nikkō, Chichibu-Tama, Fuji-Hakone-Izu and Ogasawara
national parks.   ⇨ CHICHIBU-TAMA KOKURITSU-KŌEN, FUJI-HAKONE-
IZU KOKURITSU-KŌEN, JŌSHIN'ETSU-KŌGEN KOKURITSU-KŌEN, NIKKŌ
KOKURITSU-KŌEN, OGASAWARA KOKURITSU-KŌEN

Kantō Daishinsai 関東大震災   the Great Kantō Earthquake of 1923.
an earthquake which struck on September 1, 1923, at 11:58 a.m.,
causing unprecedented damage in Tokyo and the surrounding
prefectures.   With its epicenter in the western part of Sagami Bay,
28 kilometers below the sea bottom, the quake registered a mag-
nitude of 7.9 on the Richter scale.   It killed or injured over
150,000 persons and destroyed some 575,000 houses, due to
tremors or fire.   Tokyo exprienced a massive fire which lasted
three days.   The total amount of damage was estimated as
¥550–650 billion in the yen of those days.   The aftermath of the
quake saw social upheaval, including the murder of many Koreans
by radicals because of totally untrue rumors that they had set fires.
〖注〗 unprecedented 前例がない, 空前の. epicenter 震源地. the Richter
scale 地震の大きさを表す尺度(マグニチュード). tremor 震動, 地震のゆれ.
aftermath 余波. upheaval 動乱.

Kantō Matsuri 竿頭祭   lit. the festival of the top of a bamboo pole.
the Lantern-Balancing Festival held in Akita city (August 5–7).
This festival features the manipulation of the *kantō*, a long bamboo
pole with nine cross-beams holding dozens of lighted paper lanterns.   Men from many districts compete in balancing the *kantō* on

their foreheads, shoulders or backs. The original purpose of this festival was to pray for a good rice harvest; the shape of the *kantō* symbolizes well-ripened ears of rice.

〖注〗 lantern ちょうちん. manipulation 操ること, 操作. cross-beam 横ば り. ears of rice 稲穂.

kappa 河童 lit. a river child. a mythical creature living in rivers. It is depicted as having a dish-like indentation on the top of its head containing a fluid of power. It has straight hair around this dish, the body of a turtle, the limbs of a frog, the beak of a bird of prey, and is green all over. It is an excellent swimmer. It wreaks mischief and tricks people, and is said to lose its power if the fluid in the "dish" spills or evaporates.

〖注〗 mythical creature 架空の生き物. indentation 凹み. fluid 液体. beak 口ばし. a bird of prey 肉食鳥. wreak (わるさ, おどしなどを)与える.

kappamaki かっぱ巻き a cucumber *sushi* roll; vinegared rice rolled up in a sheet of seaweed laver with a piece of cucumber at the center. It is flavored with a bit of green Japanese horseradish. Like most kinds of *sushi*, it is eaten with soy sauce. Cucumber is said to be a favorite food of the *kappa*, a mythical green creature in folklore which is said to live in rivers. ⇨ KAPPA, SUSHI

〖注〗 vinegared 酢で味をつけた. seaweed laver 海苔. green Japanese horseradish わさび. soy sauce 醬油. mythical 架空の, 想像上の. creature 生き物. folklore 民話.

karaage 空揚げ deep-frying without batter. One method of *kara-age* is to deep-fry ingredients without any coating at all, to retain natural colors and shapes. Foods cooked in this way include green beans, eggplant, potato, whole small fish, etc. Soft or juicy foods such as cut fish, chicken, etc., are usually sprinkled with starch and then deep-fried. ⇨ AGEMONO, TENPURA

〖注〗 deep-frying たっぷりの油で揚げること. batter (小麦粉などの)こねたもの. ingredient (料理の)材料.

karae 唐絵 lit. paintings of the T'ang dynasty (618–907). Chinese-style paintings of ancient times; Japanese paintings of Chinese style, as opposed to indigenous Japanese-style paintings, especially those drawn prior to the Muromachi period (1336–1568). The term *karae* came to be used to distinguish Chinese-style paintings from those of Japanese style (*yamatoe*) which emerged in the middle of the Heian period (794–1185). In the Muromachi period, *karae* referred particularly to black-and-white paintings (*suibo-*

kuga) from China or in Chinese style. Chinese-style paintings of later years are called *kanga*, a more generic term. ⇨ KANGA, SUIBOKUGA, YAMATOE

〚注〛 the T'ang dynasty 唐朝. indigenous 土着の，土地特有の. indigenous Japanese-style painting 大和絵.

Karafuto 樺太 Sakhalin; a long island situated north of Hokkaidō, close to eastern Siberia. The island was originally inhabited by settlers sent from both Japan and Russia. With the Treaty of St. Petersburg (1875), Japan gave up this island in exchange for the Kurile Islands. After the Russo-Japanese War (1904–05), by the Treaty of Portsmouth (1905) Japan gained the southern half, and benefited from oil and coal deposits, and the fishing grounds there. However, in 1947, shortly after the end of World War II, southern Sakhalin was occupied by the Soviet Union, along with the Kurile Islands. ⇨ CHISIMA-RETTŌ, HOKKAIDŌ

〚注〛 the Kurile Islands 千島列島. the Treaty of St. Petersburg (= the Sakhalin-Kurile Islands Exchange Treaty) ロシアのSt. Petersburg（今のソ連の Leningrad）で日本とロシアとの間で結ばれた「樺太千島交換条約」. the Treaty of Portsmouth 米国 New Hampshire の海港のある Portsmouth で結ばれた日露 戦争の講和条約. fishing ground 漁場.

karakasa から傘 a paper umbrella; a traditional umbrella made of oiled paper, bamboo ribs and a bamboo handle. Bamboo ribs forming straight lines at narrow intervals are fastened together at the top and strung with cotton cords. Unlike a Western-style cloth umbrella, the *karakasa* is stored with its handle down. There are roughly two types: *bangasa*, the coarse type for common use, and *janome*, the fine type for women. ⇨ BANGASA, JANOME(-GASA)

〚注〛 rib あばら骨，細い骨. coarse 粗野な，こわい.

karaoke カラオケ lit. naked orchestra. a sound system which plays tapes of music for vocal accompaniment. With a microphone attached to the machine, the user can sing along to prerecorded music. The machine is equipped with a reverberation effect system, which helps to make the user's voice sound better. *Karaoke* bars and night clubs have been popular since the late 1970s, giving people a means of releasing the tension accumulated from their daily routine work.

〚注〛 vocal accompaniment 歌の伴奏. be equipped with ～が取りつけられて いる. reverberation effect system 反響効果システム. release . . . from ～か ら解放する.

karaori 唐織　lit. Chinese weave.　a kind of brocade with heavy, elaborate patterns.　It is usually used for making garments worn by actors playing the leading female roles in Noh.　It was originally imported from China but no longer refers only to imported weaves.　⇨ NŌ

〖注〗 brocade 錦織，金襴．　heavy, elaborate pattern 大胆な，手のこんだ模様．ガ garment 衣服，上衣．　leading female role 主役の女役．

karashishi [karajishi] 唐獅子　a Chinese lion; a figure of an imaginary lion which was introduced from China by way of Korea.　It is said to protect people from evil with its fierce leonine features.　It used to be drawn on doors and screens for protection and could especially be seen in the Imperial Court.　⇨ FUSUMA, KOMAINU

〖注〗 imaginary figure 想像上の姿．　leonine 獅子の（ような）．

karate 空手　lit. empty hands.　weaponless fighting; a martial art of self-defense in which the hands, elbows, knees or feet are employed against weak spots to disable an opponent.　The art was created by combining a martial art indigenous to Okinawa called *te* and Chinese forms originating at Shaolin Temple (Shōrinji) around the sixth century and introduced into Okinawa around the 14th century.　It matured in secret over a period of several hundred years as a means of self-defense for Okinawans who were prohibited from carrying weapons. On reaching mainland Japan in the 1920s, it took on the spirit of traditional Japanese martial arts and gradually developed into a popular sport.　The basic techniques consist of the thrust with the fist, the chop with the open hand, and the kick.　To each offensive technique there is a corresponding defensive technique.　The physical strength and spiritual concentration acquired through severe training in karate enable one to render blows so powerful as to smash bricks.　Thus, in competition the goal is accuracy and effectiveness, but blows are stopped just before impact at a vital spot of the body.　⇨ BUGEI

〖注〗 martial art 武術．　indigenous 固有の．　Shaolin Temple 少林寺．thrust 突き．　chop 打ち．　kick けり．　offensive technique 攻め技．　defensive technique 受け技．　vital spot 急所．

Karatsu-yaki 唐津焼　Karatsu ceramic ware; a generic term for the ceramic ware produced in the Karatsu region of northern Kyūshū. A number of kilns were constructed by Korean potters in the 16th century, producing various kinds of ceramic ware of Korean influence.　In general, Karatsu ware is characterized by an unsophisticated, substantial appearance of grayish brown color resulting from the iron content of the clay. One kind of Karatsu ware is painted blue-green or brown under the glaze. Karatsu tea bowls in particular won wide recognition after receiving the favor of Furuta Oribe (1544-1615), a great tea master who resided for a while in Karatsu. ⇨ CHAWAN

〚注〛 ceramic 陶器(の). kiln 窯. potter 陶工. unsophisticated 素朴な. glaze 釉. Furuta Oribe 古田織部.

karayō 唐様 Chinese style; a Chinese style in art as opposed to an indigenous Japanese style. From the Kamakura period (1185-1336) on, this term has specifically referred to an architectural style; that is, the Chinese style of temple building introduced by a Zen priest from the Sung dynasty (960-1279) of China. Such a building features upward curving of the roof eaves, open transom windows, the use of brilliant colors, etc.

〚注〛 indigenous 土着の, その土地固有の. the Sung dynasty 宋朝. roof eaves 屋根の軒. transom 梁, 窓を水平に仕切る横材.

karesansui(-teien) 枯山水(庭園) a dry landscape garden; a garden composed entirely of rocks and sand. It depicts mountains and rivers, or even the ocean, symbolizing the multiplicity and vastness of nature. The rock gardens of Ryōanji Temple and Daisen'in Temple, both in Kyoto, are representative examples, showing the influence of Zen Buddhism. ⇨ SEKITEI, NIHON-TEIEN

〚注〛 landscape garden 造景庭園, 日本庭園. multiplicity 多様性, 複雑さ. Daisen'in Temple 大仙院.

karetaki 枯滝 a dry waterfall. In a dry landscape garden, a dry waterfall is often arranged with large rocks, symbolizing flowing water. ⇨ KARESANSUI(-TEIEN)

〚注〛 landscape garden 造景庭園, 日本庭園. dry landscape garden 枯山水 (庭園).

karintō 花林糖 a kind of fried cookie; finger-shaped fried cookie coated with unrefined brown sugar. The dough is mixed with starch syrup. The cookies are brittle and crunchy, similar to pretzels in texture but very sweet.

〚注〛 unrefined brown sugar 精製していない赤砂糖. dough 練り粉. starch syrup 水あめ. brittle こわれやすい, くだけやすい. crunchy かりかりいう, ざくざくいう. pretzel プレッツェル(外側に塩のついたかりかりした乾性ビスケット). texture 生地, 肌合い.

karuta 歌留多 a game of cards or cards for a game; the generic term for some card games: *iroha-garuta*, *uta-garuta* (or *hyakunin-isshu*), *hana-garuta* (or *hanafuda*), etc. The term *karuta* was borrowed from the Portuguese "carta." ⇨ IROHA-GARUTA, HYAKUNIN-ISSHU, UTAGARUTA

kashiwa-mochi 柏餅   a rice cake wrapped in an oak leaf; a traditional food, along with *chimaki*, for Boys' Day (May 5). The half-moon-shaped cake is made of boiled and pounded sweet powdered rice, and filled with red-bean paste. The oak leaf wrapping adds flavor. This leaf is not edible while the cherry leaf used to wrap *sakura-mochi* is. ⇨ CHIMAKI, MOCHI, SAKURA-MOCHI

〖注〗 oak 柏の木. red-bean paste 小豆餡.

kasuri 絣［飛白］   cloth with splashed patterns; cotton fabric designed with blurred patterns, mostly white patterns on an indigo background. White cotton threads are first tied together at certain intervals and then dyed in indigo or sometimes in other dyes; the knotted part remains white. These mottled threads are woven to form patterns of blurred, irregular shapes. The cotton thread used is thick and strong, so *kasuri* fabric is used for everyday work wear. ⇨ IYO-GASURI, KURUME-GASURI

〖注〗 splashed pattern 散らばった模様. fabric 織物. blurred pattern ぼかしの模様. indigo 藍. background 生地. knotted 縛った，結んだ. mottled まだらの.

kataginu 肩衣   the ancient-styled stiff, sleeveless jacket. It is used in a comic interlude (Kyogen) in Noh for roles such as a servant. In ancient times it was worn by lower-class people but in feudal times by warriors. ⇨ KYŌGEN, NŌ

〖注〗 stiff 角張った. comic interlude 狂言. feudal times 封建時代. warrior さむらい.

katakake 肩掛け   lit. shoulder covering. a shawl; a rectangular piece of cloth to cover the shoulders when wearing a kimono during cold weather. A variety of materials is used: wool, silk, velvet, fur, etc. One is supposed to take it off when greeting someone and when indoors.

katakana 片仮名   lit. a part or side script. the angular or straight-line form of *kana* script, one of the two sets of Japanese syllabary writing (*katakana* and *hiragana*). *Katakana* script is derived from parts of Chinese characters of the same sound, with no reference to their meaning. This syllabary is said to have been invented by Kibi no Makibi (693–755). It was first used in Buddhist scriptures as a pronunciation aid; the use of *katakana* combined with Chinese characters appeared in the ninth century. Today, *katakana* is used only for writing foreign words, technical names of flora and fauna, and the functional parts of a word on some types of documents.   ⇨ HIRAGANA, KANA

〔注〕 script 書体，筆跡． angular 角のある，角張った． syllabary 音節文字 （表），字音表． Chinese character 漢字． Kibi no Makibi 吉備真備． Buddhist scripture 仏典． flora and fauna 植物と動物，動植物． functional part of a word 語の機能的部分（名詞や語幹でない部分）．

katana 刀 a sword; a weapon always worn by samurai when outside the home, in particular, a sword longer than 60 centimeters. It has a slightly curved, hard flat blade usually with only one sharpened edge and is wielded with both hands on the haft.   Along with this long sword, a samurai usually carried a shorter one (*wakizashi*).   As a symbol of loyalty and honor, the sword was regarded as the soul of the samurai.

〔注〕 wield （刀などを）ふるう，執る． haft （刀の）つか，柄． loyalty 忠誠． honor 名誉．

katsudon カツ丼 pork cutlet on rice in a bowl; a bowl of rice topped with breaded, deep-fried pork cutlet dressed with egg.   Soy-flavored fish broth is simmered with onions and Japanese mushrooms in a small pan, over which beaten egg is poured and slices of fried cutlet are placed.   After the egg has cooked, the cutlet, together with the cooked broth and egg, is put on a bowl of hot rice. ⇨ DONBURIMONO

〔注〕 deep-fried たっぷりの油で揚げた． soy-flavored 醤油で味をつけた． fish broth （魚でとった）だし汁． simmer 煮つめる．

katsuobushi 鰹節 dried bonito or its shaved flakes; bonito cut in half and dried until it becomes like a piece of driftwood.   It is shaved into thin flakes to be used as the base for Japanese soup stock.   This creates the basic and essential flavor of Japanese cooking.   Shaved bonito flakes used to be made at home by pushing dried bonito over the blade of a shredder placed on the top of a wooden box into which the flakes fell.   Today, machine-shaved flakes are available on market.   ⇨ DASHI

〔注〕 bonito 鰹． shaved flakes フレーク状に削ったもの． driftwood 流木． stock 煮出し汁． shredder 小片に削る器具．

katsuogi 鰹木 lit. bonito wood.   short logs placed on the ridge of a shrine roof.   They are placed crosswise in a row on a long flat pole of the roof ridge. Along with *chigi*, originally they secured the roof against wind, but came to be used as ornaments symbolizing Shinto shrine architecture. They are so called because these cigar-shaped logs resemble pieces of dried bonito (*katsuobushi*). ⇨ CHIGI, JINJA, KATSUOBUSHI

〖注〗 bonito 鰹. ridge 屋根の水平の頂上［背］. crosswise 横に, 十文字に.

katsuo no tataki 鰹のたたき lit. pounded bonito. a dish of semi-raw bonito to which seasonings are added by pounding. Bonito cut lengthwise into two or four pieces is wrapped in wet straw, and then slightly grilled so that only the surface becomes scorched, with the inside remaining raw. It is cut into thin slices when served, and eaten by dipping it in soy sauce mixed with condiments such as grated ginger, grated radish, minced green onions, garlic, etc. Originally, such condiments were placed on the surface and pounded in before slicing. This dish originated in Shikoku which is known for its bonito. ⇨ DAIKON-OROSHI

〖注〗 bonito 鰹. seasoning 調味(すること), 調味料. lengthwise 長く, 縦に. scorch こげる. soy sauce 醤油. condiment 調味料, 薬味. grated ginger おろし生姜. grated radish おろし大根. minced green onions こまかく刻んだねぎ.

katsuramono [kazuramono] 鬘物 lit. a wig thing. the third group in the five categories of Noh plays. This group includes women plays in which the main character (*shite*) is a beautiful woman. Differences of age, social status, etc., are represented by wigs in exaggerated forms. ⇨ NŌ, SHITE

kawabiraki 川開き lit. the opening of a river. originally, bonfires along a river to console the dead, and eventually, fireworks displays along a river. In the 18th century, for those who died from an epidemic in Edo, a Buddhist rite was observed in which lanterns were floated down the Sumida River during the Bon season. In time, it became customary to shoot fireworks into the sky to ward off evil spirits. Today, *kawabiraki* refers to the fireworks display itself, held in July at Ryōgoku on the Sumida River and becoming popular in other districts as well. Fireworks contests may be featured. ⇨ BON

〖注〗 bonfire 大かがり火, 祝火. firework(s) 花火. epidemic 流行病. Buddhist rite 仏教儀式, 法要. lantern とうろう. afloat 漂っている. ward off さける, かわす.

kawarabuki 瓦葺き a tiled roof; a tile-covered slanting roof. Roof tiles of a traditional-style house are made of fired clay and are dark gray in color.   There are roughly three kinds of tiles: plain, ridged, and those bearing the figure of a devil.   ⇨ ONIGAWARA

〖注〗 slanting 傾斜した，勾配のある． fire（陶器などを）焼く． ridged 背になった．

kaya 蚊帳   a mosquito net; a tent made of netting, set up for keeping out mosquitoes on summer nights.   The netting is made into the shape of a square by being suspended from the ceiling at the four corners of a room.   It becomes nearly as large as the room.   There is also a smaller net like a cage for infants.

kayabuki 茅葺き   a thatched roof; roofing of thatched grass.   For common thatching, straw is used, but for better quality, grass called *kaya* (miscanthus reed) is used.   A thatch-roofed house forms a picturesque scene in the countryside.   Tearooms are thatch-roofed to suggest refined poverty and rustic simplicity.

〖注〗 thatched 茅葺きの，草葺きの． thatching 屋根葺き，屋根葺き材料． refined poverty 洗練された素朴さ，わび・さび． rustic simplicity わびれた簡素さ，わび・さび．

kayu 粥   rice gruel; rice boiled in plenty of water, usually plain with salt added but sometimes mixed with beans, potatoes or vegetables.   It is easily digested, and thus good for invalids and the elderly.   In olden days, it was often eaten as a main dish among the common people.

〖注〗 gruel かゆ状の食物． invalid 病人．

kazoedoshi 数え年   one's age as counted on New Year's Day; the older method of counting one's age.   Until the end of World War II, people were considered a year old in the year of their birth, and a year older with the coming of the New Year, that is, on January 1.   Strange as it may seem, a child who was born on December 31 became two years old the next day.   Some older people still count their age according to this old custom.

kazoku 華族   lit. the flowery family.   the nobility; a family of the nobility; the title for the nobility, one of the three social classes—*kazoku*, *shizoku* and *heimin*—categorized in 1869 shortly after the Meiji Restoration (1868).   Limited to a small number of the population, this title was conferred upon former nobles related to the Imperial Court (*kuge*) and feudal lords (*daimyō*), plus eminent persons who rendered distinguished contributions to the state.   There were five ranks (officially classified in 1884): duke (*kōsha-*

ku), marquis (*kōshaku*), count or earl (*hakushaku*), viscount (*shishaku*) and baron (*danshaku*). Under the new constitution (1940), this system was abolished. ⇨ DAIMYŌ, HEIMIN, MEIJI ISHIN, SHIZOKU

〖注〗 the nobility 貴族. the Meiji Restoration 明治維新. confer upon 授ける. feudal lord 大名. duke 公爵. marquis 候爵. count or earl 伯爵. viscount 子爵. baron 男爵.

keigo 敬語 a polite expression; a term of respect; honorific (*sonkeigo*), humble (*kenjōgo*) and formal (*teineigo*) expressions, as classified in Japanese grammar. Persons who are younger or of lower position usually use honorific expressions when addressing or referring to elders or persons of superior rank. Of course, regardless of position, honorific expressions are often used to show respect. Humble expressions are used for referring to oneself and members of one's family and relatives. Formal expressions are neutral in themselves, involving rather a matter of "register" or degree of formality and situation depending on the circumstances.

〖注〗 honorific expression 尊敬語. humble expression 謙譲語. formal expression 丁寧語. address 人を呼ぶ，人に話しかける. register 言語使用の領域. formality 形式，儀礼.

Keirō no Hi 敬老の日 Respect-for-the-Aged Day (September 15); a national holiday, set to honor the aged. The people are reminded of great contributions made by the aged to the family and society, and are encouraged to respect them and wish for their happiness and longevity. ⇨ KOKUMIN NO SHUKUJITSU

〖注〗 longevity 長寿.

kemari 蹴鞠 a kick-ball game; a game played in the court during the Heian period (794-1185). A leather ball is kicked in the air by several participants forming a circle. The ball must be kept in play as long as possible without falling to the ground. When it is played as a traditional event, the participants wear ancient costumes and shout as they did in the olden days when it was played in the Heian period. ⇨ HEIAN-JIDAI

ken[1] 県 a prefecture; a regular prefecture as an administrative division. After the Meiji Restoration, Japan was divided for administrative purposes into prefectures. Today, there are 47 prefectures which are composed of one metropolis (*to*), one district (*dō*), two metropolitan prefectures (*fu*), and 43 rural prefectures. Prefectures are subdivided into cities and counties (*gun*). The rural prefectures called *ken* are: Aomori, Iwate, Akita, Yamagata, Miyagi, Fukushima, Tochigi, Ibaraki, Chiba, Saitama, Gunma, Kanagawa, Nagano, Yamanashi, Shizuoka, Fukui, Ishikawa, Toyama, Niigata, Aichi, Mie, Gifu, Shiga, Nara, Wakayama, Hyōgo, Okayama, Hiroshima, Yamaguchi, Shimane, Tottori, Tokushima, Kagawa, Ehime, Kōchi, Nagasaki, Saga, Fukuoka, Kumamoto, Ōita, Miyazaki, Kagoshima, and Okinawa.   ⇨ DŌ², FU, GUN, TO, TO-DŌ-FU-KEN

〖注〗 administrative division 行政区画. the Meiji Restoration 明治維新. metropolis 都、大都市、首都圏. metropolitan 大都市の、首都圏の. county 郡.

ken² 間 a traditional unit for measuring length, particularly of buildings and lots.   One *ken* is six *shaku* or 1.818 meters, or the length of a *tatami*-mat (six by three *shaku*).   One square *ken* is called a *tsubo* which is the size of two *tatami*-mats.   One *ken* was originally the distance between the two main pillars of a Japanese-style room, *ken* meaning "between."   ⇨ SHAKKAN-HŌ, SHAKU, TATAMI

〖注〗 lot 敷地. square *ken* 平方間.

kendai 見台 a book stand; a stand on which the script of a narrator or the score of a musician is placed such as in Kabuki and Bunraku. It is usually a small decorative desk made of wood, about 50 centimeters high.   ⇨ BUNRAKU, KABUKI

〖注〗 script 台本. score 楽譜.

kendō 剣道 lit. the way of the sword.   Japanese-style fencing; the sport of swordsmanship derived from *kenjutsu*, one of the traditional martial arts practiced by samurai.   With the dissolution of the samurai class and a ban on the bearing of swords following the Meiji Restoration (1868), swordsmanship was transformed into an art of mainly spiritual training.   After World War II, with its competitive aspect expanded, it developed into a sport, without losing its spiritual values.   Kendoists wear traditional outfits consisting of a face mask (*men*) with a throat protector (*nodo*), chest plate (*dō*), arm guards (*kote*), waist protector (*tare*), etc.   In competition, a stab to the throat protector or a blow to one of the other parts of the protective gear with a 1.1-meter bamboo training sword results in points.   ⇨ BUGEI, KENJUTSU

〖注〗 swordsmanship 剣術. martial art 武術. dissolution 解体. the Meiji Restoration 明治維新. outfit 服装. chest plate 胴. arm guard 小手.

waist protector 垂. bamboo training sword 竹刀.

kenjutsu 剣術 lit. the art of sword. training for fencing. The sword long served as an important weapon in combat, and swordsmanship flourished from the 12th century with the rise of the samurai class. Great progress in techniques was made with the emergence of various schools, starting from the mid-Muromachi period (15th century). In the peaceful Edo period (1603-1868) in which, under a firm government, samurai no longer needed to turn to their swords for the sake of survival, *kenjutsu* took on other aspects such as spiritual enhancement, including mental preparedness for death at any moment, under the influence of Zen Buddhism. In the 18th century, protective wear and pliant bamboo swords were developed which permitted more practical training. After a ban on carrying swords was imposed in the Meiji era (1868-1912), the tradition of *kenjutsu* was continued in the sport of mental training called *kendō*. ⇨ BUGEI, KENDŌ

【注】 swordsmanship 剣術. spiritual enhancement 精神修養. mental preparedness for death 死の覚悟. pliant しなやかな. bamboo sword 竹刀. ban 禁止.

Kenkoku Kinen no Hi 建国記念の日 National Foundation Day (February 11); a national holiday in commemoration of the founding of Japan and for fostering the people's love for their country. Japanese history records that on this day in 660 B.C. the first Japanese emperor, Jinmu, acceded to the throne and founded the imperial line. Until the end of World War II this day was called *Kigensetsu*. ⇨ KOKUMIN NO SHUKUJITSU

【注】 in commemoration of 〜を記念して. foster 育てる. accede to the throne 即位する.

Kenpō Kinenbi 憲法記念日 Constitution Day (May 3); a national holiday, designated to commemorate the new constitution of Japan. The new constitution was promulgated on November 3, 1946, and came into effect on May 3, 1947. ⇨ KOKUMIN NO SHUKUJITSU, NIHONKOKU KENPŌ

【注】 commemorate 記念する. promulgate 公布する. come into effect 施行される、効力を発する.

kensho 見所 where the audience sits in the Noh theater. It was traditionally a *tatami*-mat floor with cushions (*zabuton*) provided. In recent years, chairs have been installed in most Noh theaters. A lane of white gravel separates it from the elevated stage. ⇨ NŌ,

NŌBUTAI, SHIRASU
〖注〗 white gravel 白州.

kensui 建水 a waste-water container; a vessel for disposing of water after rinsing a tea bowl in the tea ceremony. The container is made of ceramics, bronze or curved unpainted wood, and comes in a variety of shapes, usually without a lid. On very formal occasions, a newly made *kensui* of curved, unpainted wood is used, symbolizing the highest level of hospitality. ⇨ CHANOYU
〖注〗 curved unpainted wood 木地の曲物.

kentōshi 遣唐使 a delegation to the T'ang dynasty; a Japanese diplomatic delegation sent to China during the T'ang dynasty (618-907). Official diplomatic relations with China, which had been established during the previous dynasty by Shōtoku Taishi (574-622), the regent for Empress Suiko (554-628), were maintained in the T'ang dynasty but on a larger scale. Hundreds of Japanese intellectuals were officially sent to China on a regular basis and stayed for several years to study advanced Chinese culture. Starting in 630, such delegations continued for two and a half centuries until 894, when they were abolished at the suggestion of Sugawara Michizane (845-903). He felt that Japan had already absorbed enough Chinese culture and that it was time for the country to develop its own. ⇨ KENZUISHI
〖注〗 delegation 代表団, 派遣団. the T'ang dynasty 唐朝. official diplomatic relation 公式外交関係. regent 摂政.

kenzan 剣山 lit. a sword mountain. a flower holder; a metal plate with many needles for holding plants. It is used to fix stems in an arrangement using a shallow container. In arranging flowers, caution must be taken to hide the needle holder. ⇨ IKEBANA, MORIBANA, SHIPPŌ
〖注〗 metal plate 金属板.

kenzuishi 遣隋使 Japanese diplomatic delegations sent to China during the Sui dynasty (581-618). They began when Shōtoku Taishi (574-622), the regent for Empress Suiko (554-628), sent a delegation of envoys headed by Ono no Imoko (seventh century) to China in 607 to restore diplomatic relations and to study Chinese culture. Four or five such delegations were sent, and the practice was continued by the *kentōshi*, delegations to the T'ang dynasty (618-907) which followed. ⇨ KENTŌSHI
〖注〗 delegation 代表団. the Sui dynasty 隋朝. regent 摂政. envoy 公

使, 使節. the T'ang dynasty 唐朝.

kesa 袈裟 a surplice; an outer vestment worn by Buddhist priests. It is an oblong cloth garment worn diagonally, covering the right shoulder and passing under the left armpit.

〖注〗 surplice (聖職者などの)上衣. vestment おおう布, 法衣. garment 衣服. diagonally 斜めに. armpit わきの下.

kichikumono 鬼畜物 a demon play; one of the five categories of the Noh play. This group is made up of demon plays in which the main character (*shite*) is a demon. The demon may first appear in the guise of a human. Also called *kirinōmono* (an ending piece), as a play from this group is performed at the end of a program of many plays. ⇨ NŌ, SHITE

〖注〗 demon 鬼, 悪魔. main character 主役, (能の)仕手. in the guise of ～に扮して, ～に見せかけて.

kigo 季語 a seasonal word; a word or phrase expressive of the season in a haiku (17-syllable poem). A seasonal feeling must be rendered, explicitly or implicitly, in a haiku poem as one of the necessary elements. The Japanese concept of man's relationship with nature permeates each short poem of haiku. ⇨ HAIKAI, HAIKU

〖注〗 render 描写する, 表現する. explicitly あからさまに, 言葉で表現して. implicitly 含蓄的に, 言外に含んで. permeate 浸透する, ～にしみ込む.

kihachijō 黄八丈 yellow Hachijō weave; checked or striped yellow silk fabric originally developed on Hachijō Island located to the south of Tokyo in the Pacific. It is herb-dyed and hand-woven silk. Its rustic yellow comes from *kariyasu* grass available on Hachijō Island. Black, brown and reddish-yellow checks or stripes are woven into the yellow background. ⇨ IZU-SHOTŌ

〖注〗 weave 織物. silk fabric 絹織物. herb-dyed 草木染めの. rustic 素朴な, わびれた. background 生地.

kihon-kakei 基本花型 the basic styles of flower arrangement. The basic styles in flower arrangement have three main stems. The difference in the placement of the three main stems determines the type of basic style. There are three basic styles in the Ikenobō school—*chokutai* (an upright style), *shatai* (a slanting style) and *suitai* (a hanging style)—and four in the Sōgetsu school—*risshin-kei* (an upright style), *keishin-kei* (a slanting style), *heishin-kei* (a horizontal style) and *suishin-kei* (a hanging style). ⇨ IKEBANA, SHIN-SOE-HIKAE, SHIN-SOE-TAI, SHU-FUKU-KYAKU, SHUSHI

〖注〗 flower arrangement 生け花． basic style 基本型． main stem 主枝．

kiju 喜寿 lit. joyous congratulatory occasion． the celebration of one's 77th birthday; the 77th anniversary of one's life, one of the special ages to celebrate one's longevity． The Chinese character 喜 (*ki*) meaning "rejoice" or "congratulations" has the abbreviated form of 㐂 suggesting 七十七, or seventy-seven． Thus, the 77th birthday came to be called *kiju*, the *ki* combined with *ju* to mean "longevity" or "congratulations." Such a special 77th birthday is customarily honored with a party organized by relatives and acquaintances． ⇨ BEIJU, HAKUJU, KANREKI

〖注〗 longevity 長寿． Chinese character 漢字． abbreviated form 省略形．

kikkō 亀甲 a tortoise-shell motif; a hexagonal pattern, similar to a section of a honeycomb, as an abstract form of the markings of a tortoise shell． It became popular in the Edo period (1603-1868) as an auspicious symbol since a tortoise has a long life． Tortoise-shell grid designs have been adopted for traditional Japanese textiles.

〖注〗 tortoise-shell 亀の甲． hexagonal pattern 六角形の模様． honeycomb 蜂の巣． grid design 格子模様．

kiku-ningyō 菊人形 a chrysanthemum doll; life-size dolls decorated all over with chrysanthemum flowers and leaves． They usually depict historical figures and scenes． Traditional exhibitions of chrysanthemum dolls are held here and there throughout the country—such as in shrine precincts, on castle grounds, or sometimes at department stores—in autumn, particularly around November 3 (Culture Day) when chrysanthemums are at their best． ⇨ BUNKA NO HI

〖注〗 chrysanthemum 菊． life-size 実物大(の)． figure 人物． shrine precincts 神社の境内． castle grounds 城内．

Kimigayo 君が代 lit． His Majesty's Reign． the national anthem of Japan． The poem (author unknown) is a traditional 31-syllable verse (*tanka*), from the *Kokinshū*, an anthology compiled by the poet Ki no Tsurayuki (?-945) in the 10th century． It goes: "*Kimi ga yo wa／Chiyo ni yachiyo ni／Sazare ishi no／Iwao to nari te／Koke no musu made*." Translated by Basil H. Chamberlain as: "Thousands of years of happy reign be thine;／Rule on, my lord, till what are pebbles now／By age united to mighty rocks shall grow／Whose venerable sides the moss doth line." The music was composed by Hiromori Hayashi and accepted by the Imperial Household Ministry in 1880. ⇨ TANKA

〖注〗 national anthem 国歌. 31-syllable verse 31音節の詩、短歌. anthology 名詩選、詞華集. venerable 尊敬に値する. Hiromori Hayashi 林広守. the Imperial Household Ministry 宮内省.

kimon 鬼門 lit. the demon's gate. the unlucky quarter, i.e., the northeastern direction. According to the Chinese philosophy of dual cosmic forces (yin-yang), the northeast is said to be the direction from which devils come. In the construction of a house, exposure to this unlucky direction is avoided by superstitious persons. Changing one's residence in this direction may also be considered unlucky.

〖注〗 demon 鬼、悪魔. unlucky quarter 不吉な方位. the philosophy of dual cosmic forces 陰陽道. yin-yang 陰陽. exposure to the unlucky direction 不吉な方位に向けること.

kimono 着物 the national costume of Japan; Japan's traditional costume with wide square sleeves, worn with a sash (*obi*). Developed from an ancient undergarment, the kimono in its present form was established as standard wear in the Muromachi period (1336-1568). Women's kimono in particular became decorative and their sashes broader in the Edo period (1603-1868). The kimono is double-breasted and reaches the ankles. The left part is folded over the right part and the sash holds it in place. The collar extends to the waist diagonally over the chest. There are *hitoe* (unlined kimono) for summer, and *awase* (a lined kimono) and wataire (padded kimono) for the other seasons. Men's kimono usually come in dark, plain colors and the sash is narrow and simple. On formal occasions, *hakama* (a loose lower garment) is worn with it. Women's kimono come in a variety of styles, chosen to suit different occasions. They are categorized according to various overlapping classifications, by weave (*tsumugi*, *chirimen*, *ro*, etc.), color (*kuro-tomesode*, *iromuji*, etc.), pattern (*komon*, *tsukesage*, *kasuri*, etc.), length of the sleeve (*furisode*, *chū-furisode*, etc.), purpose (*hōmongi*, *mofuku*, *yukata*, etc.), etc. The selection of an appropriate sash to go with the kimono is very important. ⇨ CHIRIMEN, FURISODE, HAKAMA, HŌMONGI, IROMUJI, KASURI, KOMON, KURO-TOMESODE, MOFUKU, OBI, RO, TOMESODE, TSUKESAGE, TSUMUGI, YUKATA

〖注〗 undergarment 下着. lined 裏のついた. weave 織物、織り方.

kinai 畿内 the central provinces; the central district surrounding the former capitals of Nara and Kyoto, one of the old large administrative divisions. The name was first used in 646 during the Taika Reform, and shortly after the district was divided into four provinces—Yamashiro, Yamato, Kawachi and Settsu—with the imposition of the province (*kuni*) system. The four provinces were collectively called *shi-kinai* (the four central provinces). Later, in 716, with the addition of Izumi Province, this district came to be called *go-kinai* (the five central provinces) until the reforms of the Meiji Restoration (around 1868). This district corresponds to present-day Kyoto, Ōsaka, and surrounding prefectures.   ⇨ GOKI(NAI)-SHICHIDŌ, MEIJI ISHIN, KUNI

〖注〗 province (行政区画としての) 国，県，管区．administrative division 行政区分．the Taika Reform 大化の改新．imposition 課すこと．the Meiji Restoration 明治維新．畿内：山城，大和，河内，摂津，和泉．

kinako 黄粉   soybean flour; yellow flour made by grinding roasted soybeans. Mixed with sugar and a dash of salt, it is used as coating for rice cakes, dumplings or the like to make traditional sweets. Among them, abekawa-mochi is popular.   ⇨ ABEKAWA-MOCHI, MOCHI, WAGASHI

〖注〗 dumpling 団子．

Kinki chihō 近畿地方   the Kinki region; a region in the western part of central Honshū, one of the five geographical divisions of Honshū (the main island), the other four being the Tōhoku, Kantō, Chūbu and Chūgoku regions. The Kinki region consists of Ōsaka-*fu*, Kyoto-*fu* and the five prefectures of Nara, Wakayama, Hyōgo, Shiga and Mie. It contains four national parks—the Ise-Shima, Yoshino-Kumano, San'in Coast and Seto Inland Sea national parks.   ⇨ ISE-SHIMA KOKURITSU-KŌEN, SAN'IN-KAIGAN KOKURITSU-KŌEN, SETO NAIKAI KOKURITSU-KŌEN, YOSHINO-KUMANO KOKURITSU-KŌEN

kinpira(-gobō) 金平(牛蒡)   flavored burdock root. Thin strips or shavings of burdock root are sauteed with sesame-seed oil and then boiled in soy sauce, sweet rice wine (*mirin*) and sugar. As a finishing touch, red pepper is added to taste. When regular oil is used, sesame seeds are sprinkled on top when it is served. Carrots may be used together with the burdock.

〖注〗 flavored 風味をつけた．burdock 牛蒡．shavings 削ったもの．soy sauce 醤油．sweet rice wine 味醂．finishing touch 仕上げ．red pepper 赤唐辛子．

Kinrō Kansha no Hi 勤労感謝の日   Labor-Thanksgiving Day (November 23); a national holiday designated to remind the nation of the importance of labor and to honor working people.   Until the end of World War II, this day, called *Niinamesai* (the Harvest Festival), was observed for thanking the gods specifically for the rice harvest of the year.   ⇨ KOKUMIN NO SHUKUJITSU

Kintarō 金太郎   lit. Golden Boy.   a character in a Japanese folk tale.   He is depicted as a sturdy boy wearing only a pinafore-like cloth, often riding a bear and carrying an axe.   As a child, he lived with his animal followers in the forests of Mount Ashigara near Hakone.   As an adult he was discovered by Minamoto Yorimitsu (948-1021), a celebrated warrior, and named Sakata no Kintoki. He is said to have served him in subduing demons.   He is interpreted as a combination of two figures: one a hero appearing in the *Konjaku Monogatari* (Tales of Once Upon a Time, 31 volumes) written in the Heian period (794-1185), and the other a legendary boy born on Mount Ashigara, the son of a mountain witch.

〖注〗 folk tale 民話. pinafore 前掛け，腹掛け. Minamoto Yorimitsu 源頼光. celebrated 有名な. warrior 武士. Sakata no Kintoki 坂田公時[金時]. subdue 鎮圧する.

kirinōmono 切能物   the ending piece in a program of Noh plays; the last group of the five categories of Noh plays.   In this type of play the main character (*shite*) performs the role of a demon or an evil supernatural being.   ⇨ KICHIKUMONO, NŌ, SHIKINŌ, SHITE

〖注〗 supernatural being 超自然のもの.

Kirishima-Yaku Kokuritsu-kōen 霧島屋久国立公園   Kirishima-Yaku National Park (550.1 square kilometers), designated in 1934; a natural park, situated in southern Kyūshū, comprising parts of Miyazaki and Kagoshima prefectures.   This park consists of the Kirishima region, the Kagoshima Bay area and Yaku Island. The Kirishima volcanic range is made up of 23 peaks including Mount Karakuni (1,700 meters) and Takachiho Peak (1,574 m). According to Japanese mythology, it is to Takachiho Peak that the god Ninigi no Mikoto descended from heaven to rule the Japanese islands.   In Kagoshima Bay lies Sakurajima, an active volcano which erupts quite often, which was once an island and is now a peninsula.   Some 60 km south of the southern tip of Kyūshū is Yaku Island, with Mount Miyanoura (1,935 m) its highest peak. Hot springs abound in this park; the Ibusuki Spa features hot-sand baths.   ⇨ KOKURITSU-KŌEN

〚注〛 volcanic range 火山帯. mythology 神話. erupt 噴火する.

Kirishitan キリシタン[切支丹] Christians or Christianity in medieval Japan; the Japanese pronunciation of the Portuguese "Christan," Catholics of the 16th and 17th centuries. Christianity was introduced to Japan in 1549 when the feudal leader Oda Nobunaga (1534–82) received a mission headed by Saint Francis Xavier; it made great contributions in terms of social welfare. Despite suppression by Toyotomi Hideyoshi (1536–98), in 1605 there were some 700,000 converts, 4 percent of the population. In fear that an increase in Christians might lead to Spanish and Portuguese colonization of the country, the Tokugawa shogunate officially prohibited Christianity in 1614, and punished or persecuted followers of the faith. However, many "hidden Christians" (*kakure-Kirishitan*) remained true to their faith in secret. In 1873, during the Meiji Restoration, the prohibition on Christianity was lifted after appeals by foreign countries.　⇨ KAKURE-KIRISHITAN, SAKOKU(-SEISAKU), SHIMABARA NO RAN

〚注〛 suppression 圧迫. convert 改宗者. persecute 処刑する. the Meiji Restoration 明治維新. lift 取り除く.

kiseru 煙管 lit. a smoking pipe. a long, slender tobacco pipe. They vary in size but each consists of three parts: a pipe head with a tiny bowl (*gankubi*), a stem (*rao*) and a mouthpiece (*suikuchi*). The pipe head and mouthpiece are made of metal and the stem of bamboo or metal. *Kiseru* has been in use since the 16th century, but today they are used by only a limited number of aged people and traditional-style carpenters.

〚注〛 tiny bowl 雁首. stem 羅宇. mouthpiece 吸口.

Kiseto(-yaki) 黄瀬戸(焼) yellow Seto ceramic ware; old Seto ceramic ware which is covered with a yellow or yellowish-green glaze, produced in the 13th century. This yellowish glaze first resulted from incorrect firing; a Chinese jade celadon coloring was intended. But the effect of its uniqueness unexpectedly came to appeal to connoisseurs of ceramics.　⇨ SETO-YAKI, KOSETO(-YAKI)

〚注〛 ceramic ware 陶器. glaze 釉、つや. jade celadon color ひすい青磁色. connoisseurs of ceramics 陶芸通. connoisseur 目きき、鑑識家、通.

Kisshōten 吉祥天 Sri Lakshmi (Sanskrit); the Goddess of Beauty; a deity of fortune represented as the incarnation of beauty. She holds a gem in her hand which is said to have the power to give beauty and fortune to those who worship her. Representative images of Kisshōten include the colored statue at Jōruriji Temple, Kyoto, and the painting at Yakushiji Temple, Nara. She is sometimes included in the Seven Deities of Good Luck, to fill the vacancy when Fukurokuju and Jurōjin are regarded as one and the same. ▷ FUKUROKUJU, JURŌJIN, SHICHI-FUKUJIN

〖注〗 deity 神, 神のような人[もの]. incarnation 化身. statue 彫像. Jōruriji Temple 浄瑠璃寺. the Seven Deities of Good Luck 七福神. fill the vacancy 欠員を補充する, あきを埋める.

Kiyomizu-yaki 清水焼 Kiyomizu porcelain ware; porcelain ware first produced around Kiyomizu Temple, Kyoto, the best-known of Kyoto chinaware. The Kiyomizu kiln was constructed by Shimizu Rokubei in the 18th century, taking on the style of pottery developed by Nonomura Ninsei in the 17th century. The style established by these two men forms the mainstream of *Kiyomizu-yaki*, though many other skilled potters have produced various styles. It is characterized by an indigenous method of coloring and design, influenced by the Tosa and Kanō schools of painting. ▷ KANŌ-HA, TOSA-HA

〖注〗 porcelain 磁器. chinaware 陶磁器. kiln 窯. pottery 焼き物. Nonomura Ninsei 野々村仁清. potter 陶工. indigenous (土地, 国)固有の.

kiyomoto(-bushi) 清元(節) the Kiyomoto style of *jōruri* chanting; a style of traditional song to *shamisen* accompaniment. It was developed by Kiyomoto Enjudayū (1777-1825) and derived from *gidayū* puppet theater music. It came to serve as the narrative music for the dance in the Kabuki theater, though it has also been chanted independently. The vocalization consists of a heavily nasalized falsetto, with the pitch higher than that of other styles of *jōruri*. ▷ GIDAYŪ, JŌRURI, SHINNAI(-BUSHI), TOKIWAZU(-BUSHI)

〖注〗 chanting 単調に繰り返して歌うこと, 謡うこと. accompaniment 伴奏. Kiyomoto Enjudayū 清元延寿太夫. narrative 語り(の). vocalization 発声 (法). falsetto 裏声, 作り声. pitch 声の高低.

kizewamono 生世話物 a later genre of Kabuki plays. All of the *kizewamono* are of Kabuki origin and were produced in Edo. They are so called to distinguish them from *sewamono* (a genre of Kabuki produced in Ōsaka), most of which are of Bunraku origin. The pioneer writer of *kizewamono* was Kawatake Mokuami (1816-93). ▷ BUNRAKU, KABUKI, SEWAMONO

〖注〗 genre ジャンル, 分野.

kō 孝   ▷ KŌKŌ

kobachi 小鉢 a small ceramic bowl; a ceramic bowl for individual use at meals. It is usually about 10 to 15 centimeters in diameter, with a rather flat bottom, and is used for serving individual portions of salad, boiled foods, etc. ⇨ HACHI
〖注〗 ceramic 陶器(の). individual portion 個人の分量.

kōban 交番 lit. alternate guarding. a police box; a small police station located at a street corner for the security of a neighborhood, where a few police officers are on duty around the clock on a shift system. Along with their primary duties of maintaining security, they also give people directions, deal with lost and found articles, process traffic accidents, etc. There are some 15,600 such police boxes across the country, about 1,250 of them in Tokyo. They are also called *hashutsujo* (lit. a branch police station). Such places in rural districts are called *chūzaisho* (lit. the station of a resident officer).
〖注〗 on duty 当番で, 勤務時間中で. around the clock 24時間. on a shift system 交代制で. lost and found article 忘れ物. a branch police station 派出所. the station of a resident officer 駐在所.

kōdan 講談 epic narration; narrating historical events—particularly war tales—in a rhythmical and dignified manner before an audience. Its origins go back to the Muromachi period (1336-1568), when lectures, called *kōshaku*, on historical works were given by scholars to feudal lords and warriors. In the Edo period (1603-1868), wandering masterless samurai and former priests used this technique in telling war tales in an amusing way on the streets to earn a living. Two storytellers who worked in the precincts of Asakusa Kannon Temple in Edo gained great pupularity with their repertoires which included even stories of love and domestic affairs. In the Meiji era (1868-1912), such a method of storytelling was utilized by the government to impart to the public the meaning of the Meiji Restoration, but later it also became a means of propaganda used by the democratic movement against the government. After World War II, the popularity of *kōdan* greatly declined. ⇨ GUNKI-MONOGATARI, MEIJI ISHIN
〖注〗 epic 叙事詩の. feudal lord 大名. wandering masterless samurai 浪人. precincts 境内. the Meiji Restoration 明治維新.

kōdō 香道 the art of incense; a traditional aesthetic pastime of incense burning. It was developed in the Heian period (794-1185) and was popularly enjoyed in the Edo period (1603-1868) in order to acquire a refined sense of smell and to cultivate mental composure. Also, it was considered hospitable to scent the air of a room by burning incense when special guests were expected.

〖注〗 incense 香. aesthetic 美的な, 審美的な. pastime 娯楽, 道. mental composure 精神の平静.

Kodomo no Hi 子供の日   Children's Day (May 5); a national holiday designated after World War II for wishing all children happiness, good health and a bright future. Formerly, this day was Boys' Day (*Tango no Sekku*), Girls' Day being on March 3. Thus, along with the new holiday to celebrate all children, the traditional *Tango no Sekku* festival for boys is still widely celebrated among families with young sons.   ⇨ KOKUMIN NO SHUKUJITSU, MOMO NO SEKKU, TANGO NO SEKKU

kōenkai 後援会   a support organization, especially one for a politician; a group organized for election campaigns. The *kōenkai* plays an important role because the multi-member electoral district system tends to enhance intraparty competition. Therefore, an individual candidate is often more dependent upon his personal support organization than his party. In order to compete against other candidates from the same party, a politician must organize a support organization to win in an election. Also, the name is given to groups that financially support performers of traditional arts such as Noh and Kabuki, as well as *sumō*.

〖注〗 multi-member electoral district system 複数選挙区制. intraparty competition 党内競争.

kofukusa 古帛紗   an old-type *fukusa*; a square silk cloth used in the tea ceremony, smaller than the *fukusa*. The small cloth is used to prevent damage to precious tea-ceremony objects while they are being appreciated by the guests.   ⇨ CHANOYU, FUKUSA

〖注〗 tea ceremony 茶の湯. appreciate 鑑賞する.

kofun 古墳   a tumulus; an ancient burial mound; a mounded tomb made for powerful rulers in the earliest times of Japanese history, presumably from around the third to the sixth centuries. The huge size of the tumulus confirms the power of the ruling class of those days. They come in a variety of shapes: round, square, round at the top and square at the base, square at the head and round at the bottom, keyhole shaped, etc. A number of clay figurines and articles were buried with the corpse. Among the famous remaining *kofun* are Emperor Nintoku's tumulus in Sakai,

Ōsaka, and Emperor Ōjin's in Fujiidera, Ōsaka, the former being the largest tomb in area in the world, measuring 415 meters in length and 36 m in height.　⇨ HANIWA, KOFUN-JIDAI

〖注〗 tumulus 塚、古墳．　burial mound 埋葬塚．　round at the top and square at the base 上円下方（墳）．　square at the head and round at the bottom 前方後円（墳）．　clay figurine 埴輪．　figurine 小立像．　corpse 死体．

Kofun-jidai 古墳時代　the Tumulus period (250–552); the earliest period of Japanese history, when huge mounded earth tombs were made for powerful rulers.　This period is considered to include the age of the emergence of powerful ruling families, the establishment of the Yamato court, and the introduction of Buddhist culture. The grand scale of the tumulus confirms the absolute power of the ruling class then, and figurines and other articles buried within them give some idea of life in those days.　⇨ HANIWA, KOFUN

〖注〗 tumulus 古墳．　mound 小山にする、積み上げる、塚にする．　emergence 出現．　figurine 小立像．

kōgō 香合　an incense burner; a small container with a perforated lid in which incense is burned in the tea ceremony.　Incense burning is an important part of the tea ceremony, creating a fragrant atmosphere.　In a complete tea ceremony, incense is burned in a *kōgō* using a charcoal fire according to a prescribed manner, while in an abbreviated tea ceremony the *kōgō* is simply displayed in the alcove or the side alcove.　The type of *kōgō* and incense used differs according to the season and whether an inset hearth or brazier is used.　For example, in winter when an inset hearth is used, kneaded incense (*nerikō*) is burned in a *kōgō* of pottery or lacquered wood (in the latter case the incense is placed on a camellia leaf).　In summer when a portable brazier is used, *jinkō* (aloeswood) or *byakudan* (sandalwood) is burned in a wooden or metal *kōgō*.　⇨ CHANOYU, FŪRO, RO

〖注〗 incense 香．　perforated 穴のあいた．　prescribed 規則にかなった．　alcove 床の間．　side alcove 脇床．　inset hearth 炉．　brazier 風炉．　kneaded incense 練り香．　aloeswood 沈香．　sandalwood 白檀．

Kōhaku Utagassen 紅白歌合戦　Red-and-White Singing Competition; an annual song festival held on New Year's Eve and televised by NHK (Nippon Hoso Kyokai), the public broadcasting system. Selected popular singers form two teams, the red consisting of women and the white consisting of men, making about 20 pairs. They sing their hit songs in competition against each other.　The program ends with the singing of *Auld Lang Syne*, close to midnight when temple bells begin to ring out the old year. It has been an annual event since 1950 and has enjoyed one of the highest audience ratings annually.

〖注〗 *Auld Lang Syne*「蛍の光」. audience rating 視聴率.

koicha 濃茶 thick powdered tea; pasty green tea, which looks like spinach soup. In a complete tea ceremony, *koicha* is served in the earlier stage of the proceedings and is shared by several guests from the same tea bowl. ⇨ CHANOYU, USUCHA

〖注〗 pasty どろどろした, 粘った. tea ceremony 茶の湯. proceedings 進行, 点前.

koinobori 鯉のぼり carp streamers; a set of carp streamers hoisted on a bamboo pole for Boys' Day. Traditionally, the Festival of Boys has been celebrated on May 5 (called Children's Day today) to honor boys. A set of huge decorative carp streamers consisting of a black male carp and a red female one (and sometimes many more) are flown from a long pole set up in the yard, with the wish that boys be courageous and strong like carp. The carp is symbolic of courage because of its ability to swim up a waterfall. ⇨ KODOMO NO HI, TANGO NO SEKKU

〖注〗 streamer 吹き流し. hoist 引き上げる, 揚げる. bamboo pole 竿. waterfall 滝.

Kojiki 古事記 *The Record of Ancient Matters* (712). Japan's oldest historical account and oldest remaining book in Japanese, compiled by Ō no Yasumaro (?-723) by imperial command. Covering in three volumes the period from the creation of the Japanese islands in the mythological age to the era of Empress Suiko (554-628; r. 592-628), this work includes myths, legends, Imperial genealogy, historical events and poems, with assertions of the descendancy of the imperial family from mythological gods. Based on the oral recitation of Hieda no Are (?650-?) who had been assigned to memorize this body of works by Emperor Tenmu (622-686; r. 673-686), the account was recorded by Ō no Yasumaro and presented to Empress Genmei (661-721; r. 707-715) in 712. Unlike *Nihon Shoki* (The Chronicle of Japan, 720), *Kojiki* is written mostly in the Japanese language, but borrowing Chinese characters to phonetically represent Japanese syllables. ⇨ MAN-YŌ-GANA, NIHON SHOKI

〖注〗 imperial command 勅令. Imperial genealogy 皇室の系図.

descendancy 子孫.　Chinese character 漢字.　phonetically 発音上.

kokata　子方　a child actor or a child role; a juvenile actor cast for special roles in Noh and Kabuki plays.　He usually plays children, but sometimes is given an adult role to bring the principal actor (*shite*) out into prominence, or to add a symbolic atmosphere of innocence or nobility to a certain character.　⇨ KABUKI, NŌ, SHITE
　〖注〗 principal actor 仕手.　bring...out into prominence ～を目立たせる.

kōken　後見　stage assistants in Noh and Kabuki plays.　Dressed in black, they play important roles on the stage, helping an actor, especially the main character (*shite*) in a Noh play, by changing his costume, taking care of hand properties, or prompting him when he forgets a line.　They have more dignified roles than *kurogo* (a stage assistant attired in black), appearing with their face uncovered and in dignified costume.　⇨ KABUKI, KUROGO, NŌ, SHITE
　〖注〗 main character 主役, (能の)仕手.　hand property 小道具.　dignified 威厳のある, 堂々たる.

kokeshi　小芥子　a cylindrical wooden doll; a primitive form of doll, made of wood, consisting of a ball-shaped head and a limbless cylindrical body.　Some are made from a single piece of wood while others have a detachable head.　Most *kokeshi* have a meek feminine face, with the body painted with a simple floral or abstract design.　The making of *kokeshi* originated in the Tōhoku region, northern Honshū, as indoor work during the severe winter season.　*Kokeshi* dolls are now made in various parts of the country in distinctive local forms and are sold as souvenirs.　Recently creative, modern types of *kokeshi* dolls are also being made.
　〖注〗 cylindrical 円柱(形)の.　limbless 手足のない.　detachable とりはずしの出来る.　floral design 花の模様.　distinctive local form その土地独特の形.

koki　古稀　lit. rare from ancient times.　the celebration of one's 70th birthday; the 70th anniversary of one's birth, one of the special ages to celebrate longevity.　The term *koki*, meaning "rare from ancient times," derives from a phrase in a poem by the ancient Chinese poet Tu Fu (712-70): "Man has rarely lived to attain his 70th year of age from ancient times."　⇨ BEIJU, HAKUJU, KANREKI, KIJU
　〖注〗 longevity 長寿.　Tu Fu 杜甫.　"Man has rarely lived to attain his 70th year of age from ancient times." 「人生七十古来稀なり」.

Kokin(waka)shū　古今(和歌)集　*The Anthology of Ancient and Modern Poems* (around 905); a collection of Japanese vernacular poems, compiled in the Heian period (794-1185) by order of Emperor Daigo (885-930; r. 897-930). It is composed of 20 volumes of some 1,100 poems, most of which are *tanka*, short poems of 31 syllables. They were selected from among all known Japanese poems which had appeard since the late eighth century, by four poets designated by the emperor—Ki no Tsurayuki (?-945), Ki no Tomonori (?-?905), Ōshikōchi no Mitsune (early Heian period) and Mibu no Tadamine (mid-Heian period). The older poems include a large number whose authors are unknown, which are rather naive and candid, whereas the poems of the compilers and their contemporaries are characterized by courtly elegance and sophistication, largely reflecting the aesthetic trends of the period. The invention of the *kana* system of writing in the eighth century spurred a revival of Japanese vernacular poetry, supplementing the Chinese-style poems which comprised the mainstream of poetry at the time. ⇨ HEIAN-JIDAI, KANA, KOJIKI, TANKA

〖注〗 anthology 名詩選． vernacular 自国の． Ōshikōchi no Mitsune 凡河内躬恒． Mibu no Tadamine 壬生忠岑． contemporary 当世の人． courtly elegance 雅び． sophistication 洗練されていること，凝っていること． aesthetic 美意識の．

kokkeibon 滑稽本 lit. a comical book. a story book with humor; a genre of prose works of the late Edo period (1603-1868). The works describe humorous aspects of worldly affairs of common people. Representative tales include *Tōkaidōchū Hizakurige* (Shanks' Mare Along the Tōkaidō) by Jippensha Ikku (1765-1831) and *Ukiyodoko* (The Floating-World Hairdresser) by Shikitei Sanba (1776-1822), both retaining literary value as well. ⇨ CHŌNIN

〖注〗 genre 種類，(文学の)形式． Shanks' Mare Along the Tōkaidō 「東海道中膝栗毛」． The Floating-World Hairdresser 「浮世床」．

ḳōkō 孝行 filial piety; filial devotion; to be dutiful to parents and ancestors as an obligation. Derived from Confucianism (*Jukyō*), filial devotion has been regarded as an important moral basis of human conduct and still persists in the Japanese way of thinking. ⇨ JUKYŌ

〖注〗 filial 子の，子としての． piety 忠誠，孝心． obligation 義理，恩義． be derived from ～から出ている，～に由来する． Confucianism 儒教．

kōkō-yakyū 高校野球 high school baseball; specifically referring to the two annual high school championship tournament held at

Kōshien Stadium, Hyōgo Prefecture, in spring and summer. These tournaments began in 1924 and 1915 respectively. The National Invitational High School Baseball Tournament held in spring presently hosts 32 schools chosen by the National High School Baseball Committee from among schools nominated by district committees, based on performance during the autumn season. The National High School Baseball Championship Tournament held in summer hosts 49 schools that have won preliminary tournaments in their respective districts, held just prior to the championship tournament. The present representatives are two schools each from Hokkaidō (northern and southern Hokkaidō) and Tokyo (western and eastern Tokyo), and one each from the remaining 45 prefectures. These events attract special attention throughout the nation and enjoy wide coverage by the mass media.

〖注〗 preliminary tournament 予選大会. coverage 報道.

koku 石 a bale; a unit of measurement of capacity used in former days. One *koku* is equivalent to 180.4 liters. In feudal times this unit was significant in connection with rice; the feudal lords and officials received bales (*koku*) of rice as their annual stipend, the amount determined according to their status. ⇨ DAIMYŌ. HAN²

〖注〗 capacity 容量. feudal times 封建時代. feudal lord 大名、藩主. annual stipend 年俸.

kokubunji 国分寺 an ancient provincial temple; temples established in every province by the order of Emperor Shōmu (701-56) during the late Nara period (710-94). At the same time, *kokubunniji* (provincial nunneries) were also ordered to be built in each province. Tōdaiji Temple in Nara, still existing today, was the central temple of all the *kokubunji*, with the famous giant statue of the Great Buddha enshrined there. Most of the *kokubunji* disapeared during the Heian period (794-1185) after losing the sponsorship of the state. ⇨ KUNI

〖注〗 province (行政上区分された)国. provincial nunnery 国分尼寺. enshrine 祀る.

kokuhō 国宝 a national treasure; rare properties of highest historical value, officially designated as treasures of the country. They are selected from among important cultural properties (*jūyō-bunkazai*) and are protected under the Cultural Properties Protection Law enacted in 1950; previously they came under the National Treasures Preservation Law (1929). The categories include buildings, sculptures, paintings, archaeological articles, objects of academic value, etc. ⇨ BUNKAZAI, JŪYŌ-BUNKAZAI, JŪYŌMUKEI-BUNKAZAI, NINGEN-KOKUHŌ

〖注〗 property 財産, 資産. important cultural property 重要文化財. the Cultural Properties Protection Law「文化財保護法」. enact 施行する. the National Treasures Preservation Law「国宝保存法」. archaeological article 考古学的出土品. objects of academic value 学術の重要品.

kokumin-kyūkamura 国民休暇村 national vacation villages; resorts established in national parks and quasi-national parks, to promote the people's health. They are financed out of reserve funds of national pension and health insurance plans, and managed by the National Vacation Villages Association under the supervision of the Environment Agency of the Prime Minister's Office. Since the first one was built in 1961, the system has grown to include about 30 villages. The resorts feature camping areas, playgrounds, beaches, ski grounds, various sports and recreation facilities, as well as lodging. They are maintained either by government or local public organizations, or the National Vacation Villages Association. Some 3.5 million persons visit the villages annually, a million of whom make use of the accommodations offered. ⇨ KOKUMIN-SHUKUSHA, KOKURITSU-KŌEN, KOKUTEI-KŌEN

〖注〗 quasi-national park 国定公園. reserve fund 積立金. national pension 国民年金. the Environment Agency 環境庁. the Prime Minister's Office 総理府. accommodation 宿泊施設.

kokumin no shukujitsu 国民の祝日 a national holiday; twelve national holidays designated according to the National Holiday Act enacted in 1948 (partly amended in 1966). Schools and most offices are closed on these days. The national holidays are: *Ganjitsu* or New Year's Day (January 1), *Seijin no Hi* or Coming-of-Age Day (January 15), *Kenkoku Kinen no Hi* or the Nation's Foundation Day (February 11), *Shunbun no Hi* or Vernal Equinox Day (March 21 or 20), *Tennō Tanjōbi* or Emperor's Birthday (April 29), *Kenpō Kinenbi* or Constitution Day (May 3), *Kodomo no Hi* or Children's Day (May 5), *Keirō no Hi* or Respect-for-the-Aged Day (September 15), *Shūbun no Hi* or Autumnal Equinox Day (September 23 or 24), *Taiiku no Hi* or Sports Day (October 10), *Bunka no Hi* or Culture Day (November 3), *Kinrō Kansha no Hi* or Labor Thanksgiving Day (November 23). (See separate entries.)

〖注〗 the National Holiday Act「国民の祝日に関する法律」. enact 施行する. entry 項目.

kokumin-shukusha 国民宿舎 people's lodging houses; inexpensive public accommodations built in scenic areas, designed to promote the people's health. First planned in 1956, they have been built with financing from reserve funds of national pension and health insurance plans. There are about 350 such hotels managed by local public organizations, utilized annually by some 4.5 million persons for lodging and by about 3.5 million for taking a rest. In addition, about 160 such facilities are privately operated under the supervision of public organizations such as the National Parks Association.

〖注〗 accommodation 宿泊施設. reserve fund 積立金. national pension 国民年金. facilities 施設.

Kokumin Taiiku Taikai 国民体育大会 the National Athletic Meet; the annual sports event for amateur athletes, divided into summer, autumn and winter games, in which prefectures compete against each other. The first meet was held in 1946 near Kyoto with the purpose of bringing back the spirit of sports which was lost during the war and putting life back into the people depressed by the difficult situation after the war. The site of the games alternates among the 47 prefectures. It is held under the joint sponsorship of the Education Ministry, the Japan Athletic Association and the hosting prefecture. The prefecture with the best overall record in the three meets during the year wins the Emperor's Cup and the prefecture with the best record in women's events wins the Empress' Cup. The events include track and field, ball games, winter sports, etc., as well as traditional sports such as judo and *kendō*.

〖注〗 the Japan Athletic Association 日本体育協会. hosting 主催の. track and field 陸上競技.

kokuritsu-kōen 国立公園 national parks; national parks designated by the government. Specifically, they are designated by the National Park Council, and administered by the Environmental Agency of the Prime Minister's Office. The first ones, the Seto Inland Sea and Unzen National Parks, were designated in 1934. As of 1984, when the parks system marked its 50th anniversary, there were 27 such parks: (from north to south) Rishiri-Rebun-Sarobetsu (Hokkaidō), Shiretoko (Hokkaidō), Akan (Hokkaidō),

Daisetsuzan (Hokkaidō), Shikotsu-Tōya (Hokkaidō), Towada-Hachimantai (Aomori, Akita, Iwate), Rikuchū-kaigan (Iwate, Miyagi), Bandai-Asahi (Yamagata, Niigata, Fukushima), Nikkō (Fukushima, Tochigi, Gunma, Niigata), Jōshin'etsu-kōgen (Gunma, Niigata, Nagano), Chichibu-Tama (Saitama, Tokyo, Yamanashi, Nagano), Ogasawara (Tokyo), Fuji-Hakone-Izu (Kanagawa, Yamanashi, Tokyo, Shizuoka) Chūbu-sangaku (Niigata, Toyama, Nagano, Gifu), Minami-Alps (Nagano, Yamanashi, Shizuoka), Hakusan (Toyama, Ishikawa, Fukui, Gifu), Ise-Shima (Mie), Yoshino-Kumano (Mie, Nara, Wakayama), San'in-kaigan (Kyoto, Hyōgo, Tottori), Daisen-Oki (Tottori, Okayama, Shimane), Seto Naikai (Wakayama, Hyōgo, Okayama, Hiroshima, Yamaguchi, Tokushima, Kagawa, Ehime, Fukuoka, Ōita), Ashizuri-Uwakai (Kōchi, Ehime), Aso (Kumamoto, Ōita), Unzen-Amakusa (Nagasaki, Kumamoto, Kagoshima), Saikai (Nagasaki), Kirishima-Yaku (Miyazaki, Kagoshima), Iriomote (Okinawa). (See separate entries.)

〖注〗 the National Park Council 国立公園審議会. the Environmental Agency 環境庁. the Prime Minister's Office 総理府.

Kokusai Kankō Shinkōkai 国際観光振興会 Japan National Tourist Organization (JNTO); a quasi-governmental organization established in 1959 to promote international tourism. Funded in part by the government under the supervision of the Ministry of Transport, the JNTO is also partially supported by travel-related organizations and businesses. Special subsidies are granted by the government, for example, when an exposition is held. Activities of the JNTO include disseminating Japanese travel information overseas, making arrangements for foreigners traveling in Japan, facilitating Japanese travel abroad, etc. There are 16 overseas branch offices in about a dozen countries, several of which are in the U.S. The JNTO set up the Japanese Convention Bureau (1965) to hold international conventions and has opened Tourist Information Centers in Tokyo (1962), Kyoto (1964) and Narita (1978) to assist foreign tourists with travel information and arrangements.

〖注〗 quasi-governmental organization 準政府機関, 特殊法人. the Ministry of Transport 運輸省. subsidy 助成金. exposition 博覧会. disseminate 宣伝する, 普及する. the Japanese Convention Bureau 日本コンベンションビューロー, 日本国際会議事務局. Tourist Information Center 総合観光案内所.

Kokutani 古九谷 old Kutani porcelain ware; one type of Kutani porcelain ware, first produced in the mid-17th century at Kutani in the province of Kaga, presently in Ishikawa Prefecture. While the body of new Kutani is white and smooth, that of old Kutani is grayish and coarse in texture, and covered with a bubbled glaze. Old Kutani has decorative designs of flowers, birds or landscapes in colors of green, red, yellow, brown and purple, with the edge accentuated in brownish red. The design and color, influenced by the Kanō school of painting, emerged in the Muromachi period (1336-1568). Genuine old Kutani ware is difficult to come by today. ⇨ KANŌ-HA, KUTANI-YAKI

〖注〗 porcelain 磁器. province 地方の諸国, (行政のために分けた)国. texture 生地, 肌合い. glaze 釉. come by 手に入る.

kokutei-kōen 国定公園 quasi-national parks; semi-national parks designated by the Environmental Agency of the Japanese government and administered by prefectural authorities. The designation started in 1950 with Biwako and Sado-Yahiko-Yoneyama quasi-national parks. There are 54 such areas (as of 1984). They are: (from north to south) Abashiri (Hokkaidō), Niseko-Shakotan-Otaru-kaigan (Hokkaidō), Hidaka-sanmyaku-Erimo (Hokkaidō), Ōnuma (Hokkaidō), Shimokita-hantō (Aomori), Tsugaru (Aomori), Hayachine (Iwate), Kurikoma (Iwate, Miyagi, Akita, Yamagata), Minami Sanriku-Kinkazan (Miyagi), Zaō (Miyagi, Yamagata), Oga (Akita), Chōkai (Akita, Yamagata), Echigo-sanzan-Tadami (Fukushima, Niigata), Suigō-Tsukuba (Ibaraki, Chiba), Myōgi-Arafune-Saku-kōgen (Gunma, Nagano), Minami Bōsō (Chiba), Meiji-no-mori-Takao (Tokyo), Tanzawa-Ōyama (Kanagawa), Sado-Yahiko-Yoneyama (Niigata), Noto-hantō (Toyama, Ishikawa), Echizen-Kaga-kaigan (Ishikawa, Fukui), Wakasa-wan (Fukui, Kyoto), Yatsugatake-Chūshin-kōgen (Yamanashi, Nagano), Tenryū-Okumikawa (Nagano, Shizuoka, Aichi), Ibi-Sekigahara-Yōrō (Gifu), Hida-Kisogawa (Gifu, Aichi), Aichi-kōgen (Aichi), Mikawa-wan (Aichi), Suzuka (Mie, Shiga), Murō-Akama-Aoyama (Mie, Nara), Biwako (Shiga, Kyoto), Meiji-no-mori-Minoo (Ōsaka), Kongō-Ikoma (Ōsaka, Nara), Hyōnosen-Ushiroyama-Nagisen (Hyōgo, Tottori, Okayama), Yamato-Aogaki (Nara), Kōya-Ryūjin (Nara, Wakayama), Hiba-Dōgo-Taishaku (Tottori, Shimane, Hiroshima), Nishichūgoku-sanchi (Shimane, Hiroshima, Yamaguchi), Kitanagato-kaigan

(Yamaguchi), Akiyoshidai (Yamaguchi), Tsurugisan (Tokushima, Kōchi), Muroto-Anan-kaigan (Tokushima, Kōchi), Ishizuchi (Ehime, Kōchi), Kitakyūshū (Fukuoka), Genkai (Fukuoka, Saga, Nagasaki), Yaba-Hita-Hikosan (Fukuoka, Kumamoto, Ōita), Iki-Tsushima (Nagasaki), Kyūshū Chūōsanchi (Kumamoto, Miyazaki), Nippo-kaigan (Ōita, Miyazaki), Sobo-Katamuki (Ōita, Miyazaki), Nichinan-kaigan (Miyazaki, Kagoshima), Atsumi-guntō (Kagoshima), Okinawa-kaigan (Okinawa), Okinawa-senseki (Okinawa). ⇨ KOKURITSU-KŌEN, SHIZENKŌEN HŌ

〖注〗 quasi- 準～. the Environmental Agency 環境庁. administer 管理する. prefectural authorities 都道府県の行政当局.

kōkyo 皇居 the Imperial Palace. It was originally called Edo Castle and was built in 1457 by Ōta Dōkan (1432-86), a warlord of the Muromachi period (1336-1568). Tokugawa Ieyasu (1542-1616), the first Tokugawa shogun, made this castle the headquarters of the shogunate in 1590. Upon the Meiji Restoration (1868), Emperor Meiji moved there from Kyoto in 1869 when the name of Edo was changed to Tokyo. Since then the Imperial Family has lived there except during six years of repairs after it was destroyed by fire in 1873. The palace is surrounded by wide moats, walls of massive rocks, and beautiful pine trees. The front entrance is famous for its double bridge (*nijūbashi*). ⇨ MEIJI ISHIN, TOKUGAWA-BAKUFU

〖注〗 warlord 武将. headquarters 本拠. shogunate 幕府. the Meiji Restoration 明治維新. moat 濠.

komainu 狛犬 a lion-dog; a pair of statues of guardian dogs placed at a shrine. They are usually made of stone and are placed at the sides of the entrance to a shrine or the approach to the oratory in the shrine precincts. It is said that they protect the shrine against evil spirits with their fierce leonine countenance. With their roots in China, they are sometimes called *karashishi* ("Chinese lions"); *Karashishi* refers to any such figure including those painted on screens, scrolls, etc. ⇨ JINJA, KARASHISHI

〖注〗 approach 参道. oratory 拝殿. shrine precincts 神社の境内. leonine countenance 獅子のような表情. Chinese lion 唐獅子. screen 屏風. scroll 巻物.

komon 小紋 lit. small crests. a pattern on kimono fabric, made up of the repetition of small motifs. Thick paper is cut to make a pattern of small motifs. The stencil thus made is pasted on silk

fabric to be dyed.   The size of the motif varies, ranging from a
life-size flower to a small grain.   The fabric of the finest pattern
is called *same-komon* (a shark-skin pattern), which was first used
to make the ceremonial attire of samurai (*kamishimo*) in the Edo
period (1603–1868).   Soon the kimono fabric was widely used by
women in Edo, thus giving rise to the name *Edo-komon*.   *Komon* of
various kinds are still widely favored for their subdued elegant
atmosphere, and their wide use, from informal to semiformal.   ⇨
EDO-KOMON

〚注〛 crest 紋, 家紋. fabric 織物. motif 繰り返しの意匠. stencil 型紙.
life-size 実物大の. ceremonial attire 式服, 儀式用正装. give rise to 生じる,
由来する. subdued おさえた, 渋い.

komusō 虚無僧   a strolling priest; a mendicant monk of the Fuke
sect, a branch of Zen Buddhism.   First appearing in the Muromachi period (1336–1568), they strolled from door to door asking for
alms by playing *shakuhachi* (a vertical bamboo flute).   They wore
a huge sedge-basket hat covering the entire head and face.   Later,
in feudal days, most of them are said to have been wandering
masterless samurai, thus usually carrying a sword at their side.   ⇨
SHAKUHACHI

〚注〛 stroll 歩きまわる, さまよう. mendicant monk 物乞いをする僧, 托鉢僧.
Fuke sect 普化宗. alms 布施, 施し. sedge-basket hat 菅でできた籠のような
帽子. feudal days 封建時代. wandering masterless samurai 浪人, 主人がな
くさまよっている侍.

kondō 金堂   lit. a golden hall.   the main building of a grand Buddhist temple.   It is the most important structure among several in
the compounds of a grand temple, and is where the principal
Buddhist image is enshrined.   It is so called because the inside of
the building used to be painted gold.   ⇨ GARAN, HONDŌ, HONZON
〚注〛 compounds 敷地, 境内. principal Buddhist image 本尊. enshrine
祀る.

konnyaku こんにゃく   devil's tongue; square cakes or noodle-like
strings made from the starch of devil's tongue or arum root.   The
gelatinous starch is mixed with limewater to coagulate it.   Thus,
before cooking, it should be washed well or boiled in water and
drained to remove the lime residue.   It comes in two textures, an
unrefined dark one and a refined white one.   *Konnyaku* is generally used in *oden* (Japanese hodgepodge), *nabemono* (pot dish),
etc.   The fine noodles of the white type are called *shirataki* (lit.

white cascade), and are an indispensable ingredient for *sukiyaki*.
⇨ ODEN, NABEMONO, SHIRATAKI

〖注〗 devil's tongue こんにゃく. arum アルム芋(サトイモ科), こんにゃく芋.
limewater 石灰水. coagulate 凝固させる. lime residue 石灰のかす. texture 生地, きめ. ingredient (料理の)材料.

Kōrai-seiji 高麗青磁 Koryo celadon ware; celadon ware originating
in China, and transmitted via Korea during its Koryo dynasty
(918-1392) to Japan in the Kamakura period (1185-1336). The
body has carved designs with whitish inlaid slips. The surface is
coated with grayish-green celadon glaze. After firing, the surface
takes on finely crackled patterns. ⇨ SEIJI

〖注〗 celadon 灰(淡)緑色, 青磁. the Koryo dynasty (朝鮮の)高麗朝. carved design 彫り模様. inlaid はめこんだ, ちりばめた, 象眼の. glaze つや, 釉.
crackled pattern ひび入りの模様.

kōro 香炉 an incense burner; a small container, usually with a
perforated lid, in which incense is burned. The container is made
of pottery, metal or lacquered wood. First used for burning
incense as part of Buddhist rituals, *kōro* have been made in various
artistic shapes, differing according to purpose—for use as a religious offering, for scenting clothes and rooms, for the aesthetic
appreciation of the incense itself, for creating a fragrant atmosphere in the tea ceremony, etc. The *kōro* used in the tea ceremony
is called *kōgō*. ⇨ KŌDŌ, KŌGŌ

〖注〗 incense 香. perforated 穴のあいた. ritual 儀式. religious offering お
供え. aesthetic appreciation 美的鑑賞.

koromogae 衣替え changing of clothes; the custom of changing to
clothes appropriate for the season. Traditionally, the two major
dates for this are June 1 for wearing cool clothes and October 1 for
warm clothes, regardless of the temperature or weather. This
custom is still observed by those who enjoy the coming of seasonal
changes. Often school or official uniforms are light-colored during
the summer period, and black or navy blue during the winter
period.

Koseto 古瀬戸 Old Seto ceramic ware; glazed ceramic ware first
produced by Katō Tōshirō at Seto, Aichi Prefecture, in the 13th
century. It was the first form of ceramics to take on ash glaze, the
colors being yellow, red-brown and black. ⇨ SETO-YAKI

〖注〗 ceramic ware 陶器. glazed 釉のついた. Katō Tōshirō 加藤藤四郎.
ash glaze 灰釉.

koshihimo 腰紐 a waist string; a cord tied around the waist, used under the sash (*obi*) for fixing a kimono in place. It is not unusual for a dozen cords to be used to maintain the shape of a formal kimono. ⇨ KIMONO, OBI
〖注〗 cord 紐. sash 帯.

kotatsu 火燵 a foot warmer; a traditional heating unit composed of a low table made of a latticed wooden frame and a coverlet. A charcoal fire used to be provided underneath in a fireproof clay pot filled with ashes or in a box set in the floor. Today, it is more commonly found in the form of a table with a special electric heating device attached underneath, which is called *denki-gotatsu* (an electric foot warmer).
〖注〗 unit 設備一式. latticed wooden frame 格子になった木わく. coverlet 掛け布団, 覆い. charcoal fire 炭火. fireproof 防火になった. clay pot 粘土製のつぼ.

koto 琴 a Japanese zither; the most popular traditional musical instrument played widely, especially by women, even today. It is made of paulownia wood and is about 180 centimeters in length and 30 to 40 cm in width. It has 13 strings, each stretching over a bridge, which are plucked with small plectrums attached to the thumb and two forefingers of the right hand.
〖注〗 zither ツィター(琴に似た水平な弦楽器). musical instrument 楽器. paulownia 桐. bridge (弦楽器の)こま. pluck (弦楽器などを)かき鳴らす. plectrum ばち.

kōtō-gakkō 高等学校 1) (in the postwar school system) a senior high school; an upper secondary school; the three-year school following the three-year junior high school and followed by a four-year college or two-year junior college. It is part of the 6-3-3-4 system adopted under the School Education Law established in 1947. It is classified into two courses, general and vocational. 2) (in the prewar school system) a higher school; a post-secondary school; the three-year school following the five-year middle school and followed by the three-year university. Those who completed four out of five years of middle school were qualified to take admission exminations. These schools were organized in 1894 with the issuance of the Higher School Order, but under the new school system they were incorporated into some universities as the preliminary two-year division of general studies within the university. The school consisted of a humanities and a science department, and served to prepare students for entering imperial universities.   ⇨ CHŪGAKKŌ, GAKKŌ KYŌIKUHŌ, KYŌIKU KI-HONHŌ, SENMON-GAKKŌ, TEIKOKU-DAIGAKU

〖注〗 the School Education Law「学校教育法」. vocational 職業の、職業教育の. admission examination 入学(許可)試験. issuance 発布. the Higher School Order「高等学校令」. the preliminary two-year division of general studies 最初の2年間の教養課程. humanities department 人文学部.

kōtō-jogakkō 高等女学校   a girls' high school; the four- or five-year secondary school for girls, equivalent to middle school for boys, in the prewar school system.   *Kōtō-jogakkō* were organized in 1899 with the issuance of the Girls' High School Order. After graduating from a girls' high school, women had opportunities to enter several kinds of institutions of higher education for women—higher professional school (*senmon-gakkō*), ordinary normal school (*shihan-gakkō*), higher normal school for women (*joshi kōtō shihan-gakkō*), private college for women (*joshi-daigaku*), etc. Women were not expected to go to state universities prior to the postwar educational reform.   ⇨ CHŪGAKKŌ, SENMON-GAKKŌ

〖注〗 issuance 発布. the Girls' High School Order「高等女学校令」. institution 機関. higher professional school 専門学校. normal school 師範学校. higher normal school for women 女子高等師範学校.

kotsuzumi 小鼓   a shoulder drum; a small hourglass-shaped drum, made up of a hollow wooden body (called *dō*) with a horse-skin leather cover at each end. Two vermilion cords are used, one for keeping the body and the covers together by passing it through the holes on both covers, and the other for adjusting the sound by winding it over the middle of the body laced with the other cord. The drum is placed on the right shoulder with the left hand holding the cords, and is struck with the tip of the middle and ring fingers of the right hand. The cover should be slightly moistened with a small piece of wet Japanese paper to maintain an echoing sound. The pitch is controlled by squeezing the cords. *Kotsuzumi* is an important instrument along with *ōtsuzumi* (a large hand drum) in the instrumental ensembles (*hayashi*) of the Noh and Kabuki theaters and related Japanese dance forms.   ⇨ HAYASHI, KABUKI, NŌ, ŌTSUZUMI, TSUZUMI

〖注〗 hourglass-shaped 砂時計型の. vermilion 朱色. pitch 音の高低. instrumental ensemble 楽器の合奏、囃子.

kouta 小唄   lit. a short song. a traditional song or ballad sung to the accompaniment of *shamisen*. It is commonly performed by geisha as well as many amateur performers, and may accompany traditional dances.   ⇨ SHAMISEN

〖注〗 ballad 伝承的叙事詩または歌謡. accompaniment 伴奏.

kōyadōfu 高野豆腐 lit. Mount Kōya bean curd. freeze-dried soybean curd; dried *tōfu* with a fine sponge-like texture made by freezing and drying. It was invented centuries ago by Buddhist monks who lived on Mount Kōya, which becomes snowbound in winter. The bean curd is frozen and, then after dehydration, becomes sponge-like. It is generally prepared for cooking by soaking it in hot water, squeezing the water out, and then simmering it in seasoned fish broth.   ⇨ TŌFU

〖注〗 bean curd 豆腐. freeze-dried 凍らせてから乾燥させた. texture きめ、質. dehydration 脱水、乾燥. simmer 煮つめる. seasoned 味をつけた. fish broth 魚のだし汁.

ku 区 a ward; an urban district, a subdivision of a large city. For example, Tokyo city proper is divided into 23 wards; each has its own self-governing administrative organ but is also administered by the metropolitan government.

〖注〗 Tokyo city proper 東京23区. self-governing administrative organ 自治行政機関. metropolitan 首都圏の.

kuchitori 口取り an appetizer; a side dish; an assortment of delicacies artistically arranged, usually on a lacquered plate. It is served with Japanese rice wine or clear soup as the first course of a large dinner.

〖注〗 appetizer 食欲をそそるもの、前菜. side dish 副食. course 一品(dinnerのひと皿ひと皿).

Kudara 百済 the Korean kingdom of Paekche; the Japanese pronunciation of the name Paekche. It occupied the southwest part of the Korean Peninsula from the early fourth century until 660. Many things Chinese were introduced to Japan through this Korean kingdom, some with Korean influence as well.

〖注〗 Paekche 百済.

kuge 公家 court nobles; the imperial family and its direct descendants in the Nara (646-794) and Heian (794-1185) periods; court-related nobles from the Kamakura period (1185-1336) on. In feudal times, this term came to be used in particular to distinguish all court-related nobles from high-ranking feudal lords (*buke*) serving the shogunate.

〖注〗 feudal times 封建時代． feudal lord 武家，大名． shogunate 幕府．

kūkan 空間 a space; negative space. The effect of space or negative space in works of Japanese art is considered very important; for example, the space created between the branches in a flower arrangement, the white part left undrawn in a Japanese painting, etc. This concept is attributed to the value of "nothingness" in Zen philosophy. ⇨ IKEBANA, MA, SUMIE, ZENGA

〖注〗 flower arrangement 生け花． be attributed to ～に由来する． nothingness 無，空．

kumadori 隈取り the exaggerated makeup in Kabuki. The muscles and nerves of the face are accented in heavy red and indigo or black to represent the nature of the character and emotions —usually red to symbolize righteousness and indigo or black to symbolize viciousness. ⇨ KABUKI

〖注〗 indigo 藍色． righteousness 善． viciousness 悪．

Kume-tsumugi 久米紬 pongee textile of Kumejima (Kume Island). *Kume-tsumugi* is a resist-dyed pongee textile produced on the volcanic island of Kume, west of the main island of Okinawa. Designs are painted on a paper pattern, and the dye patterns are thereby worked out. Silk threads are dyed individually before weaving, using dyes produced locally. The resulting textile has neither an obverse nor a reverse side. The threads are woven on a handloom. One *tan* (34 centimeters by 10.6 meters) takes over a month to produce. Dyed pongee of the Ryūkyū Islands is said to be among the world's finest. ⇨ TAN, TSUMUGI

〖注〗 pongee 絹紬（柞蚕から取った糸で織った絹織物）． resist-dyed（部分的に）防染剤を使って染めた． obverse 表，前面． handloom 手織りばた．

kuni 国 a province; administrative divisions of the country, established by the Taika Reform (645–46). With this reform, the country was divided into 58 provinces and three islands, each of which was entrusted to a provincial governor (*kokushi*). Though the system underwent several changes over time, it continued until the Meiji Restoration when the country was officially divided according to the prefecture system (1871). The divisions of *kuni* under the eight regions (the central provinces and the seven districts) just before the prefecture system was adopted were: 66 provinces and two islands (since 824), to which 11 provinces in Hokkaidō were added in 1869.

Kinai (5) — Yamashiro, Yamato, Kawachi, Izumi, Settsu

Tōsandō (8) — Ōmi, Mino, Hida, Shinano, Kōzuke, Shimotsuke, Dewa, Mutsu

Tōkaidō (15) — Iga, Ise, Shima, Owari, Mikawa, Tōtōmi, Suruga, Kai, Izu, Sagami, Kazusa, Shimofusa, Hitachi, Awa, Musashi

Hokurikudō (7) — Wakasa, Echizen, Etchū, Echigo, Kaga, Noto, Sado

San'indō (8) — Tanba, Tajima, Inaba, Hōki, Izumo, Iwami, Oki, Tango

San'yōdō (8) — Harima, Bizen, Bitchū, Bingo, Aki, Suhō, Nagato, Mimasaka

Nankaidō (6) — Kii, Awaji, Awa, Sanuki, Iyo, Tosa

Saikaidō (11) — Chikuzen, Chikugo, Buzen, Bungo, Hizen, Higo, Hyūga, Satsuma, Ōsumi, Iki (Island), Tsushima (Island)

Hokkaidō (11) — Oshima, Shiribeshi, Ishikari, Teshio, Kitami, Iburi, Hidaka, Tokachi, Kushiro, Nemuro, Chishima

⇨ DŌ¹, GOKI(NAI)-SHICHIDŌ, HOKKAIDŌ, KINAI, TŌKAIDŌ

〖注〗 administrative division 行政区画. the Taika Reform 大化の改新. province（行政区画としての)国, 県, 管区. entrust 委任する. provincial governor 国司. the Meiji Restoration 明治維新. the central provinces and the seven districts（五)畿内七道.

kura 蔵 a storehouse. In the compounds of a traditional-style home of the upper class is found a thick-walled fireproof earthen building, usually white or black but sometimes black and white in design. In it, important or rare goods are stored.

〖注〗 compounds 敷地. fireproof 耐火の. earthen building 土蔵.

kurofune 黒船 a black ship; European ships which appeared off the Japanese coast during the Tokugawa period (1603-1868), so called because they looked black. In particular, it refers to the fleet of American ships led by Commodore Matthew C. Perry which anchored off Uraga at the entrance of Tokyo Bay in July 1853 with the mission of asking Japan to open relations with the United States. ⇨ NICHIBEI SHŪKŌ TSŪSHŌ JŌYAKU, NICHIBEI WA-SHIN JŌYAKU, SAKOKU(-SEISAKU)

〖注〗 fleet 艦隊. commodore 提督, 艦長. mission 使命.

kurogo [kuroko] 黒衣 [黒子] lit. a man attired in black. a stage assistant attired and hooded in black so as to be inconspicuous. They are seen most commonly on the stage in Bunraku and Kabuki. On the Bunraku stage, the second and third puppeteers are usually dressed in black. On the Kabuki stage, *kurogo* serves

to help actors change clothes and to bring props to the stage.　⇨
BUNRAKU, KABUKI

〖注〗 attire 装わせる. inconspicuous 出しゃばらない, 目立たない. puppeteer 人形遣い. prop 小道具.

kuro-tomesode 黒留袖　a black formal silk kimono; the most formal
kimono for married women, worn on especially auspicious occasions. It has five white family crests (*kamon*) on it—one on the
back, one on each upper part in front and one on each sleeve, and
a lavish picturesque design on its lower front, in gold, silver and
other colors, with embroidery added. At weddings, married
female relatives of the bride and bridegroom customarily wear
black *tomesode*.　⇨ IRO-TOMESODE, TOMESODE

〖注〗 on auspicious occasion めでたい機会. family crest 家紋. embroidery
縫取り, 刺しゅう.

Kurume-gasuri 久留米絣　Kurume cotton fabric; cotton fabric with
splashed patterns produced at Kurume, Kyūshū, since the late 18th
century. The designs of this fabric are mostly of white patterns
on indigo; white cotton threads are dyed in indigo with parts tied to
be left undyed, and then woven into fabric. The cloth is tough
enough for repeated washings and thus suitable for everyday
kimono for work.　⇨ KASURI, KYŪSHŪ

〖注〗 fabric 織物, 布. splashed patterns 飛び散った模様. indigo 藍(色).

Kusanagi no Tsurugi 草薙の剣　the Grass-Cutting Sword; one of the
three treasures or regalia of the Japanese imperial throne, the
other two being the Sacred Mirror and the Comma-Shaped Gem.
Legend has it that Susanō no Mikoto killed an eight-headed dragon
and found a sword in its body. He offered it to the Sun Goddess,
Amaterasu Ōmikami. Early Japanese history records that with
this sword Yamato Takeru no Mikoto, one of the ancestors of the
Imperial Family, cut burning grass set afire by an enemy and
succeeded in escaping from danger. This story gave rise to the
name "Grass-Cutting Sword." It is enshrined at Atsuta Shrine in
Nagoya.　⇨ MAGATAMA, SANSHU NO JINGI, YATA NO KAGAMI

〖注〗 the three treasures or regalia 三種の神器. regalia 王位の標章. the
Sacred Mirror 八咫の鏡. the Comma-Shaped Gem 勾[曲]玉. Legend has it
that... 伝説によると. the eight-headed dragon 八岐大蛇(やまたのおろち).
give rise to ～を生じる, 引きおこす. enshrine 祀る.

Kutani-yaki 九谷焼　Kutani porcelain ware; porcelain ware
produced around Kutani in Ishikawa Prefecture from the mid-17th

century. Kutani ware is roughly divided into two types—Old Kutani and new Kutani. Genuine Old Kutani ware, produced by Gotō Saijirō (1655-1704) in the early stage (spanning about 40 years), is thick and coarse in texture. After his death, the making of high quality Kutani ware discontinued. In the early 19th century, a new type of Kutani ware, in the form of all sorts of daily articles, emerged and came into general use. Unlike the old type, it is thin and fine in texture, similar to Imari ware. Both types are bright and decorative in color scheme and design. The pictures used are largely influenced by the Kanō school of painting of the Muromachi period (1336-1568). ⇨ KANŌ-HA, KOKUTANI

〖注〗 porcelain ware 磁器. genuine 真正の, 本物の. texture 生地, 肌合い. color scheme 配色.

kyōdai 鏡台 a mirror stand; a stand with a mirror mounted on a small dressing table or chest of drawers holding cosmetics. It came into use during the Muromachi period (1336-1568). The traditional *kyōdai* is used with one seated on one's knees. A modern one is often equipped with a three-faced mirror and a stool, which is called *sanmenkyō*. A *kyōdai* is customarily included in the furniture for a bride to take along to her new home.

〖注〗 mount のせる. be seated on one's knees 正座する.

kyōgen 狂言 lit. crazy words. a traditional form of drama reflecting everyday and social conditions, often making use of mime and comical situations. In addition to performing in complete Kyogen plays, Kyogen actors may occasionally take roles in a Noh play or perform "Kyogen interludes" between two acts of a Noh play which often interpret the drama in common language. ⇨ AI-KYŌGEN, NŌ

〖注〗 mime 物まね. interlude 幕間, 間狂言, 幕間の演芸.

Kyōiku-chokugo 教育勅語 the Imperial Rescript on Education; the rescript issued by Emperor Meiji in 1890 to clarify the foundation of moral principles of education and the nation's way of life. The moral principles, stemming from the ideas of Confucianism, center around the virtues of justice, benevolence, loyalty and filial piety; the aim was to indoctrinate the nation to be loyal to the throne and to be filial to superiors, parents and ancestors. This rescript was read aloud by principals at school ceremonies. In 1948, shortly after the end of World War II, it was abolished. ⇨ JUKYŌ, KŌKŌ, ON

【注】 rescript 勅語，勅令． stem from ～から由来する，起こる，発する． Confucianism 儒教． virtue 美徳，価値． benevolence 慈悲． loyalty 忠誠． filial piety 孝行． indoctrinate 教える，吹き込む．

kyōiku-kanji 教育漢字 Chinese characters for education (996 characters since 1968); essential Chinese characters which must be learned in the six years of elementary school. In 1946, as one of the postwar reforms of the writing system, the Cabinet officially listed 1,850 Chinese characters for daily use as selected by the Council on National Language (Kokugo Shingikai). In 1981, the number of characters for daily use was raised to 1,945. Of them, 881 had been designated as educational Chinese characters in 1948, and later 996 after a 1968 amendment. ⇨ JŌYŌ-KANJI, KANJI

【注】 Chinese character 漢字． the Council on National Language 国語審議会． amendment（法）改正．

Kyōiku Kihonhō 教育基本法 the Fundamental Law of Education (1947); the law outlining the basis of education, enacted shortly after World War II in accordance with the democratic spirit of the Constitution of Japan (1947). It consists of 11 articles, which provide the aim of education, educational principles, equal opportunity in education, compulsory education, co-education, school education, social education, political education, religious education and school administration, plus additional rules. This basic law was followed by a series of detailed laws and regulations, including the School Education Law, Private School Law, Social Education Law, etc. ⇨ GAKKŌ KYŌIKUHŌ, NIHONKOKU KENPŌ

【注】 the Constitution of Japan「日本国憲法」． 11 articles 11条． school administration 学校行政． the School Education Law「学校教育法」． the Private School Law「私立学校法」． the Social Education Law「社会教育法」．

Kyōto-gozan 京都五山 the five principal temples of the Rinzai sect of Zen Biddhism, located in Kyoto. They are the Tenryūji, Shōkokuji, Kenninji, Tōfukuji and Manjuji temples. They rank under Nanzenji Temple (ranking highest) and Daitokuji Temple (ranking second) in this sect. This hierarchical order was designated by the shogun Ashikaga Yoshimitsu (1358-1408) in 1386. ⇨ GOZAN, KAMAKURA-GOZAN, RINZAISHŪ

【注】 the Rinzai sect 臨済宗． hierarchical order 位階序列． 京都五山：天龍寺，相国寺，建仁寺，東福寺，万寿寺．

kyōtsū-ichiji(-shiken) 共通一次(試験) the Joint First-Stage Achievement Test; the preliminary examination for selecting applicants to national and other public universities. This examination was launched in 1979 in an attempt to alleviate the keen competition to enter select universities and to assess upper secondary school performance. This examination is conducted once a year in January simultaneously throughout the country and is administered by the National Center for University Entrance Examination, under the supervision of the Ministry of Education. The subjects covered are Japanese, a foreign language, mathematics, science and social studies (four subjects for some colleges). Second-stage entrance examinations are conducted by individual universities, and final decisions are based on a combined evaluation of the two.

〖注〗 preliminary examination 予備試験. alleviate 緩和する. the National Center for University Entrance Examination 国立大学入試センター. the subjects covered 科目範囲, 該当科目.

Kyō-yaki 京焼　Kyoto chinaware; the generic term for porcelain and ceramic ware produced in and around Kyoto, as represented by Kiyomizu ware and Awata ware. Nonomura Ninsei (1596-1660) contributed greatly to the development of the Kyoto faience and raised Japanese ceramics to an art.　⇨ AWATA-YAKI, KIYOMIZU-YAKI

〖注〗 chinaware 陶磁器製品. porcelain ware 磁器. ceramic ware 陶器. Nonomura Ninsei 野々村仁清. faience 釉で着色した陶磁器.

kyū 灸　moxibustion; moxa treatment; one of the traditional medical treatments of Japan introduced from China. "Moxa" comes from the Japanese word *mogusa* (mugwort in English). A tiny cone, the size of a rice grain, of dried fiber from the undersurface of a mugwort leaf is burned on the skin at one or more of about 360 therapeutic points (*tsubo*) on specific meridians called *keiraku*, linked to pain. There is said to be a particular connection between these therapeutic points and various symptoms. This treatment has been used since ancient times and is still popular for soothing certain pains and relieving fatigue.　⇨ HARI(-CHIRYŌ), KANPŌI, SHIATSU

〖注〗 moxa もぐさ, よもぎ(=mugwort). undersurface 葉裏の表面. therapeutic point つぼ. therapeutic 治療(上)の. meridian 経絡. symptom 病の症状. soothe やわらげる.

kyūdō 弓道　lit. the way of the bow. archery as a sport; the art or sport of shooting arrows at a target derived from *kyūjutsu*, a traditional martial art. *Kyūdō* developed as a means of developing mental discipline after the Meiji Restoration (1868). Later, following World War II, it was recognized as a sport with the establishment of the All Japan Kyūdō Federation (1949). Influenced by Zen concepts, the sport maintains the original principles of cultivating concentration and mental composure as well as a competitive aspect. The bow is made of strips of wood and bamboo glued together, having a length of 2.21 meters with the grip located below center. The arrow is made of bamboo and is about half the length of the bow. The archer is clad in a white *kyūdō* garment and black *hakama* trousers, usually with a three-fingered archer's glove (*yugake*) on the right hand. Shooting is done according to a solemn ritual, *shahō-hassetsu* (lit. eight parts in shooting). ⇨ KYŪJUTSU

〖注〗 target 的. martial art 武芸、格闘技. the Meiji Restoration 明治維新. the All Japan Kyūdō Federation 全日本弓道連盟. mental composure 精神の落ち着き. grip 握り部. garment 衣服. archer's glove 弽 (ゆがけ).

kyūjutsu 弓術 lit. the art of the bow. archery as a traditional martial art. Archery has a long history in Japan, with records showing that the bow and arrow had already become the most important weapon in the days of the first Japanese emperor Jinmu (seventh century B.C.). With the introduction of Chinese culture in the third century, the art underwent a major change in taking on a spiritual aspect. During the civil wars at the end of the Heian period (794-1185) many experts emerged, including Nasu no Yoichi (12th century) and Minamoto no Yoshiie (1039-1106), trained in both horseback and standing archery. It also played an important role during the days of civil wars from the late Kamakura period (1185-1336) through the Muromachi period (1336-1568), while undergoing technical development. Although archery lost its value as a means of warfare with the introduction of firearms in the mid-16th century, the art became more important as a form of spiritual training under the influence of Zen Buddhism. After the Meiji Restoration (1868) it developed into a sport as *kyūdō*. ⇨ KYŪDŌ

〖注〗 martial art 武芸、格闘技. civil wars 内戦. firearm 鉄砲.

Kyūshū 九州 one of the four major islands of the Japanese archipelago, the other three being Honshū, Hokkaidō and Shikoku. It is situated to the southwestern tip of Honshū with which it is connected by a 3.6 kilometers undersea tunnel and a bridge.

Kyūshū comprises seven prefectures—Fukuoka, Saga, Nagasaki, Ōita, Kagoshima, Kumamoto and Miyazaki—and covers an area of about 44,000 square kilometers including small islands belonging to the given prefectures. ⇨ HOKKAIDŌ, HONSHŪ, NIHON-RETTŌ, SHIKOKU

〖注〗 the Japanese archipelago 日本列島.

M

ma 間 a pause; an interval; a silent interval or pause in Japanese drama and music. It is an aesthetic concept of Japanese performing arts, making best use of the effect of timing and silence to give one relief from heightened tension and to make the imagination work to the full. To be sensitive to what is implied rather than to what is explicitly expressed is expected in the appreciation of Japanese arts, although silence may often be boring to foreign audiences. ⇨ KŪKAN

〖注〗 aesthetic concept 美的概念. performing arts 舞台芸術, 芸能. explicitly 明白に, あからさまに.

magatama 勾玉[曲玉] lit. a crooked gem. a comma-shaped gem; beads used to make necklaces in the earliest period of Japanese history. They were made of jade, agate, amber, crystal or clay, measuring one to five centimeters in length. The shape is said to have derived from the canine tooth of a certain animal. A *magatama* of pedigree has been preserved in the imperial family, which is said to have been handed down from emperor to emperor tracing back to the Sun Goddess, Amaterasu Ōmikami. This is one of the three treasures of the Japanese imperial throne, the others being the Sacred Mirror enshrined at Ise Shrine in Ise and the Grass-Cutting Sword at Atsuta Shrine in Nagoya. ⇨ KUSANAGI NO TSURUGI, SANSHU NO JINGI, YATA NO KAGAMI

〖注〗 jade ひすい. agate めのう. amber 琥珀. canine tooth 犬歯. pedigree 由緒, 系図. imperial throne 皇位. the Sacred Mirror 八咫鏡. enshrine 祀る. the Grass-Cutting Sword 草薙の剣.

mage 髷 traditional hairstyles; a chignon for women and a topknot for men. In feudal days both men and women had to dress their hair according to their particular status. There were many kinds of *mage* hairstyles especially for women—*maru-mage*, *shimada-mage*, *momoware*, *chōcho-mage*, etc.—in the past. Today *mage* can be seen only on special occasions such as at weddings, during the

New Year holidays, in traditional dramas, etc., and are usually wigs.　⇨ CHONMAGE, MARUMAGE, MOMOWARE, SHIMADA(-MAGE), TA-KASHIMADA

〖注〗 chignon 束髪の髷. topknot 髪の房, ちょん髷. feudal days 封建時代.

mai 舞　dance; a term referring to traditional dance forms such as the controlled, sedate and stylized Noh dance.　⇨ NŌ

〖注〗 sedate 静かな, 落ち着いた. stylized 様式化した.

maiko 舞子〔舞妓〕　dancing girls in Kyoto; young apprentice geisha. They are seen strolling around the Gion district in Kyoto, wearing an elaborate traditional coiffure, and a colorful kimono with a long sash (*obi*) hanging from the back. They are trained in dancing, singing, playing *shamisen* (a string instrument) and manners for entertaining guests, in an effort to become accomplished geisha. Like geisha, they are available for Japanese-style parties or banquets.　⇨ DARARI NO OBI, GEISHA

〖注〗 apprentice 徒弟, 見習(生). stroll ぶらぶら歩く, ぶらつく. traditional coiffure 伝統的な髪型. string instrument 絃楽器. accomplished 完成した, 堪能な, たしなみのある.

makie 蒔絵　inlaid lacquer; a method of sprinkling lacquer ware with gold and silver dust or chips in various designs. The art originated in the Heian period (794-1185) and flourished up to the Muromachi period (1336-1568).

〖注〗 inlaid (金などを)散りばめる, はめこんだ. lacquer ware 漆器.

makunouchi(-bentō) 幕の内(弁当)　a variety box lunch; a variety of foods arranged in a wooden box. It consists of small rice balls sprinkled with black sesame seeds and an assortment of bits of fish, meat, egg and vegetables, boiled, broiled or pickled. Originally it was eaten in a theater between acts of a Kabuki play, which gave rise to the term *makunouchi* (within a tent or a theater).

〖注〗 black sesame seeds 黒ごま. assortment 各種取り合せもの, 詰め合せ. act (芝居の)一幕. give rise to を生じる, 引き起こす.

Makura no Sōshi 枕草子　*The Pillow Book* (around 1000); a collection of random notes or light essays written by Sei Shōnagon (late 10th century) in the Heian period (794-1185). The title derives from the idea of casual notes being made in the bedroom and possibly kept in the drawer of a wooden pillow. This collection, consisting of over 300 paragraphs or fragments, constitutes Sei Shōnagon's memoirs of the days when she served as lady-in-waiting to Empress Teishi. She depicts the empress, and court life and events spontaneously with witty criticism, interspersed with descriptions of the changing seasons. The style is vivid and rhythmical, distinctively revealing her personality—sharp, sensitive and high-spirited. She is regarded as one of the two most talented women writers to emerge in the Heian period, the other being Murasaki Shikibu (?978-?1016) of *The Tale of Genji*. ⇨ GENJI MONOGATARI, HEIAN-JIDAI

〖注〗 random notes 想いいずるままに記したもの, 随筆. memoir 回想録. lady-in-waiting 宮廷に仕える婦人. spontaneously ～が散りばめてある、～がそ ここに配されている.

makuuchi 幕内 lit. within a tent. the highest division in professional *sumō*, also called *makunouchi*. This division is limited to not more than 38 wrestlers. The ranks of the champion class are *yokozuna* (grand champion), *ōzeki* (champion), *sekiwake* (junior champion) and *komusubi* (junior champion, second class). The latter three are called *san'yaku* collectively. The next class is the *maegashira*, with rankings from one down to 13-15 depending upon the number of wrestlers in the champion class and in the division altogether. Each rank is further divided into east and west with the east ranking higher. Since the method of promotion to *yokozuna* and *ōzeki* differs from the system of promotion for other ranks, the number of wrestlers for each of the champion class ranks is not fixed. ⇨ ŌZEKI, ŌZUMŌ, SUMŌ, YOKOZUNA

〖注〗 grand champion 横綱. champion 大関. junior champion, second class 小結.

mamemaki 豆まき the bean-throwing ceremony; an event observed on the evening of *Setsubun* falling on February 3 or 4, the day before the first day of spring according to the lunar calendar. The head of the family throws roasted dried soybeans inside and outside the home in order to bring in good fortune and drive away evil spirits, shouting "*Fukuwauchi, oniwasoto!*" (In with good luck; away with demons!). Many shrines and temples also hold ceremonies in which men born under the particular zodiac sign of the year (*toshi-otoko*) are selected as bean throwers, and people crowd the grounds to try to catch the thrown beans which are said to bring good fortune. ⇨ SETSUBUN

〖注〗 the lunar calendar 太陰暦. evil spirits 悪霊. zodiac 十二支、十二宮.

mandara 曼陀羅[曼荼羅] a mandala (Sanskrit), meaning "circle"

or "collection"; an assembly of divinities; a graphic representation of the stages to the realm of enlightenment, used particularly in esoteric Buddhism. The mandala bears a number of images or symbols of deities (some have over 1,000) arranged symmetrically, with the most perfect (or enlightened) in the center and the most imperfect beings (or stages) at peripheral positions. The Shingon sect explains that the chart symbolizes the two dimensions of cosmic life, unity and diversity, emphasizing the harmony between them. The chart is used as an aid in meditation to attain enlightenment. Japan's oldest existent one (early ninth century), though badly worn out, is at Daigoji Temple, Kyoto. ⇨ SHINGON-SHŪ

〖注〗 divinity 神格, 天上の人. graphic representation 図案で表したもの. realm of enlightenment 悟りの境地. esoteric Buddhism 密教. deity 神, 神のような人[もの]. peripheral position 周辺の位置. cosmic life 宇宙の生命. unity and diversity 単一性と多様性. meditation 黙想, 座禅. attain enlightenment 悟りに達する.

manekineko 招き猫 a beckoning cat; a porcelain figure of a cat with one paw raised. It is a pose for calling in good fortune. It is believed that if this figure of a beckoning cat is placed in front of stores and inns, it will draw many customers, thus bringing prosperity. It originated during the Edo period (1603-1868) from a story about a real cat which brought prosperity to a declining temple by beckoning people passing by in a storm, among whom there was the feudal lord of Hikone, who later became the patron of the temple.

〖注〗 beckon 招く. porcelain figure 磁器の像. paw (動物の)足. feudal lord 大名.

manjū 饅頭 a bean-jam bun; a bun stuffed with sweetened bean paste. The bun is generally made of wheat flour, but sometimes mixed with rice or buckwheat flour. It is usually steamed, but sometimes steamed and then baked. ⇨ AN, WAGASHI

〖注〗 bean jam 餡. bun 丸パン. stuff 詰める. sweetened bean paste 餡. buckwheat flour 蕎麦粉.

Man'yō-gana 万葉仮名 Man'yō-style script; method of writing the Japanese language by borrowing Chinese characters, as used for recording the poems in the *Man'yōshū* (The Collection of Ten-Thousand Leaves, eighth century). A Chinese character is used for each syllable of the same sound in Japanese, with no reference to its original meaning. Through simplification and modification, this method of writing led to the invention of two Japanese phonetic alphabets—*katakana* and *hiragana*—in the Heian period (794–1185). ⇨ HIRAGANA, KANA, KATAKANA

〖注〗 script 書体，筆跡．　Chinese character 漢字．　modification 修正．　phonetic alphabet 音標文字表．

Man'yōshū 万葉集 *The Collection of Myriad Leaves* (eighth century); the oldest remaining anthology of Japanese poetry, presumably compiled by Ōtomo no Yakamochi (?718–85) in the Nara period (646–794). Consisting of 20 volumes, the work contains over 4,500 poems—some 4,200 are *tanka* (short poems of 31 syllables; 5-7-5-7-7), and the rest are *chōka* (long poems; repetitions of 5-7 syllables ending with 5-7-7), *sedōka* (38-syllable poems; 5-7-7-5-7-7), Chinese poems, etc. The poems are written in Chinese characters used to phonetically represent Japanese syllables, giving rise to the term *Man'yō-gana*. Covering the period from 347 to 759, the works are selected from writers of all classes, from emperors to the lowly. Among them are such celebrated poets as Kakinomoto no Hitomaro, Yamabe no Akahito, Yamanoue no Okura and Ōtomo no Yakamochi. The poems are generally naive, candid and masculine in tone, and express optimistic sentiments toward nature and man in ancient Japan. ⇨ MAN'YŌ-GANA, TANKA

〖注〗 anthology 名詩選集．　Chinese character 漢字．　the lowly 身分の低い人々．

manzai¹ 万歳 lit. ten thousand years. a pair of entertainers who sing and dance during the New Year period. Clad in ancient costumes, the pair go from door to door, singing and dancing merrily to the accompaniment of their hand drums (*tsuzumi*), wishing families a happy new year in return for a tip. The *manzai* performers from the Mikawa district in Aichi Prefecture are well-known as they were particularly patronized by the Tokugawa shogunate during the Edo period (1603–1868). ⇨ MANZAI², TSUZUMI

〖注〗 clad 装った．　to the accompaniment of ～に合わせて，～の伴奏で．　hand drum 鼓．　patronize 後援する．

manzai² 漫才 a comic dialogue; a witty stage dialogue; a popular form of vaudeville entertainment performed by a pair of comedians. A pair of comedians engages in fast dialogue, one deliberately mistaking what his partner is saying, thus moving the audience to laughter. *Manzai* is usually performed in colloquial

Ōsaka dialect on topics derived from daily life, sometimes accompanied by instruments such as an accordion or *shamisen* (three-stringed instrument). With its roots in traditional local folk *manzai* where a pair of comedians go from door to door at New Year's, modern *manzai* appeared as a stage form, influenced by the classical comic Kyogen, in the Ōsaka district in the mid-Meiji era (1868-1912). In the early Shōwa era (1926-   ), it established its reputation as one of the principal plebian entertainments, due to the emergence of intellectual *manzai* writers from top universities. Modern *manzai* came to be written as 漫才 to distinguish from the original *manzai* (万歳). ⇨ KYŌGEN, MANZAIᴵ

〖注〗 vaudeville 寄席演芸. deliberately わざと. stage performance 舞台演芸. plebian 庶民の.

maruhonmono 丸本物 lit. a piece from a complete Bunraku score. Kabuki plays of Bunraku origin. The stage performance is accompanied by *gidayū* chanting and *shamisen* music, which are elements from the Bunraku puppet theater. *Kanadehon Chūshingura* (The Treasury of Loyal Retainers, 1748), *Sugawara Denju Tenarai Kagami* (The Secrets of Sugawara's Calligraphy, 1746), etc., from this genre of Kabuki are still popularly performed today. ⇨ BUNRAKU, GIDAYŪ, KABUKI

〖注〗 Bunraku score 浄瑠璃の楽譜. accompany 伴奏する. *gidayū* chanting 義太夫（節）を謡うこと. The Treasury of Loyal Retainers「仮名手本忠臣蔵」. The Secrets of Sugawara's Calligraphy「菅原伝授手習鑑」.

marumage 丸髷 lit. a round chignon. the *marumage* hairstyle, a traditional coiffure developed during the Edo period (1603-1868). The style is made up of an elevated oval-shaped chignon, a small front tuft, and puffed-out back and side locks. It was widely worn by married women until the end of the Meiji era (1868-1912). The size of the oval chignon was reduced with age. ⇨ MAGE

〖注〗 coiffure 髪型, 髪の結い方. chignon 束髪の髷. tuft（髪などの）束. lock 髪の房.

maru-obi 丸帯 lit. a circle sash. a wide decorative *obi* (kimono sash), used only for ceremonial occasions. a reversible woman's *obi* made of a single piece of thick silk cloth, folded in half and sewn. It is distinguished from others by the designs in that it decorate the entire length of the *obi*, inner and outer surface, and can be tied into various forms. It is about four meters long and a little over 30 centimeters wide, longer and wider than the usual *obi*.

This type of *obi* is worn with a very formal kimono, such as *furisode* (a long, hanging sleeve kimono for young women), *tomesode* (a ceremonial kimono for married women), etc. A lavishly decorated *maru-obi* is used for a bridal costume. ⇨ FU-RISODE, KIMONO, OBI, TOMESODE

〖注〗 lavishly 華麗に

Mashiko-yaki 益子焼 Mashiko earthenware; folk pottery produced in the village of Mashiko in Tochigi Prefecture. The clay at Mashiko being rich in iron ore, ware from this area takes on a quality of rustic simplicity. The surface is usually glazed in brown or persimmon red. Firing was started by Ōtsuka Keisaburō in the early 1850s, and a variety of daily household utensils—water jars, mortars, bowls, clay pots, etc.—have been made in the folkcraft style. The most well-known recent potter of Mashiko was Shōji Hamada (1894–1978), who was officially designated an "intangible cultural property" (*mukei-bunkazai*) and devoted himself to preserving the tradition of Mashiko handmade folk-art pottery. ⇨ MUKEI-BUNKAZAI, NINGEN-KOKUHŌ

〖注〗 folk pottery 民芸陶磁器. iron ore 鉄鉱石. rustic simplicity わび、さび. glaze つやを出す、上薬をかける. Ōtsuka Keisaburō 大塚啓三郎. mortar すり鉢. potter 陶工、陶芸師. Shōji Hamada 浜田庄司.

masu 升[枡] a square measuring box; a wooden box used for measuring grain and liquid. There are three kinds of boxes, which measure 0.18, 0.9 and 1.8 liters respectively. It is uniquely constructed with the technique of dovetailing where no nails or adhesives are employed. A new one made of fragrant cypress wood is also used for drinking saké. ⇨ GŌ, SAKE, SHŌ

〖注〗 dovetail ありつぎにする(木組で両方の板の凹凸をつくってはめこむ). adhesive 粘着剤. cypress 檜.

matcha 抹茶 powdered green tea; foamy or pasty green tea made from powdered tea, served mainly in the tea ceremony. Unlike other kinds of green tea, *matcha* is not brewed, but is prepared by beating the powder and hot water with a bamboo whisk. Two kinds are made in the tea ceremony, *koicha* (thick, pasty tea) and *usucha* (thin, foamy tea); each is served according to its own prescribed form. *Matcha*, also called *hikicha*, is often used in traditional Japanese sweets as well. ⇨ CHA, CHANOYU, CHASEN, HIKICHA, KOICHA, USUCHA

〖注〗 foamy 泡立つ. tea ceremony 茶道. brew (煮溶かして)飲み物を作る、

（茶など）煎じる，茶を入れる．　bamboo whisk 茶筅．　prescribed form 前もって
規定されている型．

matsu no uchi 松の内　lit. inside the pine.　the New Year holidays
during which pine decorations (*kadomatsu*) are placed at gates.
The period was from January 1 to January 15 formerly, and
recently is until January 7.　After the last day of this period, New
Year decorations are removed.　Customarily, New Year greetings
will no longer be exchanged, though New Year cards may be
mailed until January 15.　⇨ GANJITSU, KADOMATSU, NENGAJŌ, SAN-
GANICHI

matsutake 松茸　*Tricholoma matsutake*; *Armillaria edodes*; a pine
mushroom; an edible fungus growing at the foot of Japanese red
pine trees (*akamatsu*).　In autumn it grows from an underground
mycelium of a red pine tree during a limited period of a few weeks.
It consists of a long, thick whitish stem and a brown cap which is
first rounded and later spreads open like an umbrella, spanning 10
to 15 centimeters in diameter.　With its exquisite fragrance,
matsutake is highly praised as an autumnal delicacy.　Unlike *shiitake*, it cannot be artificially cultivated, nor can it be preserved by
drying.　It is slightly broiled over a charcoal fire, boiled together
with other ingredients, or served as the main ingredient of seasoned
rice (*matsutake-gohan*).　⇨ SHIITAKE
〔注〕　fungus 菌類．　mycelium 菌糸体．　exquisite 微妙な，絶妙な．　delicacy
珍味．　ingredient （料理の）材料．　seasoned rice 味つけごはん．

mawari-butai 回り舞台　a revolving stage.　It is used as a device on
the Kabuki stage for the rapid shifting of scenes.　The time
between acts is shortened because the scene can be prepared
behind the stage.　⇨ KABUKI
〔注〕　revolving 回転式の．　shifting 転換，移り変わり．　scene 舞台．

mawashi 回し　a *sumō* wrestler's loincloth; a piece of cloth used as
a combination of belt and loincloth by *sumō* wrestlers.　A long
piece of cloth five to 14 meters long and 50 to 80 centimeters wide
is folded four to six times into a long strip, tightly wrapped over
the groin once and around the waist five to six times, and then tied
together at the back.　There are three kinds.　The *tori-mawashi* is
worn during a bout—that for *sekitori* (upper-division wrestlers) is
of silk and generally dark blue or purple while that for lower-
division wrestlers is of cotton and limited to dark blue.　The
keshō-mawashi worn during the ceremonial *dohyōiri* (entering the

ring) is of silk and has an additional part that looks like an apron,
which is embroidered with elegant designs unique to each wrestler.
The *keiko-mawashi* worn during practice is of cotton, white for
sekitori and black for others. ⇨ DOHYŌIRI, SEKITORI, SUMŌ

〖注〗 loincloth 回し、腰布. groin 股. embroider 刺しゅうをする.

Meiji 明治 the Meiji era; the appellation of the era when Emperor
Meiji (1852-1912), the grandfather of the present Emperor, Hirohito, was on the throne. Starting with the Imperial Restoration
(*Meiji Ishin*) in 1868 and ending in 1912, it lasted 45 years, followed
by the Taishō era (1912-1926). The year 1868 corresponds to the
first year of Meiji, and the year 1912 to the 45th year of Meiji and
at the same time to the first year of Taishō. ⇨ GENGŌ, MEIJI ISHIN,
TAISHŌ, TENNŌ

〖注〗 appellation 名称、呼称. on the throne 即位している. the Imperial
Restoration 王政復古、明治維新.

Meiji Ishin 明治維新 the Meiji Restoration (1868; 1841-77 or 1854-
71 centering around 1868); the restoration of supremacy of the
emperor, and the political and social reformation for the purpose of
modernizing Japan carried out under Emperor Meiji (1852-1912;
r. 1867-1912). With the opening of its doors to the world in 1858
after 220 years of isolation, Japan realized the need to establish a
modern government to cope with world capitalism. As a result of
strong demand from imperial loyalists of the lower samurai class,
the last shogun Tokugawa Yoshinobu (1837-1913) stepped down in
1867. With Emperor Meiji on the throne, a number of innovative
reforms were carried out in an attempt of consolidate national
unity and modernization. Among the main reforms were: the
proclamation of the Five Imperial Oaths for the new regime (1868),
the transfer of the capital from Kyoto to Edo and the changing of
its name to Tokyo (1868), the return of lands from feudal lords to
the Emperor (1869), the separation of legislature, administration,
and judiciary (1869), the opening of a railroad between Tokyo and
Yokohama (1872), the abolition of the feudal domain system and
adoption of the prefectural system (1871), the promulgation of the
government order on education (1872), and the promulgation of
the Meiji Constitution (1889). ⇨ GOKAJŌ NO GOSEIMON, HAN²,
KYŌIKU-CHOKUGO, MEIJI, MEIJI KENPŌ, SAKOKU (-SEISAKU), SHŌGUN

〖注〗 the restoration of supremacy of the emperor 王政復古. isolation 孤立、
鎖国. imperial loyalist 尊皇派の人. step down 地位を退く. on the throne

即位している．　the Five Imperial Oaths「五箇条の御誓文」．　feudal lord 大名，藩主．　legislature 立法．　judiciary 裁判権，司法．　the feudal domain system 幕藩体制．　promulgation 発布．　the government order 政令．

Meiji Kenpō 明治憲法　the Meiji Constitution of Japan; the former constitution of Japan, which was officially called *Dainippon-teikoku Kenpō* (the Constitution of the Great Japanese Empire) when it was in effect.　This constitution, drafted in secret by then Prime Minister Hirobumi Itō (1841-1909) and his colleagues and approved by Emperor Meiji (1852-1912), was promulgated in 1889.　It was composed of 76 articles under seven chapters and owed much to the constitutional theory of Germany, but was centered around the absolute authority of the emperor.　It also referred to the rights and duties of the people, the bicameral national assembly, the judicial system, etc.　This constitution was abolished soon after World War II and replaced by the present constitution.　⇨ MEIJI ISHIN, NIHONKOKU KENPŌ

〚注〛　the Great Japanese Empire 大日本帝国．　in effect 実施されている，効力がある．　draft 起草する．　colleague 同僚，仲間．　promulgate 発布する，施行する．　76 articles under seven chapters 7 章76条．　rights and duties 権利と義務．　bicameral national assembly 二院制の国会．　the judicial system 司法制度．

meishi 名刺　a calling card; a business card; a name card used for self-introduction as well as for business purposes.　On a typical *meishi* are one's name, address, phone number and, most important, one's group affiliation with one's specific title or status.　The Japanese frequently exchange *meishi* to clarify their social group and status, when they want to get acquainted with one another.

〚注〛　affiliation 所属．

men(rui) 麺(類)　noodles; the generic term for noodles, including Chinese noodles.　Japanese noodles can be divided roughly into two categories—*udon* (white noodles made from wheat flour) and *soba* (brownish noodles made from buckwheat flour).　Making a noisy, slurping sound while eating the noodles or drinking the soup is considered appropriate in Japan.　⇨ SOBA, SŌMEN, UDON

〚注〛　generic term 総称．　buckwheat flour 蕎麦粉．　slurping sound するするという音，すする音．

menko 面子　a card game played by children or the card used in such a game.　The card is usually a round or rectangular piece of cardboard, with one side picturing popular figures such as famous samurai, *sumō* wrestlers or, nowadays, cartoon characters. The object of the game is to flip over the opponent's card laid on the ground by slapping one's own card on it. If one succeeds, he or she gets to keep the flipped card, as with marbles. The game itself is said to have already existed in the Edo period (1603-1868) with pieces of wood, clay, earthenware, lead, etc., also used as *menko* cards. *Menko* is also called *betta* or *patchin* in some districts.

〖注〗 flip ひっくりかえす. slap 投げつける. marble ビー玉.

mezashi 目刺し lit. passing through the eyes. salted dried sardines. Several sardines are fixed in a row by means of a rice straw or bamboo skewer passed through the eyes. They are soaked in salted water overnight and dried in the sun. There are two methods of drying—half-drying and complete drying. They are then broiled over a direct fire, and go well with white rice.

〖注〗 bamboo skewer 竹串.

miai 見合い lit. mutual seeing. an arranged meeting of a potential match. In the traditional way of finding a spouse, a go-between arranges an opportunity for two people to "see" each other, usually accompanied by their parents. From this time on, if the two so wish, they will date for a period of time to get more acquainted and make a decision on whether they wish to marry or not. ⇨ MIAI-KEKKON, NAKŌDO, YUINŌ

〖注〗 spouse 配偶者. go-between 仲人.

miai-kekkon 見合い結婚 an arranged marriage; a marriage arranged by match-making through a go-between and parents. If an arranged meeting (*miai*) through a go-between results in success, both parties will prepare themselves for marriage following an engagement ritual of exchanging betrothal gifts (*yuinō*). In *miai-kekkon*, emphasis is often placed more on the family than on the individual. Today it is said that the proportion of arranged marriages to love marriages is almost even. ⇨ MIAI, NAKŌDO, YUINŌ

〖注〗 go-between 仲人. arranged meeting お見合い. engagement ritual 婚約の儀式. betrothal gifts 婚約の贈物, 結納.

michiyuki[1] 道行き lit. going on the street. a type of light coat worn over a kimono outdoors. It also serves to protect the kimono from dust. Unlike *haori* (an overgarment), it has to be taken off indoors. ⇨ HAORI, KIMONO

michiyuki[2] 道行き lit. going on the street. a traveling scene on the

Kabuki or Bunraku stage, often including a dance. Mainly it refers to a trip of a pair of runaway lovers or of those who try to commit double suicide, thus often implying a sad ending. In Noh, the *michiyuki* is a song chanted by the secondary character (*waki*) as he travels from one place to another, describing the scenery he is passing by or explaining the direction he is heading for. ⇨ BUNRAKU, KABUKI, NŌ, WAKI

【注】 runaway lovers 駆け落ちの恋人達.

midarebako 乱れ箱 lit. a messy case. a clothes tray; a shallow container to temporarily hold clothing and accessories just after removal. It is made of lacquered wood or braided split bamboo, and measures about a meter by 45 centimeters, just the size to hold a folded kimono. It used to be placed in the corner of a Japanese-style room. It may still be found at some Japanese inns. ⇨ RYOKAN, ZASHIKI

【注】 removal 除去, 脱ぎさること. braided split bamboo 割竹で編んだもの.

mie 見得 a pose; a Kabuki pose. At the climax of an act, a Kabuki actor remains still for a moment to express his emotions, holding a rigid and sedate pose and letting his eyes speak for his inner feelings. This pose is emphasized by the sound of clappers or other musical instruments. ⇨ KABUKI

【注】 rigid 厳正な, 動かない. sedate 落ちついた, 静かな. clappers 拍子木. musical instrument 楽器.

mikado 御門 lit. an honorable gate. the honorable gate of the Imperial Palace; the ancient honorific title used to address and refer to the emperor, i.e., Your Majesty and His Majesty. It was used because to use his name directly was considered impolite. Today this term is obsolete; it sounds too elegant. The term *tennō-heika* or *heika* is commonly used by the Japanese people. ⇨ HEIKA, TENNŌ

【注】 honorific title 敬称. address 呼びかける. Your Majesty 陛下 (呼びかけるとき). His Majesty 陛下 (言及するとき). obsolete すたれた, 旧式の.

mikkyō 密教 lit. secret teachings. esoteric Buddhism; sects of Buddhism which emphasize mystical teachings and practices. In esoteric Buddhism, all phenomena in the universe are considered a manifestation of a central being — Buddha Dainichi, the Great Illuminator. He embraces other Buddhas and all human beings. Sakyamuni Buddha is the other aspect of Dainichi or the expounder of his existence, according to different sects. Devoted believers aspire to become Buddhas themselves, in paradise or on earth, upon attaining enlightenment through severe esoteric practices such as meditation, prayer, fasting, ascetic rituals, etc. The origins of esoteric Buddhism can be traced back to the early stages of Buddhism in India, namely Tantric Buddhism which incorporates indigenous magical elements and the worship of numerous deities as well. Two major branches were introduced to Japan through China in the ninth century—the Shingon sect founded by Kūkai (774-835) and the Tendai sect founded by Saichō (767-822). In the Heian period (794-1185) these sects flourished, with the incorporation of indigenous Shinto elements. Their mysticism and symbolism had a great influence on the development of Buddhist arts. ⇨ BUKKYŌ, SHINGONSHŪ, SHINTŌ, TENDAISHŪ

〖注〗 esoteric 秘教の、内密の. manifestation 現れ、顕現. illuminator 照らすもの. expounder 解説者、使わされた者. enlightenment 悟り. ascetic ritual 苦行の儀式、修験. Tantric タントラの(ヒンズー教のTantra派の). indigenous その土地固有の. deity 神、神のような人〔もの〕.

miko 巫女 a shrine maiden; girls who serve the deity of a shrine by offering prayers and receiving oracles. They wear white kimono and a long red pleated skirt (*hakama*). On special occasions, they perform the sacred *kagura* dance of dedication to the deity to bless worshipers. A certain type of *miko* is said to be endowed with the power to communicate with the deity and the spirits of the dead. ⇨ JINJA, KAGURA

〖注〗 deity 神、神のような人〔もの〕. offer prayers 祈禱する. oracle 神託、神のお告げ. pleated skirt 袴. dedication 奉納. be endowed with ～が与えられている、～を授かっている.

mikoshi 御輿〔神輿〕 a portable shrine; a sacred palanquin bearing the emblem of the deity enshrined in it. This miniature shrine, resting on two or four long poles, is made of black lacquered wood with gilted decorations and has a phoenix affixed to the roof. On festive occasions of the local shrine, a number of young men and boys wearing *happi* coats and short white pants carry it on their shoulders, proceeding through the streets from and to the local shrine, shouting "*wasshoi, wasshoi, wasshoi!*" This vigorous shouting is said to ward off evil spirits. ⇨ HAPPI, JINJA

〖注〗 palanquin かつぎかご. the emblem of a deity 神のしるし. deity 神、神のような人〔もの〕. enshrine 祀る. gilt 金箔の、金色の. phoenix 鳳凰鳥. affix とりつける. ward off 追い払う.

mikudarihan 三下り半   lit. three lines and a half.   a note of divorce. In the Edo period (1603-1868), there was a standard format in writing a note of divorce—in three and a half lines—which gave rise to this idiomatic expression, used metaphorically even today. In those days, only the husband could take the liberty of divorcing his wife, and not vice versa.

〖注〗 a note of divorce 離婚状． format 用式，書式． give rise to ～を生じる，引き起こす． metaphorically 隠喩的に，比喩的に． take the liberty of～ing 勝手に～する，自由に～する． vice versa 逆に，反対に．

Minami-Arupusu Kokuritsu-kōen 南アルプス国立公園   Southern Alps National Park (357.5 square kilometers), designated in 1964; a natural park situated in central Honshū, encompassing mountainous parts of Nagano, Shizuoka and Yamanashi prefectures.   Like Chūbu-sangaku (Northern Alps) National Park, this region contains a number of towering mountains, including Mount Shirane (3,192 meters, Japan's second-highest mountain after Mount Fuji), Mount Akashi (3,120 m), Mount Senjō (3,033 m), Mount Koma (2,966 m), etc.   These mountains are noted for their alpine plants, primeval forests, granite cliffs, deep ravines, etc.   ⇨ CHŪBU-SANGAKU KOKURITSU-KŌEN, KOKURITSU-KŌEN

〖注〗 alpine plant 高山植物． primeval forest 原始林． granite cliff 花崗岩でできた崖． ravine 峡谷，渓谷．

mino 蓑   a straw raincoat; a cape made of rice straw, formerly worn in rainy or snowy weather.   The straw is arranged so that it forms layers and covers the entire body.   It is made up of two parts: the lower part is tied at the waist like a skirt and the upper part is draped around the shoulders like a cape.

〖注〗 drape 掛ける，包む．

Mino-gami 美濃紙   Mino (rice) paper; hand-made Japanese paper produced in former Mino Province, presently around Mino in Gifu Prefecture.   Long fibers from paper bushes or paper mulberries are cut irregularly, to make a paper of a uniquely beautiful texture. Mino paper is the strongest of Japanese paper and too hard for moths to eat; thus it has been used in particular for documents, special books, paper for sliding doors (*shōji* and *fusuma*), etc.   ⇨ FUSUMA, SHŌJI, WASHI

〖注〗 province (行政のために分けた)国，諸地方． paper bush 三椏． paper mulberry 楮． texture 生地，肌合い． sliding door すべる戸(障子，襖など)．

Mino-yaki 美濃焼   Mino ceramic ware; a generic term for ceramic ware produced at Mino, around present-day Tajimi in Gifu Prefecture. During the days of civil strife in the 16th century, many potters moved to Mino from Seto (in Aichi Prefecture). Protected by the ruling feudal lord, Oda Nobunaga (1534–82), they produced a variety of ceramic ware of rustic type, including superb tea utensils. Skills in making yellow and black Seto ware were brought to Mino, resulting in the production of the renowned Shino and Oribe ware. All of these products contributed greatly to the tremendous development of ceramics from the Momoyama period (late 16th century) to the early Edo period (17th century). ⇨ ORIBE-YAKI, SHINO-YAKI

〖注〗 ceramic ware 陶器. the days of civil strife 戦国時代, 波乱の世. potter 陶工. feudal lord 大名. rustic さびれた. tea utensil 茶道具.

minshuku 民宿 lit. lodging at a private home. private homes that offer rooms and meals to travelers at a reasonable price. They are usually run by ordinary families, particularly farmers, as a side business. Travelers can enjoy rural life in an ordinary house, with *tatami*-mat rooms and a Japanese bath, and everyday meals of the locality. *Minshuku* are registered at the Japan Minshuku Association. Brochures and information are available through the Japan Travel Bureau, the Japan National Tourist Organization, and other large travel agencies.

〖注〗 locality 地方性, 地方特有. the Japan Minshuku Association 日本民宿協会. the Japan Travel Bureau 日本交通公社. the Japan National Tourist Organization 日本旅行協会. travel agency 旅行代理店, 旅行会社.

min'yō 民謡 a folk ballad; a folk song; songs of unknown origin handed down by oral tradition in rural communities. Many of these songs reflect daily life of people working together in the field, at sea, etc. There are also songs connected with rituals and festivals, accompanying dances such as songs for Bon dances. *Min'yō* are generally characterized by repeated refrains, echoed exclamations, simple rhythms, etc. They gradually came to be sung to the accompaniment of traditional instruments, such as drums, *shamisen* (a three-stringed instrument), *shakuhachi* (a bamboo flute), etc. Today many of these folk songs are artistically arranged by professionals. ⇨ BON-ODORI, SHAKUHACHI, SHAMISEN

〖注〗 ballad 伝承的に歌われる素朴な叙情詩. ritual 祭事, 儀式. to the accompaniment of ～の伴奏で.

mirin 味醂 Japanese cooking wine; sweet rice wine, used only for seasoning dishes. It is made from *shōchū* (a strong distilled alcoholic beverage), glutinous rice and yeast. The alcohol content is about 15 percent, but during the process of cooking, most of the alcohol is eliminated. It is used in many traditional dishes to add flavor, a sweet taste and luster. ⇨ SHŌCHŪ

〖注〗 season 味をつける. distilled 蒸留した. alcoholic beverage アルコール飲料. glutinous rice 糯米. alcoholic content アルコール含有量. luster つや.

Mishima-yaki 三島焼 Mishima ceramic ware; a Mishima-style tea bowl. It is Korean-style ware with an incised, rope-pattern design on both the inner and outer surface, with a translucent glaze. The ware came to be called *Mishima* because the design was traced to that of the calendar of Mishima Shrine in Shizuoka Prefecture.

〖注〗 ceramic ware 陶器(製品). incised 切りこんだ, 刻みこんだ. translucent 半透明の. glaze つや, 釉.

miso 味噌 *miso* paste; soybean paste; a brownish paste made from soybeans, rice or wheat fermented with salt and malt. Together with soy sauce, *miso* is an indispensable seasoning in traditional Japanese cuisine. It is used for making *miso* soup and for flavoring fish, meat and vegetables, and also for preserving fish and pickling vegetables since *miso* keeps them from spoiling for several years. The color and taste vary according to the locality. The dark-colored *miso* contains more soybeans, the lighter more rice. The one containing more malt tastes mild and sweet. ⇨ MISOSHIRU

〖注〗 ferment 発酵する. malt 麦芽.

misoshiru 味噌汁 *miso* soup; soybean-paste soup; a thick brownish soup made of soybean paste and other ingredients. It is a popular soup usually served with a Japanese-style meal, especially at breakfast. The soup is flavored with fish stock. Some typical ingredients for the soup served at breakfast are bean curd (*tōfu*), soft seaweed (*wakame*), shellfish and seasonal vegetables. For the evening meal, the ingredients become more varied, sometimes including fish, pork, etc. Excess boiling of the soup may spoil the flavor of *miso*. ⇨ AKADASHI, MISO

〖注〗 ingredient (料理の)材料. fish stock (魚からの)だし. bean curd 豆腐.

mitomein 認印 an unregistered seal; a personal seal for everyday use. A family usually has several unregistered private seals to be used for daily affairs of little official or legal importance, such as withdrawing money, receiving registered mail, etc. Seal-affixing serves as a substitute for signing one's name in Japan; using an unregistered seal may be considered equivalent to signing just one's initials. A seal of this kind can easily be bought at stationery shops or the like unless the family name is uncommon. ⇨ HAN,[2] INKAN, JITSUIN

〖注〗 withdraw money お金を（銀行などから）引き出す． registered mail 書留郵便． seal-affixing 捺印． substitute 代わり． stationery shop 文房具店．

mitsumame 蜜豆 lit. honey beans. cubes of Japanese gelatin (*kanten*) in syrup, mixed with sweet beans and fruit. Sometimes a scoop of red-bean jam (*an*) or a scoop of ice cream is placed on top. ⇨ AN, KANTEN

〖注〗 cube 立方体． a scoop of ひとすくいの． red-bean jam 餡．

miyabi 雅び courtly refined elegance; an aesthetic sensibility cultivated in the court culture of the Heian period (794–1185), elegant, refined, aristocratic and feminine in tone. With the development of the syllabary writing system (*kana*) in the Heian period, many talented women emerged from the aristocracy as writers and poets, represented by Murasaki Shikibu of *The Tale of Genji*. They contributed greatly in cultivating *miyabi* sensibility, which was enhanced to become the aesthetic standard of that age. This quality has since been inherited as a traditional element of Japanese art and literature. ⇨ HEIAN-JIDAI, KANA

〖注〗 courtly 王朝の，宮廷の． refined 洗練された． aesthetic sensibility 美的感覚． syllabary writing system 仮名，音節を基盤とした書体． the aristocracy 貴族階級． enhance 強める，（価値を）引き上げる．

miyamairi 宮参り visiting a Shinto shrine; in particular, a newborn child's first visit to the local tutelary Shinto shrine. The day for this rite varies according to districts, but in most cases it is held on the 30th, 75th or 100th day after birth. Dressed in its best kimono, the baby is taken to the shrine by its mother or grandmother, or formerly perhaps a midwife who assisted at its birth. A Shinto priest performs a ceremony of purification and blessing by reciting Shinto prayers and waving over the baby's head a sacred staff strung with white paper streamers. This signifies recognition by the gods of the baby as a being to protect. ⇨ GOHEI, JINJA, UJIGAMI

〖注〗 tutelary Shinto shrine 守護の神社，氏神． midwife 産婆． purification

清め，お祓い．a sacred staff strung with white paper streamers 御幣，ぬさ．

mizuage(-hō) 水揚げ(法) methods of raising water into stalks; treatment for preservation of cut flowers. The methods include cutting the stem in water, pumping water into the stalk, singeing the cut end, etc. ⇨ IKEBANA

〖注〗 stalk 茎，葉柄．singe 焦がす，(表面を)軽く焼く．cut end 切り口．

mizuhiki 水引 lit. to draw water. a paper cord used for binding up a gift. The cord is made up of a set of five paper strings stuck together, looking like a stream of water. Each half of the cord is of different colors. One of gold and silver is for especially auspicious occasions, such as weddings; one of red and white for ordinary congratulatory and courtesy gifts; one of black and white for funeral offerings. Ways of tying the cord differ according to the occasion. Iida in Nagano Prefecture is best known for its production of *mizuhiki*. ⇨ NOSHI, NOSHIGAMI

〖注〗 cord ひも．auspicious occasion めでたい時，祝いの機会．courtesy 儀礼の．funeral offering 葬式に贈るもの，香典．

mizusashi 水指[水差] a water jar; a water receptacle used in a tearoom. It is usually made of china, but Sen no Rikyū (1512-91), the great tea master of the 16th century, used one made of plain, curved wood. The water is used to wash the tea bowl and to be added to the iron kettle. ⇨ CHANOYU, CHASHITSU

〖注〗 jar 広口のびん，つぼ．receptacle 入れ物，容器．curved wood 木地曲．iron kettle 茶釜．

mizutaki 水炊き boiled chicken; chunks of chicken boiled in water (or fish broth) in an earthen pot at the table. Both the soup and the chicken are placed in a small bowl and eaten with a mixture of soy sauce, bitter-orange juice (*ponzu*) and condiments. Recently soybean curd (*tōfu*), mushrooms and other vegetables are often added to the pot. ⇨ DASHI, TŌFU

〖注〗 chunk 厚切り，塊り．fish broth 魚の煮出し汁，だし．soy sauce 醤油．bitter orange 橙．bitter-orange juice 橙をしぼった汁，ポンズ．condiment 調味料，薬味．soybean curd 豆腐．

mizuya 水屋 lit. a water room. a small pantry adjoining the tearoom; the tearoom kitchen where utensils are kept, washed and arranged for the tea ceremony. The pantry has a recessed area a meter or so wide and about 60 centimeters deep, equipped with, a few shelves and a bamboo-drain sink. For the use in an informal tearoom with no such adjoining pantry, there are cupboards for tea utensils, such as the *oki-mizuya* (a movable cupboard-type *mizuya*) and *dōko* (a small built-in cabinet), serving as a substitute for the *mizuya*. Tea utensils are placed in the most convenient manner according to prescribed rules. ⇨ CHANOYU, CHASHITSU

〖注〗 pantry 配膳室. tea utensil 茶道具. recessed 入りこんだ. bamboo-drain sink 竹のすの子を敷いた流し. small built-in cabinet 洞庫.

mizuyōkan 水羊羹　soft sweet bean-paste jelly. Like *yōkan*, it is made of bean paste, sugar and agar-agar. But *mizuyōkan* is softer, as it contains more water (*mizu*). It is pleasant to the palate when served cold in hot weather. It is usually placed on a green leaf for seasonal aesthetic charm. Today, canned or plastic-packed *mizuyōkan* is also available. ⇨ AN, YŌKAN

〖注〗 bean paste 餡. agar-agar 寒天. palate 舌, 味覚. seasonal aesthetic charm 季節感.

mochi 餅　a rice cake; a rice cake made from glutinous rice, having a sticky consistency. Steamed rice is pounded in a mortar and made into flat round cakes or flat square sheets. It is a traditional custom to eat *mochi* on New Year's Day since it is regarded as a good omen. It is used in clear soup or in sweet red-bean soup. It is also broiled and seasoned with soy sauce. ⇨ KAGAMI-MOCHI, MOCHITSUKI

〖注〗 rice cake 餅. glutinous rice 糯米. consistency 濃度, 粘度. pound 搗く, たたく. mortar 臼. good omen 吉兆, 幸運. sweet red-bean soup 汁粉. season 味をつける. soy sauce 醬油.

mochitsuki 餅搗き　making rice cake; pounding steamed rice into rice cake. Steamed glutinous rice is pounded many times with a pestle in a big wooden mortar until it takes on a sticky consistency. The soft *mochi* thus made is rolled into round cakes, or is spread into a large square to be cut into smaller square pieces after it hardens. Formerly, *mochitsuki* was done in most households with the New Year holidays approaching. Today, in cities and towns, people order their *mochi* from rice and confectionery shops. ⇨ KAGAMI-MOCHI, MOCHI

〖注〗 pound たたく, 搗く. glutinous rice 糯米. pestle きね. mortar 臼. sticky consistency べとべとした質, 粘性. household 家族, 所帯. confectionery 菓子屋.

mofuku 喪服　mourning wear; a black formal kimono or dress worn at a funeral or a memorial service. A mourning kimono is made of silk fabric such as *habutae* (soft silk) or *chirimen* (silk crepe)

for autumn, winter and spring, or *ro* (silk gauze) for summer.   On
pure black, it has five white family crests (*kamon*)—one on the
back, one on each side of the upper front and one on each sleeve.
The sash (*obi*) and other accessories must also be black, and the
under-collar (*han'eri*), the undergarment (*juban*) and the socks
(*tabi*) must be pure white.   Today men usually wear a black
Western-style suit with a black tie on such occasions.   ⇨ CHI-
RIMEN, HAN'ERI, JUBAN, KAMON, KIMONO, OBI, RO, TABI
〖注〗 memorial service 法事. silk fabric 絹織物. soft silk 羽二重. silk
crepe 縮緬. silk gauze 絽. family crest 家紋. under-collar 半衿. undergarment 襦袢.

mokugyo 木魚 lit. a wooden fish. a wooden gong struck con-
tinuously while a Buddhist sutra is chanted.   It is roughly round in
shape and hollow inside.   It is said that, inspired by a passage
about fish in a Buddhist sutra, a Chinese priest made a gong in the
shape of a fish, though the *mokugyo* may appear more like a skull
than a fish.
〖注〗 gong 銅羅，打つと音が出るもの. Buddhist sutra 仏教のお経. chant
(単調に)歌う，吟唱する.

mokuhanga 木版画 a woodblock print. It is the joint work of a
painter, an engraver and a printer.   Printing by means of engrav-
ing woodblocks can be traced back to the seventh century.   But
toward the end of the Tokugawa period (1603-1868) *ukiyoe*
painters such as Katsushika Hokusai (1760-1849), Andō Hiroshige
(1797-1858), etc., produced masterpieces with this form, depicting
landscapes and the life of the people.   Since then Japan has been
famous for its woodblock prints.   ⇨ UKIYOE
〖注〗 woodblock 木版. trace back たどる.

momiji-oroshi 紅葉おろし tinted grated radish; Japanese radish
grated with red pepper mixed in.   It is made by inserting a dried
red pepper into a block of Japanese radish before grating.   With
its slightly hot taste, it is good as a condiment for *tenpura,
nabemono,* etc.   ⇨ DAIKON-OROSHI, OROSHI
〖注〗 tinted 色のついた. grate おろす. Japanese radish 大根. condiment
薬味.

Momo no Sekku 桃の節句 lit. the peach-blossom festival. the
Dolls' Festival or Girls' Festival held on March 3, when peach
blossoms are at their best.   Traditionally, dolls have been displayed together with peach blossoms, symbolic of happiness in

marriage, and feminine virtues such as gracefulness, tenderness, etc. More commonly called *Hina Matsuri*. ⇨ HINA MATSURI, HINA-NINGYŌ

〖注〗 the Dolls' Festival 雛祭り. feminine virtue 女性の美徳, 女らしさ.

Momotarō 桃太郎   Peach Boy; a character in one of Japan's five most famous folk tales.   He was born from a huge peach floating down a stream, which was found by the wife of an old woodcutter as she was doing her wash on the bank.   Adopted by the couple, he grew to be big and strong.   One day, he set out to conquer an island of ogres, accompanied by a dog, a monkey and a pheasant. He returned to his parents in triumph, bringing back myriad treasures.   This tale can be traced back to the Muromachi period (1336-1568) but with a slightly different plot.   The present version became popular in the Edo period (1603-1868).

〖注〗 character 人物. folk tale 民話. woodcutter 木こり. adopt 養子にする. an island of ogres 鬼が島. in triumph 勝利を得て, 意気揚々と. be traced back to ～にまでたどる, ～にさかのぼる. the present version 現代版.

momoware 桃割れ   lit. a split peach. the *momoware* hairstyle, a type of traditional coiffure developed during the Edo period (1603-1868).   It is characterized by puffed-out side locks and a chignon resembling a split peach.   It was common among girls in their teens in the Meiji era (1868-1912).   Even today, kimono-clad girls may sometimes be seen wearing this style during the New Year season.   ⇨ MAGE

〖注〗 coiffure 髪型, 髪の結い方. lock 髪の房. chignon 束髪の束.

Momoyama-jidai 桃山時代   the Momoyama period (around the end of the 16th century); a period of about 35 years during the end of which Toyotomi Hideyoshi (1536-98) reigned over the country. The name Momoyama came from one of his headquarters, Fushimi-Momoyama Castle (presently called Fushimi Castle) built on a hill near Fushimi in 1594.   Together with the previous Azuchi period, this period is more commonly called the Azuchi-Momoyama period (1568-1603). ⇨ AZUCHI-JIDAI, AZUCHI-MOMO-YAMA-JIDAI

〖注〗 headquarters 本部, 本拠.

monaka 最中   lit. in the midst. bean-jam wafers; a kind of sweet made of two wafers stuck together with a sweet bean-paste jam filling.   As with many foods in Japan, the *monaka* has a seasonal aspect.   Originally it was made in a round shape which suggested "a full moon in the midst of autumn," thus giving rise to its name. Today, however, *monaka* come in various shapes.   ⇨ AN

〖注〗 bean jam 餡. wafer ウエハース. filling つめもの. give rise to ～を生じる、引き起こす.

Monju (Bosatsu) 文珠(菩薩)   Manju sri (Sanskrit); the bodhisattva of wisdom; an enlightened being of wisdom.   His image appears as one of the two attendants to Buddha Sakyamuni, often riding on a lion.   Born in India shortly after Sakyamuni's death, he is said to have played an important role in compiling Buddhist scriptures. He was respected for his extraordinary intellect and wisdom.   In Japan he is commonly believed to give children wisdom.   A Japanese proverb goes, "Out of the counsel of three comes the wisdom of Monju," the English counterpart of which might be "Two heads are better than one."   ⇨ BOSATSU

〖注〗 bodhisattva 菩薩. enlightened being 悟りを開いた人. attendant お伴、従者. Sakyamuni 釈迦. scripture 聖典、経典. "Out of the counsel of three comes the wisdom of Monju." 「三人寄れば文珠の知恵」. counterpart 相当するもの、対の一方.

monme 匁[文目]   a traditional unit for measuring weight.   One *monme*, about 3.75 grams, is one-thousandth of a *kan*.   In medieval times, the *monme* was also a minor monetary unit equivalent to one-sixtyth of a small gold coin.   As with the *kan*, the monetary *monme* is considered to have become a standard weight.   ⇨ SHAKKAN-HŌ

〖注〗 minor monetary unit 小貨幣単位. small gold coin 小判.

monpe(i) もんぺ(い)   women's work pants; a trousers-like garment gathered at the ankles and made of kimono cloth, worn over the half-kimono.   It was widely used during World War II, and even now by elderly women when working in the field, especially in northern Japan.

〖注〗 garment 衣服.

moribana 盛り花   lit. piled-up flowers.   a style of flower arrangement using a shallow container.   The container can be a shallow basin, a flat plate or a low compote.   Usually a metal holder—a *kenzan* (a holder with needle points) or a *shippō* (a holder with holes)—is used to fix the flowers in place.   With a narrow compote, the stems are arranged in the center.   With a wide basin they are usually arranged at one corner so that the cool atmosphere of the water can be appreciated as well.   This is one of the most popular styles of arrangement today, another one being the *nageire* style (throw-in style), and was introduced late in the Meiji era (1868-1912) by Unshin Ohara (1861-1914) to allow more creative and artistic arrangements to fit both modern and traditional environments. Free abstract arrangements developed from this form after World War II. ⇨ IKEBANA, KENZAN, NAGEIRE, SHIPPŌ, SUIBAN

〖注〗 shallow basin 水盤. compote 足のついた花器や皿. Unshin Ohara 小原雲心.

mori-soba 盛り蕎麦 piled-up buckwheat noodles; buckwheat noodles served on bamboo ware, with no seaweed laver sprinkled on top, unlike *zaru-soba*. It is often served on a split-bamboo rack on a square, lacquered wooden frame. *Mori-soba* comes with a tiny dish of Japanese horseradish and minced green onions, which are added to a cup of dip made of soy sauce and fish broth. The noodles are eaten by dipping into this sauce. ⇨ NORI, SOBA, ZARU-SOBA

〖注〗 buckwheat noodle 蕎麦. seaweed laver 海苔. split-bamboo rack 割り竹のすのこ. lacquered wooden frame 漆塗りの木わく. Japanese horseradish わさび. minced green onions きざみねぎ, さらしねぎ. condiment 薬味. soy sauce 醬油. fish broth 魚のだし汁.

mugicha 麦茶 barley tea; a tea made by boiling roasted barley in water. Roasted barley is simmered for a few minutes, the barley is discarded, and then the tea is chilled. It is a popular summer drink, served in place of hot green tea. ⇨ CHA

〖注〗 barley 大麦. simmer 煮つめる. discard 捨てる.

mukei-bunkazai 無形文化財 intangible cultural properties; cultural assets of traditional and artistic value, having intangible forms (drama, music, handicraft skills, etc.). Especially important skills are designated as important cultural properties (*jūyōmukei-bunkazai*) and are protected by the government. ⇨ BUNKAZAI, JŪYŌ-BUNKAZAI, JŪYŌMUKEI-BUNKAZAI, NINGEN-KOKUHŌ

〖注〗 intangible 無形の, 触れることができない. property 資産, 財産. assets 資産, 財産. handicraft 手工芸.

mukoyōshi 婿養子 an adopted son-in-law; a son-in-law taken into a family as the husband to a daughter. He changes his surname to his wife's and becomes the nominal heir to head her family's household. In Japan, adoption has been practiced not for welfare purposes, but for the continuation of the family name. Thus there

have also been cases of adoption of both a son and his wife.
〖注〗 nominal heir 名目上の相続人. adoption 養子にすること.

mukōzuke 向附 lit. a dish served on the far side. a simple dish
placed beyond the bowls of rice and soup on the diner's individual
tray in a formal Japanese dinner. It is usually a dish of raw fish
or vinegared vegetables arranged in a small ceramic container
suiting the season. ⇨ SASHIMI, SUNOMONO
〖注〗 raw fish 刺身. vinegared vegetables 野菜の酢の物. ceramic container 陶器の入れ物.

murahachibu 村八分 lit. eight parts rejected from the village.
ostracism from a village; social alienation; rejection from a group
or community. A sanction of this kind was customarily applied as
a heavy punishment, particularly in the Edo period (1603-1868), to
those who violated rules and regulations, or to those who were
regarded as dangerous to the community, often involving an entire
family. Some were totally rejected and condemned to exile;
others were subjected to restrictions on involvement in community
affairs except on two occasions, fires and funerals. Japanese, who
are largely interdependent within groups, such treatment was
extremely harsh. A feeling of aversion to ostracism still remains
in modern Japanese society.
〖注〗 ostracism 追放, 社会的追放. social alienation 社会からの疎外. sanction 制裁. heavy punishment 重い罰. violate 犯す, 違反する. condemn to
exile 流刑に処す. be subjected to 服従させられる, 蒙らせる. interdependent
相互依存の. aversion 嫌悪.

Muromachi-bakufu 室町幕府 the Muromachi shogunate (1336-
1568 or 1573); the government of the Ashikaga shogun, established
in 1336 by Ashikaga Takauji (1305-58) with its headquarters in
Kyoto. In 1378 the third shogun Yoshimitsu (1358-1468) built the
so-called "flowering palace," also used as administrative headquarters, in the Muromachi district of Kyoto, hence the name
Muromachi-bakufu. Despite the establishment of centralized government by Yoshimi-tsu, about half a century later the shogun's
power declined with the Ōnin Revolt (1467-77), which broke out in
Kyoto in connection with problems of succession. In addition, the
arts-oriented Ashikaga shoguns found themselves militarily vulnerable in coping with provincial feudal lords. The shogunate was
overthrown by a provincial feudal lord, Oda Nobunaga (1534-82),
in 1573 at the time of the 15th shogun Yoshiaki (1537-97). ⇨

ASHIKAGA-BAKUFU, MUROMACHI-JIDAI, SHŌGUN

〚注〛 "flowering palace"「花の御所」． administrative headquarters 政治の本
拠． vulnerable 弱みのある． provincial feudal lords 諸国の大名．

Muromachi-jidai 室町時代 the Muromachi period (1336-1568 or
1573); the period of the Ashikaga shogunate government established by Ashikaga Takauji (1305-58) at Muromachi, Kyoto.
Many of the 15 Ashikaga shoguns were men of aesthetic taste.
Fostered by the shoguns, arts in many fields blossomed—gardening, architecture, flower arrangement, tea ceremony, Noh drama,
etc. On the other hand, this period was fraught with disturbances,
especially in the latter half, eventually leading to the Age of Civil
Wars (1467-mid-16th century). It was during this period that the
Portuguese first came to Japan (1543), bringing tobacco, firearms
and Christianity. ⇨ ASHIKAGA-BAKUFU, SENGOKU-JIDAI

〚注〛 the Ashikaga shogunate government 足利幕府． a man of aesthetic
taste 風流人． fraught with ～を含む，に満ちた． the Age of Civil Wars 戦国
時代． firearm 鉄砲，小銃．

musha-ningyō 武者人形 a warrior doll; dolls in armor representing
famous feudal generals and other historical or legendary heroic
figures. As a traditional custom since the 16th century, on Boys'
Day (May 5) such dolls are displayed on tiers, together with articles
used by samurai including swords, helmets, armor, banners, etc.
These dolls portray such historical figures as Katō Kiyomasa
(1562-1611) who single-handedly slew a ferocious tiger during the
Korean invasion; Toyotomi Hideyoshi (1536-98), the son of a poor
farmer who became a generalissimo; as well as such legendary
heroes as Kintarō, a strong boy who had animal followers;
Momotarō, who was born from a peach and conquered fiends, etc.
⇨ KINTARŌ, KODOMO NO HI, MOMOTARŌ, TANGO NO SEKKU

〚注〛 armor 甲冑，よろい． feudal general 封建武将． heroic figure 英雄．
tier 段． banner 旗． slew slay の過去形(=kill)． ferocious 恐ろしい，どう猛
の． generalissimo 征夷大将軍． fiend 悪魔，鬼．

musha-shugyō 武者修行 training as warriors; specifically, travels
undertaken by swordsmen in feudal times to discipline themselves
as warriors through hardship. At the same time, through such
travels, many graduates of schools of swordsmanship found opportunities to place themselves in the service of a feudal lord. ⇨
DAIMYŌ, KENJUTSU

〚注〛 warriorship 武士道，武術． swordsman 剣士，剣術家． feudal times 封

建時代．　swordsmanship 剣道，剣術．　feudal lord 大名．

mushimono 蒸し物　steamed foods; fish, shellfish, egg or vegetables cooked in steam and served hot.　There are basically two kinds —one steamed individually in small cups like *chawanmushi* and the other steamed with salt in a large steamer.　⇨ CHAWANMUSHI

〖注〗　steamer 蒸し器．

Myōō 明王　a conquering deity; an incarnation of Dainichi Nyorai or an attendant deity to Dainichi Nyorai.　With his fierce expression and with various kinds of weapons in his hand, he is said to vanquish all evils that might appear along the path to salvation. There is usually a halo of flames behind his head.　Representative kinds of Myōō are Fudō Myōō, Aizen Myōō, etc.　⇨ DAINICHI NYORAI, FUDŌ MYŌŌ

〖注〗　deity 神，神のような人［もの］．　incarnation 化身．　attendant deity 従者の神［神のようなもの］．　vanquish 征服する，打ち勝つ．　the path to salvation 救いに至る道．　halo of flames 炎の光輪．

N

nabemono 鍋物 a generic term for a pot dish; meat, fish, soybean curd and vegetables cooked in a pot (or pan) at the table. It is eaten from the pot while cooking. *Sukiyaki, yosenabe* and *mizutaki* are some examples. ⇨ MIZUTAKI, SUKIYAKI, YOSENABE

〖注〗 soybean curd 豆腐.

Nabeshima-yaki 鍋島焼 Nabeshima porcelain ware; porcelain ware first made under the supervision of the Nabeshima family, the rulers of Saga in northern Kyūshū, in the 17th century. Originally, Nabeshima ware was not for sale, but rather for the clan lord to use as gifts, and was therefore made very carefully and in limited numbers. It has a very smooth and lustrous texture. The design —mainly gorgeous flowers and birds—is painted clearly and realistically with colors raised above the surface of the glaze. Of the different types of Nabeshima ware—colored *Nabeshima* (*iro-Nabeshima*), celadon *Nabeshima* (*Nabeshima-seiji*), blue-and-white *Nabeshima* (*sometsuke-Nabeshima*), etc.—colored *Nabeshima* is considered the finest. ⇨ SEIJI, SOMETSUKE

〖注〗 porcelain ware 磁器. clan lord 藩主. lustrous texture 光沢のある地. glaze 上薬, 釉. celadon 青磁. blue and white 染付け(藍色の模様を焼きつけた陶磁器).

nabeyaki-udon 鍋焼きうどん pot-boiled noodles; noodles boiled in an earthen pot with soy-sauce-flavored fish broth, served piping hot in the pot. Shrimp *tenpura,* an egg, mushroom, slices of fish-paste cake, wheat-gluten bread (*fu*), slices of bamboo shoot and bits of green vegetables are arranged on top. ⇨ FU, TENPURA, UDON

〖注〗 soy-sauce-flavored 醤油で味つけをした. fish broth 魚の煮出し汁, だし. piping hot しゅうしゅういうほど熱い. fish-paste cake 蒲鉾. wheat-gluten bread 麦のグルテン質から作ったパン状のもの, 麩. bamboo shoot 竹の子.

nagahibachi 長火鉢 an oblong brazier; a rectangular wooden brazier with drawers, used to warm one's hands. It is usually made of *keyaki* (zelkova) wood. One section is depressed, the inside of

which is lined with copper, and filled with ash and charcoal to heat
water for tea or to warm sakê (rice wine). The other section is
covered with a *nekoita*, or board on which tea cups or pots can be
placed.   ⇨ HIBACHI

〖注〗 oblong 長方形の. brazier 火鉢. drawer 引き出し. zelkova 欅.
line 張る，裏打ちをする.

nagajuban 長襦袢 a long undergarment; a kimono-size undergarment worn under a kimono by both men and women. A woman's
nagajuban is of a bright color, often brighter than the kimono. It
has a silk collar or neckband which is interchangeable to harmonize with the kimono.   ⇨ HAN'ERI, JUBAN, KIMONO

〖注〗 undergarment 下着. silk collar or neckband 半衿.

nagashibina 流し雛 dolls to be drifted away; an ancient purification ritual of setting dolls adrift on a river. Dolls made of straw
or paper were floated down rivers together with offerings such as
food, flowers, etc. This was to purify people by transferring evil
spirits to these dolls. This ritual can still be observed in some
districts. The origin of *hina*-dolls, lavishly dressed today, can be
traced back to such simple dolls of religious significance.   ⇨ HINA
MATSURI, HINA-NINGYŌ

〖注〗 purification 清め，禊. ritual 儀式. adrift 漂って.

nagauta 長唄 lit. a long song. a long epic song or ballad chanted
to the accompaniment of *shamisen*, and often drums and flutes as
well. It developed as major music for dances performed in the
Kabuki theater. Such ballads also came to be sung to the *shamisen* independently in a chamber.   ⇨ KABUKI, SHAMISEN, SHAKUHA-
CHI

〖注〗 epic 叙事詩(の). ballad 伝承的物語詩. chant 詠唱する. to the accompaniment of ～の伴奏に合わせて.

nagaya 長屋 a row-house; a small traditional tenement house
generally used by humble people. It is a traditional type of apartment house, wooden and generally one-storied, and long and narrow in structure. The small apartments are connected in a line
under a single roof. Such structures were typical of urban housing
in poorer sections of towns in the Edo period (1603-1868). Due to
the Great Kantō Earthquake of 1923 and World War II, many have
been replaced by more modern apartment houses and condomin-
iums.   ⇨ KANTŌ DAISHINSAI

〖注〗 tenement 家屋，借家. condominium 分譲アパート，(敷地共有の)分譲マ

ンション.

nageire 投げ入れ the thrown-in style of flower arrangement; flowers arranged in a tall vase without a metal holder (*kenzan*), but usually with a fixture made of twigs. In this type of arrangement, flowers should be arranged in a vase as naturally as possible. In fact, vase arrangements require more skill than the *moribana* type. ⇨ IKEBANA, MORIBANA

〖注〗 flower arrangement 生け花. metal holder 金属の花留め(剣山や七宝). fixture 花留め. twig 小枝.

naginata 長刀 a Japanese halberd, or the martial art in which such a halberd is used. The weapon consists of a curved single-edged blade attached to the end of a long wooden shaft. It was commonly used on the battlefield along with the sword and spear from the late Heian period (794-1185), particularly by monk soldiers. With the development of spearing techniques and the introduction of firearms from abroad in the latter half of the Muromachi period (1336-1568), it went out of use. In the Edo period (1603-1868) it was revived as a means of self-defense for women of the samurai class. Thus the martial art of using a *naginata* with a substitute blade of bamboo, which was established as a means of spiritual training in the Meiji era (1868-1912), developed as a sport chiefly for women. In competition the contestants are clad in an outfit similar to that for *kendō,* consisting of a face mask, chest protector, arm guards and a waist protector, with the addition of shin guards. Points are acquired by stabbing or striking a part of the opponent's protective gear other than the waist protector. ⇨ KENDŌ

〖注〗 halberd 長い刀, 鉾槍. martial art 武芸, 格闘技. shaft やりの柄, 取っ手. spear 槍, 槍を使う. monk soldiers 僧兵. firearm 鉄砲. face mask 面. chest protector 胴. arm guard 小手. waist protector 垂れ. shin 向うずね. protective gear 防具.

Nagoya-obi 名古屋帯 a Nagoya sash; one type of women's *obi*, which originated around Nagoya during the Taishō era (1912-1926). This type of *obi* is made up of one part about 30 centimeters wide and the other part folded in half. The former part is for forming a drum bow at the back and the latter goes around the waist. It comes in a variety of fabrics—silk, cotton, synthetic fiber, etc.—with a variety of patterns which are woven, painted or embroidered. This *obi* is suitable with many kinds of semiformal

and informal kimono, but not with a very formal kimono.　⇨
KIMONO, OBI

〖注〗 drum bow お太鼓. synthetic fiber 合成繊維. embroider 刺しゅう
する.

naishinnō 内親王 an imperial princess; the honorific title for princesses of the Imperial Family.　Formerly it was used as a title for
the sisters and daughters of the emperor.　Today, it is the title of
the daughters of the emperor and the daughters of the male heirs
to the throne.　The princes of the imperial family bear the honorific title of *shinnō*.　⇨ SHINNŌ

〖注〗 honorific title 敬称. a heir to the throne 皇位継承者.

nakōdo 仲人 a go-between; a matchmaker; a person or a couple,
who arranges a marriage for a young couple.　In a traditional
arranged marriage, a go-between introduces the two parties and if
they decide to marry, he or she will be entrusted with the affairs of
the wedding and serve as a consultant throughout their marriage.
Even in the case of a love match, a young couple and their parents
will ask someone, such as a superior or a close friend, to act as a
ceremonial go-between.　One reason is that customarily the seats
next to the bride and groom at the wedding reception are reserved
for the *nakōdo* couple.　⇨ MIAI, MIAI-KEKKON

〖注〗 entrust 任せる.

namaage 生揚げ half-fried soybean curd; a thick slice of soybean
curd lightly deep-fried.　It is usually boiled in soy sauce, sugar,
sweet rice wine and fish broth, and is popular as an ingredient of
oden (Japanese hodgepodge).　⇨ ABURA(A)GE, ODEN, TŌFU

〖注〗 soybean curd 豆腐. deep-fry 油をたっぷりつかって揚げる. soy sauce
醤油. sweet rice wine 味醂. fish broth 魚の味のだし. ingredient 調理の
材料.

namagashi 生菓子 unbaked sweets; a moist cake; a generic term
for traditional sweets usually made from bean paste and/or glutinous rice.　There are several categories: bean-paste cake, steamed
cake, jellied cake, etc.　Most are formed into dumplings, often in
the shape of flowers, leaves, etc., expressive of a particular season.
These sweets go well with green tea, and are called *omogashi* when
served in the tea ceremony.　⇨ OMOGASHI, WAGASHI

〖注〗 glutinous rice 糯米. dumpling 団子. tea ceremony 茶の湯.

namasu 膾 a kind of salad; a dish of sliced raw seafood and/or
vegetables seasoned with vinegar.　The vinegar dressing is sea-

soned with sugar, or sugar and soy sauce, and may be flavored with
sesame seed or *yuzu* citron.

〚注〛 season 味をつける. sesame seeds ごま.

nanakusa 七草 the seven herbs or grasses; the seven herbs of spring
(*haru no nanakusa*) or the seven grasses of autumn (*aki no
nanakusa*). The seven herbs of spring are *seri* (Japanese parsley),
nazuna (shepherd's purse), *gogyō* (cutweed), *hakobe(ra)* (chickweed), *hotokenoza* (henbit), *suzuna* (turnip leaves) and *suzushiro*
(garden radish leaves). The seven grasses of autumn are *hagi*
(Japanese bush clover), *obana* (flowering eulalia), *kuzu* (pueraria),
nadeshiko (wild pink), *ominaeshi* (patrinia), *fujibakama* (eupatorium) and *kikyō* (*platycodon grandiflorum* or althea). The former
have to do with food for health; the latter are selected for their
flowers to represent the season. ⇨ AKI NO NANAKUSA, HARU NO
NANAKUSA

nanakusa-gayu 七草粥 seven-herb rice gruel; rice gruel cooked
with some or all of the seven herbs of spring—*seri, nazuna, gogyō,
hakobera, hotokenoza, suzuna* and *suzushiro*. Traditionally it is
made on January 7, and is believed to remove evil from the body
and prevent illness. ⇨ HARU NO NANAKUSA, NANAKUSA

〚注〛 herb 薬草. gruel かゆ, かゆ状のもの. the seven herbs of spring 春の
七草.

nanbanjin 南蛮人 lit. southern barbarians. early European visitors coming from the southern seas. The term was used to refer
to the Europeans—Portuguese, Spanish, Dutch and English—who
came to Japan by way of the seas south of Japan in the late 16th
and early 17th centuries. ⇨ NANBANMONO

〚注〛 barbarian 野蛮人、異邦人.

nanbanmono 南蛮物 lit. southern barbarian things. European
things; articles brought in from Europe, especially Portugal and
Spain, in the 16th and 17th centuries. The arrival of Portuguese
ships in the late Muromachi period in the 16th century enabled the
Japanese to come into contact with European articles. They were
called southern barbarian things in those days because they came
to Japan by way of the sea south of Japan. The articles included
wool fabric, calico, ceramic ware, gold and silver braid, etc.
Japanese-made articles with designs of Portuguese or Spanish
influence are also called *nanbanmono*. ⇨ NANBANJIN

〚注〛 barbarian 野蛮人. wool fabric 毛織物. calico 更紗. ceramic ware

陶器．braid 紐．

Nanbokuchō-jidai 南北朝時代 the Nanbokuchō period (1333-92); the period of division of the imperial throne into the northern and southern courts. Emperor Godaigo (1288-1339) and his successors, driven out of Kyoto by the Ashikagas, maintained the Southern court at Yoshino while the Ashikagas set up a new Northern court in Kyoto, a puppet court with a relative of Godaigo installed as emperor, to make his shogunate official. This was an era of strife between the two courts, which was eventually ended by the restoration of the legitimate sovereign. One school of historians maintains that this era be considered a part of the Muromachi period (1336-1568). ⇨ ASHIKAGA-BAKUFU, MUROMACHI-JIDAI

〖注〗 the imperial throne 朝廷，天皇の座．puppet court 傀儡朝廷．restoration 返還．legitimate 合法的な，正統の．sovereign 支配，統治権．

nanga 南画 the southern school of Chinese painting. It originated during the Southern-Sung dynasty (1127-1279) of China and was introduced to Japan during the Kyōhō era (1716-36). Generally a landscape is depicted, mostly in black India ink in various shades. Often a poem is written on the white part. Also called *bunjinga*, or literati painting, it was developed by scholars of the Chinese classics. ⇨ SUIBOKUGA

〖注〗 India ink 墨．various shades さまざまな濃淡．literati 文学者たち，文人（literatusの複数）．scholars of the Chinese classics 漢学者．

naniwabushi 浪花節 Naniwa-style of reciting epics; a combination of story-telling and singing to the accompaniment of *shamisen* (a three-stringed instrument). This style was developed by Naniwa Isuke in Ōsaka late in the Edo period (1603-1868) and was first performed on the street. It was adopted for variety shows in the Meiji era (1868-1912). The themes of the stories are derived from legends, historical events, literary works, social situations, etc., often depicting conflicts between obligation and human feelings. Also called *rōkyoku*. ⇨ SHAMISEN

〖注〗 epic 叙事詩，物語り．to the accompaniment of ～の伴奏で，～に合わせて．Naniwa Isuke 浪花伊助．variety shows 寄席．conflicts between obligation and human feelings 義理人情の葛藤．

Naoki-shō 直木賞 the Naoki Literary Prize; a prestigious literary prize awarded to works with entertaining elements in addition to literary value. It was established in 1935 by the writer Kan Kikuchi (1888-1948) in memory of Sanjūgo Naoki (1891-1934).

The prize was first administered by the Bungeishunju Ltd. and from the seventh prize (1938) it was taken over by the Japan Literature Promotion Association (Nihon Bungaku Shinkokai). Since 1935, the prize has been awarded twice a year, excluding several years during and after World War II. Recipients are selected, by outstanding writers and critics, from among writers whose works have appeared in newspapers or magazines. The selected works are published in the *Ōru Yomimono* magazine. ⇨ AKUTAGAWA-SHŌ

〖注〗 literary value 文学的価値. Sanjūgo Naoki 直木三十五. take over 引き継ぐ. the Japan Literature Promotion Association 日本文学振興会.

Nara-jidai 奈良時代 the Nara period (646-794); the period during which the capital was Nara (710-84) and Nagaoka (784-94), where the Imperial Court was located. In 710, the capital Heijōkyō was built in Nara—the first stationary capital in Japanese history. It lasted for 74 years under eight successive emperors (though the last emperor Kanmu (737-806) was in Nagaoka as well for 10 years). The Nara period was characterized by the development of Buddhism, and Buddhist arts and structures, as well as the establishment of a law-abiding centralized country. ⇨ BUKKYŌ, HEIJŌKYŌ, RITSURYŌ, TAIKA NO KAISHIN

〖注〗 the Imperial Court 皇居. stationary 固定した, 長期の. structure 建造物. law-abiding 法律に従う.

narazuke 奈良漬け saké-flavored pickles; vegetables pickled in saké lees, originally developed around Nara. Most commonly used are cucumbers, cucumber melons, eggplant and various kinds of radish. They are pickled first with salt for one or two months and then in saké lees for several months. To bring out more flavor, sugar, *mirin* (sweet seasoning wine) and fresh saké lees are added several times during the process. ⇨ MIRIN, SAKE, TSU-KEMONO

〖注〗 lees (酒類の)残りかす. cucumber melon まくわ瓜.

naruto(-maki) 鳴門(巻き) lit. a whirlpool roll. a kind of steamed fish-paste cake shaped like a long cylinder with grooves on the surface. When it is sliced at an angle, a red design in the form of a whirl appears. It is often used to decorate the top of noodles in a bowl or as an ingredient in soup. The term was derived from the Naruto Straits, in the Inland Sea of Seto, where the stream flows rapidly, forming whirls. ⇨ SETO NAIKAI, UDON

〖注〗 whirlpool うず巻き． (steamed) fish-paste cake 蒲鉾． cylinder 円柱．
groove 細いみぞ． at an angle 斜めに． whirl うず． ingredient （料理の）材
料． the Naruto Straits 鳴門海峡．

natsume 棗 a lacquered tea caddy; a jujube-shaped lacquer caddy to
hold powdered green tea used to make foamy green tea (*usucha*).
A tea caddy of pure black lacquer finish is very formal and traditional, though tea caddies of various colors and designs have come
into use recently. ⇨ CHAIRE. USUCHA
〖注〗 lacquered 漆を塗った． tea caddy 茶入れ． jujube なつめ（の木）．
powdered green tea 抹茶． foamy green tea 泡立った抹茶，薄茶． pure black
lacquer （漆の）真塗．

nattō 納豆 fermented soybeans; steamed soybeans with a slimy
consistency, fermented with the *natto* bacillus. Traditionally, it
was made by wrapping soybeans in straw where the *natto* bacillus
generates.   The bacillus softens the protein in soybeans and makes
it more digestible by producing enzymes. Today, the bacillus in
the straw is separated and cultured to prevent contamination by
other organisms. *Nattō* is regarded as a health food. It is usually
eaten with soy sauce, mustard, minced green onions, etc.
〖注〗 ferment 発酵する． slimy ねばねばした． consistency 濃度，粘度．
natto bacillus 納豆菌． enzyme 酵素． culture 培養する． contamination 汚
染． soy sauce 醬油． minced green onions きざみねぎ，さらしねぎ．

nawashiro 苗代 a rice nursery; a nursery bed for rice seedlings.
Rice seedlings grown in nursery beds are transplanted to large
paddy fields. ⇨ TAUE
〖注〗 nursery 苗木畑，苗床． seedling 苗，苗木． transplant 移植する．
paddy field 田んぼ，水田．

Nebuta Matsuri ねぶた祭 the Dummy Festival at Aomori and
Hirosaki, Aomori Prefecture (August 3 to 7). *Nebuta* (called
neputa in Hirosaki) are dummies made of paper on bamboo
frames, often lighted by candles inside. On these festive days,
huge lighted *nebuta*, some as wide as the street, depicting legendary
figures and animals, are placed on floats and carried through the
streets at night, with people dancing alongside. The festival is
said to have originated some ten centuries ago to celebrate the Ezo
(presumably the Ainus) conquest in which *nebuta* were successfully
used to trick the enemy.
〖注〗 dummy 飾り人形，マネキン，模造品． legendary figure 伝説上の人物．
float 浮遊物，山車． the Ezo conquest 蝦夷征伐．

Negoro-nuri 根来塗 Negoro lacquer ware; red-and-black lacquer articles produced in Negoro, Wakayama Prefecture. The wooden body is first coated with black lacquer, and then with a coral-red lacquer. This lacquer ware is strong and practical. Repeated daily use adds rustic beauty to the ware, the black undercoating seen through. The technique was developed in the 13th century by priests at Negoro Temple, where they made such ware for their own daily use. ⇨ NURIMONO, SHIKKI, URUSHI

〖注〗 lacquer ware 漆器. coral-red 珊瑚色の赤. rustic beauty さびれた美しさ, 素朴な美.

nemawashi 根回し lit. to make more roots grow around the trunk of a tree. informal discussions held prior to a formal decision being made in order to obtain a consensus. One or two years before transplanting a large tree, the ground around its trunk is dug up and the roots are trimmed in order to make new roots. This term came to be used figuratively, referring to a decision-making process widely followed in business. Plans are thrashed out behind the scenes among the persons concerned, involving both management and labor, so that at formal meetings they can be unanimously agreed upon with no confrontation. ⇨ RINGISEI

〖注〗 transplant 植えかえる. figuratively 比喩的に. decision-making process 意思決定過程. thrash out 徹底的に案を練る. unanimously 満場一致で. confrontation 対立.

nenbutsu 念仏 a Buddhist invocation, particularly to Amitabha (the Lord of Infinite Light) in the Jōdo and related sects. It is composed of six Chinese characters, "*na-mu-a-mi-da-butsu,*" meaning "I pray to Buddha Amitabha" (namu=I pray; amida=Amitabha; butsu=Buddha). It originally referred to meditation on Buddha Amitabha by invoking his name. It gradually came to also refer to repeated chanting of the name of Amitabha. In the late Heian period (794-1185), Priest Hōnen (1133-1212), founder of the Jōdo sect, stressed the need for sincere repetition of this phrase, in place of elaborate rituals and philosophies, in order to be reborn in the Pure Land. ⇨ BUKKYŌ, DAIMOKU, JŌDOSHŪ

〖注〗 invocation 祈願. Amitabha 阿弥陀. Chinese character 漢字. ritual 儀式. the Pure Land 浄土.

nengajō 年賀状 a New Year's greeting card; greeting cards sent to wish happiness throughout the new year. It has long been a custom for the Japanese to exchange greetings with relatives and close acquaintances by paying visits during the New Year holiday period. With the launching of postal services at the beginning of the Meiji era (1868-1912), such greetings came to be extended to a larger number of people by means of *nengajō*. Unlike Christmas cards, New Year greetings are made by means of official post cards or other post cards of a standard size. Since 1949, New Year's lottery post cards have been issued annually by the Postal Ministry. The greetings may be written in calligraphy, conveyed by means of creative designs, or printed with a few personal comments added. Those marked with the word *nenga* and brought to the post office one or two weeks before the end of the year are delivered on January 1. ⇨ GANJITSU, OTOSHIDAMA-TSUKI NENGAHAGAKI

〖注〗 postal service 郵便事業. New Year's lottery post card お年玉つき年賀はがき. calligraphy 書道.

nenkō-joretsu 年功序列 the seniority system; ranking according to seniority or length of experience; priority given to the aged over the younger. Traditionally in Japan, the aged are to be respected because of their experience and wisdom. This idea, stemming from Confucianism, is deeply ingrained both in the family and in society, thus forming a so-called vertical structure. This is also applied to the system of employment in terms of ranking and salary, which are based on seniority and length of service. ⇨ JUKYŌ, NENKŌJORETSU-CHINGINSEI, SHŪSHIN-KOYŌSEI(DO)

〖注〗 seniority 年長, 先輩. stem from 〜から由来する. Confucianism 儒教. ingrain 〜を植えつけられている, 深く浸み込んでいる. vertical structure 縦構造. length of service 勤続年数.

nenkōjoretsu-chinginsei 年功序列賃金制 the seniority system in wages; the wage system based on seniority, and length of service and experience. Customarily in most Japanese firms, pay is raised on the basis of age and the number of years of employment in the company, so is the amount of payment on retirement. The young, newly employed are underpaid regardless of their ability and productivity. However, a steady increase in pay is secured even in adverse times for those who make a commitment to one company, based on the fixed-wage system regulated according to educational background, kind of work, sex and, above all, length of service. Adopted shortly after World War I during a serious labor shortage, this method worked well partly because it met the employee's financial needs with the advancement of age. At the same time, it eventually led to the development of the lifetime employment system, and fostered loyalty to the firm and, in effect, the growth of industry. ⇨ NENKŌ-JORETSU, SHŪSHIN-KOYŌSEI

〖注〗 seniority 年長、先輩. length of service 勤続年数. the amount of payment on retirement 退職金の額. adverse times 不況時. commitment 献身. the fixed wage system 固定賃金制. the lifetime employment system 終身雇用制度.

nenneko(-banten) ねんねこ(半天) a coat worn by a nursemaid; a kind of padded or lined short coat worn in winter by a woman carrying a baby on her back. The coat is loose enough to cover both mother and child.

〖注〗 nursemaid 子守. padded 綿の入った. lined 裏地のついた. carry a baby on one's back 赤ちゃんをおんぶする.

netsuke 根付け a toggle for attaching things to a sash; a small ornament, formerly used as an accessory on a man's sash for hanging personal things. It was fitted with a cord for fastening a purse, tobacco pouch, writing kit, etc., to the sash. It was in itself an art object, of elaborately carved ivory, wood, stone, metal, etc. To wear a *netsuke* was a vogue among the commoners, as it was the only luxury they could indulge in freely during the latter part of the Edo period (1603-1868) when attire was strictly regulated according to status. *Netsuke* came to be regarded as good-luck charms as well. The designs depict a variety of subjects associated with the culture of the Edo period. ⇨ EDO-JIDAI

〖注〗 toggle 留め木. tobacco pouch 煙草入れ. writing kit 矢立. carve 彫る. attire 服装. charm お守り.

niboshi 煮干し anchovies or finger-sized small sardines, boiled and dried. They are used to add flavor to boiled vegetables or *miso* soup. Sometimes they are used in place of *katsuobushi* (bonito flakes). ⇨ KATSUOBUSHI, MISOSHIRU

〖注〗 anchovy カタクチ鰯、小さい鰯. bonito flakes 鰹の削り節.

Nichibei Shūkō Tsūshō Jōyaku 日米修好通商条約 the Japan-U.S. Treaty of Amity and Commerce; the treaty between Japan and the U.S. signed in July 1858 by the Shimoda official of the Tokugawa shogunate government (1603-1868) and the first U.S. consul Townsend Harris. Effective July 4, 1859, it consisted of 14 articles concerning the exchange of currency, the exchange of consuls, the residence of Americans in Japan, regulations governing trade, etc.

The signing of this treaty eventually led to the opening of Japan's doors to the world after a period of seclusion lasting about 220 years.　⇨ NICHIBEI WASHIN JŌYAKU, SAKOKU(-SEISAKU), TOKUGAWA-BAKUFU

〖注〗 amity 親善，友好関係．the Tokugawa shogunate government 徳川幕府．consul 領事．effective 施行される，効力をもつ．article 条項．the exchange of currency 通貨交換．seclusion 鎖国．

Nichibei Washin Jōyaku 日米和親条約 the Japan-U.S. Treaty of Amity; the first treaty between Japan and the United States, signed in 1854 by the Tokugawa shogunate government (1603-1868) and Commodore Matthew C. Perry of the United States.　With this treaty, Japan opened the port of Shimoda at the tip of the Izu Peninsula and that of Hakodate in Hokkaidō to Americans, after a period of seclusion lasting 220 years during which the Dutch were the only Europeans allowed to land on Japan's shores.　This treaty is also called *Kanagawa Jōyaku* (the Kanagawa Treaty of Amity) because it was signed at Kanagawa.　⇨ NICHIBEI SHŪKŌ TSŪSHŌ JŌYAKU, SAKOKU(-SEISAKU), TOKUGAWA-BAKUFU

〖注〗 amity 親善，友好関係．the Tokugawa shogunate (government) 徳川幕府．Commodore 提督，艦長．seclusion 隔離，鎖国．Japan's shores 日本の陸地．

Nichigin 日銀　⇨ NIHON GINKŌ

Nichirenshū 日蓮宗 the Nichiren sect of Buddhism; a Buddhist sect founded by the priest Nichiren (1222-82) in the middle of the Kamakura period (1185-1336).　Aggressive in spirit and critical of the established religions and politics, he was subjected to persecution by other religious sects and exiled by the Kamakura shogunate government (1185-1336).　His teachings, based on the Lotus Sutra (*Hokekyō*), stress the practical application of esoteric Buddhism.　He taught that eternal Buddhahood would be revealed to believers even during their lifetime if they recited with all sincerity the phrase *"Namu myōhō rengēkyō"* (Hail! The Sutra of the Lotus of the Wonderful Law).　Today, the Nichiren sect is said to have some thousands of temples and millions of adherents, with its headquarters at Kuonji Temple on Mount Minobu near Mount Fuji.　⇨ DAIMOKU

〖注〗 persecution 迫害．exile 流刑に処す．Lotus Sutra 法華経．eternal Buddhahood 永遠の仏性．sutra お経．lotus 蓮．adherent 信者．headquarters 本部．

nigiri-meshi 握り飯 a rice ball; rice in round or triangular shape, rolled with both hands. It is covered with a dried seaweed-laver sheet (*nori*) or sprinkled with sesame seeds, etc., the center being filled with a pickled plum, codfish roe, salty salmon or spicy boiled foods. This is a popular food for picnics or traveling, the Japanese counterpart of the Western sandwich. Also called *onigiri* or *omusubi*. ⇨ NORI, TSUKUDANI, UMEBOSHI

〖注〗 dried seaweed laver 海苔. sesame seeds ごま. pickled plum 梅干. codfish roe 鱈子. spicy boiled food 香のきいた煮つめもの, 佃煮. counterpart 相当するもの.

nigiri-zushi 握り鮨 vinegared rice balls; a bite-size rectangular rice ball topped with a piece of seafood, generally raw but sometimes cooked. It is rolled with one hand by an expert, requiring special skill to produce a superb taste. A variety of seafoods are used: *maguro* (tuna), *ika* (cuttlefish), *awabi* (abalone), *akagai* (ark shell), *aoyagi* (round clam), *ikura* (salmon eggs), *uni* (sea-urchin), *tako* (octopus), *ebi* (shrimp), *anago* (conger eel), *shako* (mantis shrimp), *kohada* (gizzard shad), etc. The latter five are usually cooked. *Wasabi* (green horseradish) is spread under the topping. One can order either an assortment of them, or one by one, choosing according to preference. It is recommended that a sweetened-omelet *nigiri* be eaten last to rid the mouth of a fishy smell. *Nigiri* are eaten after dipping them in soy sauce. Vinegared sliced ginger is usually served as a condiment. ⇨ SHŌYU, SUSHI, SUSHIYA, WASABI

〖注〗 assortment 取り合わせ. soy sauce 醤油. condiment 薬味.

Nihon Bengoshi Rengōkai 日本弁護士連合会 the Japan Federation of Bar Associations; an organization for the attorney-at-law, established in 1949 under the Attorneys Law (*Bengoshi Hō*). There are 52 bar associations, three in Tokyo and one for each for the jurisdictions of the district courts. Those who have passed the state law examination (*Shihō-Shiken*) and have completed two years of training at the Legal Training and Research Institute (Shihō Kenshūjo) are required to register at one of the local bar associations before practicing law. Approximately 12,500 attorneys are on the roll (vs. 600,000 in the U.S.). A 1955 amendment bared new foreign attorneys from admission to the bar associations. However, the special law concerning the handling of the legal practice by foreign lawyers was enforced on April 1, 1987, and foreign lawyers are scheduled to be enrolled under the conditions permitted by the said law.　⇨ SHIHŌ KENSHŪJO, SHIHŌ-SHIKEN

〖注〗 federation 連合会． bar association 弁護士会． attorney 代理人，弁護士． attorney-at-law 弁護士(米)． the Attorneys Law「弁護士法」． the Legal Training and Research Institute 司法研修所． register 登録する． on the roll 名簿に記載されている． amendment 法改正． bar さえぎる，禁じる． enroll 登録する，名簿に記入する．

Nihon Bōeki Shinkōkai 日本貿易振興会　Japan External Trade Organization (JETRO); an official organization serving to promote international trade. Taking over the functions of the Japan Export Trade Research Association (established in 1951), this organization was developed in 1958 with a government outlay of ¥2 billion, under the supervision of the Ministry of International Trade and Industry. Branch offices (over 50) have been established in important overseas business centers. They research and investigate foreign markets, introduce export businesses to Japanese firms, advertise Japanese goods, arrange for Japanese participation in world trade fairs, etc. In recent years, trade friction has led JETRO to work to open Japanese markets to foreign imports as well.

〖注〗 take over 受け継ぐ． the Japan Export Trade Research Association 海外市場調査会． government outlay 国庫支出． the Ministry of International Trade and Industry 通商産業省． world trade fair 国際見本市． trade friction 貿易摩擦．

Nihongi 日本紀　　⇨ NIHON SHOKI

Nihon Ginkō 日本銀行　the Bank of Japan; the central bank of Japan, the government's financing institution, supervised by the Ministry of Finance, the Japanese counterpart of the U.S. Federal Reserve Bank. It was established in 1882, funded mainly by the government, upon the recommendation of Finance Minister Masayoshi Matsukata (1835-1924) in an attempt to deal with excessive and varied issues of currency and a shortage of liquid capital for businesses. At present, along with its functions concerning the issue of convertible notes, the bank is in charge of accounting governmental revenue and expenditure, financing the government, dealing with deposits and loans for commercial banks, controlling foreign exchange, etc. In 1970 it joined the Bank of International Settlements.

〖注〗 financing institution 金融機関． the Federal Reserve Bank 連邦準備銀

行．　Masayoshi Matsukata 松方正義．　issue of currency 通貨発行．　liquid capital 流動資本．　function 役割，活動．　convertible note 兌換紙幣．　revenue 歳入．　expenditure 支出．　deposit 預金．　commercial bank 市中銀行．　foreign exchange 外国為替．　the Bank of International Settlements 国際決済銀行．

Nihon Ikueikai 日本育英会　the Japan Scholarship Foundation; a non-profit quasi-governmental foundation for student financial aid, supervised by the Ministry of Education.　Beneficiaries of the loan-scholarships are selected on the basis of scholastic performance and degree of financial need.　There are two types: ordinary loans and special loans.　The latter are for students of superior ability and a part of it need not be repaid.　The ordinary, no-interest loans must be repaid within 20 years after completion of studies.　Those who engage in specified teaching careers for a certain number of years are exempt from repayment.　The monthly amounts granted vary: ¥7,000 (public high school, ordinary loans), ¥18,000 (private high school, ordinary), ¥18,000 (public university, ordinary), ¥27,000 (private university, ordinary), ¥70,000 (doctoral candidates), etc., as of 1983.

〖注〗　scholarship 奨学金，奨学制度．　non-profit 非営利．　quasi-government 半官，準政府(の)．　beneficiary 受益者．　performance 業績，成績．　repay 返金する．　no-interest loan 無利子の貸付．　teaching career 教職．　be exempt from ～を免除される．

Nihonkoku Kenpō 日本国憲法　the Constitution of Japan; the Constitution of 1947; the present constitution, promulgated on November 3, 1946, and put into effect on May 3, 1947.　Soon after the end of World War II, in October 1945, the U.S. Occupation authorities ordered the Japanese government to reform the Meiji Constitution for the establishment of a democratic country.　Based on a draft presented by the authorities, the new constitution was completed in March 1946 after bilateral negotiations.　The new constitution consists of a preamble and 11 chapters (103 articles) concerning the Emperor, renunciation of war, rights and duties of the people, the Diet, the Cabinet, the judiciary, finances, local self-government, amendments, supreme law and supplementary provisions.　The basic democratic principles contained in it can be summarized as: sovereign power resting with the people, a desire for peace by renouncing war, and the guarantee of fundamental human rights.
⇨ MEIJI KENPŌ

〖注〗 promulgate 公布する． be put into effect 効力を発する，発布される．
the U.S. Occupation authorities アメリカ占領軍当局． draft 草案． bilateral
negotiation 二国間の交渉． preamble 前文． renunciation of war 戦争放棄．
the judiciary 司法． finance 財政． local self-government 地方自治．
amendment 改正． supreme law 最高裁判所(法)． supplementary provision
補則．

Nihon-rettō 日本列島 the Japanese islands; the Japanese archipelago. It consists of four major islands—Honshū, Hokkaidō, Shikoku and Kyūshū—plus over 3,900 small islands, including Okinawa.
The total area covers about 380,000 square kilometers. The
greater part of this area lies in the temperate zone with the
northern part, Hokkaidō in particular, in the subarctic zone and the
small southern islands—the Ryūkyū Islands (Okinawa) and Amami
Islands—in the subtropical zone. Thus, the Japanese islands
stretch from north to south in the form of an arc, from 45°31′ north
to 20°25′ north in latitude. ⇨ HOKKAIDŌ, HONSHŪ, KYŪSYŪ, SHIKO-
KU
〖注〗 the temperate zone 温帯． the subarctic zone 亜寒帯． the subtropical
zone 亜熱帯． latitude 緯度．

nihon-ryōri 日本料理 Japanese cooking [cuisine]; the generic
term for Japanese-style dishes. Some of the important factors in
Japanese cooking are to cook so as not to lose or distort the
original natural flavor, to arrange the food artistically in harmony
with the plate it is served on and to choose materials and wares to
match the season. Traditional Japanese cooking is intended to
appeal to the eye as well as to the palate.
〖注〗 cuisine 料理． distort そこなう． original natural flavor そのものも
つ自然の風味． palate 舌、味覚．

Nihon-sankei 日本三景 Japan's outstanding scenic trio; the three
most beautiful landscapes, officially designated in Japan. They
are: Amanohashidate, on Miyazu Bay on the Japan Sea coast north
of Kyoto for its sand bar covered with pine trees, which looks like
a bridge leading to the sky; Matsushima, near Sendai in Miyagi
Prefecture for its more than 250 pine-clad islands dotting Matsushima Bay; and Itsukushima (also called Miyajima), in Hiroshima
Bay in Hiroshima Prefecture, for its combination of the Inland Sea
and a shrine structure jutting out into the sea and for its huge
vermilion shrine gate in the sea.
〖注〗 sand bar 砂州、砂嘴． pine-clad 松でおおわれた、松で装った． dot 点在

させる．vermilion 朱（色）．

Nihon-sankōen 日本三公園 the three most celebrated parks of Japan. They are Kenrokuen Park in Kanazawa, Ishikawa Prefecture; Kōrakuen Park in Okayama, Okayama Prefecture; and Kairakuen Park in Mito, Ibaraki Prefecture. These parks are huge landscape gardens for strolling, which were formerly estates of influential feudal lords. Kenrokuen Park （101,000 square meters) built in 1819 by the feudal lord Maeda Norihiro features three artificial hills, two ponds, a cascade, etc., and is renowned for its abundant Japanese irises, azaleas and cherry blossoms. Kōrakuen Park （115,000 sq. m) built in 1700 by the feudal lord Ikeda Tsunamasa is situated along the Asahi River. In the compound are tea ceremony houses, a few ponds with cascades, etc. The landscape changes every season with its pine, plum, cherry and maple trees. Unlike the other two gardens, the landscape of Kairakuen Park （75,400 sq. m) is natural. The park is particularly renowned for its plum trees which number about 3,000. It was built in 1842 by the feudal lord Tokugawa Nariaki as a retreat. ⇨ KAIYŪSHIKI-TEIEN, NIHON-TEIEN

〖注〗 celebrated 有名な． landscape garden for strolling 回遊式庭園． estate 所有地． feudal lord 大名． Maeda Norihiro 前田斉広． artificial hill 築山． cascade 小滝，人工滝． Japanese iris 菖蒲． azalea つつじ． Ikeda Tsunamasa 池田綱政． the Asahi River 旭川． compound 敷地，囲われた区域． Tokugawa Nariaki 徳川斉昭． retreat 保養地，隠遁所． 日本三公園：兼六園，後楽園，偕楽園．

Nihon Shoki 日本書紀 *The Chronicle of Japan* （720); the second-oldest remaining historical work （after the *Kojiki*) and the first of six official histories of Japan compiled by Prince Toneri （676-735), Ō no Yasumaro （?-723) and others under Imperial supervision. The compilation was begun by order of Emperor Tenmu （622-686; r. 673-686) and completed during the reign of Emperor Genshō （680-748; r. 715-724), requiring over 30 years of endeavor. This project was attributed to a rise in national consciousness stimulated by the growing power of Japan's neighbors, China and Korea. Written in Chinese, the work consists of 30 volumes. It is arranged in chronological order, the first two volumes dealing with the mythological age, and the rest devoted to historical events centering on the Imperial Family from the reign of the first emperor, Jinmu （? enthroned 660 B.C.) to that of Empress Jitō （645-703;

r. 690-697) and contains quotations from Chinese and Korean historical works. Unlike in the *Kojiki*, emphasis is placed on contemporary historical details. This is generally regarded as the most reliable historical accout of ancient Japan. ⇨ KOJIKI

〖注〗 chronicle 年代記．　Imperial supervision 勅撰．　be attributed to ～に由来する．　chronological order 年代順．　contemporary historical details 当時の詳しい歴史的事項．

nihonshu **日本酒** Japanese rice wine; alcoholic beverage made from fermented rice and water. This term is used to distinguish rice wine from Western kinds of alcoholic beverages. More commonly called sakê. ⇨ SAKE

〖注〗 beverage 飲み物．　ferment 発酵させる．

nihon-teien **日本庭園** a Japanese garden; a traditional type of garden representing a natural landscape or symbolizing the grandeur of nature in a limited space. The garden is laid out asymmetrically, using rocks, sand, ponds, streams, bridges, stone lanterns, evergreens, etc. Flowers are sometimes avoided in formal gardens, since they wither. There are two categories of such gardens: the hilly and flat garden, each having three styles—formal, semiformal and informal. Representative types of Japanese gardens, viewed historically, include the pond garden in which the aristocracy enjoyed boating in the Heian period (794-1185), the dry landscape garden (*karesansui*) for Zen contemplation in the Kamakura (1185-1336) and Muromachi (1336-1568) periods, the tea garden (*chatei*) surrounding a tea hut in the Muromachi period and the strolling garden (*kaiyūshiki-teien*) of influential feudal lords in the Edo period (1603-1868). ⇨ CHATEI, KAIYŪSHIKI-TEIEN, KA-RESANSUI(-TEIEN), SHIN-GYŌ-SŌ, TSUKIYAMA-TEIEN

〖注〗 asymmetrically 非対称的に，均整をさけて．　stone lantern 石燈籠．　hilly garden 築山庭園．　flat garden 平庭．　formal, semiformal and informal 真・行・草．　the pond garden in which the aristocracy enjoyed boating 池泉舟遊式庭園．　dry landscape garden 枯山水．　contemplation 黙想．　strolling garden 回遊式庭園．　feudal lord 大名，藩主．

Nihon Yushutsunyū Ginkō **日本輸出入銀行** the Export-Import Bank of Japan; a government institution involved in matters concerning international loan financing, supervised by the Ministry of Finance. The bank was established in 1950 with the name Japan Export Bank and totally funded by the government, for the purpose of promoting exports by financially aiding corporations. In 1952 it took its present name and also became involved in import financing to adjust the country's balance of payments.　In 1957 its functions were expanded, to financing Japanese overseas investments.　At present, it extends loans to foreign governments and corporations as well.

〖注〗 loan financing 融資.　the Japan Export Bank 日本輸出銀行.　balance of payments（国際）収支.　overseas investment 海外投資.

nihyakutōka 二百十日 the 210th day; a stormy day in autumn. Falling on September 1, the 210th day is counted from the first day of spring—the day after *Setsubun*—according to the lunar calendar. Rice begins to ripen ; in some districts rice harvesting might begin. It is also at this time of the year that strong typhoons appear in the southern seas threatening to hit Japan, thus giving rise to the fear that the ripening crops might be damaged.　⇨ SETSUBUN

〖注〗 the lunar calendar 太陰暦.　crop 収穫.

nijiriguchi 躙り口 lit. a crawling entrance.　a small entrance to the tearoom.　It is intended as a partition between the tearoom and the outside world and to inculcate a feeling of humility to high and low alike.　It is only about a meter in height, and so, in passing through it, the guests have to maneuver themselves while sitting Japanese-style, with their heads lowered.　⇨ CHANOYU, CHASHITSU

〖注〗 crawl はう、ひざで歩く.　partition 区分、仕切り.　inculcate 説く、刻みつける.　maneuver 巧みに操る、動かす.

Nikkō Kokuritsu-kōen 日光国立公園 Nikkō National Park (1,407 square kilometers), designated in 1934; a natural park situated in central Honshū, encompassing parts of Tochigi, Gunma, Fukushima and Niigata prefectures.　Located some 145 kilometers northeast of Tokyo, this park is accessible from the city in less than two hours by the fastest limited express train.　The greatest attraction of the area is Tōshōgū Shrine, which was completed in 1663 and dedicated to Tokugawa Ieyasu (1542-1616), founder of the Tokugawa shogunate (1603-1867).　In addition, there are many other temples and shrines of historical importance, including Rinnōji Temple.　This park is also renowned for its varied scenery: Lake Chūzenji with the Kegon waterfalls and a sacred vermilion bridge; the volcanoes, Mount Nantai (2,484 meters) and Mount Nasu (1,917 m) with the hot springs scattered around them; Oze Marshland, which abounds with *mizubashō* (water-banana plant) and other varieties of flowers; and the Kinu River running through

rich forests which are especially spectacular in autumn.   A saying goes, "Never say *kekkō* (magnificent) until you have seen Nikkō."
⇨ KOKURITSU-KŌEN

〖注〗 encompass 取りまく，囲む． dedicate to ～に捧げる． the Tokugawa shogunate 徳川幕府． vermilion 朱色． hot spring 温泉． Oze Marshland 尾瀬沼． abound with ～に富む． water-banana plant 水芭蕉． "Never say *kekkō* until you have seen Nikkō." 「日光を見ぬうちは結構というな」．

ningen-kokuhō 人間国宝   living national treasures; human national treasures; persons officially designated as "bearers of important intangible cultural properties".   The Japanese government honors and protects those who preserve the traditional spirit and skills of Japan's time-honored arts and crafts, according to the Cultural Properties Protection Law promulgated in 1950.   As of 1984, about 150 persons under 65 general categories have been recognized as *ningen-kokuhō*.   They are artists and craftsmen specializing in pottery, dyeing, lacquer ware, textile-weaving, sword-forging, doll-making, etc., as well as actors and musicians, particularly in Noh, Kabuki and Bunraku.   They are granted an annual stipend of ¥1.5 million (as of 1984).   ⇨ BUNKAZAI, JŪYŌMUKEI-BUNKAZAI, MUKEI-BUNKAZAI

〖注〗 bearers of important intangible cultural properties 重要無形文化財保持者． time-honored 由緒ある． the Cultural Properties Protection Law 「文化財保護法」． promulgate 発布する． pottery 陶芸． dyeing 染色． lacquer ware 漆器． textile-weaving 織物． sword-forging 刀の鋳造． annual stipend 年俸．

Niō 仁王［二王］   the two Deva kings; a pair of guardian divinities of a temple.   Statues of them stand at the sides of a temple gate or a Buddhist image.   Their task is to guard the temple or the Buddhist image from evil spirits with their fierce countenances.   They are also referred to as Kongō-Rikishi: one is Kongō with his mouth open as if saying "a" (あ) which implies "beginning," and the other, Rikishi, has his mouth closed as if saying "n" (ん) which implies "end," these implications having to do with Buddhist doctrines.   The most well-known are the pair at the gate of Tōdaiji Temple, Nara, made by Unkei (?-?1223) in the Kamakura period (1185-1336).   ⇨ BUTSUZŌ, CHŪMON², GARAN

〖注〗 deva (インド神話の)提婆，天神，(ゾロアスター教)悪魔． guardian divinity 守護神． Buddhist image 仏像． countenances 表情．

Nishijin-ori 西陣織   Nishijin brocade; Nishijin silk fabric; a generic term for silk fabrics produced in the Nishijin district of Kyoto since the end of the eighth century. The term Nishijin (lit. western camp) recalls the civil strife of the 15th century. This fabric was particularly favored by the imperial court and the nobility, and the industry was supported by the Tokugawa shogunate (1603-1868). The varieties of Nishijin include brocades, damasks, silk satin, silk crepe, etc. ⇨ TOKUGAWA-BAKUFU

〖注〗 brocade 錦、錦織. silk fabric 絹織物. western camp 西陣. civil strife 内戦. the nobility 貴族、貴族階級. damask どんす、綾織りの布. silk crepe 縮緬.

nishikie 錦絵 lit. a brocade picture. a multicolored woodblock print; brocade-like pictures reproduced in woodblock prints with the theme of the floating world, such as flowers, beauties, Kabuki actors, customs, etc. This type of colored picture as such was first achieved by the painter Suzuki Harunobu (1725-70) in the middle of the 18th century. It soon gained popularity in Edo with the development of the unique technique through the cooperation of painter, engraver and printer. Other well-known painters include Utagawa Toyokuni (1777-1835), Katsushika Hokusai (1760-1849), etc. ⇨ MOKUHANGA, UKIYOE

〖注〗 woodblock print 木版. the floating world 浮き世. engraver 彫り師.

nishiki-ori 錦織 Japanese brocade; thick silk fabric with raised patterns woven with threads of gold, silver and other colors. This fabric is used to make *obi* (a sash for kimono), Noh costumes, and articles of interior decoration. The Nishijin district of Kyoto is well-known for its time-honored production of brocade weave, specifically called Nishijin brocade. ⇨ NISHIJIN-ORI

〖注〗 brocade 錦. time-honored 由緒ある. Nishijin brocade 西陣織.

nisshōken 日照権 a right to sunshine; a right to have sunshine fall on a residence. The growing emergence of tall buildings, which obstructed sunlight from smaller residences, led to a social controversy over the right to sunshine in the early 1970s. Sunshine is regarded as especially important in the humid climate of Japan. The Japanese have traditionally used sunshine to dry laundry and air bedding.

〖注〗 emergence 出現、発生. obstruct 妨害する. social controversy 社会の論議.

nō 能 a Noh drama; a traditional dance-drama form developed by Kan'ami, and refined by his son Zeami in the 14th century. It is characterized by highly stylized acting, unique vocalization, wooden masks and elaborate costumes, and above all its symbolism, and severely simple settings and performance style. A Noh play is brought into perfect harmony when three performance styles—*utai* (dramatic chant), *mai* (refined dance) and *hayashi* (drums and flute) —are blended into one. The themes are derived from religion, folk myths, classical poetry and historical tales. ⇨ AIKYŌGEN, HAYASHI, MAI, NŌBUTAI, UTAI

【注】 folk myth 民衆神話. stylized 様式化された. vocalization 発声. setting 舞台装置, 背景. blend into one 一つにとけ合う.

nobori 幟 a banner or a streamer; long narrow vertical banners such as those presented to actors by their fans and patrons. They are often displayed in front of the traditional theater where the actors perform. Other traditional uses of *nobori* include the war banners carried into battle and the carp banners displayed on Boys' Day in May. ⇨ KOINOBORI, TANGO NO SEKKU

【注】 vertical 縦の. banner 旗. carp banner 鯉のぼり.

nōbutai 能舞台 a Noh stage. The stage consists of a floor of plain cypress wood with five pillars to support the roof. A Noh stage has four sections—the square main stage floor for acting, the space for the orchestra behind the acting area (*atoza*), the right side for the chorus (*jiutaiza*) and entrance corridor (*hashigakari*). On the wall at the back is painted a single dignified pine tree. ⇨ ATOZA, HASHIGAKARI, JIUTAIZA, KAGAMIITA, NŌ, NŌGAKUDŌ

【注】 cypress 檜. dignified 荘重な.

nodate 野点 an open-air tea ceremony; a tea ceremony conducted in natural surroundings. A straw mat or a carpet is spread out on the ground where the ceremony is to be held. A spot in the ground is dug up to make a hearth for the teakettle. When possible, water from a running stream is used for preparing the tea. Thus harmony with nature is pursued in serene surroundings. On the other hand, party-style open-air tea ceremonies are also held, in places where many people gather, such as for cherry-blossom or moon viewing. Often a huge umbrella made of paper and bamboo is set up at the site. ⇨ CHANOYU

【注】 tea ceremony 茶道. straw mat 筵. hearth 炉. teakettle 茶釜. cherry-blossom or moon viewing 花見や月見.

nōgaku 能楽 Noh and Kyogen are collectively referred to as *nōgaku*. Often the same meaning as Noh. ⇨ KYŌGEN, NŌ

nōgakudō 能楽堂   a Noh theater. Originally Noh was performed on an outdoor stage with white gravel spread on the ground between the stage and audience to make use of the reflection of the sunlight. In the modern Noh theater, *nōgakudō*, the stage, the dressing room and the seats for the audience are inside the same building which accommodates a few hundred people. The stage made of plain cypress wood has a roof supported by five pillars, retaining the original outdoor characteristics. White gravel is also still used.   ⇨ NŌ. NŌBUTAI

〖注〗 white gravel 白州. plain wood 白木.

nōgyō-kyōdō-kumiai 農業協同組合   agricultural cooperatives; an autonomous cooperative organization established in 1947 with the promulgation of the Agricultural Cooperative Societies' Act, for the purpose of improving farmers' social and economic status, and promoting agricultural productivity. Postwar agricultural land reforms enabled tenant farmers to become independent, land-owning farmers, most of whom voluntarily joined this organization for assistance in various ways. Today, with a membership of several million and with local cooperatives in most farming communities, the *nōkyō* (abbreviated name for this organization) is one of the largest organizations in Japan. Its main functions include the collective distribution of agricultural products, the lending of machinery and facilities, the provision of credit and loans, mutual aid for health and disasters, as well as technical instruction in farming.

〖注〗 autonomous 自治の. promulgation 施行, 発布. the Agricultural Cooperative Societies' Act「農業協同組合法」. agricultural land reform 農地改革. tenant farmer 小作農. function 役割, 活動. collective distribution 協同集配, 総合的流通. credit and loans 信用貸付. mutual aid 共済.

nōkan 能管   a Noh flute; the horizontal flute used in the Noh theater. It has seven finger-holes and is uniquely constructed from strips of bamboo turned inside out.   ⇨ HAYASHI. NŌ

〖注〗 strips of bamboo 竹を細く割ったもの.

nōkyō 農協   ⇨ NŌGYŌ-KYŌDŌ-KUMIAI

nōmen 能面   a Noh mask. It is made of wood—usually Japanese cypress—and is painted in layers. Masterpieces of Noh masks handed down for generations are very much valued. However, it is a great actor on the stage that can give life to a Noh mask.   ⇨ NŌ

〖注〗 Japanese cypress 檜. masterpiece 傑作.

noren 暖簾 a sign curtain of a shop; a short cloth hung at the entrance of a traditional shop or restaurant. A typical *noren* is made of cotton cloth dyed in indigo, bearing the name or the crest of the shop in white, and is slit at intervals so that people can enter. Originally, a short white curtain hung at the entrance used to keep the street dust out of a shop. *Noren* often serves as a symbol to reflect the long-standing tradition and reputation of the shop. A similar type of curtain is used at the entrance of the kitchen or the like in homes. ⇨ KAMON

〖注〗 indigo 藍(色). crest (家)紋. long-standing 長年の.

nori 海苔 *Porphyra tenera*; seaweed laver; a dried laver sheet; a type of dark brown algae which is dried into thin black sheets. The dried sheet is eaten after lightly parching it over a charcoal fire or gas flame. The standard size of a sheet is about 20 by 20 centimeters. A whole sheet is usually used to wrap rice in making *nori*-roll *sushi*. Packaged *nori* of a smaller size is popularly served with the traditional Japanese breakfast. *Nori* is used to add flavor to a variety of dishes. ⇨ NORIMAKI(-ZUSHI), SUSHI

〖注〗 algae 藻, 海藻(algaの複数). parch あぶる. charcoal fire 炭火. flavor 香, 風味.

norimaki(-zushi) 海苔巻き(鮨) seaweed-roll *sushi*; vinegared rice rolled in a sheet of seaweed laver with various ingredients in the center. These ingredients include egg, mushroom, dried gourd, greens, etc., but sometimes only boiled dried gourd or cucumber is used. It is served cut into bite-size pieces. ⇨ KANPYŌ, NORI, SUSHI

〖注〗 seaweed laver 海苔. ingredient (料理の)材料. dried gourd 干ぴょう. greens 緑の野菜.

noshi 熨斗 a courtesy emblem on a gift; a thin strip of dried abalone folded in red and white paper. It is attached to the upper right-hand corner of the wide strip of white paper put around a gift, as a sign of sincerity and expression of congratulations. The combination of the colors, red and white, signifies auspiciousness. The use of dried abalone has its origin in warriors' victory parties, at which they ate slices of dried abalone with saké. ⇨ NOSHIGAMI

〖注〗 courtesy emblem 儀礼のしるし. abalone あわび. fold in 中に折りたたむ. auspiciousness 慶事, めでたいこと. warrior さむらい.

noshigami 熨斗紙 white gift paper with a courtesy emblem on it; a wide strip of paper used to cover a gift as a symbol of courtesy. A courtesy emblem *(noshi)* is pasted on the upper right-hand corner of the paper. This paper is attached either over the wrapping paper or under it (directly over the box), depending on the custom of the district. A gift-binding cord *(mizuhiki)* is used to bind the paper over the box. An informal *noshigami* has printed *noshi* and *mizuhiki* on it. On the paper, one is supposed to write the reason for giving the gift above the *mizuhiki* and the name of the sender beneath. ⇨ MIZUHIKI, NOSHI

〖注〗 courtesy emblem 儀礼のしるし，熨斗．gift-binding cord 贈り物を結ぶ紐，水引．

nuitori 縫い取り embroidery; embroidered fabric; the art or work of embroidering fabric for the kimono and *obi,* traditionally done by hand. Patterns on the fabric for formal or semiformal wear, particularly *obi*, are often embroidered by hand with threads of gold, silver or other colors, to add a touch of resplendence. Japanese embroidery threads are delicate and thin. ⇨ KIMONO, OBI

〖注〗 embroidery 刺しゅう，縫い取り．fabric 織物．resplendence 華麗さ，まばゆさ．

nukamiso 糠味噌 rice-bran paste; fermented rice-bran paste mixed with salt, which is used for pickling vegetables. It has a very strong odor, but gives vegetables a delicate taste, and contains a lot of vitamin B and enzymes. The bran paste must be stirred every day to allow the bacteria to work properly. Maintaining the characteristic flavor and taste of the rice-bran paste for pickling has long been a measure of a good housewife. ⇨ NUKA(MISO)-ZUKE, TSUKEMONO

〖注〗 rice bran 米糠．fermented 発酵した．enzyme 酵素．

nuka(miso)-zuke 糠(味噌)漬け vegetables pickled in salty rice-bran paste. There are two kinds—one which is left in the bran paste for a long time, producing long-lasting well-preserved pickles; the other is kept in the bran for only a day or so and must be eaten soon. Semi-dried Japanese radish is often used for the former, and seasonal vegetables such as cucumber, eggplant and cabbage for the latter. ⇨ NUKAMISO, TSUKEMONO

〖注〗 pickle 漬ける．rice-bran paste 糠味噌．bran ふすま，糠．pickle 漬物．Japanese radish 大根．

nureen 濡縁 lit. a wet veranda. a short veranda in traditional Japanese architecture. It is made of wood jutting out a bit, usually opening onto a garden, and is not protected by rain shutters (*amado*). It also serves as a bench.   ⇨ AMADO

〖注〗 jut out 突き出る，張り出る．

nurimono 塗り物 a generic term for lacquered objects; a japan article; a variety of articles made of wood coated with lacquer. The sap from the bark of the Japanese lacquer tree (*Rhus vernici-flua*) is used to produce a polished, lustrous finish on the surface of wood or the like. Lacquered objects include desks, vases, boxes, the outer frame of sliding doors (*fusuma*), etc., as well as a variety of table ware called *shikki*. They are often inlaid with ivory, shell or metal (gold and silver). The art of lacquering bloomed in Japan, thus giving rise to the term "japan" meaning "lacquer." The humid climate of Japan helps keep the coating from wearing off. ⇨ FUSUMA, MAKIE, SHIKKI, URUSHI

〖注〗 japan 漆(器)． sap 樹液． bark 樹皮． lacquer tree (=*Rhus vernici-flua*) 漆の木． finish 仕上り． sliding door ふすま． inlay はめこむ． give rise to 生じる，由来する． wear off はがれる，あせる．

Nyorai 如来 Tathagata (Sanskrit); one who has attained perfection or enlightenment; one of the names of Buddha, meaning "an enlightened one." Nyorai was originally synonymous with Buddha and is usually used as an honorific title by adding it to the names of specific kinds of Buddha—e.g. Shaka Nyorai, Amida Nyorai, Dainichi Nyorai, etc.   ⇨ AMIDA(NYORAI), DAINICHI NYORAI

〖注〗 enlightenment 悟り． enlightened one 悟りを開いた人． honorific title 敬称．

nyūdō 入道 lit. entering the way. a person or the title of a person who has become a Buddhist priest or nun. This title used to be given to those who pursued the spiritual path or entered the Buddhist priesthood, thus being released from secular life, their heads shaven. It was used in particular to indicate retired emperors and nobles who entered Buddhist life.   ⇨ BUKKYŌ

〖注〗 nun 尼僧． spiritual path 霊的な道． Buddhist priesthood 僧職． secular life 俗世．

O

obi 帯 a sash for a kimono; a broad sash tied in a decorative bow at the back, worn with a kimono. From the Tokugawa period (1603–1867), the *obi* for women, which was a simple waistband before, developed into the broad decorative sash of today, although those for men are still simple. The average length of a woman's *obi* today is a little over four meters. There are various kinds such as *fukuro-obi, maru-obi, Nagoya-obi, hitoe-obi,* etc., chosen according to the season, occasion and kind of kimono being worn. The *obi* is regarded as the central element of the kimono ensemble. ⇨ FUKURO-OBI, KIMONO, MARU-OBI, NAGOYA-OBI

〖注〗 decorative bow はでやかなお太鼓．waistband 腰紐．

obiage 帯揚げ a sash bustle; a decorative piece of cloth used with the *obi* when wearing a kimono. The bustle is usually made of soft silk, solid in color with woven designs or simply designed with dapples made by tie-dyeing, and is about 30 centimeters wide. It serves as a decoration between the upper edge of the *obi* and the kimono, and also covers the bow pad under the bow or the drum of the *obi* at the back. ⇨ KIMONO, OBI

〖注〗 bustle あて布．solid in color 無地．dapples made by tie-dyeing 絞り．drum 帯の太鼓の部分．

obidome 帯留め an *obi* buckle; a sash brooch; a brooch-like ornament attached to the *obijime* (sash cord). It is made of metal, wood, ivory or gems and is elegantly designed. An *obijime* is passed through this buckle, which is centered at the front of the *obi*. It is not appropriate for formal or serious occasions. ⇨ OBI, OBIJIME

obidome(-gane) 帯留め（金） a metal *obi* clip; a metal clip for keeping a kimono sash in place. It is useful in holding the *obi* knot tight at the back, so as to keep the bow pad (*obimakura*) from falling off. A real expert in tying an *obi* will not use one, however. ⇨ KIMONO, OBI, OBIMAKURA

〖注〗 bow pad 帯枕.

obiita 帯板 an *obi* board; a board used under the front of an *obi* (kimono sash) to prevent wrinkles. It is made of plastic or hard paper covered with soft silky cloth or the like, and is slightly bent to fit the body. Sometimes there is a pocket on the side facing the body. ⇨ OBI

〖注〗 wrinkle しわ.

obijime 帯締め a sash cord; a cord or narrow band used with the *obi* (sash) when wearing a kimono. It is usually made of silk, decoratively braided flat or round, and holds the *obi* in place. It is passed through the bow or drum of the *obi* at the back and tied at the front. It serves as an indispensable accessory, thus requiring careful selection in order to match the color of the *obi*. ⇨ KIMONO, OBI

〖注〗 braid 編む, 組紐にする. drum 帯のお太鼓の部分.

obimakura 帯枕 a pad for an *obi* (sash); a thick pad for holding up the bow or the drum part of the *obi* at the back when wearing a kimono. It is placed on a metal clip or on the knot made by tying the *obi* to add thickness to the drum-shaped bow. The ends of the string attached to the pad are tied at the front and tucked into the *obi*. The pad and string are concealed with a decorative piece of cloth (*obiage*). ⇨ OBI, OBIAGE, TAIKO

〖注〗 drum 帯の太鼓の部分. metal clip 帯留め金. knot 結び目.

obon お盆 ⇨ BON

ochazuke お茶漬け ⇨ CHAZUKE

oden おでん Japanese hodgepodge, usually served together with hot mustard as a condiment. A variety of foods—soybean curd, cuttlefish, hard-boiled eggs, devil's tongue (*konnyaku*), Japanese radish, rolls of kelp, many kinds of fish-paste cake, etc.—are boiled together in a large pot with seasoned fish broth. As a typical accompaniment of sakē, *oden* are served at street stands. ⇨ KONNYAKU, TŌFU, YATAI

〖注〗 hodgepodge ごった煮, 濃いシチュー(=hotchpotch). condiment 薬味. soybean curd 豆腐. cuttlefish いか. devil's tongue こんにゃく. Japanese radish 大根. rolls of kelp 昆布巻. fish-paste cake 蒲鉾, さつま揚げの類. seasoned 味のついた. fish broth 魚でとっただし汁. accompaniment of sakē 酒の肴. street stand 屋台.

ōfurisode 大振袖 lit. large swinging sleeves. a silk kimono with full-length hanging sleeves. These sleeves are very long, reaching to the hem of the kimono, almost touching the ground.   This type of kimono, usually lavishly decorated with traditional designs and colors, is worn by young unmarried women on very formal occasions, such as weddings, coming-of-age ceremonies, New Year celebrations, etc.   A bride also wears a kimono of this type of superb quality.   The sash (*obi*) that goes with this kimono is either the *maru-obi* or *fukuro-obi* tied in an especially elaborate fashion. ⇨ FUKURO-OBI, FURISODE, KIMONO, MARU-OBI, OBI

〖注〗 swinging ゆれる． coming-of-age ceremony 成人式． superb quality 極上の質．

Ogasawara Kokuritsu-kōen 小笠原国立公園   Ogasawara National Park (61 square kilometers), designated in 1972; a natural park located some 1,000 kilometers south of Tokyo, comprising the Ogasawara chain of about 30 volcanic islands, plus Kita Iōjima to the south.   Chichijima (lit. Father Island), the main island of the group, can be reached in about 30 hours by ferry from Tokyo. These islands boast a variety of semitropical plants.   The surrounding waters have tropical fish, coral reefs, green sea turtles, etc.   ⇨ KOKURITSU-KŌEN, OGASAWARA-SHOTŌ

〖注〗 semitropical plant 亜熱帯植物． tropical fish 熱帯魚． coral reef 珊瑚礁． green sea turtle 青海亀．

Ogasawara-shotō 小笠原諸島   the Ogasawara Islands (60 square kilometers); a group of small islands located some 1,000 kilometers south of Tokyo.   The group consists of about 30 small islands, the main ones being Chichijima (lit. Father Island) and Hahajima (lit. Mother Island).   Discovered in 1593 by Ogasawara Sadayori, the islands were officially claimed by Japan in 1862 by the Tokugawa shogunate (1603-1868).   Since 1880, the islands have been under the jurisdiction of the Tokyo metropolitan government, excluding the postwar period of U.S. occupation from 1945 to 1968 (though the occupation of the Japanese archipelago ended in 1951).   The entire group of islands along with Kita Iōjima were designated as Ogasawara National Park in 1972.   ⇨ OGASAWARA KOKURITSU-KŌEN

〖注〗 Ogasawara Sadayori 小笠原貞頼． under the jurisdiction of ～の管轄内に． the Tokyo metropolitan government 東京都庁． U.S. occupation 米国による占領． the Japanese archipelago 日本列島．

ōgi 扇   a folding fan; generally the same as *sensu*.   *Ōgi* specifically refers to the bigger type of folding fan, which is used for dance or decoration and is regarded as an art object rather than a practical thing. ⇨ SENSU

Ogura-hyakunin-isshu 小倉百人一首 a hundred poems of a hundred poets; a collection of a hundred 31-syllable poems (*tanka*), used in a poem-matching card game. It is said to have been compiled in the early Kamakura period (1185-1336) from among poems of famous poets from the seventh to the 13th centuries by Fujiwara Sadaie (1162-1241) at a villa near Mount Ogura in Kyoto (thus giving rise to its name). The collection became very popular in the Edo period (1603-1868) when it was used for a card-matching game, a game which has since been widely enjoyed during the New Year holidays. It is more commonly called simply *hyakunin-isshu*. ⇨ HYAKUNIN-ISSHU, KARUTA, TANKA, UTAGARUTA
〖注〗 31-syllable poem 短歌. poem-matching card game 歌合わせ遊び. give rise to 生じる，ひき起こす.

ohaguro お歯黒[鉄漿] teeth dyed black; the custom of dyeing teeth black practiced in olden days, mainly by women. The black dye is an oxidized mixture of iron shavings melted in vinegar and powdered gallnuts. Around the ninth century, tooth blackening came into fashion among Heian court ladies and some men. In the Muromachi period (1336-1568), it became popular even among commoners and was done from the age of puberty. In the Edo period (1603-1868), married women were required to dye their teeth black. The custom is no longer practiced.
〖注〗 oxidized mixture 酸化化合物. iron shavings 鉄を削ったもの. gallnut (植物の茎，葉の)虫こぶ，没食子. puberty 年ごろ，思春期.

Oharame 大原女 an Ohara woman; women from Ohara Village in the vicinity of Kyoto. They have a custom of carrying heavy loads on their heads. They may be seen carrying flowers and vegetables for sale in and around Kyoto. With a piece of white cloth covering their heads, they wear an indigo cotton kimono with sleeves tucked up by red strings (*tasuki*) and white cloth wrapped around the legs and arms. ⇨ KIMONO, TASUKI
〖注〗 in the vicinity of ～の付近に. heavy loads 重い荷物. indigo 藍色. tuck up まくし上げる.

ohitashi お浸し   ⇨ HITASHIMONO

Ōhi-yaki 大樋焼 Ōhi ceramic ware; Kanazawa Raku ware; ceramic ware originally produced at Ōhi in Kanazawa in present-day Ishikawa Prefecture around the 17th century. Using the techniques of the Raku ware of Kyoto, Mikawa Chōzaemon, a potter for the feudal lord Maeda, began making tea utensils, particularly tea bowls, of an original design.　It is thick and covered with a deep brown or brownish yellow glaze.　It also reflects influences of old Kutani ware, developed earlier in the same district.　⇨ KOKUTANI, RAKU-YAKI

〖注〗 Mikawa Chōzaemon 三河長左衛門．　potter 陶工．　feudal lord 大名．　tea utensil 茶道具．　glaze 釉，釉をつける．

ojigi お辞儀　a bow; to bow as a polite greeting.　Shaking hands is not a traditional custom in Japan.　Instead, there are bows of various degrees of profundity, made sitting on one's knees or standing.　The most profound bow while standing is made by bending the upper body to hip level, which, until the end of World War II, was the required form for salutations to the emperor.　When seated on the *tatami* floor of a Japanese-style room, the formal bow is made by placing one's hands side by side on the floor and bowing until the head approaches the hands.　⇨ SAIKEIREI, TATAMI, ZASHIKI

〖注〗 profundity 丁重さ，いんぎんさ．　sit on one's knees 正座する．　profound 丁重な．　salutation 敬礼，挨拶．

Ojiya-chijimi 小千谷縮　Ojiya crepe linen fabric; fabric made from twisted ramie threads, woven in the Ojiya district of Niigata Prefecture.　Fine ramie is produced in this district, tempered by its rigorous climate, with deep snow in winter and high humidity in summer.　Fine ramie thread is tightly twisted and woven into a thin crepe fabric which is porous, sweat-absorbing and does not cling to the skin—ideal for summer kimono.　Along with *Echigo-jōfu* (also produced in this district), the skill of making *Ojiya-chijimi* is designated as an intangible cultural property (*mukei-bunkazai*) by the government.　⇨ ECHIGO-JŌFU, KIMONO, MUKEI-BUNKAZAI

〖注〗 crepe 縮み．　linen fabric 麻織物．　ramie ラミー（繊維をとるアジア産の植物）．　temper 練る，適度に柔軟になる．　porous 多孔性の．　cling to ～にへばりつく．　intangible cultural property 無形文化財．

okazu おかず　lit. a number of (side dishes).　dishes other than rice at a meal.　Japanese meals include a number of side dishes.　They are usually served in small individual portions, on appropriate ware.

okiagari-koboshi 起き上がり小法師　a tumbling *daruma* doll; a red round papier-mâché doll with no limbs, weighted at the bottom. When knocked over, the doll immediately swings back upright. Thus, it is regarded as a symbol of good luck, symbolizing the idea that, despite repeated ups and downs, eventually success will come. Like regular *daruma* dolls, tumbling ones are often sold without the eyes painted in, letting the purchaser paint in one eye when he embarks on something difficult and then the other after he has successfully completed the task. The *daruma* doll derives from a Zen priest who lost his limbs after sitting in meditation for nine years. ⇨ DARUMA, ZAZEN

〖注〗 tumble ころがる. papier-mâché 張り子(の). knock over つき倒す. embark 船出する, 着手する. sit in meditation 座禅する.

Okina 翁 lit. an old man. a piece of a Noh play. It was originally performed by a priest in an ancient religious service praying for peace and a good harvest, and later adopted in Noh. It is now performed as an opening rite for purification in Noh programs only on special occasions. ⇨ NŌ

〖注〗 religious service 宗教的儀式. opening rite 開演の儀式. purification 清め.

Okinawa 沖縄 Okinawa Island of the Ryūkyū archipelago; Okinawa Prefecture (capital: Naha). Okinawa is the main and largest island of the Ryūkyū archipelago which stretches 1,300 kilometers from Kyūshū to Taiwan. Okinawa is also the name of the prefecture which includes most of the archipelago. The name Okinawa first appeared in Japanese documents in the eighth century. The earliest residents of Okinawa were cave dwellers occupying the islands 32,000 years ago, but little is known about them. Okinawa's cultural development shows a mixture of Japanese, Chinese, Korean, Melanesian and Southeast Asian influences. Much of Okinawa's early history consists of struggles among petty local lords. The island was finally united in 1422 under the Shō dynasty. This dynasty lasted, for a time under a system of dual sovereignty with tribute paid to both Satsuma (present-day Kagoshima Prefecture) and China, until the Meiji government of Japan established Okinawa as a prefecture in 1879. During the early 1900s, large numbers of Okinawans emigrated to Hawaii, Brazil and Peru. The last days of World War II saw a massive assault on Okinawa by the Allied Forces, lasting 82 days. Following the war, the United States occupied the island. The San Francisco

Peace Treaty of 1951 recognized Japan's "residual sovereignty" over Okinawa, although reversion did not take place until 1972. The 1945–72 government of Okinawa was called the "United States Civil Administration of the Ryūkyū Islands." U.S. military forces still occupy large areas of Okinawa, under terms of the reversion treaty. Okinawa is mountainous, having a total area of 2,245 square kilometers, with fairly constant warm weather and lush subtropical greenery. The 1980 population was 1.1 million. Okinawa's economy is mainly supported by tourism, agriculture and the U.S. military. ⇨ RYŪKYŪ-SHOTŌ, SHŌ-ŌCHŌ

〖注〗 archipelago 列島. the Shō dynasty 尚王朝. tribute 貢物. assault 襲撃. residual sovereignty 残留統治. reversion 返還. "United States Civil Administration of the Ryūkyū Islands"「アメリカ合衆国施政権下の沖縄」. lush subtropical greenery 緑の亜熱帯植物が繁茂していること.

Okinawa-jōfu 沖縄上布 ramie cloth of Okinawa; a dyed textile, a specialty of the Miyako and Yaeyama Islands of Okinawa. *Okinawa-jōfu* is a type of fine ramie cloth of various colors and designs developed in a region of the Ryūkyū Islands. The *jōfu* of the Miyako Islands is indigo-dyed in an elaborate *kasuri* (thread-resisting) process, featuring patterns of tiny blurred crosses which make up larger designs. The Yaeyama islanders produce a *jōfu* textile with small brown patterns rub-dyed on a white background. Yonaguni Island, one of the Yaeyama Islands, features *jōfu* with simpler striped or checked patterns. ⇨ JŌFU, KASURI

〖注〗 ramie イラクサ種の植物. the Yaeyama Islands 八重山諸島. indigo-dyed 藍染めの. Yonaguni Island 与那国島.

Okinawa-shikki 沖縄漆器 Okinawa lacquer ware; various utensils, containers, boxes, furniture and other objects made of wood covered by a protective layer of lacquer (*urushi*) varnish. Okinawa lacquer ware differs from that of the other Japanese islands mainly in that the wood used is from the diego tree (a short tropical tree with a light gray bark and scarlet flowers). Lacquer ware techniques were introduced from China around 1640. The wood is made into bowls, trays, and other objects which are then sanded smooth. The lacquer is then applied in layers. It penetrates and seals the wood, thereby increasing the durability of the ware. Multilayered lacquer is polished and sometimes even carved. Mother-of-pearl inlay is often added. Okinawa lacquer ware is among the most sought after, and is noted for its unique decorative style. ⇨ OKINAWA, SHIKKI, URUSHI

〖注〗 lacquer varnish 漆塗り． mother-of-pearl inlay 真珠貝のはめこみ，蒔絵．

okonomiyaki お好み焼き lit. a pancake of your choice. a Japanese-style pizza; a flat pancake made of batter and various ingredients. The ingredients—vegetables, egg, meat, seafoods, ginger, etc.—are chosen according to one's taste. The pancake is cooked on a broad iron plate, usually in front of the customer, and is covered with a thick spicy sauce when served.

〖注〗 batter (小麦粉の)こねたもの． ingredient 料理の材料．

Oku no Hosomichi 奥の細道 *The Narrow Road of the Deep North* (1694); a travel diary interspersed with haiku (17-syllable poem), written by Matsuo Bashō (1644-94), the great haiku master. For inspiration, Bashō journeyed throughout the country, in search of communion with nature and relics of previous days. From March to September 1689, he underwent a pilgrimage from Edo to the northern provinces with a disciple, Kawai Sora (1649-1710). They traveled by way of the Hokuriku district, terminating their journey at Ōgaki in present-day Gifu Prefecture. He then spent four years (1690-94) in writing this small book based on his experiences. Many of his finest haiku were composed during this journey, the longest one he had undertaken, covering 2,400 kilometers. During this pilgrimage, he developed a quality for his haiku, known as *sabi* —rustic simplicity, or the tranquil beauty to be found in desolation, age and solitude. ⇨ HAIKAI, HAIKU, SABI

〖注〗 be interspersed with そこここに配されている． communion 深くかかわること． relics 遺跡． pilgrimage (名所旧跡などへの)行脚． disciple 弟子． Kawai Sora 河合曽良． desolation すたれていること，さびれていること．

omikuji お神籤 lit. a divine lottery. a written oracle; a piece of paper on which one's fortune is written, sold at some shrines. After drawing one stick from a box of them, one is given a piece of paper matching the number on the stick. The paper will read: great luck (*dai-kichi*), luck (*kichi*), small luck (*shō-kichi*) or ill fate (*kyō*), with a short explanation added. Customarily, after reading their fortune, people tie the paper to a branch of a tree in the shrine precincts, praying either that a good prediction may come true or that ill fortune may be driven away by the spiritual power of the deity. ⇨ JINJA

〖注〗 oracle 神託，お告げ． precincts 境内，敷地． deity 神，神のような人 [もの]．

ōmisoka 大晦日　lit. the grand last day.　the last day of the year
(December 31).　People are found busy clearing up matters from
the passing year in order to greet the new year in a pleasant frame
of mind, and preparing special foods and decorations for the New
Year holidays.　Many eat buckwheat noodles (*toshikoshi-soba*) in
the evening.　"Buckwheat noodles" is *soba* in Japanese, which is
the homophone for *soba* meaning "close" i.e., it is close to the New
Year.　At midnight, temple bells peal 108 strokes (*joyanokane*) to
mark the passing of the old year.　⇨ JOYANOKANE, TOSHIKOSHI-
SOBA

〖注〗 buckwheat noodles 蕎麦.　homophone 同音異義語.　peal 鐘が鳴りひ
びく，とどろく.

omizutori お水取り　the drawing of holy water; the water-drawing
ceremony observed as a Buddhist rite at the Nigatsudō Hall of
Tōdaiji Temple, Nara (February 20 to March 15, especially March
13), first observed in the eighth century.　Eleven priests, fasting
from February 20, conduct Buddhist rites during the nights of
March 5, 6, 7, 12, 13 and 14.　On the night of the 12th to the dawn
of the 13th, starting with the waving of huge torches, they go to
draw holy water from the Wakasa Well near the Nigatsudō Hall
and offer it to the image of the Eleven-Faced Kannon Bodhisattva.
This first water of spring is believed to have healing powers.　This
event is said to mark the beginning of spring.　⇨ JŪICHIMEN-
KANNON

〖注〗 draw 引き出す.　Buddhist rite 仏教の儀式.　fast 断食する.　torch
松明.　Eleven-Faced Kannon Bodhisattva 十一面観音菩薩.

omogashi 主菓子　a wet cake or moist sweets; a cake usually served
with thick green tea (*koicha*) in the tea ceremony.　It is made from
bean paste and/or glutinous rice, formed into dumplings in the
shape or with designs of flowers, leaves, etc.　Types expressive of
the season are carefully chosen for the tea ceremony.　Moist cakes
for daily use are more commonly called *namagashi*.　⇨ CHANOYU,
KOICHA, NAMAGASHI

〖注〗 glutinous rice 糯米.　dumpling 団子.　tea ceremony 茶の湯.

omozukai 主遣い[面使い]　the leader of the puppeteer trio in Bunraku.　He manipulates the puppet's head and right arm and hand
while the *ashizukai* manipulates the legs and the *hidarizukai* the left
arm and hand.　The *omozukai* appears with his face uncovered; the
other two wear hoods over their heads.　⇨ ASHIZUKAI, BUNRAKU,

HIDARIZUKAI

〖注〗 puppeteer 人形遣い． puppeteer trio（文楽の）三人遣い． manipulate 操る．

on 恩 benevolence; a debt of gratitude; a sense of gratitude or indebtedness felt by a beneficiary toward his or her benefactor, which permeates human relations in Japan. The concept of gratitude or repayment of favors existed indigenously from ancient times as seen in folk tales such as *Urashima Tarō*, *Shitakiri Suzume* (Tongue-Cut Sparrow), etc. The concept was combined with Buddhism which dictates that benevolence as bestowed by Buddha is limitless and cannot be repaid but with gratitude. In the Kamakura period (1185-1336), the notion of *on* took on concrete form in vertical social relationships between a lord and his vassals. Vassals had to repay a lord for land and protection with loyalty and sacrifice. In the Tokugawa feudal society (1603-1868), benevolence conferred by superiors imposed compelling obligation on the part of inferiors. To respect *on* is still regarded as a virtue and a beneficiary of *on* is expected to respond with loyalty and sincerity. ⇨ OYABUN-KOBUN, SHITAKIRI SUZUME, URASHIMA TARŌ

〖注〗 gratitude 恩恵，感謝． indebtedness 負債のあること，恩を受けていること． beneficiary 恩恵を受ける者，受益者． benefactor 恩恵を施す者，恩人． permeate 浸透する． repayment 返済，恩返し． indigenously（土地）固有のものとして． bestow 授ける． vassal 家臣，領臣． confer 授ける． obligation 義理，恩義．

onbu おんぶ a piggyback ride; to carry a child on the back papoose-style. Customarily in Japan, a baby is carried tied onto its mother's back using a long sash. The baby faces the mother's back with its legs spread and its hands on her shoulders. In cold seasons, a coat specially designed for this purpose is worn to cover the baby and mother. This custom related to child-rearing may foster a feeling of security but at the same time an attitude of dependency. ⇨ AMAE

〖注〗 piggyback 背負って． on the back papoose-style インディアンの赤ん坊のように後向きに背負わせて． papoose アメリカインディアンの赤ん坊． child-rearing 子育て．

onigawara 鬼瓦 lit. a devil tile. an ornamental tile placed at the ridge end of a tiled roof. The design may be that of the head of a devil or some such form. A ridge-end tile with no such design also came to be called *onigawara*.

〖注〗 ridge end 屋根の棟の端.

onigiri お握り ⇨ NIGIRI-MESHI

onjōshugi 温情主義 lit. the principle or attitude of warm-heartedness. paternalism; the principle of caring for and directing subordinates with affection in the manner of a father toward his children. Paternalism has been a feature of the vertically structured grouping in Japanese society since feudal times, fostered by the relationship between feudal lords and their retainers. To this day, it persists as seen in the relationship of a *senpai* (senior) and *kōhai* (junior) in a clique, the *oyabun* (parent role) and *kobun* (child role) among gangsters, and even in modern companies between an employer and his employees. It is considered a virtue for a person of higher status to give his subordinates moral support and protection and to foster loyalty and dependency, thus strengthening vertical ties in a group. ⇨ OYABUN-KOBUN, SENPAI, TATE-SHAKAI
〖注〗 subordinate 部下. vertically structured 縦構造になっている. feudal lord 大名. retainer 家臣. clique 派閥, 徒党. moral support 精神的支え. loyalty 忠誠心.

onnagata 女方[女形] a female role; a Kabuki female impersonator. Since the Tokugawa shogunate (1603-1868) prohibited females from appearing on the stage, males acted the female roles and continue to do so today. These actors or roles are called *onnagata* or *oyama*. With successful impersonations, they often look more feminine than real women because of the symbolism in the art of Kabuki. ⇨ KABUKI, ONNA-KABUKI
〖注〗 impersonator 扮装者, 演技者. female impersonator 女に扮する役者, 女方.

onna-kabuki 女歌舞伎 female Kabuki; the forerunner of modern Kabuki, which was developed in the 17th century by a woman called Izumo no Okuni. It was soon banned by the Tokugawa shogunate (1603-1868). The result was the modern type of Kabuki performed exclusively by men. ⇨ KABUKI, ONNAGATA

onsen 温泉 a hot spring; a spa; a thermal mineral spring, or a resort with such springs. With its many volcanoes, Japan abounds in natural hot springs, with such resorts (or spas) numbering over 2,000. Springs of hot water or gas with a temperature of over 25 degrees C. and with specified mineral content are designated as hot springs, according to the Hot Spring Law of 1948. Both open-air and indoor bathing are enjoyed. Since ancient times, the Japanese have enjoyed hot springs for medicinal purposes as well as relaxation. Dōgo Spa in Shikoku maintains a monument erected by Prince Shōtoku (574–622). Among well-known hot-spring resorts are: Noboribetsu (Hokkaidō), Jōzankei (Hokkaidō), Zaō (Yamagata Prefecture), Akakura (Niigata Prefecture), Shiobara (Tochigi Prefecture), Nasu (Tochigi Prefecture), Kusatsu (Gunma Prefecture), Asama (Nagano Prefecture), Atami (Shizuoka Prefecture), Itō (Shizuoka Prefecture), Shirahama (Wakayama Prefecture), Arima (Shimane Prefecture), Dōgo (Ehime Prefecture), Beppu (Ōita Prefecture), Unzen (Nagasaki Prefecture), Ibusuki (Kagoshima Prefecture), etc.

〖注〗 spa 温泉地. thermal 熱の. content 含有物.

Oribe-yaki 織部焼　Oribe ceramic ware; ceramic ware made according to the designs of Furuta Oribe (1544–1615), one of the direct disciples of Sen no Rikyū (1521–91), founder of rustic tea ceremony. Influenced by the Portuguese who came to Japan in the 16th century, the ware often has geometrical designs and is made using an iron glaze.

〖注〗 ceramic ware 陶器(製品). geometrical 幾何学的な. glaze 釉, つや.

origami 折り紙　the craft of paper-folding; the traditional art of making various shapes by folding squares of paper, without using scissors or paste. Square, colored pieces of paper are folded into birds, animals, flowers, furniture and many other things. Most popular is the folded crane *(orizuru)*, a symbol of happiness. This art can be traced back to the Heian period (794–1185) and became popular in the middle of the Edo period (1603–1868) with the mass production of paper. It is not only an entertaining pastime, but can also serve an educational purpose.

〖注〗 craft 手工芸, 手細工, 芸術. folded crane 折り鶴. be traced back to ～にさかのぼる, に起源をたどる. pastime 趣味, 娯楽.

oroshi 下ろし　a grater or grated vegetables. Commonly it refers to grated Japanese radish *(daikon)* which is often used as a condiment for *tenpura*, pot dishes *(nabemono)*, etc. It helps digestion with a substance called diastase.　⇨ DAIKON-OROSHI, NABEMONO, TENPURA

〖注〗 grate おろす. Japanese radish 大根. condiment 薬味. substance 成分.

osechi-ryōri 御節料理　lit. dishes on seasonal festive occasions (also the original meaning). special dishes for the New Year; a variety of foods artistically arranged in a set of layered lacquer boxes, usually served with herb wine (*toso*) during the New Year holidays. A formal traditional set consists of four boxes: the first box (on the top) is arranged with appetizers (*kuchitori*), including herring roe (*kazunoko*), black soybeans (*kuromame*), candied dried small sardines (*tatsukuri*), sliced fish cake (*kamaboko*), mashed sweet beans or chestnuts (*kinton*), etc.; the second contains broiled foods (*yakimono*), such as seabream (*tai*) or lobster (*ebi*); the third, boiled foods (*nimono*) such as kelp rolls (*kobumaki*) and many kinds of vegetables; the fourth, vinegared foods (*sunomono*) made of vegetables, sometimes with fish.   Many of these foods have a symbolic meaning, celebrating the New Year and wishing happiness.   For example, herring roe implies prosperity for descendants; *tatsukuri* (small sardine) is a homonym for "cultivating fields"; *kobu* (kelp) and *tai* (seabream) rhyme with "rejoice" (*yoro-kobu*) and "celebration" (*mede-tai*) respectively.   Today, *osechi* includes new types of cuisine such as Chinese or Western dishes as well.   ⇨ GANJITSU, JŪZUME, KAMABOKO, KUCHITORI, SANGANICHI, SUNOMONO, TATSUKURI, TOSO, YAKIMONO²

〖注〗 lacquer 漆.   homonym 同音異義語.   cuisine 料理.

oseibo お歳暮   ⇨ SEIBO

oshibori お絞り   a wet wrung hand towel; a damp towel served at restaurants or homes so that guests may wipe their hands or faces before eating.   It is the size of a face towel or wash cloth, and served rolled up on a small tray made of bamboo, glass or metal, and served hot in cold weather and cool in hot weather.   Those served at restaurants are often wrapped in plastic.

〖注〗 wrung 絞った, ねじった.   damp しめった.   wash cloth 浴用[洗面用]タオル, 皿洗い用ふきん.

Ōshima-tsumugi 大島紬   Ōshima pongee; a type of hand-spun raw silk fabric, produced on Amami Ōshima Island in Kagoshima Prefecture.   Rough and uneven silk threads are soaked in and rubbed with mud so as to take on a rustic brown color.   It takes about a month to hand-weave enough fabric to make one kimono. *Ōshima-tsumugi* is one of the most expensive fabrics, but it is not supposed to be worn on formal occasions.   ⇨ KIMONO, TSUMUGI

〖注〗 pongee 絹紬.   silk fabric 絹織物.   rustic さびれた, 素朴な.

oshizushi 押し鮨   pressed *sushi*; rectangular cuts of pressed vinegared rice.   It is topped with a variety of ingredients—fish, egg, vegetables—which are cooked. This is a kind of Ōsaka-style *sushi,* as opposed to Edo-style *sushi*, which uses mostly raw fish as ingredients. ⇨ SUSHI

〖注〗 ingredient（料理の）材料.

otaiko お太鼓 ⇨ TAIKO

otoshidama お年玉 lit. the year's gem. a monetary gift given to children, or young employees in small businesses, at the New Year. Children receive it from parents or relatives upon the occasion of visits to extend New Year's greetings. Formerly the custom of the New Years' *otoshidama* was quite different. In the late Muromachi period（1336-1568）, there was a custom of exchanging gifts among nobles and warriors, and distributing rice cakes among commoners. Prior to that, offerings to deities at shrines and temples, such as rice cakes, were distributed among worshipers as a token of blessings for the new year. ⇨ GANJITSU

〖注〗 offering お供え. deity 神、神としてあがめられる人［物］. a token of blessings 祝福のしるし.

otoshidama-tsuki nengahagaki お年玉つき年賀はがき a New Year's lottery post card; official New Year's post cards with a lottery number printed at the bottom of the address side. Since 1949 such post cards have been issued annually in November by the Postal Ministry. Part of the income is used for social welfare. Prizes range from electric appliances to postage stamps. The drawing is conducted on January 15 and televised. The period of exchanging winning post cards for prizes is from January 20 to July 19. ⇨ GANJITSU, NENGAJŌ

〖注〗 lottery くじ. social welfare 社会福祉. electric appliance 電気器具. drawing くじをひくこと.

ōtsuzumi 大鼓 a large hand drum; a large hourglass-shaped drum, made up of a hollow wooden body（called *dō*）with a horse-skin leather cover at each end. Two cords are used, a vermilion one for keeping the body and the covers together, and the other one of different material for adjusting the sound. The drum is placed on the left thigh close to the side bone, with the left hand holding the cords, and is usually struck with the tip of the middle finger （nowadays, often with a special sack on it）of the right hand. The covers are dried by a heater to maintain an echoing sound. The pitch is controlled by squeezing the cords. *Ōtsuzumi* is similar in construction to but larger than *kotsuzumi*（a small shoulder drum）.

Both instruments are important in the instrumental ensembles (*hayashi*) of the Noh and Kabuki theaters and related Japanese dance forms. Also called *ōkawa*. ⇨ HAYASHI, KABUKI, KOTSU-ZUMI, NŌ, TSUZUMI

〖注〗 hourglass-shaped 砂時計型の. vermilion 朱色. pitch 音の高低. instrumental ensemble 楽器の合奏, 囃子.

oyabun-kobun 親分子分 lit. parent role and child role. a parent-child relationship between a superior and his subordinates; a pattern of superior-inferior relations within a group, deriving from the feudal system of Japan. The *oyabun,* a boss with a "parent" status, and *kobun*, his subordinates with "children" status, are tied to each other, economically and socially. The former takes care of the latter in everything, providing security and protection just as a parent does for a child. In return, the dependent *kobun* are obliged for benevolence received and are expected to respond with loyalty and sacrifice. Even today, such relations persist within organizations, although perhaps only implicitly, but remain quite strong in gangster groups. ⇨ ON

〖注〗 superior-inferior relation 上下関係. feudal system 封建制度. benevolence 慈悲心, 恩. obligation 義務, 義理. loyalty 忠誠. implicitly 表面化せずに. gangster やくざ.

oyako-donburi 親子丼 lit. parent and child on rice in a bowl. chicken and egg on rice; a bowl of rice topped with cooked egg and slices of chicken, onion and mushroom. Seasoned with soy sauce, sugar and sweet wine, chicken and vegetables are simmered, over which a beaten egg is poured. After the egg is cooked, the ingredients are placed on a bowl of rice. Pieces of seaweed laver may be added as a garnish when served. ⇨ DONBURI, DONBURIMONO

〖注〗 season 味をつける. soy sauce 醬油. sweet wine 味醂. simmer 煮つめる. ingredient (料理の)材料. seaweed laver 海苔. garnish 飾り.

oyama 女形 ⇨ ONNAGATA

ōzeki 大関 a *sumō* champion; the second highest rank in *sumō*. To be promoted to this rank a *sekiwake* (junior champion) must finish with a good record in at least two consecutive tournaments, the standard being to win some 31-32 bouts out of a possible 45 during three consecutive tournaments. An *ōzeki* gets demoted after two consecutive losing records. An *ōzeki* facing such a possibility with a losing record in the previous tournament is called a *kadoban-ōzeki*. A demoted *ōzeki* may regain the rank if he wins 10 or more bouts in the next tournament. ⇨ ŌZUMŌ, SUMŌ

〖注〗 junior champion 関脇. consecutive 連続の. bout 試合, 勝負. demote 位を下げる.

ōzumō 大相撲 a grand *sumō* tournament; major professional *sumō* tournaments held for a period of 15 days every two months. There are six such tournaments: the *ichigatsu-basho* (January tournament) or *hatsu-basho* (New Year's tournament) held in Tokyo; the *sangatsu-basho* (March tournament) or *haru-basho* (spring tournament) held in Ōsaka; the *gogatsu-basho* (May tournament) or *natsu-basho* (summer tournament) held in Tokyo; the *shichigatsu-basho* (July tournament) or *Nagoya-basho* (Nagoya tournament) held in Nagoya; the *kugatsu-basho* (September tournament) or *aki-basho* (autumn tournament) held in Tokyo; and the *jūichigatsu-basho* (November tournament) or *Kyūshū-basho* (Kyūshū tournament) held in Fukuoka, Kyūshū. All begin on the Sunday closest to the 10th of the month, and close with the *senshūraku* (the final day of a tournament), also falling on a Sunday. During this period wrestlers in the *makuuchi* and *jūryō* divisions wrestle every day, while those of lower divisions play every other day for a total of seven bouts. Lower-ranking wrestlers compete first, with higher-ranking wrestlers following and the *yokozuna* coming last. The wrestler with the best win-loss record wins the tournament. A playoff is held if there is a tie. ⇨ JŪRYŌ, MAKUUCHI, SUMŌ, YO-KOZUNA

〖注〗 New Year's tournament 初場所. bout 試合, 勝負. playoff 優勝決定戦. tie 同点, 引き分け.

P

pachinko パチンコ　Japanese pinball; a game in which the player tries to shoot steel balls into winning holes in an upright pinball machine.　The player buys steel balls and loads them into a tray from which the balls roll into the machine.　He or she controls a lever which shoots the balls to the top of the game board studded with pegs that change the course of the ball as it drops to the bottom.　When a ball goes into one of several winning holes on the board, new balls are released into the tray.　The other balls are collected into the machine through an opening at the bottom of the game board.　The player can exchange the balls for prizes ranging from food to leisure goods, according to the number of balls won. *Pachinko* first saw commercial success in Nagoya after World War II and soon caught on throughout the country.

〖注〗 load 積む, 載せる.　peg くぎ, くさび.　release 放つ.

puro-yakyū プロ野球　Japanese professional baseball.　Baseball was first introduced in Japan in 1873, and the first professional game was played in 1934.　Although pro ball caught on only after World War II, the game has since become Japan's most popular spectator sport.　Presently there are two major leagues, each having six teams owned by large corporations.　They are the Chūnichi Dragons, Hanshin Tigers, Hiroshima Carp, Taiyō Whales, Yakult Swallows and Yomiuri Giants of the Central League, and the Hankyū Braves, Kintetsu Buffaloes, Lotte Orions, Nankai Hawks, Nippon Ham Fighters, and Seibu Lions of the Pacific League.　After 130 regular season games, the pennant winners of the two leagues battle it out for the championship in the Japan Series, the counterpart of America's World Series.　Unlike in the U.S., tied games do not go into extra innings after a certain time limit, and thus can end up in a draw.　Up to two players of foreign nationality are allowed to play on each major league team.

〖注〗 counterpart 相当するもの.　foreign nationality 外国籍.

R

rakugo 落語 lit. telling with a drop. comic monologue; humorous storytelling performed by a professional raconteur. Seated on his knees, a raconteur relates a story with dramatic use of his hands and facial expressions, and a fan (and sometimes a towel). The monologue is marked by humorous anecdotes, a plebian style of talking, ample use of puns and, most important, a witty surprise ending with unexpected twists in the plot called *ochi* (lit. drop) along the way. The origin of *rakugo* can be traced back to civil-war days in the 16th century when warlords were entertained by comic storytellers. Such storytelling spread to the common people in the Edo period (1603-1868), with humorous topics coming from everyday life. Today, there are roughly two categories of *rakugo*: classical *rakugo*, whose repertory was fixed in the Meiji (1868-1912) and Taishō (1912-1926) eras, and modern creative *rakugo*. ⇨ YOSE

〖注〗 raconteur 噺家, 話のたくみな人. anecdote 逸話. plebian 庶民の. pun しゃれ, 語呂合わせ.

Raku-yaki 楽焼 Raku earthenware; a soft and thick kind of pottery made by hand, without using a wheel. It is fired at low temperature, after which a glaze, primarily lead oxide, is applied. Raku ware originated with Sen no Rikyū (1521-91) who had tea bowls fired to his taste by potters from Korea. It has been greatly favored by tea-cult devotees for its rustic quality. There are roughly two kinds—black *Raku* and red *Raku*.

〖注〗 earthenware 土器, 陶器. pottery 陶器(類). wheel (製陶用の)ろくろ. glaze 釉, 上薬. lead oxide 酸化鉛. apply 上薬[釉]をつける. fire (陶器などを)焼く. potter 陶工. tea-cult devotees 茶人. rustic quality さびれたおもむき, さび.

rangaku 蘭学 Dutch studies; Western studies, especially medicine, in the Dutch language, in the Edo period (1603-1868). During the period of national seclusion (1639-1854), the Dutch were the only

Europeans allowed to trade with Japan, and then only at a specified place, Dejima in Kyūshū. Western medicine and other scientific subjects drew the attention of some Japanese scholars in the late 17th and early 18th centuries. Supported by the eighth Tokugawa shogun, Yoshimune (1684-1751), scholars in Dutch studies, through strenuous efforts, produced dictionaries and translations on scientific subjects. Among the noted scholars were Arai Hakuseki (1657-1725), Aoki Kon'yō (1698-1769) and Sugita Genpaku (1733-1817). Philipp Franz Jonkheer Balthasar von Siebold (1796-1866), a German physician who came to Japan in 1823, contributed greatly to this academic movement. ⇨ DEJIMA, SAKOKU(-SEISAKU)

〖注〗 medicine 医学.   national seclusion 鎖国.

ranma 欄間   a kind of transom; the space between the ceiling and the lintel beam above the sliding doors of a traditional Japanese room. The transom is made of wood or bamboo, sometimes covered with rice paper, and has ornamental open-work.

〖注〗 transom 窓を水平に仕切る横材.   lintel beam 鴨居.   sliding door すべり戸(襖や障子).   rice paper 和紙.   ornamental open-work 透かし彫りの装飾意匠.

renga 連歌   a linked verse; a series of stanzas; a verse of five-seven-five syllables alternating with seven-seven syllables, composed jointly by more than two persons. It appeared around the 11th century and flourished in the 14th century as an intellectual pastime especially among the literati and priests. The five-seven-five syllable part later developed into the *haikai* poem. ⇨ HAIKAI

〖注〗 stanza (詩の)連, (詩の構成単位の)節.   syllable 音節.   intellectural pastime 知的娯楽.   literati 文学者たち, 文人たち(literatusの複数).

renju 連珠   Japanese tick-tack-toe; a simplified version of *go* commonly called *gomoku-narabe*. The game is played with black and white *go* stones on a board bearing a grid of 15 by 15 lines. The stones are placed on the intersections with black going first. The object of the game is to place five stones in a row either along one of the lines or diagonally. Since the game is more involved than tick-tack-toe, a row of stones generally has to be blocked at two places. A line of three stones and a line of four blocked at a single spot are called *katsuren* (lit. alive row). To win, one must make two *katsuren* simultaneously in one turn. Since going first is considered advantageous, to even things out, the player with black is limited to making a double *katsuren* of three and four. ⇨ GO

【注】 tick-tack-toe 三目並べ. simplified version 簡素版. intersection 交差点.

ri 里 a unit for measuring distance in the old Japanese scale system. One *ri* is 3.93 kilometers. This unit is now only used by a small portion of elderly people. The metric system was officially adopted after World War II. ⇨ SHAKKAN-HŌ

【注】 unit 単位. scale system 計量法. the metric system メートル法.

rikka 立華 the standing form of flower arrangement; a classical style of arrangement of flowers with a composition of seven (or nine) main branches. It is characterized by a fixed form of arrangement to symbolize the laws of nature in microcosm, i.e., a peak, hill, waterfall, village, valley, a sunny side and a shaded side. This style originated in the 15th century and flourished in the 16th and 17th centuries. Today's *rikka* arrangement comprises nine main branches. ⇨ IKEBANA, MORIBANA, NAGEIRE

【注】 fixed form 定型. microcosm 小宇宙. sunny side 陽. shaded side 陰.

Rikuchū-kaigan Kokuritsu-kōen 陸中海岸国立公園 Rikuchū Coast National Park (123.5 square kilometers), designated in 1955; a coastal natural park, extending along the Pacific coast of northern Honshū, in Iwate and Miyagi prefectures. This park stretches some 180 kilometers, with Miyako City at its center. It is characterized by massive, rugged coastlines, featuring terraced shores, sandy beaches, steep cliffs, sea-eroded grottoes, etc. Wild birds such as black-tailed sea gulls, stormy petrels, etc., are protected as "natural monuments." ⇨ KOKURITSU-KŌEN, TENNEN-KINENBUTSU

【注】 rugged coastline リアス式海岸線. terraced shore 段丘海岸. sea-eroded 海水で浸食した. grotto 洞窟. black-tailed sea gull 海猫. stormy petrel 海燕. natural monument 天然記念物.

rikyū 離宮 a detached Imperial Palace; an imperial villa; an imperial villa located outside the grounds of the permanent imperial palace. There are two imperial villas at present: the Katsura Imperial Villa built originally in the 17th century and repaired in 1983, and the Shugakuin Imperial Villa built in the mid-17th century, both in Kyoto. The present state guesthouse (Geihinkan; reconstructed in 1974) at Akasaka in Tokyo was formerly a detached imperial palace (the Akasaka Rikyū). It was built in 1907, modeled after Buckingham Palace, primarily for the use of the crown prince at the time (later, Emperor Taishō, father of the present emperor).

〖注〗 detached 離れた． the Katsura Imperial Villa 桂離宮． the Shugakuin Imperial Villa 修学院離宮． state guesthouse 迎賓館．

ringisei 稟議制 a collective, participative style of decision-making; a process of reaching a consensus by circulating a document. It usually originates at the bottom of an organization, passing up to the top, thereby involving everyone concerned in the decision-making process. This style of decision-making is said to be typical of Japanese organizations, and can be attributed to the group orientation of the Japanese. ⇨ NEMAWASHI

〖注〗 decision-making process 意思決定過程． be attributed to ～に由来する． group orientation 集団志向．

Rinzaishū 臨済宗 the Rinzai branch of Zen Buddhism; one of the two major branches of the Zen sect, the other being the Sōtō branch. It was founded by Lin-chi (died 867)—called Rinzai in Japan—during the T'ang dynasty (618-907) of China. In the late 12th century, Eisai (1141-1215), who studied in China, introduced Rinzai Zen to Japan. He built Kenninji Temple (1202) in Kyoto and Jufukuji Temple (1200) in Kamakura as its headquarters. Over the years this branch has been subdivided into more than a dozen branches. A difference between Rinzai Zen and Sōtō Zen is that the former is characterized by a positive approach to self-realization stressing *kōan* (catechistic questions) while the latter values meditation and tranquillity of mind. ⇨ SŌTŌSHŪ, ZAZEN, ZEN[1], ZENSHŪ

〖注〗 Lin-chi 臨済のもとの中国発音． the T'ang dynasty 唐朝． Eisai 栄西． Kenninji Temple 建仁寺． Jufukuji Temple 寿福寺． headquarters 本処地， 総本山． subdivide 細分化する． self-realization 自己完成，悟り． catechistic questions 公案． meditation 黙想，座禅． tranquillity of mind 心の平静．

rinzu 綸子 figured satin; silk satin fabric with repeated small crest-like patterns woven into it. The satin is smooth and lustrous, dyed plain or printed with colored figures. An elaborate silk fabric, it is made into formal kimono and *obi* (sash), and luxurious bedding. First produced in Kyoto in the Muromachi period (1336-1568), this type of weave developed in Komatsu near Kanazawa, in present-day Ishikawa Prefecture, under the protection of the local feudal lord. *Komatsu-rinzu* is still renowned for its superb quality. ⇨ KIMONO, OBI

〖注〗 figured satin 模様のついた繻子． fabric 織物． crest-like pattern 紋様

の柄．　weave 織り．　feudal lord 大名，藩主．

Rishiri-Rebun-Sarobetsu Kokuritsu-kōen 利尻礼文サロベツ国立公園　Rishiri-Rebun-Sarobetsu National Park (212.2 square kilometers), designated in 1974; a natural park located in northernmost Hokkaidō.　This park comprises the Sarobetsu Plain on the mainland of Hokkaidō, and Rishiri and Rebun islands off the coast of the Sea of Japan.　The Sarobetsu Plain features natural fields of subarctic wild flowers, such as rhododendrons, sweet briers, day lilies, etc.　Rishiri Island has a conic volcano, Mount Rishiri.　The waters in this park area contain rich fishing grounds.　⇨ HOKKAIDŌ, KOKURITSU-KŌEN

〖注〗 the Sarobetsu Plain サロベツ原野．　subarctic 亜寒帯．　rhododendron シャクナゲ属の植物．　sweet brier 浜茄子．　day lily (ここでは)蝦夷萱草等．conic volcano 円錐火山．　fishing ground 漁場．

risshū 立秋　the beginning of autumn in the lunar calendar.　It falls around August 7 in the present calendar.　Severe summer heat still lingers in most parts of the Japanese archipelago on this day.　But customarily, seasonal terms used in greetings are related not to midsummer, but to late summer or early autumn, although such expressions as "lingering summer heat" may often be added.　⇨ RISSHUN

〖注〗 the lunar calendar 太陰暦．　linger 長びく，だらだら続く．　the Japanese archipelago 日本列島．　lingering summer heat 残暑．

risshun 立春　the beginning of spring in the lunar calendar.　It falls on February 4 or 5 in the present calendar.　Formerly the new year began on this day.　Traditional annual events to mark the change of season are still observed.　For example, on the eve of the first day of spring, bean-throwing rituals are held at homes and at shrines and temples.　⇨ MAMEMAKI, RISSHŪ, SETSUBUN

〖注〗 lunar calendar 太陰暦．　annual event 年中行事．　bean-throwing ritual 豆まきの儀式．

ritsuryō 律令　criminal law and administrative law; the code consisting of criminal law (*ritsu*) and civil law (*ryō*) modeled after that of T'ang China and enforced from the late seventh century. Beginning with the Ōmi Code (671), the code was completed in the form known as *Taihō Ritsuryō* (701) after several revisions.　Based on Confucian doctrine, the laws established a centralized system of government stressing imperial authority, which required military service, tax payments, etc.　With repeated modifications, the main body of the Taihō Code remained in effect until the Meiji Restoration (1868). ⇨ JUKYŌ, MEIJI ISHIN, TAIKA NO KAISHIN

〖注〗 criminal law 刑法，律．　adminstrative law 行政法，令．　code 法典，法律．　civil law 民法，令．　T'ang China 中国の唐朝．　enforce 施行する．　the Ōmi Code「近江令」．　Confucian doctrine 儒教の教義．　military service 兵役．　modification 修正．　the Meiji Restoration 明治維新．

ro¹ 炉　an inset hearth; a square brazier—about a half a meter square—sunk in the floor by removing a corner of the *tatami*.　It is used to hold an iron kettle on a tripod for the tea ceremony during winter, while the portable fire brazier is used during the warmer seasons.　⇨ CHANOYU, CHASHITSU, FŪRO, KAMA

〖注〗 inset はめこむ．　hearth 炉床．　brazier 火鉢．　iron kettle 茶釜．　tripod 三脚．　portable fire brazier 持ち運びできる炉，風炉．

ro² 絽　a kind of silk gauze; thin silk fabric with mesh lines.　The lines run like narrow stripes either vertically or horizontally.　As it is cool due to the porous mesh, the fabric is appropriate for summer.　Kimono of this fabric is worn from June to September.　⇨ KIMONO

〖注〗 gauze 薄織りの布．　silk fabric 絹織物．　porous 多孔性の．

robuchi 炉縁　the frame for an inset hearth; a square frame fitted around the inset brazier sunk in the *tatami*-mat floor of a room for the tea ceremony.　The *robuchi* is made of lacquered wood with designs, or of plain wood, taken from a mulberry, Japanese cedar or chestnut tree.　It is about 40 centimeters square, inside which a teakettle is placed for the tea ceremony.　⇨ CHANOYU, CHASHITSU, KAMA, RO

〖注〗 inset hearth（床に）はめこんだ炉．　brazier 火鉢，炉．　tea ceremony 茶道．　mulberry tree 桑の木．　Japanese cedar 檜．　teakettle 茶釜．

rōchū 老中　　⇨ RŌJŪ

roji 露地[露路]　lit. the ground of dew.　a tea garden, or a pathway leading to the tearoom in a tea garden.　The *roji* is divided into two areas—the outer *roji* which includes the area close to the entrance to the garden with a waiting chamber and the inner *roji* which includes the path leading to the tearoom and its surrounding area.　There are usually stone lanterns, stepping stones and a stone water basin.　The *roji* symbolizes the passage into the realm of meditation, where the landscape is arranged so as to induce tranquillity of mind, preparing the guests to enjoy the tea ceremony.　⇨ CHANOYU, CHASHITSU

〖注〗 pathway 通路, 小道. waiting chamber 待合. stone lantern 石燈籠. stepping stones 飛び石. stone water basin つくばい. passage 通路. the realm of meditation 瞑想境. tranquillity of mind 心の平静.

rōjū 老中 members of the Council of Elders in the Tokugawa shogunate government (1603-1868). Four of the five council members were chosen from among hereditary feudal lords (*fudai-daimyō*) having a revenue of more than 25,000 *koku* of rice. In turns, each served the shogun for about a month. ⇨ DAIMYŌ, FUDAI-DAIMYŌ, KOKU, SHŌGUN

〖注〗 hereditary feudal lord 譜代大名. revenue 年収, 歳入. *koku* 石(約180.4リットル).

rokki 六輝 ⇨ ROKUYŌ

rokkoyō 六古窯 the six old kilns; the six time-honored kilns well-known since the Kamakura period (1185-1336). The six are: Seto Kiln and Tokoname Kiln in the present Aichi Prefecture, Echizen Kiln in Fukui Prefecture, Shigaraki Kiln in Shiga Prefecture, Tanba Kiln in Kyoto Prefecture, and Bizen Kiln in Okayama Prefecture. ⇨ BIZEN-YAKI, ECHIZEN-YAKI, SETO-YAKI, SHIGARAKI-YAKI, TANBA-YAKI, TOKONAME-YAKI

〖注〗 kiln (焼き物を焼く)窯. time-honored 昔からの, 由緒ある. 六古窯：瀬戸, 常滑, 越前, 信楽, 丹波, 備前.

Roku-Kannon 六観音 the Six Kannon Bodhisattvas; the six representative types of the Deity of Mercy worshiped in esoteric Buddhism. In the Tendai sect, they are Shō Kannon, Jūichimen Kannon, Senju Kannon, Nyoirin Kannon, Batō Kannon and Fukū-kenjaku Kannon. In the Shingon sect, Fukūkenjaku Kannon is replaced by Juntei Kannon. Most or some of these are worshiped in other major sects of Buddhism as well. ⇨ BATŌ KANNON, JŪI-CHIMEN KANNON, KANNON BOSATSU, SENJU KANNON, SHINGONSHŪ

〖注〗 Bodhisattva 菩薩(すでに仏性に達しているのに, 人々が救われるのを助けるために, 涅槃に入らない存在). the Deity of Mercy 観音. deity 神, 神のような人[もの]. esoteric Buddhism 密教.

rokuyō 六曜 the six-day week; a period comprising six days on the lunar calendar, used in divination. The six days of the cycle are *senshō* (a day of luck in the morning but ill fortune in the afternoon), *tomobiki* (a day of luck in the morning and evening, but ill fortune at noon; also a day when friends are attracted), *senpu* (a day of luck in calmness, particularly in the afternoon), *butsumetsu* (a day of ill fortune in everything), *taian* (a day of great luck in everything) and *shakkō* (a day of caution against encountering ill fortune). These six days are still listed today as a supplement on most calendars. The significance of the days is customarily observed for special occasions. Weddings are often held on *taian* days and are avoided on *butsumetsu* days; funerals are avoided on a *tomobiki* day. Such observance became popular in the Edo period (1603-1868). The six divisions are said to have derived from the Chinese philosophy of cosmic dual forces, appearing in the T'ang dynasty (618-906). The divisions were first used to indicate the time of day. ⇨ BUTSUMETSU, TAIAN

〖注〗 lunar calendar 太陰暦. divination 占い. supplement 付け加え. observance 慣習, 従うこと. cosmic dual forces 宇宙の二元力, 陰陽. the T'ang dynasty 唐朝. 六曜：先勝, 友引, 先負, 仏滅, 大安, 赤口.

rōkyoku 浪曲 ⇨ NANIWABUSHI

rōmaji ローマ字 the romanization of the Japanese syllabic alphabet; a method of writing the Japanese language in Roman letters. Each script of the Japanese syllabic alphabet can be transcribed in the Roman alphabet, mostly with one or two consonants followed by a vowel (except for the *a, i, u, e, o* and *n* sounds). Beginning with the romanization developed by Jesuit missionaries in the 16th century, there have been various systems. The most commonly used at present is the Hepburn system (*Hebon-shiki*; also called the standard system or *hyōjun-shiki*), established by James C. Hepburn (1815-1911), an American missionary and founder of Meiji Gakuin University. Another common one is the official system (*kunrei-shiki*; derived from the Japanese system or *Nippon-shiki*), established in 1937 and officially authorized in 1954. The latter is now taught in elementary schools because it is governed by rules and easy to learn. However, the Hepburn system is more compatible with the Japanese sound system, and thus is more widely used. For example, たちつてと (Japanese syllabic script) appears as:

```
[ta  tʃi  tsu  te  to]  (phonetic transcription)
 ta  ti   tu   te  to   (kunrei system)
 ta  chi  tsu  te  to   (Hepburn system)
```

〖注〗 romanization ローマ字化. script 書体, 筆跡. transcribe 書き写す, 音標文字で書く. consonant 子音. vowel 母音. Jesuit missionary イエズス伝道会の宣教師. be compatible with ～に適合する, 調和する.

rōnin 浪人 lit. a wandering samurai. a student who has not yet been admitted to the college of his choice. Many students who have failed the entrance examination to the college of their choice attend preparatory schools for a year or sometimes even several years.   These students are called *rōnin*, using the term for wandering samurai of feudal times who had lost their masters.   ⇨ JUKU, YOBIKŌ

〖注〗 preparatory school 予備校. feudal times 封建時代.

Roppō Zensho 六法全書 *The Complete Collection of the Six Major Codes*; a book comprising the six major codes—the Constitution, Civil Code, Criminal Code, Commercial Code, Code of Civil Procedure and Code of Criminal Procedure—in addition to important parts of subsidiary statutes, government orders, local ordinances, etc.   The collection of legislation is contained in a huge volume, the *Hōrei Zensho* (The Complete Collection of Statutes and Subsidiary Legislation, 1867–today); treaties in force are contained in the *Genkō Jōyaku Shūran* (The Collection of Treaties in Force). Called a bible for the legal profession, the *Roppō Zensho* is made up of the minimum essentials, but also covers important legislation in all fields of law.   Smaller editions, the *Kihon Roppō* (A Basic Collection of the Six Codes) and *Shō Roppō* (A Small Collection of the Six Codes), are commonly used by law students.   One scholar traces the origin of the "six codes" to the *Criminal Codes of Six Volumes* of T'ang dynasty (618-907) of China (the oldest collection of recorded Oriental codes and perhaps the world's oldest collection of recorded criminal codes), and maintains that the "six codes" may have been combined with the *Zensho* (the complete collection) of the above *Hōrei Zensho*.

〖注〗 code 法典. the Civil Code「民法」. the Criminal Code「刑法」. the Code of Civil Procedure「民事訴訟法」. the Code of Criminal Procedure「刑事訴訟法」. subsidiary statute 付随的法令. government order 政令. local ordinance 地方条令. legislation 法律, 法規.

Rushana Butsu 盧遮那仏 Buddha Vairocana; the Great Buddha of the Universe or Light, illuminating creation.   He is believed to be the perfect being, from whom everything comes and who is omnipresent in the universe. Some sects of Buddhism consider Gautama Sakyamuni the manifestation of this being. Representative statues of Rushana Butsu include the Great Buddha of Kamakura and that of Nara.   In esoteric Buddhism, he is called Dainichi Nyorai.   ⇨ BUKKYŌ, DAIBUTSU

〖注〗 omnipresent 遍在している. Gautama Sakyamuni 釈迦牟尼. manifestation 出現.　esoteric Buddhism 密教.

Ryōbu Shintō 両部神道　double-aspect Shinto; a syncretic mixture of Buddhism and Shintoism.　In an attempt to make Buddhism more acceptable to the Japanese who worshiped Shinto gods, Buddhist priests such as Gyōki (670-749), Kūkai (774-835), Saichō (767-822), etc., evolved the idea that the indigenous gods of Shinto were temporary manifestations of various Buddhist divinities. The Shingon sect of Buddhism, with its central element of mysticism, served well to combine the Shinto religion and Buddhism. With the movement to revive pure Shintoism at the end of the Edo period (1603-1868) and with the official adoption of Shinto as the state religion at the Meiji Restoration (1868), Ryōbu Shinto was rejected.　⇨ BUKKYŌ, MEIJI ISHIN, SHINGONSHŪ, SHINTŌ

〖注〗 syncretic 諸派統合的な.　indigenous 土着の.　temporary manifestation 一時的な現れ.　Buddhist divinity 仏, 仏性を備えた人格.　mysticism 神秘主義.　the Meiji Restoration 明治維新.

ryokan 旅館　an inn; a traditional lodging house for travelers.　It looks like a large ordinary house, usually with a sedate landscape garden.　One takes off one's shoes when entering; a pair of slippers is provided for use in the corridors.　The rooms have *tatami*-mat floors, sliding doors, and an alcove decorated with a hanging scroll and a flower arrangement, as in a guest room in a traditional Japanese house.　At such inns, one can relax in *yukata* (a simple cotton kimono), together with *tanzen* (a padded kimono) in the cold season, after enjoying a hot bath.　⇨ KIMONO, TANZEN, TATAMI, YUKATA

〖注〗 lodging house 宿泊の家.　sedate 落ちついた, 静寂な.　landscape garden 風景庭園.　sliding door 障子, ふすま.　alcove 床の間.　hanging scroll 掛け軸.

ryokucha 緑茶　green tea or green tea leaves; beverage prepared by steeping green tea leaves in hot water.　Green tea is more commonly called just *cha* or *ocha* (a more polite form) as a generic term, it being the most popular beverage among Japanese.　The term *ryokucha* is used to specifically distinguish it from black tea which is also popular today.　Green tea is made from the same kind of tea leaves as black tea; however, it is not fermented but rather processed by steaming and drying, so it thus remains green. There are various kinds of green tea such as *gyokuro, sencha, bancha,* etc.　⇨ BANCHA, CHA, GYOKURO, SENCHA

〖注〗 beverage 飲み物. steep 浸す. ferment 発酵する.

ryōtei 料亭 lit. a cuisine house. Japanese restaurants of the highest level. They are constructed as large luxurious traditional houses with many *tatami*-mat guest rooms, both large and small. The rooms are refined and often face a tranquil landscape garden, separated only by a sliding door. *Ryōtei* are used for parties, private talks, etc., as well as for the sheer enjoyment of Japanese cuisine of the finest quality served with saké and traditional hospitality. Geisha are available for entertainment. The Akasaka district close to the Diet Building in Tokyo is well-known for its numerous fine *ryōtei*. ⇨ GEISHA, ZASHIKI

〖注〗 cuisine 料理. tranquil landscape garden 閑静な日本庭園. sliding door 障子.

Ryūkyū-akae 琉球赤絵 Okinawan red-enameled ceramic ware. This style originated in China and was introduced to Okinawa during the period of Chinese influence (12th to 16th centuries). *Ryūkyū-akae* is marked by an incised design with an overglaze. ⇨ AKAE, OKINAWA, RYŪKYŪ-SHOTŌ

〖注〗 incised design 刻みこみ模様. overglaze 上薬, 上塗り.

Ryūkyū-garasu 琉球ガラス Ryūkyū glassware; decorative vases, bottles and other glass objects made in Okinawa. This art form has prospered mainly since World War II. Rather than using new glass, Ryūkyū glassware is made by melting or refashioning discarded bottles. The original bottles are heated to around 1,000 degrees C. Colors are achieved by adding various chemicals. Decorative bottles, vases, jars, bunches of glass grapes, glass flowers, etc., are popular with tourists from the mainland as well as overseas. Many of these glass objects are also exported. ⇨ OKINAWA, RYŪKYŪ-SHOTŌ

〖注〗 discarded bottle 捨てびん, 空きびん.

Ryūkyū-shotō 琉球諸島 the Ryūkyū Islands; a chain of over 70 islands stretching southwest from Kyūshū for about 1,200 kilometers; also called Nansei-shotō. Ryūkyū is the Japanese pronunciation of the Chinese name Liu-ch'iu (Liugiu) used during the Ming dynasty (1368-1644) to refer to Okinawa and its surrounding islands. The islands are subtropical and usually ringed by coral reefs. Many are beautiful and have become important tourist attractions. The Ryūkyūs saw some of the fiercest fighting of World War II. The islands northeast of Okinawa are administered by Kagoshima Prefecture, while Okinawa and the islands to the southwest comprise Okinawa Prefecture.　⇨ OKINAWA

〖注〗　the Ming dynasty 明朝．　coral reef 珊瑚礁．

S

sabi 寂 lit. patina; agedness; solitary look. rustic simplicity; the quiet beauty of things in a state of natural decay; active appreciation of the value of things seemingly negative, such as rusticity, agedness, loneliness, deficiency, etc., an aesthetic concept fostered under the influence of Zen in the Muromachi period (1336-1568). This concept has become one of the most important and lasting elements in traditional Japanese arts and literature, and has been particularly esteemed in the tea ceremony. It is what simple, rustic tea utensils acquire after repeated use over a long period of time, gradually and naturally taking on a withered and wasted look which bears richness in historical associations and spiritual connotations. In the early Edo period (1603-1868), Matsuo Bashō (1644-94) and his followers valued the concept of *sabi* as an ideal in *haikai* (17-syllable poem), in the context of tranquil beauty in desolation and solitude. This quality is depicted well in the following *haikai*.

Kono kido ya	This castle gate
Jō no sasarete	Remains locked—
Fuyu no tsuki.	The winter moon, now.
(Enomoto Kikaku, 1661-1707;	(Translated by S.K.)
a disciple of Bashō)	

⇨ CHANOYU, HAIKAI, WABI, WABI-SABI, ZEN[1]

〖注〗 patina 古さび，古色． agedness 年月を経ていること． solitary look 孤独な様子，寂しい様子． aesthetic concept 美的概念． tea ceremony 茶道． tea utensil 茶道具． withered ひからびた． wasted すたれた，使い古した． connotation 含蓄，深い意味． tranquil 静かな． desolation 荒涼たること，寂しさ． solitude 孤独，寂しさ． disciple 弟子．

sadō 茶道 the way of tea; the tea ceremony. The same as *chanoyu*, but the term *sadō* has a more philosophical and spiritual connotation with an emphasis on self-realization as well as aesthetic entertainment. The way of tea is based on the Zen concept of the greatness to be found in imperfection. The ceremony first developed from a kind of tea-drinking ritual conducted in front of the image of Buddha by Zen monks. It reached perfection, both spiritually and aesthetically, in the 16th century under the great tea master, Sen no Rikyū (1521-91). ⇨ CHANOYU, WABICHA

〖注〗 connotation 含蓄，深い意味．self-realization 悟り．aesthetic entertainment 美的趣味．Zen concept 禅の思想．ritual 儀式．image of Buddha 仏像．Zen monk 禅僧．

Sadogashima 佐渡が島 Sado Island (858 square kilometers); an island in the Sea of Japan, north of Niigata City. This island is the largest after the four major islands of Japan, with a population of some 100,000, and is under the administration of Niigata Prefecture. It can be reached in about two hours by ferry, or 20 minutes by air, from Niigata. Points of interest include scenic sites in Senkaku Bay and along the Sotokaifu coast, and remains of gold mines opened in 1601, as well as demonstrations of the Sado folk dance and song. In addition, there are numerous historical landmarks in connection with exiles in the medieval age, including such celebrated persons as Nichiren (1222-82), founder of the Nichiren sect of Buddhism; Zeami (1363-1443), a Noh actor and playwright exiled because of his confrontation with other Noh authorities; and Emperor Juntoku (1197-1242), who tried to restore imperial rule during the time of the Kamakura shogunate (1185-1336). ⇨ NICHIRENSHŪ, NŌ

〖注〗 point of interest 見どころ．scenic site 風光明媚な地．the Sotokaifu coast 外海府海岸．remains of gold mine 金鉱跡．Sado folk dance and song 佐渡おけさ．historical landmark 史跡．exile 流刑(に処する)．celebrated 有名な，著名な．playwright 劇作家．

Saga-nishiki 佐賀錦 Saga brocade weave; brocade developed in the Saga district of Kyūshū. Beautiful patterns are woven by inserting the weft strip through the warp, traditionally by hand. The warp is of threads made from gold and silver; the weft is of silk yarn in gold, silver or other colors. This brocade is used for bags, purses, *zōri* (sandals worn with kimono), *obi* (a sash for kimono), etc. ⇨ NISHIKI-ORI

〖注〗 brocade 錦．textile 織物．weft 横糸．warp 縦糸．

Saikai Kokuritsu-kōen 西海国立公園 Saikai National Park (246.5 square kilometers), designated in 1955; a natural park situated in Nagasaki Prefecture, in northwestern Kyūshū. This park embraces the northwestern coast of the Matsuura Peninsula and some 350 islands. The Gotō Islands consist of five large islands and some 150 small ones, and the Kujūku (lit. 99) Islands which comprise nearly 200 volcanic islets. This park is characterized by subtropical vegetation, rugged coastlines and rich fishing grounds. Close to the park area on the peninsula lies Sasebo City, a naval base since 1886, and on Hirado Island is Hirado City, though not belonging to this park, which was the first port to be opened to foreign traders in the mid-16th century. ⇨ KOKURITSU-KŌEN, KYŪ-SHŪ

〖注〗 subtropical vegetation 亜熱帯植物. rugged coastline リアス式海岸. fishing ground 漁場. naval base 海軍基地.

saikeirei 最敬礼 the most deep bow; a polite bow made by bending at the hips. Formerly, especially during World War II, the people of the nation were required to make a *saikeirei* to the emperor or his portrait to show their loyalty. ⇨ OJIGI, TENNŌ

〖注〗 loyalty 忠義, 忠誠.

saisen 賽銭 money offerings; money, usually coins, offered to a shrine or a temple. Before praying at a shrine or a temple, people toss an offering into the offertory chest placed in front of the oratory. ⇨ SAISENBAKO

〖注〗 offering お供え, 奉納(物). toss 投げる. offertory chest 賽銭箱. oratory 拝殿.

saisenbako 賽銭箱 an offertory box; a rectangular wooden chest, usually topped with bars, for money offerings, which is placed in front of the oratory at a shrine or a temple. Before praying to the deity, people toss in a small offering, generally coins, into this chest. ⇨ SAISEN

〖注〗 offertory 献金, 奉納. offering 奉納(物), 供え物. oratory 拝殿. deity 神, 神のような人[物]. toss 投げる.

sake 酒 Japanese rice wine; a clear alcoholic beverage made from fermented rice and water. Saké has an alcoholic content of 18 to 19 percent. It is usually drunk warm at about 50 degrees C., although some prefer it cold. At the table it is served before the rice course, together with various dishes, in a small ceramic bottle (*tokkuri*) and then poured into a small saké cup (*sakazuki* or *choku*). Like wine in French cooking, saké is also used as a seasoning for soups and boiled dishes. Unlike Western alcoholic beverages, however, it can rarely be preserved for over a year.

Today, saké is officially categorized into three grades: *tokkyū-shu* (special grade), *ikkyū-shu* (first grade) and *nikyū-shu* (second grade). Saké is believed to have first appeared in the Nara period (646–794). ⇨ CHOKU

〖注〗 alcoholic beverage アルコール飲料. ferment 発酵した. alcoholic content アルコール含有料. seasoning 調味料.

sakekasu 酒糟 rice-wine lees; the residue left after saké (rice wine) is made. It is used for pickling vegetables or preserving fish. Such vegetables and fish are called *kasuzuke* ⇨ SAKE

〖注〗 rice wine 日本酒. lees (酒などの)糟. residue 残りかす. pickle 漬ける.

sakoku(-seisaku) 鎖国(政策) the policy of national seclusion; national isolation policy; the seclusion policy imposed from 1638 to 1853 by the Tokugawa shogunate government (1603–1868) in an attempt to unify the nation. Influence on the people by Catholic missionaries and traders from Spain triggered the shogunate fear of a Spanish invasion. Thus, the third shogun, Tokugawa Iemitsu (1604–51), officially closed the country to all foreigners except for a limited number of Chinese and Dutch traders; the Dutch were allowed to reside only at Dejima located at the western tip of Kyūshū. The Japanese were not allowed to have any interest in foreign countries or their cultures for nearly two and a half centuries until the arrival of Commodore Perry from the United States. As one result, peace during this long period permitted the development of Japan's own culture. ⇨ DEJIMA, NICHIBEI SHŪKO TSŪSHŌ JŌYAKU, NICHIBEI WASHIN JŌYAKU, TOKUGAWA-BAKUFU

〖注〗 national seclusion 国の隔離, 鎖国. impose 課す. trigger 引き金となる, 原因となる. commodore 提督, 艦長.

sakura-mochi 桜餅 a cherry-blossom sweet; a pinkish ball of glutinous rice, filled with sweet bean-paste, and wrapped in a cherry leaf, fresh or brined. The cherry leaf is edible. This sweet is enjoyed for its color and fragrance in the cherry-blossom season. ⇨ AN, MOCHI

〖注〗 glutinous rice 糯米. sweet bean-paste 餡. brine 塩水につける. fragrance 芳香.

sakura-zensen 桜前線 the cherry-blossom front; the front of the blooming of cherry blossoms, moving from south to north through Japan. The front appears in the southern part of the country at the end of March, passes through the central part around the beginning of April, and moves northward. This indicates the coming of the height of spring in each region. The national flower of Japan, the cherry blossom is appreciated by the people with special affection, partly because of the short life of its bloom, lasting for only a few days. The time of cherry blossoms is symbolic of children's entering school.   ⇨ HANAMI

samisen 三味線   ⇨ SHAMISEN

sanbō 三方   lit. three sides.   a wooden tray stand; a square tray stand made of unpainted Japanese cypress wood with four supporting panels under the tray.   Three of the sides—the front, right and left—have cut-out patterns.   The tray is used for placing offerings to Buddhist and Shinto deities, and for presenting gifts in ceremonies conducted in the context of Shintoism, such as betrothal gift exchanges.   Formerly gifts offered to nobles and superiors were customarily placed on such a tray.   ⇨ SHINTŌ, YUINŌ

〖注〗 unpainted Japanese cypress 白木の檜. cut-out patterns 切り抜き模様. offering 奉納(物)，供え物. deity 神，神のような人[もの]. betrothal gift exchange 結納.

sanganichi 三が日   the first three days of the year; holidays for New Year celebration.   Most people do not engage in business during this period, but spend the days visiting shrines to pray for good luck for the new year, exchanging greetings among friends and relatives, enjoying specially prepared foods, playing New Year games, etc., although January 1 is the only day of this period recognized as a national holiday.   ⇨ GANJITSU

sangen 三弦[三絃]   ⇨ SHAMISEN

San'in-kaigan Kokuritsu-kōen 山陰海岸国立公園   San'in Coast National Park (90 square kilometers), designated in 1963; a natural park extending some 77 kilometers along the Japan Sea coast, from Amino in Kyoto Prefecture to the Tottori Sand Dunes in Tottori Prefecture.   The coast offers scenic variety with bays, inlets, caves, rocky cliffs and sand dunes.   Black pines are distinctive feature of the area.   ⇨ KOKURITSU-KŌEN

〖注〗 Amino 網野. the Tottori Sand Dunes 鳥取砂丘.

sanjaku(-obi) 三尺(帯)   a kimono waistband; an unsewn *obi* of soft material such as silk crepe.   It is often decorated with white dapple patterns made by tie-dyeing.   It is worn by men, or young boys and girls with ordinary everyday kimono.   ⇨ CHIRIMEN, KIMONO, OBI

〖注〗 unsewn 縫っていない. silk crepe 縮緬. dapple patterns 班点模様、ま
だら模様. tie-dyeing 結び染め、しぼり染め.

sanjūnotō 三重の塔 a three-storied pagoda; a three-storied tower-
like structure erected in the precincts of a Buddhist temple. It is
made of wood with three tiled roofs placed one above the other.
The ashes or relics of Buddha or Buddhist saints are enshrined in
the foundation stone or in an altar on the first floor. The Japanese
pagoda is said to be a transformed grave marker, with its origins
tracing back to the Indian stupa. The famous three-story pagoda
of Yakushiji Temple, Nara, may appear to have six-stories, with
smaller eaves protruding under each of the three roofs. ➪ GARAN,
GOJŪNOTŌ, TERA, TŌ

〖注〗 pagoda (東洋の)塔. precincts 境内. one above the other 上に重なり
合って. relics 遺物. enshrine 祀る. altar 祭壇. grave marker 墓標.
trace back to ～にさかのぼる、～にまでたどる. stupa 仏舎利塔、卒塔婆.
eaves 軒. protrude 突き出す、はみ出る.

sankinkōtai 参勤交代 alternate attendance; the system of alternate
residence of feudal lords in Edo, enforced from 1635 to 1862. For
the purpose of controlling feudal lords across the country, the
Tokugawa shogunate compelled them to reside both in Edo and in
their domains alternately for a specified length of time, usually a
year or two, making their wives and children live in Edo as
hostages. Feudal lords headed for Edo with long processions of
retainers to domonstrate their power. People encountering such a
procession were required to make a deep bow on the ground. This
system eventually caused financial difficulty for the feudal lords,
due to tremendously accumulating expenses for traveling for many
days back and forth. ➪ DAIMYŌ, TOKUGAWA-BAKUFU

〖注〗 alternate 交代性の. attendance 奉仕、近侍. feudal lord 大名. the
Tokugawa shogunate 徳川幕府. domain 領地. retainer 家来、家臣.

sankyoku 三曲 lit. trio music. the trio ensemble of *koto* and
shamisen [*sangen*] music with the addition of a third melodic
instrument, usually the *shakuhachi*. ➪ KOTO, SHAKUHACHI, SHAMI-
SEN

〖注〗 trio 三つ組の. ensemble 合奏、合唱.

sanninzukai 三人遣い a trio of puppeteers consisting of *omozukai*
(a head manipulator), *hidarizukai* (a left-arm manipulator) and
ashizukai (a leg manipulator). They work as a team in manipulat-
ing a single Bunraku puppet. ➪ ASAHIZUKAI, HIDARIZUKAI, OMOZU-

KAI

〖注〗 puppeteer 人形遣い. manipulator 操る人.

Sanriku chihō 三陸地方   the Sanriku region; a region on the Pacific side of northern Honshū. Formerly, Sanriku referred to the provinces of Mutsu, Rikuchū and Rikuzen in northern Honshū. Today, the area comprising Aomori, Iwate and Miyagi prefectures is called Sanriku *chihō*. Much of the coast of this area, with its varied scenic beauty, is included in Rikuchū Coast National Park.
⇨ HONSHŪ, RIKUCHŪ-KAIGAN KOKURITSU-KŌEN

〖注〗 province 地方の諸国, (行政目的で分けた)国.

sansankudo 三三九度   lit. three-by-three, or nine times. the saké-drinking ritual in a traditional Shinto wedding ceremony. The bride and bridegroom take three sips each of rice wine from three lacquered saké-cups of different sizes, nine times in all. This signifies the nuptial pledge between the two in the presence of a Shinto god. ⇨ SHINTŌ

〖注〗 ritual 儀式. nuptial pledge 結婚の誓い.

sanshō 山椒   Japanese peppertree; toothache tree; pepper made from the nut and leaves of the toothache tree. The powder is used to garnish barbecued eels, etc. The fresh leaves are used in clear soups, and vinegared or seasoned foods.

〖注〗 Japanese peppertree 山椒. toothache tree 山椒属の木. garnish つまを添える. barbecued eel 鰻の蒲焼. vinegared or seasoned foods 酢の物や和物.

Sanshu no Jingi 三種の神器   the Three Divine Treasures; the Three Regalia of the Japanese Imperial Throne. They are the Sacred Mirror (*Yata no Kagami*), the Comma-Shaped Gem (*magatama*) and the Grass-Cutting Sword (*Kusanagi no Tsurugi*). Japanese mythology says that Amaterasu Ōmikami (the Sun Goddess) bestowed the three regalia on her grandson Ninigi no Mikoto as tokens of his mission to rule the Japanese islands when he descended from heaven. History relates that these three objects have been passed down through the centuries to the present emperor from Ninigi no Mikoto's grandson, the first emperor Jinmu, and have often been cited to prove that the line of emperors has been maintained, unbroken, since antiquity. ⇨ KUSANAGI NO TSURUGI, MAGATAMA, YATA NO KAGAMI

〖注〗 regalia 王位の標章. imperial throne 皇位. the Sacred Mirror 八咫の鏡. the Comma-Shaped Gem 勾[曲]玉. the Grass-Cutting Sword 草薙の剣.

bestow 授ける. token しるし. mission 使命.

sansui 山水   lit. mountains and water. a landscape; the scenic beauty of mountains and rivers. This phrase has multiple connotations in landscape painting, landscape gardening, etc., symbolizing the multiplicity and vastness of nature with such a simple expression.   ⇨ NIHON-TEIEN, SANSUIGA

〖注〗 connotation 含蓄, 意味合い. multiplicity of nature 森羅万象.

sansuiga 山水画   lit. pictures of mountains and water. monochromatic paintings of landscape. This style of painting first flourished in the Muromachi period (1336-1568), influenced in terms of technique and scheme by Chinese artists of the Sung dynasty (960-1279). The brush work owes much to the techniques of calligraphy, with bold stylized lines and the effect of gradated shades of black and white. The pictures thus drawn do not reproduce landscapes photographically, but rather attempt to represent the grandeur of nature. Human figures, if any, are depicted as small and insignificant beside awesome landscapes. The two most distinguished *sansuiga* painters were Shūbun (?-?1450) and Sesshū (1420-1506), the former largely influenced by the Chinese style and the latter cultivating a uniquely Japanese style.   ⇨ FUDE, SHODŌ, SUIBOKUGA, SUMIE

〖注〗 monochromatic 単色の. scheme 構図. the Sung dynasty 宋朝. brush work 筆の扱い. calligraphy 書道. stylized 様式化した. gradated shades ぼかした濃淡. human figure 人物(像). Shūbun (天章)周文. Sesshū 雪舟(等陽).

sarakin サラ金   lit. salaried men's financing. loan-sharking; a consumer financing business which provides cash at high interest rates to individuals without security or mortgage. Replacing premodern pawnshops at street corners, these firms offer emergency financing mainly to salaried workers and housewives with modest incomes, at tremendously high interest rates through a loophole in the law restricting interest rates. They often resorted to harsh means in collecting the money back. The ease of borrowing cash without security promoted the rapid growth of this industry in the early 1980s, causing tragedy for a number of ignorant overborrowers (called "loan-shark hell"). Thus, the Sarakin Control Law was enacted in November 1983, providing the ceiling of 73 percent per annum on interest rates until 1986, restrictions on collection methods, etc.

〖注〗 financing 融資. shark 鮫, 高利貸しをする, 詐欺をする. interest rate 利子率. security 保証, 担保. mortgage 抵当. pawnshop 質屋. modest income 少ない収入. loophole in the law 法律の抜穴. loan-shark hell 借金地獄. the Sarakin Control Law「サラ金規制法」. enact 施行する. per annum 一年につき. restrictions on collection methods 集金方法の規制.

sarugaku 猿楽 lit. monkey music. a prototype of the Noh drama and the Kyogen farce. It is a form of entertainment of great antiquity —perhaps dating back to the 10th century —which seems to have been a lively mixture of song and dance combined with a certain amount of humorous mimicry and remarks. With a dramatic element gradually added, it came to form one of the bases of the Noh drama.   ⇨ KYŌGEN, NO

〖注〗 prototype 原型. farce 道化芝居, 笑劇. of great antiquity 大昔からの. mimicry まね, 模倣. remark せりふ, 寸言.

Sarukani Kassen 猿蟹合戦 *The Battle Between the Monkey and the Crab*; the story of the crab's revenge, one of Japan's five most famous folk tales. A monkey trades his persimmon seed for a crab's rice ball. When the seed grows into a tree full of ripe persimmons, the monkey comes along to eat the sweet fruit and throws green ones at the crab, who gets seriously injured. The crab's children, with the help of their friends—chestnuts, a mortar and hornets—take revenge on the monkey and make him apologize. The original story appeared in the late Muromachi period (16th century).

〖注〗 folk tale 民話. persimmon seed 柿の種. rice ball お握り. mortar 臼. hornet 大蜂.

sasadango 笹団子 a dumpling wrapped in bamboo leaves. The dumpling is made by steaming powdered glutinous rice with minced moxa (mugwort) leaves mixed in, and has a filling of sweet red-bean paste. The large dried leaves of bamboo grass used for wrapping give the dumpling fragrance and help preserve it. This is a specialty of Niigata Prefecture.   ⇨ AN

〖注〗 dumpling 団子. powdered glutinous rice 糯米の粉. minced moxa こまかく切ったよもぎ. mugwort よもぎの一種. filling つめもの. sweet red-bean paste あずき餡. specialty 特産物.

sashiko 刺し子 quilting or quilted materials; cloth patterned with stitching. The most common is indigo cotton cloth with repeated patterns made by stitching with white threads. Quilting gives the material warmth, strength and durability as well as beauty. Such needlework originally developed in Takayama, deep in the mountains of Gifu Prefecture, where fine textiles were rarely available. The patterned stitching on judo outfits (white stitching on white cloth) is one type of *sashiko*.

〖注〗 indigo 藍(色). durability 耐久性. outfit 服装, 服装一式.

sashimi 刺身 sliced raw fish. It is served on a plate artistically arranged with garnishes such as shredded white radish, seaweed, fragrant leaves, etc., and eaten by dipping it in a small dish of soy sauce mixed with horseradish (*wasabi*) or ginger. Among many kinds of fish served in this way, some of the most popular are tuna, seabream, flatfish, bonito, lobstar, cuttlefish, etc. Raw fish is sliced in different ways to bring out different flavors: *hirazukuri* (slicing it flat, about one centimeter thick and several cm long), which is the most common; *sogizukuri* (scraping it into very thin pieces); *kakuzukuri* (cutting it into cubes); *kawazukuri* (slicing retaining the skin), *ikezukuri* (slicing of a living fish), etc. ⇨ IKEZUKURI, WASABI

〖注〗 garnish (料理の)つま. shredded white radish 大根を細く切ったもの. seaweed 海藻. fragrant leaves 香りのある葉(しそなど). seabream 鯛. flatfish 平目. bonito 鰹. cuttlefish いか.

Satsuma-jōfu 薩摩上布 Satsuma ramie fabric; fabric made from ramie, produced at the southern tip of Kyūshū, around the area formerly called Satsuma Province. The material is woven into a thin fabric with splashed patterns—white patterns on indigo, or indigo patterns on white. It is one of the most desired and expensive fabrics for making summer kimono. ⇨ JŌFU, KIMONO

〖注〗 ramie からまし, まお, アジア産イラクサ科マオ属の低木(皮から繊維をとる). fabric 織物. splashed patterns かすり模様. indigo 藍.

Satsuma-yaki 薩摩焼 Satsuma ceramic ware; a cream-colored variety of pottery produced in the Satsuma district of Kyūshū since around the end of the 16th century. It was originally decorated with monochrome glazes, and later with overglaze enamels and gilding.

〖注〗 ceramic ware 陶器(製品). pottery 陶器(類). monochrome 単色, 白黒. glaze 釉, つや. overglaze (陶磁器の)二重塗り, 重ね塗り. enamel (陶磁器の)上薬[釉]. gilding 金箔張り.

sawari 触り[佐和利] lit. touch. an emotional point which borders on pathos, expressed not by words but by psychological description. This technique is very effectively used when accompanied by *jōruri* music in a Bunraku puppet play or a Kabuki play of Bunraku puppet origin. Also the term is used for the buzzing sound of the strings on a *biwa*, which is imitated by the *shamisen*. ⇨ BIWA, BUNRAKU, JŌRURI, KABUKI, SHAMISEN

〖注〗 pathos 情緒, あわれを感じさせる力. accompany 伴う, 伴奏する. puppet 操り人形. buzz ぶんぶんいう, 低い震動音をたてる. string 弦.

seibo 歳暮 a year-end gift; gifts sent as a token of gratitude in return for special favors received over the year or in the past. The Japanese seek to clear all matters of the old year before the advent of the new one, including obligations or appreciation. Formerly they expressed thanks for past favors in person with a small gift. In some districts, there was a custom of presenting fish or rice cakes to a daughter-in-law's parents for an inquiry about health at the year's end. In recent years, boosted by commercialism and taking advantage of the bonus paid around this time of the year, this practice has become increasingly lavish. *Seibo* are sent not only by individuals but also by businesses to retain firm ties. More commonly called *oseibo*. ⇨ CHŪGEN

〖注〗 token of gratitude 感謝のしるし. clear 片づける, 後始末をする. obligation 恩. boost あおる, 奨励する. lavish ぜいたくな, 華やかな. retain firm tie 固い絆を保つ.

seii-taishōgun 征夷大将軍 lit. a great general to subdue barbarians. generalissimo; general. 1) First given to Ōtomo Otomaro in 794, this title was granted to those generals who were sent to northern Honshū to subdue the Ezo race (presumably the Ainus) or rebellions. It was eliminated after 811. 2) Without reference to its original meaning, this title was granted to Minamoto Yoritomo (1147-99) by Emperor Gotoba (1180-1239) when he established the Kamakura shogunate (1185-1336). Thereafter, the head of military governments took this title, but were more commonly called shogun. The Minamoto, Ashikaga and Tokugawa families in succession held power under this title until the Meiji Restoration (1868). ⇨ ASHIKAGA-BAKUFU, KAMAKURA-BAKUFU, SHŌGUN, TOKUGAWA-BAKUFU

〖注〗 subdue 征服する, 鎮圧する. barbarian 異民族. Ōtomo Otomaro 大伴弟麻呂. rebellion 反乱者. the Kamakura shogunate 鎌倉幕府. the Meiji Restoration 明治維新.

seiji 青磁 celadon porcelain ware; green ceramics with a glassy glaze. It is thick and often has relief designs under the glaze.

Celadon ware originated in China, and pieces made during the T'ang (618–907) and Sung (960–1279) dynasties are most highly valued. Generally, Chinese celadon are sage green or gray green and have large crackles, while Japanese ones are pure or bluish green and are seldom crackled. ⇨ HAKUJI

〖注〗 celadon 淡緑色，灰青色，青磁．porcelain ware 磁器(製品)．glassy glaze 透明な釉．relief design 浮き彫り模様．the T'ang dynasty 唐朝．the Sung dynasty 宋朝．crackles ひび，ひび模様．

Seijin no Hi 成人の日 Coming-of-Age Day (January 15); a national holiday, designated after World War II to honor youths who have reached the age of 20 since the previous January 15. Their communities honor them with a ceremony on this day. At the age of 20, youths gain the right to vote and are allowed to drink and smoke. On the other hand, they are officially regarded as adults with responsibilities in society. ⇨ KOKUMIN NO SHUKUJITSU

Sekigahara no Tatakai 関ヶ原の戦い the Battle of Sekigahara (1600); the decisive battle fought at Sekigahara, in present-day Gifu Prefecture, between Tokugawa Ieyasu (1542–1616) and vassals of the deceased Toyotomi Hideyoshi (1536–98), which eventually led to the establishment of Tokugawa's supremacy. After the death of Hideyoshi, his son Hideyori (1593–1615) took over, but power was actually held by Ishida Mitsunari (1560–1600), one of Hideyoshi's close retainers. He feared Ieyasu as a threat to the Toyotomi family and attempted to overthrow him. The battle divided the country, with most feudal lords throughout the country taking sides. The battle resulted in a decisive victory for Ieyasu's force of 80,000 men (called the East Army) over the larger force of 130,000 men of Mitsunari's (called the West Army). ⇨ DAIMYŌ, TOKUGAWA-BAKUFU

〖注〗 decisive battle 天下分け目の戦い．vassal 臣下，家臣．supremacy 主権，覇権．take over 受け継ぐ．retainer 家来，家臣．feudal lord 大名．

sekihan 赤飯 red-bean rice; rice steamed together with red beans, which is prepared for auspicious occasions such as festivals and birthdays. The red beans give the white rice a reddish-pink coloring, the color of joy. Both regular rice and glutinous rice can be used, the latter being also called *okowa*.

〖注〗 red bean あずき．prepare 調理する．auspicious occasion めでたい機会．glutinous rice 糯米．

sekimori-ishi 関守石 a barrier stone; a stone placed on a stepping stone here and there in a Japanese tea garden. It is a small, round, fist-sized stone tied with straw cord in the shape of a cross. When a tea ceremony is to be held, the stone is used to indicate to guests seeking the teahouse that it is the wrong direction. ⇨ CHANOYU, CHASHITSU, CHATEI

〖注〗 barrier 障害, 関門. stepping stone 飛び石. fist-sized こぶし大の. straw cord 縄. tea ceremony 茶の湯.

sekitei 石庭 a rock garden; a garden made of rocks and sand, which symbolize mountains and rivers in a natural landscape. Ryōanji Temple has a world-famous rock garden, composed of only white sand and 15 stones, which is symbolic of Zen Buddhism. ⇨ KA-RESANSUI(-TEIEN), NIHON-TEIEN, ZEN¹, ZENSHŪ

sekitori 関取 *sumō* wrestlers of the *makuuchi* and *jūryō* divisions. In the hierarchical society of *sumō*, there exists a distinct difference in terms of treatment and privileges between *sekitori* and wrestlers of lower rank. *Sekitori* receive salaries while other wrestlers receive money in the form of allowance from their stable-masters. In the ring they are allowed to tie their hair in an elegantly puffed-out ginkgo-leaf knot (*ōicho-mage*) and wear silk loincloths (*tori-mawashi*), while lower-ranking wrestlers are restricted to simply tied top-knots and black cotton loincloths. Outside of the ring the lower-ranking wrestlers must tend to their stablemate *sekitori* and perform all kinds of chores, from helping the *sekitori* with their loincloths to preparing meals. Thus, becoming a *sekitori* and maintaining this status is considered a primary goal in *sumō*. ⇨ JŪRYŌ, MAKUUCHI, SUMŌ, SUMŌBEYA

〖注〗 hierarchical society 序列社会. allowance 手当, 小遣い. stable-master 親方. ginkgo-leaf knot 大銀杏髷. loincloth 取り回し. top-knot 丁髷. stablemate 部屋仲間. chores 雑用.

sekku 節句 a seasonal festival; originally indicating the five representative festive days coming with the seasons, also called "*go-sekku*" (five festive days). The five are the Day of the Young Herbs (*Wakana no Sekku*) falling on January 7, Girls' Festival (*Hina Matsuri* or *Momo no Sekku*) on March 3, Boys' Festival (*Tango no Sekku*) on May 5 (now Children's Day), Star Festival (*Tanabata Matsuri*) on July 7, and Chrysanthemum Festival (*Kiku no Sekku*) on September 9. The custom of observing these festivals dates back to the early Tokugawa period; the Girls' Festival, Boys' Festival and Star Festival are still widely celebrated today.

⇨ HINA MATSURI, MOMO NO SEKKU, TANABATA MATSURI, TANGO NO SEKKU

【注】 festive day 祭日，節句．　date back to（ある時期から）始まる，さかのぼる．　五節句：若菜の節句，桃の節句［雛祭り］，端午の節句，七夕祭り，菊の節句．

sen 銭　sen, the minor monetary unit of Japan; 100th of one yen. It used to be minted, but is no longer in circulation. Today, this unit is used in the calculation of interest, exchange rates, etc. Idiomatic expressions using the term *sen* still survive, rather than the term yen, as in "to spend every *sen*," "It's not worth a mere one *sen*," etc.　⇨ EN

【注】 monetary unit お金の単位．　in circulation 流通している．　interest rate 利息の率．　exchange rate 為替レート．

senbazuru 千羽鶴　one thousand paper cranes; a string of a thousand folded paper cranes, popularly used as a gift in praying for someone's recovery from illness. Each crane is made with square, colored pieces of paper without using scissors or paste. A thousand or so cranes are fitted on a string in the fashion of a lei. The crane is a symbol of celebration and longevity, and thus the *senbazuru* symbolizes a thousand prayers or prayers from myriad well-wishers.　⇨ ORIGAMI, TSURU-KAME

【注】 folded (paper) crane 折り鶴．　fit on うまくはめる，うまくつなぐ．　lei レイ（首にかける花などをつないだ輪）．　longevity 長寿．　well-wisher 幸福を祈る人．

senbei 煎餅　Japanese crackers; sweetened or salted crackers made from wheat flour or rice. There are roughly two kinds. One type is made from wheat flour, mixed with sugar, eggs, spices, seasonings, etc. The dough is pressed flat in iron molds, and baked. The other is made from rice, either rice cakes or steamed rice flour. Dried and baked to a crisp, the crackers are seasoned with salt or spiced soy sauce, and dried by baking them again. Some are wrapped in seaweed laver. The kinds composed of small cubes or pellets are also called *arare*, meaning "hail." The size and shape of *senbei* vary greatly from locality to locality.　⇨ MOCHI, NORI

【注】 seaweed laver 海苔．　pellet 小球．

sencha 煎茶　lit. infused tea.　green tea leaves of medium grade and medium size. (Tea leaves come in a wide range of grades and sizes.) Boiling-hot water is not used to steep the tea leaves. Instead, boiled water is kept in the kettle or placed in a ceramic

container until it cools to about 80 degrees C, before it is poured
over the leaves in a teapot.   It is steeped for half a minute or so.
To use the leaves a second time, the tea must be drained to the last
drop.   Tea of the first serving is sweet; on the second serving, it is
bitter yet tasty.   *Sencha* is the most commonly used tea in everyday life and is also appropriate for guests.   ⇨ CHA, RYOKUCHA

〚注〛 infused 煎じた. steep 浸す. drain 水をきる.

Sengoku-jidai 戦国時代   the Civil War Age (1467-1568); the period
of continuous civil wars during the latter half of the Ashikaga
shogunate (1336-1568).   Disturbances began with the Ōnin Revolt
(1467-77) which broke out in Kyoto in connection with succession
problems of the Ashikaga shogunate, and continued for about a
century, with the country divided up among provincial rulers.   In
1573, Oda Nobunaga (1534-82) terminated the long civil wars and
restored order to the country.   However, it was Toyotomi Hideyoshi (1536-98), one of his vassals, who actually unified the country
in 1590, since Nobunaga suffered a revolt by another vassal in
which he met his end.   ⇨ ASHIKAGA-BAKUFU

〚注〛 civil wars 内戦. the Ashikaga shogunate 足利幕府. disturbance 動
乱, 混乱. the Ōnin Revolt 応仁の乱. succession problem 継承問題. provincial 地方諸国の. vassal 臣下.

Senju Kannon 千手観音   the Thousand-Handed Kannon Bodhisattva; the Deity of Mercy having 1,000 hands with an eye on the
palm of each hand.   The hands and eyes are believed to have the
power to save human beings with the hands signifying "countless
gracious acts" and the eyes "powers to illuminate countless
affairs."   The statues in Tōshōdaiji and Fujiidera temples, made in
the Nara period (646-794), have exactly 1,000 hands.   The ones
made in later years have only 40 besides the main two hands, but
each hand is said to save 25 people or 25 situations—therefore,
making the total 1,000 (40 × 25), which also signifies countless-
ness.   ⇨ BOSATSU, KANNON (BOSATSU)

〚注〛 bodhisattva 菩薩. the Deity of Mercy 観音. countless gracious acts
無限の慈悲. illuminate 照らす.

Senke 千家   the Sen family; the Senke schools of tea ceremony, with
their origins in the great tea master Sen no Rikyū (1521-91).
After the death of Rikyū, during the generation of his grandsons,
the way of tea split into the three Senke schools (called *San
Senke*): the Omote Senke, Ura Senke and Mushanokōji Senke

schools. The first two are the leading schools of tea ceremony even today. ⇨ CHANOYU, SADŌ, WABICHA

〚注〛 tea ceremony 茶の湯． tea master 茶人，茶の師匠． leading school 代表的流派．

senmon-gakkō 専門学校 1)（since 1976）a higher special training school; a private vocational institution offering college-level courses in specialized fields（computer, foreign language, etc.）, authorized by the Ministry of Education. This is one of the three types of courses among special training schools（*senshū-gakkō*）inaugurated in 1976 under a 1975 amendment to the School Education Law（1947）. 2)（in the prewar school system）a training college; a higher professional school; professional or technical academic institutions ranking below the university. Those who graduated from middle school（*chūgakkō*）and girls' high school（*jogakkō*）were entitled to apply for an additional three years of study. With the postwar school reform, most of these training colleges became four-year colleges and universities. ⇨ CHŪGAK-KŌ, GAKKO KYŌIKUHŌ, KŌTŌ-JOGAKKŌ, SENSHŪ-GAKKŌ

〚注〛 vocational 職業的な，職業教育の． institution 機関． special training school 専修学校． inaugurate 開始する． amendment 法改正． the School Education Law「学校教育法」． be entitled to ～する権利がある，～する資格がある．

senpai 先輩 a senior（person）; superiors among those who belong to a group. Customarily, a person who has started a career or activity earlier and achieved a degree of respect is expected to teach his juniors（*kōhai*）strictly but affectionately in the manner of a big brother. The juniors, as subordinates, are expected to show respect for their seniors. Such a vertical relationship may develop among those who share a feeling of belonging, such as to a school, and is especially evident in club activities. Very often seniors and juniors remain interdependent even after they graduate from school.

〚注〛 subordinate 部下． vertical relationship 縦関係． feeling of belonging 所属感． interdependent 相互依存的．

senryū 川柳 a short humorous poem; a humorous or witty 17-sylla-ble verse, usually composed in colloquial language. It is often ironical in nature, revealing the foibles of people and society, but provoking laughter. Unlike haiku, also a 17-syllable verse, *senryū* does not have a seasonal aspect. Around the middle of 18th century, *senryū* flourished among the townspeople, Karai Senryū (1718–90) being a representative composer. ⇨ HAIKAI, HAIKU

〖注〗 verse 詩. ironical 風刺的な, 皮肉な. foible 弱点, うぬぼれている点. provoke 刺激する, ひきおこす. Karai Senryū 柄井川柳.

senshū-gakkō 専修学校 a special training school; private vocational institutes authorized by the Ministry of Education. These institutes were inaugurated in 1976 under a 1975 amendment to the School Education Law (1947), in addition to those schools already defined by this law. The courses are classified into three types: the upper secondary course, the advanced or college course, and the general subject course (preparatory for a college-level course). Schools offering upper secondary-level courses are known as *kōtō senshū-gakkō* (lit. vocational high school) and those offering college-level courses as *senmon-gakkō* (lit. professional school). Private institutes that do not meet required standards are called *kakushu-gakkō* (miscellaneous school). ⇨ GAKKŌ, KYŌIKUHŌ, SENMON-GAKKŌ

〖注〗 vocational 職業的, 職業教育の. institute 訓練機関, 専門学校. inaugurate 開始する. amendment 法改正. the School Education Law「学校教育法」. upper secondary course 高等学校の程度に応ずる高等課程. advanced or college course 大学の程度に応ずる専門課程. general subject course 一般課程. preparatory 準備の. required standard 要求にかなった規準. miscellaneous school 各種学校.

sensu 扇子 a folding fan; a fan made of paper pasted on a thin split-bamboo frame. It can be folded into the shape of a stick. When unfolded, it has a semi-circular shape. On the paper is drawn a picture or calligraphy. It is used not only for fanning oneself in summer, but also a symbol of friendship, respect or good wishes. Formerly a *sensu* was often given to a friend embarking on a trip. It is still exchanged as one of the traditional engagement gifts. When invited to a tea ceremony, one is expected to carry a very small folding fan of a type used exclusively for the occasion. ⇨ CHANOYU, ŌGI

〖注〗 split-bamboo frame 割竹の枠. semi-cirlular shape 半円の形. calligraphy 書道. embark 出発する, 始める. engagement gift 結納品. tea ceremony 茶道.

sentō 銭湯 lit. a pay bath. a public bathhouse. Public bathhouses become particularly popular in the Edo period (1603–1868) in the town of Edo where commoners were not allowed to have private baths due to the fear of fires. They also served as gathering places where townsfolk could chat with friends and strangers. Even today, though most homes have private baths, some prefer going to a public bath to enjoy the ample water there and to chat. A bathhouse can easily be identified by its huge chimney rising high above the surrounding houses. It is divided into two parts, one for men and the other for women, with a dressing room and bathing room in each. The bathing room is equipped with a large, deep tub usually designed for more than a dozen people, smaller tubs with medicinal water, and a series of hot and cold taps on the wall, as well as a washing area. As in private Japanese-style baths, one must thoroughly wash and rinse the body before getting into the tub of hot water. No soaping is permitted in the tub. ⇨ FURO

〖注〗 townsfolk 町人. dressing room 脱衣所, 着替え室. medicinal 薬効のある, (病気を)いやす. tap 水道の蛇口.

seppuku 切腹 lit. cutting the belly. ceremonial suicide by cutting the abdomen. This was formerly, especially in feudal times, committed by samurai when dishonored or condemned to death. For samurai an execution was considered a disgrace; thus *seppuku* was viewed as an honorable way of dying. With a dagger or a sword, the person would rip open his abdomen, an assistant cutting off his head to terminate his suffering. The *seppuku* of the 47 loyal retainers in 1703 is one of the most well-known examples: they were compelled to commit *seppuku* shortly after avenging the death of their master. In 1970, an internationally renowned novelist Yukio Mishima (1925-70) committed this ritual suicide in public, attributable to his failure to restore the absolute place of the emperor and Japan's old samurai values, as well as his possessed aesthetic concept about death. ⇨ HARAKIRI

〖注〗 belly 腹部. feudal times 封建時代. condemn to death 死刑に処す. execution 処刑. disgrace 不名誉. dagger 短剣. rip open 切り開く. the rite of cutting off his head 介錯. retainer 家臣. avenge あだを討つ. aesthetic concept 美意識.

seriage 迫り上げ a movable platform on a Kabuki stage. It is a small platform on which an actor is raised onto or lowered from the stage. Sometimes this platform raises a group of actors from beneath the stage. ⇨ KABUKI

〖注〗 platform 高台.

sesshō 摂政 a regent or regency; a regent for an emperor who is still a minor or who is in ill health, or for a female sovereign. Prince Shōtoku (574-622) is regarded as the first real *sesshō,* serving his aunt, Empress Suiko (554-628, r. 592-628). Fujiwara Yoshifusa (804-72) acted as the first regent from outside the imperial family. The next regent, Fujiwara Mototsune (836-891), who served the young emperor Yōzei (r. 876-84), retained this position even after the emperor came of age, assuming the title of *kanpaku* (chief adviser of an adult emperor). Thereafter, both the *kanpaku* and *sesshō* positions were held by descendants of Mototsune until the Meiji Restoration (1868), although their political power declined after the Heian period (794-1185). The Imperial Household Act, enacted in 1889 (amended in 1947) after the Meiji Restoration, provides that the Crown Prince shall act as regent; accordingly, the present Emperor was regent while his father Emperor Taishō was ill. ⇨ KANPAKU, SHIKKEN

〖注〗 regent 摂政職にある人. regency 摂政の職. minor 未成年. sovereign 統治. Fujiwara Yoshifusa 藤原良房. Fujiwara Mototsune 藤原基経. the Meiji Restoration 明治維新. the Imperial Household Act「皇室典範」. enact 制定する. provide 規定する.

setomono 瀬戸物 lit. a product of Seto. chinaware produced in and around Seto in Aichi Prefecture. Generally the same as *Seto-yaki.* The term *setomono* is also often used as a general term for chinaware or pottery produced in any district. ⇨ SETO-YAKI

〖注〗 chinaware 陶磁器(製品). pottery 陶器類, 製陶法.

Seto Naikai 瀬戸内海 the Inland Sea of Seto; the inland sea surrounded by Kyūshū, Shikoku and the western part of Honshū. It covers an area of some 9,500 square kilometers, dotted with over 1,000 small islands including Awaji Island and Shōdo Island. It connects with the Pacific Ocean through the Kii Channel to the east and the Bungo Channel to the west, and also connects with the Japan Sea to the extreme west through the Kanmon Straits. Along the coast are such large cities as Ōsaka, Kōbe, Hiroshima, etc. Because of the spectacular sights along the coastline, this area was one of the first to be designated as a national park in 1934, along with Unzen National Park in Kyūshū. ⇨ SETO NAIKAI KOKURITSU-KŌEN

〖注〗 be dotted with ～が点在する. the Bungo Channel 豊後水道. the Kanmon Straits 関門海峡.

Seto Naikai Kokuritsu-kōen 瀬戸内海国立公園 Inland Sea National Park (629.5 square kilometers); a natural park embracing the Inland Sea of Seto (9,500 sq. km) and the surrounding coasts of western Honshū, Shikoku and Kyūshū. Scenes of the waterway dotted with over 1,000 small islands, combined with the rugged coastline with a variety of pine trees, are spectacular throughout the park, including Miyajima, one of the three most beautiful sights of Japan. Voyages by cruise ships, hydrofoils and ferryboats are available. This park was one of the first two to be designated as national parks in 1934. ⇨ KOKURITSU-KŌEN, NIHON-SANKEI, SETO NAIKAI

〖注〗 be dotted with 〜が点在する． rugged coastline ぎざぎざの海岸線，リアス式海岸． the three most beautiful sights of Japan 日本三景． cruise ship 遊覧船． hydrofoil 水中翼船．

Seto-yaki 瀬戸焼 Seto chinaware; Seto pottery; a generic term for ceramic and porcelain ware produced in the Seto district of Aichi Prefecture. The Seto district is Japan's largest and perhaps oldest pottery-producing area, thus giving rise to the common term *setomono* (lit. Seto things) for pottery. Katō Tōshirō, known as the founder of glazed ceramics at Seto, brought back glazing techniques from China in the Kamakura period (1185–1336). Since then, Seto has produced various kinds of glazed ceramic ware, ranging from high-quality tea utensils to everyday kitchen ware, including Shino, Oribe, and Ofuke ware. Seto succeeded in developing various glazes; ash glaze was followed by transparent yellow glaze, opaque brown glaze, dark amber glaze, etc. After Katō Tamikichi began producing porcelain, particularly *sometsuke* (indigo design under glaze), at Seto in the early 19th century, the mainstream of Seto ware has been porcelain ware with a glassy glaze. ⇨ ORIBE-YAKI, SETOMONO, SHINO-YAKI, SOMETSUKE

〖注〗 pottery 焼き物． ceramic ware 陶器． porcelain ware 磁器． Katō Tōshirō 加藤藤四郎． glaze 釉，釉を塗る． tea utensil 茶道具． Ofuke ware 御深井焼． ash glaze 灰釉． transparent 透明な． opaque 不透明な． dark amber glaze 飴色の釉． Katō Tamikichi 加藤民吉．

setsubun 節分 the point of change of seasons; the day before the first day of each season. Nowadays, it more commonly refers to the day before the first day of spring, the last day of the year in the old lunar calendar, falling on February 2 or 3 on the present calendar. On the evening of this day, a festive ceremony of bean-throwing (*mamemaki*) is held in homes, and at shrines and

temples, in the belief that it will bring in good fortune and drive out evil spirits.   A twig of Japanese holly (*hiiragi*) together with the head of a sardine may be seen hung at the entrances of some houses to shut out evil spirits.   ⇨ MAMEMAKI, SHUNBUN (NO HI)
〚注〛 the lunar calendar 太陰暦. bean-throwing 豆まき. twig 小枝. Japanese holly ひいらぎ.

setsugekka 雪月花 snow, the moon and blossoms; an aesthetic phrase referring to the manifestations of the beauty of nature, changing from season to season. The Japanese are sensitive to the changing of the seasons, as exemplified by snow, the moon and cherryblossoms. Such seasonal feelings are reflected in art and literature, as well as in the Japanese way of life.
〚注〛 aesthetic phrase 美意識の語句. manifestation 現れ.

setsuwa-bungaku 説話文学 tale literature; a generic term referring to anecdotal literature derived from legend, myth and folklore; specifically, collections of folk stories as one genre of medieval narrative literature. As opposed to aristocratic narrative literature, which flourished in the early medieval period, this genre derived from tales handed down in the oral tradition by the common people. It is generally characterized by a secular, anecdotal or entertaining, as well as didactic, quality.   The stories reflect the customs, beliefs and everyday life of the common people of ancient times, although some tales are borrowings from China and India. Beginning with *Nihon Ryōiki* (A Japanese Chronicle of Miracles, early ninth century) with a Buddhist quality and written in Chinese, scores of collections were compiled in the Heian (794-1185) and Kamakura (1185-1336) periods. Particularly well-known are *Konjaku Monogatari* (Tales of Once Upon a Time, 1120) comprising over 1,000 tales, and *Uji Shūi Monogatari* (A Collection of Tales from Uji, early 13th century) consisting of 196 tales (author unknown for both).
〚注〛 anecdotal 逸話の. be derived from ～に由来する. folklore 民話. genre (文学, 芸術などの)ジャンル, 類型. narrative literature 物語文学.   oral tradition 口承による言い伝え. secular 世俗的な. didactic 教訓的な, 説教的な. A Japanese Chronicle of Miracles「日本霊異記」.

sewamono 世話物 a genre play; Kabuki and Bunraku plays that deal with the everyday life of the common people, especially in the Edo period (1603-1868). Chikamatsu Monzaemon (1653-1724) wrote a number of excellent genre dramas for the puppet stage: e.g.

Shinjū Ten no Amijima (A Double Suicide at Amijima), *Meido no Hikyaku* (An Attempt to Elope to the Other World). ⇨ BUNRAKU, JIDAIMONO, KABUKI, KIZEAWAMONO

〖注〗 genre 風俗を描いた. puppet stage（文楽）人形芝居. A Double Suicide at Amijima「心中天網島」. An Attempt to Elope to the Other World「冥途の飛脚」.

sha 紗 a kind of silk gauze; thin porous silk fabric used for summertime kimono. A solid-color weave is typical of *sha,* but there are also *sha* of patterned weave of a single color or multi-colored ones. The fabric is made into semiformal or informal kimono for both men and women for use at the height of summer. ⇨ KIMONO

〖注〗 gauze 薄織り, 紗, 絽. porous 多孔性の. silk fabric 絹織物. solid-color 単色, 無地. patterned weave 柄織り.

shabu-shabu しゃぶしゃぶ thinly sliced tender beef and various vegetables cooked in a pan. Very thinly sliced beef, soybean curd, mushrooms, Chinese cabbage, green onion, leafy spring chrysanthemum, etc., are prepared on a large platter. The ingredients are swished portion by portion in the boiling soup stock in a pan on the table. Then it is dipped in special sauces made of *miso* paste, soy sauce, sesame seeds or pasted nut, citron or lemon juice, etc.

〖注〗 tender beef やわらかい牛肉. soybean curd 豆腐. Chinese cabbage 白菜. green onion 長ねぎ. leafy spring chrysanthemum 春菊. platter 大皿. ingredient 成分,（料理の）材料. swish 振り回す. portion by portion 少しずつ. boiling soup stock 煮えたぎるスープ種. soy sauce 醤油. citron 柑橘類.

shakkan-hō 尺貫法 the system of traditional units of weights and measures; the traditional system of measuring, with the *shaku* as a standard of linear measurement, *kan* of weight, etc. Weights and measures were first systematized by the Code of Taihō (701), but the measures changed over time and varied depending on the district. It was not until 1891 that they were standardized, as shown in the table below. The metric system was officially adopted in 1924, but the old system predominated in everyday life and business as in measuring grains or wine, building houses, making kimono, etc. From 1966, the metric system was strictly enforced for official use. ⇨ CHŌ, GŌ, HYŌ, KAN, KEN, KOKU, MONME, RI, SHAKU, SUN, TSUBO

〖注〗 linear measurement 線上の寸法・尺度. the Code of Taihō「大宝律令」. table 表. the metric system メートル法. predominate 優勢となる.

enforce 施行する，（法的に）実施する．

	shakkan system	metric system
length & distance	1 *sun*	A. 3.03 centimeters B. 3.79 cm
	1 *shaku* (10 *sun*)	A. 30.3 cm B. 37.9 cm
	1 *ken* (6 *shaku* of A)	1.818 meters
	1 *jō* (10 *shaku*)	3.03 m
	1 *chō* (60 *ken*)	109.09 m
	1 *ri* (36 *chō*) etc.	3.927 kilometers
area	1 *tsubo* (6×6 *shaku*)	3.306 square meters
	1 *se* (30 *tsubo*)	99.175 sq. m
	1 *tan* (10 *se*)	991.75 sq. m
	1 *chō* (10 *tan*) etc.	9,917.5 sq. m
capacity	1 *gō*	180.39 cubic centimeters
	1 *shō* (10 *gō*)	1.8039 liters
	1 *to* (10 *shō*)	18.039 *l*
	1 *hyō* (4 *to*)	72.156 *l*
	1 *koku* (10 *to*) etc.	180.39 *l*
weight	1 *monme* 1 *kan* (1,000 *monme*) etc.	3.75 grams 3.75 kilograms

shakkei 借景 lit. a borrowed landscape. natural scenery serving as a backdrop for a garden. In traditional garden design, the beautiful natural surroundings—trees, hills and mountains—beyond the garden's actual borders, are often effectively used as a backdrop to form an integral part of the garden. The beautiful shape of Mount Hiei seen beyond the hedge of Entsūji Garden in Kyoto is an example of such "borrowed scenery."

〖注〗 backdrop（舞台正面の）背景幕，（一般に）背景． integral 全体構成の．
hedge 生垣． Entsūji Garden 円通寺の庭．

shaku 尺 a traditional unit for measuring length or distance. Ten
sun make one *shaku*. There are two different scales for *shaku:*
one is 30.3 centimeters and the other, formerly used for measuring
cloth, is about 1.25 times the length of the regular one (37.9 cm).
Since measuring sticks for the former were originally made of
metal, they were called *kanejaku* (lit. metal *shaku*), while the latter,
being made of a piece of whale whisker, were called *kujirajaku* (lit.
whale *shaku*). ⇨ SHAKKAN-HŌ, SUN

〖注〗 scale 尺度． measuring stick ものさし． whale whisker 鯨のひげ．

shakuhachi 尺八 a Japanese flute; a vertical flute with five holes,
four in front and one at the back, made from a bamboo stem near
the root. The term *shakuhachi* derives from its length—one *shaku*
and eight (*hachi*) *sun*, about 55 centimeters. Today's common
type has four or so bamboo joints, though formerly a type of
bamboo stem with one joint was also popular. It produces a deep
plaintive sound in many varieties through various combinations of
fingering and blowing techniques. It is used for classical solo
pieces, in the *sankyoku* trio with *koto* and *shamisen* [*sangen*], and
as an accompaniment for folk music. ⇨ KOTO, MIN'YŌ, SANKYOKU,
SHAMISEN

〖注〗 vertical 縦の． a bamboo stem with one joint 一節切（ひとよぎり）（の尺
八）． plaintive 悲しげな，哀愁のこもった． derive from ～に由来する． finger 指で演奏する． solo piece 独奏曲目． trio 三人の，三つ組の． ensemble
合奏，合唱． accompaniment 伴奏．

shamisen 三味線 a three-stringed instrument; a traditional
Japanese banjo-like musical instrument with three strings which
was introduced to Japan in the 16th century from the Ryūkyū
Islands. The body is covered with catskin. The *shamisen* is
played with a triangular ivory plectrum (*bachi*) by plucking the
three strings; the heavier the string, the deeper the tone given. It
is used for the music accompanying Bunraku and Kabuki as well as
other narrative kinds of folk music, and a wide variety of dance
and vocal styles. There are various sizes for the differing styles,
ranging from the smaller one used for *kouta* songs to the larger,
deeper-pitched instrument used in Bunraku, known as *futo-jamisen*.
Shamisen is also called *sangen* (lit. three strings), particularly
among professionals. ⇨ BACHI, BUNRAKU, JABISEN, KABUKI, KOUTA

〖注〗 instrument 楽器． plectrum ばち． pluck はじく． accompany 伴う，
伴奏する． narrative 叙事詩風の． deep-pitched 低音の．

shamoji 杓文字 a serving spoon; a big spoon used for dishing out
rice or soup. The one used for rice is flat and usually made of
wood or bamboo, or more recently plastic; the one for soup is a
semi-spherical dipper and usually made of metal. *Shamoji* is the
term commonly used among housewives, while the more formal
term is *shakushi*.

〖注〗 serving spoon 給仕用スプーン． dish out（料理を）取り分ける． dipper
すくう物，ひしゃく．

share 洒落 an improvised witty remark; a play on words, particularly referring to puns. For example, a word or phrase is used in
such a way as to suggest another meaning or application, and is
meant to be misinterpreted; as a result, a humorous effect is
achieved. The great number of homophones found in the Japanese
language renders a wide range of puns. In a broader sense, allu-
sions and parodies may be considered *share*. ⇨ KAKEKOTOBA,
MANZAI, RAKUGO

〖注〗 improvise 即興する． pun しゃれ，語呂合わせ． homophone 同音異義
語． render 表現する，描写する． allusion ほのめかし，あてつけ，隠喩．

shari¹ 舎利 lit. human ashes or bones. white rice grains or boiled
white rice. This term is used at *sushi* restaurants in particular,
referring to rice for *sushi*. In making *sushi* rice, a sheet of kelp
（*konbu*）is placed on top of the rice in water until it begins to boil,
which brings flavor to the rice. When done, the rice still piping hot
is placed in a shallow wooden tub and sprinkled with vinegar
dressing, made with salt, sugar and *mirin*（seasoning wine）. Then
the rice is mixed carefully not to bruise the grains and make them
stick together. It must be cooled very quickly with a hand fan.
⇨ SUSHI

〖注〗 shallow wooden tub 半切（はんぎり），半桶．

shari² 舎利 Sarira（Sanskrit）; Buddha's bones, particularly Sakyamuni's bones. After Sakyamuni died and entered permanent
Buddhahood, his disciples divided his bones among themselves, and
built stupas in which to enshrine them. In Japan, the stupa developed into the multistoried pagoda where Sakyamuni's bones or
ashes called *shari* are enshrined. The bones are also called *bus-
shari*（Buddha's *shari*）to distinguish them from ordinary human
bones. ⇨ GOJŪNOTŌ, SANJŪNOTŌ, TŌ

【注】 Buddhahood 仏性, 仏陀としての境地, 悟りの境地. disciple 弟子.
stupa 仏舎利塔, 卒塔婆. enshrine 祀る. multistoried pagoda 多重塔.

shiatsu(-ryōhō) 指圧(療法)   finger-pressure therapy; one of the
traditional methods of medical treatment in Japan, originally
introduced from China. Even today, it is widely practiced for
curing certain pains and minor diseases, and is especially effective
for fatigue. Some parts of the body where specific points underlie,
called *tsubo* (acupuncture points), are pressed quite strongly with
the fingers, usually the thumbs. This stimulates the nervous system and the circulatory system to work better.   ⇨ KANPŌI
【注】 therapy 療法. specific point 特定の点, つぼ. acupuncture point つ
ぼ. the nervous system 神経組織. the circulatory system 循環組織.

shibuuchiwa 渋団扇   a tannin-coated paper fan; a flat paper fan,
round or square in shape, coated with persimmon tannin. The
frame, including the handle, is made of bamboo over which strong
tannin-coated paper is pasted and lacquered persimmon-red. It is
stronger than an ordinary unpainted fan, and so it was formerly
used to fan fires in the kitchen. Today, it may be found at *yakitori*
restaurants or the like.   ⇨ UCHIWA
【注】 tannin-coated タンニン(渋)を塗った. persimmon tannin 柿の渋.

shichidō-garan 七堂伽藍   seven temple buildings; a grand Buddhist
temple having a complete set of seven structures in its compounds.
The seven structures are: a main hall, a pagoda (one or two), a
lecture hall, a belfry, a library, a dormitory and a refectory (or a
middle gate). Early great temples built by the end of the Nara
period (646–794) were composed of seven structures and were laid
out according to a fixed pattern. A typical remaining example is
Hōryūji Temple, Nara, built in 607.   ⇨ CHŪMON², GARAN, HONDŌ,
SHŌRŌ, TERA, TŌ
【注】 compound 囲いをした区域, 境内, 敷地. pagoda 塔. lecture hall 講堂.
belfry 鐘楼. library 経蔵. dormitory 僧房. refectory (寺院, 大学などの)
食堂. middle gate 中門.

Shichi-fukujin 七福神   the Seven Deities of Good Luck; a group of
legendary divinities consisting of one goddess (Benten) and six
gods (Bishamon, Ebisu, Daikoku, Hotei, Fukurokuju and Jurōjin).
One version regards Fukurokuju and Jurōjin as the same; in this
case Kisshōten (a goddess) is included in the seven. According to
legend, on New Year's Eve a ship bearing the seven deities and
treasures comes to Japan from afar, bringing good luck for the

coming year. The seven deities each have different roles in making people happy. ⇨ BEN(ZAI)TEN, BISHAMON(TEN), DAIKOKU (TEN), EBISU, FUKUROKUJU, HOTEI, JURŌJIN, KISSHŌTEN

〖注〗 deity 神，神のような人［もの］． legendary divinity 伝説上の聖なる人物． one version 一説． 七福神：弁（財）天，毘沙門天，恵比須，大黒天，布袋，福禄寿，寿老人（又は吉祥天）．

shichigosan 七五三 lit. seven-five-three. the celebration for children of seven, five and three years of age, observed on November 15. Girls of seven, boys of five, and both boys and girls of three are taken by their parents either to their local guardian shrine or to a noted shrine, such as Meiji Shrine, to express gratitude to the gods for their growth and to pray for further blessings. Most of the children are dressed up in colorful traditional costumes, although Western clothing is increasingly seen. After a rite of blessing by a shrine priest, they are given candy called *chitoseame* (lit. thousand-year candy) which is said to promise them a long life. This celebration became a custom in the Edo period (1603–1868), and spread throughout the country since various districts already had ways of their own in celebrating the stages of children's growth. ⇨ CHITOSEAME, JINJA, UJIGAMI

〖注〗 local guardian shrine その土地の守護神社． rite of blessings 祝福の儀式． shrine priest 神主． stage 段階，節目．

shichimi-tōgarashi 七味唐辛子 lit. seven flavors. seven-spice powder; a mixture of seven or so kinds of spices, including hot red pepper (*tōgarashi*). In addition to red pepper, the dried ground spices include *sanshō* pepper, sesame seeds, poppy seeds, seaweed laver, etc. The blend is left to individual taste, but nowadays ready-made mixtures are available. *Shichimi-tōgarashi* is used as a flavoring to sprinkle over hot noodles, as a condiment for pot dishes, and also as a seasoning for barbecued meat and fish. ⇨ SANSHŌ

〖注〗 hot red pepper 赤唐辛子． seaweed laver 海苔． condiment 薬味． seasoning 調味料．

shichirin 七輪 a clay cooking stove; a portable charcoal stove, made of clay or the like. It was a handy device for boiling and broiling, and particularly suitable for broiling fish and meat over a direct fire. A paper fan is used for kindling the fire instead of a bellows. It is disappearing from daily life in cities. ⇨ SHIBU-UCHIWA, UCHIWA

〖注〗 charcoal fire 炭火. kindle 火をつける. bellows ふいご.

Shigaraki-yaki 信楽焼 Shigaraki ceramic ware; ceramic ware first produced at the beginning of the 16th century at Shigaraki in the present-day Shiga Prefecture. This ware is thick and sturdy with a transparent dark blue glaze shading into brown and yellowish red. It was highly appreciated for its rustic appearance by such famous tea masters as Takeno Jōō (1502-55) and Sen no Rikyū (1521-91). Shigaraki water jars are particularly valued for use in the tea ceremony. ⇨ CHANOYU

〖注〗 ceramic ware 陶器. sturdy がん健な, がん強な. transparent 透明な. glaze つや, 上薬[釉]. rustic わびれた, 粗野な. Takeno Jōō 武野紹鷗. tea ceremony 茶の湯, 茶道.

Shihō Kenshūjo 司法研修所 the Legal Training and Research Institute; Japan's only professional law institute, which trains prospective lawyers, judges and public prosecutors. University law departments offer a B.A. degree; their graduate divisions are mainly for those seeking university appointments. Those planning to practice law must pass the state law examination (*shihō-shiken*) for admission to the two-year course at the Legal Training and Research Institute. After passing the final examination upon completion of the course, the graduates can practice law in the field of their choice. An agency of the Supreme Court, this state-owned institute was founded in 1947 with the enforcement of the new constitution. ⇨ SHIHŌ-SHIKEN

〖注〗 institute 研修所. prospective 将来の, 見込みのある. public prosecutor 検察官. B.A. degree 学士号. graduate division 大学院部. practice law 法律に関する職業をもつ. the state law examination 司法試験. the Supreme Court 最高裁判所. enforcement 施行.

shihō-shiken 司法試験 a state law examination; a national examination for selecting those who are qualified to take part in licensed legal professions. This examination is conducted annually by the Law Examination Control Committee (Shihō-shiken Kanri Iinkai) of the Ministry of Justice. It is designed for selecting candidates for the two-year course at the Legal Training and Research Institute (Shihō Kenshūjo), Japan's only professional law institute, which trains new lawyers, judges and public prosecutors. This entrance examination is taken mostly by undergraduates and graduates of the law department of universities, but can be taken by anyone who holds Japanese citizenship. The passing rate is extremely low, annually accounting for a mere several hundreds out of 20,000 to 30,000 applicants.   ⇨ SHIHŌ KENSHŪJO

〖注〗 licensed legal profession 免許を持った法律に関する職業. the Law Examination Control Committee 司法試験管理委員会. the Legal Training and Research Institute 司法研修所. public prosecutor 検察官. undergraduate 四年生までの大学生. passing rate 合格率.

shihō-shoshi 司法書士   a judicial scrivener; a quasi-legal profession specializing in the documentation of contracts and legal registration.   Since the number of attorneys is rigorously restricted in Japan, much routine legal documentation and registration is handled by judicial scriveners at low fees.   There are some 90,000 scriveners (as of 1983) who are licensed by state examination (since 1979); most have undergraduate law degrees.

〖注〗 judicial 司法の. scrivener 公証人、筆稿者. quasi-legal profession 準法的専門職. the documentation of contracts 契約書作成. legal registration 法的登記. attorney 弁護士(=attorney-at-law). undergraduate law degree 四年生の法学士号.

shiitake 椎茸   *Cortinellus shiitake*; Japanese mushroom; *shiitake* mushroom.   It is an edible mycorrhizal fungus grown on decaying logs of varieties of Japanese oak such as *shii* (pasania), *nara* (*Quercus serrata*), *kunugi* (*Quercus acutissima*), *kuri* (Japanese chestnut tree), etc.   Each mushroom consists of a brown flat cap with white undersurface gills and a short stem.   It is used for its fragrant woody aroma and flavor in a wide range of cooking—for *sushi*, pot dishes, boiled dishes, soup, etc.   Both fresh mushrooms (*nama-shiitake*) and dried ones (*hoshi-shiitake*) are available.

〖注〗 mycorrhizal 菌根の. fungus 菌類. pasania 椎. gills ひだ. fragrant 芳ばしい. aroma 芳香.

shijuku 私塾   a private academy of the Edo period (1603-1868).   Along with the official schools for the warrior class run by the shogunate or feudal lords, a variety of private schools were founded by temples and individuals, most of which were open to commoners as well.   The number of *shijuku* totaled 437 in 1829, growing to 1,528 in 1867.   The subjects offered ranged from the basics such as reading and arithmetics to advanced studies in medicine, Dutch or Western studies, Confucianism, etc.   Some of the *shijuku*—such as the Shōka Sonjuku founded in 1856 by Yoshida Shōin (1830-59), Rangaku-juku (the present Keiō-Gijuku University) founded in 1858 by Yukichi Fukuzawa (1835-1901)

—surpassed official academies and produced many eminent personages with liberal ideas.　⇨ JUKYŌ, RANGAKU

〖注〗 warrior class 武士階級. shogunate 幕府. feudal lord 大名，藩主. Confucianism 儒教. surpass（他に）まさる，（他をしのいで）すぐれる.

shikibuton 敷布団　a mattress stuffed with cotton. It is spread directly on the *tatami*-mat floor. Over it, a larger covering *futon* is used, sometimes together with a blanket.　⇨ FUTON, KAKEBUTON, TATAMI

〖注〗 stuff 詰める.

shikinō 式能　a formal Noh program. It includes one play from each of the five categories of Noh plays with Kyogen pieces performed in between; a first group god piece（*wakinōmono*）, a second group warrior ghost piece（*shuramono*）, a third group wig piece（*katsuramono*）, a fourth group piece（*yobanmemono*）, and an ending piece（*kirinōmono*）.　⇨ KATSURAMONO, KIRINŌMONO, NŌ, SHURAMONO, WAKINŌMONO, YOBANMEMONO

〖注〗 piece 作品. god piece 脇能物. warrior ghost piece 修羅物. wig piece 鬘物. fourth group piece 四番目物. ending piece 切能物.

shikiri 仕切り　a ritual performed by *sumō* wrestlers before a bout to enhance concentration by pressuring the opponent. It is performed after the sequence of *chirichōzu*（hand ritual）, salt tossing and *shiko*（stomping）. The wrestlers first face each other squatting on their heels at the center of the ring and proceed to squat with their fist clutched on their respective white *shikiri* lines. They then slowly rise to their feet while staring at each other. This mental battling takes place a few times until the referee indicates that time is up, with the salt tossing ritual performed during the intervals. The bout begins from a squatting position. The time limit for the *shikiri* is four minutes for the *makuuchi* division, three for the *jūryō,* and two for the remaining lower divisions.　⇨ CHIRICHŌZU, JŪRYŌ, MAKUUCHI, SHIKO, SUMŌ

〖注〗 ritual 儀式. bout 試合. hand ritual 塵手水. stomping 四股. squat しゃがむ.

shikishi 色紙　a square card used for pictures, poems or calligraphy. It is a thin paper board, white for pictures and calligraphy, and white or slightly tinted for poems. The space left unused on a *shikishi* is regarded as aesthetically important. Standard sizes are about 25 by 27 or 18 by 20 centimeters.　⇨ KŪKAN, SHODŌ

〖注〗 calligraphy 書道. aesthetically 美学上.

shikken 執権   a regent for a shogun; shogunal regency held by the Hōjō family in the Kamakura period (1185-1336). Hōjō Tokimasa (1138-1215), who played an important role in the founding of the Kamakura shogunate, was the first to receive this title in 1203 when the son of his daughter and the first shogun Minamoto Yoritomo, Minamoto Sanetomo (1192-1219), took over as the third shogun at the age of 11. After the Hōjōs eliminated their political rivals and succeeded in having Sanetomo assassinated, they established a government with the *shikken* (with this title in 1213) as the de facto ruler under a puppet shogun. This position was passed down through the Hōjō family, which held power until the fall of the Kamakura shogunate in 1336. ⇨ KAMAKURA-BA-KUFU, SESSHŌ

〖注〗 regent 代理統治者(摂政, 執権など). shogunal regency 幕府のための代理統治, 執権. assassinate 暗殺する. de facto 事実上の. puppet shogun 傀儡将軍, 操られている将軍.

shikki 漆器   lacquer ware; japan ware; tableware made of lacquer-coated wood. Lacquer, obtained from the sap of the Japanese lacquer tree (*Rhus verniciflua*), is applied to a wooden base to give a smooth, lustrous surface, also enabling the ware to be cleaned easily. Famous types include Aizu lacquer ware made in Fukushima Prefecture, Wajima and Yamanaka lacquer ware of Ishikawa Prefecture, and Shunkei lacquer ware manufactured at Hida in Gifu Prefecture and at Noshiro in Akita Prefecture. Cheap lacquered tableware of today may have a plastic base and is often hardly distinguishable from the real thing. ⇨ AIZU-NURI, NURI-MONO, SHUNKEI-NURI, TSUGARU-NURI, TSUISHU, URUSHI, WAJIMA-NURI

〖注〗 lacquer 漆. japan 漆, 漆器. sap 樹液. Japanese lacquer tree 漆の木 (=*Rhus verniciflua*).

shiko 四股   a basic traditional exercise done by *sumō* wrestlers. From a standing position with the legs parted, a wrestler raises his stretched right leg sideways as high as he can while putting his hands on his knees and leaning his upper body to the left, then bringing his foot down hard to the ground. He proceeds to the same with the left leg to complete a round of *shiko*, which is then repeated again and again. *Shiko* is done prior to a *sumō* bout as part of a ritual to drive away evil spirits that may be lurking in the ring. ⇨ DOHYŌ, SUMŌ

〖注〗 bout 勝負, 試合. ritual 儀式. lurk 潜む.

Shikoku 四国 the smallest of the four major islands of the Japanese archipelago, the other three being Honshū, Hokkaidō and Kyūshū. It comprises four (*shi*) prefectures—Tokushima, Ehime, Kagawa and Kōchi—covering an area of about 18,800 square kilometers including small islands belonging to the prefectures. Its southern coast faces the Pacific Ocean; the northern coast looks toward Honshū across the Inland Sea of Seto. ⇨ HOKKAIDŌ, HONSHŪ, KYŪSHŪ, SETO NAIKAI

〖注〗 the Japanese archipelago 日本列島. the Inland Sea of Seto 瀬戸内海.

Shikotsu-Tōya Kokuritsu-kōen 支笏洞爺国立公園 Shikotsu-Tōya National Park (983.3 square kilometers), designated in 1949; a natural park situated to the south of Sapporo, in southern Hokkaidō. It includes three caldera lakes, around which a number of active volcanoes and hot springs are located. Around Lake Shikotsu are Mount Eniwa (1,320 meters), Mount Tarumae (1,024 m), etc., and to the north, Mount Yōtei (1,893 m), Jōzankei Spa, etc. To the south of Lake Tōya are Mount Usu (725 m), Mount Shōwa Shinzan (408 m), Tōya Spa, etc. In the southern part of the park, Noboribetsu Spa is located near Lake Kuttara. With its well-equipped lodging facilities and good ski slopes, this park is a popular one as it is easily accessible from Sapporo and other cities. ⇨ HOKKAIDŌ, KOKURITSU-KŌEN, ONSEN

〖注〗 caldera カルデラ(火山の火口のくぼ地). hot spring 温泉. Jōzankei Spa 定山渓温泉. Lake Kuttara 倶多楽湖. lodging facility 宿泊施設. accessible 接近できる.

shikunshi 四君子 lit. four noble men. a set of four noble plants. They are the plum blossom, bamboo, chrysanthemum and pine (originally orchid, in China). These plants, often combined as a set, have been used as traditional subjects of paintings and designs for other artistic objects.

〖注〗 plum blossom 梅の花. chrysanthemum 菊. orchid 蘭.

Shimabara no Ran 島原の乱 the Shimabara Uprising (1637–38); a rebellion by Christians and farmers against local authorities and the Tokugawa shogunate (1603–1868), along the Shimabara Peninsula. Headed by Amakusa Shirō (1621–38), some 35,000 oppressed Christians and farmers rose in protest against their local lord, Matsukura Shigemasa (?–1630), because of his overtaxation, and the Tokugawa shogunate for its policy of suppressing Christianity. Despite initial success, the rebellion was crushed by a huge army of 100,000 men sent from the shogunate, led first by Itakura Shigemasa (1588-1638), and then Matsudaira Nobutsuna (1596-1662). This incident eventually led to intensified suppression of Christianity, and finally resulted in the country's closing its doors to the world in 1639. ⇨ KAKURE-KIRISHITAN, KIRISHITAN, SAKOKU(-SEISAKU), TOKUGAWA-BAKUFU

〖注〗 uprising 反乱. rebellion 反乱. the Tokugawa shogunate 徳川幕府. oppressed 困窮した. local feudal lord その土地の大名. Matsukura Shigemasa 松倉重政. overtaxation 重税を課すこと. the policy of suppressing Chiristianity キリスト教禁圧政策. Itakura Shigemasa 板倉重昌. Matsudaira Nobutsuna 松平信綱.

shimada(-mage) 島田(髷) the *shimada* hairstyle; a traditional coiffure developed during the Edo period (1603-1868). It is made up of a plectrum-shaped chignon with puffed-out front, back and side locks. First worn by a courtesan at Shimada on the Tōkaidō Highway, it came to be a hairstyle for young single women of marriageable age. After marriage, they changed their hairstyle into *marumage*. Today kimono-clad young women may be seen wearing this style during the New Year holidays. An elaborate variation of this style, the *takashimada*, is usually worn by brides in a traditional-style wedding. ⇨ KIMONO, MAGE, MARUMAGE, TAKA-SHIMADA

〖注〗 coiffure 髪型. plectrum-shaped ばちの形をした. chignon 束髪のまげ. lock 髪の房. courtesan 遊女. elaborate variation 変形した手のこんだ型.

shimai 仕舞 an abbreviated performance of a Noh dance; a classical dance taken from Noh dramas and performed in plain costume. It consists of only an important passage of a Noh drama and is performed usually only by the principal actor (*shite*), accompanied by a stage chorus (*jiutai*) usually without any instrumental music. The performer is not dressed in formal Noh costume but in formal kimono and *hakama* (pleated long skirt), and holds a fan (*ōgi*) in one hand. *Shimai* is performed not only by professionals but also by amateurs. ⇨ HAKAMA, JIUTAI, KIMONO, NŌ, ŌGI, SHITE

〖注〗 the principal actor 仕手. stage chorus 地謡.

shimekazari 注連飾り ⇨ SHIMENAWA-KAZARI

shimenawa 注連縄 a sacred straw rope; a straw rope used in Shintoism to indicate sacredness. The rope is made of plaited greenish rice straw from which tufts of straw and pieces of white paper (called *gohei*) hang. Within the Shinto shrine it is used to indicate sanctified objects and areas. On New Year's Day a special type of *shimenawa* festoon is often hung at the entrance to a house as a symbol of purification. ⇨ GOHEI, JINJA, SHIMENAWA-KAZARI, SHINTŌ

〘注〙 plaited 編んだ． tuft 房，束． pieces of cut white paper 御幣． sanctified 神聖化した，清めた． festoon 飾りづな．

shimenawa-kazari 注連縄飾り　a decorated sacred straw festoon; a decorative type of sacred straw festoon (*shimenawa*), used on New Year's Day. It is hung above the entrance to a house to purify the home for the new year. Greenish rice straw is twisted and tied into a specific shape, to which pieces of white paper (*gohei*), a bitter orange (*daidai*), fern leaves, sometimes a lobster, etc., are attached as decorations; these decorations are symbolic of purity, prosperity from generation to generation (*daidai*), good fortune and longevity, respectively. ⇨ GANJITSU, GOHEI, SANGANICHI, SHIMENAWA

〘注〙 festoon 飾りづな． sacred straw festoon 注連飾り． pieces of white paper 御幣． bitter orange だいだい． longevity 長寿．

shimofuri(-niku) 霜降り(肉)　lit. fallen frost meat. marbled beef; quality beef with white streaks of fat, giving a marble-like appearance. This kind of beef is produced through a unique method of raising cattle which are kept in stalls. The excellence in quality is said to be a result of feeding the cattle beer and giving them a daily massage. This beef, thinly sliced, is best used in *sukiyaki*. ⇨ SUKIYAKI

〘注〙 marbled 大理石模様の，まだらの． quality beef 高級牛肉． streak 縞． stall 牛舎，畜舎．

shimoza 下座　a seat of least honor; the seat of a lower-ranking position in a room. For example, in a traditional Japanese room, it is situated nearest to the entrance and farthest from the alcove (*tokonoma*), in front of which the seat of honor (*kamiza*) is situated. ⇨ KAMIZA, TOKONOMA

〘注〙 the seat of honor 栄誉ある席，上座．

shincha 新茶　new tea leaves; newly picked tea of the year. The season for tea-leaf picking comes at the very beginning of May, when the tea is at its best—in the lunar calendar it falls on the 88th day (May 1 or 2 in the present calendar) from the beginning of spring. Green tea made from new leaves is refreshing and fragrant, and tastes sweet and mild, though it may lack a bitter taste. The new leaves begin to appear on the market in the middle of May.　⇨ CHA, HACHIJŪHACHI-YA, RYOKUCHA

〖注〗 tea-leaf picking 茶摘み． the lunar calendar 太陰暦． fragrant 芳ばしい，香りが良い．

shinden-zukuri 寝殿造り palace-style residential architecture; an architectural style, developed in the Heian period（794-1185）and favored by the aristocracy． It involves a distinctive form—single-storied, unpainted and with Japanese cypress bark roof shingles． The mansion estate centered around the chief dwelling, or *shinden*, which faced south onto an open court． Two wide covered corridors（*watadono*）link the main building with its east and west subsidiary living quarters（*tainoya*）． Narrow corridors extend southward from these annexes, forming a U-shape around the court． The Shishinden Hall of the Old Imperial Palace, Kyoto, is an existing representative example of this kind of architecture.

〖注〗 the aristocracy 貴族階級． Japanese cypress bark 檜の皮． shingle 屋根板． mansion estate 屋敷． chief dwelling 本殿，寝殿． court 中庭． subsidiary living quarters 対屋（左右の別棟の建物）． the Shishinden Hall 紫宸殿． the Old Imperial Palace 京都御所．

Shingonshū 真言宗 lit. the True Word Sect． the Shingon sect of Buddhism; one of the two sects of esoteric Buddhism in Japan, the other being the Tendai sect． At the beginning of the ninth century, shortly after the emergence of the Tendai sect, the Shingon sect was founded by the priest Kūkai（774-835）, popularly known as Kōbō Daishi, who while in China had studied esotericism of Indian origin． In 817 he built Kongōbuji Temple on Mount Kōya in present-day Wakayama Prefecture and in 823 was granted Tōji Temple in Kyoto by Emperor Saga（786-842）, both of which have served as headquarters of the sect's different branches． The Shingon sect focuses on the three mysteries—the body, words and the Buddha—teaching that harmony of these elements is the foundation of life and that it can be attained by everyone through esoteric Shingon rituals.　⇨ MIKKYŌ, TENDAISHŪ

〖注〗 esoteric Buddhism 密教． emergence 台頭，出現． esotericism 秘法． Kongōbuji Temple 金剛峰寺． headquarters 本部，本山． ritual 儀式．

shin-gyō-sō 真・行・草 elaborate, intermediate and abbreviated; formal, semiformal and informal; block, semi-cursive and cursive; the three basic styles for traditional artistic works, including land-

scape gardening, flower arrangement, painting, calligraphy, etc.
⇨ IKEBANA, NIHON-TEIEN

〚注〛 elaborate 精巧な, 手のこんだ. intermediate 中間の. abbreviated 簡略化された. landscape gardening 造園. flower arrangement 生け花.

shinjūmono 心中物 double suicide pieces in Kabuki and Bunraku plays. They were made popular by Chikamatsu Monzaemon (1653-1724), a distinguished playwright of the 17th century. Pieces still popularly staged include *Shinjū Ten no Amijima* (A Double Suicide at Amijima), *Sonezaki Shinjū* (A Double Suicide at Sonezaki), etc. Double suicides were not unusual in feudal days, for people could not marry outside their social class. ⇨ BUNRAKU, KABUKI

〚注〛 double suicide 心中. playwright 劇作家. feudal days 封建時代.

Shinkansen 新幹線 the New Trunk Line; the bullet train; high-speed train service operated originally by the Japanese National Railways (JNR) and since 1987 by private corporations. In 1964, the year of the Tokyo Olympics, the bullet train (which runs at a top speed of 210 k.p.h.) went into operation on the New Tōkaidō Trunk Line (Tōkaidō Shinkansen), covering a distance of 515 kilometers between Tokyo and Ōsaka. It takes three hours 10 minutes by Hikari (Light) runs, with stops at Nagoya and Kyoto, and four hours 10 minutes by Kodama (Echo) runs, with stops at 11 stations. In 1972 the line was extended to Okayama, and in 1975 to Hakata in northern Kyūshū, some 1,069 km from Tokyo, taking some nine hours by Hikari runs. Two more lines were opened in 1982: the Tōhoku Shinkansen between Tokyo and Morioka, Iwate Prefecture, and the Jōetsu Shinkansen between Tokyo and Niigata, Niigata Prefecture.

〚注〛 bullet 弾丸. the Japanese National Railways (JNR) 日本国有鉄道(国鉄). go into operation 開通する.

Shin-Kokin(waka)shū 新古今(和歌)集 *The New Anthology of Ancient and Modern Poems* (1205); a collection of *tanka*, 31-syllable poems, compiled in the Kamakura period (1185-1336), under the supervision of the retired Emperor Gotoba (1180-1239; r.1183-1198). The set is composed of 20 volumes of 1,980 poems, selected by several poets including Fujiwara Teika (1162-1241) and Fujiwara Ietaka (1158-1237), from among all known 31-syllable poems from the *Man'yōshū* (The Collection of Myriad Leaves, eighth century) onward, with special emphasis on contemporary ones. Major poets included are Kakinomoto no Hitomaro (seventh or eighth century), Ki no Tsurayuki (?-945), Priest Saigyō (1118-1190), Fujiwara Teika, Fujiwara Ietake, as well as Emperor Gotoba himself. Though covering a great range of poetic styles, the general tone of the collection, particularly of the contemporary works, is characterized by technical refinement, retrospective sentiment, and subtle symbolism with understated elegance. ⇨ KAMAKURA-JIDAI, KOKIN(WAKA)SHŪ, MAN'YŌSHŪ, TANKA

〖注〗 anthology 名詩選集. technical refinement 技巧が洗練されていること. retrospective sentiment 回顧的感情. subtle symbolism with understated elegance 幽玄.

shinnai(-bushi) 新内(節) the Shinnai style of *jōruri* chanting; a style of traditional song sung to *shamisen* accompaniment. Developed by Tsuruga Shinnai (1714-74), it was first adopted for the Kabuki stage, but gradually broke away and developed as narrative chamber music for entertainment. Most *shinnai* pieces sound plaintive and sentimental. ⇨ GIDAYŪ, JŌRURI, KABUKI, KIYOMOTO (-BUSHI), SHAMISEN, TOKIWAZU(-BUSHI)

〖注〗 chanting 単調にくりかえして歌うこと, 謡うこと. accompaniment 伴奏. Tsuruga Shinnai 鶴賀新内. narrative 語り(の). chamber music 室内音楽, お座敷音楽. plaintive もの悲しい, あわれな.

shinnō 親王 an imperial prince; an honorific title for princes of the imperial family. For example, the Crown Prince (*Kōtaishi Denka Tōgū*) is also called Akihito Shinnō (Prince Akihito), when his name is used. Formerly, *shinnō* was used as a title for the brothers and sons of the emperor. Today, it is the title for the sons and direct male descendants of the emperor. The princesses of the imperial family bear the honorific title of *naishinnō*. ⇨ NAISHINNŌ, TENNŌ

〖注〗 honorific title 敬称.

shi-nō-kō-shō 士農工商 warriors, farmers, artisans and merchants; the four classes of people in society, as officially established in the Edo period (1603-1868). A striking distinction was made between the ruling warrior class and the commoners of the other three classes. The system was abolished at the time of the Meiji Restoration (1868). ⇨ EDO-JIDAI, MEIJI ISHIN, TOKUGAWA-BAKUFU

〖注〗 warrior 武士. artisan 職人. striking distinction きわだった区別. the Meiji Restoration 明治維新.

Shino-yaki 志野焼　Shino ceramic ware; ceramic ware fired in the Mino region, presently Gifu Prefecture.　It has an opaque, bubbly, pale cinnamon glaze, with orange brown burns from the kiln fire, and is delicately but hastily decorated with dark brown floral or abstract patterns.　The rough and rustic quality of such tea bowls endears them to tea enthusiasts.　Genuine Shino ware is hand-made.

〖注〗 ceramic ware 陶器製品．　fire（陶器などを）焼く．　opaque 不透明な，光沢のない．　bubbly 泡の多い．　pale cinnamon 淡いシナモン色．　glaze 釉．　kiln 窯．　hastily 急いで，あっさりと．　rough and rustic quality 素朴でひなびた味，わび・さびの趣．　endear 愛させる，慕わせる．

shinpan-daimyō 親藩大名　a kin feudal lord; a Tokugawa-related *daimyō*; feudal lords from Tokugawa-lineage families, one of the three classifications of feudal lords during the Edo period (1603-1868), the other two being *fudai-daimyō* (hereditary feudal lords) and *tozama-daimyō* (outside feudal lords).　Among a total of 250-300 *daimyō*, there were only some 20 *shinpan-daimyō*, who enjoyed high status in connection with shogunate governmental affairs.　They also had the responsibility of monitoring *tozama-daimyō*, in cooperation with *fudai-daimyō*.　The first Tokugawa shogun, Ieyasu (1542-1616), appointed three of his sons as special *shinpan-daimyō* to govern Owari, Kii and Hitachi provinces respectively.　Their families and descendants were privileged with the possibility of being successors to the shogun when he had no heir, and were thus called the three honorable families (*gosanke*).　⇨ DAIMYŌ, FUDAI-DAIMYŌ, GOSANKE, KUNI, TOZAMA-DAIMYŌ

〖注〗 feudal lord 大名．　lineage 血統，家柄．　outside feudal lord 外様大名．　hereditary feudal lord 譜代大名．　the three honorable families 御三家．

shin-soe-hikae 真・副・控　the main, second and third branches of a flower arrangement; the names for the three principal stems in the Sōgetsu school—the longest stem, the second longest stem and the shortest stem, forming the main triangular lines of a flower arrangement.　The *soe* is about three-fourths of the length of the *shin*, and the *hikae* is about one-half to three-fourths of the *soe*.　Called *shin-soe-tai* in the Ikenobō school and *shu-fuku-kyaku* in the Ohara school.　⇨ IKEBANA, KIHON-KAKEI, SHIN-SOE-TAI, SHU-FUKU-KYAKU, SHUSHI

〖注〗 principal stem 主枝．

shin-soe-tai 真・副・体　the main, second and third branches of a flower arrangement; the names for the three principal stems of flower arrangement in the Ikenobō school—the longest stem, the second longest stem and the shortest stem, forming the main triangular lines of a flower arrangement.   The *soe* is three-fourths of the length of the *shin*, and the *tai* is about one-half to three-fourths of the *soe*.   Called *shin-soe-hikae* in the Sōgetsu school and *shu-fuku-kyaku* in the Ohara school.   ⇨ IKEBANA, KIHON-KAKEI, SHIN-SOE-HIKAE, SHU-FUKU-KYAKU, SHUSHI

〖注〗 principal stem 主枝.

Shintō 神道 lit. the way of gods.   Shinto; Shintoism; the indigenous folk religion of Japan, characterized by the worship of myriad deified nature spirits, mythological ancestors and historical figures. Rooted in the beliefs of the agricultural people of ancient Japan, Shinto involves fertility rites as well as purification for protection from evil spirits.   Natural phenomena were the first objects of worship and gradually shrines came to be constructed.   The introduction of Buddhism and Confucianism from China led to the designation of the term Shinto for combined indigenous beliefs. Shinto has survived in combination with Buddhism.   In the 17th century, it was revived as a national religion, with the Sun Goddess Amaterasu Ōmikami considered the original ancestor of the Imperial Family and the most important deity.   From the Meiji era (1868–1912) until the end of World War II (1945), shrine Shinto, as distinguished from sectarian Shinto, was adopted as the official state religion in an attempt to boost patriotism.   At present, Shinto can roughly be divided into imperial Shinto, shrine Shinto, sectarian Shinto and local community Shinto.   ⇨ AMATERASU ŌMIKAMI, BUKKYŌ, JINJA, JUKYŌ

〖注〗 indigenous（土地）固有の. deified 神格化した. fertility rite 豊じょう を祈る祭事. purification 浄め. Confucianism 儒教. deity 神, 神のような 人[もの]. sectarian Shinto 教派神道. patriotism 愛国心.

shiohigari 潮干狩り lit. hunting on the ebb.   shellfish gathering at low tide.   It is a popular seasonal recreation enjoyed in April or May when the sea is no longer very cold.   Edible shellfish are dug for in the sand using a small rake, clams (*asari* and *hamaguri*) being the most common.

〖注〗 on the ebb 引き潮の時. at low tide 潮が低い時. clam 浅蜊, 蛤等.

shioyaki 塩焼き salt-broiling; broiling with salt, usually referring to fish.   Fish sprinkled with salt is broiled until the skin becomes crisp. Sweetfish (*ayu*), seabream (*tai*), mackerel pike (*sanma*), horse mackerel (*aji*), etc., are good for *shioyaki*. A whole fish is often skewered before broiling, so as to create a graceful shape. ⇨ YAKIMONO[1]

〚注〛 sweetfish 鮎. seabream 鯛. mackerel pike 秋刀魚. horse mackerel 鰺. skewer 串をさす.

shippō 七宝 a frog; a metal plant holder with no needles, used for arranging flowers in a shallow basin. This metal holder has open sections to secure the ends of the stems into position. The Ohara school considers this open-type holder preferable to the needle-point holder. ⇨ IKEBANA, KENZAN, MORIBANA, SUIBAN

〚注〛 frog 花器の水の中におく花を留める金具(剣山, 七宝). metal plant holder 金具の花留め. needle-point holder 剣山.

shippō(-yaki) 七宝(焼) cloisonné (ware); the art of enameling on a metal base of copper or silver. *Shippō* literally means "seven gems"—i.e., gold, silver, coral, agate, emerald, crystal and pearl. Vases, plates and other ornaments take on a gem-like surface of various colors through this enameling art. The design is formed by wires of silver, gold or brass to make a multitude of cells on the metal base. These cells are filled with enamel of various colors containing silica niter, lead oxide, etc. Then, the object is fired at a high temperature and polished. First introduced from China around the 16th century, the art has developed in Japan in its own way.

〚注〛 enamel 上薬をかける, ほうろう彩飾する. metal base 金属の台. coral さんご. agate めのう. emerald 緑玉石. plate 皿. a multitude of 無数の. cell 組織の穴. silica niter 珪酸硝石. lead oxide 酸化鉛.

shirasu 白州 a white sandbar; white sand or gravel, such as in a dry landscape garden. The surface of the white gravel is often raked carefully in parallel lines to represent the waves of the ocean, as seen in the Ryōanji rock garden in Kyoto.

〚注〛 sandbar 砂州. gravel 砂利. dry landscape garden 枯山水(庭園). rake 熊手でかく. parallel lines 平行線.

shirataki 白滝 lit. a white cascade. fine translucent noodles made from the starch of devil's tongue or arum root. The gelatinous starch is mixed with limewater to coagulate it. Thus, before cooking, it should be washed well or boiled in water and drained to remove the lime residue. It is an indispensable ingredient for *sukiyaki*, and is also used in other kinds of pot dishes. ⇨ KON-

NYAKU, NABEMONO, SUKIYAKI

〖注〗 cascade 小滝, 人工滝. translucent 半透明の. devil's tongue こんにゃく. arum アルム属の植物. gelatinous ゼラチン質の. limewater 石灰水. coagulate 凝固する. lime 石灰. residue 残り, 残りかす. ingredient (料理の)材料.

Shiretoko Kokuritsu-kōen 知床国立公園 Shiretoko National Park (397.3 square kilometers), designated in 1964; a natural park situated in northeastern Hokkaidō, covering the Shiretoko Peninsula, which juts out into the Sea of Okhotsk. The mountainous backbone of this peninsula is made up of a number of volcanoes and caldera lakes. The mountains are covered with primeval forests of spruce and fir, and are inhabited by wild animals such as brown bears, northern foxes (*kitakitsune*), etc. ⇨ HOKKAIDŌ, KOKURITSU-KŌEN

〖注〗 jut out 突き出る, 張り出る. caldera lake 火山の火口からできた湖. primeval forest 原始林. spruce 蝦夷松. fir 樅.

shiro 城 a castle; a fortress-like structure constructed by feudal lords around the 16th century. Originally, it was a kind of wooden stockade built as a fortification upon a hilltop. Gradually, grand ones, which included many structures within their compounds, were constructed to serve as a symbol of the authority of feudal lords. Besides a multistoried towering donjon (*tenshukaku*), a great castle features large moats surrounding the entire compound, high stone walls, watchtowers, residences for the lord and his family, warriors' quarters, etc. Very few original castles remain in existence, but many have been restored to their original appearance using modern construction methods. Existing original castles include Himeji Castle (in present-day Hyōgo Prefecture), Inuyama Castle (Aichi Prefecture), Hikone Castle (Shiga Prefecture) and Matsumoto Castle (Nagano Prefecture). ⇨ DAIMYŌ

〖注〗 fortress 要塞. feudal lord 大名. stockade 防御柵, 柵で作った囲い. fortification 防御物, 要塞. compound 敷地, 囲われた地域. donjon 天守閣. watchtower 火の見やぐら. warriors' quarters 武士の宿所.

shirozake 白酒 lit. white liquor. a sweet mild whitish rice wine. Boiled rice is mixed with rice malt and *mirin* (sweet seasoning wine) or *shōchū* (distilled spirit) and left to ferment for 20 to 30 days. It is then mashed and a whitish liquid is squeezed out. The alcohol content of this beverage is less than 10 percent. Traditionally on Girls' Day (March 3), parties are held where this beverage is offered to dolls on display, and to daughters and their guests. ⇨ HINA MATSURI, HINA-NINGYŌ, MIRIN, SAKE, SHŌCHŪ

〖注〗 distilled spirit 蒸留酒. ferment 発酵する.

shiruko 汁粉 sweet red-bean soup; sweet bean-paste soup containing a piece of rice cake. *Azuki* beans are soaked in water overnight, and then boiled and simmered over low heat until they become soft. The soft beans are then strained to remove the skin. The creamy bean paste thus made is heated in a mixture of water, sugar and a dash of salt, with a piece of rice cake or sometimes a few rice-flour dumplings. Sweet red-bean soup with whole beans is called *zenzai*. ⇨ AN, ZENZAI

〖注〗 sweet bean paste 餡. simmer 煮つめる. strain 濾して除く. a dash of 一つまみの. dumpling 団子.

shirumono 汁物 a generic term for Japanese soup. Roughly there are two kinds—clear soup (*sumashi*) and soybean-paste soup (*misoshiru*). ⇨ MISOSHIRU, SUIMONO

shirushi-banten 印半天 a traditional livery jacket; a kimono-style work jacket with a mark on the back. Usually this jacket is of strong, coarse cotton cloth of indigo color with a white trademark on it. The mark, a Chinese character or other design, tells where the person wearing it is employed. This type of jacket is still worn by carpenters and by employees at traditional shops. ⇨ HANTEN, HAPPI, KIMONO

〖注〗 livery そろいの服, (使用人の)仕着せ, 同業の制服. indigo 藍(色). Chinese character 漢字.

Shitakiri Suzume 舌切り雀 *Tongue-Cut Sparrow*; one of Japan's five most famous folk tales. An honest old man kept a sparrow, which ate up rice starch prepared by his greedy wife to be used for washed clothes. The outraged wife cut the sparrow's tongue off with a pair of scissors, and the bird flew away in tears. The old man went out to look for the sparrow and found it in a bamboo grove. He was welcomed by the sparrow and offered two boxes of which he was to choose one. He chose the lighter one and found it full of treasures. The old woman then went to the sparrow's home and brought back the heavier box, out of which appeared ghosts and strange creatures. The original tale is found in *Uji Shūi Monogatari* (A Collection of Tales from Uji, 13th century).

〖注〗 folk tale 民話. rice starch ごはんで作った糊. outraged かっとなった. bamboo grove 竹やぶ.

shite 仕手 the main actor or protagonist in a Noh play. The *shite* almost always wears a Noh mask while the *shitezure* (his assistant) may occasionally wear one. The *shite* is accompanied by a *tsure* (companion), *tomo* (attendant) or *kokata* (juvenile actor), and portrays various kinds of characters including a god, an old man, a ghost, a warrior or even a beautiful woman.   ⇨ KOKATA, NŌ, TOMO, TSURE

〖注〗 protagonist（劇の）主役，主人公，（特にギリシャ劇の）主役，（能の）仕手．companion 仲間，（能の）連．attendant 従者，（能の）供．juvenile actor 年少の役者，子方．warrior さむらい．

Shitennō 四天王 the Four Guardian Kings; the Four Devas; a group of four deities guarding the Buddhist world in four directions. Of the four deities, Tamonten is said to be guarding the north, Zōchōten the south, Jikokuten the east and Kōmokuten the west. The statues of the four often stand guarding Nyorai or Bodhisattva, as seen in the Golden Hall of Hōryūji Temple. They are depicted with fierce, severe expressions, and are shown standing firmly on a pedestal of demons.   ⇨ BOSATSU, NYORAI

〖注〗 guardian 守護（の），保護（の）．deva（インド神話の）堤婆神，善霊;（ゾロアスター教）悪魔．deity 神，神のようなもの．bodhisattva 菩薩．the Golden Hall 金堂，本堂．pedestal 台座．四天王：多聞天，増長天，持国天，広目天．

Shizenkōen Hō 自然公園法 the Natural Park Law; a law enacted in 1949 to protect natural parks designated by the government. Prior to this law, the National Park Law had been in effect since 1934 to protect national parks. It was partially revised in 1949 in order to broaden its scope to cover a new project of quasi-national parks, and renamed. National parks are designated and administered by the Ministry of Health and Welfare; quasi-national parks are designated by this ministry but are administered by prefectural governments.   ⇨ KOKURITSU-KŌEN, KOKUTEI-KŌEN

〖注〗 enact 法律にする，（法令を）発する．the National Park Law「国立公園法」．in effect 実施されて，（法律が）有効で．quasi-national park 国定公園．the Ministry of Health and Welfare 厚生省．prefectural government 都道府県行政機関．

shizoku 士族 the samurai class; families of samurai origin; the title for the samurai class, one of the three classes—*kazoku*, *shizoku* and *heimin*—established in 1879, shortly after the Meiji Restoration (1868). This title was conferred upon former samurai and their descendants. They ranked between the nobility (*kazoku*) and the commoners (*heimin*). Like *kazoku*, this class included only a small number of the population, first accounting for about 1.9 million and later on showing a considerable decline. Under the present constitution, these class divisions have been abolished. ⇨ HEIMIN, KAZOKU, MEIJI ISHIN

〖注〗 the Meiji Restoration 明治維新． confer 授与する．

shō¹ 升 a traditional unit for measuring capacity (1.8 liters). This is still used for measuring rice, soy sauce, Japanese rice wine, etc. There is a traditional square measuring box holding one *shō*, usually made of Japanese cypress, for rice. Japanese rice wine and soy sauce are generally contained in one-*shō* bottles. ⇨ GŌ, SHAKKAN-HŌ

〖注〗 unit for measuring capacity 容量単位． soy sauce 醬油． Japanese rice wine 日本酒． measuring box 量をはかる容器，桝． cypress 檜．

shō² 笙 a Japanese mouth organ; an organ-like wind instrument made up of 17 slender bamboo pipes of various sizes and a lacquered box into which the performer blows. It is about 50 centimeters long. It was introduced from China in the seventh century and is used primarily in Gagaku (court music and dance). ⇨ GAGAKU

〖注〗 wind instrument 吹奏楽器，管楽器． lacquered box 漆塗りの箱．

shōbuyu 菖蒲湯 a Japanese-iris bath. Leaves of Japanese iris or sweet flag (*shōbu*) are steeped in the tub as one of the traditional customs observed on Boys' Day (May 5), which was originally called the Iris Festival (*Shōbu no Sekku*). Japanese iris leaves, very fragrant in this season, are said to have the medicinal effect of preventing disease, as well as the spiritual power to ward off demons with their shape resembling swords. The word *shōbu* (Japanese iris) is a homonymn of *shōbu* meaning "victory or defeat"; thus *shōbu* plants are regarded as especially appropriate for Boys' Day. ⇨ KODOMO NO HI, TANGO NO SEKKU

〖注〗 Japanese iris 菖蒲(=sweet flag)． steep 浸す． ward off 追い払う． homonymn 同音異義語．

shō-chiku-bai 松竹梅 pine, bamboo and Japanese plum branches. The three form a traditional combination of auspicious significance, each symbolizing longevity, constancy and purity. The combination of these plants is particularly associated with the New Year, and are thus used in New Year decorations—in gate decorations (*kadomatsu*), in flower arrangements, etc. The designs of utensils and even those of cakes for the New Year may include one of these patterns or a combination of the three.　⇨ KADOMATSU

〖注〗 Japanese plum branch 梅の枝．　auspicious significance 祝いの意味，めでたい意味．　longevity 長寿．　constancy 不変，貞節．　gate decoration 門松．flower arrangement 生け花，華道．

shōchū 焼酎 lit. burning liquor. a distilled alcoholic beverage made from grain or sweet potatoes.　Grain such as rice, millet, molasses, rye, barley, corn, or sweet potatoes are fermented with the aid of malted rice.　The alcoholic content varies from 20 to 45 percent.　*Shōchū* is served either cold or warmed like sakê.　It is considered a low-grade liquor, but is also used as the base in making high-quality fruit liquor such as plum wine.　⇨ SAKE, UMESHU

〖注〗 distilled 蒸留した．　alcoholic beverage アルコール飲料．　millet きび，あわ．　molasses 糖密．　barley 大麦．　ferment 発酵する．　malted rice こうじ．　alcoholic content アルコール含有量．　plum wine 梅酒．

shochūmimai 暑中見舞い midsummer greetings; an inquiry about health at the height of summer, either by sending a letter or by visiting with a small gift.　These greetings are exchanged during the 18 days before the coming of autumn according to the lunar calendar, falling around August 7 on the present calendar.　Since it is more customary to send gifts during the *chūgen* period (from the beginning of June to the middle of July), sending only cards is more common for this greeting.　⇨ CHŪGEN, SHOCHŪMIMAI-JŌ

〖注〗 inquiry 問合わせ，お伺い．　the lunar calendar 太陰暦．

shochūmimai-jō 暑中見舞状 a midsummer greeting card; a card or letter inquiring about one's health sent at the height of summer.　These greetings are exchanged during the 18 days before the coming of autumn in the lunar calendar, falling around August 7 on the present calendar.　After this period, it is the custom to use the expression "lingering summer heat" in referring to the weather.　Seasonal greeting cards with a small refreshing picture on them are sold, although many people make their own.　From around the middle of June the Ministry of Posts and Telecommunications issues official post cards bearing seasonal designs.　⇨ SHOCHŪ-MIMAI

〖注〗 the lunar calendar 太陰暦．　lingering summer heat 残暑．　the Ministry of Posts and Telecommunications 郵政省．

shodō 書道 calligraphy; the method of writing with a brush and *sumi* or dark Japanese-type India ink. It is regarded as an art as well as a means of communication. The characters take on beauty only when they are written with harmony of mind and body. Attention is paid to the shades of the ink and the movement of the brush strokes, along with the forms of characters.

〖注〗 India ink 墨. character 文字. the shades of ink 墨の濃淡. brush strokes 筆致.

shōgi 将棋 Japanese chess; a board game for two players, with the object of checkmating the opponent's king. The game is played on a board of 81 squares (nine by nine) with 20 pieces each of eight different ranks. Initially, the *fuhyō* (nine pieces) are placed in the third row, the *hisha* in the second space from the right behind a *fuhyō*, the *kakugyō* opposite the *hisha* in the same second row. In the first row on both sides of the king in the center are the *kinshō*, *ginshō*, *keima* and *kyōsha*. The *fuhyō* can move only one space forward. The *hisha* moves as a rook, the *kakugyō* as a bishop. The king moves one space in any direction, the *kinshō* one space in any direction except diagonally backward, the *ginshō* one space in any direction except backward or sideways, the *keima* a combination of two spaces forward and one to either side, the *kyōsha* any number of spaces forward. There are two notable differences between chess and *shōgi*. One is that a piece that penetrates the opponent's three-row territory can be promoted by turning the piece over. The king and the *kinshō* cannot be promoted, but the *fuhyō*, *ginshō*, *keima* and *kyōsha* can become *kinshō*, and to the *hisha* and *kakugyō* can be added the movements of a king. The other difference is that, once captured, a piece can be used by the captor. The piece can be put on any unoccupied space as one move.

〖注〗 board game 盤を使ったゲーム. checkmate 王手詰め. bishop (チェスの)ビショップ. rook (チェスの)ルーク. penetrate 進入する. territory 陣地. captor 捕獲者. 駒名：歩兵, 飛車, 角行, 王将, 金将, 銀将, 桂馬, 香車.

shōgun 将軍 a general; a generalissimo; the abbreviated term for *seii-taishōgun*, originally used for a great general to subdue the Ezo race (presumably the Ainus) or rebellions in the Heian period (794-1185), then used as a formal title for a shogunate general. The term shogun came to be more commonly used with the establishment of the shogunate government, as the title of the ruler of the Kamakura (1185-1336), Ashikaga (1336-1568) and Tokugawa

(1603–1868) shogunates. ⇨ AINU, SEII-TAISHŌGUN

〖注〗 generalissimo 最高司令官，大将軍． great general to subdue the Ezo race 蝦夷を制圧する大将軍（征夷大将軍）． shogunate 将軍の． shogunate government 幕府．

shoin-zukuri 書院造り the study-room style of residential architecture; a style of architecture developed in the Azuchi-Momoyama period (1568–1603), reaching perfection in the early Edo period (17th century). Developed first for samurai residences and priests' quarters, this style provided for a main room with *tokonoma* (an alcove), *chigaidana* (a side alcove with staggered shelves) and *shoin* (a built-in desk). The rooms, with *tatami* (a rush mat) floors, were divided by decorated *fusuma* (sliding screen doors). Superb examples may be seen at the Kōjōin Guest Hall (1601) of Onjōji Temple in Shiga Prefecture and Ninomaru Palace (1626) of Nijō Castle in Kyoto. This style is the basis of present-day Japanese-style residential architecture. ⇨ CHIGAIDANA, FUSUMA, TATAMI, TOKONOMA

〖注〗 quarters 宿所，住居． alcove 床の間． staggered shelves 違い棚． built-in desk 造りつけの机，書院． rush mat 畳． sliding screen door ふすま． the Kōjōin Guest Hall 光浄院客殿． Onjōji Temple 園城寺．

shōji 障子 a paper sliding door; a sliding screen covered with white Japanese paper on thin wood laths admitting a soft diffused sunlight or moonlight to the room. It serves as a kind of curtain, as a substitute for windows, or as a partition between rooms in Japanese homes. The size of a *shōji* is about the same as the *tatami*—about 180 centimeters in height and 90 cm in width. Some *shōji* are fitted with glass at eye level when one is seated on the *tatami* floor. ⇨ FUSUMA, TATAMI

〖注〗 laths 木ずり，下地の細い木片． diffused 放たれた，広がった． partition 仕切り，区画．

shōjin-ryōri 精進料理 lit. a diet in pursuing the way to enlightenment. a vegetarian diet; dishes for those who abstain from fish and meat, first developed in temples. The protein source is primarily soybeans and soybean products—*tōfu* (soybean curd), *aburage* (fried soybean curd), *nattō* (fermented soybeans), etc. The restriction on materials has resulted in elaborate methods of cooking and arrangement, and has influenced Japanese cuisine as a whole. ⇨ ABURA(A)GE, NATTŌ, TŌFU

〖注〗 diet 食品，食物． pursue the way to enlightenment 精進する． enlight-

enment 悟り． vegetarian 菜食主義者(の)． abstain from ～を控える，～を断
つ． soybean curd 豆腐． fried soybean curd 油揚げ． fermented soybeans
納豆． cuisine 料理．

Shōjō Bukkyō 小乗仏教 lit. Lesser Vehicle Buddhism. Hinayana
Buddhism; the older of the two large categories of Buddhism, the
other being Mahayana Buddhism (*Daijō Bukkyō*). It is prevalent
mainly in Sri Lanka, Burma, Thailand, etc. The teachings stress
personal salvation to nirvana by attaining a state of enlightenment
through severe moral and intellectual self-training. ⇨ BUKKYŌ,
DAIJŌ BUKKYŌ

〖注〗 Mahayana Buddhism 大乗仏教． prevalent 広く行きわたる． personal
salvation 個人の救済． nirvana 涅槃． the state of enlightenment 悟りの
境地．

shōkyaku 正客 the guest of honor; the principal guest at a tea
ceremony. He or she plays an important role in the proceedings,
for each guest follows the manners of this principal guest.

〖注〗 tea ceremony 茶の湯． proceedings 進行，仕方．

Shō-ōchō 尚王朝 the Shō dynasty (1406–1879) of the Chūzan kingdom of Okinawa. The island of Okinawa was united by King Shō
Hashi (1372–1439) of Chūzan during the first Shō dynasty
(1406–1469), a line of seven kings. This was followed by the
second Shō dynasty (1470–1879), a line of 19 kings. King Shō
Shin (ruled 1477–1526) ensured lasting peace by forcing local rulers
and petty lords to live in the capital city of Shuri. Shō Shin also
took over control of the religious hierarchy by making his sister
chief priestess. By the mid-16th century, the Shō dynasty had
spread its rule throughout the four major island groups of the
Ryūkyūs. Contact with China brought major new influences, and
Chinese visitors likened Okinawa to a flower in full bloom. In
1609, Satsuma (present-day Kagoshima Prefecture) conquered
Okinawa, but allowed the Shō dynasty to continue. The kingdom
entered a period of dual sovereignty, paying tribute to both China
and Satsuma. By the late 17th century, the Shō dynasty had
recovered its glory and led Okinawa into a second golden age.
The Shō dynasty was abolished with the establishment of Okinawa
as a prefecture in 1879 by the Meiji government. ⇨ OKINAWA,
RYŪKYŪ-SHOTŌ

〖注〗 religious hierarchy 宗教の位階制度． dual sovereignty 二重統治． tribute 貢物．

shōrō 鐘楼　a belfry; a bell tower; a structure in which a temple bell (*tsurigane*) is hung together with a huge wooden hammer.　It has a simple frame construction made of four pillars and a tiled roof, with no walls.　It stands in the compounds of large temples, often on an elevated place.　⇨ GARAN, SHICHIDŌ-GARAN, TERA, TSURIGANE
　〖注〗 frame construction わく組, 構造.　compounds 敷地.

Shōwa 昭和　the Shōwa era.　The appellation of the era of the present emperor (Hirohito).　The era started in 1926 when the present emperor was enthroned.　The year 1985 corresponds to the 60th year of Shōwa.　⇨ GENGŌ
　〖注〗 appellation 呼称.　enthrone 即位させる.

Shōwa Kenpō 昭和憲法　　⇨ NIHONKOKU KENPŌ

shōyu 醤油　soy sauce; a dark brown sauce made from fermented soybeans and wheat, mixed with a special yeast in brine.　This is the most basic seasoning, used in a wide variety of cooking.　Though it was first introduced from China, Japan developed its own techniques with the sauce, starting in the 16th century.　There is a light soy sauce (*usukuchi-shōyu*) and a dark sauce (*koikuchi-shōyu*).　The former is favored in the Kyoto-Ōsaka area, particularly for clear soup.　The latter is more widely used in other districts though there are local variations.　In addition, there is a thick, very dark soy sauce called *tamari* made mainly of fermented soybeans, which is used as a dip for raw fish (*sashimi*), or for marinating fish or meat.　⇨ SASHIMI
　〖注〗 fermented 発酵した.　brine 塩水.　seasoning 調味料.　local variations その土地特有の種類.　marinate 調理の前にソースなどに漬ける.

Shūbun (no Hi) 秋分(の日)　Autumnal Equinox Day (September 23 or 24), one of the national holidays; the middle day of the autumn Buddhist week beginning on or around September 21.　On this date, day and night are equal in length as the sun crosses directly above the equator.　According to Buddhist belief, this is the day when the dead can cross the river leading to eternal paradise.　Thus it is the custom on this day (or any day of this week) for Buddhists to pay a visit to their ancestor's graves and observe worship services at home or at temples.　It is said that no summer heat lingers past the equinox day.　⇨ HIGAN, SHUNBUN(NO HI)
　〖注〗 equinox 昼夜平分時(点), 彼岸の中日.　the equator 赤道.　eternal paradise 永遠の楽園, 極楽.　worship service 法要.　the equinox day 彼岸(の中日).　No summer heat lingers past the equinox day.「暑さ(寒さ)も彼岸まで」.

shu-fuku-kyaku 主・副・客 the subject, the secondary and the object branches; the names for the three principal stems of flower arrangement in the Ohara school—the longest stem, the second longest stem and the shortest stem forming the main triangular lines of a flower arrangement. The *fuku* is three-fourths of the *shu*, and the *kyaku* is one-half to three-fourths of the *fuku*. Called *shin-soe-tai* in the Ikenobō school and *shin-soe-hikae* in the Sōgetsu school. ⇨ IKEBANA, KIHON-KAKEI, SHIN-SOE-HIKAE, SHIN-SOE-TAI

〖注〗 subject branch 主体となる枝, 主. secondary branch 副体となる枝, 副. object branch 客体となる枝, 客. principal stem 主枝.

shugendō 修験道 mountain asceticism; a religious body pursuing asceticism in deep mountains. It derives principally from the esoteric Buddhism of the Shingon and Tendai sects, and partially from shamanistic aspects of Shintoism and the cosmic principles of Chinese Taoism. It is characterized by disciplinary regimens, communion with nature, the casting of spells, peculiar rituals, etc. Emerging from the austere practices of Buddhist hermits, with no individual founder, in the early Heian period (794-1185), it flourished during the Heian and early Kamakura (1185-1336) periods, gradually assuming the form of a religious sect. By the early Edo period (1603-1868), it had split into two branches—the Tōzan branch associated with the Shingon sect and the Honzan branch associated with the Tendai sect. Surviving today, Shugendō training areas are located on Mount Ōmine (on the border of Nara and Wakayama prefectures), on the Three Dewa Mountains (Yamagata Prefecture), etc. ⇨ BUKKYŌ, SHINGONSHŪ, SHINTŌ, TENDAISHŪ, YAMABUSHI

〖注〗 asceticism 修行, 苦行. esoteric Buddhism 密教. shamanistic シャーマニズム的, 呪術による神秘的交霊的な. Taoism 道教. disciplinary regimen 厳しい修行. in communion with nature 自然と合体して. casting of spells まじないをかけること. ritual 儀式. austere practice 厳しい修行. hermit 隠遁者. the Tōzan branch 当山派. the Honzan branch 本山派. the Three Dewa Mountains 出羽三山.

shūgibukuro 祝儀袋 lit. a congratulatory envelope. a money-gift envelope; an envelope for money used as a congratulatory gift or gratuity. It is made of white rice paper folded in a specific way or else in the form of a regular envelope, with a congratulatory emblem (*noshi*) and gift-binding cord (*mizuhiki*) attached to or printed on it. One with a gold-and-silver cord is for weddings, while a red-and-white cord is appropriate for other happy occasions like having a child, entering an upper school, etc., or to indicate appreciation. ⇨ MIZUHIKI, NOSHI

〖注〗 gratuity 心付け, 祝儀. rice paper 和紙. congratulatory emblem お祝いのしるし, 熨斗. gift-binding cord 水引.

shugo 守護 a safeguard; the head of provinces; the title for an administrative official under the Kamakura (1185-1336) and Muromachi (1336-1568) shogunate governments. When Minamoto Yoritomo (1147-99) organized a military government at Kamakura, he established this post along with *jitō* (the head of estate) throughout the country with the approval of the emperor. The *shugo* were at first appointed to take charge of security in the provinces, gradually taking over political affairs from *kokushi* (the governor of the province appointed directly by the Imperial Court). ⇨ BAKUFU, JITŌ

〖注〗 province 地方, (行政区画としての)国. shogunate government 幕府. estate (大きな)地所, 不動産. security affairs 安全に関する事柄. take over 受け継ぐ. governor 統治者, 長官.

shukke 出家 lit. leaving home. a hermit life; to enter a secluded life devoted to religious pursuits in Buddhism. This custom was very common even among laymen in the middle ages of Japan. Some, purely for the purpose of spiritual realization, entered Buddhist religious orders to be free from worldly desires; others escaped the bonds of society and led a secluded life to devote themselves to literary or aesthetic diversions. ⇨ BUKKYŌ

〖注〗 hermit 隠者, 世捨人. secluded 人里はなれた. layman 俗人. spiritual realization 霊的な悟り. Buddhist religious orders 僧職. worldly desires 煩悩. literary or aesthetic diversions 文学的審美的趣味.

shukuba-machi 宿場町 a post-station town; towns developed as relay stations along major roads. These towns developed rapidly along the five major roads (*gokaidō*) extending from Edo in the Edo period (1603-1868), when the system of alternate attendance (*sankinkōtai*) in Edo was imposed on feudal lords by the Tokugawa shogunate (1603-1868). The 53 post stations on the Tōkaidō Highway are still well-known as depicted on woodblock prints by Andō Hiroshige (1797-1858). Centering around the main official inn (*honjin*) where the feudal lord and his retainers stayed, minor official and other inns and shops lined the main road of each post-station town. ⇨ GOKAIDŌ, SANKINKŌTAI, TŌKAIDŌ-

GOJŪSANTSUGI

【注】 post station 宿場. relay station 中継駅. the five major roads 五街
道. alternate attendance 参勤交代. feudal lord 大名. the Tokugawa shogunate 徳川幕府. woodblock print 木版画. main official inn 本陣.
retainer 家臣. minor official inn 脇本陣.

shūmei 襲名 to inherit a name; succession to a hereditary name in
the pursuit of an art. In particular, it refers to a stage name in
time-honored performing arts such as Kabuki, Bunraku, etc. A
family's illustrious name is bestowed on a gifted performer who is
accomplished enough to hand its traditional artistic spirit and skills
down to the next generation. It usually involves blood ties, but not
necessarily. A name-inheriting ceremony, accompanied by a
series of stage performances with the participation of other major
actors, is held not only to honor the recipient, but also in recognition of the artistic heritage of the family. When the full name is
assumed, an ordinal number is used before the name along with the
term for "generation," as in "Jūni-daime Ichikawa Danjūrō" (lit.
the 12th Generation Ichikawa Danjūrō; i.e., Ichikawa Danjūrō XII).
⇨ BUNRAKU, KABUKI

【注】 hereditary 世襲の. time-honored 由緒ある、伝統的な. performing art
舞台芸術. illustrious 有名な、輝かしい. recipient 受ける人. ordinal number 序数.

Shunbun (no Hi) 春分(の日) Vernal Equinox Day (March 20 or
21), one of the national holidays; the middle day of the spring
Buddhist week beginning on or around March 21. On this date,
day and night are equal in length as the sun crosses directly above
the equator. According to Buddhist belief, this is the day when the
dead can cross the river leading to eternal paradise. Thus, it is the
custom on this day (or any day of this week) for Buddhists to pay
a visit to their ancestors' graves and observe worship services at
home or at temples. It is said that no winter cold lingers past the
equinox day. ⇨ HIGAN, SHŪBUN (NO HI)

【注】 vernal 春の. equinox 昼夜平分時(点)、彼岸の中日. the equator 赤道.
eternal paradise 永遠の楽園、極楽. worship service 法要. the equinox day
彼岸の(中日). No winter cold lingers past the equinox day.「(暑さ)寒さも彼
岸まで」.

Shunkei-nuri 春慶塗 Shunkei lacquer ware; wooden ware thinly
coated with a brownish translucent lacquer, so thinly that the
beauty of the texture of the wood can also be appreciated. It was

originally made in the Muromachi period (1336–1568) by a lacquer-
er named Shunkei at Sakai, near Ōsaka, and called Sakai Shunkei,
as distinguished from the Shunkei ware made at Hida and Noshiro
—called *Hida Shunkei-nuri* and *Noshiro Shunkei-nuri* respectively.
⇨ NURIMONO

〖注〗 lacquer ware 漆器. coat 塗る. translucent 半透明の. texture of
wood 木目. Hida Shunkei-nuri 飛騨春慶塗. Noshiro Shunkei-nuri 能代春
慶塗.

shuramono 修羅物 a warrior ghost piece; the second group of the
five categories of the Noh play. In this play the main actor (*shite*)
plays the ghost of a warrior, and battle scenes are depicted. ⇨ NŌ,
SHIKINŌ, SHITE

〖注〗 warrior さむらい. piece 作品. the main actor 仕手.

Shūsen Kinenbi 終戦記念日 the anniversary of the end of World
War II (August 15); Surrender Day in Japan, the day called V-J
(Victory Over Japan) Day in the U.S. In commemoration of the
victims of World War II and in hope of everlasting peace, memorial
services are observed around the country.

〖注〗 surrender day 降伏の日. in commemoration of ～を記念して，～をし
のんで. memorial service 記念式典，記念礼拝.

shushi 主枝 the main branches; the three principal stems in a flower
arrangement. They are the longest, the second longest and the
shortest stem, each referred to differently by the different schools
—*shin-soe-tai* in the Ikenobō school, *shin-soe-hikae* in the Sōgetsu
school and *shu-fuku-kyaku* in the Ohara school. Basically,
Japanese flower arrangement is composed of three principal stems
or three parts—symbolic of heaven, man and earth—to which
subordinate stems are added. ⇨ IKEBANA, JŪSHI, SHIN-SOE-HIKAE,
SHIN-SOE-TAI, SHU-FUKU-KYAKU

〖注〗 flower arrangement 生け花. principal stem 主枝. subordinate stem
従枝.

shūshin 修身 lit. self-discipline. moral education in the elementary
school curriculum, conducted until the end of World War II. The
textbook used for this subject contained an abundance of stories to
indoctrinate the importance of filial piety, loyalty to one's master,
sacrifice for the emperor, and patriotism, and was based largely on
Confucianism and Shintoism. This subject was abandoned with
the end of World War II. ⇨ JUKYŌ, KŌKŌ, SHINTŌ

〖注〗 indoctrinate 教えこむ. filial piety 孝行心. Confucianism 儒教.

Shintoism 神道.

shūshin-koyōsei(do) 終身雇用制(度) the lifetime employment system; the career-long employment system; employment with a single company until the age of retirement (55-65). This system came to be widely adopted shortly after World War II to save on time and costs for beginners' in-service training necessary with the development of new technology. This method turned out to well suit the Japanese, group-oriented and ingrained with a traditional sense of loyalty and commitment. Combined with the seniority system in wages, the lifetime employment system has become anchored among most large firms, benefiting both management and employees with the growth of productivity and job security for individuals even in adverse times. However, temporary or part-time workers and employees of many smaller firms are not covered by the system. ⇨ NENKŌ-JORETSU, NENKŌJORETSU-CHINGINSEI

〘注〙 the career-long employment system 定年までの雇用制度. in-service training 社内訓練. group-oriented 集団志向の. ingrained with ～に深く根ざしている，～に浸みこんでいる. a sense of loyalty 忠誠心. the seniority system in wages 年功序列賃金制. anchor 錨をおろす，根をおろす. job security 職の安定. adverse times 不況時.

soba 蕎麦 buckwheat noodles; long thin brownish noodles made from buckwheat flour with egg and yam starch added. They are eaten either hot in soup or as a cold dish with a dip. Minced green onions and other spices are used as condiments. ⇨ MEN(RUI), MORI-SOBA, UDON, ZARU-SOBA

〘注〙 buckwheat flour 蕎麦粉. yam starch 山芋の澱粉. minced 細かく刻んだ. minced green onions さらしねぎ，きざみねぎ. condiment 薬味.

soba-choko [soba-choku] 蕎麦猪口 a buckwheat-noodle cup; a porcelain cup used for serving a kind of sauce as a dip for buckwheat noodles. It is about the size of a regular coffee cup but with a flat bottom and no handle. A set consists of five cups. ⇨ CHOKU, SOBA

〘注〙 buckwheat noodles 蕎麦. porcelain 磁器(の).

sōgō-shōsha 総合商社 a general trading company; large Japanese firms operating with a worldwide trading network including Japan. A *sōgō-shōsha* deals with diversified goods and services in multilateral fields, ranging from instant noodles to tanks. Its distinctiveness has grown from the dependence of the Japanese economy on foreign natural resources and foreign markets. With one of its roots deriving from the exports and imports sector of prewar *zaibatsu* combines, today a tremendous number of *sōgō-shōsha* are bolstering the Japanese economy. The sales of the largest 10 together usually account for over one-third of the Japanese GNP.

〖注〗 diversified goods 多様な商品. multilateral 多角的な、多様な. natural resources 自然資源. combine 企業合同. bolster 支える、活気づける.

sōkaiya 総会屋 racketeers at stockholders' general meetings; professional filibusterers hired to manipulate an annual general meeting to the company's advantage. Their services consist of causing confusion in the proceedings of such meetings in an attempt to block individual stockholders from exercising their rights. Their attendance is legal since in most cases they hold a few shares. Under the Commercial Code, Article 497 (amended in 1981), both *sōkaiya* who extort money and companies that hire them are punishable, subject to imprisonment not exceeding six months or a fine not exceeding ￥300,000.

〖注〗 racketeer 脅迫者、ゆすり. stockholder 株主. filibusterer 議事進行妨害者. munipulate 操る. proceedings 議事. share 分担所有、株. the Commercial Code, Article 497 商法497条. extort 強奪する、ゆすりとる. imprisonment not exceeding six months 6か月以下の懲役. fine 罰金.

sōkyoku 箏曲 a generic term for *koto* music. ⇨ KOTO

sōmen そう麺 very thin noodles; a kind of thin white vermicelli made of wheat flour. In summer, it is most commonly served in a large glass bowl containing water and a few ice cubes. A few vegetables or fruits, such as tomatoes, cucumbers, and a cherry or the like float on the surface of the water to add a refreshing touch. They are eaten, dipped in a sauce made of soy sauce and fish broth, together with condiments such as grated ginger and minced green onions. In winter, they are served with ample hot soup in a ceramic bowl, garnished with greens, mushrooms, and shrimps or the like. ⇨ DASHI, MEN(RUI)

〖注〗 vermicelli 極細のスパゲティ. soy sauce 醤油. fish broth 魚のだし汁. condiment 薬味. grated ginger おろし生姜. minced green onions さらしねぎ、きざみねぎ.

sometsuke 染め付け lit. dyed ware. blue-and-white porcelain ware; white porcelain ware with a design in indigo under the glaze. Indigo pigment is applied directly on the biscuit and the ware is then glazed. The shades of blue vary depending on the firing temperature. Introduced from China, this type of decoration was employed first at Arita, Kyūshū, in the 17th century, and then spread to Kyoto, Kutani in present-day Ishikawa Prefecture, Seto in present-day Aichi Prefecture, etc. ⇨ ARITA-YAKI, KUTANI-YAKI

〖注〗 porcelain ware 磁器. indigo 藍(色). glaze 釉. pigment 絵の具, 色素. biscuit 素焼き.

soroban 算盤 a Japanese abacus; a traditional calculator, made of a wooden frame with beads on fixed sticks. Each vertical column is worth nine (or 10) units with one bead representing five units in the upper section and four (or five) beads, each representing one, in the wider lower section. One unit on a column represents a number 10 times that of one on a column next to it on the right. The *soroban* is still used, even though it has been largely replaced by electronic calculators and computers, and a single-unit combination of a *soroban* and a calculator are also available. The *soroban* used to be taught at most primary schools. Calculation can be done with amazing speed even by schoolchildren, sometimes more rapidly and accurately than with an electronic calculator.

〖注〗 vertical column 縦の棒. single-unit combination of a *soroban* and a calculator そろばんと計算機が一つに組み合わさったもの.

sōsho 草書 lit. grass writing. the cursive style of writing letters and characters; the most abbreviated style among the three styles of writing Japanese, the other two being *kaisho* (block style) and *gyōsho* (semi-cursive style). The term in particular refers to calligraphy. *Sōsho* is more an artistic form than one of practical use, and is reminiscent of flowing reeds. ⇨ GYŌSHO, KAISHO, SHODŌ

〖注〗 calligraphy 書道. reminiscent of ～を思わせる.

sotoba 卒塔婆 a stupa (Sanskrit); a dagoba or pagoda; a grave monument in the shape of a mound or a tower. Originally it was built to enshrine the bones or relics of Buddha Sakyamuni or Buddhist saints in India. Multistoried pagodas in Japan and China are modified versions of the Indian stupa. In Japan it also refers to long flat wooden boards standing around gravestones, specifically called *ita-sotoba* (a board stupa), bearing the posthumous name of the deceased and a phrase from a Buddhist sutra. ⇨ TŌ

〖注〗 stupa 仏舎利塔, 卒塔婆. dagoba (=pagoda) (東洋の)塔. grave monument 墓標. mound 小高い山. enshrine 祀る. relic 遺物. posthumous 死後の. Buddhist sutra お経.

Sōtōshū 曹洞宗 the Sōtō branch of Zen Buddhism; one of the two major branches of the Zen sect, the other being the Rinzai branch.

It was founded in China by Tung-shan (807-69) and his disciple
Ts'ao-shan (839-901) during the T'ang dynasty (618-907). Having studied in China, Dōgen (1200-53) introduced Sōtō Zen to Japan
in 1228. Its headquarters are Eiheiji Temple in Fukui Prefecture
and Sōjiji Temple in Kanagawa Prefecture. A difference between
Sōtō Zen and Rinzai Zen is that the former values meditation and
tranquillity of mind while the latter stresses a positive approach to
self-realization, emphasizing *kōan* (paradoxical catechetical question). ⇨ RINZAISHŪ, ZAZEN, ZENSHŪ
〖注〗 Tung-shan 慧能. Ts'ao-shan 良价. disciple 弟子. the T'ang
dynasty 唐朝. Eiheiji Temple 永平寺. Sōjiji Temple 総持寺. meditation
黙想, 座禅. the tranquillity of mind 心の平静. self-realization 自己完成, 悟
り). catechetical question 公案.

sudare 簾 a reed or bamboo blind; a shade made of reeds or split
bamboo, bound with strings. In summer, it is hung up in place of
a sliding door (*shōji* or *fusuma*), or it is suspended from just below
the eaves, in front of open windows and doors. It admits fresh,
cool breezes into the room and provides shade from the hot sun.
Today cheaper plastic ones are also available. ⇨ FUSUMA, SHŌJI
〖注〗 reed 葦(あし, よし). split bamboo 割り竹. sliding door 障子やふす
ま. eaves 軒.

sugegasa 菅笠 a sedge hat; a flat-cone shaped hat made of dry
sedge grass with a frame made of bamboo. It was worn by
farmers working in the fields and by travelers on foot and was
popular in the Edo period (1603-1868). It is still used in some
rural districts.
〖注〗 sedge すげ風の植物. cone shape 円錐型.

sugoroku 双六 Japanese parcheesi; a game played on a large piece
of paper, a simplified version of the board game. On the paper is
a series of pictures. After throwing a die, each player moves one's
piece according to the number indicated, with the goal of advancing
to the final picture quicker than one's opponents. This is one of
the traditional games played by children during the New Year
holidays.
〖注〗 parcheesi インドすごろく. die さいころ, さい.

suiban 水盤 a water basin; a shallow flower container or a basin
with a flat bottom. Flowers are arranged in such a way that the
surface of the water can be enjoyed. It is usually used for
moribana (piled-up flowers) and floating flower arrangements. ⇨

IKEBANA, MORIBANA, UKIBANA

〖注〗 basin 水鉢. floating flower arrangement 浮き花.

suibokuga 水墨画 lit. water and India-ink painting. a monochrome painting; a black-and-white painting; a picture basically in shades of black and white, drawn in India ink. Sometimes very pale colors may be partially added. Like calligraphy, it is drawn with a brush, and the beauty of the strokes of the brush is appreciated. Black India ink made from charcoal soot is used by diluting it with water so as to make a gradation of shades. The profound effect of that left undrawn, delineated by simplified lines, dots and splashes, has much to do with Zen perception. This painting style was developed in the 14th and 15th centuries by Zen monks such as Josetsu, Shūbun, Sesshū, etc., whose works were essentially Chinese in style and religious in implication. After Sesshū, the Japanese-style monochrome painting emerged in the early Edo period (1603-1868), as represented by Nōami, Geiami, Sōami, etc., whose works emphasized the aesthetic phase of Zen. *Suibokuga* is generally synonymous with *sumie*, but the former has a connotation of Chinese style while the latter is of Japanese style. ⇨ SHODŌ, SUMI, SUMIE, ZEN[1]

〖注〗 India ink 墨. monochrome 単色画, 白黒画. calligraphy 書道. strokes of the brush 筆致, 筆跡. charcoal soot 炭のすす. dilute うすめる. gradation of shades 陰影の段階, 色の濃淡. profound effect 深みのある効果, 微妙な効果. delineate 輪郭を描く. Josetsu 如拙. Shūbun 周文. implication 含蓄, 意味合い. Nōami 能阿弥. Geiami 芸阿弥. Sōami 相阿弥. aesthetic phase 美的側面. connotation 内的意味.

suimono 吸い物 Japanese broth; a clear soup seasoned with fish broth, salt, soy sauce and sweet rice wine. Ingredients include chicken, *tōfu*, a variety of seafoods, and seasonal vegetables. The ingredients are often cooked separately and placed in a lacquered bowl, into which the soup is poured, so as to keep the soup clear. *Yuzu* (citron peel), *kinome* (young leaves of Japanese pepper) and *mitsuba* (trefoil) may be added for their delicate flavor.

〖注〗 season 味をつける. fish broth 魚のだし汁, だし. soy sauce 醤油. sweet rice wine 味醂. ingredient (料理の)材料. citron peel ゆずの皮片.

suiteki 水滴 lit. drops of water. a tiny water container, one of the utensils used in calligraphy. To produce the black India ink used in calligraphy, one rubs an ink stick (*sumi*) back and forth on an inkstone (*suzuri*), using a small amount of water. A *suiteki* has a small hole from which water can be poured drop by drop. It is usually made of ceramic or metal. Artistically shaped and decorated, it is appreciated as an art object as well. ⇨ SHODŌ, SUMI, SUZURI

〖注〗 calligraphy 書道. ink stick（棒形の）墨. inkstone 硯. ceramic 陶器.

sukiyaki 鋤焼き beef and vegetables boiled in soy-flavored sauce; thinly sliced beef cooked in a shallow iron pan, with various other ingredients: soybean curd, *shirataki*, mushroom, long green onion, etc. The ingredients are put in a cast-iron pan over a hot fire at the table and are seasoned with soy sauce, sweet rice wine（*mirin*）, sugar, etc. The piping-hot foods are picked directly from the pan while they are boiling, and dipped into a small bowl of raw egg. ⇨ MIRIN, SHIITAKE, SHIRATAKI, SHŌYU

〖注〗 soy-flavored sauce 醤油で味をつけたソース. ingredient 成分，（料理の）材料. soybean curd 豆腐. long green onion 長ねぎ. cast-iron pan 鋳鉄製の鍋. season 味をつける. soy sauce 醤油. sweet rice wine 味醂. piping hot しゅうしゅういうほど熱い.

sumi 墨 an India ink stick or India ink made from an India ink stick. The stick is made from a mixture of plant soot and glue. The solid stick is scraped in water on an inkstone. The black ink thus made is used for calligraphy and monochromatic painting. ⇨ SHODŌ, SUIBOKUGA, SUZURI

〖注〗 India ink stick（棒形の）墨. India ink 墨（汁）. soot すす. scrape こする，こすりおとす. inkstone 硯. calligraphy 書道. monochromatic painting 単色画，墨絵.

sumie 墨絵 an India-ink painting; a monochromatic painting; a black-and-white painting. ⇨ SUIBOKUGA, SUMI

〖注〗 India ink 墨. monochromatic 単一色の.

sumō 相撲 Japanese wrestling; a traditional national sport in which two wrestlers, with their hair in a topknot and wearing only a loincloth, try to force each other out of a ring or to touch the ground with a part of the body other than the soles of the feet. With the announcement of the wrestlers' names, two wrestlers enter the ring to perform pre-bout rituals. They first do the *chirichōzu*, an act of vowing to fight fairly with all their might, and then go to their respective corners to grab a handful of salt which they toss toward the center of the ring to purify it. They proceed to do the *shiko* (stomping) to show their fighting spirit, followed by the repetition of *shikiri* (toeing the mark), to build up concentration, and more salt tossing.   When the referee announces that time is up, the two face each other in a crouching position with their fists to the ground and then charge at each other for a battle that is usually shorter than the pre-bout rituals.   After the bout, the wrestlers and referee make a simple simultaneous bow and the loser makes a quick departure, whereas the winner remains and takes a sitting position at the edge of the ring while the referee calls his name out as the winner.   He then steps down to the side of the ring where he offers *chikaramizu* (lit. strength water) to the next wrestler to occupy the corner.   This form of wrestling is said to have originated in ancient times and become a professional sport during the Edo period (1603–1868).   ⇨ CHIRICHŌZU, DOHYŌ, MAWA-SHI, ŌZUMŌ, SHIKIRI, SHIKO, SUMŌBEYA

〖注〗 topknot ちょんまげ． loincloth 回し，褌． pre-bout ritual 試合前の儀式． stomping 四股． toeing the mark 仕切り． referee 行司． crouching position かがむ姿勢． departure 退場．

sumōbeya 相撲部屋 a *sumō* stable. Professional *sumō* wrestlers belong to one of many stables headed by a retired high-ranking wrestler where they live together, with the exception of married wrestlers of high rank. A stable usually consists of training quarters with a dirt floor, personal quarters for the stable master (*oyakata*), separate rooms for *sekitori* wrestlers, a large room shared by the other wrestlers, a large bathroom, a reception room, etc. Under a strict hierarchy for the purpose of developing discipline, junior wrestlers must perform all domestic chores and attend senior wrestlers. In return, senior wrestlers take on the responsibility of training their juniors. During tournaments, stablemates are not required to compete against each other.   ⇨ SEKITORI, SUMŌ

〖注〗 stable 馬小屋． training quarters 稽古場． dirt floor 土間． hierarchy 序列制． chores 雑用． attend 世話をする，つき添う．

sun 寸 a traditional unit for measuring length. One *sun* is one-tenth of a *shaku*. As with *shaku*, there are two different scales for *sun*. One is 3.03 centimeters; the other, formerly used by measuring cloth, is 3.79 cm, about 1.25 times the length of the regular one. ⇨ SHAKKAN-HŌ, SHAKU

sunomono 酢の物 a type of salad; sliced vegetables and seafoods (raw or boiled in water) dressed with vinegar and some other seasonings—salt, sugar, soy sauce, sesame seeds, etc. It is usually tastefully arranged and served in small portions.

〖注〗 dress（料理を）仕上げる. seasoning 調味料. soy sauce 醬油. tastefully 上品に.

sushi 鮨 vinegared rice with fish and vegetables; a popular and unique Japanese dish delicately seasoned with vinegar, salt, sugar and sweet rice wine, in the form of rolls, slices, oval-shaped balls, etc. The varieties are too numerous to list. Fish, shellfish, egg or vegetables, raw or cooked, are placed on small balls of rice, rolled up with rice in seaweed laver, or mixed with rice. It is usually eaten with soy sauce and a dab of grated horseradish. ⇨ CHIRASHI-ZUSHI, INARI-ZUSHI, NIGIRI-ZUSHI, NORIMAKI(-ZUSHI)

〖注〗 season 味をつける. vinegar 酢. sweet rice wine 味淋. shellfish 貝. raw 生の. roll up in 巻きこむ. seaweed laver 海苔. soy sauce 醬油. a dab of 少量の. grated horseradish おろしたわさび.

sushiya 鮨屋 a *sushi* shop; a small restaurant serving *sushi* at a wood counter. A combination of *sushi* is also served in lacquered boxes or on plates at the table. But the characteristic feature of a *sushi* shop is the counter where the guest is served *sushi* directly on the lacquered part of the counter after pointing out one by one the kinds he would like to try. Two rice balls topped with fish or the like usually constitute a single order. ⇨ NIGIRI-ZUSHI, SUSHI

〖注〗 lacquered box 漆器の箱.

suteteko すててこ men's long underwear; a pair of long drawers, worn by men under trousers and over underwear. They are of plain cotton cloth, usually white, extending down to the knees. The younger generation prefers not to wear them, regarding them as unfashionable. The aged may wear them at home in the place of trousers during hot weather.

〖注〗 drawers ズボン下.

suzuri 硯 an inkstone; a rectangular stone block used for calligraphy. It has a depression at one end to hold water. India ink for calligraphy is made by rubbing an India-ink stick on an inkstone. ⇨ SHODŌ, SUMI

〖注〗 depression 凹み. calligraphy 書道. India-ink stick （棒形の）墨.

suzuribako 硯箱 an inkstone box; a case containing a set of calligraphy utensils. It is made of wood, lacquered or engraved, and artistically designed. The utensils include an inkstone, an India ink stick, a few writing brushes, etc. ⇨ FUDE, SHODŌ, SUMI, SUZURI

〖注〗 inkstone 硯. calligraphy 書道. engrave 彫りものをする.

T

tabakobon 煙草盆 a smoking tray; a square wooden lidless box with a handle, for keeping smoking utensils in.　It contains a small earthen pot with hot charcoal in it.　It was popularly used in the Edo period (1603-1868).

〚注〛 lidless 蓋のない.　earthen pot 土器の壺.

tabi 足袋 Japanese-style socks; socks with the toes split, the big toe separated from the others, worn with Japanese sandals or wooden clogs.　They are made of cotton, silk or velvet, and fastened on the inner ankle with three or four tiny metal clasps.　Formally, *tabi* are pure white.　Colored ones are also casually worn: black or indigo for men and brighter colors for women.　⇨ GETA, KIMONO, ZŌRI

〚注〛 Japanese sandals 草履.　wooden clogs 下駄.　metal clasp 金具の留め, こはぜ.

tachiai 立合い the instant a *sumō* bout is begun; the moment when two *sumō* wrestlers spring at each other from a crouching position with their fists touching the *shikiri* line.　Unlike other sports where the referee signals when the game is to begin, in *sumō* the referee simply urges the wrestlers to take up their starting positions.　It is up to the wrestlers themselves when to begin.　As they stare at each other, sitting on their heels, they slowly draw back their hips and lower their fists to the *shikiri* line, seeking the psychological moment for them to touch the line and spring at each other while trying to get the edge in the jump.　If an overanxious wrestler makes a false start before his opponent touches the *shikiri* line, the *tachiai* is done over again.　It is often said that how well a wrestler does at the *tachiai* determines the outcome of the match.　⇨ ŌZUMŌ, SHIKIRI, SUMŌ

〚注〛 bout 試合, 勝負.　crouching position しゃがんだ姿勢.　referee 行司.

tachiyaku 立役 a player of male roles as opposed to female roles in Kabuki (in Kabuki all roles are played by males).　Also refers to the principal male role in a play: the *tachiyaku* is usually a virtuous and serious person. The villain, or the enemy role, is called *akkatsura* which literally means "red-faced". ⇨ KABUKI

〔注〕 principal male role 主役の男役. virtuous 正義感のある，徳の高い. villain 悪い奴.

taian 大安 a great lucky day; the luckiest day during a period comprising six days on the lunar calendar. Deriving from the Chinese philosophy of cosmic dual forces, the cycle of six divisions came to be applied to fortune-telling and is still observed for special occasions. A *taian* day is chosen for weddings, moving, starting long journeys, etc. ⇨ BUTSUMETSU, ROKUYŌ

〔注〕 the lunar calendar 太陰暦. cosmic dual forces 宇宙の二元力，陰陽. the cycle of six divisions 六曜，六輝. fortune-telling 運命鑑定.

Taiiku no Hi 体育の日 Sports Day; Health-Sports Day (October 10); a national holiday, established for promoting the health of the people, both mentally and physically. On this day, people are encouraged to enjoy sports for good health. Customarily, at this time of the year, many schools and some communities hold athletic meets (*undōkai*). ⇨ KOKUMIN NO SHUKUJITSU

Taika no Kaishin 大化の改新 lit. "Great Change" Renovation. the Taika Reform (645); the great political reform of the Taika era (645-50), aimed at the establishment of a centralized country under imperial rule. During the preceeding eras, powerful local clans (*uji*) had often threatened the imperial throne. Externally, neighboring China had established the huge centralized T'ang dynasty. Thus, partisans of the imperial family keenly felt the vulnerability of the rulers of the country. Together with the Crown Prince Naka no Ōe (later Emperor Tenchi, r. ca. 661-71), innovative reformers headed by Nakatomi (later Fujiwara) no Kamatari (614-69) eliminated the most powerful clan, the Soga family, which had been interferring with administration, and thereby established imperial supremacy. Making possible the enthronement of Emperor Kōtoku (r. 645-54) and moving the capital to Naniwa (present-day Ōsaka), the partisans carried out reforms following the example of the T'ang dynasty. The reforms consisted of four articles, summarized as follows: 1) abolishment of private possession of hereditary lands and workers, 2) establishment of the system of "central provinces (*kinai*) and local provinces (*kuni*)" to administer the country, 3) mandatory registration of the population for the allotment of land, and 4) introduction of a new system of taxes to be paid in both products and labor. ⇨ GOKI(NAI)-SHICHIDŌ, KINAI, KUNI, UJI

〖注〗 renovation 改新、改革. local clan 氏. the T'ang dynasty 唐朝. partisan 支持者. vulnerability 弱みのあること、攻撃されやすいこと. enthronement 皇位につくこと. article 条(項). central provinces 畿内. local province 国. mandatory 強制的な、義務の. registration 戸籍の登録. allotment 割り当て、配分.

taiko¹ 太鼓 a stick drum; a musical percussion instrument of cylindrical shape. The body is usually made of wood, hollow inside, covered at both ends with leather. It is placed on a stand in front of the drummer and struck with thick wooden sticks called *bachi*. Japanese *taiko* come in various sizes, ranging from one meter to about 30 centimeters in diameter. A huge barrel-shaped one is used for festivals. In Noh, small ones are played. On Kabuki stages, *taiko* of various sizes appear, most likely played in rhythmic and rapid dance passages. ⇨ BACHI, KABUKI, NŌ

〖注〗 musical percussion instrument 打楽器. cylindrical shape 円柱形. stand 台. passage (芸術、文などの)一部、一節.

taiko² 太鼓 lit. a drum. a drum bow; a type of *obi* (sash) fixed at the back of a kimono in such a way that it looks like a drum. This is the most popular form of tying an *obi* worn by women both young and old, and is appropriate for both ordinary and semi-formal kimono. Tying must be done carefully so that the design on the *obi* will form a whole picture on the drum part. For young women, the drum bow is made bigger especially on formal occasions. More commonly called *otaiko*. ⇨ KIMONO, OBI

〖注〗 bow 結んだもの.

tairō 大老 lit. a great senior. the senior minister of the Tokugawa shogunate government (1603–1868). He was the top-ranking official who directly assisted and advised the shogun, from 1638, a few decades after the establishment of the Tokugawa shogunate government, until its fall. The *tairō* was chosen from among hereditary feudal lords. ⇨ DAIMYŌ, TOKUGAWA-BAKUFU

〖注〗 senior minister 年輩の閣僚. hereditary feudal lord 譜代大名.

Taishakuten 帝釈天 Sakra devānām Indra (Sanskrit); in the Brahminism of India, a brave deity who fought against the demon deity Asura; in Japan, a guardian deity who protects the land of Buddhism. He is usually depicted as wearing armor under a long

Chinese-style garment. The image of him at Tōji Temple, a masterpiece made in the early Heian period (794–1185), is depicted as seated on an elephant. ⇨ ASHURA, BUKKYŌ

〖注〗 Brahminism バラモン教. deity 神, 神のような人[もの]. guardian deity 守護神. armor 冑. garment 上衣.

Taishō 大正 the Taishō era; the appellation of the era of the former emperor, Taishō Tennō (1879–1926); the era from July 30, 1912, to December 25, 1926, lasting about 15 years. The year 1912 corresponds to the first year of Taishō and at the same time to the 45th year of Meiji (the era before Taishō); the year 1926 corresponds to the 15th year of Taishō and to the first year of Shōwa (the present era). ⇨ GENGŌ, TENNŌ

〖注〗 appellation 呼称.

taiyaki 鯛焼き lit. a baked seabream. a fish-shaped pancake stuffed with sweet red-bean paste. It is baked on hot iron plates with shallow depressions shaped like fish. It is primarily sold at street stands and is eaten while still hot. ⇨ AN

〖注〗 seabream 鯛. stuff 詰める. sweet red-bean paste あずきの餡. depression 凹み. street stand 屋台.

takakura 高倉 an elevated storehouse for grain and/or other agricultural products. The *takakura* is a ruggedly and ingeniously constructed storehouse found since ancient times in the fields of Okinawa. Its design and construction are strikingly similar to those of such storehouses found in Southeast Asia, particularly Indonesia. The storehouse consists of a thatched roof and wooden walls, with a trapdoor in the floor, all rat-proof, standing on vertical support posts. It is between two and six meters in height. The structure is circular in Okinawa, but square, hexagonal or circular on the Amami Islands. Farmers rest in the shade or sit out rainstorms in the space between the floor and the ground. Although decreasing in number due to the modernization of farming, the *takakura* is still found in remote rural areas of Okinawa. ⇨ OKINAWA, RYŪKYŪ-SHOTŌ

〖注〗 ruggedly 素朴に, 粗野に. ingeniously 巧妙に. thatched roof 茅葺きの屋根. trapdoor はねあげ戸. rat-proof ねずみの入らない. vertical support post 縦の支柱. hexagonal 六角形の.

takarabune 宝船 a treasure ship; the ship loaded with the Seven Deities of Good Luck who carry treasures. This ship has a large square sail with the Chinese character *takara* 宝 (treasure) written on it.   The treasures they carry include a treasure hammer, sacred keys for treasure storage, scrolls of longevity, bales of rice, etc. Legend has it that on New Year's Eve, this ship will come to Japan from afar, bringing good luck for the coming year.   There used to be a belief that a picture of this ship placed under the pillow on New Year's Eve would ensure the first dream of the new year to be a happy one, with the result of happiness throughout the year.   ⇨ GANJITSU, ŌMISOKA, SHICHI-FUKUJIN

【注】 the Seven Deities of Good Luck 七福神.   Chinese character 漢字. treasure hammer 宝の小槌.   treasure storage 宝の蔵.   scrolls of longevity 長寿の巻物.   bales of rice 米俵.   Legend has it that... 伝説によると.

Takasago 高砂 a typical Noh song for wedding ceremonies; the Noh song of twin pine trees at Takasago—symbolic of a happy devoted couple—chanted at weddings.   Inspired by twin pine trees clinging to each other found at Takasago in Hyōgo Prefecture, the celebrated Noh writer Zeami (1363-1443) created the play *Takasago* depicting the story of a happy couple, Jō and Uba—the Japanese version of Darby and Joan.   Traditionally, a passage from this play, beginning with "*Takasago ya, kono urabune ni, ho o agete. . .* (Hoist our sail on a boat in the inlet of Takasago, and put out into the sea of life. . .)" should be chanted solemnly at wedding ceremonies.   Nowadays, this happy passage is often sung at the receptions as well.   There is also an ornament depicting the aged couple Jō and Uba under twin pine trees, symbolic of a happy, lifelong marriage.   ⇨ NŌ, UTAI

【注】 a happy devoted couple 相思相愛の幸せな夫婦.   chant 歌う、詠唱する. celebrated 有名な.   Jō (尉)能楽で翁、老翁をかたどった能面.   Uba (姥)老女. Darby and Joan むつまじい老夫婦(1735 Gentleman's Magazine に出た詩の中 の老夫婦).   passage 作品の一部、文章の一節.

takashimada 高島田 the *takashimada* hairstyle; a coiffure developed during the Edo period (1603-1868), a variation of the *shimada* hairstyle.   It consists of a highly set plectrum-shaped chignon and puffed-out front, back and side locks, with ornaments added.   It was first worn by court attendants.   Among many other *shimada* styles, this is the most elaborate and elegant, and has been worn by brides in traditional-style weddings since the early Meiji era (1868-1912).   ⇨ MAGE, SHIMADA

【注】 coiffure 髪型.   variation 変形したもの.   plectrum-shaped ばちの形を した.   chignon 束髪のまげ.   lock 髪の房.

Takatori-yaki 高取焼　Takatori ceramic ware; ceramic ware originally produced at kilns around the foot of Mount Takatori, Fukuoka Prefecture, Kyūshū.　These kilns were started by Korean
potters brought to Japan by the feudal lord Kuroda Nagamasa
(1568-1622).　Later, under the supervision of Kobori Enshū
(1579-1647), a master of the tea ceremony and garden designer,
the kilns produced a number of kinds of excellent tea ware.　This
ware has a lustrous glaze of brown, yellow, bluish gray or purple-
black.
〖注〗 ceramic ware 陶器．kiln（焼き物を焼く）窯．potter 陶工．feudal
lord 大名．tea ceremony 茶道．glaze 上薬[釉]．

take no kawa 竹の皮　a bamboo sheath; dried sheaths of young
bamboo culms.　Formerly these were very often used for wrapping
foods such as rice balls, sweets, meat, etc., but only rarely nowadays.　They were also woven into sandals.
〖注〗 sheath さや．culm（竹，稲などの）節があって中空の茎．rice ball お
握り．

takezaiku 竹細工　bamboo craft; bamboo works; articles, house-
wares and other products made of dried bamboo stems.　Bamboo
has served as the material for a variety of goods in Japan.　The
larger bamboos are used as poles, water pipes, etc., or are made
into vases by being cut at the joints; the smaller ones are made into
tobacco-pipe stems, flutes, picture frames, walking sticks, etc.
Split bamboo and thinly stripped bamboo are handled artistically
by experts and made into various kinds of crafts including not only
articles for daily use but also artistic ornaments, flower containers,
tea-ceremony utensils, etc.　⇨ CHANOYU, HANAIRE, KAKI
〖注〗 water pipe 樋．joint 節．split bamboo 割いた竹．stripped bamboo
ひも状にした竹．tea-ceremony utensils 茶道具．

takiginō 薪能　bonfire Noh; open-air performances of Noh plays by
torchlight.　Originally in the Muromachi period (1336-1568), Noh
performance was presented at Kōfukuji Temple, Nara, where a
Buddhist rite was conducted at night in February with an open-air
bonfire kindled.　Gradually, any open-air Noh performance by the
light of bonfires presented at temples and shrines came to be called
takiginō, regardless of the season.　Today, Kōfukuji Temple hold
such an annual event in May.　Other famous examples can be seen
at Heian Shrine in Kyoto in June and at Meiji Shrine in Tokyo in
November.　⇨ NŌ

〖注〗 bonfire 大かがり火． torchlight たいまつの明り． dedicate 奉納する．

takoyaki たこ焼き octopus dumplings. Cooked on a griddle, these dumplings consist of wheat flour, bits of octopus (called *tako* in Japanese), green onion, cabbage, dried bonito shavings and ginger, and are eaten with a spicy sauce. They are usually sold at street stands.

〖注〗 griddle （料理用）鉄板． dumpling 団子． green onion 長ねぎ． street stand 屋台．

takuan 沢庵 pickled radish; Japanese radish pickled yellow in rice bran. In a large wooden tub each layer of radishes is covered with a mixture of rice bran, salt and spices, and heavy weights (usually stones) are placed on top. It takes from one to a few months until the bran ferments and the radish is made tasty. It was so named after Priest Takuan who invented it in the 17th century. Also called *okōko* colloquially. ⇨ NUKA(MISO)-ZUKE, TSUKEMONO

〖注〗 Japanese radish 大根． rice bran 米糠． ferment 発酵する．

takuhaibin 宅配便 door-to-door express delivery service; commercial service offering special delivery of small packages, from a door or pickup station to the receiver's door. Due to its promptness and careful handling, the Yamato Transport Company, which started such a service in 1976, caught public attention and experienced unexpected success. Soon, dozens of such firms emerged, and surpassed the government-run postal system and the Japanese National Railways in this field. In less than a decade, a huge delivery networks has developed with well over 200,000 pickup stations (as opposed to about 5,700 offices of the postal system). Pickup stations are located at neighborhood supermarkets, rice stores, liquor stores, etc. Such firms' trade marks are often animals, such as a pelican, elephant, dog or a cat carrying a kitten.

〖注〗 delivery service 配達業． special delivery 特別配達，速達便． pickup station 取り次ぎ所． firm 会社． postal system 郵便制度．

takuhatsu 托鉢 religious mendicancy. Buddhist monks undergoing training go out on a round of alms-begging as a means of mental discipline. They give prayers at doors and in return receive rice or small amounts of money as alms. *Takuhatsu* are rarely seen nowadays other than as a part of ascetic training for Zen monks.

〖注〗 mendicancy こじき生活，物もらい生活． Buddhist monk 仏僧． go on a round 巡回にでる． alms 施し，喜捨． ascetic training 苦行．

Tanabata (Matsuri) 七夕(祭り) the Star Festival held on the night of July 7; the festival held in celebration of a legend of two stars, which originated in China. According to legend, two stars in love, Kengyū (Altair or Cowherd Star) and Shokujo (Vega or Weaver Star), residing on opposite sides of the Milky Way, were allowed to meet just once a year, on the evening of July 7. On the occasion of this festival, fresh bamboo branches are set up outside homes, from which long slips of paper and colorful paper decorations are hung. On the slips of paper are written romantic poems and wishes. The Star Festival in Sendai is especially spectacular, and is held annually on August 6, 7 and 8 (July 7 of the lunar calendar). Main streets are filled with huge bamboo branches decorated with fancy colorful streamers and other oddities.

〔注〕 Altair(=Cowherd Star) アルタイル(わし座 Aquila の主星)，牽牛星. Vega(=Weaver Star) ベガ(琴座の一等星)，織女星. the Milky Way 天の川. a long slip of paper 短冊. the lunar calendar 太陰暦.

Tanba-yaki 丹波焼 Tanba ceramic ware; ceramic ware produced in Tanba Province (today an area covering parts of Kyoto and Hyōgo prefectures). The ware is reddish brown in color and coarse in texture, with a natural glaze developed in the firing process. Utensils for the tea ceremony and vases of Tanba produced in the Momoyama period (late 16th century) are still highly admired by tea devotees. ⇨ CHANOYU, HANAIRE

〔注〕 ceramic ware 陶器. texture 生地, 肌合い. natural glaze 自然釉. utensil for the tea ceremony 茶道具. devotee 献身者, 通の人.

Tango no Sekku 端午の節句 the Iris Festival; the Boys' Day; the Boys' Festival held on May 5, in the season when Japanese Irises are at their best. This day has traditionally been celebrated by families having young sons with the wish that their boys be courageous. Carp streamers (*koinobori*), symbolic of courage, are hoisted high on a pole. Historical warrior dolls are displayed on tiers set up in the alcove. Traditional treats for this special day, *chimaki* and *kashiwa-mochi*, are prepared. Japanese iris leaves (*shōbu*) are used to decorate roofs and are put in a hot bath as a charm against evil spirits and diseases; thus, this day was originally called *Shōbu no Sekku* (Iris Festival). After World War II, May 5 was designated as a national holiday called Children's Day (*Kodomo no Hi*) to honor both boys and girls. ⇨ CHIMAKI, KASHIWA-MOCHI, KODOMO NO HI, KOINOBORI, MUSHA-NINGYŌ, SHŌBUYU

〖注〗 Japanese iris 菖蒲． carp streamer 鯉のぼり． hoist かかげる． warrior doll 武者人形． tier 段． treat ごちそう，もてなし． alcove 床の間． charm お守り．

tanka 短歌 lit. a short poem. a 31-syllable poem; a traditional verse form, consisting of five lines of 5-7-5-7-7 syllables. *Tanka* is said to have derived from the ancient *chōka* (a long poem) consisting of long, unfixed repetitions of a 5-7 syllable pattern ending with extra seven syllables. The pattern of 5-7-5-7-7 syllables became dominant with the *Man'yōshū* (The Collection of Ten-Thousand Leaves, eighth century). Ever since, it has been the principal classical poetic form, remaining very popular even today. Unlike the epical *chōka*, the *tanka* is lyrical and evokes emotions. The Heian period (794-1185) saw the development of the aristocratic florid *tanka* tradition, as seen in the *Kokinshū* (An Anthology of Japanese Poetry, Ancient and Modern, around 905) and the *Shin-Kokinshū* (A New Anthology of Japanese Poetry, Ancient and Modern, completed in the late 12th and early 13th centuries). In modern times, *tanka* has attempted to cover a wide range of trends in expressions and themes, though some schools retain a somewhat courtly tradition. The following is one of the most famous *tanka*, composed in the Heian period.

> *Hito wa isa*
>   *kokoro mo shirazu*
>   *furusato wa,*
> *Hana zo mukashi no*
>   *ka ni nioi keru*
> (by Ki no Tsurayuki, ?868-945)
> How the village friend may meet me
>   I know not, but the old plum flowers
> Still now with their fragrance greet me
>   Kindly as in the bygone hours
> (translated by Heihachirō Honda)

⇨ MAN'YŌSHŪ, KOKIN(WAKA)SHŪ, SHIN-KOKIN(WAKA)SHŪ, WAKA

〖注〗 derived from ～から由来する． long poem 長歌． epical 叙事(詩)的な． lyrical 叙情(詩)的な． evoke 呼びおこす． florid 華麗な．

tanmono 反物 kimono fabric; a roll of cloth for one kimono. So called because kimono fabric is sold in lengths of *tan*, which measures about 12 meters in length and 30 centimeters in width, which is traditionally thought to be enough to make a kimono.

Quality *tanmono* usually come in rolls by the *tan*.   ⇨ KIMONO

〖注〗 fabric 織物. quality 上等品(の).

tansu 簞笥 a chest of drawers; a piece of furniture for storing kimono and accessories. It is made up of several drawers and a cabinet. Some *tansu* also have a double-leafed hinged door. The best kind is made of paulownia wood—good in humid weather to protect clothes, especially kimono, from the humidity. The *tansu* is customarily included among the furniture for a bride to take along to her new home.   ⇨ KIMONO

〖注〗 double-leafed hinged door 観音開きのとびら. paulownia 桐.

tanuki-soba [tanuki-udon] 狸蕎麦 [狸うどん] lit. raccoon noodles. a bowl of buckwheat noodles [or white wheat noodles] in a fish broth seasoned with soy sauce. Pieces of crispy *tenpura*-batter crust, some greens, etc. are arranged on top. The crusts are considered disguised *tenpura*. According to Japanese legend, the raccoon tricks people in the disguise of something else.   ⇨ SOBA, TENPURA, UDON

〖注〗 buckwheat noodles 蕎麦. fish broth 魚でとっただし汁. season 味を つける. soy sauce 醬油. *tenpura*-batter crust てんぷらの衣. in the dis- guise of ～に扮して, ～に化けて.

tanzaku 短冊 a long, narrow piece of paper; a thick piece of paper used for writing poems, particularly *tanka* (31-syllable poem). Fixed on a special type of board, it is often displayed on a pillar in a Japanese-style room. The paper is generally slightly tinted or speckled with dust of gold or silver color. The standard size is about 30 by six centimeters.   ⇨ TANKA

〖注〗 speckle 斑点をつける.

tanzen 丹前 a padded kimono; a kind of thick padded gown in the shape of a kimono, worn for warmth and relaxation. It is pro- vided for guests at Japanese inns in winter and usually worn over a simple cotton kimono (also provided) after taking a bath.   ⇨ KIMONO, RYOKAN

〖注〗 padded 綿の入った.

tasuki 襷 a cord for holding up kimono sleeves. It is passed over the shoulders and under the armpits crossing at the back. It keeps the sleeves of the kimono from getting soiled and allows freedom of movement of work.

〖注〗 cord 紐. armpit わきの下. get soiled 汚れる.

tatami 畳 a straw mat; thick, rectangular mats used as floor coverings in a traditional Japanese room. The mat is made of tightly woven rice-straw covered with woven rush grass with the edges hemmed with cloth. A standard mat is about 180 by 90 centimeters and about five cm thick. The area of a Japanese-style room is usually measured by the number of *tatami* it contains —e.g. a four-and-a-half mat room, a six-mat room, an eight-mat room, etc. Slippers should not be worn on *tatami* although they are used on wooden floors.

〖注〗 floor covering 床をおおうもの. tightly woven かたく編んだ. rush grass 藺草. a four-and-a-half mat room 四畳半の部屋.

tate-shakai 縦社会 a vertical society; a social structure of hierarchical groupings as seen in Japanese society. This term drew special attention in the late 1960s when anthropologist Chie Nakane (1926-) analyzed the vertical principle central to Japanese society in her *Tate-shakai no Ningen Kankei* (1967, Human Relations in a Vertical Society). She maintains that "the principle of the Japanese social structure can be seen clearly portrayed in the household structure" where, with the household head at the top, the members form hierarchical rankings, remotely with the head of a small community as well, attributable to the need for cooperation in farming. Thus, even today within both informal groups and formal organizations, vertical links appear based on direct personal relations—employer and employee, senior and junior, veteran worker and newcomer, etc. The members of a group are tightly knit by paternal concerns and personal loyalty crossing status lines, thus encouraging a sense of belonging, making distinctions between insiders (we) and outsiders (they). From ancient times Japanese society as a whole was vertically divided into classes with the imperial family at the top. This was especially clear in feudal times, when society was artificially divided into distinct classes —warriors, farmers, artisans and merchants—on a hereditary basis. Nevertheless, direct vertical relations involving mutual benefits within a group, such as lord-retainer relations, assumed actually more importance, Nakane points out. With the fall of the feudal government and especially after World War II, the hereditary factor has been replaced by a status system determined by educational or economic background, and Japanese society as a whole is now rather egalitarian, in contrast to the intra-structure of a group. ⇨ ICHIZOKU-RŌTŌ, ONJŌSHUGI, SHI-NŌ-KŌ-SHŌ

〘注〙 hierarchical 序列的. anthropologist 人類学者. household structure イエ的構造. attributable to 〜に由来するとされる. paternal concern 父親的気づかい, 温情. loyalty 忠誠. warriors, farmers, artisans and merchants 士農工商. on a hereditary basis 世襲に基づいて. lord-retainer relation 主従関係. egalitarian 平等主義の. intra-structure 内部構造.

tatsukuri 田作り lit. tilling a paddy-field. small dried sardines; dried finger-sized sardines, cooked as one of the traditional New Year dishes. The dried sardines are also used as a fertilizer, bringing a good harvest of rice. They are also good for the health because of their high calcium content. Thus, they are eaten and offered to the gods during the New Year period. Usually, the sardines are roasted and then seasoned with soy sauce and sugar. ⇨ OSECHI-RYŌRI

〘注〙 till 耕す. paddy-field 田んぼ. calcium content カルシウム含有物. soy sauce 醬油.

taue 田植え rice-transplanting; the planting of rice seedlings in wet paddy-fields. Seedlings or rice plants are grown in nursery beds. The transplanting work is done during the rainy season, usually from around June 12 to mid-July. The seedlings are traditionally planted in straight rows by hand. Recently mechanical planters and planting tractors have been developed for this purpose. ⇨ INEKARI, TSUYU

〘注〙 seedling 苗, 苗木. wet paddy-field 水田. nursery bed 苗床.

tebako 手箱 lit. a hand box. a wooden box in which to keep stationery, letters and other personal articles. It is usually about 30 centimeters wide, 40 cm long and ten cm high, large enough to accommodate a few things. The wood is lacquered and decorated with a graceful design, sometimes with gold or silver lacquer, or mother-of-pearl inlay. This type of box first came into vogue among the nobility in the Heian period (794-1185), but can now be commonly found. ⇨ MAKIE, NURIMONO

〘注〙 stationery 文房具. personal article 身の回り品. accommodate 収納する. lacquer 漆を塗る, 漆. mother-of-pearl 真珠貝. inlay はめ込む, はめこみ細工. the nobility 貴族, 貴族階級.

teikoku-daigaku 帝国大学 an imperial university; national universities designated according to the Law of the Imperial University established in 1886 (the 19th year of Meiji). They were the following: Tokyo Imperial University (established in 1877), Kyoto Imperial University (1897), Tōhoku Imperial University (1907),

Kyūshū Imperial University (1910), Hokkaidō Imperial University (1918), Ōsaka Imperial University (1931) and Nagoya Imperial University (1939) (in Japan proper); in addition, Keijō Imperial University in Korea and Taihoku Imperial University in Taiwan, under Japan's colonial governments. After World War II, *teikoku* meaning "imperial" was dropped from their names. They came to be called *kokuritsu-daigaku* (national university).

〚注〛 Japan proper 日本本土. Japan's colonial governments 日本植民地政府.

teishoku 定食 a set meal; a fixed menu; a table d'hôte at a Japanese restaurant. A typical Japanese *teishoku* includes a bowl of rice, *miso* soup, pickles and the main dish of the day (fish or meat). It is popular with the lunchtime crowd, because it is served quick, and is much economical compared with separate dishes. ⇨ MISOSHIRU, TSUKEMONO

〚注〛 table d'hôte 定食.

teishu 亭主 lit. a host. 1) a husband or the head of a family. It implies an authoritative place over his wife or the other family members. Also, this term is used to refer to one's own husband or master in a fairly rude way. 2) a host or hostess in a tea ceremony, one who receives guests and provides hospitality in the tea ceremony. He or she has the important task of selecting the tea utensils to be used, along with the hanging scroll and flower arrangement, to suit the season and create a harmonious atmosphere. During the ceremony, the *teishu* presents tea, or tea and a simple meal, according to prescribed manners, with the help of an assistant (*hantō*). Special attention is paid so that all the guests can experience and share the spirit of the tea ceremony—harmony, reverence, purity and tranquillity. ⇨ CHANOYU, IKEBANA, KAKEJI-KU, WA-KEI-SEI-JAKU

〚注〛 tea ceremony 茶の湯. tea utensil 茶道具. hanging scroll 掛け軸. flower arrangement 生け花. prescribed manners 定められた作法. hantō 飯頭. harmony, reverence, purity and tranquillity 和敬清寂.

tekka-donburi 鉄火丼 lit. iron-fire rice in a bowl. vinegared rice covered with slices of raw tuna—red as molten iron (*tekka*) —served in a bowl (*donburi*). A few slices of vinegared ginger and a bit of grated Japanese horseradish are arranged at the center of the fish. Black seaweed laver is spread beneath the tuna. As with most *sushi*, it is eaten with soy sauce. ⇨ DONBURI, DONBURI-

MONO, SUSHI

〖注〗 slices of raw tuna まぐろの刺身． molten 溶解した，火に溶けた． grated Japanese horseradish おろしわさび． seaweed laver 海苔． soy sauce 醬油．

tekkamaki 鉄火巻き lit. iron-fire roll. a kind of rolled *sushi*; vinegared rice rolled up in a sheet of seaweed laver with a piece of raw tuna in the center. It is flavored with a bit of green horseradish. Like most kinds of *sushi*, it is eaten with soy sauce. The red tuna is likened to hot iron. ⇨ NORI, SUSHI, WASABI

〖注〗 seaweed laver 海苔． green horseradish わさび． soy sauce 醬油．

temae 点前 the tea ceremony procedure; the procedure of preparing and serving tea in the tea ceremony. The procedure is distinguished according to whether foamy thin tea or thick pasty tea is made and whether a portable brazier or stationary brazier is used. ⇨ CHANOYU, FŪRO, KOICHA, RO, USUCHA

〖注〗 tea ceremony 茶道． procedure 手順，作法． foamy thin tea 泡立っている抹茶，薄茶． thick pasty tea どろどろ粘った抹茶，濃茶． portable brazier 持ち運びできる火鉢，風炉． stationary brazier 備えつけた火鉢，（はめこみの）炉．

Tendaishū 天台宗 the Tendai sect of Buddhism; one of the two major sects of esoteric Buddhism in Japan, the other being the Shingon sect. This sect was founded at the beginning of the ninth century, in the early Heian period, by the priest Saichō (767–822) who had studied in China. He built Konponchūdō on Mount Hiei, which later became the main building of Enryakuji Temple, the headquarters of this sect. The teachings are based on the *Hokekyō* (Lotus Sutra), emphasizing salvation through meditation and wisdom; mystic rites are also performed. This sect was later divided into three branches, with their headquarters at Enryakuji, Onjōji and Saikyōji temples. ⇨ SHINGONSHŪ

〖注〗 esoteric Buddhism 密教． Konponchūdō 根本中堂． headquarters 本部，本山． salvation 救い． meditation 黙想，座禅． mystic rite 神秘的儀式． Onjōji Temple 園城寺． Saikyōji Temple 西教寺．

tendon 天丼 a bowl of *tenpura* and rice; a bowl of rice topped with a few pieces of *tenpura*, usually prawns. Sometimes the *tenpura* may include vegetables or various kinds of fish. A sauce made from fish broth, soy sauce and sweet rice wine (*mirin*) is poured over the rice. It is usually served with a small dish of pickles. ⇨ DASHI, MIRIN, TENPURA

〖注〗 prawn 大正えび，中位のえび． fish broth 魚のだし汁，だし． soy sauce 醤油． sweet rice wine 味醂．

tengu 天狗 a red-faced, long-nosed goblin; a mythical being which is said to have dwelt deep in the forests and mountains. This goblin has a body like a human, is clad in black kimono, but has an extremely long nose and wings on his back. He holds a fan made of feathers that enables him to fly. ⇨ KIMONO

〖注〗 goblin 鬼，化物． mythical being 想像上の存在，神話的な存在． be clad in ～を着ている．

Tenjin(-sama) 天神(様) the deified spirit of Sugawara Michizane (845–903); the guardian deity of studies, in particular calligraphy. Sugawara Michizane, a renowned scholar in the Heian period (794–1185), was favored by the emperor, becoming a high-ranking imperial minister. Jealousy among other ministers resulted in his exile to Kyūshū. After his death all his honors were restored. He is enshrined at Kitano Tenmangū Shrine in Kyoto and his spirit is revered at many other shrines called "such-and-such Tenjin," as at Yushima Tenjin in Tokyo's Bunkyō Ward. Today these shrines are visited by many students wishing for success in their entrance examinations. ⇨ SHODŌ

〖注〗 deify 神聖化する，神として祀る． guardian deity of studies 学問の守護神． calligraphy 書道． high-ranking imperial minister 宮中の高官． exile 流刑，追放． enshrine 祀る．

Tenmoku-jawan 天目茶碗 a Tenmoku tea bowl, used in the tea ceremony. It is a heavy cone-shaped bowl of blue, black and dark brown. It was named after Mount Tenmoku in China where Zen priests practiced austerity, from which they brought tea bowls of this kind back to Japan.

〖注〗 tea ceremony 茶道． cone-shaped 円錐形の． austerity 耐乏，難行苦行．

tennen-kinenbutsu 天然記念物 natural monuments; animals, plants, and geologic and mineral formations, officially protected under the Cultural Properties Law (1950). Most are administered by the Agency for Cultural Affairs of the Education Ministry, but others are administered by local governments. Prior to this, natural monuments had been protected under the Law for the Preservation of Historical Sites, Places of Scenic Beauty and Natural Monuments (1919). Protected species of animals include the Japanese crested ibis (*toki*), the Japanese crane (*tanchōzuru*), the Japanese serow (*kamoshika*) and the giant salamander (*san-*

shōuo). Protected plants include the ball-shaped moss (*marimo*) in Lake Akan in Hokkaidō, the Japanese sago palm (*sotetsu*) in Kagoshima and Miyazaki prefectures, etc., as well as primeval forests and individual old trees.　The geologic formations include the Shūhōdō limestone grotto at Akiyoshi Plateau in Yamaguchi Prefecture, the geyser at Onikōbe in Miyagi Prefecture, etc.

〖注〗 geologic and mineral formation 地質鉱物構成．the Cultural Properties Law「文化財保護法」．the Agency for Cultural Affairs 文化庁．the Law for the Preservation of Historical Sites, Places of Scenic Beauty and Natural Monuments「史跡名勝天然記念物保護法」．primeval forest 原始林．limestone grotto 鐘乳石の洞窟．geyser 間欠温泉．

tennō 天皇　the Emperor of Japan.　The Emperor of Japan is believed to have direct lineage from Amaterasu Ōmikami, the Sun Goddess of the age of Japanese mythology.　The present emperor, Hirohito, is said to be the 124th monarch in an unbroken line of emperors starting with Jinmu, who founded the country in 660 B.C., and became the first *tennō*.　Until the end of World War II, the Emperor had been regarded as sacred and inviolable, but the new constitution adopted in 1947 states: "The Emperor shall be the symbol of the state and of the unity of the people, deriving his position from the will of the people with whom resides sovereign power."　⇨ NIHONKOKU KENPŌ

〖注〗 direct lineage 直系．mythology 神話．the unbroken line of emperors 万世一系の天皇．sacred and inviolable 神聖で侵すべからざる．derive... from から由来する．reside 備わっている，（権利などが）帰属する．sovereign power 支配権．

Tennō Tanjōbi 天皇誕生日　the Emperor's Birthday (April 29); a national holiday celebrating the birthday of the present emperor Hirohito, born on April 29, 1901.　On this day, the compounds of the Imperial Palace are open to the public.　The Emperor, Empress, and other members of the Imperial Family appear on the balcony of the palace to greet the public and receive their good wishes.　This day was formerly called *Tenchōsetsu*.　⇨ IPPANSAN-GA, KOKUMIN NO SHUKUJITSU, TENNŌ

〖注〗 compounds 敷地．the Imperial Palace 皇居．

tenpura 天婦羅　a variety of deep-fried foods; Japanese fritters of seafoods (mostly prawns) and vegetables.　The ingredients are dipped in a batter of wheat flour mixed with egg, and deep-fried in vegetable oil.　They are eaten hot, dipped in a sauce made from soy sauce, sweet rice wine and fish broth.　Grated Japanese radish, or sometimes grated ginger, is mixed into the dip.　⇨ TENTSUYU

〖注〗 deep-fried たっぷりの油で揚げた.　fritter フリッター(練り粉にくるんで揚げた料理).　prawn 車えび, 中位のえび.　ingredient 成分, (料理の)材料. batter 練り粉, 小麦粉を練ったもの.　soy sauce 醬油.　sweet rice wine 味□. fish broth 魚の煮出し汁.　grated Japanese radish 大根下し.　grated ginger おろし生姜.

tenpura-soba〔tenpura-udon〕天婦羅蕎麦〔天婦羅うどん〕 *tenpura* noodles; a bowl of buckwheat noodles [white wheat noodles] in soup, with one or two prawn *tenpura* on top.　*Yuzu* citron peel and bits of greens such as spinach or trefoil leaves may be added.　The soup, a fish stock, is seasoned with soy sauce.　The noodles are eaten with minced green onions and *shichimi-tōgarashi* (a spice of seven seasonings including red pepper).　⇨ SHICHIMI-TŌGARASHI, SOBA, TENPURA, UDON

〖注〗 buckwheat 蕎麦.　spinach ほうれん草.　trefoil leaves 三つ葉.　season 味をつける.　minced green onions さらしねぎ, きざみねぎ.

Tenpyō-bunka 天平文化　the culture of the Tenpyō era (729-49) during the Nara period (646-794); the culture of aristocrats strongly influenced by Buddhism and T'ang civilization, which bloomed in the capital of Nara during the reign of Emperor Shōmu (r. 724-49).　The aims of the policy of centralization, conducted in accordance with the Code of Taihō (701), were realized in this era, eventually bringing prosperity to the aristocracy.　Promoted by the emperor, numerous temples were built, including Tōdaiji Temple dedicated to the Buddha Vairocana, Tōshōdaiji Temple housing the statue of the Chinese priest Ganjin (688-763), etc. Many of the paintings, other works of art, and daily articles of the period of Buddhist or T'ang influence are still preserved in almost perfect condition in the Shōsōin Repository, Nara.　At the same time, this era also saw the rise of national consciousness, with the appearance of compilations of historical legend—*Kojiki* (Records of Ancient Matters, 712) and *Nihon Shoki* (Chronicles of Japan, 720)—as well as the oldest anthology of poems, the *Man'yōshū* (The Collection of Ten-Thousand Leaves, 20 volumes, eighth century).　⇨ BUKKYŌ, NARA-JIDAI

〖注〗 T'ang civilization 唐文明.　the Code of Taihō 大宝律令.　the aristocracy 貴族階級.　dedicate 奉納する.　the Buddha Vairocana 毘盧遮那仏. the Shōsōin Repository 正倉院.　compilation 編纂.

tentsuyu 天つゆ *tenpura* sauce; sauce made from fish broth, soy sauce and sweet rice wine brought to a boil. It is used as a dip when eating *tenpura* (deep-fried foods), mixed with grated Japanese radish. ⇨ TENPURA
〖注〗 fish broth 魚の煮出し汁, だし. soy sauce 醤油. sweet rice wine 味醂. bring to a boil 沸騰させる. grated Japanese radish 大根おろし.

tenugui 手拭い a kind of hand towel; a Japanese towel of rough cotton cloth with a simple design usually in white and indigo. It came into use during the Kamakura period (1185-1336) chiefly as a head covering; in the Tokugawa period (1603-1868) it came to be used for wiping the hands and washing the body in the bath as well.
〖注〗 rough cotton cloth 粗い綿布. indigo 藍色.

tenuguikake 手拭い掛け a towel rack; a stand to hang a wet towel on. It stands about 60 centimeters high, and is made up of two vertical poles with crossbars at the top and at the center. The material used is usually lacquered wood. Such racks may be found in the rooms of Japanese-style inns. ⇨ RYOKAN, TENUGUI
〖注〗 vertical pole 縦の棒. crossbar 横木. lacquered wood 漆塗りの木.

teppanyaki 鉄板焼き foods grilled on an iron sheet; meat and vegetables cooked on an iron griddle set in a table or on an iron-sheet counter. Electric griddles are also used today. Thinly sliced meat and seafoods—chicken, beef, shrimp, squid, clams, etc.—are served on a large platter together with vegetables such as green peppers, onions, mushrooms, etc. Diners seated around the table pick out what they want and cook it themselves. The foods are then dipped in a sauce and mixed with condiments such as minced green onions, grated radish, etc. The sauce itself is a mix of soy sauce and ingredients such as sesame seeds, red pepper, Japanese lemon juice (*ponzu*), etc.
〖注〗 griddle 鉄板. squid いか. platter 大皿. green pepper ピーマン. dip 浸す, つける. condiment 薬味. minced green onions 刻みねぎ, さらしねぎ. grated radish 大根おろし. soy sauce 醤油. ingredient (調理の)材料, 成分.

tera 寺 a temple; a Buddhist temple where images of the Buddha are enshrined and worshiped. The compound of a temple comprises some or all of the following structures: a main hall, a lecture hall, a belfry, a pagoda and priests' quarters. The style of temple architecture is of Chinese origin, and more remotely of Indian origin, though it has been Japanized to a considerable degree.

Many temples have graveyards within or adjacent to their compounds. ⇨ GARAN, SHICHIDŌ-GARAN

〖注〗 image of the Buddha 仏像. enshrine 祀る. compound 境内，敷地，囲
われている区域. lecture hall 講堂. belfry 鐘楼. pagoda 塔. priests'
quarters 僧房. adjacent to 〜の隣に，〜の近くに.

terakoya 寺小屋 a temple school; private schools operated at Buddhist temples in the Edo period (1603-1868). These schools offered opportunities for elementary education to children of the common people, particularly for boys aged 10 to 15. They were
mainly taught the three Rs—reading, writing and arithmetic
(mostly how to use the abacus). Such institutions disappeared
with the Meiji Restoration (1868) when a new school system was
officially adopted. ⇨ MEIJI ISHIN, SOROBAN

〖注〗 three Rs (reading, 'riting and 'rithmetic) 読み，書き，算術. abacus そ
ろばん. institution 機関. the Meiji Restoration 明治維新.

teriyaki 照り焼き glazed broiled fish or meat; fish or meat broiled
after being marinated in a mixture of soy sauce, sugar and sweet
rice wine. Sometimes, the sauce mixture is boiled until thick to
pour over the fish or meat again before serving. Chicken and
yellowtail fish are especially good done in *teriyaki* style.

〖注〗 glazed 照りをつけた. marinate (肉・魚などを)下地ソースにつける.
soy sauce 醤油. sweet rice wine 味淋. yellowtail fish ぶり.

tetsubin 鉄瓶 an iron kettle; a teapot-shaped kettle made of iron.
The *tetsubin* is portable and has a spout and a handle, while
chagama, the iron kettle used in the tea ceremony, is much bigger
with no spout or handle. Water boiled in an iron kettle brings out
the subtle flavor of Japanese tea. *Tetsubin* are chiefly produced in
Kyoto, Ōsaka and Iwate prefectures. The Morioka district of
Iwate Prefecture is especially well-known for its production of iron
kettles called *Nanbu-tetsubin*. ⇨ CHAGAMA, CHANOYU

〖注〗 kettle 湯わかし. spout (水さしなどの)つぎ口. iron kettle 茶釜. tea
ceremony 茶道. subtle flavor 微妙な風味.

to 都 the metropolis; the metropolitan capital district; the Tokyo
metropolis (Tokyo-*to*), one of the administrative divisions of
Japan. Tokyo-to is presently composed of 23 wards (*ku*), 26
cities, and a number of towns and villages, plus the Ogasawara
Islands and the Izu Islands, both groups situated to the south of
Tokyo in the Pacific. ⇨ IZU-SHOTŌ, OGASAWARA-SHOTŌ, TO-DŌ-FU-
KEN

〖注〗 metropolis 主要都市，首都圏．the Tokyo metropolis 東京都．metropolitan 主要都市の，首都圏の．administrative division 行政区分．

tō 塔 a pagoda or stupa; a multistoried tower-like structure built over bones, ashes or relics of the Buddha or a Buddhist saint. A typical pagoda in Japan has three or five stories, with three or five square roofs placed one above the other. They are mostly made of wood, though some smaller ones are made of stone or metal. The oldest existent one is the Five-Storied Pagoda at Hōryūji Temple, which was first constructed at the beginning of the eighth century. ⇨ GARAN, GOJŪNOTŌ, SANJŪNOTŌ, SHARI, SHICHIDŌ-GARAN, TERA

〖注〗 pagoda（東洋の）塔．stupa 仏舎利塔，卒塔婆．multistoried 幾重にもなった．relic 遺物．one above the other 重なり合って．

tobiishi 飛石 stepping stones; flat stones placed on a path in a Japanese landscape garden. They are arranged not only as a path but also as an important part of the landscape. The stones should be of various sizes and forms, and blend naturally with the scheme of the garden. There should be balance in irregularity but without geometrical symmetry. ⇨ NIHON-TEIEN

〖注〗 path 通り路．landscape garden 造景庭園．symmetry 均斉，対称．

to-dō-fu-ken 都道府県 *to, dō, fu* and prefectures; metropolitan Tokyo, Hokkaidō, and metropolitan and rural prefectures. For administrative purposes, the Japanese archipelago is divided into 47 sections: one *to*（Tokyo）, two *fu*（Ōsaka and Kyoto metropolitan prefectures）, one *dō*（Hokkaidō）and 43 *ken*（rural prefectures）. Collectively they are called *to-dō-fu-ken*. ⇨ DŌ, FU, KEN, TO

〖注〗 metropolitan 主要都市の，首都の．metropolitan prefecture 大都市の県（府）．the Japanese archipelago 日本列島．

tōfu 豆腐 soybean curd; bean curd made from soybean milk coagulated with bittern. *Tōfu* is thought to have originated in China during the Han dynasty（206 B.C.-A.D. 220）and been brought to Japan in the late Heian period（794-1185）. It is like a smooth fragile pudding in texture, sold usually in rectangular cakes weighing about 300 grams. There are basically two types of *tōfu* distinguished by texture: "cotton" *tōfu*（*momen-dōfu*）and "silk" *tōfu*（*kinugoshi-dōfu*）, the latter being smoother and more fragile. *Tōfu* is made by boiling crushed soybeans, and then squeezing out the soy milk which is coagulated with bittern in molds. The cut cakes are kept in cold water. *Tōfu* is eaten with soy sauce or *miso* with some condiments, and is also used in soup and pot dishes. *Tōfu* is low in calories, rich in protein, and cholesterol-free.　⇨ MISO, NABEMONO

〖注〗　curd 凝乳．　coagulate 凝固する．　bittern にがり．　the Han dynasty 漢朝．　texture きめ．　soy milk 豆乳．　mold 型，流し型．　condiment 薬味．　cholesterol-free コレステロールをつくらない．

Tōhoku chihō 東北地方　the Tōhoku region; the region covering northern Honshū, one of the five geographical divisions of Honshū (the main island), the other four being the Kantō, Chūbu, Kinki and Chūgoku regions.　The Tōhoku region consists of the six prefectures of Aomori, Iwate, Miyagi, Fukushima, Akita and Yamagata. It is also known as the Ōu region in a historical context.　It contains four national parks—Towada-Hachimantai, Rikuchū Coast, Bandai-Asahi and Nikkō national parks.　⇨ BANDAI-ASAHI KOKURITSU-KŌEN, NIKKŌ KOKURITSU-KŌEN, RIKUCHŪ-KAIGAN KOKURITSU-KŌEN, TOWADA-HACHIMANTAI KOKURITSU-KŌEN

〖注〗　historical context 歴史的意味あい．

Tōkaidō¹ 東海道　lit. the Eastern Sea Road.　the Tōkaidō Highway; one of the five great roads which formerly connected the provinces with Edo, the headquarters of the Tokugawa shogunate (1603–1868).　The Tōkaidō Highway started from Nihonbashi in Edo (present-day Tokyo) and extended to Kyoto, for about 518 kilometers along the Pacific side of Honshū.　It is famous for its 53 posting stations depicted in Hiroshige's woodblock prints.　As National Highway No.1, the Tōkaidō still exists, though its appearance is quite different now; close by, the Old Tōkaidō train line still runs (extending to Kōbe).　⇨ GOKAIDŌ, KUNI, TŌKAIDŌ-GOJŪSANTSUGI

〖注〗　province 地方の諸国，（行政目的で分けた）国．　posting station 宿場，宿駅．　woodblock print 木版画．　the Old Tōkaidō train line 在来東海道本線．

Tōkaidō² 東海道　the Tōkaidō Region; the area along the southern coast of the Pacific side of the mainland, one of the eight large administrative units established under the Code of Taihō (promulgated in 701).　It comprised 13 provinces in 701 and 15 provinces in 771.　The provinces were: Iga, Ise, Shima, Owari, Mikawa, Tōtōmi, Suruga, Kai, Izu, Sagami, Kazusa, Shimōsa, Hitachi, plus Awa and Musashi.　⇨ GOKI(NAI)-SHICHIDŌ, RITSURYŌ, TAIKA NO KAISHIN, TŌKAIDŌ¹

〖注〗　adminitrative unit 行政単位．　the Code of Taihō「大宝律令」．　promul-

gate 施行する，発布する． province 地方の諸国，(行政目的で分けた)国． 東海
道諸国：伊賀，伊勢，志摩，尾張，三河，遠江，駿河，甲斐，伊豆，相模，上総，
下総，常陸，安房，武蔵．

Tōkaidō-gojūsantsugi 東海道五十三次　the 53 relay posting stations
on the Tōkaidō Highway.　The Tōkaidō was one of the great
roads connecting the provinces with Edo, the headquarters of the
Tokugawa shogunate (1603-1868).　Starting from Nihonbashi in
Edo and extending to the then capital of Kyoto (about 518 kilometers) along the Pacific side of Honshū, the Tōkaidō had 53
posting stations between Edo and Kyoto in the Edo period
(1603-1868).　The 53 stages are well-known through color woodblock prints by Andō Hiroshige (1797-1858).　The 53 stations
were: Shinagawa, Kawasaki, Kanagawa, Hodogaya, Totsuka,
Fujisawa, Hiratsuka, Ōiso, Odawara, Hakone, Mishima, Numazu,
Hara, Yoshiwara, Kanbara, Yui, Okitsu, Ejiri, Fuchū, Maruko,
Okabe, Fujieda, Shimada, Kanaya, Nissaka, Kakegawa, Fukuroi,
Mitsuke, Hamamatsu, Maisaka, Arai, Shirasuka, Futakawa, Yoshida, Goyu, Akasaka, Fujikawa, Okazaki, Chiriyu, Narumi, Miya,
Kuwana, Yokkaichi, Ishiyakushi, Shōno, Kameyama, Seki, Sa-
kanoshita, Tsuchiyama, Minakuchi, Ishibe, Kusatsu, Ōtsu.　⇨
MOKUHANGA, SHUKUBA-MACHI, TŌKAIDŌ[1]

〖注〗 relay 中継(の)． posting station 宿場，宿駅． province (行政上分けた)
国． headquarters 本拠． the then capital 当時の首都． stage 宿場，足場．
woodblock print 木版画．

Toki no Kinenbi 時の記念日　the Time Day (June 10); a day commemorating time and timepieces.　This day has been observed
since 1920 to mark the introduction of clocks and to encourage
punctuality in daily life.　Japan's first water clock was introduced
from China and installed in the Imperial Court in 660.　Modern
types of clocks were brought by the Portuguese in 1551.

〖注〗 commemorate ～を記念する． timepiece 時計． install とりつける．
the Imperial Court 宮中．

tokiwazu(-bushi) 常磐津(節)　the Tokiwazu style of *jōruri* chanting; a style of traditional song to *shamisen* accompaniment.　It was
developed by Tokiwazu Mojidayū (1709-81) within the framework
of traditional *gidayū* puppet theater music, and developed particularly as the narrative music for dance on the Kabuki stage,
although it has also been chanted independently.　The vocalization
is characterized by the use of falsetto.　Compared with other

styles of *jōruri* chanting, it sounds less nasal and is delivered more naturally and rhythmically.   ⇨ BUNRAKU, GIDAYŪ, JŌRURI, KABUKI, KIYOMOTO(-BUSHI)

〖注〗 chanting 単調に繰り返して歌うこと、謡うこと. accompaniment 伴奏. Tokiwazu Mojidayū 常磐津文字太夫. narrative 語り(の). vocalization 発声(法). falsetto 裏声、作り声.

tokobashira 床柱 the main alcove pillar in a Japanese-style guest room.   The wood of this pillar is different from the other pillars to avoid monotony in the room.   It is carefully selected and is usually of natural shape with knots and slightly crooked lines.   ⇨ TO-KONOMA, ZASHIKI

〖注〗 alcove 床の間. knot こぶ、まるい木の目. crooked line 曲がった線.

Tokoname-yaki 常滑焼 Tokoname earthenware; earthenware produced around Tokoname in Aichi Prefecture since the Heian period (794-1185).   A typical ware is reddish-brown in color, usually without an artificial glaze on the surface although some kinds of larger water jars are covered with natural ash glaze. Small teapots (*kyūsu*) of Tokoname earthenware without glaze are widely favored.

〖注〗 earthenware 土器. artificial glaze 人工的な上薬、人工的光沢. natural ash glaze 自然灰釉. small teapot 急須.

tokonoma 床の間 an alcove; a recessed place in the guest room of a Japanese-style house.   It is a place of honor where a hanging scroll and a vase of arranged flowers, or an artistic ornament, are displayed.   Its origins lie in the private altar of a Buddhist's house where a low table with candles, an incense burner and flowers were placed before a Buddhist scroll hung on the wall (Kamakura-Muromachi periods).   Today, the *tokonoma* is generally used for aesthetic purposes, to create peace of mind.   In the tea ceremony, it is customary for guests to appreciate the hanging scroll and flower arrangement in the *tokonoma*.   ⇨ CHANOYU, IKEBANA, KAKE-JIKU, ZASHIKI

〖注〗 alcove 壁の凹ませてある所、部屋の凹んだ所、床の間. recessed 凹んだ、引っこんだ. a place of honor 正面の座、上座. hanging scroll 掛け軸. arranged flowers 生けた花. altar 祭壇. incense burner 香炉. aesthetic 美的な.

tokoroten ところ天 gelidium jelly; vermicelli-like strips of gelatin made from seaweed.   It is served in a tangy soy sauce.   Grated ginger is sometimes used as a condiment.

〚注〛 vermicelli 細いめん類.　seaweed 海藻.　tangy 味がぴりっとする.
soy sauce 醤油.　grated ginger おろし生姜.　condiment 香辛料, 薬味.

Tokugawa-bakufu 徳川幕府　the Tokugawa shogunate (1603-1868);
the government of the Tokugawa shogun, with its headquarters in
Edo.　It was established by Tokugawa Ieyasu in 1603, and lasted
until the restoration of imperial rule in 1868 (the Meiji Restoration)
carried out by Tokugawa Yoshinobu (or Keiki) (1837-1913), the
15th Tokugawa shogun.　During the Tokugawa regime, a firm
system of feudalism was enforced in an attempt to secure complete
unification of the nation and the country was closed to foreigners.
Also called *Edo-bakufu*.　⇨ EDO-JIDAI, MEIJI ISHIN
　〚注〛 shogunate 幕府.　headquarters 本部.　the restoration of imperial rule
大政奉還.　the Meiji Restoration 明治維新.　the Tokugawa regime 徳川政
体.　feudalism 封建主義.　enforce 施行する, 強要する.

Tokugawa-jidai 徳川時代　the Tokugawa period (1603-1868); the
period in which the Tokugawa shogunate government controlled
the nation.　More commonly called *Edo-jidai* (the Edo period) in
historical contexts.　⇨ EDO-JIDAI, TOKUGAWA-BAKUFU
　〚注〛 historical context 歴史的意味.

tome 留め　a plant holder.　In flower arrangements, artificial
methods of support are necessary to secure the branches and
flower stalks in place in a vase.　Among the various devices used
are the cross-bar fixture, the T-shape fixture, the vertical type or
the bent fixture.　Such fixtures are usually made with twigs.　⇨
IKEBANA, NAGEIRE
　〚注〛 flower stalk 花の茎.　cross-bar fixture 十字留め.　T-shaped fixture
丁字留め.　vertical type 縦型.　bent fixture まげ留め.

tomesode 留袖　ceremonial kimono for women; a very formal silk
kimono worn by women on auspicious occasions such as weddings.
The most formal one is black with five family crests (*kamon*) on
it—one on the back, one on each side of the upper front and one on
each sleeve.　Recently a light-colored *tomesode* (*iro-tomesode*) has
also been in vogue.　The black one is for married women while the
colored one for both married and unmarried.　Both of these
tomesode kimono have a gorgeous picturesque design on the lower
part, the front and often the hem as well, in gold, silver and other
colors, with embroidery added.　Traditionally, when a daughter
gets married, *tomesode* is prepared by her parents, with her future
husband's family crests on.　⇨ IRO-TOMESODE, KAMON, KIMONO,

KURO-TOMESODE, NUITORI

〖注〗 on auspicious occasions めでたい機会. family crest 家紋. embroidery 刺しゅう, 縫い取り.

tomo 供 an attendant; a servant; an attendant to the main character (*shite*) in a Noh play. A *tomo* plays such minor roles as a lady in waiting, a swordbearer, etc. ⇨ NŌ, SHITE

〖注〗 lady in waiting 侍女. swordbearer 刀持ち.

tonarigumi 隣組 a neighborhood group; the smallest unit, consisting of about a dozen families, within a larger community of groups (*chōnaikai* in towns; *sonkai* in villages), organized during World War II by the order of the government. The system was intended to aid in controlling the nation and in distributing rationed goods. It was abolished with the end of the war in 1945. However, the larger community group system is retained for various purposes.

〖注〗 rationed goods 配給品.

torii 鳥居 lit. bird dwelling. a shrine archway or gate; a gate at the entrance to a Shinto shrine to mark the boundary of sacred precincts. It is made of stone or wood, consisting of two standing pillars, with two horizontal beams, one a little above the other. It is said to have originated as a perch for sacred birds within the shrine precincts. ⇨ JINJA

〖注〗 archway 通路のアーチ. precincts 境内. horizontal beam 水平な梁. perch とまり木.

tori no ichi 酉の市 lit. the cock fair. an annual fair held at Ōtori shrines during November on the days of the cock (one of the 12 signs of the zodiac). Ōtori shrines, whose headquarters are located in Sakai City, Ōsaka, are dedicated to Yamato Takeru no Mikoto, a deity of war; today the shrines are worshiped by merchants praying for good fortune. The chief feature of the fair is the sale of bamboo rakes decorated with good-luck symbols: ornaments representing gold coins, cranes and tortoises, pine trees, figures of the Seven Gods of Good Fortune (*shichi-fukujin*), etc. These rakes are believed to rake in good fortune. The most famous fair is the one held at Ōtori Shrine in Asakusa, Tokyo. ⇨ JINJA, JŪNISHI, SHICHI-FUKUJIN

〖注〗 12 signs of the zodiac 十二支. headquarters 本部. be dedicated to ～に献げられている, ～を祀る. deity 神, 神のようなもの. figures of the Seven Gods of Good Fortune 七福神の像. rake in かき入れる, 手に入れる.

Tosa-ha 土佐派 the Tosa school of painting; a school of indigenous painting (*yamatoe*) carried on through generations by a family of court painters from the middle of the Muromachi period (1336-1568) to the end of the Edo period (1603-1868). This family can be traced back to Fujiwara Motomitsu of the 11th century. The name Tosa is attributed to Fujiwara Yukihiro (13th century), a supervisor for the imperial painting and later a provincial official of Tosa in Shikoku. The school retained the native style of painting, characterized by simple, delicate brush lines and historical or legendary subjects. It is said to have exerted great influence on the *ukiyoe* genre of later years. Particularly distinguished painters of the Tosa school were Tosa Mitsunobu (1434-1528) and Tosa Mitsuoki (1617-91), who were noted for their illustrated scroll paintings (*emaki*). ⇨ EMAKI, UKIYOE, YAMATOE

〖注〗 indigenous 土地固有の, 土着の. Fujiwara Motomitsu 藤原基光. Fujiwara Yukihiro 藤原行廣. a supervisor for the imperial painting 絵所預. Tosa Mitsunobu 土佐光信. Tosa Mitsuoki 土佐光起. illustrated scroll painting 絵巻.

Tōsansai 唐三彩 lit. T'ang three colors. three-colored pottery, originally produced during the T'ang dynasty (618-907) of China. Three-colored ceramic articles that have been unearthed are mostly funeral articles—jars, dishes, and figurines of humans and animals. They have a dappled glaze of three colors: white, bluish-green and yellowish-brown. The Shōsōin Imperial Repository in Nara preserves many indigenous articles of three-colored pottery closely resembling those of the T'ang dynasty.

〖注〗 pottery 陶磁器. the T'ang dynasty 唐朝. ceramic article 陶器用品. figurine 小立像. dappled 斑の. glaze 釉. the Shōsōin Imperial Repository 正倉院. indigenous 土着の, 土地固有の.

toshikoshi-soba 年越しそば buckwheat noodles customarily eaten on New Year's Eve. *Soba*, meaning buckwheat noodles, is the homophone for *soba* meaning "close"—i.e., it is now close to the New Year. ⇨ ŌMISOKA, SOBA

〖注〗 buckwheat noodles 蕎麦. New Year's Eve 大晦日. homophone 同音異義語.

Tōshōgū 東照宮 a Tōshōgū shrine; shrines dedicated to Tokugawa Ieyasu (1542-1616), founder of the Tokugawa shogunate (1603-1868). The term *Tōshō* (lit. the Illuminator of the East) is derived from Ieyasu's posthumous title, Tōshō Daigongen (the Great Manifestation of the Illuminator of the East), granted by the

Imperial Court. His remains were first buried at Mount Kunō in Shizuoka Prefecture and in 1617 transferred to Nikkō, Tochigi Prefecture. Construction of the present mausoleum was started in 1634. With over a dozen structures, including gates, a belfry, tower, storehouses, etc., Tōshōgū Shrine at Nikkō represents the most elaborate architecture in the country, characterized by lavish decorations with gilt, paintings and carvings. There are many other Tōshōgū shrines built on a smaller scale in honor of Ieyasu by feudal lords in their domains, including the ones in Nagoya (1619) and Ueno (1627), as well as the one built at Mount Kunō (1617). ⇨ NIKKŌ KOKURITSU-KŌEN

〖注〗 dedicate 捧げる、奉納する. illuminator 照らす者. posthumous 死後の. manifestation 出現. remains 遺体. mausoleum 霊廟. belfry 鐘楼. gilt 金箔. carving 彫り物. feudal lord 大名. domain 領地、藩.

toso 屠蘇 spiced rice wine; sweet saké flavored with spicy herbs —*nikkei* (cassia bark), *sanshō* (Japanese pepper), *kikyō* (Japanese bellflower), *bōfū* (sand trefoil), etc. *Toso* is served to celebrate New Year's Day, in a decorative lacquered teapot and saké cup. It is believed that *toso* has the power to drive away evil and to invite health for the year. ⇨ GANJITSU, SAKE, SANGANICHI

〖注〗 cassia bark 肉桂. Japanese pepper 山椒. Japanese bellflower 桔梗. sand trefoil 防風. lacquered 漆塗りの.

Towada-Hachimantai Kokuritsu-kōen 十和田八幡平国立公園 Towada-Hachimantai National Park (854.1 square kilometers), designated in 1936; a natural park situated in northern Honshū, straddling the borders of Aomori, Akita and Iwate prefectures. This park centers around Lake Towada and the Hachiman Plateau. Lake Towada (60 sq. km) is an old crater lake, dotted with pine-clad isles and rimmed with mixed forests of pines, maples and many other types of trees. The lake is particularly well-known for its dazzling autumnal tints blending with the blue of the lake. The Hachiman Plateau (410 sq. km) features a number of volcanoes, such as Mount Iwate (2,041 meters), Mount Hachiman (1,613 m), Mount Koma (1,637 m), etc., and thus is scattered with hot springs. ⇨ KOKURITSU-KŌEN, ONSEN

〖注〗 straddle 股にかける. crater lake 噴火口からできた湖. be dotted with 〜が点在する. pine-clad 松の木でおおわれた. rim ふちどる. autumnal tints 秋の紅葉. hot spring 温泉.

tozama-daimyō 外様大名 an outside feudal lord; feudal lords who

were not hereditary vassals of the shogunate, one of the three kinds
of feudal lords (*shinpan-daimyō*, *fudai-daimyō* and *tozama-daimyō*)
during the Tokugawa period (1603-1868). These feudal lords did
not side with the Tokugawas in the Battle of Sekigahara (1600),
but later submitted to them with the establishment of the Tokugawa shogunate government. They were not allowed to take part
in government affairs, located in the domains, remote from Edo.
Later, toward the Meiji Restoration (1868), they came to the fore
to restore the imperial rule by overturning the Tokugawa shogunate.   ⇨ DAIMYŌ, FUDAI-DAIMYŌ, SEKIGAHARA NO TATAKAI, SHINPAN-
DAIMYŌ, TOKUGAWA-BAKUFU

〖注〗 feudal lord 大名. hereditary vassal 世襲的家臣. shogunate 幕府.
domain 領地. the Meiji Restoration 明治維新.

tsubo 坪 a traditional unit for measuring area. It is used popularly
even today, particularly for measuring floor space and land area.
One *tsubo* is 6 by 6 *shaku*, about 1.8 by 1.8 meters (3.3 square
meters). This is the size of two *tatami* mats.   ⇨ SHAKKAN-HŌ,
SHAKU, TATAMI

〖注〗 unit for measuring area 面積を計る単位.

Tsuboya-yaki 壺屋焼 ceramic ware of Tsuboya, Okinawa.
Tsuboya ware is basically an Okinawan modification of 17th-
century Korean ceramics. In 1617 a Korean potter settled at
Tsuboya, near Naha, establishing a kiln there and becoming a
subject of the King of the Ryūkyūs. The potter had been brought
to Satsuma by Shimazu forces during Hideyoshi's invasion of the
Korean Peninsula. Okinawans proved to be apt pupils and thus
Tsuboya ware came into being. Interest in this ware appeared in
mainland Japan mainly after World War II, in large part due to
the famed potter of Mashiko, Shōji Hamada (1894-1978).   ⇨
MASHIKO-YAKI, OKINAWA, RYŪKYŪ-SHOTŌ

〖注〗 ceramic ware 陶器. modification 修正, 変化. kiln 窯. Shōji
Hamada 濱田庄司.

Tsugaru-nuri 津軽塗 Tsugaru lacquer ware; lacquer ware originating in the Tsugaru area in the present Aomori Prefecture in the
middle of the Edo period (1603-1868). This ware has a bumpy
surface mottled with multicolored spots. On the wooden base as
many as 20 coats of lacquer of different colors are applied one over
another. Then the layered lacquer is scraped here and there with
a special spatula so that depressions are made showing the layers

of differently colored lacquer. ⇨ NURIMONO, SHIKKI, URUSHI

【注】 lacquer ware 漆器. bumpy surface でこぼこの表面. mottle まだらにする，雑色にする. lacquer 漆. scrape けずる. spatula へら. depression 凹んだところ.

tsuishu 堆朱 lit. heaped vermilion. red, laminated lacquer ware. Patterns such as flowers, birds, landscapes, etc., are carved in relief on a wooden base, to which as many as 100 vermilion coatings are elaborately applied. This art developed in China during the Sung dynasty (960-1279) and was brought to Japan during the Muromachi period (1336-1568). *Tsuishu* produced in Murakami in Niigata Prefecture is highly esteemed. ⇨ NURIMONO, SHIKKI, URU-SHI

【注】 vermilion 朱色. laminate 箔にする，塗りを重ねる. carve 彫る. relief 浮き彫り（品）. coating 塗り. the Sung dynasty 宋朝.

tsukemono 漬物 pickles; vegetables preserved in brine and/or a pickling base. Pickles serve as an important side dish in a Japanese meal. There are numerous kinds of pickles, those of each district, even each home, having their own unique taste. According to the base used, they are classified into *nukazuke* (rice-bran pickles), *misozuke* (bean-paste pickles), *shiozuke* (salt pickles), *kasuzuke* (saké-lees pickles), etc., all having varying pickling periods, ranging from overnight for fresh vegetables to a few months for *umeboshi* (pickled plum), *takuan* (pickled radish), etc. ⇨ NUKA(MISO)-ZUKE, TAKUAN, UMEBOSHI

【注】 brine 漬物用の塩水. rice-bran 糠の. bean-paste 味噌の. saké-lees 酒粕の.

tsuke-obi つけ帯 a fixed sash for a kimono; a ready-tied *obi*, with the bow and the sash as separate pieces. With this, one can avoid difficulty in tying the *obi* in a bow at the back, which requires special skill. This *obi* is worn casually with an informal kimono and is not appropriate for very formal wear. Children's *obi* are usually of this type. Also called *keisō-obi* (lightly worn *obi*). ⇨ KIMONO, OBI

【注】 bow 結び目，お太鼓. lightly worn *obi* 軽装帯.

tsukesage 付下げ a formal or semiformal kimono with vertical patterns; women's silk kimono with patterns flowing toward the shoulder, or hanging from the shoulder, at both the front and back. The fabric is carefully designed (often hand-painted) so that the patterns are not turned upside down when it is made into a kimono.

Tsukesage with a picturesque design and a family crest at the back is worn on formal occasions; those with modest designs are used on semiformal occasions such as social visits, parties, etc.   ⇨ HŌMON-GI, KIMONO

〖注〗 family crest 家紋.

tsukimi 月見   moon viewing; the traditional custom of enjoying the full moon in midautumn.   A special moon-viewing event is traditionally held, on August 15 in the lunar calendar, falling around September 29 on the present calendar, when the harvest moon is at its best.   It is an occasion for people to pray to the moon for a good harvest of rice.   People used to offer rice dumplings to the moon together with the seven grasses of autumn, particularly pampas grass (*susuki*) and bush clover (*hagi*).   Moon viewing was also an elegant pastime for enjoying a poetic atmosphere.   Its origin dates back to the 10th century when nobles and men of letters were invited to the court by Emperor Godaigo (897-930) and composed short poems while looking at the full moon.   ⇨ AKI NO NANAKUSA, JŪGOYA

〖注〗 the lunar calendar 太陰暦.   rice dumpling お団子.   the seven grasses of autumn 秋の七草.   pampas grass 薄.   bush clover 萩.   pastime 娯楽. men of letters 文人.

tsukimi-soba [tsukimi-udon] 月見蕎麦 [月見うどん]   lit. moon-viewing noodles.   a bowl of *soba* or *udon* noodles in soup flavored with fish and soy sauce.   A raw egg (though partly cooked from the heat of the boiling-hot noodles) is placed sunny-side up, giving rise to its name *tsukimi* (moon viewing), since the egg resembles the moon.   ⇨ SOBA, UDON

〖注〗 moon viewing 月見.   soy sauce 醬油.   boiling hot 湯気の出るように熱い.   sunny-side up 目玉の方を上にして.   give rise to 起こる，生じる.

tsukiyama-teien 築山庭園   a hilly garden; a Japanese landscape garden containing artificial hills and ponds.   Famous examples of this kind of garden include Suizenji Garden (1632) in Kumamoto and Rikugien Garden (1702) in Tokyo.   ⇨ HIRA-NIWA, NIHON-TEIEN

〖注〗 landscape garden 造景庭園.   Suizenji Garden 水前寺庭園.   Rikugien Garden 六義園.

tsukubai 蹲踞   lit. crouching.   a stone basin; a stone water basin set near the tearoom in a tea garden.   The *tsukubai* consists of a stone washbasin and some other stones arranged around it.   The guests at a tea ceremony crouch (*tsukubau*) and wash their hands with the water of the basin using a ladle before entering the tearoom. There are some basins into which water flows through a bamboo pipe.　⇨ CHATEI

〖注〗 basin (水)鉢. washbasin 手水鉢. tea ceremony 茶の湯. crouch かがむ, つくばう. bamboo pipe 竹の筧.

tsukudani 佃煮 lit. boiled foods from Tsukuda. foods boiled down in soy sauce, sugar or starch syrup, etc., for preserving. Ingredients include shellfish, small dried fish, chopped seaweed, etc. They go well with hot rice. They were so named because this method of preserving foods began as a means of using fish left unsold at Tsukuda Shrine in Edo (the present Tokyo) in the Edo period (1603-1868).

〖注〗 boil down 煮つめる. soy sauce 醤油. starch syrup 水あめ. ingredient (料理の)材料.

tsuma つま[妻] garnish; ornamental vegetables served with meat or fish. With sliced raw fish, thinly shredded Japanese radish (sometimes with carrot) and certain kinds of seaweeds are served to aid digestion and enhance the appearance of the dish. They are eaten together with the meat or fish.

〖注〗 garnish 料理に装飾的に添えるもの, つま. sliced raw fish 刺身. Japanese radish 大根. seaweed 海藻. enhance 増す, (値うちを)引きあげる.

tsume 詰め the last guest in a tea ceremony. He or she takes the last seat in the tearoom, and plays an important role in assisting the host in many ways. Usually called *o-tsume* in polite form.　⇨ CHASHITSU, TEISHU

〖注〗 tea ceremony 茶の湯.

tsumugi 紬 Japanese pongee; fabric woven from hand-spun threads of raw silk. The threads used are left natural and uneven, thus taking on a rustic texture. A kimono made of this fabric is highly valued and extremely expensive, but it is not worn on formal occasions. Famous kinds include *Ōshima-tsumugi*, *Yūki-tsumugi*, *Ueda-tsumugi*, etc., each having a unique design and texture.　⇨ KIMONO, ŌSHIMA-TSUMUGI, YŪKI-TSUMUGI

〖注〗 pongee 絹紬, 柞蚕糸から織った絹織物. fabric 織物. hand-spun thread 手でつむいだ糸. rustic texture 素朴な生地.

tsuno-kakushi 角隠し lit. a horn concealer. the bride's head covering; an oblong white cloth worn on the traditional coiffure by a bride at her wedding. It is said to hide the horns of jealousy which women might possess, and to assure that the bride will not have horns of jealousy after marriage. It also symbolizes humility in the nuptial pledge before gods.

〖注〗 oblong 矩形(の). coiffure 髪型. nuptial 婚礼の.

tsure 連   a companion; the tritagonist in a Noh play. He functions as an assistant performer to the main actor (*shite*) and the secondary actor (*waki*) in a Noh play. ⇨ NŌ, SHITE, WAKI

〖注〗 companion 仲間, (能の)連. tritagonist 三番目に重要な役, (能の)連. main actor 主役, (能の)仕手.

Tsurezure-gusa 徒然草   *Essays in Idleness* (around 1331); a collection of essays written by Yoshida Kenkō (1282-1350) in the Kamakura period (1185-1336). This collection consists of 243 separate sections with a short preface, each section varying in length from one sentence to a few pages. They are random notes of "all trivial thoughts that happen to come to mind" as the author writes in the opening sentence, all in a lucid and flowing style. The subjects include descriptions of the changing seasons, episodes of human interest, observations on the aristocracy, suggestions on how to live, thoughts on artistic pursuits, etc., which reflect the diversity of his thinking, based on Confucianism, Taoism, Shintoism and especially Buddhism. As a Buddhist monk living in seclusion, with a pessimistic view of the world, he is detached and observes life and things objectively, but at the same time is very much involved in human affairs. ⇨ BUKKYŌ, JUKYŌ, SHINTŌ

〖注〗 "all trivial thoughts that happen to come to mind" 「つれづれなるままに心にうつりゆくよしなしごと」. lucid and flowing style 澄んで流れるような文体. artistic pursuit 芸術の追求. Confucianism 儒教. Taoism 道教. live in seclusion 脱俗的な生活をする. detached 超然としている.

tsuridōrō 釣り燈籠   a hanging lantern; a small hanging lantern made of iron or bronze. It is usually a quaint old rusty lantern hanging by a chain from a corner of the eaves of a traditional Japanese-style house. It not only lights up the garden but also adds charm to the surroundings. ⇨ TŌRŌ

〖注〗 quaint 風変わりでおもしろい, 古風で趣のある. eaves 軒.

tsurigane 釣り鐘   a hanging bell; a bell hanging in a belfry in the compounds of a temple. It is struck from the outside by a huge suspended wooden hammer drawn back and forth, sometimes by several people. The peals of a temple bell are said to ward off evil. Compared with a church bell, a Japanese temple bell gives a longer peal in a very low key. ⇨ SHŌRŌ, TERA

〖注〗 belfry 鐘楼. compounds 敷地, 境内. peal 響き. ward off 追い払う. key 音程.

tsuru-kame 鶴亀 the crane and the tortoise; a traditional combination symbolic of longevity. Both are said to have long lives, as a Japanese proverb goes, "A crane lives a thousand years and a tortoise ten thousand years." A picture or an ornament which depicts this combination is displayed as a sign of good luck and longevity on occasions such as weddings, celebrations for the aged, etc.

〖注〗 longevity 長寿. "A crane lives a thousand years and a tortoise ten thousand years."「鶴は千年, 亀は万年」.

tsuyu 梅雨 the rainy season. This season begins around June 10 and lasts until the middle of July. It is caused by the meeting of a cold high atmospheric pressure front over the Sea of Okhotsk and a warm high atmospheric pressure front over the Pacific. The weather is usually humid and gloomy during this season. Yet, the season is necessary for rice planting. Also called *baiu* (plum rain) because Japanese plums ripen at this time of the year. ⇨ BAIU, TAUE

〖注〗 high atmospheric pressure 高気圧. Japanese plum 梅.

tsuzumi 鼓 a generic term for Japanese hand drums. Older forms (called *ko*) are still used in Gagaku court music. There are *ko-tsuzumi* (a small hand drum) and *ō-tsuzumi* (a large hand drum). Both became the principal rhythm instruments of the *hayashi* ensemble accompanying Noh dances. Later, these two drums were used in Kabuki, especially in the *nagauta hayashi* which often accompany Japanese dance performances separate from the Kabuki drama. ⇨ GAGAKU, HAYASHI, KABUKI, KOTSUZUMI, NAGAUTA, NŌ, ŌTSUZUMI

〖注〗 ensemble 合奏, 合唱. accompany 伴う, 伴奏する.

tsuzure-obi 綴れ帯 a sash (*obi*) of tapestry weave; a designed tapestry *obi*, hand-woven with silk threads. It is woven with the use of a tiny tool attached to the fingernails by raking the weft yarns one by one through the warp yarns, producing elaborate designs. A tremendous number of days are required for completing a single *obi*. This kind of *obi* is the most gorgeous and luxurious of all *obi*, and thus it is worn with a wedding costume. This method of tapestry weave has a long history of 1,300 years in Japan as evidenced by an example preserved in the Shōsōin Imperial Repository (before the eighth century) in Nara. ⇨ OBI

〖注〗 tapestry 綴れ織, 綴れ錦. rake 手でかき集める. weft yarn 横糸. warp yarn 縦糸. repository 貯蔵所.

U

uchikake 打掛け[裲襠]　a long ceremonial overgarment; a formal gown worn over a bride's wedding kimono. It has a thick edge and is made of brocade or figured satin with decorative patterns. Derived from a ceremonial garment worn by women of the high-ranking samurai class in the Muromachi period (1336-1568), it was first adopted as wedding attire by wealthy townsfolk in the Edo period (1603-1868). Nowadays it is very popularly worn at traditional-style weddings.　⇨ KIMONO

〖注〗 overgarment 上にはおる衣服．figured satin 模様入りしゅす織り．attire 装い，盛装．townsfolk 町人．

uchiwa 団扇　a round paper fan with a bamboo handle; a flat paper fan used to keep oneself cool and also to kindle a fire in place of a bellows. It is made by pasting paper on a thin frame of finely split bamboo. While the *sensu*, or folding fan, is appropriate with formal wear, the *uchiwa* is for home wear, especially the *yukata*.　⇨ SENSU, YUKATA

〖注〗 bellows ふいご，火ふき．folding fan 扇子．

udon うどん　noodles; white noodles made from wheat flour, thicker than *soba* (buckwheat noodles). The flour is kneaded, then rolled out and cut into long strips, which are dried up for preservation. *Udon* is eaten like *soba* with a dip or in a soup with minced green onions, but is almost always served hot.　⇨ SOBA

〖注〗 knead 練る，こねる．roll out ひきのばす．minced 細かく刻んだ．minced green onions さらしねぎ，きざみねぎ．

uji 氏　a clan; a group consisting of kindred families, plus non-kindred subordinate families in ancient times. The most influential family ruled over the rest of the kin, each family further controlling minor subordinate families including workers and servants. They all formed a single clan (*uji*) with a hierarchical system among themselves. The clan had its own tutelary shrine. According to Japanese history, the present imperial family (*Tennō*

family) is traced back to the ruling family of the Yamato group.
⇨ TENNŌ

〖注〗 kindred 親戚. subordinate family 家臣，家来の家族. kin 血縁，親族.
hierarchical system 位階制度，序列制度. tutelary shrine 守護神社.

ujigami 氏神 the deity of a clan(*uji*); a shrine or its deity worshiped
for protection by the members of a clan or community. In ancient
times, all the members of a clan belonged to a particular shrine
where the spirit of one of their ancestors was enshrined as a
guardian deity. Later on, a small shrine, or its deity, of a local
community (originally called *chinju*) also came to be called *ujigami*. ⇨ CHINJU, JINJA, UJI

〖注〗 enshrine 祀る. guardian deity 守護神.

ukai 鵜飼 cormorant fishing; the ancient method of catching *ayu*
(river smelt) by using tamed cormorants. The most famous and
festive display can be observed on the Nagara River, Gifu Prefecture, almost every night from May 11 to October 15. Cormorant-
fishing masters (*ushō*) in ancient costume handle about a dozen
cormorants harnessed with long leashes on a boat bearing a basket
of torches. The cormorants capture the fish with their beaks but
are forced to disgorge the fish because of rings around their necks
which prevent them from swallowing. This scene can be enjoyed
from the river bank or from a hired boat in which the guests are
entertained with foods and drinks.

〖注〗 cormorant 鵜. river smelt 鮎. cormorant-fishing master 鵜匠. har-
ness 馬具をつける，ひもをつける. leash 綱. torch たいまつ，かがり火. disgorge 吐き出す.

ukibana 浮き花 floating flowers; the floating style of flower
arrangement. This flower arrangement is intended not only for
appreciating the flowers but at the same time for enjoying the
feeling of coolness created by the surface of the water. Water
plants are most suitable for such arrangements. ⇨ IKEBANA

〖注〗 flower arrangement 生け花.

ukiyoe 浮世絵 lit. pictures of the floating world. a genre of painting and woodblock prints developed in Japan from the 17th through
the 19th centuries. The subjects depict landscapes, actors and the
world of pleasures—entertainment quarters and women. The
great artists of this category include Andō Hiroshige (1797-1858)
for his 53 views of the Tōkaidō Highway, Katsushika Hokusai
(1760-1849) for Mount Fuji, Kitagawa Utamaro (1753-1806) for

beautiful women, and Tōshūsai Sharaku (18th century) for Kabuki actors. ⇨ EDO-JIDAI, MOKUHANGA, TŌKAIDŌ-GOJŪSANTSUGI

【注】 the floating world 浮世. genre 風俗画. woodblock print 木版画. entertainment quarters 娯楽街, 花柳界. the 53 views of the Tōkaidō Highway 東海道五十三次.

ukiyozōshi 浮世草子 lit. novels of the floating world. a genre of literature which flourished in the Edo period (1603-1868). The stories depict various aspects of the society of those days very realistically, ranging from the rigid outlook of staid samurai to the mundane and sensual lives of the townspeople. Ihara Saikaku (1642-93) is a representative writer of this kind of literature.

【注】 genre ジャンル, 分野. staid 落ち着いた, 真面目な. mundane 世俗的な.

umeboshi 梅干し a pickled plum; pickled Japanese plums, usually light brown or reddish in color. They are made by salting and sun-drying plums a few times. To obtain the red color, the red leaves of beefsteak plants (*shiso*) are pickled with the plums. The pickling is done around mid-June when the plums are ripe, and the pickles are mature by September. They can be preserved many years. *Umeboshi* aids digestion and also works as a germicidal agent. It is used in rice-balls (*nigiri-meshi*) or as a garnish on rice in lunch boxes. ⇨ NIGIRI-MESHI

【注】 Japanese plum 梅. beefsteak plant 紫蘇. mature 熟成する. germicidal agent 殺菌剤. garnish 飾る, (料理のつまに)添える.

umeshu 梅酒 plum wine; liquor made from Japanese plums. *Shōchū* liquor is poured over green Japanese plums and sugar (or rock sugar) placed in alternating layers in a large glass jar. The jar is sealed tight and stored in a dark place, and the wine can be drunk after a few months. But, to bring out its taste, it should be aged at least a year. By adding water and ice, it becomes a refreshing summer "health" drink. The plums are also edible. ⇨ SHŌCHŪ

【注】 rock sugar 氷砂糖. age 熟成する.

unadon 鰻丼 an abbreviation and common term for *unagi-donburi,* eel on rice in a bowl; charcoal-broiled barbecued eel and rice served in a bowl. A special sauce is poured over it and powdered *sanshō,* a kind of Japanese pepper, is often sprinkled on top. ⇨ DONBU-RIMONO, SANSHŌ, UNAGI NO KABAYAKI

【注】 abbreviation 省略語. eel 鰻. charcoal-broiled 炭火で焼いた.

unagi no kabayaki 鰻の蒲焼 barbecued eel; split eel broiled on bamboo skewers over a charcoal fire or a gas flame. It is basted a few times with a boiled mixture of eel stock (made from the head and bones of the eel), soy sauce, sugar and sweet rice wine. Powdered *sanshō*, a kind of pepper, is often sprinkled over the eel when it is eaten on rice. ⇨ SANSHŌ, UNADON

〖注〗 bamboo skewer 竹串. split eel 開いた鰻. baste たれをかける. soy sauce 醤油. sweet rice wine 味淋.

Unzen-Amakusa Kokuritsu-kōen 雲仙天草国立公園 Unzen-Amakusa National Park (255 square kilometers), designated in 1934; a natural park covering parts of Nagasaki, Kumamoto and Kagoshima prefectures in western Kyūshū. In addition to the Shimabara Peninsula where Unzen is located, this park includes some 100 islands, centering around the Amakusa Islands. The peninsula and islands are surrounded by the Ariake Sea, Chijiwa Bay, Shimabara Bay, the Yatsushiro Sea and Amakusanada Sea. The Unzen region, featuring the active Fugen volcano of Mount Unzen, is particularly famous for its bubbling hot sulphur springs. The Amakusa Five Bridges built in 1966 link the peninsula with the Amakusa Islands. It was on Shimabara Peninsula that Japanese Christian armies fought against Tokugawa shogunate armies in 1637, while on the Amakusa Islands many hidden Christians adhered to their religion in secret during the 250 years of the official prohibition of Christianity (1614-1873). ⇨ KAKURE-KIRISHITAN, KOKURITSU-KŌEN, KYŪSHŪ, SHIMABARA NO RAN

〖注〗 Chijiwa Bay 千々石湾. the Yatsushiro Sea 八代海. hot sulphur spring 硫黄温泉. the Amakusa Five Bridges 天草五橋.

urabon 盂蘭盆 the Bon Festival; the Buddhist All Souls' Day (July 13-15 or 16, or August 13-15 or 16). The term *urabon* derives from the Sanskrit *ullambana* meaning "severe suffering." During this period, prayers and feasts are offered to the dead so that they may be relieved from suffering. This practice started in the seventh century and continues today. It is also a festive time of reunion for living as well as departed members of the family. It is more commonly called *Bon* or *Obon*. ⇨ BON

〖注〗 reunion 再会. departed member 死者.

Urashima Tarō 浦島太郎 a Japanese folk tale character; the Japanese counterpart of Rip Van Winkle. One day, Urashima Tarō, a young fisherman, saved a turtle that was being bullied by children. The next day, the turtle invited him to the Dragon

Palace at the bottom of the sea, where a beautiful princess lived. Heartily welcomed by those at the palace, he spent what he thought was three years there. When he decided to return home, the princess handed him a box, telling him never to open it. Upon reaching his native village, he found everything had changed. At a loss, he opened the box only to find smoke rise from it, which turned him into a wizened old man. What he thought had been three years had actually been 300. There are many versions of the story, with slight variations. This tale dates back to ancient times, appearing in the *Nihon Shoki* (The Chronicle of Japan, 720), *Man'yōshū* (The Collection of Ten-Thousand Leaves, eighth century) and *Tango Fudoki* (The Record of Tango Province, eighth century). ⇨ FUDOKI, MAN'YŌSHŪ, NIHON SHOKI

〖注〗 counterpart 相対物、よく似たもの. bully いじめる、おどす. the Dragon Palace 龍宮. secret box 玉手箱. wizened しなびた.

urushi 漆 lacquer; japan; a resinous varnish obtained from the sap of the Japanese lacquer tree, *Rhus verniciflua*. It is used as a coating to add a lustrous finish to the surface of wooden articles (nowadays, plastic articles as well) such as trays, soup bowls, chopsticks, etc. The art of lacquering bloomed in Japan, thus giving rise to the term "japan" meaning lacquer. ⇨ NURIMONO, SHIKKI

〖注〗 resinous 樹脂質の. varnish ワニス、ニス、天然樹液. sap 樹液. *Rhus verniciflua* (=Japanese lacquer tree) 漆の木. coating 上薬、上塗り. lustrous finish 光沢のある仕上り. give rise to ~を生じる、~を引き起こす.

usucha 薄茶 thin powdered tea; foamy green tea served in the tea ceremony. The amount of tea powder used for a cup of tea is about a tea scoop and a half. About three and a half mouthfuls of hot water makes one serving. It is prepared in individual bowls for each guest, whereas a cup of thick powdered tea (*koicha*) is shared by several guests. *Usucha* is served at a later stage of the proceedings in the formal tea ceremony when both *koicha* and *usucha* are served. ⇨ CHANOYU, CHASHAKU, KOICHA, MATCHA

〖注〗 powdered tea 抹茶. foamy green tea 泡立ったお茶、薄茶. tea ceremony 茶の湯. tea scoop 茶杓. thick powdered tea 濃茶. proceedings 手順、作法の順序.

utagaruta 歌がるた a set of cards of a poem-matching game; a poem-matching game. A set consists of two decks of cards, reading cards and cards to be picked up. On the reading card is a

31-syllable poem—originally the first 17 syllables of the poem —composed of five lines with 5-7-5-7-7 syllables respectively; on the cards to be picked up only the last 14 syllables are written. The object of the game is to gather more cards than the other players by picking up the cards that match the ones read out.   The most popular and time-honored set of *utagaruta* is *Ogura-hyakunin-isshu*, more generally called just *hyakunin-isshu*.   ⇨ HYAKUNIN-ISSHU, KARUTA, OGURA-HYAKUNIN-ISSHU

〖注〗 poem-matching game 歌合わせの遊び.   deck (トランプ, かるた等の)一組.   31-syllable poem 31音節の詩, 短歌.   time-honored 由緒ある, 伝統的な.

utai 謡 the chanting of a Noh passage; the vocalization of Noh chanting, sometimes performed independently by amateur performers.   Formally referred to as *yōkyoku*.   ⇨ NŌ, YŌKYOKU

〖注〗 chanting 歌うこと, 吟ずること.   passage (作品の)一節.   vocalization 声を出すこと, 発声.

utakai-hajime 歌会始 the New Year Imperial poetry party; the 31-syllable poem (*tanka*) recitation party held annually at the Imperial Court at the beginning of the year.   This function has been held since ancient times, but it was not until the second year of Meiji (1869) that it came to be an annual New Year event for the imperial family.   Poems by members of the imperial family, and others selected from compositions by the public, are recited in a ceremonial way by specialists.   The theme for the poems is announced the previous year and anyone may submit a poem for consideration, even from abroad.   ⇨ CHOKUDAI, KŌKYO, TANKA

〖注〗 31-syllable poem 短歌.   recitation 吟唱.

W

wa 和 harmony; unity; concord; a harmonious integration among human beings, or between an individual and his surroundings. From ancient times in Japanese society, this concept has been highly esteemed as one of the supreme values, socially and ethically, for a peaceful and orderly life among people. In the Constitution of 17 Articles (604), the regent Prince Shōtoku (574-622) stressed *wa* as the basic principle of human behavior. The concept of *wa* also exists in the tea ceremony as one of the essential elements; here it can be interpreted as man's harmonious unity with nature and the universe, as well as harmony among the people participating in the tea ceremony. ⇨ JŪSHICHIJŌ NO KENPŌ, CHANOYU

〖注〗integration 融合. concept 物の考え方, 概念. esteem 尊ぶ, 大切にする. the Constitution of 17 Articles「十七条の憲法」. regent 摂政.

wabi 佗 lit. loneliness; insufficiency. refined poverty; a humble life in solitude with nature as a companion; to lead a solitary life, contemplating nature and appreciating the spiritual and aesthetic values underlying insufficiency, a way of life idealized with the development of the rustic tea ceremony around the 16th century. Prior to that time, *wabi* had been associated with the hermit's humble life in seclusion, a life of resignation. Under the influence of Zen Buddhism, Sen no Rikyū (1521-91) and other tea masters brought more positive and profound meaning to the concept of *wabi* as an important element of the tea ceremony. In a tea hut, humble and withered, one is expected to contemplate the boundless universe and to experience unlimited spiritual richness. In the 17th century, Matsuo Bashō (1644-94) produced *haikai* short verses expressive of the tranquil beauty of loneliness and barrenness as suggested in the following. (Translation: Kenneth Yasuda)

Kare-eda ni   On a withered bough
Karasu no tomaritaru ya   A crow alone is perching;

Aki no kure   Autumn evening now.

Along with *sabi,* the concept of *wabi* has become deeply rooted in Japanese aesthetics.   ⇨ CHANOYU, HAIKAI, SABI, SADŌ, WABICHA, WABI-SABI, ZEN[1]

【注】 contemplate 観照する． aesthetic value 美的価値． rustic tea わび茶． hermit 隠者, 世捨人． seclusion 閑居, 隠遁． resignation 諦め, 悟り． profound 意味の深い． barrenness 貧弱． withered 枯れた, わびれた．

wabicha 侘茶 lit. poverty tea. the rustic tea ceremony; the simple, rustic tea ceremony developed to completion by Sen no Rikyū (1521-91). While the shogun Toyotomi Hideyoshi (1536-98) injected luxury into the tea ceremony, using expensive imported Chinese tea utensils in decorative reception rooms, Murata Jōkō (1422-1502), having a background in Zen Buddhism, maintained a simple style. Adopting his style, Takeno Jōō (1502-55) began developing the rustic tea ceremony and Sen no Rikyū brought it to completion. Basing their ideas on Zen philosophy, the two tea masters sought spiritual richness and profundity, strenuously avoiding superficial gorgeousness. They used utensils made of bamboo and roughly fired, misshapen earthenware, and conducted the ceremony in a withered, rustic thatched hut. From this developed the concept of *wabi*, an aesthetic quality involving poverty, simplicity, rusticity, etc., which became deeply rooted in Japanese culture. The principles of the rustic tea ceremony—harmony, reverence, purity and tranquillity—as taught by Sen no Rikyū have been handed down in the tea ceremony to the present. ⇨ CHANOYU, CHASHITSU, SADŌ, WABI, WABI-SABI, WA-KEI-SEI-JAKU, ZEN[1], ZENSHŪ

【注】 inject 注入する． tea utensil 茶道具． profundity 意味深さ． withered 枯れた, わびれた． thatched hut 茅葺き小屋． rusticity わびれていること． harmony, reverence, purity and tranquillity 和敬清寂．

wabi-sabi 侘・寂 refined poverty and rustic simplicity; active aesthetic appreciation of poverty, deficiency, rusticity, loneliness, etc. *Wabi* and *sabi* are related terms, often used jointly to denote a profound aesthetic concept deeply rooted in traditional Japanese culture since late medieval times. In particular, the concept expressed by these two terms together constitutes the essence of the tea ceremony, reflecting the spirit of Zen. They are also used synonymously or interchangeably. In formal use, *wabi* has more subjective and personal connotations, referring to a preference for a humble and solitary way of life, while *sabi* is more objective and detached, and is applied to art objects and poems, such as rustic tea utensils taking on a patina by use and age or the tranquil beauty suggested by a *haikai* (17-syllable poem). In short, the former has spatial and environmental connotations and the latter those of time and agedness. ⇨ CHANOYU, HAIKAI, SABI, WABI, WABICHA, ZEN¹

〖注〗 aesthetic 美的な． rusticity わびれていること． profound 意味の深い． connotation 含蓄． detached 超然とした． rustic tea utensil さびれた茶道具． patina 古さび，古色． tranquil 静寂な． spatial 空間的． agedness 年月を経ていること．

wagashi 和菓子 the generic term for Japanese-style confectionery. The main ingredients used are rice flour, wheat flour, red beans, agar-agar, egg, sugar, etc. There are two kinds—moist (*yōkan, manjū,* etc.) and dry (*senbei, higashi,* etc.) ⇨ HIGASHI, MANJŪ, SENBEI, YŌKAN

〖注〗 ingredient 成分，(料理の)材料． red bean あずき． agar-agar 寒天，天草．

wagon 和琴 a Japanese zither; a six-stringed zither, made of a board about 180 centimeters long and 20 cm wide. It is the forerunner of the present *koto* (13-stringed zither) and is still used in court music (Gagaku). ⇨ GAGAKU, KOTO

〖注〗 zither ツィター(横になった弦楽器)． forerunner 前身．

wagoto 和事 lit. a soft thing. a feminine style of Kabuki acting, as opposed to *aragoto* (a masculine style). Love scenes and scenes dealing with affairs of everyday life, acted in an elegant and delicate style, belong to this category. Female impersonators (*onnagata*) play an important role in this genre. Sakata Tōjūrō (1645-1709) developed this style of acting in Kyoto in the Genroku era (1688-1704). Kabuki in the Kyoto and Osaka area has since maintained this tradition, while that of Edo is characterized by a masculine style of acting. ⇨ ARAGOTO, GENROKU-JIDAI, KABUKI, ONNAGATA

〖注〗 masculine 男性的な． female impersonator 女形． Sakata Tōjūrō 坂田藤十郎．

Wajima-nuri 輪島塗 Wajima lacquer ware; lacquer ware produced since the mid-Edo period in Wajima in the present Ishikawa Prefecture. It consists chiefly of articles for domestic use, such as soup bowls, trays, chopsticks, etc., and is widely used because of its durability. Some bear beautiful gold inlay work.

〔注〕 lacquer 漆. articles for domestic use 家庭用品. chopsticks 箸. durability 耐久性, 堅牢. gold inlay work 沈金.

waka 和歌 lit. a Japanese poem. the generic term for indigenous poems inherited from ancient times, as opposed to Chinese-style poems. In a broader sense, *waka* involves several kinds of classical poetry: *chōka* (a long poem) with many unfixed repetitions of 5-7 syllables ending with an extra 7; *sedōka* (a head-repeated poem) with a 5-7-7-5-7-7 syllable pattern; *tanka* (a short poem) with a 5-7-5-7-7 syllable pattern, etc., sometimes also including haiku with 5-7-5 syllables. In a narrower sense, *waka* refers to *tanka*. The *tanka* form was fixed around the time of the compilation of the *Man'yōshū* (The Collection of Ten-Thousand Leaves, eighth century). Since the Heian period (794-1185), the term *waka* has generally been synonymous with *tanka*. ⇨ TANKA

〔注〕 indigenous 土着の, 固有の. unfixed repetitions 長さが一定せずに繰り返されること. head-repeated poem 旋頭歌.

wa-kei-sei-jaku 和敬清寂 harmony, reverence, purity and tranquillity. Sen no Rikyū's four basic principles for the tea ceremony. These four principles have been regarded as the fundamentals of the rustic tea ceremony. ⇨ CHANOYU, WABICHA

〔注〕 harmony 調和, 和. reverence 尊敬, 敬. purity 純粋, 清. tranquillity 静寂, 寂. tea ceremony 茶の湯. fundamentals 根本事項, 基礎となる事柄.

waki 脇 lit. side. the second actor, or deuteragonist, in a Noh play. He usually performs the role of a priest, a worrior, a minister or an imperial messenger, with no mask or makeup. His function is to call the attention of the audience to the main actor (*shite*). ⇨ NŌ, SHITE

〔注〕 deuteragonist 2番目に重要な役, (特にギリシャ劇の) 2番目役, (能の) 脇. minister 大臣. imperial messenger 朝廷からの使者. main actor 主役, (能の) 仕手.

wakinōmono 脇能物 the god-related plays in Noh; the first group in the five categories of the Noh play. In this type of play the main actor (*shite*) plays a god or the messenger of a god. ⇨ NŌ, SHIKINŌ, SHITE

〔注〕 main actor 主役, (能の) 仕手.

wakō 倭寇[和寇] Japanese pirates; Japanese bandits who infested the coasts of China and the Korean Peninsula from the 13th to the 16th centuries. They were originally private traders, based along the Inland Sea of Seto and northern Kyūshū. With the declining authority of the Muromachi shogunate (1336-1568) and Chinese restrictions on foreign trade, they resorted to piracy. After Toyotomi Hideyoshi (1536-98) imposed a ban on their activities, the number of *wakō* drastically declined.　⇨ MUROMACHI-BAKUFU

【注】 pirate 海賊.　bandit 強盗.　infest 〜にはびこる.　the Inland Sea of Seto 瀬戸内海.　ban 禁止.

wan 椀　a small wooden bowl; a wooden bowl usually with a lid, used for soup or other liquid dishes.　On the wooden base, vermilion or black lacquer is applied, often with designs.　The wood used is *keyaki* (zelkova), *buna* (Japanese beech) or *tochinoki* (horse chestnut tree).　⇨ NURIMONO, SHIKKI

【注】 vermilion lacquer 朱色の漆.

waribashi 割箸　splittable chopsticks; disposable chopsticks made of plain wood; a piece of wood that can be easily split into two sticks.　It is usually wrapped in paper.　Most restaurants have their own wrappers with the restaurant's name and phone number printed on them.　At cheap restaurants, a bunch of bare *waribashi* in a chopstick holder may be provided on each table.　⇨ HASHI

【注】 disposable 使い捨て出来る.　chopstick holder 箸立て.

warishita 割り下　soy-sauce flavored seasoning; a boiled mixture of fish-flavored soup stock, soy sauce and sweet rice wine.　It is used as a dip for fried foods, noodles, etc.　⇨ TENPURA

【注】 soy-sauce flavored 醤油で味をつけた.　seasoning 調味料.　fish-flavored 魚の風味のついた.　soup stock スープ種, 煮出し汁.　sweet rice wine 味醂.

wasabi わさび　Japanese horseradish; a very hot aromatic green spice, made from the root of the *wasabi* plant.　This plant grows along very clear waters in mountains.　As a condiment, the root is grated, but these days canned powdered *wasabi* is also available. It is put in *sushi*, in soy sauce for *sashimi* (raw fish), or in the dip for noodles.　It is also used for making spicy pickles.　⇨ SASHIMI, SUSHI

【注】 aromatic 芳香のある.　condiment 薬味.　grate おろす.　soy sauce 醤油.　dip つけ汁.

washi 和紙　Japanese paper; rice paper, as it is generally called by foreigners.　In fact, *washi* is not made from the rice plant, but from the bark of the paper-mulberry (*kōzo*) or that of the paper bush (*mitsumata*).　Cut fibers of these plants are immersed in water mixed with paste and then pressed into thin sheets.　The paper is very strong and absorbs moisture, so it is used for sliding doors (*shōji* and *fusuma*), as well as for many kinds of writing paper. ⇨ FUSUMA, MINO-GAMI, SHŌJI

〖注〗 rice paper 日本紙． immerse 浸す． sliding door 障子，襖．

washoku 和食 Japanese-style dishes or menu. The same as *nihon-ryōri*. ⇨ NIHON-RYŌRI

Y

Yabatai(-koku) 耶馬台(国)〔邪馬台(国)〕 the Yabatai empire of ancient Japan; the oldest empire, which is said to have emerged in the second or third century. It is quoted in the Chinese book *Wêi zhĭ wō rén zhuǎn* (?third century) as being the most influential empire in the Japanese islands, ruled by Queen Pimiko and having subdued several minor countries. There are two theories as to its location, one indicating the Kyūshū district and the other the Yamato district of central Honshū. Its relation with the courts of the Nara period (646–794), of which historical records remain, is not yet clear. ⇨ YAMATO, YAMATO-CHŌTEI

〖注〗 Pimiko〔Himiko〕卑弥呼. *Wêi zhĭ wō rén zhuǎn*「魏志倭人伝」.

yabuiri 薮入り lit. entering the bush. apprentice's holidays, traditionally observed on January 16. On this day, apprentices and servants working in towns would get permission to return to their homes in the country. This custom remains today in the form of people returning to their hometowns during the New Year holidays and during the Bon season in summer. ⇨ BON

〖注〗 apprentice 丁稚.

yabusame 流鏑馬 archery on horseback; a traditional form of archery from the back of a galloping horse. Originally it was a Shinto rite for forecasting harvests, and was later adopted by the samurai class to foster chivalry in Japan's medieval age. It is now demonstrated as a traditional festive event at some shrines, among which the festival at Tsurugaoka Hachiman Shrine at Kamakura offers the most famous performance of *yabusame* on September 15 or 16. Participants in colorful medieval hunting costumes shoot at a target with bow and arrow as they pass by on a horse galloping at full speed. ⇨ HACHIMANGŪ, KYŪDŌ, KYŪJUTSU

〖注〗 archery 弓術. gallop 馬に乗ってギャロップで走る, 疾走する. Shinto rite 神道の儀式. chivalry 武士道. hunting costume 狩衣.

yakatabune 屋形船 a house-shaped boat; a roofed boat. In the

Heian period (794-1185), such boats were used by nobles for sightseeing. In the Edo period (1603-1868), lavishly decorated *yakatabune* were owned privately by wealthy townsfolk; rental boats were available for sightseeing purposes as well. Today, such boats may be occasionally seen for seasonal events, such as on the Sumida River for watching fireworks displays while enjoying food and drink. ⇨ KAWABIRAKI

〖注〗 lavishly はでに，気前よく． townsfolk 町人． rental boat 貸しボート． firework 花火．

yakimono[1] **焼き物** a generic term for a broiled dish; fish, meat or vegetables broiled or grilled over a charcoal fire or an open gas fire. There are several methods of broiling and seasoning—salt broiling (*shioyaki*), soybean-paste broiling (*misoyaki*), soy-sauce broiling (*teriyaki*)—among which salt broiling is traditionally the most popular. Bamboo or metal skewers are often used to maintain the shape of the fish. ⇨ SHIOYAKI, TERIYAKI

〖注〗 season 味をつける． soybean paste 味噌． soy sauce 醬油． skewer 串．

yakimono[2] **焼き物** lit. a fired thing. Generally, *yakimono* refers to any ceramic and porcelain ware, but more specifically, it means pottery, distinguished from porcelain. The spirit of the tea ceremony—rustic simplicity and refined elegance—exerted great influence on the development of ceramics as an art.

〖注〗 ceramic ware 陶器製品． pottery 陶磁器． porcelain 磁器． tea ceremony 茶の湯． rustic simplicity さびれた簡素さ，わび・さび． refined elegance 洗練された優雅さ，幽玄． exert 及ぼす． ceramics 製陶法．

yakiniku 焼き肉 broiled or grilled meat; thinly sliced beef or pork broiled on a grill or an iron plate. It is dipped or marinated in soy sauce mixed with spices including garlic, ginger, red pepper, etc. This sauce is found in great variety on the market. Vegetables such as onions, green peppers and mushrooms may be broiled together with the meat.

〖注〗 dip 浸す． marinate ソースにつける． soy sauce 醬油． green peppers ピーマン．

yakitori 焼き鳥 barbecued chicken; chunks of chicken or chicken parts arranged on bamboo skewers and broiled over a charcoal fire (or a gas fire). They are dipped in a specially prepared sweetened barbecue soy sauce, either before or after broiling. Often vegetables such as green onions, green peppers, etc., are arranged between the chunks.

〖注〗 chunk 塊, 厚切れ. chicken parts 鶏の臓. bamboo skewer 竹串. charcoal fire 炭火. soy sauce 醬油. green pepper ピーマン.

yakudoshi 厄年 a person's unlucky or critical ages; years in life when men and women should take special precautions concerning their health and behavior. It is generally believed that men's critical ages are 25, 42 and 60, and women's are 19, 33 and 49. In particular, 42 for men and 33 for women are regarded as the most critical. One interpretation suggests this is because 42 can be pronounced *shi-ni*, homophonously suggesting the word "die" (*shinu*), and 33 *san-zan*, meaning "terrible" or "disastrous" (*san-zan*). Upon reaching *yakudoshi*, superstitious persons will pray for exorcism at shrines and temples, and refrain from starting anything new. At any rate, since these ages (though based on the shorter life span of olden days) are likely to be turning points in life, mentally and physically, it is considered that extra precautions are called for.

〖注〗 homophonously 同音異語的に. exorcism 厄払い. life span 寿命. turning point 転機.

Yakushi (Nyorai) 薬師(如来) the Buddha Yakushi; the Healing Buddha; the Buddha of Medicine. He is said to have made 12 promises to relieve people of physical illness and spiritual suffering, by providing them with sacred medicine. His image is depicted as holding a bottle of medicine in one hand though over time the bottle has disappeared in some works. The famous Yakushiji Temple in Nara was dedicated to the Buddha Yakushi in 697 by Emperor Tenmu (r. 673-87), in prayer for his empress' recovery from illness. ⇨ NYORAI

〖注〗 dedicate to ～に捧げる.

Yakushi-sanzon 薬師三尊 the Yakushi Triad; a set of three statues consisting of the Buddha Yakushi (the Healing Buddha) and his two attendants. The Buddha Yakushi is in the center, usually seated cross-legged on a pedestal, accompanied by bodhisattvas at his side—the Sunlight Bodhisattva (Nikkō Bosatsu) on the left and the Moonlight Bodhisattva (Gakkō Bosatsu) on the right. The Yakushi Triad enshrined in the main hall of Yakushiji Temple (first built in 680) is a famous example made in the Nara period (646-794). ⇨ BOSATSU, YAKUSHI (NYORAI)

〖注〗 triad 三つ組. attendant 付添人, 従者. be seated cross-legged あぐら

をかいて座る，脚を組んで座る．　pedestal 台座．　Bodhisattva 菩薩．　enshrine
祀る．

yamabushi 山伏　a mountain ascetic; a priest wandering in deep
mountains to pursue asceticism (*shugendō*).　Undergoing disciplinary regimens in communion with nature, they gain miraculous
powers in performing magic rituals.　Their beliefs can be traced
back to the esotericism of the Shingon and Tendai sects of Buddhism, but also have links with shamanistic elements of Shintoism
and the cosmic principles of Chinese Taoism.　They commonly
had long hair and went unshaven, wearing a black cap, a kimono-
style jacket and baggy trousers, with a huge Buddhist rosary and a
long staff held in the hand, and a conch-shell trumpet hung from the
neck.　They were active in the Heian (794-1185) and early Kamakura (1185-1336) periods.　In later periods, some of them lived in
villages to practice exorcism and couduct magic rituals for healing.
Yamabushi survive today, though they are small in number, practicing asceticism on Mount Ōmine (on the border of Nara
and Wakayama prefectures), on the Three Dewa Mountains
(Yamagata Prefecture), etc., and also ministering among people.
▷ BUKKYŌ, SHINGONSHŪ, SHINTŌ, SHUGENDŌ, TENDAISHŪ

〖注〗　ascetic 修行者，修験者．　asceticism 修行，苦行．　disciplinary regimen
厳しい修行．　in communion with nature 自然と合体して．　magic ritual 魔法
の儀式，呪術．　esotericism 密教的要素．　shamanistic element シャマニズム的
要素，呪術による神秘的交霊的要素．　Taoism 道教．　Buddhist rosary 数珠．
conch-shell　trumpet 法螺貝のラッパ．　exorcism 厄払いの儀式や呪文．　the
Three Dewa Mountains 出羽三山．　minister 布教する．

Yamatai-koku 耶馬台国　　▷ YABATAI(-KOKU)

Yamato 大和　an ancient name of Japan.　Specifically it refers to
the country as ruled by the Yamato imperial court which appeared
in the Yamato district (the present Nara district) around the second
or third century.　▷ YABATAI(-KOKU), YAMATO-CHŌTEI

〖注〗　the Yamato Imperial Court 大和朝廷．

Yamato-chōtei 大和朝廷　the Yamato court; the earliest court of
the Japanese empire on record, which ruled central Japan with its
seat in the present Nara district (still also called the Yamato
district).　Definite evidence of the time of its foundation remains
to be established.　According to the *Kojiki* (The Record of Ancient
Matters), a book of mythology compiled in 712, the imperial court
was founded in Yamato in 660 B.C.　Archaeologists claim that it

was probably founded in the Tumulus period (third to sixth centuries), when a number of scattered clans were united by some powerful clans competing with each other, and then these by the most influential Yamato family. One theory is that the headquarters of Queen Pimiko in third-century Japan mentioned in an ancient Chinese record (third century) was actually the Yamato Court. During the rule of this court, the hereditary emperor system was established, which continues to this day. After the Taika Reforms of 645, the country became a law-abiding state setting the foundations for the centralized government of the Nara period (646-794). ⇨ KOFUN-JIDAI, NARA-JIDAI, TAIKA NO KAISHIN, YABATAI(-KOKU), YAMATO

〖注〗 The Record of Ancient Matters「古事記」. archaeologist 考古学者. the Tumulus period 古墳時代. clan 氏. Pimiko[Himiko] 卑弥呼. law-abiding 法律に従う，法律を順守する.

yamatoe 大和絵 indigenous Japanese paintings; a style of painting expressive of native Japanese tastes and sentiments, as opposed to Chinese-style paintings. The term came into use in the mid-Heian period (794-1185) to distinguish such paintings from those of Chinese style which developed along with the spread of Buddhism. *Yamatoe* is characterized by simple and delicate lines, the subjects being historical themes, legendary figures or seasonal landscapes unique to Japan. Such paintings were drawn on sliding doors and screens. This style was also used to illustrate narrative scrolls (*emaki*), exemplified by *Genji Monogatari Emaki* (Scrolls of the Tale of Genji), *Shigisan Engi Emaki* (The Scroll of the Legends of Mount Shigi), etc. *Yamatoe* was further developed by painters of the Tosa school in the Muromachi (1336-1568) and Edo (1603-1868) periods. Japanese-style painting of later years and up to the present is called *Nihon-ga*, a more generic term. ⇨ EMAKI, KANGA

〖注〗 indigenous 土地固有の，土着の. legendary figure 伝説上の人物. sliding door 襖. narrative scroll 絵巻.

yamato-mai 大和舞 the Yamato dance; originally the generic term for indigenous Japanese dance, specifically an ancient ritual folk dance of the Yamato district, in present-day Nara Prefecture. Performed quietly and solemnly by several persons in a circle, this folk dance was believed to invoke the spirit of the land. It has been preserved over the years at Kasuga Shrine in Nara. ⇨ YAMATO

〖注〗 indigenous 土着の，土地特有の． ritual 儀式の． solemnly 厳かに．
invoke 呼び出す．

yaoyorozu no kamigami 八百万の神々 lit. eight-hundred myriad
gods. a countless number of deities or all sacred beings, particularly in the context of polytheistic Shintoism. In a narrow sense,
this term refers to a great number of gods that appear in Shinto
mythology, the supreme one being Amaterasu Ōmikami, the Sun
Goddess. Shintoism, with its beginnings in nature worship, person-
ifies all phenomena of nature. Thus, natural objects—mountains,
trees, water, wind, fire, etc,—can be identified as deities when an
awe-inspiring quality is felt from them. In a broader sense,
humans are also included among *kami* when they are deified and
enshrined, such as emperors, heroes, scholars, religious persons,
warriors and soldiers, etc. ⇨ AMATERASU ŌMIKAMI, JINJA, SHINTŌ
〖注〗 polytheistic 多神教の． personify 擬人化する． awe-inspiring 畏敬の念
をおこす． enshrine 祀る．

yarimizu 遣り水 a water conduit; an artificial stream running
through a Japanese landscape garden. It flows murmuring over
small pebbles in the stream bed and creates an atmosphere of
coolness both to the eyes and to the ears. It was considered one of
the essential elements of a garden laid out to enhance tranquillity,
in the residences of the nobility in the Heian period (794-1185).
⇨ NOHON-TEIEN
〖注〗 conduit 樋． landscape garden 造景庭園． stream bed 流れの底． tranquillity 静寂． the nobility 貴族階級．

yatai 屋台 a street stall; a roofed open-air stall selling cheap dishes.
They are moved on carts and set up mostly at night on streets in
busy quarters. During festivals such stalls are set up in rows in
and around the precincts of a shrine or temple. Types of food
offered include *oden* (Japanese hodgepodge), *yakitori* (barbecued
chicken), *takoyaki* (dumplings with a bit of octopus inside), grilled
corn on the cob, various kinds of noodles and less traditional fare
such as hot dogs. Some *yatai* appearing at a place on a regular
basis provide stools or benches where workers, tempted by the
smell, drop by to enjoy food together with sakê at low cost. ⇨
ODEN, SAKE, TAKOYAKI, YAKITORI
〖注〗 stall 屋台，露店． precincts 境内． hodgepodge ごった煮． corn on the
cob 穂軸つきとうもろこし． fare メニュー，食物．

Yata no Kagami 八咫鏡 lit. an octagonal mirror. the Sacred

Mirror, one of the three treasures or regalia of the Japanese imperial throne, the other two being the Comma-Shaped Gem and the Grass-Cutting Sword. This mirror is enshrined at the Inner Shrine of Ise and is believed to represent the sacred body of Amaterasu Ōmikami (the Sun Goddess), the original ancestor of the Imperial Family. Japanese mythology has it that the mirror was cast by the gods to induce the Sun Goddess to come out from a cave where she was hiding. ⇨ KUSANAGI NO TSURUGI, MAGATAMA, SANSHU NO JINGI

〖注〗 octagonal 八辺形. regalia 王権, 王位の標章. the three regalia 三種の神器. the Comma-Shaped Gem 勾玉. the Grass-Cutting Sword 草薙の剣. enshrine 祀る.

yatsuhashi 八つ橋 lit. eight bridges. a zigzagging bridge made of wooden planks in a Japanese garden. Japanese irises are usually planted alongside the bridge, a popular motif taken from *The Tale of Ise* of the Heian period (794–1185). A brittle cinnamon-flavored biscuit, a well-known type of confectionery made in Kyoto, was inspired by this kind of bridge.

〖注〗 zigzagging 稲妻形の, Z字形の. plank 板, 厚板. Japanese iris あやめ. brittle カリカリした.

Yayoi-jidai 弥生時代 the Yayoi period (ca. 200 B.C.–A.D. 250); a prehistoric period, also known as the latter half of the neolithic period. The name *Yayoi* takes rise from the pottery of the period, first discovered in Yayoichō, Tokyo. It was during this period that people first formed farming communities and ruling families gradually emerged. In addition to pottery, they also began to use bronze and iron tools. ⇨ JŌMON-JIDAI, YAYOISHIKI-DOKI

〖注〗 the neolithic period 新石器時代. earthenware 土器.

yayoishiki-doki 弥生式土器 Yayoi-style earthenware; earthenware made in the Yayoi period (ca. 200 B.C.–A.D. 250), the latter half of the Japanese neolithic period. So called because pieces were first excavated in Yayoichō, Tokyo, in 1884. Generally it is reddish brown in color and simple in design, such as having a slight comb-like pattern on a smooth surface. It has an emphasis on form while Jōmon-style earthenware of the preceding period has more decoration. ⇨ JOMONSHIKI-DOKI, YAYOI-JIDAI

〖注〗 earthenware 土器. the neolithic period 新石器時代. excavate 発掘する.

yobanmemono 四番目物 lit. the fourth group piece. the fourth group in the five categories of a Noh play. It deals with various subjects covering a wide range. ⇨ NŌ, SHIKINŌ

yobikō 予備校 a preparatory school; a private cram school for students preparing for college entrance examinations. These schools usually offer curricula for both part-time and full-time students—for regular high-school students, and for students called *rōnin* who have failed to enter the college of their choice and want to prepare for another try. ⇨ JUKU, RŌNIN

〖注〗 preparatory 準備の, 予備の. cram school 塾, つめこみ学習塾. the college of their choice 自分の志望の大学.

yōkan 羊羹 sweet bean-paste jelly; bean-jam jelly; confectionery made of bean paste, sugar and agar-agar. It is usually molded into long rectangles, or packed in cans. Besides red beans, kidney beans, mottled kidney beans, green peas, etc., are also used as the main ingredient. Some *yōkan* are flavored with tea, citrus fruits, etc. Some are mixed with chestnuts, whole or mashed. As for texture, there are *neri-yōkan* (kneaded *yōkan*), *mushi-yōkan* (steamed *yōkan*) and *mizu-yōkan* (water *yōkan*). *Neri-yōkan* can be preserved for over a month when packed tightly. ⇨ AN, KANTEN, MIZUYŌKAN, NAMAGASHI

〖注〗 sweet bean-paste 餡. bean-jam 餡. confectionery 菓子, 糖菓. agar-agar 寒天. mold 型に入れて造る. red bean 小豆. kidney bean 隠元豆. mottled kidney bean 鶉豆. ingredient (料理の)材料. citrus fruit 甘橘類. texture きめ. kneaded 練った.

yokozuna 横綱 a grand champion; the highest rank in *sumō*. To be promoted to this rank an *ōzeki* must either win two consecutive tournaments or at least come out with records that can be considered good. The imposition of such severe conditions is natural since a *yokozuna* may not be demoted to a lower rank. The only change he might experience is that of position within the ranks of *yokozuna*. A *yokozuna* is seen as a contender for the championship in every tournament, so if he begins to do poorly and cannot live up to his title he is expected to voluntarily retire from the ring. ⇨ ŌZEKI, ŌZUMŌ, SUMŌ

〖注〗 consecutive 連続の. imposition 課すこと. demote 階級を下げる, 地位を下げる. contender 競争者, 優勝をねらえる者.

yōkyoku 謡曲 lit. song music. the lyrics delivered in a chanting form in the libretto used in the Noh drama, to which the Noh dance is performed. Popularly referred to as *utai*. ⇨ NŌ, UTAI

〖注〗 lyric 叙情詩. chanting form 謡の様式. libretto（歌劇，ミュージカルなどの）本文や歌詞，台本.

yomihon 読本 lit. a reading book. a story book; a literary genre of the late Edo period (1603-1868). This genre includes didactic stories, historical semi-fiction, Chinese tales, etc., most with the theme that virtue will be rewarded and vice will be punished. Well-known works include *Nansō Satomi Hakkenden* (The Biographies of Eight Dogs) by Takizawa Bakin (1767-1845), *Ugetsu Monogatari* (The Tales of Rain and the Moon) by Ueda Akinari (1734-1809), etc. ⇨ EDO-JIDAI

〖注〗 genre（文学などの）分野. didactic 教訓的な. Virtue will be rewarded and vice will be punished. 勧善懲悪.

yoritsuki 寄付 a waiting room or arbor for the tea ceremony. It is generally a small room consisting of three *tatami* mats. The guests assemble there and then walk along the garden path to a bench where they wait for the host. ⇨ CHANOYU

〖注〗 arbor あずまや，休憩小屋. tea ceremony 茶の湯. garden path 庭の通路，露地.

yose 寄席 lit. seats for gathering. a variety-show house; a small theater featuring traditional variety shows—*rakugo* (comic story-telling), *manzai* (comic dialogue), *kōdan* (storytelling), *naniwabushi* (story-singing), etc. Starting in the Akasaka district of Edo in the mid-Edo period (1603-1868), they became very popular among the townsfolk and the number of such theaters soon grew. They are equipped with a small stage, in front of which the audience sits on a *tatami*-mat floor, retaining an atmosphere of old Edo. Traditional variety shows are still enjoyed, particularly on TV, though *yose* houses are decreasing in number. ⇨ KŌDAN, MANZAI², NANIWABUSHI, RAKUGO

〖注〗 townsfolk 町人.

yoshido 葦戸[蘆戸] a reed door; a screen or sliding door, made of reed with a wooden frame. In summer, ordinary sliding doors (*shōji* or *fusuma*) may be replaced by the *yoshido*, permitting the breeze to pass through. ⇨ FUSUMA, SHŌJI

〖注〗 reed 蘆，葦. sliding door すべり戸，障子，ふすま.

Yoshino-Kumano Kokuritsu-kōen　　吉野熊野国立公園 Yoshino-Kumano National Park (585.5 square kilometers), designated in 1936; a natural park situated on the Kii Peninsula in central Honshū, comprising part of Mie Prefecture, and most of Nara and

Wakayama prefectures. The northern region is mountainous and famous for its cherry trees. Deep in the mountains stand a number of temples and shrines of historical importance. Mount Yoshino (455 meters) and Mount Ōmine (1,719 m) in particular were formerly associated with the practice of asceticism of the Shingon sect. The southern Kumano region features rivers and ravines including the Kumano River and Doro Gorge, and long rugged coastlines.

〖注〗 the practice of asceticism 修験行. ravine 峡谷. the Doro Gorge 瀞峡. rugged coastline リアス式海岸.

yōshoku-shinju 養殖真珠 cultured pearls; pearls artificially cultivated using pearl oysters or the like. A few round beads coated with a thin membrane are inserted into a living oyster to act as an irritant. The oysters are placed in wire baskets, which are hung from rafts and left to float in the sea for a few years. The beads come out as perfectly spherical pearls taking on the same luster as that of natural pearls. The method was first successfully employed by Kōkichi Mikimoto (1858-1954) in 1893 at a tiny island (now called Pearl Island) in Toba Bay, Mie Prefecture, where demonstrations of pearl culture are conducted. Today Mie Prefecture, especially Ago Bay, boasts two-thirds of total pearl production. Other producing areas are on the coast of the Inland Sea of Seto and some coastal regions of Kyūshū.

〖注〗 cultivate 養殖する. pearl oyster 真珠貝, あこや貝. membrane 粘膜. irritant 刺激物.

yuba 湯葉 lit. leaves of hot water. soybean-milk skin, usually dried; soy-milk film produced in the process of making soybean curd. When soy milk is boiled and before coagulant is added, a thin skin forms on the surface. This skin is carefully scooped up and then dried. It is regarded as a delicacy and is used as an ingredient in soup and traditional dishes. Kyoto-style cuisine features raw *yuba* dishes. In other districts, raw *yuba* is hard to come by as it spoils easily.

〖注〗 soy milk 豆乳. soybean curd 豆腐. coagulant 凝固剤. delicacy 珍味. ingredient (料理の)材料. cuisine 料理. come by 手に入る.

yudōfu 湯豆腐 boiled soybean curd; cubes of bean curd boiled in water in an earthenware pot, usually prepared at the table. A sheet of kelp placed at the bottom of the pot adds flavor to the water. *Yudōfu* is eaten piping hot with soy sauce and condiments

—minced green onions, grated ginger, dried bonito flakes, red pepper, etc. ⇨ KATSUOBUSHI, SHICHIMI-TŌGARASHI, TŌFU

【注】 soybean curd 豆腐. earthenware 土器. kelp seaweed 昆布. piping hot 非常に熱い，ぽっぽいうほど熱い. soy sauce 醤油. condiment 薬味. minced green onions さらしねぎ，刻みねぎ. grated ginger おろし生姜. dried bonito flakes 鰹の削り節.

yūgen 幽玄 understated elegance; subtle profundity; symbolic beauty of subtlety and profundity, aesthetic sensibility which was highly valued in the medieval age of Japan. The connotation of this subtle and profound beauty involves a variety of qualities: elegance, tranquillity, spirituality, mystique, eternity, etc. When it is expressed in art and literature, the surface takes on elaborate simplicity, but with profound significance beneath, limitless in terms of time and space. Artists and poets of those days pursued this in an attempt to suggest something limitless with minimal expression, whether by words or actions. What one feels as the essence of Noh best conveys the implication of *yūgen*. ⇨ HIGA-SHIYAMA-BUNKA, MUROMACHI-JIDAI, NŌ

【注】 understated elegance おさえた優雅さ. subtle profundity 微妙な深みのあること. aesthetic sensibility 美的感覚. connotation 含蓄，暗示するもの. tranquillity 静寂. mystique 神秘. eternity 永遠性. implication 意味，含蓄.

yuinō 結納 an engagement gift; betrothal gifts exchanged between the two families of the prospective bride and bridegroom. The exchange rite is conducted in a ceremonial way, with the parents of the prospective bridegroom visiting the prospective bride's house. The gifts brought by the former used to consist of folding fans, casks of rice wine, rolls of kimono fabric, etc. But today, money, wrapped in red and white folded paper tied decoratively with gold and silver strings, is usually presented. In return, a portion of it is used to buy something for the bridegroom. ⇨ KIMONO, MIZUHIKI, NOSHIGAMI

【注】 betrothal 婚約. prospective 将来の，見込みのある. rite 儀式. folding fan 扇子. cask of rice wine 酒樽. gold and silver strings 金銀の水引.

yukata 浴衣 lit. a bathrobe. an informal, light, unlined, cotton kimono worn in summer. It most commonly bears plain designs dyed in shades of indigo or simple patterns in white and indigo. It is used for relaxation and as sleepwear, and is especially enjoyed after a bath. Japanese inns provide them for guests. ⇨ KIMONO, RYOKAN

〖注〗 unlined 裏地のない. shades of indigo 藍の濃淡.

yukimidōrō 雪見燈籠 a snow-viewing stone lantern; a short, three or four-legged stone lantern with a broad roof. It serves as an aesthetic object in a Japanese landscape garden. Aesthetic-minded persons used to insert candles into the lanterns for viewing snow-covered landscapes at night, hence the name. ⇨ NIHON-TEIEN, TŌRŌ

〖注〗 lantern 燈籠. aesthetic object 鑑賞物. landscape garden 風景庭園. aesthetic-minded 風流の心のある.

Yūki-tsumugi 結城紬 Yūki hand-spun silk; a type of hand-spun silk for kimono, originally produced in the city of Yūki in Ibaraki Prefecture. The thread is reeled off waste cocoons and woven by hand with immense care, requiring long hours of work to produce a seemingly rough texture. In particular, special skills are required to produce elaborate *kasuri* (splashed blurred) patterns. The fabric takes on an exquisite rustic elegance. In spite of its beauty, it is not made into formal wear. ⇨ KASURI, KIMONO, KUME-TSUMUGI, ŌSHIMA-TSUMUGI, TSUMUGI

〖注〗 silk fabric 絹織物. reel off (繭から)糸を巻きとる. waste cocoon あまり物の繭, 雑繭. rough texture 粗野な生地. exquisite 絶妙な, 優雅な. rustic elegance さびれた優雅さ, 飾らない美しさ.

yunomi 湯飲み a teacup; a ceramic cup used for drinking green tea in daily life. It is much smaller than the one used for powdered green tea (*matcha*) in the tea ceremony. *Yunomi*, like all other tableware in Japan, is sold in sets of five—not six—without saucers, but sometimes with lids. When green tea is served, a *yunomi* is placed on a wooden or metal coaster. ⇨ CHA

〖注〗 ceramic 陶器の. powdered green tea 抹茶. coaster 茶托.

Yūzen(-zome) 友禅(染) Yūzen-style dyeing; a pictorial silk fabric dyed in the Yūzen fashion, which is said to have been developed by Miyazaki Yūzensai (?1680-?1710) in Kyoto in the Edo period (1603-1868). The pictorial design is made by the paste-resist method of dyeing by applying rice starch paste on brush-work painting and then dyeing the background. This method captures the air of real paintings. Originally the design was hand-painted, and those of high-quality products still are today. In former days, long strips of colorful Yūzen fabric could be seen being washed (to remove the paste) in the Kamo River in Kyoto. ⇨ KAGA-YŪZEN

〖注〗 pictorial 絵画的な. silk fabric 絹織物. paste-resist 糊の防染剤.

Z

zabuton 座布団 a kneeling cushion; a floor cushion for individuals; a square cushion used when sitting on one's knees on a *tatami*-mat floor. It is made of silk or cotton and stuffed with cotton wool or synthetic fibers, its standard size measuring about 60 by 55 centimeters square. It is almost always offered to guests in a Japanese-style room. The use of *zabuton* became popular among commoners during the Edo period (1603-1868) in place of the small straw mat commonly used earlier. ⇨ TATAMI

〖注〗 sit on one's knees ひざを折って座る. cotton wool 綿. synthetic fibers 合成繊維.

zaibatsu 財閥 lit. a financial clique. the big financial and industrial combines of Japan, which had developed by the 1920s and were dissolved shortly after World War II. These combines, represented by the four giant family-dominated groups—Mitsui, Mitsubishi, Sumitomo and Yasuda—controlled the upper level of the Japanese dual economy, with their stockholding companies embracing affiliates in the fields of banking, manufacturing, shipbuilding, mining, etc. Under the order of the postwar U.S. Occupation authorities, which feared the restoration of military-related activities, the holding companies of *zaibatsu* combines were dissolved and broken up into component corporate companies. Later, however, those component companies developed into new industrial groups issuing their own stock. Besides these Big Four, new rising *zaibatsu* developed during World War II, mainly associated with military industries. ⇨ BATSU, SŌGŌ-SHŌSHA

〖注〗 clique 派閥. combine 企業合同. dissolve 解体させる. family-dominated 一族中心の，一族が優勢を持つ. stockholding company 持株会社. affiliate 子会社，支社. the U.S. Occupation authorities 米占領軍当局. component 構成部分(の). corporate company 企業会社.

zaru-soba 笊蕎麦 buckwheat noodles on bamboo ware; buckwheat noodles with pieces of seaweed laver sprinkled on top, served on bamboo ware. The ware usually consists of a square, lacquered wooden frame on top of which a split-bamboo rack is placed. *Zaru-soba* comes with a tiny dish of Japanese horseradish and minced green onions as condiments, which are added to a cup of dip made of soy sauce and fish broth. Buckwheat noodles of the same type with no seaweed laver on top are called *mori-soba*. ⇨ MORI-SOBA, NORI, SOBA

〖注〗 buckwheat noodles 蕎麦. bamboo ware 竹の食器. seaweed laver 海苔. lacquered wooden frame 漆塗りの木枠. split bamboo rack 割り竹のすのこ. Japanese horseradish わさび. minced green onions さらしねぎ, 刻みねぎ. condiment 薬味. soy sauce 醤油. fish broth 魚のだし汁.

zashiki 座敷 a reception room; Japanese-style guest room with *tatami* mats on the floor and a *tokonoma* (alcove) at one side. The *zashiki* emphasizes space and avoids gaudy displays. An ideal *zashiki* has no furniture, the only decoration being a flower arrangement or an ornament, and a hanging scroll, placed in the alcove. In reality, however, to have such space is considered a luxury in average city homes. Instead of chairs, cushions called *zabuton* are offered for guests to sit on. ⇨ KAKEMONO, KŪKAN, TATAMI, TOKONOMA, ZABUTON

〖注〗 alcove 床の間. flower arrangement 生け花. ornament 飾り物. hanging scroll 掛け軸.

zazen 座禅 sitting meditation; silent meditation in the lotus position as practiced in Zen Buddhism. Zen disciples sit in meditation for many hours, silent and motionless, with their eyes almost closed, their legs crossed and their backs straight, in an effort to enter a state of nothingness and attain enlightenment. If a disciple becomes drowsy or is distracted in the meditation hall, a monk keeping watch strikes him with a wooden rod. ⇨ ZEN¹, ZENSHŪ

〖注〗 meditation 黙想, 座禅. lotus position 正座, 仏が蓮の台座に座っている様な姿勢. disciple 弟子, 修行僧. attain enlightenment 悟りに達する. drowsy 眠い. distract 気を散らす. monk 僧.

Zen¹ 禅 the essence of Zen Buddhism; an abbreviation of *zenna* (禅那), transliterated from the Sanskrit word *dhyāna* which denotes meditation, contemplation, concentration, etc. Originally in India *dhyāna* was a method of self-discipline to discover one's being. It developed into a sect of Buddhism in China, and was brought to Japan in the 12th century where it matured. Not only did Zen Buddhism become one of Japan's major religions, but its essence permeated deeply into the culture. "The object of Zen," according to internationally renowned Zen scholar Daisetz T. Suzuki, "consists in acquiring a new viewpoint for looking into the essence of things."* The state of *satori* (enlightenment or inward awakening) is said to be attained in a flash by direct intuition, not by intellect or words, through the practice of meditation and self-discipline. *Satori* is a state of nothingness in the mind, in an affirmative sense, by which one can observe freely the essence of life and the nature of one's being, free of obstacles. Zen was first welcomed by warriors who sought the composure of the mind in preparation for death, as well as to train themselves in military skills requiring self-discipline and concentration. Subsequently the spirit of Zen came to form the core of martial arts—archery, swordsmanship, judo, etc. At the same time, Zen priests and devotees had tremendous influence on the arts and literature. Consequently, Zen became a lasting aesthetic element in Japanese culture. For example, in the tea ceremony one can experience the infinity of the universe in a small tea hut and penetrate the infinite beauty to be found in old rustic tea utensils. A Zen garden represents the grandeur of nature or the universe in a small space. In black and white painting, a few simple dots and lines depict something subtle with the blank white area expressing even more. A haiku poem expresses profound meaning, having an evocative power through a mere 17 syllables. In short, "nothingness" permits an infinite number of meanings. However, Zen is above explanation with words. ⇨ BUKKYŌ, BUSHIDŌ, CHANOYU, HAIKU, JŪDŌ, KENDŌ, KYŪDŌ, SADŌ, ZAZEN, ZENGA, ZENSHŪ

* D.T. Suzuki: *Introduction to Zen Buddhism*, Grove Press Inc., New York, 1964

〔注〕 abbreviation 省略語. meditation 瞑想, 座禅. contemplation 瞑想, 観想. self-discipline 自己鍛練. enlightenment 悟り. inward awakening 内的めざめ. intuition 直感. composure of the mind 心の平静. devotee 帰依者, 道を追求する人. infinity 無限. evocative 喚起する.

zen² 膳 a dining tray; individual table-like trays with legs used for meals. It is about 30 centimeters high and 45 cm square. Bowls and dishes of food and chopsticks are placed on this "table." Today it is used mostly on special occasions or at traditional Japanese restaurants. In some rural districts, it is still used in everyday life, each person having his or her own individual lacquered table. ⇨

HONZEN-RYŌRI

〖注〗 chopsticks 箸． lacquered 漆を塗った．

zenga 禅画 Zen painting; a simple monochromatic painting suggesting the essence of the concept of Zen. Specifically, it refers to brush paintings of India ink drawn by Chinese and Japanese Zen monks, in which their Zen enlightenment is expressed. The painting is characterized by its extremely simple form, often made up of only dots and lines of a few brush strokes drawn in black India ink in the corner of a sheet of white paper, with the white part largely left untouched—letting nothingness or this void express something limitless, according to Zen concepts.   ⇨ SUIBOKUGA, SUMI, SUMIE, ZEN¹

〖注〗 monochromatic 単色の． India ink 墨． enlightenment 悟り（の境地）． brush stroke 筆の跡． void 空，無，中味のないこと．

Zenshū 禅宗 Zen Buddhism; the Zen sect of Buddhism. Having originated in India, it was taken to China by Bodhidharma early in the sixth century. In Japan, three branches of Zen Buddhism were founded by two Japanese priests who had studied in China and one Chinese priest. The branches were the Rinzaishū introduced in 1191 by Eisai (1141-1215), Sōtōshū in 1228 by Dōgen (1200-1253), and Ōbakushū in 1654 by Ingen (1592-1673) from the Ming dynasty (1368-1644); the last one has been incorporated in large part into the Rinzaishū. Basically, in Zen Buddhism neither sermons nor the worship of images of the Buddha are stressed. Rather, enlightenment is said to be attained, not through outward teaching or intellectual theory, but through personal experience and direct intuition by means of an austere life and long hours of silent meditation. Zen Buddhism has exerted a great influence on Japanese art and culture.   ⇨ BUKKYŌ, RINZAISHŪ, SŌTŌSHŪ, ZAZEN, ZEN¹

〖注〗 sect 宗派，分派． the Ming dynasty 明朝． sermon 説教． the worship of images 仏像崇拝． enlightenment 悟り． intuition 直観． austere 厳しい，耐乏の． meditation 黙想，座禅．

zenzai 善哉 a thick kind of sweet red-bean soup; sweetened bean-paste soup which includes a piece of rice cake. Red beans (*azuki*), soaked in water overnight, are boiled and simmered over low heat until they become soft. In the sweetened soup, a dash of salt is added and a piece of rice cake, or sometimes rice-flour dumplings. *Zenzai* is made up of whole beans, while *shiruko* is from strained beans.　⇨ AN, SHIRUKO

〖注〗 red bean 小豆. bean paste 餡. rice cake 餅. simmer 煮つめる. a dash of salt ひとつまみの塩. rice-flour dumpling 米の粉の団子. strain 濾過する.

zōgan-zaiku 象眼細工[象嵌細工] lit. elephant-eye craft. damascene; an inlaid work with gold and silver on a metal base, made into jewelry and ornaments.　A metal base is engraved to make a floral geometric design made up of lines in the shape of an elephant's eye, and is then inlaid with gold and sterling silver.　The metal surface is lacquered in black and then polished with charcoal until the gold and silver design comes out.

〖注〗 damascene 象眼細工, 波模様. inlaid work はめこみ細工. engrave 彫り込む. sterling silver 純銀.

zōni 雑煮 a soup with rice cake; a special rice-cake soup served to celebrate the New Year.　Boiled together with the rice cake are slices of chicken or fish-paste cake, and vegetables such as trefoil leaves, rapeseed leaves, mushrooms, bamboo shoots, etc., with citron peel added for flavor.　Usually a clear soup, but sometimes *miso* soup, is used.　Each district boasts its own specialty.　⇨ KAMABOKO, MISOSHIRU, MOCHI, SUIMONO

〖注〗 ingredient （料理の）材料. fish-paste cake 蒲鉾. trefoil leaves 三つ葉. rapeseed leaves 菜種の葉, 小松菜. bamboo shoot 竹の子. citron peel ゆずの皮片.

zōri 草履 a pair of Japanese sandals; low sandals consisting of a flat sole with a V-shaped thong passing between the big toe and the second toe.　They are made of leather, cloth or vinyl, which covers the base of cork or rubber.　Those of straw are called *wara-zōri*, but are now rarely used.　⇨ GETA, HANAO, TABI

〖注〗 sole 足底. thong 紐, 鼻緒.

zōsui 雑炊 lit. boiled rice with miscellaneous things.　a hodgepodge; a kind of porridge of rice, vegetables, etc.　Rice is boiled in an ample amount of soup seasoned with soy sauce.　When cooked, it is mixed with seafoods or an egg, and some vegetables.　Trefoil leaves may be used to add flavor.　When leftover rice is used, the starch is usually removed by rinsing.

〖注〗 hodgepodge ごった煮. porridge 粥. season 味をつける. soy sauce 醤油. trefoil leaves 三つ葉. leftover 残り物.

SETSUKO KOJIMA

Graduated from the Department of English Literature at Nanzan University (BA), Japan. Graduate study in TEFL Program, Department of English, California State University, San Francisco (MA), USA. Presently an instructor of English at Aoyama Gakuin University, School of Law (Atsugi and Tokyo) and at Aoyama Gakuin Woman's Junior College, Department of English (Tokyo). Co-author of *A Cultural Dictionary of Japan* (The Japan Times, Ltd.), *A Classified English Dictionary for Tourist Guides* (ibid.), *Study Guide to the National Examination of Guide Interpreters* (Kenkyusha Publishing Co.), "S(Inanimate)+V+O" in *English for Specific Purposes* (Oregon State University Press).

GENE A. CRANE

Graduated from Kansas State Teachers College (BSE), USA. Graduate TESOL study done at Aoyama Gakuin University (International Division), Tokyo; Temple University, Tokyo; Newport University, Tokyo. Presently an instructor at Aoyama Gakuin University, School of International Politics, Economics and Business (Atsugi campus, Japan). Also teaching at Keio University (Tokyo), NHK Bunka Center (Tokyo), etc. Editor/writer for educational radio, NHK Broadcasting Corp. Former vice-president of the Association of Foreign Teachers in Japan, 1983-87. Co-author of *English Grammar Guide* (Asahi Press), *Practical English Writing* (Gakushobo), and others.